THE GUNNERS
A HISTORY OF NEW ZEALAND ARTILLERY

ALAN HENDERSON, DAVID GREEN AND PETER COOKE

A RAUPO BOOK
Published by the Penguin Group
Penguin Group (NZ), 67 Apollo Drive, Rosedale,
North Shore 0632, New Zealand (a division of Pearson New Zealand Ltd)
Penguin Group (USA) Inc., 375 Hudson Street,
New York, New York 10014, USA
Penguin Group (Canada), 90 Eglinton Avenue East, Suite 700, Toronto,
Ontario, M4P 2Y3, Canada (a division of Pearson Penguin Canada Inc.)
Penguin Books Ltd, 80 Strand, London, WC2R 0RL, England
Penguin Ireland, 25 St Stephen's Green,
Dublin 2, Ireland (a division of Penguin Books Ltd)
Penguin Group (Australia), 250 Camberwell Road, Camberwell,
Victoria 3124, Australia (a division of Pearson Australia Group Pty Ltd)
Penguin Books India Pvt Ltd, 11, Community Centre,
Panchsheel Park, New Delhi – 110 017, India
Penguin Books (South Africa) (Pty) Ltd, 24 Sturdee Avenue,
Rosebank, Johannesburg 2196, South Africa

Penguin Books Ltd, Registered Offices: 80 Strand, London, WC2R 0RL, England

First published by Penguin Group (NZ), 2008
10 9 8 7 6 5 4 3 2 1

2008 © Crown Copyright

Cover Image: Oil painting by
Peter McIntyre. *Archives
New Zealand, AAAC 898,
NCWA 299*

Designed by Suzanne Wesley
Maps by Blackant Productions
Printed in China by Nordica

All rights reserved. Without limiting the rights under copyright reserved
above, no part of this publication may be reproduced, stored in or
introduced into a retrieval system, or transmitted, in any form or by any
means (electronic, mechanical, photocopying, recording or otherwise),
without the prior written permission of both the copyright owner and
the above publisher of this book.

ISBN 978 07900 1141 7

A catalogue record for this book is available
from the National Library of New Zealand.

www.penguin.co.nz

Contents

Organisational Charts and Tables   4
Foreword   5
Acknowledgements   7
Introduction   9
Glossary   15

1. Early Artillery in New Zealand   17
2. The Years of Transformation, 1899–1914   56
3. Artillery Comes of Age: The First World War   82
4. Retrenchment and Modernisation, 1919–39   157
5. Battle Rejoined: The Second Divisional Artillery, 1940–41   190
6. Perfecting the Art: Syria to Trieste, 1942–45   243
7. Pacific Theatre and Home Defence, 1939–45   309
8. Cold and Hot Wars, 1946–72   359
9. Towards a New Role, 1972–2006   433

Notes   468
Bibliography   499
Index   508

Organisational Charts and Tables

Artillery Volunteer Corps, 1886	48
Artillery Units in New Zealand, 1900-1914	67
New Zealand Artillery at Gallipoli, 1915	155
New Zealand Divisional Artillery, Western Front, 1917-18	156
Reorganisation of Artillery Units, 1920s	160
Coastal and Anti-Aircraft Units, 1937	168
Divisional Artillery Order of Battle, 1941	202
Field and Anti-Tank Units, North Africa	225
Artillery in New Zealand, World War Two	356
3 New Zealand Division Artillery Units and Coast Defence in Pacific	358
Artillery in New Zealand, 1956	369
New Zealand Artillery in Korea	386

Foreword

I am delighted to have been asked to provide the foreword to this valuable and comprehensive history of the Royal New Zealand Artillery. A strong bond exists between all gunners and the links between our regiments are strong and enduring. Those links were forged in times of adversity, and since the South African War in 1900 we have shared operational experience, serving the guns in many conflicts, with New Zealand gunners showing great gallantry and élan. More recently we have served alongside each other in Bosnia-Herzegovina and Afghanistan, where the ties have been renewed.

We value the friendship and camaraderie of our Kiwi counterparts and share much in terms of tradition, heritage and ethos, which is best summed up by our shared motto:

'Quo fas et gloria ducunt – Whither honour and glory lead.'

General Sir Alex Harley KBE CB
Master Gunner St James's Park

Acknowledgements

This book has been some time in the making. It was conceived by the Royal Regiment of New Zealand Artillery's Regimental Fund Committee in 1997 to mark the 2002 anniversary. The Committee commissioned the Historical Branch of the Department of Internal Affairs to prepare a scoping study. Subsequently an advisory committee was established by the Chief of General Staff to represent the Regiment during the project, which the Historical Branch (now the History Group, Ministry for Culture and Heritage) was contracted to produce. In 1999 Alan Henderson began research and writing; he moved on to other employment after writing drafts of all but the first and last chapters. Peter Cooke and David Green were then hired to finish the book. Peter wrote chapter 9, most of the technical and biographical boxes and organisational charts, supplemented Alan's narrative with material from diaries and interviews, and researched the illustrations. David wrote chapter 1 (including its biographies), filled some gaps elsewhere and revised the whole manuscript. Anna Rogers then edited the text with an expert eye for redundancy and infelicity.

Many people helped the book to reach publication. The New Zealand Defence Force has provided generous financial and other support. All the members of the advisory committee gave welcome guidance and encouragement, including valuable suggestions on the draft chapters as they appeared. Sadly, four members of the committee have since died. Initially it was chaired by Brigadier Lindsay (Lin) Smith, who played a key role in establishing the project. Lieutenant-General Sir Leonard Thornton, a strong advocate for the project, Brigadier John (Blackie) Burns, who provided judicious advice as research and writing proceeded, and Major-General Ron Hassett, a long-standing supporter of New Zealand Army history, also died during the course of the project. Brigadiers Ray Andrews, then Colonel Commandant of the Regiment, became chairman of the advisory committee in 2002. He was succeeded in 2004 by Brigadier Graham Birch who, along with Brigadiers John Valintine and Geoff Hitchings, Colonels John Horsford, Herbert Jones, Don Kenning, and Ralph Porter, successive representatives of 16 Field Regiment, and John Crawford, New Zealand Defence Force Historian, comprised the committee during the project's latter stages. The authors are also grateful to the many other retired and serving gunners who have made significant contributions. Those interviewed are acknowledged in the bibliography.

At the Ministry for Culture and Heritage, Acting Chief Historian Claudia Orange and Chief Historian Jock Phillips provided essential oversight. The General Editor (War History), Ian McGibbon, and the current Chief Historian, Bronwyn Dalley, have provided much perceptive advice and encouragement. The staff of numerous libraries and archival institutions, including Archives New Zealand, the Alexander Turnbull Library and the New Zealand Defence Force library, have been of assistance. Fran McGowan, Research and Library Adviser in the Ministry for Culture and Heritage, was unfailingly helpful in seeking out sources for the authors, as were Windsor Jones and Dolores Ho at the Kippenberger Military Archive, Waiouru. Several people generously shared their knowledge of coastal fortifications: Peter Corbett of the Hauraki Gulf, Peter Wilkins of Lyttelton Harbour and Laurie Stewart of Otago Harbour.

Suzanne Wesley designed the book, which was expertly put together by Sam Hill and the team at Reed. Ross Armstrong compiled the index. The authors are grateful to everyone who has helped them in their labours.

Introduction

The Royal Regiment of New Zealand Artillery celebrated its centenary in 2002. In the course of its first 100 years – during which artillery dominated the battlefield as never before – New Zealand's gunners served with distinction in two world wars and two major Asian conflicts, and made numerous other military and peacetime contributions. For much of this century the Royal New Zealand Artillery was the core of New Zealand's regular army. But gunnery in this country has deeper roots nourished by older British Empire-wide traditions. When the first Royal Artillerymen arrived in New Zealand in 1845, cannon had already been used here, by both Maori and Pakeha, for decades, on land and round the coasts. And when the Royal Artillery itself was created as a standing corps in 1716, British artillery was already centuries old.

This book chronicles the use of artillery in New Zealand and by New Zealand soldiers from 1642 to 2003, and tells the story of gunners in many guises: Maori, Royal Artillerymen, regulars, volunteers, conscripts. About half the text covers New Zealand artillerymen fighting overseas, especially in the two world wars and Korea, when artillery played a crucial role thanks to technological and doctrinal developments summarised in these pages. New Zealand's gunners prepared for battle within imperial and alliance contexts that were variously enabling and constraining. This account of New Zealand's artillery corps and its performance in the field also explores what it was like to be a gunner: to train and exercise with (sometimes imaginary) guns and other corps; to fire and to come under fire; to move the guns by hand, horse, tractor or aircraft; to feel exhilaration, fear and remorse; to enjoy time out of the line. In this way it supplements the previous official and unofficial histories of campaigns and units, which cover operations in more detail.

The earliest 'artillery' was mechanical, using the spring of a bow, the counterweight of a siege engine.[1] In the modern sense of using gunpowder to propel shot, artillery originated in Europe in the fourteenth century. For the next 300 years these weapons – clumsy, immobile, expensive, almost as dangerous to operate as to face – were used strategically, to attack or defend centres of population and power; siege warfare was their raison d'être. The expense and difficulty of manufacturing them was a significant factor in the early growth of nation states. Between 1382 and 1388 alone the English Crown bought 87 cannon at the then massive cost of nearly £1800. Casting guns was a near-occult process, and early gunnery acquired a religious mystique that was enhanced by the practice of blessing them. Losing guns in battle has never been a purely military setback.[2]

Professional cadres of artillerymen appeared early in the sixteenth century. Typically, the members of London's Honourable Artillery Company, founded in 1537, were initially mainly archers. Henry VIII strengthened his status as a Renaissance prince by rapidly expanding his artillery train and encouraging a cannon-founding industry. During the reign of Elizabeth I, English cast-iron cannon became renowned. After winning the Civil War, Cromwell's Commonwealth ordered 3000 cannon from local foundries for its navy and new standing army as it moved to unite the British Isles and lay the foundations for great-power status.

The use of guns as mobile field weapons was pioneered by the Swedish artillery under Lennart Tortensson during the Thirty Years War (1618–48). The effect was mainly psychological – the difficulty of moving such heavy pieces continued to inhibit warfare until the War of the Spanish Succession (1701–14), when the Duke of Marlborough brought light artillery forward to support infantry movements. In 1685 James II had raised companies of Fusiliers to guard his artillery train (guns and engineers) – and to prevent its civilian drivers running away. In this period the artillery (the 'Scientific Corps') was the responsibility of a Board of Ordnance under a Master-General. Fortuitously, Marlborough held both this position and that of Captain-

General, the commander in the field, so it was at his initiative that a permanent artillery train was established in 1716.³ Previously artillery trains had been disbanded once wars ended, a practice shown up by the Jacobite Rebellion of 1715, which erupted too rapidly for artillery to be assembled. Marlborough's foresight bore fruit at Culloden in 1746, when devastating artillery fire ended the Second Jacobite Rebellion. Many Royal Artillery officers were promoted from the ranks, and with the founding of the Royal Military Academy at Woolwich in 1741 artillerymen became professionals in a way officers in most other corps were not.

During the Seven Years War (1756–63), Frederick the Great enhanced mobility by creating horse artillery, with crews riding on horseback or the gun-limbers rather than marching alongside. The Prussian monarch also developed the concept of indirect fire, using howitzers to attack troops hidden by landscape features. Under the direction of Napoleon Bonaparte, himself an innovative artillery officer, large batteries shattered infantry squares during the Napoleonic Wars (1796–1815), causing more than half the casualties in some battles. From 1803, shrapnel – a hollow sphere filled with shot packed around an explosive core – supplemented the less lethal established projectiles: round-shot, grape and canister. The development of rifling of gun-barrels then gave small arms greater accuracy over longer distances, allowing infantry to regain the initiative until this technology was applied successfully to artillery later in the nineteenth century.

Royal Artillerymen came to New Zealand in the 1840s armed with unreliable Congreve rockets and inaccurate muzzle-loading guns. They were technically in the service of the East India Company, whose conquest of India had recently been confirmed by two 'Sikh Wars' notable for the largest ever artillery battles between European and indigenous forces. These were near-run conflicts, but there would be no similar balance of forces in the New Zealand Wars. The most successful Maori leaders realised that their only hope was to inflict unacceptable British losses in wars of attrition. For their part, the British sent some of their best officers and men, and the latest technologies and tactics. Rifled breech-loading guns were used on land for the first time in Taranaki in 1861; and though some modern pa proved able to stand up to big guns, mortars – with their higher arc of fire – were found to be more effective.

With the colony secure internally, the settler government looked to its defence. In return for Royal Navy command of the high seas, the colonies were responsible for defending themselves against raiding vessels. This brought into play two archetypal features of imperial military organisation: volunteerism and coastal defence. The world's largest empire could not be defended by regulars alone and the post-Crimean War emphasis on part-time soldiering soon reached New Zealand. Stiffened by a small regular cadre, citizen soldiers (volunteers or sometimes conscripts) were to flesh out New Zealand's armed forces, including the more technical arms such as artillery, for the next century and a half. But coastal defence was expensive; and big guns and the technology supporting them all too soon became obsolete.

On land, rifling and the invention of successful breech-loading mechanisms enabled mobile artillery units to bring down more rapid bursts of effective fire at longer ranges in the colonial wars of the late nineteenth century. The 1880s saw two major innovations in ammunition technology. First, the replacement of black powder with 'smokeless' nitrocellulose explosive ('cordite') further increased ranges. It was harder to find an explosive more powerful than gunpowder with which to fill shells, but in 1888 British scientists discovered that melted picric acid crystals could withstand the shock of being fired from a gun. This 'Lyddite' (named for the Kent town near where it was tested) was eventually superseded by TNT, a very stable high explosive (HE) initially used in shells just before the First World War, during which HE superseded shrapnel in field artillery shells. Lyddite and TNT were particularly well suited to the purposes of medium and heavy artillery, and in the armour-piercing shells of the coastal artillery.

The second key development was hydraulic and hydro-pneumatic buffers which absorbed recoil and kept guns stable, so they did not have to be manhandled back into position after each shot. Recoil systems, quick-action breech mechanisms and fixed ammunition (with charge and shell loaded in one piece) were the major elements of the quick-firing field guns that originated with the French 75-mm gun of 1897. Once gun carriages remained stable during firing, it became practical to fit armoured shields to protect gun crews from rifle fire. But direct fire against enemy infantry would become increasingly unusual as the potential of coordinated indirect fire – 'the most important innovation in artillery practice for 300 years'[4] — was realised. The South African War (1899–1902) saw the birth of coordinated fire control by a Commander, Royal Artillery, which was to become standard practice. Though New Zealand's main contribution to this conflict was mounted riflemen, experienced volunteers joined artillery units formed in the theatre.

The increasing pre-eminence and sophistication of the artillery arm had been reflected in its numerical dominance of the regular army established by New Zealand's Defence Act of 1886. But accelerated technological innovation also brought issues of cost and obsolescence which would constrain New Zealand's use of artillery throughout the twentieth century. As the great powers stumbled towards the Great War, it was clear that New Zealand's key military contribution would be manpower: sending an expeditionary force of mounted rifleman and artillery to Europe. To meet imperial standards, the volunteers were replaced in 1911 by a Territorial Force of conscripts.

Field artillery reached its battlefield apotheosis during the First World War. The effectiveness of indirect fire was enhanced by dial sights that allowed individual guns to be aimed at targets invisible from the gun line. A revolution in doctrine, tactics and operational communications, command and control, meant massive volumes of shells could be brought down on the enemy at short notice, or to support infantry in creeping barrages. Trench mortars also came into their own, and field guns remounted on improvised carriages became the first significant anti-aircraft artillery. The importance of surveying, wire-cutting and counter-battery work were also learnt through bitter experience on the Western Front, and field telephones became indispensable. Using artillery to deliver chemical weapons added to the horrors of trench warfare. New Zealand's field and howitzer brigades, fighting alongside units of the Royal Artillery — half a million strong by 1918 — played their part in all these developments.

The British Army, like others, paid a heavy price for entering the Great War with a doctrine of taking the offensive under virtually all circumstances. No longer could specialised military education be seen as necessary only for officers, or regarded as less important than character and breeding. New Zealand sent officer cadets to the Royal Military College of Australia at Duntroon, and young officers to the School of Artillery established between the wars at Larkhill on England's Salisbury Plain; other ranks were trained at Trentham. In the 1930s artillery was mechanised: horses were replaced by tractors, trucks and purpose-built 'quads'.

Anti-aircraft artillery was refined between the wars, and during the Second World War it was aided by radar and supplemented by rockets. By 1945, anti-aircraft fire control was almost completely automated. Guns to support and destroy tanks were also developed. In mobile Second World War battles, self-propelled guns mounted on tank chassis, and radio communications, were essential. Multiple rocket launchers came into their own on the Eastern Front. The Second New Zealand Expeditionary Force's field, anti-aircraft and anti-tank regiments again operated within a wider British Army context. During the war of movement in North Africa, they made significant contributions to Eighth Army tactics. In anticipation of New Zealand Army experience later in the century, the Third Division in the Pacific was integrated into a much larger American military effort, and applied their skills in a jungle setting. By the time coast gunners at home received their new weapons the Japanese threat they were supposed to repel had receded.

Though it has retained its intrinsic function of concentrating fire at short notice in support of infantry and armour, since 1945 artillery has been joined in this role by increasingly sophisticated aircraft and missiles. Coastal artillery was rendered obsolete by the new scale of threat from the air. Though the Korean War generally reprised the weapons and tactical doctrines of the Second World War, for New Zealand it marked two shifts in emphasis: towards alliance with the United States, and towards making proportionately larger artillery contributions to the localised conflicts in which the Cold War sporadically turned hot. This partly reflected a post-1945 political imperative to make a visible (and effective) contribution without suffering substantial casualties. Field guns and frigates were essential to this: both were deployed in Korea, the latter in Malaya, the former in South Vietnam. Medium artillery could not be retained because of its prohibitive expense for a small nation that was becoming increasingly independent of the great powers as the Cold War thawed.

As ever, armed conflict in the twenty-first century will be fuelled by both ideas and economics, and facilitated by technological innovation. This may be an era of small wars and peacekeeping missions, but the globalisation of communications poses new threats. The 'war on terror' has its changing front lines, but there are no longer any truly secure rear areas. In these circumstances, factors such as civilian morale may be of unparalleled significance. Yet the traditional military role of protecting a country's civilians is timeless. There will always be a call for soldiers on foot – to patrol, occupy, consolidate – and hence a need for artillery (in whatever form) to support and protect them. In providing such support and protection around the world, New Zealand's gunners have lived up to the regiment's battle honour, 'Ubique' (everywhere).[5]

Glossary and Abbreviations	
AA, 'ack-ack'	anti-aircraft
(A)QMG	(Assistant) Quartermaster-General
ATL	Alexander Turnbull Library, Wellington
BC	Battery Commander
Beach platform	platforms on which field guns were mounted to improvise fixed coastal defences
BL	breech-loading
BLHP	breech-loading gun on hydro-pneumatic mounting
BOP	Battery Observation Post
cal(s)	calibres(s)
case shot	bullets or other small metal objects packed in a thin metal case which disintegrates on firing
CMT	Compulsory Military Training
CO	commanding officer
CRA	Commander, Royal Artillery
enfilade	fire directed along a line, e.g. a trench
examination battery	battery positioned to intercept unidentified ships entering a port
FPDA	Five Power Defence Arrangements
HAA	heavy anti-aircraft
HE	high explosive

HEAT	high explosive anti-tank ammunition
HEP	high explosive, plastic
HESH	high explosive squash head ammunition
hutchie	hut improvised from materials such as shell cases, cartridge cases and timber
infantillery	gunners serving as infantry for want of guns
LAA	light anti-aircraft
LAD	Light Aid Detachment
LCI	landing craft, infantry
MDS	Main Dressing Station
ML	muzzle-loading
NCO	non-commissioned officer
OCTU	Officer Cadet Training Unit
OP	Observation Post
pr	pounder
premature	explosion in the breech or barrel as a gun is loaded or fired
proof	test-fire guns
QF	quick-firing
RBL	rifled breech-loading
RHA	Royal Horse Artillery (UK)
RMT	Reserve Mechanical Transport (Company)
RNZA	Royal (Regiment of) New Zealand Artillery
shaft-draught	system for moving guns in which a horse is harnessed between two shafts attached to the front of the limber
shorts	shells which fall short of their target
swivel gun	a small gun able to traverse an arc; often used at sea
WAAC	(New Zealand) Women's Auxiliary Army Corps
YMCA	Young Men's Christian Association

1

Early Artillery in New Zealand

The story of artillery in New Zealand is as old as that of Europeans in these islands. This chapter covers the period up to the end of the nineteenth century. Cannon arrived by sea from Europe but were soon dragged across the beach, adopted by Maori for Maori ends. Once New Zealand became a British colony, cannon became instruments of imperial subjugation, though the locals proved unexpectedly adept at countering them. When the Maori were finally defeated, the great guns were turned around to face the ocean and a possible new generation of European invaders. Even after this threat proved chimerical many Volunteers spent much of their leisure time training enthusiastically to meet it, motivated by patriotism and camaraderie.

First Contact
On 19 December 1642, Abel Janszoon Tasman's Dutch East India Company ships *Heemskerck* and *Zeehaen* struck Ngati Tumatakokiri waka with canister shot after the fatal skirmish in Golden Bay that decided him against landing.[1] James Cook's Royal Navy bark *Endeavour* carried 4-pr carriage guns and swivel guns on its first voyage to the Pacific, and fired them several times to terrify threatening Maori in 1769. In the same year Jean François Marie de Surville had a Ngati Kahu chief 'in ecstasies' by preparing and firing one of the French warship *St Jean Baptiste*'s 36 guns. In 1772, the *Mascarin* and *Marquis de Castries* fired shots into Nga Puhi pa and sank waka in the Bay of Islands after their commander Marion du Fresne and many of his crew were killed by local Maori.

Ships' guns were fired often in the subsequent decades – usually to demonstrate European power, sometimes with lethal intent. In 1815 the Reverend Samuel Marsden threatened to bombard Rangihoua when he was prevented from visiting his new mission's dying protector, the Nga Puhi chief Ruatara. After James Busby was appointed British Resident in New Zealand, imperial authority was asserted more strongly. In March 1834 a British warship trained its guns on a Bay of Islands pa during a property dispute. Six months later, HMS *Alligator* and the barque *Harriet* bombarded a Taranaki pa with round shot and rockets for three hours during a mission to rescue a captive Pakeha family. A week later, a shore party dragged a 6-pr naval gun nearly 2 miles to fire at a pa. This was the first significant formal British use of artillery in New Zealand. The following year, Additional British Resident (and Hokianga timber magnate) Thomas McDonnell used his private eleven-gun battery to foil a kidnap attempt by Maori allied to rival settlers. With no central authority, other settlers also took precautions. In 1835, for example, Otago whalers Edward and Joseph Weller armed their ship with swivel guns. In the 1830s, several Pakeha-Maori traders mounted gun batteries at their trading stations. Maketu's Phillip Tapsell boasted a battery of twelve carronades, but these failed to prevent his trading station being sacked in 1836.

MAORI ARTILLERY

During the Musket Wars of the 1820s and 1830s, many iwi obtained heavy weapons in their ceaseless quest for mana and the lead in local arms races.[2] The first were acquired by plunder. In 1827, Nga Puhi leader Hongi Hika used cannon taken from the *Boyd* in 1809 against the Whangaroa people who had originally appropriated them. Two years later, carronades and swivel guns captured from the trading vessel *Haweis* were used by Ngati Awa to successfully defend Whakatane against Ngai Te Rangi attack. The Ngai Tahu chief Tuhawaiki is said to have stolen a heavy gun from a European vessel in 1824.

In the 1830s, cannon were acquired through trade. James Clendon paid for a Bay of Islands property in 1830 in part with a carronade. Under attack by Ngati Toa in the early 1830s, Ngai Tahu exchanged land for arms, including two 12-pr carronades. Land sales subsequently financed other Ngai Tahu cannon purchases. For his part, Ngati Toa chief Te Rauparaha apparently exchanged Cloudy Bay land he had taken from Ngai Tahu for an 18-pr carronade in 1832. In the same year, the Pakeha-Maori Dicky Barrett and Jacky Love were among those manning several small cannon and a swivel gun which helped Te Atiawa to repel a Waikato attack on Ngamotu. Nga Puhi brought ten 'great guns' and an English gunner on an expedition against Ngai Te Rangi at Tauranga, buying more from Tapsell on arrival; the defenders also had guns. The trade was not entirely one-way. In 1835, Te Atiawa gave two cannon to the captain of the *Lord Rodney* as part-payment for enabling their invasion of the Chatham Islands. Iwi also traded cannon with each other. Wanganui Maori are said to have acquired a gun, a keg of powder and 20 cannonballs from Te Rangihaeata at Kapiti in exchange for four canoeloads of pigs.

Some heavy guns became spoils of war because they were difficult to move quickly. Occasionally they were spiked to prevent use by an enemy. By 1839, 37 chiefs had between them acquired about 80 ships' cannon, most deployed in the new musket/gunfighter pa that had made inter-iwi warfare prohibitively costly in both lives and resources. Cannon also added mana on solemn occasions, being fired at tangi and haihunga (exhumation ceremonies).[3] Their practical value was less certain, given their immobility, slow rate of fire, the difficulty of obtaining ammunition (frequent use of stones or scrap iron as scattershot damaged them) and the need for training in their use. Wanganui's gun, for instance, apparently toppled over the first time it was fired and was left where it lay.

In the early years of British colonisation, artillery reassured settlers fearful of attack by Maori. In March 1840, New Zealand Company ships fired cannon during a parade in Wellington Harbour to demonstrate who was in charge. After the Wairau incident in June 1843, in which Ngati Toa wiped out a party of Nelson settlers who unwisely attempted to enforce a dubious land purchase, two Company 18-prs were dragged up the hill above the junction of Willis Street and Lambton Quay in Wellington, and an earthwork fort with 18-pr carronades was built on the future site of Christ Church Cathedral, Nelson. More positions were constructed in Wellington after Kororareka, in the Bay of Islands, was sacked in 1845.[4]

THE NORTHERN WAR (1845–46)

Governor Robert FitzRoy's small military force had little artillery but was backed up by the personnel and guns of visiting Royal Navy ships.[5] When Kororareka was attacked by Nga Puhi in March 1845, its defences included four land-based cannon (one of which was captured) and the eighteen guns of the sloop *Hazard*, which bombarded the town after it fell. The May attack on Hone Heke's Puketutu pa was supported by the spectacular but ineffective fire of two naval Congreve rocket tubes.

The remainder of the campaign saw big guns deployed with mixed results. At Ohaeawai, 400 unconcentrated rounds delivered over a week by a cobbled-together battery manned by a scratch force of largely untrained gunners did little damage and caused few casualties among defenders sheltering in bomb-proof covered pits.[6] The artillerymen also attempted chemical warfare, constructing from old shell cases 'stench balls' containing a 'poisonous substance' that was expected to 'deprive the rebels of all animation'.[7] Despite this innovation, Nga Puhi routed a storming party, causing heavy casualties. The pa's defences included four old iron ship's guns which fired scrap metal. There were no Royal Artillery in Australasia, but a temporary corps of soldiers drilled to use guns was formed in Sydney. By October, nineteen volunteer artillerymen were serving with Colonel Henry Despard's forces.

MOVING THE GUNS

In the 1840s one artillerymen thought New Zealand 'the worst country I ever saw for field operations', with its almost impenetrable forest, 'precipitous' hills, and lack of roads. On one journey the Deputy Assistant Quartermaster-General encountered an artillery officer – 'the most travel-worn object one can imagine, his clothes in tatters and cased in mud from head to foot'. His 'bush costume' comprised 'a blue serge shirt, coarse trowsers, hobnail boots, and a cabbage-leaf hat or cap'.[8]

It took great effort in 1846 to haul two small mortars up to Horokiri Hill, near Porirua:

> [E]very man carr[ied] three shells and a fifteen-pound bag of powder;... taking it ... turn about ... to carry the heavy parts of the apparatus.... We were obliged to make frequent halts, and had the greatest difficulty in

ascending some of the steep and slippery hills, the men not unfrequently coming down with their loads, which ... gave us the extra work of taking them up a second time. We had a few shot-boxes of shells, some of which went to pieces from the repeated tumbles; and we had to divide them amongst us, carrying them in the bosoms of our blue frocks.

Moving bigger guns was a nightmare. During the Northern War, rain 'so churned up the single track that it took all morning to cover [5 miles], with soldiers and sailors pulling on drag ropes to supplement the efforts of the bullocks harnessed to the drays on which the guns were placed'. Negotiating the forests below Ruapekapeka 'required between fifty and sixty men to each gun..., on account of the heavy trees it was necessary to cut down in making the road, and the steepness of the hills'.

The return trip was little easier. Most of the men carried a shot each as well as their knapsacks; others lugged boxes of shells in pairs, or mortars in groups of four. One man lost part of his leg when the gun carriage his section was dragging ran over him. An officer had to set fire to fern near the ammunition to persuade the troops to keep moving. Spirits rations helped them endure this twelve-hour march.

The invasion of Waikato in the 1860s posed different problems. During General Duncan Cameron's advance up the Waipa River in January 1864, the guns were taken apart at Ngaruawahia, shipped to Whatawhata and then reassembled. Bullocks were more useful than horses on unmetalled roads, and easier to feed. It took two days for six-strong bullock teams to drag three 12-prs the 12 miles to Te Rore along 'narrow paths, and roads hurriedly made by the engineers [with] any number of steep ascents and descents.... [O]ften the guns were in imminent danger of being upset down places from which it would have taken hours to extricate them'. Transport shortages meant spare wheels could not be carried.

Temporary bridges over creeks were cobbled together from any materials to hand. The guns had to be manhandled over these bridges and the more difficult pinches by men also carrying a blanket, carbine and change of clothes. After dark on the second day they reached a wide creek with soft banks. Sailors helped the gunners to dismantle the guns and lug them across a canoe doing duty as a bridge. After reassembling the guns they trekked 3 miles more to camp.

Travelling by sea was also hazardous. Three 12-prs were shipped from Onehunga to New Plymouth in March 1863. Guns could be taken to pieces. The horses had to be placed in slings, driven into the water and towed 500 yards by boats to the ship, where they were hoisted on board and stowed away in the hold or on deck. After the ship anchored about three-quarters of a mile from the beach at the open roadstead of New Plymouth, the horses were hoisted overboard and towed ashore by surfboats, two to each boat. Some panicked, and one drowned.[9]

In November 1845, New Zealand's first detachment of regular artillerymen arrived – a dozen men of the East India Company's artillery. It took them more than a month to haul thirteen pieces (including three 32-prs weighing 1½ tons and several Coehorn mortars)[10] up to Nga Puhi leader Kawiti's new fighting pa, Ruapekapeka. Kawiti had a 12-pr and a 4-pr, but their usefulness, as at Ohaeawai, was limited by a shortage of projectiles. After Ruapekapeka's outer defences were damaged by a bombardment during which Kawiti's larger gun was disabled by a direct hit, Nga Puhi abandoned the pa. With the Northern War now effectively over, Kawiti acknowledged the significance of British artillery: 'had they nothing but muskets, the same as ourselves, I should [still] be in my *pa*'.[11] As in all the inter-racial conflicts of this period, there was a fundamental asymmetry in the resources available to the protagonists.

No. 2 Company, 6 Battalion Royal Artillery arrived via Sydney on the steamship HMS *Driver* after the war ended.[12] During fighting with Ngati Toa around Wellington in the winter of 1846, they converted a ship's longboat into a gunboat by improvising a breastwork of bedding and mounting a 12-pr carronade and a brass gun. The artillerymen later bombarded Te Rangihaeata's position in the Horokiri Valley at long range with two small mortars, to little effect. In 1847 they saw action with two 12-prs at Wanganui.

Further Royal Artillery detachments arrived during the 1850s; that from 3 Company, 7 Battalion in 1859 was accompanied by women and children.[13] This was a decade of uneasy peace during which artillerymen drilled endlessly and filled in time lacquering gun barrels and painting field carriages. A trial using pohutukawa to make howitzer carriages proved unsuccessful.[14] Officers studied fighting pa, sometimes in the field. In Taranaki in 1858, Sergeant William Marjouram judged that 'when artillery is brought to bear upon these defences, they [will] soon give way'.[15] He was about to be proved wrong.

THE TARANAKI WAR (1860–61)

The first Taranaki War marked the beginning of the main phase of the New Zealand Wars. The guns then in Royal Artillery service – as they had been since the Napoleonic Wars – were smooth-bore 6-, 9- and 24-prs, Coehorns and Royal Mortars, supplemented by naval 68-prs.[16] Tactical thinking initially failed to keep pace with the 1860s revolution in the design of field artillery. Smooth-bored muzzle-loading cannon of limited range and accuracy were superseded by rifled breech-loaders such as the Armstrongs first used in Taranaki in 1861. These new weapons would eventually have a devastating effect on infantry. In New Zealand, however, the mixture of new and old weapons was used in a traditional way: relatively close-range bombardments of fortified positions (the strengths and weaknesses of which were often disguised) intended to soften up defences and defenders before an infantry assault. As the action at Gate Pa was to show in 1864, this process was no more guaranteed to work against Maori than it was in Europe.

The Taranaki War began with a howitzer bombardment of Kingi's 'L-pa' at Te Kohia in March 1860. The artillery was reinforced by a detachment of 3 Battery, 12 Brigade in April. Two howitzers were used to soften up a purpose-built Te Atiawa/Ngati Maniapoto position at Puketakauere in June. The attack was repulsed with heavy casualties because the obvious stockade served mainly to divert attention from the key defences – rifle pits roofed with split timber covered with earth and fern, under which the defenders were safe from all but direct hits. The infantry's retreat was covered by the howitzers, which discouraged pursuit with case-shot.[17]

After further abortive attempts to provoke a decisive battle (and much tedious and occasionally dangerous escort duty by the artillery), General Thomas Pratt's troops embarked on a classic siege-warfare technique: digging protected trenches towards the enemy's lines until the latter had to be evacuated. At Waitara, eight redoubts were built at intervals along these saps. By March 1861, some of the cannon fire from these was being provided by three rifled Armstrong guns which, along with four heavy mortars, had just arrived from Woolwich with Captain Henry Mercer's 3 (soon restyled C) Battery of 4 Brigade Royal Artillery.[18] This was the first use of breech-loading, composite-cast artillery against a trench system.[19] A few days later, with the British sap about to reach the crucial Te Arei pa, a truce was negotiated.

THE WAIKATO WAR (1863–64)

Determined to break Maori resistance, Governor George Grey assembled an army that eventually numbered 12,000,[20] 450 of whom would be Royal artillerymen. The units involved were C Battery, 4 Brigade, and 3 Battery, 12

Brigade (the renamed 3 Company, 7 Battalion), which was replaced in 1864 by I Battery, 4 Brigade.[21] In preparation for an invasion of Waikato, artillerymen built roads, bridges and redoubts, carted provisions (these duties continued throughout the campaign) and practised bombarding model pa erected at Point Chevalier from plans made during the Northern War. Useful breaches proved difficult to make.[22] The gunners and drivers of Captain Mercer's C Battery also drilled as cavalry. In autumn 1863 they were sent to Taranaki but saw no action. General Cameron's first New Zealand action, the capture of an incomplete pa at Katikara on 4 June, was notable for the despatch of guns and ammunition from New Plymouth several hours ahead to avoid delaying the main body of troops.

The long-awaited invasion of Waikato began in July. The King Movement forces mounted three old ship's guns in their first completed defensive line at Meremere. These weapons, acquired from a trader in the 1830s, had been hauled and rafted from the coast: a former East India Company gunner had apparently provided the instructions for their use. An effective bombardment could have sunk steamers and delayed the British advance, but the guns' age and lack of shot prevented this. A direct hit on the gunboat *Pioneer* by a 7-pound grocer's weight damaged only a cask of beef. General Cameron's resources at Meremere included several 40-pr Armstrongs firing short-fuse shells which burst in the air over the defences.

The first major battle, an attack on a second defensive line at Rangiriri in November 1863, began with a bombardment by three field pieces and the 12-pr Armstrong guns of two gunboats which did little damage to the earthworks. In one of several unsuccessful assaults on the central redoubt, 36 Royal Artillerymen armed with revolvers suffered six casualties. Some of the survivors then threw shells over a high parapet after lighting improvised fuses. Two artillerymen were awarded VCs.[23] After Rangiriri was captured the Armstrongs were barged upriver to Ngaruawahia. The Kingitanga's next defensive line included two old ship's guns which had been carried overland from Kawhia many years earlier, then canoed to Te Rore when Paterangi was fortified. Loaded with pieces of bullock chain and scraps of iron and secured to tree trunks sunk in the ground with aka vines, the guns were not fired because Cameron, at night, outflanked the formidable Paterangi defences – judged by one officer to be stronger and more skilfully designed than the Redan in the Crimea.

The attack on Hairini soon afterwards was notable for the unusual firing of 6-prs over the heads of advancing infantry. The Royal Artillery Mounted Corps then 'pursued as far as the ground admitted, and sabred some few of the enemy'.[24] The final set-piece battle in Waikato followed the Kingite decision in March 1864 to fortify a site at Orakau. A bombardment by 6-pr Armstrong guns made little impression on these earthworks, and howitzers or mortars could not be brought up in time. Shells were again thrown by hand into the pa, and the mounted corps pursued escaping Maori.

With the Kingitanga preparing another defence line in the upper Waikato, a strong British force under Cameron moved to the Bay of Plenty to disrupt the flow of supplies and reinforcements.[25] On 29 April they attacked Ngai Te Rangi forces entrenched in the Gate Pa, Tauranga, after a concentrated artillery bombardment by eight mortars, two 24-pr howitzers, two 32-pr naval cannon and five Armstrong guns. One of the last was 'probably the heaviest gun ever used on shore against tribesmen', a 110-pr mounted on a ship's traversing platform. After a day firing heavily at close range onto a small target, the guns had made a breach and flattened the visible defences. But because of their flat trajectory many of the shells had overshot the pa; its internal structure remained intact and at most fifteen of the garrison had been killed. The remainder reappeared 'as if vomited from the bowels of the earth' to rout the 300-strong assault party, which became disorientated in the smoke-filled tunnels and suffered 100 casualties. This stunning defeat was avenged within two months at nearby Te Ranga, where Ngai Te Rangi were surprised in an incomplete pa.

Imperial troops were redeployed to south Taranaki in early 1865 to oppose adherents of the new Pai Marire creed. To improve mobility Cameron took into the field only two 6-pr Armstrongs, which could be manhandled over the many steep-sided stream banks.[26] A year later, his successor General Trevor Chute attacked south Taranaki iwi with a force that included 33 Royal Artillery and three small field guns. Although efforts to have an artillery corps included in the Colonial Defence Force had been rejected, its successor, the Armed Constabulary, included artillery detachments. These were armed with the small field guns that the British batteries had left in the colony on their departure in 1866. In the developing tradition of colonial improvisation, the Armed Constabulary's artillerymen also acted as infantry, labourers – building roads through the North Island 'bush', and the barracks and stables at their redoubts – and farmers at remote posts. At Taupo, their main occupation was road-building, at which they became expert.[27]

COLONIAL ARTILLERY IN THE NEW ZEALAND WARS

Auckland Coastguard and Onehunga Naval Volunteers saw action in the Firth of Thames and on the southern shore of Manukau Harbour in 1863, apparently fighting as infantry.[28] Colonial and pro-government Maori (kupapa) forces bore the brunt of fighting against 'rebels' from 1865 as the colony implemented a policy of self-reliance. They mostly, at least in theory, adopted 'bush-scouring' techniques which capitalised on the increased reliability and range of breech-loading rifles and carbines. There was little scope for artillery in the bush. At Opotiki in spring 1865, however, Whakatohea emplaced and loaded – but did not fire – an old ship's cannon against a colonial/kupapa force sent to avenge the murder of the missionary Carl Sylvius Völkner. The naval 6-pr employed by their opponents was scarcely more sophisticated: it 'made a wild screeching noise as its charge of chain-shot and bits of old iron flew over the heads of the troops'.[29] In November 1865, a 6-pr firing salmon tins filled with shrapnel encouraged the surrender of the Pai Marire defenders of a pa at Waerenga-a-Hika in Poverty Bay.

Most of the battles against Titokowaru and Te Kooti were also fought in places inaccessible for artillery, which neither Maori leader possessed. After the colonials' defeat at Moturoa by Titokowaru in November 1868, Armstrong guns were brought out of the Wairoa redoubt to cover the retreat.[30] In January 1869 a Coehorn mortar, conveyed from Gisborne with great difficulty, bombarded Te Kooti's hilltop position at Ngatapa, apparently inflicting many casualties. Firing at a high fixed angle (45°), this was much more effective than the Armstrongs against well-dug-in opponents. In February 1869, light Armstrongs and Coehorns bombarded Titokowaru's formidable pa at Tauranga-ika, to little effect.[31]

COASTAL DEFENCES: THE 1850s AND 1860s

As fighting against Maori wound down in the early 1870s, military and political attention shifted to the defence of the colony against external attack.[32] The main responsibility for protecting New Zealand against this unlikely possibility lay with the Royal Navy. Five guns were stored at Auckland's Point Britomart by 1842, when a salute was fired after Governor William Hobson's death. In the early 1850s, the colony's only land defences were eight 24-prs, a 32-pr and a 12-pr which had been mounted at Point Britomart during the Northern War. In 1852, the British Army officer commanding Auckland's artillery detachment considered that a raid by an enemy frigate could be repulsed only if two more batteries of heavy guns were emplaced on the North Shore. At Wellington, a battery on Pipitea Point would protect the inner harbour; guns at the heads would be too vulnerable to capture.

From 1854, it was clear that any such works would have to be funded by the new settler government; then Britain would supply the guns (though this promise proved difficult to keep). During the Crimean War (1854–56), earthworks were erected to protect the Point Britomart batteries. The need for more batteries on the Waitemata Harbour was reaffirmed, but they were too expensive. As war between Britain and France seemed likely in the late 1850s, the resident Royal Engineers officer recommended positioning new coastal artillery batteries in refurbished fortifications, and creating volunteer artillery, engineer and rifle corps to man them. For the next two decades this pattern would be repeated: perceived external threat, assessment of defence needs which were rejected as too expensive, and the end of the 'war scare'. The clearest threat to New Zealand's security still seemed to come from within. In addition, innovations such as rifled guns and iron-clad warships were bringing the effectiveness of heavy guns into question, and underwater mines might even make them obsolete.

RUSSIAN SCARES: 1870–85

By 1870, the guns at Point Britomart had been dismantled, and the colony was defended only by two 40-pr Armstrongs mounted on Auckland's North Head. (One was destroyed when its breech block blew out in 1878; the other remained in service into the twentieth century.)[33] In the early 1870s several experts recommended differing combinations of big guns, mines, gunboats and torpedoes. Nothing was done, even after Auckland's '*Kaskowiski*' hoax in 1873 drew attention to the colony's vulnerability to Russian raiders.[34]

By the time Britain seemed likely to be drawn into the Russo-Turkish War in early 1878, New Zealand was linked to 'Home' by telegraph. The immediacy of ominous news heightened fears in a colony still without big guns. In May, George Grey (now Premier) accepted British advice to obtain 22 7-inch and 64-pr guns to protect the four main centres, at a cost (including the necessary works) of £44,000. The war scare was over by the time the guns arrived, and they went into storage. The focus of the force then shifted to south Taranaki, where fighting against the Maori passive resistance movement based at Parihaka seemed imminent. The field force there was issued with two mortars.[35]

Finding trained men to work the big guns and protect them from attack would be difficult. The New Zealand Constabulary Force, formed in 1877 by combining the Armed Constabulary with the civil police forces of the former provinces, had a 320-strong field force, but this remained focused on suppressing Maori unrest. If the new guns had been emplaced in 1878, they would have been manned by partially trained and weakly coordinated members of the Volunteer Force.

In 1880, Colonel Peter Scratchley produced one of a series of reports on New Zealand's defences. Deciding that any attack was likely to be made by only one or two cruisers, opposed by at best a similar Royal Navy force, he proposed land batteries at the four main centres, 'and possibly Invercargill', which would operate 'in combination with offensive and defensive torpedoes' (torpedo boats and mines) and be protected by 'a nucleus of permanently enrolled men … supplemented by a sufficient force to complete the gun detachments and garrison the works at the time of the attack'. Twenty-five men of the Reserve Branch of the New Zealand Constabulary Force, appropriately trained, would provide this nucleus in each main centre, supplemented by a 100-strong naval brigade. The guns would be the 22 already in the colony.[36]

Little happened initially, apart from the ordering of four torpedo boats and the establishment of an artillery depot at Mount Cook, Wellington in 1882. After a leading defence expert, Sir William Jervois, became Governor

Weapons – Coast Defence

Muzzle-loading was the age-old way to get the propellant charge and round (in that order) into a gun. As calibres increased, charges grew in size and cast-iron guns were not strong enough to withstand the pressures created. Spurred by the Crimean War, Sir W.G. Armstrong developed a breech-loading mechanism. The first, a 40-pr, was introduced in 1860. But the breech block tended to blow out and Britain returned to muzzle-loading, introducing the 64-pr and 7-inch RML guns in 1865. In 1878 – the last year they were made – New Zealand bought this style of muzzle-loading weapons. The rifled barrel sat in an iron carriage that would slide when the gun was fired on 'dwarf' central pivot traversing platforms. Recoil was inhibited by friction plates and a hydraulic buffer cylinder.

Name	RML 64-pr 64 cwt Mk III	RML 7 in 7 tons Mk IV
Entered NZ service	1878	1878
Role	coast defence	coast defence
Calibre	6.3 in	7 in
Range	4000 yds	5500 yds
Weight	3.2 ton barrel	7 ton barrel
Projectile	65 lb, 10 lb charge	112 lb, 30 lb charge
Remarks	This type of gun fired common, AP or segmented projectiles, using separately loaded bag charges. Mounted in the forts from 1885, it was declared obsolete in 1904 but was still being used for drill in the 1910s.	

The term 'BL' originally distinguished breech-loading from muzzle-loading (ML) guns. After muzzle-loaders were finally dispensed with the abbreviation was applied to guns in which the charge was loaded separately from (and after) the shell ('bag-loading'), to distinguish them from those with one-piece ammunition. The bag containing the propellant charge was made of cloth and designed to be completely consumed in the explosion that pushed the projectile out of the barrel. When the British Committee on Ordnance recommended a return to breech-loading in 1879, Sir W.G. Armstrong offered a BL 6-inch design, the first gun in service with an interrupted screw breech, which was accepted in 1882. New Zealand ordered these and the scaled-up 8-inch version four years later. Both were mounted on hydro-pneumatic carriages which 'disappeared' into a shielded pit for reloading. They were made by Armstrong's Elswick Ordnance Works near Newcastle.

Name	Ordnance BL 6-inch EOC 5 tons	BL 8-inch EOC 13 tons
Entered NZ service	1886	1886
Role	coast defence	coast defence
Calibre	6 in	8 in
Range	8800 yds	9000 yds
Weight	4.45 ton barrel plus hydro-pneumatic 'disappearing' mount (14.3 tons)	13.28 ton barrel
Projectile	100 lb Common, AP	180 lb Common, AP
Remarks	By modern standards these were cumbersome weapons, but they were revolutionary compared with the muzzle-loaders purchased a decade earlier. With 15° of elevation, these were obsolete by 1914, but some of the 6-inch version remained in service until 1943.	

There were quick-firing (QF) guns in New Zealand forts from 1886, and by the end of the century quick-firing field artillery was also in service. QF guns had light and simple breech mechanisms that could be unlocked and opened for the round to be loaded in a single rapid movement. The breech was sealed by the base of the cartridge, which contained the propellant charge. The cartridge was usually integral with the projectile (i.e. fixed or one-piece ammunition), though some QF guns later used by New Zealanders, such as the 4.5-inch howitzer and 25-pr gun, used a separate brass cartridge that was loaded second. QF guns were quick to traverse (or lay) and had built-in (or on-board) recoil systems that brought them back for the next round quickly. The QF concept applied to the lighter guns in the coastal batteries, the 6- and later 12-pr Nordenfelts; the heavier 6-inch and 8-inch were BL guns. The Nordenfelt design originated in Sweden but was manufactured under licence by Britain (and Spain). Both had 20° of elevation.

Name	QF 6-pr Nordenfelt Mk I	QF 12-pr 12-cwt Mk I
Entered NZ service	1886	1898
Role	coast defence & field gun	coast defence
Calibre	2.24 in, 42 cals	3 in, 40 cals
Range	4500 yds	8000 yds
Weight	3355 lb	9240 lb
Projectile	6 lb with 8 oz charge	12.5 lb with 2 lb charge
Remarks	The 6-pr QF guns remained in service until the Second World War, the 12-pr until the late 1950s. The 6-pr also had a field carriage. A few Hotchkiss 6-pr QF guns, with very similar specifications, were also in use.	

Officers and NCOs with their guns at Fort Britomart, Auckland, 1860s. Russian smooth-bore 18-pr at left, 5.5-inch Royal Mortars in front.
Graham Birch collection.

in 1883, Colonel Henry Cautley was appointed to take charge of defence works.[37] The two-stage programme Cautley promulgated in January 1885 was overtaken two months later by the last and greatest Russian scare. The bulk of the field force was taken off roadmaking for 'training in garrison gun-drill, torpedo instruction, and the formation of earthworks in connection with the defences at the principal ports'. The colony thus acquired its first full-time artillerymen ('an excellent … force of 120 men', including 86 transferees from the field force), equipped with the guns procured in 1878, which were at last being mounted under Cautley's supervision. (In some cases these improvised earthworks would hinder the construction of permanent works on the same sites.) Furthermore, 'a complete armament of guns of the very newest type' (thirteen 6-inch and ten 8-inch breech-loaders) were ordered from Armstrong's – though, as the war scare abated, New Zealand's Agent-General in London was told there was no rush. With eight converted 64-prs also sent over from Sydney, the harbour defence budget for 1885/6 was a whopping £200,000. By autumn 1886, the artillery corps, despite having been 'chiefly employed on [constructing] the works since last spring', was 'competent to train Artillery Volunteers to the use of garrison guns'.[38]

Armed Constabulary gunners drill with 64-prs at Mt Cook barracks, Wellington, 1880s.
1/1-025889, Alexander Turnbull Library, Wellington.

Since mid-1885 the colony had possessed a 'rudimentary' defence system: four guns on North Head and two on Resolution Point (Parnell) in Auckland; four on the Miramar Peninsula and two at Kaiwharawhara in Wellington; three at Lyttelton; and three at Taiaroa Head and two at Ocean Beach in Dunedin. Emplacements for the new muzzle-loaders, mounted on disappearing carriages, were constructed from early 1886 under the supervision of Cautley's successor, Major E.M. Tudor Boddam. Over the next two years, two 6-inch guns were emplaced on Takapuna Point in Auckland; one on the Miramar Peninsula and two at Ngauranga in Wellington; and two at Ocean Beach, plus a 7-inch gun at Taiaroa Head, in Dunedin. A fort at Ripapa Island in Lyttelton Harbour would contain two 8-inch and two 6-inch guns.

Artillery Volunteers

By 1886 New Zealand had had artillery volunteers for a quarter of a century.[39] The concept of volunteering had been revived in Britain after the Crimean War. As tension in Taranaki grew, the Militia Act 1858 provided for the formation of volunteer units. The number of volunteer companies grew from three in early 1860 to 132 in 1872. Thirty-two were formed in 1860 alone. An attempt to raise a volunteer artillery corps in Auckland in 1858 was stymied by a lack of guns; it became the Auckland Volunteer Rifle Company instead. Naval artillery corps were raised in Auckland and Nelson in 1860. Naval artillery units had naval ranks and uniforms, made use of small boats and trained with naval personnel, but in other respects resembled shore-based artillery volunteers. The Auckland Volunteer Coast Guard and Nelson Volunteer Naval Artillery soon lapsed (at least as artillery) because of a shortage of guns or inefficient administration. Christchurch had a volunteer artillery unit by 1862, and the Lyttelton Volunteer Artillery was established in 1865.[40]

The Volunteer Force Act 1865 provided explicitly for artillery units. This and a new Militia Act were the legal basis for the defence of the colony by citizen soldiers once imperial troops were withdrawn, while the Armed Constabulary Act 1867 provided for professional soldier/police. All three bodies (the militia effectively lapsed in the early 1870s) were designed to protect Pakeha settlers against Maori.

> ### Weapons – Field Artillery
>
> The first guns used in the New Zealand Wars were cast-iron smooth-bores, but by 1860 a new generation of built-up rifled guns had appeared. Sir W.G. Armstrong had perfected the technique of winding white-hot wrought iron around a cylindrical rod to form a very strong barrel. Rifling imparted a spin that gave the shell greater range and accuracy. Shells were coated in lead to conform to the rifling grooves, and given the elongated shape that has been used ever since. Though the breech mechanism was prone to fail, the Armstrong field guns served well in New Zealand, the 12-pr for more than 40 years. The term RBL was introduced for the first generation of rifled breech-loading guns after a second generation, known as BL guns, appeared in the 1880s (by which time all guns were rifled).
>
> | Name | RBL 6-pr | RBL 9-pr | RBL 12-pr 8 cwt |
> | --- | --- | --- | --- |
> | Entered NZ service | 1861 | 1886 | 1861 |
> | Role | light field | light field | medium field |
> | Calibre | 2.5 in | 3 in | 3 in; 28 cals |
> | Range | 3000 yds | 3000 yds | 3400 yds |
> | Weight | 3 cwt barrel | 6 cwt barrel | 8 cwt barrel |
> | Projectile | 6 lb | 9 lb | 12 lb |
> | Charge | 12 oz | 18 oz | 24 oz |
> | Remarks | Fired common, shrapnel or segment projectiles, using separately loaded bag charges. The 6- and 12-prs were in service from the New Zealand Wars; from 1886 eighteen old 9-prs were purchased to arm volunteer artillery corps. | | |

By mid-1866, New Zealand's 2817 volunteers included 80 navals in Auckland, and a total of 135 artillerymen in Nelson, Canterbury and Otago.[41] In 1868, the Auckland Navals drilled with two 24-pr howitzers, while the Dunedin Artillery had three Armstrong guns. Wellington and Lyttelton also now had volunteer artillery companies.[42] Over the next decade corps were raised in Thames, Gisborne, Napier, Westport, Timaru, Oamaru, Port Chalmers, Invercargill and Queenstown. By 1871, artillery (including naval) units had 789 of the colony's 6367 adult volunteers (12.4 per cent), the bulk of whom would always be riflemen, who were much easier to equip and train.

Dunedin's L Battery gunners drill on a 7-inch/7-ton RML gun mounted on a centre pivot; Saddle Battery, Taiaroa Head, c.1890.
Port Chalmers Museum.

The artillery component would grow steadily, however.

Volunteer numbers fluctuated – and units appeared and disappeared – in response to perceived threats, conditions of service, economic circumstances, facilities and counter-attractions. Lyttelton had enough artillery volunteers to man two batteries from 1866 until 1868, but none from 1875. Their demise was offset by the formation of the Timaru Artillery in 1871, which added to the 'spirit of rivalry' in Canterbury that 'tends to be of service to all'. During the 1870s Volunteering took off in the more populous and less threatened South Island. By 1878, artillery and navals were 1069 of 5508 volunteers (19.4 per cent); 614 of them were in the South Island. In 1881, despite the tensions in Taranaki, the proportions were similar: 1059 of the 1767 artillery and navals (now a quarter of all volunteers) were South Islanders. When volunteer numbers reached 8253 in 1886 after the latest 'Russian scare', the strength of the naval and field artillery was 2023, 56 per cent of them in South Island units.[43]

In the early years instructors and guns were few and premises sometimes unsatisfactory. In Dunedin in 1870, the 'shed' used by the artillery was 'very unsafe for the guns and stores; the rain pours in at every seam…. The weight of the guns has caused the flooring and piles to give away.' Nevertheless, the Dunedin Artillery remained very efficient, while the Naval Volunteers had made 'good practice with their howitzers'. The quality of a unit's facilities was important: membership of the Bluff Navals increased significantly after their new hall opened.[44]

By 1872, the colony's defence establishment included a Sergeant of Artillery in Auckland and an Artillery Instructor in Wellington. The Inspector of Volunteers hoped to re-equip the volunteer artillery with 6-pr Armstrongs in place of the ex-Royal Artillery howitzers that were used by most, including the naval corps. Instead, in 1878 the 22 'large guns' were ordered from England; Colonel G.S. Whitmore anticipated that 'the Artillery Volunteers will necessarily have much more work to do, and greater responsibility'. At this time, seventeen Armstrongs, nine 24-pr howitzers and six ancient smooth-

6-inch Armstrong disappearing gun in the twilight of its service at Fort Jervois, Ripapa Island, Lyttelton Harbour, 1943.
Royal New Zealand Artillery Old Comrades' Association.

bore 'Iron Guns, various' were issued to the volunteers. Some could not be fired often. In 1879, Oamaru's artillery volunteers were allotted 'five rounds each of shot and shell and ten rounds of blank' for their 24-pr, 'Moses'.[45]

Other essentials were also sometimes lacking. In 1886, both horses and harness had to be hired – and the harness then repaired with rope and fencing wire – for each parade by Christchurch's E Battery, whose lack of guns and therefore practical training provoked the *Volunteer and Civil Service Gazette* to complain that 'our Artillery men don't know a sponge from a handspike'. The field movements of a standard six-gun battery could be demonstrated only by manoeuvring working models built by a sergeant-major. In 1891 the field artillery still had both 'obsolete guns and grossly sub-standard harness'; they were forced to use 'dray ropes as traces and clothes-lines for reins'.[46]

Many artillery units trained attached cadet units after the 1877 Education Act required all boys in public schools to receive military instruction. Communities responded by sponsoring shooting prizes. In 1876, one town made the gaffe of presenting a colour to the local artillery unit.[47]

Following the 1878 war fears, Whitmore reformed the volunteer artillery into a regiment, 'with the same uniform and system throughout'. This 'regiment' existed only on paper, and standardisation remained wishful thinking, except that batteries were now designated by letters, a system that still survives. Though a new battery was formed in Poverty Bay, eight of the twelve batteries were located in the South Island, where more than 60 per cent of the colony's males now lived.[48]

Volunteer units were part-funded by annual capitation grants from central government. Initially payments were made per unit. From 1865 a sum was paid for each 'efficient' man (for artillery corps, with their greater and more complex responsibilities, this fluctuated between £1 5s and £3 with economic and political circumstances). In the late 1860s, the central government also gave prize money for gunnery competitions. Changing minimum and maximum numbers of men were stipulated for units; those for artillery were generally higher because of the manpower needed to work with heavy guns. In 1898, for the first time, individuals were paid directly.[49]

Corps had to maintain a minimum (but varying) number of 'efficient' members and carry out specified tasks to receive capitation funding or even

9-pr breech-loading Armstrong with I Battery volunteer, Oamaru, 1890s.
North Otago Museum.

remain in existence. During periods of retrenchment and declining rolls such as the late 1880s, non-commissioned officers (NCOs) became adept at massaging their unit's returns. Men could leave easily after completing a year's service; or they were discharged if they stopped attending parades. In 1886 the average length of service in Christchurch's E Battery was two years, four months. Much time was spent giving new recruits basic training.

Funds were also raised by fining members for disciplinary infractions. From 1885, absence without leave from a parade cost Auckland's O Battery men between 1s and 3s, depending on rank. Enforcing such rules risked resignation by offenders, which could endanger a unit's continued existence. Officers were expected to contribute personally to company funds – in 1886 the CO of the Thames Navals advanced his unit almost £100. Assuming personal financial liabilities compromised the quality of leadership officers could provide.

Officers were or aspired to be gentlemen, sometimes by autosuggestion: one B Battery officer elevated himself from 'clerk' to 'gentleman' (via 'accountant') in the roll book within four years. Without strong institutional mechanisms, genuine social status did help to enforce authority. The election of officers was often criticised as subversive of discipline, but there seemed no feasible alternative. Neither men nor officers could be compelled to serve; each group had to be comfortable with the other; and most officers had to be both willing and able to part-fund their units. Inevitably, there were tensions – and conversely, close relationships across ranks – that would have sorely tested the chain of command in the event of war.

Given the scant financial reward involved, most volunteers regarded their obligations as limited, and felt they should have some say in how they performed their duties. In 1898, for example, the Wellington Navals refused to attend their Easter Camp – the key event of the volunteer year – because they thought too much was being asked of them. Officers often responded pragmatically to breaches of discipline: when two of Auckland's three garrison artillery units refused to man the coastal fortifications one cold, wet night, medical certificates were submitted (and apparently accepted).[50]

Training and Entertaining

Amateur soldiering filled much the same role as organised sport would in the future. Volunteer artillery batteries provided a group with which to identify, a touch of excitement, a useful way of occupying leisure time and a vigorous social life.[51]

Many instructors were former Royal Artillery personnel of varying quality. Wellington's, for example, was judged to be 'very defective in … the rudiments of his duty, owing perhaps to his having … served in the tailors' shop of his battery'. Some hours after their first public demonstration, the Lyttelton Artillery Volunteers' instructor, by now drunk, fired a shell from its Armstrong gun which hit a barque. Man and gun were both put out of action – the former permanently by a conviction, the latter until a Dunedin firm could make a copy of a missing part.[52]

Volunteers usually drilled indoors one evening a week. The less frequent daylight training and camps were compromised if employers would not release men, and by distractions like race meetings. Artillery units often had to form scratch gun crews from whoever turned up. Naval artillery trained with the crews of visiting warships in gun drill, repelling boarders and boarding, and entered cutter races in the summer.

Encampments lasting several days were first held in Canterbury. One of the largest, drawing 2500 men from throughout the South Island, took place at Oamaru over Easter 1886, soon after the Russian scare. Its premise was 'a naval attack … at an hour suited to the convenience of … visitors' – military exercises made great spectator sport. While mines and torpedo boats impeded the invaders, two guns emplaced at the port, and ten field guns, countered their fire. Monday's manoeuvres were on land: 'the guns covered the infantry movement with a tremendous fire', but the artillery suffered the weekend's only injury when a gun carriage lost a wheel while crossing wet ground. Most later encampments were more modest affairs, although an 1891 'raid' on Oamaru by HMS *Curaçoa* thrilled holidaymakers with the spectacle of 'artillery dashing along in clouds of dust'.[53]

Sham fights occasionally became more realistic. At the 1865 Christchurch encampment the Lyttelton Artillery wielded iron stakes to defend their guns,

Dunedin's B Battery, Field Artillery Volunteers, ready to serve their 12-pr Armstrongs at an Easter camp at St Clair beach, 1888.
c/n E529/25, Hocken Library, University of Otago.

and three years later Christchurch artillery volunteers peppered tardy cavalry with tussock and fine gravel when they eventually charged, 'causing them to retire in great confusion'. At subsequent Canterbury encampments, shot and shell was fired out to sea, or at flagpoles.[54]

Official duties and social activities were often combined. In 1886 the Wellington Navals combined their annual field-gun firing with their annual picnic. The following year they hired professional entertainers, but usually they amused themselves – in 1896, with swimming, sailing and rowing. They also organised displays, in 1881, for example, drilling before 1000 spectators. Prizes were awarded for firing, mounting and dismounting artillery, cutlass drill and smartest No. 1 man. Competition strengthened bonds among personnel. In 1871, the Christchurch Artillery Volunteers held a rifle shoot between teams of married and single men. The prize was supper at the Golden Age hotel; 20 wives and friends watched the shooting before enjoying a cold collation. A camp of Christchurch's E Battery at New Brighton one weekend in 1895 featured parades, gun drills, and fire discipline and field movement exercises. There were also two concerts, a dance, and cricket and cribbage competitions with local residents.[55] Such camps did much to compensate for the expense and other frustrations of volunteering.

Artillery bands frequently played in public, often to raise funds. In the late 1860s, Lyttelton's artillery hired a bandmaster on a salary of £100 and mounted a promenade concert series. In the 1880s, the Christchurch Artillery's fife and drum band gave concerts and played at the opening of the Christchurch Exhibition; Auckland's Artillery Band – already two decades old – played in Albert Park on Saturday afternoons. The Thames Naval Artillery's band became the unit's most important function. In Oamaru, the Caledonian Society's band was attached to the rifle company in 1878 for capitation purposes – whereupon the artillery volunteers formed a rival band and induced some of the star performers to switch allegiance.[56]

Social gatherings were held on diverse pretexts. E Battery even performed the farce *Mad As A Hatter* at Sunnyside Asylum. In 1893 it took part in both a combined ball in the Oddfellows' Hall and a concert at the Theatre Royal which attracted a full house. The following year it joined in a military concert to assist the unemployed. Christchurch's 1883 artillery fête was illuminated by arc lights until the dynamo failed and the show had to be cancelled. The Petone Navals held concerts and balls in their own 'very fine Drillshed' while their 64-pr rusted away on the windswept beach nearby.[57]

Artillery units also performed more serious duties – searching for a murderer in Auckland, hauling a 24-pr up Wellington's Mount Victoria with block and tackle, firing salutes on occasions like the Queen's Birthday. Wellington's D Battery formed a guard of honour and fired a seven-gun salute whenever its CO returned from visits 'Home' – until the Governor asked ironically which 'distinguished officer' was being so honoured. More officially, D Battery fired a salute at the funeral of the Atiawa chief Te Puni in 1870, and at state openings of Parliament later in the decade. Horses and guns were a risky combination. Wanganui's official welcome for Governor and Lady Bowen in 1871 was marred when the horses drawing the official carriage took fright at the salute and bolted. After the groom eventually regained control, Their Excellencies – shaken, if not stirred – insisted on alighting.

Auckland's Artillery Band with their instruments, 1885.
Courtesy of The Artillery Band Association (Inc.).

Massed guns could certainly be deafening: the full battery salute celebrating the arrival of the railway at Featherston in 1878 was heard in Greytown, 8 miles away. The guns at Wellington's Fort Buckley fell silent from the turn of the century after rail travellers were scared out of their wits.[58]

By the late 1880s, many Volunteer units were as much 'well dressed drinking clubs' as military units. Since both spare time and money were required, most volunteers were middle-class. But the membership of individual units also reflected their social setting: most Lyttelton Navals were wharfies, tradesmen or seamen.[59] The Volunteers' splendid uniforms – scarlet or blue serge Garibaldi jackets with blue serge pants – were tailored locally once a textile and garment industry was established.

Parihaka

Despite their vigorous contributions to the social life of their communities, the volunteers' raison d'être was to provide military protection. Fears of further fighting with Maori arose periodically during the 1870s. Following the killing of a Pakeha labourer working inside the King Country in 1873, blockhouses armed with swivel guns were constructed along a new military road in Waikato.

Nearly 150 men of the Wellington and Thames naval brigades volunteered for service when a contingent to join imperial forces fighting against the Boer republics was suggested in 1881. Nothing came of this, but then in early October there were new rumours of impending fighting against Maori resisting the occupation of confiscated land in south Taranaki.[60] Several volunteer units, including artillery, quickly offered their services. Among the 33 called out for 'Actual Service' on 27 October were the Nelson and Wellington batteries. The latter, however, refused to participate when they learned they would have to act as infantry. The Nelsonians embarked after a torchlight procession – with their 6-pr Armstrong gun but without some of their comrades, who had been kept home by their wives.[61] The prophet Tohu warned the Parihaka people that 'the south wind was bringing soldiers and cannon'.

The volunteers camped at Rahotu, and artillery including the Wellington Navals followed the advance on nearby Parihaka early on 5 November. After the community's leaders were arrested, the Armstrong gun was hauled up to

The Lyttelton Naval Artillery encamped in 1898 at Fort Jervois, Ripapa Island, Lyttelton Harbour.
CD 10, IMG 0033, Christchurch City Libraries.

'Fort Rolleston' overlooking the village to discourage any further resistance. None came, and the artillery volunteers soon went home to enthusiastic welcomes and six weeks' pay. The Nelsonians were the last to leave, on 18 November. About 1100 volunteers had served at Parihaka.[62]

Both Naval Reservists and the Permanent Artillery would be involved in the operations which dissuaded Te Kooti from returning to Poverty Bay in 1889.[63] Then, in 1898, violence threatened during the so-called Dog Tax Rebellion of Hokianga's Te Mahurehure hapu. This time 120 men of the Permanent Force, with two Nordenfelt field guns and two Maxim machine guns, were sent to restore order. The gunboat *Torch* also lay off Rawene, but no shots were fired and calm soon returned. When it seemed that a Volunteer unit might be required, men as far away as Christchurch's E Battery offered their services.[64]

REORGANISATION

The speed with which the Volunteers had assembled at Parihaka was thought to have had 'an excellent effect on the Native mind, ... convincing them that, in an emergency, the Constabulary can be reinforced with little delay'. However, a Board of Officers noted in March 1882 that 'the defects and deficiencies of the present organization are patent' – and had been pointed out repeatedly by inspecting officers. It recommended disbanding the batteries at Gisborne and Queenstown, and one of the two at Invercargill, while creating a second battery at Auckland. Each remaining battery should have enough men to operate three actual field guns rather than the notional six which none ever had. All 534 artillery personnel ('formed into one regiment as at present') should be part of a 'First Line' of volunteers at the chief ports comprising 2572 officers and men. Naval volunteers would form part of an 1827-strong 'Second Line' who would be paid less, enrolled for one rather than three years and not liable for compulsory daylight drills. The Volunteer Force should be led by a Commandant who would double as military secretary to the Defence Minister; 'if possible, an officer of the Royal Artillery should be selected, as the main defence of the ports ... must consist of artillery batteries' manned by men of a new permanent force.[65]

In the short term, few of these recommendations were adopted. In 1883, it was decided that the naval volunteers would 'be reconstructed as Naval Artillery Volunteers, on the Home system, to be trained at the four principal ports in the working of the heavy batteries about to be erected'. The two varieties of artillery units had 1164 of the 2760 key personnel (42.2 per cent) comprising what were now called the 'Garrison Corps'. These were distinguished from the 'Country Corps', effectively a reserve force.[66]

In 1885 the Commander of the Colonial Forces, Whitmore, reported that the 'Field Artillery' remained 'miserably ill supplied with field guns'. Whitmore now divided the artillery volunteers – 'a splendid body of men' – into two brigades: L, N and O batteries (at Port Chalmers, Lyttelton and Auckland respectively) would become garrison batteries; the others would become field batteries to protect the new harbour defences.[67]

PROFESSIONALS AND VOLUNTEERS

In the mid-1880s, the colony had at last decided to erect coastal defences at the major cities. These would be manned by a small professional cadre supported by a larger auxiliary force of volunteers. Alternative proposals were rejected, not least because of the strong political and public support for volunteering. New Zealand's defence system would therefore remain militarily ineffective.

The 1885 Russian scare stimulated the creation of an army with artillery at its core, and the 1886 Defence and Police Force Acts completed the separation of the military and civilian coercive authorities. The Defence Act created a

Permanent Militia whose members would initially be those of 'any engineer, artillery, mounted infantry, or torpedo corps ... forming part of the reserve force of the Constabulary'. Police would be recruited only from the Permanent Militia, for which they would constitute a trained reserve. From 1890 police were required to perform ten days' artillery drill each year. Garrison artillery made up one-third of the Permanent Militia's initial strength of 350. A 50-strong field artillery unit, divided between Auckland and Wellington, was commanded by Major F.J.W. Gascoigne.[68]

Volunteer numbers and enthusiasm were swollen first by the war scare and then by the prestige acquired when the big guns were installed. In 1887 new regulations required artillery recruits to receive ten hours' gun drill in addition to the 30 hours' squad drill given to all recruits. Though the quality of the 1885 defences was debated, the number of guns already in the colony or on order meant that completing the fortification programme was politically unavoidable, and another £120,000 was voted in 1886/7. But enthusiasm and the economy were both declining, and in late 1887 Major-General H. Schaw was asked to assess 'the lowest absolute number of men ... required to keep the forts in order'. Had it been acted on, his scheme would have halved the size of the colony's military. When Whitmore resigned as Commandant in 1887, he was not replaced. Lieutenant-Colonel Arthur Hume, the Inspector of Prisons, was now also Inspector of Volunteers.[69]

Whitmore had noted in 1886 that 'the artillery officers have practically no instruction', nor even textbooks 'of a simple character'. It would be a decade until George Richardson, on secondment from the Royal Artillery, wrote the latter, but in 1888 detailed instructions for gun drill by Garrison and Naval Artillery volunteers were stipulated. That year the Permanent Militia was 'largely reduced' in numbers, partly by absorbing the Field Artillery into the garrison and regular artillery. Overseeing prison labour on the fortifications remained the 'chief duty' of the artillery, who had 'done their best to become effective' – 'no guns in the world could be better kept than those under their charge'. The volunteer artillery had 'begun to qualify themselves for work with heavy guns'. Whitmore recommended that some of these in the main centres 'be afforded encouragement to devote more time to the practical part of harbour defence', since 'the prescribed number of drills does not suffice to make ... artillery-men'.[70] This hint that the government should provide increased funding in return for increased volunteer service was not taken up.

In 1889, district establishments for volunteers were set for the first time. Auckland, Wellington and Dunedin would each have three Naval Artillery, one Garrison Artillery and one Field Artillery Corps (as well as one Mounted and six Rifle Corps); Christchurch would have one of each artillery unit. That year's review concluded that there were too many Field artillerymen; their guns were obsolete and lacked ammunition, and other equipment was also deficient. The Garrison and Naval Artillery were too numerous, performed similar duties and should be amalgamated. Most Navals now had no connection with the sea, and 'a considerable proportion have never practised with the guns they would have to serve in time of war'. The Permanent Artillery, on the other hand, were 'a fine body of men, well drilled and instructed', albeit still needing 'more gun-practice'.[71]

The 1890s

During the 1890 Maritime Strike, Permanent Militia personnel replaced the policemen who were assigned to strike duty after the deployment of unarmed regulars on Wellington's wharves proved provocative. On the other hand, members of the Westport Naval Artillery band led a march by striking seamen in Westport. The Minister of Defence, William Russell, threatened to abolish the band if there was any repetition of such behaviour. These were probably not the only volunteers sympathetic to the strikers. Potential disaffection was avoided by swearing in 'substantial numbers' of willing volunteers as special constables. Most of the specials at Lyttelton had volunteer artillery experience, and they were led by artillery officers.[72]

When the new Liberal government took office in 1891, the harbour defence scheme had been virtually completed, at a cost of £416,000. Two 6-inch guns were in place on Bastion Point in Auckland, while Fort Jervois on Ripapa Island was now the most powerful battery in the country. The works

Main Artillery Volunteers Corps and types (field, garrison and naval), 1886

Permanent Militia

<u>New Zealand Garrison Artillery</u>
Auckland GA Battery
Wellington GA Battery
Lyttelton GA Battery
Dunedin GA Battery

<u>New Zealand Field Artillery</u>
one battery

<u>New Zealand Regiment of Artillery Volunteers</u>

<u>1st (North Island) Brigade</u>

		Year formed	Year dissolved (if known)
A Battery	Auckland	1864	
D Battery	Wellington	1867	
F Battery	Napier	1869	1898
J Battery	Cook County	1878	1889
O Battery	Parnell	1886	1891

<u>2nd (South Island) Brigade</u>

B Battery	Dunedin	1864	
C Battery	Timaru	1866	1897
G Battery	Invercargill	1866	1898
E Battery	Christchurch	1867	
H Battery	Nelson	1867	
I Battery	Oamaru	1875	1897
K Battery	Invercargill	c.1879	
L Battery	Port Chalmers	c.1879	
M Battery	Queenstown	1879	1890
N Battery	Lyttelton	1885	

<u>Naval Artillery Volunteers Corps</u>
Auckland NAV
Dunedin NAV
Port Chalmers NAV
Thames NAV   1900

	Year formed	Year dissolved (if known)
Wellington NAV		
Lyttelton NAV		
Petone NAV		
Wanganui NAV		1898
Bluff NAV		1898
Oamaru NAV		1895
Ponsonby NAV		
Westport NAV		1895
Timaru NAV		1897
Napier NAV		1897
Onehunga NAV		1889
Greymouth NAV		1893
Waitemata NAV		1889

were manned efficiently by the small Permanent Artillery cadre. Colonels F.J. Fox and A.P. Penton, the two Royal Artillerymen who commanded the New Zealand forces during the 1890s, were to give yet more contradictory advice about the coastal defences, confirming the Liberals' inclination to leave well (or ill) alone in the absence of any tangible threat to the colony. Relatively minor improvements included mounting more guns in Auckland and Wellington. The works' existence provided some deterrence against attack, and, more importantly, reassured the public, though the batteries never fired a shot in anger.[73]

There was some revitalisation of the Volunteer Force during the decade, cautiously encouraged by Defence Minister Richard Seddon, who had been an NCO in a Melbourne volunteer artillery corps. Seddon distrusted professional soldiers and failed to appreciate the potential impact of advances in military technology and thinking. He strove to keep defence spending as low as possible, seeing little political benefit in tackling defence problems – at least in peacetime.

The poor quality of their equipment continued to inhibit the Volunteers' effectiveness. By 1893, the ex-Royal Artillery guns of the field artillery were 'in a terribly bad state, some being unsafe to fire, while the wheels, limbers, and woodwork in some cases are absolutely rotten'.[74]

Training remained rudimentary, though in 1892 Wellington's D Battery devised a four-month programme which moved from gun and small arms drill through gun aiming and positioning to detachment drills and battery exercises. Travelling instructors provided periodic training, but there was sometimes friction between these NCOs and corps' officers. Combined operations could only be practised at the annual regional encampments. In 1893, the newly appointed Commandant, Fox, could find only 142 'fairly-efficient gunners' among the 1185 Naval Artillery Volunteers. 'The field batteries are all inefficient, and amongst the Garrison Artillery Volunteers there are but 20 capable gunners.' Fox dismissed some of the Naval Artillery units as good infantry corps (or bands) who knew 'nothing' of gun-drill. Some of their guns were moved rarely – or could not be moved safely.[75]

The only remedy was 'to curtail the artillery defence as far as possible, and to put forward inducements to the men of the Artillery Volunteers, and so interest them in their work, that more trained men shall be forthcoming'. 'Inducements' in the form of increased capitation funding or partial payment in return for increased service had been suggested before, but foundered on grounds of expense. Capitation payments had been halved to £1 10s in 1887, and restored to only £2 in 1889. Artillery volunteers resented receiving the same payment as riflemen despite their higher expenses.[76]

The naval artillery was now divided into two branches. Units outside the main centres, which had proliferated because of their glamour, became rifle corps 'in name as well as practice' over the next five years. In Timaru, for example, the Naval Artillery Volunteers raised in 1884 became the Timaru Port Guards in 1897, when they were issued with Martini Henry rifles and joined the South Canterbury Infantry Battalion. Napier's F Battery became the Napier Guards. Despite their numbers in Wellington, an 1896 exercise showed that 'under the existing arrangements, the forts guarding the city could not be properly garrisoned'.[77]

Following political criticism of his attacks on individual officers, Fox resigned as Commandant without even formally taking up the position – but was then reappointed as Military Adviser to carry out many of its duties. Useful field and naval artillery manuals were produced in 1894 and 1895.

Regulations of 1882 had laid down syllabuses in which volunteer officers were to be examined before their commissions were confirmed, but the School of Instruction set up at Mount Cook in 1885 had closed within three years for want of adequate resourcing.[78]

Following the general government retrenchment of 1888, the Permanent Militia comprised at most 191 artillerymen, 51 of them in the Torpedo branch, plus officers. When Fox inspected them in 1893, the establishment was down to 142 'very highly trained' men, who were also 'well educated, intelligent, and drawn from a very superior class'. By 1896 the number of volunteers had fallen in five years from 6700 to under 5000, and there were 26 fewer units. That year the Permanent Militia was expanded from 208 to 270 men, with the Artillery receiving most of the increase. In 1897, the Artillery branch was redesignated No. 1 Service Company of the renamed Permanent Force (the Torpedo branch became No. 2). Policemen were no longer 'trained in the Forts'; their role as reserve gunners was over.[79]

Training such a small and widely dispersed force was difficult. In 1893, Fox instructed naval and garrison artillery units to focus on their specialist training when they went into camp, 'rather than wasting their time doing infantry drill and joining sham fights' (which, of course, were what both volunteers and the public enjoyed most). The officers running Easter encampments attempted to practise more realistic scenarios. In 1895, fourteen-day camps for naval and garrison artillery corps were introduced. Men trained in the mornings and evenings and on weekends while continuing their civilian jobs.[80]

Officers generally relied on whatever training they had received before joining the colonial forces. None of the garrison artillery officers serving in 1899 had undertaken 'a detailed course of instruction' – and the government declined an offer from New South Wales to put officers or men through their three-month gunnery course. The only instruction was provided by the NCOs periodically brought out from Britain. Officers' clubs obtained instructional material for garrison libraries and heard papers on topics such as 'Practical Field Works'.[81]

When a contingent was invited to Queen Victoria's Diamond Jubilee celebrations in England in 1897, the new Commandant, Penton, sought artillery instruction for its Permanent Militia component. The government responded to this risk of increased expense by withdrawing Permanent Militiamen from the contingent. However, at the Imperial Conference coinciding with the Jubilee, Seddon expressed the hope that a New Zealand artillery unit might soon be exchanged with a British one. Though this proved impractical, in 1898 two young lieutenants were sent to England for training.[82]

By 1901, with the stimulus of the South African War, the colony had 17,000 Volunteers. Patriotic fervour saw the fifteen artillery units dwarfed

Torpedomen training at Shelly Bay, Wellington, c.1900.
Royal New Zealand Artillery Old Comrades' Association.

by 71 companies of mounted rifles and 117 infantry corps. The School of Instruction had been re-established, new field guns ordered, and in Wellington horses had been obtained – 'the first step towards making our field artillery mobile'. A national (khaki) uniform had at last been approved. 'For the first time in its history the Volunteer Force resembled an "Army"', both literally and organisationally.[83]

When an English journal surveyed the state of New Zealand's military at the turn of the century it described the Permanent Artillery's main task as 'to train instructors to instruct the Volunteers'. Among the latter, the field batteries, tasked with protecting the harbour defences, were the weakest – the gunners had 'little or no practice with the guns', still the 'obsolete and worn out' Armstrongs. The naval artillery – mostly 'men employed among shipping' – helped the permanent garrison artillery to work the guns and lay mines. As ever, 'the capitation grant barely covers the cost of uniforms'.[84] The next decade would see a major overhaul of this system.

Coast defence training at Wellington in the 1890s involved aiming at this 'fly-by-wire' model warship. 1994.2363/5, Kippenberger Military Archive, Army Museum Waiouru.

Edmond Tudor Boddam

Edmond Meyer Tudor Boddam served in New Zealand as Defence Engineer and commanded the garrison artillery, torpedo corps and engineer components of the Permanent Militia for fewer than three years – the crucial period when the fortifications were finally built.[85] Born in 1850 into a family that had strong connections with both the army and India, in 1869 he became a cadet in the Royal Regiment of Artillery, serving as a lieutenant in India from 1873 to 1875. From the late 1870s he redesigned Hobart's defences, forming and commanding the Tasmanian Torpedo Corps in 1883.

In 1885 Boddam was transferred to New Zealand, promoted to lieutenant-colonel and made Engineer of Defences. He had not only to design new works, but also modify partly finished ones to accommodate the new breech-loading hydro-pneumatic 'disappearing guns'. Economic constraints encouraged innovation. For example, substituting concrete for brick in gun emplacements required fewer skilled workmen, an important consideration as most of the work was done by prisoners. He designed works on a modular basis – generic gun pits, magazine blocks and tunnels could be fitted together to form a fort suited to each site.

G.S. Whitmore, the Commander of the Colonial Forces – a man not noted for generosity towards subordinates – praised Boddam as

> an officer of singular energy, ability, and versatility of talent. Works on so large a scale were probably never attempted in so many distant places by any Government with so small an amount of supervision, and the incessant labour ... got through by him, is almost incredible .... [T]o carry out all he undertakes, with such materials as are to hand, requires a fertility of resource and ingenuity few possess.[86]

When in May 1886 Boddam also took command of the garrison artillery, torpedo corps and engineers, he was already closely involved in their selection, supervision and training. He was now in effect Director of New Zealand's artillery — the senior serving staff officer — on a salary of £500.[87]

Boddam was dismissed from his positions in early 1888, a high-level casualty of the retrenchment of the Permanent Militia. He returned to Tasmania, where in September 1889 he became Supervising Engineer in the Public Works Department's Fortifications Branch. He continued to write and speak about coastal defences. In 1896 he made false claims as a publicist for one of several rival mining and railway ventures in north-west Tasmania. Boddam returned to England and died in London in 1918.

FREDERICK GASCOIGNE

The varied career of Frederick John William Gascoigne (Gascoyne) included being the only colonist to command New Zealand's permanent force of field artillery in the nineteenth century.[88] The son of an officer in India he resolved to become a soldier after hearing artillery fire during the first Sikh War. Accompanying his family to New Zealand in 1852, he farmed at Motueka and on his relative Donald McLean's run in Hawke's Bay. He worked as a sawmiller, drover and gold prospector before being commissioned in the Colonial Defence Force.

In 1865, Gascoigne fought Pai Marire adherents on the East Coast. He helped organise the Poverty Bay force which pursued Te Kooti in July 1868, and led the defence of Turanganui after the Matawhero killings. Belatedly commissioned as a captain in the Armed Constabulary, Gascoigne took part in the attacks on Ngatapa, the pursuit of Titokowaru after Tauranga-ika, and the later operations against Te Kooti. Then (with his wife Marion) he took charge of Armed Constabulary outposts across the central North Island, supervising road-building and drilling.

Gascoigne was based at Alexandra (Pirongia) as the King Country was opened to Pakeha; in 1883 he defused a Maori raid on the town. Transferred to Opunake in 1885, he was promoted to major and policed protests by Te Whiti's followers. In 1887 he took command of the field artillery branch of the Permanent Militia in Wellington, which was helping to construct the coastal fortifications under Boddam's supervision. Gascoigne's position disappeared when the field and garrison artillery were combined in 1888. He moved to Auckland as sheriff, then was given charge of the government arms store and magazine. From 1891 he was resident magistrate in the Chatham Islands. Attempts to reduce drinking and curb the power of runholders won him few friends, but he did improve local public amenities.[89] Ill-health forced Gascoigne to retire to his Hastings smallholding in 1897. He died in 1926.

Major Frederick Gascoigne, the first colonial artillery commander.
T.W. Gudgeon, The Defenders of New Zealand.

2

THE YEARS OF TRANSFORMATION, 1899–1914

In the first fifteen years of the new century New Zealand's artillery took on the form and roles that would broadly endure for more than 50 years. At the start of this period New Zealanders served overseas as gunners for the first time, in support of imperial forces in South Africa, and within a decade the volunteer artillery units had been replaced by territorial units under a new system of compulsory military training. The regular force artillery cadre was redesignated the Royal New Zealand Artillery (RNZA), and its role took on new importance as the training of territorials began in earnest. The acquisition of modern field and coastal guns reflected the political priority given to defence preparations as international developments became more disturbing. The increasing professionalisation of the RNZA and the establishment of well-trained and increasingly well-equipped citizen artillery units came none too soon. The regiment's experienced personnel, regular and territorial, would be responsible for training and leading the artillery units that would serve in conflicts ahead.

GUNNERS IN SOUTH AFRICA

The ability of citizen soldiers to become effective gunners was demonstrated in South Africa,[1] though artillery formed only a small part of New Zealand's contribution. A handful of young officers were seconded to Royal Artillery units for experience, but this country, like the Australian colonies, concentrated on sending men who could ride well and shoot straight. Canada, in contrast, despatched potentially self-contained forces that included three batteries of 18-prs.[2] When war broke out between the British authorities in the South

African colonies and the Boer republics of the Transvaal and Orange Free State on 11 October 1899, the first New Zealand contingent of 215 mounted rifles was already undergoing basic training at Karori. A machine-gun battery of 39 men and four Hotchkiss guns was included in the Second Contingent, which left Wellington on 20 January 1900.[3] The guns, with pack-saddle equipment so they could move with mounted infantry units, were donated by the manufacturers, the English company of Armstrong, Elswick.[4] The battery, held up at Cape Town by an injury to their temporary commanding officer, Captain N.L.D. Smith, and by a shortage of gunners, did not depart for the front until 1 May. In their first operation on the march to Kroonstadt in the

Members of the Second Contingent to South Africa train with Hotchkiss machine guns at Newtown Park, Wellington, 1900.
6666 1/1, Alexander Turnbull Library, Wellington.

Transvaal, the limitations of the Hotchkiss guns soon became apparent. The unwieldy machine guns were too heavy for long-distance movement over the veldt on packhorses and they were outranged by the Boers' Mauser rifles, so the battery was disbanded; the machine-gunners became mounted riflemen.[5]

After a disastrous start to the war, imperial forces had relieved the besieged towns of Kimberley and Ladysmith and captured the Orange Free State capital of Bloemfontein in February and March 1900. The relief of Mafeking on 17 May, and the fall of Johannesburg and the Transvaal capital Pretoria by early June, seemed to promise an early end to the war. Its last conventional action was fought in November at Rhenoster Kop, near Pretoria, but the Boers now turned to guerilla warfare, demanding renewed efforts by the New Zealanders and other imperial mounted infantry units.

In the meantime, in May 1900, the Fourth and Fifth New Zealand Contingents had landed in Beira, Portuguese East Africa, and after some delay travelled by train to Marandellas, Southern Rhodesia, to join the Rhodesian Field Force (RFF) led by Sir Frederick Carrington. While the New Zealanders were encamped at Marandellas, volunteers were called to form artillery batteries for service with the RFF. Captain C.T. Major offered his 100-strong 11 Company of the Fifth Contingent as a unit for conversion to artillery. Other New Zealanders joined a composite No. 2 Battery, 2 Brigade RFF, which would travel far and wide over the next six months without seeing action.[6] Augmented by more New Zealand volunteers and renamed the No. 1 New Zealand Battery, Major's men were equipped with six 15-pr Armstrong guns and other artillery equipment and received ten days' intensive training before setting out on 14 June. After a 'long and arduous trek' over 'heavy and sandy' roads, the battery reached Bulawayo on 10 July.[7] At the beginning of August it formed part of Carrington's 'Flying Column', engaged in suppressing Boer resistance east of Mafeking. The battery's heaviest action took place on 5 and 6 August, during an attempt to relieve the British garrison at Elands River. Two sections of the New Zealand gunners fired from dawn to dusk before executing a fighting withdrawal, with rearguard actions at Marico River, Zeerust and Ottoshoop, as the column and the civilian inhabitants of the towns fell back on Mafeking.

While the left section of the battery remained at Mafeking for the next three months to bolster the garrison, the other two sections set out once again on 14 August as an element of 2 Brigade, RFF, within General Carrington's division. Ottoshoop was taken on 16 August, and the battery then participated in heavy fighting that drove the Boers out of Malmani and Buffelshoek. Subsequently it was engaged in raids and patrols in the Zeerust and Lichtenburg districts. From the end of October the sections of the battery were deployed separately, sometimes with units of the New Zealand Mounted Rifles and sometimes attached to British units. Among many operations, sections took part in operations to defend Zeerust and to occupy Lichtenburg and surrounding districts, and in the attack on Stenbockfontein. For a time the right section was besieged in Zeerust, while the left section helped to defend Lichtenburg against a determined Boer assault in March 1901. The battery had varied roles over late 1900 and early 1901: for example, one gun crew served in February and March on an armoured train shuttling between Mafeking and Vryburg.[8] The withdrawal of the Fifth Contingent units to Worcester, Cape Colony, in May led to the disbanding of No. 1 New Zealand Battery. Four of its members had lost their lives (one in action), and four more would succumb later (three to disease, and one after joining the Seventh Contingent).[9] Over the next half-century New Zealand gunners would have much experience operating within mobile expeditionary forces alongside imperial units.

The South African War also saw the beginnings of artillery techniques that would be refined on the battlefields of the First World War. At Ladysmith in February 1900, British forces under General Sir Redvers Buller adopted new offensive tactics suited to the magazine rifle and defensive entrenchments. As the historian of the South African War, Thomas Pakenham, puts it:

> Buller realised that the old three-act, one-day battle … had been killed stone-dead…. New infantry tactics had begun to emerge: better use of ground, more individual initiative, much more skill in taking cover. The artillery's role was being revolutionized; instead of merely supplying the first act in the … drama, the gunners would be in demand, day after day, throwing a creeping barrage ahead of the advancing infantry.

At Ladysmith, 'a curtain of shell fire' advanced 100 yards ahead of the 'creeping infantry'. Buller pioneered the infantry use of cover between advances 'in rushes' that were coordinated with artillery barrages.[10] Though engagements in the later stages of the war were more fluid than the set-piece reliefs of besieged towns, the importance of properly coordinating artillery and infantry was recognised – and not only for the successful prosecution of infantry assaults. Hard lessons were learnt at Colenso in December 1899 and on the Modder River in March 1900 when the Boers caught batteries in the open in front of the British infantry.

THE ROYAL NEW ZEALAND ARTILLERY

Although New Zealand's artillery units were based on the concept of citizen soldiers and commanded and manned by volunteers, a professional artillery cadre was essential for effective training and the maintenance of standards. In January 1903 the two branches of the New Zealand Permanent Force were redesignated to reflect their established roles, and at the same time granted royal patronage. With effect from 15 October 1902, No. 1 Service Company became the Royal New Zealand Artillery, while No. 2 Company became the Royal New Zealand Engineers (RNZE).[11] Only the permanent force artillery received the 'Royal' designation, the field and garrison artillery volunteers being known as the New Zealand Field Artillery Volunteers (NZFAV) and New Zealand Garrison Artillery Volunteers (NZGAV) respectively; in 1921 both became NZA. On active service in the two world wars, the restriction of the 'Royal' designation to the regulars seemed unfair, but their embarrassment was probably more acute than any sense of grievance felt by the hostilities-only or territorial men. In the field the distinction was academic: RNZA and NZ(F)A personnel served alongside each other interchangeably.

For the RNZA regulars and their RNZE counterparts, the established routine of duty continued despite their more formal corps designations: 'artillery and submarine-mining duties, annual courses of instruction, and instruction of Volunteers'. In May 1907, following a review of the defence of British ports, and with plans in hand for greatly improved gun defences at New Zealand's main ports, the government agreed to imperial advice and approved the discontinuation of mine defences. The main role of the Corps of Royal New Zealand Engineers (which had always been associated with coastal, particularly mine defences, and was not a field engineering corps) was now reduced to maintaining, and training volunteers to operate, the searchlights at the forts. The RNZE was accordingly disbanded and its personnel transferred into the RNZA, reintegrating for now the lineage of the main branches of the Permanent Force. The establishment of the RNZA Gunnery Section was 200 all ranks, while the RNZA Electric Light Section (ex-RNZE) was 55-strong; the distinction between the two sections would be dropped in 1926, by which time the Corps of New Zealand Engineers had been reinstated.[12] With the implementation of the territorial scheme in 1911, the New Zealand Staff Corps (officers) and the New Zealand Permanent Staff (warrant officers and NCOs) were established and, to the gunners' displeasure, given precedence over the existing RNZA.[13]

Advances in artillery equipment and techniques meant it was essential for regular officers and some NCOs to attend courses at the Royal Artillery School of Gunnery, at Shoeburyness on the Thames Estuary. In 1901 two officers and six NCOs of No. 1 Company began the long course of gunnery at the school, and over the following years attendance became common practice for RNZA officers about two years after receiving their commissions. From 1911 when, on Lord Kitchener's recommendation, there were ten New Zealand cadets in the inaugural intake of the Royal Military College at Duntroon, Canberra, many RNZA officers would begin their professional training alongside their Australian colleagues, graduating as lieutenants.[14] In this period, and in peacetime throughout the twentieth century, the RNZA served as training and cadre personnel for the volunteer units.

THE LAST YEARS OF THE VOLUNTEERS

The South African War reinforced New Zealand's confidence in the concept of the citizen soldier as the contingents acquitted themselves well on the veldt. The unconventional nature of the second stage of the war was suited to the riding, hunting and bushcraft skills possessed by many of the New Zealanders (and the Boers). The war also spurred enlistment in Volunteer units in New Zealand, but without proper equipment and training their usefulness was questionable.

Both the field and coastal artillery units were manned by volunteers. From 19 December 1902, these units were reorganised into five field batteries and a single regiment of garrison artillery, made up of ten companies of garrison artillery volunteers formed into four 'divisions', at Auckland, Wellington, Lyttelton and Dunedin/Port Chalmers, with a further company at Westport. (In 1904 the Westport battery was converted to a field battery, designated I Battery, FAV, 'having regard to the work it may be called upon to perform'.)[15] The garrison artillery companies were redesignated in 1907, and an additional company created in Wellington. These were now numbered from 1 to 3 or 1 to 2 within each division.

The changes of 1902–03 meant that the various units of Naval Artillery Volunteers, and the Devonport Coast Guard Artillery Volunteers, were redesignated as companies of the NZGAV. They were allowed to retain their traditional names informally, but for administrative and operational purposes they were referred to by their new designations.[16] The Devonport unit had lavish facilities – 'its own rifle range and a suite of orderly rooms and barracks … as well as a parade ground which is brilliantly illuminated on drill nights

E Battery's guard makes an impressive showing at a camp at the Heathcote Hotel, near Christchurch, 1901. *1990.597, Kippenberger Military Archive, Army Museum Waiouru.*

with a number of powerful incandescent gas lamps.'[17] The so-called 'naval' officers exchanged their ranks for the Army equivalents. The commander of each naval artillery battery was redesignated from the special rank of 'lieutenant commanding' to the equivalent military rank of 'captain'.[18] Each artillery division was placed under the command of a Volunteer lieutenant-colonel (for divisions consisting of only two batteries, a major), assisted by an adjutant, a pay- and quartermaster (one officer), a divisional sergeant-major and a divisional quartermaster-sergeant.[19] The standard establishment of the 1902–03 companies was one captain (the company CO), five lieutenants, one company sergeant-major, one company quartermaster-sergeant, eight sergeants, eight corporals, six bombardiers, two trumpeters and 175 gunners.[20] The field batteries, also commanded by a Volunteer captain, usually comprised three or four officers and a total of 60 to 70 warrant officers, NCOs and other ranks. By 1904, the actual strength of the six field batteries was 404 Volunteers, while the nine companies of the garrison artillery had 884 officers and men out of the 18,490 Volunteers of all corps, including cadet corps (2887) and defence rifle clubs (2542).[21]

The Commandant of the New Zealand Forces, Major-General James Babington, who pushed through these changes, stressed that they had 'not in any way interfered with the individuality' of the various units, which were allowed to retain their idiosyncratic uniforms.[22] Indeed, the individualism and pride of the companies fuelled an acrimonious dispute over the appointment of one of the divisional commanders. When a non-artillery volunteer officer was made commander of the Auckland Garrison Artillery Division, the CO of one of the three companies threatened legal action against the Defence Department on the grounds that the appointment had not been made under the relevant regulations. The appointment was annulled, but the complainant was further aggrieved when a more junior officer was appointed to the position. This led to a virtual mutiny, threats by members of two of the companies to disband and the charging of the officer who had complained.[23] The independent spirit of the volunteer units was also demonstrated when the officers of the Wellington Naval Artillery Company resigned over a proposal to form an additional battery in the city.

Like many of his predecessors, Babington condemned 'most strongly'

This North Island Permanent Artillery rugby team, c. 1901, includes a number of Maori players. *Royal New Zealand Artillery Old Comrades' Association.*

the election of volunteer officers by their units. 'Apart from its evil effects on discipline, it does not secure in many cases the most suitable men for the position ..., and corps suffer in efficiency in consequence.'[24] Indiscipline within Volunteer artillery batteries posed risks for civilians, particularly during shoots. Officers of Wellington's D Battery resigned and the Defence Department removed some of its guns after an incident in 1903. 'The department would be doing a service to the community if it took away the three remaining guns', the *Otago Daily Times* considered. Eight shells had landed in Ohariu Valley after overshooting the hill on which their target was placed. Five exploded, and some fell close to houses or within a flock of sheep. '[T]he battery practice put the settlers to considerable risk.' A man on the roof of a house under construction found 'three shells ... whizzing over his head, each of them landing within 150 yards of the building'. Another shell passed within 30 yards of his mother's house, a mile from the target. Problems within the corps continued, and the traditional firing on Wellington Anniversary Day had to be suspended in 1905 after settlers in Stokes Valley, to which the firing range had been shifted, voiced their opposition. The battery commander was advised to 'deceive the men of his Corps by telling them all on parade that the practice was unavoidably postponed' until Easter, when its safety could be monitored by regular instructors.[25]

The Garrison Artillery Volunteers were the best prepared of the Volunteer units. Unlike most others, they showed good attendance at evening parades and the week of intensive training required annually, as well as the Easter 'manoeuvres'. In 1905–06, for example, all nine GAV companies undertook sixteen days' training, enjoying realistic and conveniently located instruction on the guns and in the forts they would man in an emergency. Moreover, the high proportion of RNZA personnel in the Permanent Force ensured there was a solid cadre of garrison artillery professionals to train and work with these Volunteers. Commandants routinely noted the GAVs' high state of readiness. In 1905, for example, Babington reported that all companies were efficient: 'In some the shooting was good, in others very good'. Nevertheless, there had been two serious mistakes in fire discipline and drill during that year's manoeuvres: 'firing at the tug-boat in Dunedin, and opening the breach [sic] immediately after a misfire, in Wellington'.[26] These were rare mistakes, however, in a corps noted for its enthusiasm and technical skill.

The batteries of the Field Artillery Volunteers were incapable of field service at short notice, and much of their training was carried out in drill halls rather than on firing ranges. As Babington's predecessor, Colonel Arthur Penton, noted in 1901, 'Field-guns without mobility are useless, and unless the Government intends to seriously consider the question of making the field artillery a really mobile force it will only be a waste of money their making any further purchases'. A start was made by allocating the Wellington battery a small permanent force cadre and two teams of six horses, to enhance training for the volunteers and as a first step towards establishing truly mobile field batteries able to serve at short notice. Nevertheless, the field batteries continued to suffer from insufficient ammunition and a lack of field training. Babington thought the batteries capable of effective direct fire; but 'should they be required to fire from behind cover, either at ordinary or concealed targets, they would be practically useless'. In 1906 the batteries were given directors and gun arcs, but their use could not be taught in drill sheds, where only direct laying could be practised. In the Easter manoeuvres that year, however, some batteries carried out firing from behind cover. D Battery also experimented with using a field telephone for 'flank observation'; all the batteries were later equipped with field telephones.[27]

The first NZFAV tournament was held at the Addington Showgrounds in Christchurch on Boxing Day 1904, with detachments from the South Island batteries and Wellington's D Battery competing in events that included harnessing, casualty assistance and a competition in which, when an alarm was sounded, an unharnessed detachment in bivouac was required to harness its horses, limber its gun, gallop 100 yards and fire a round. The winner was No. 1 Detachment of Christchurch's E Battery.[28] Babington soon instigated a more meaningful and demanding contest, introducing 'challenge shields' for each volunteer corps, beginning with the GAV and FAV in 1906. Based on the results of the thorough and careful examination for efficiency held at each unit's annual training camp, the inaugural winner of the Garrison Artillery Challenge Shield was No. 6 Company (the 'Petone Navals', which in 1907 claimed a world record after hitting the target with all 40 rounds fired during a shoot at Fort Kelburn); D Battery was awarded the Field Artillery Challenge Shield.[29]

Despite considerable improvement in the standard of volunteer training in the first decade of the century, with more realistic field exercises and more demanding examination of units, the heterogeneous and usually undermanned volunteer units were sadly deficient overall as a potential fighting force. By 1909–10, the General Officer Commanding (GOC) considered that only the artillery Volunteers (garrison and field) and the Volunteer field engineers were receiving a satisfactory standard of instruction.[30] And the field artillery continued to be hampered by a lack of assigned horses and very limited field training. The GAV, by contrast, was ready for active duty.[31]

Rearming the Field Artillery

New Zealand's Field Artillery Volunteers lagged behind their British counterparts in the adoption of modern guns. Rearmament with the 15-prs began when Wellington's D Battery received four guns in 1900, followed the next year by Auckland's A Battery. The Christchurch and Dunedin batteries had followed suit by 1904, when the obsolete 9-pr RBL Armstrong guns were finally retired. At first only three-gun 15-pr batteries were possible, and the

Artillery Units in New Zealand, 1900–1914[32]

Lineage	1903[33]	1907	1911
AUCKLAND	Auckland Division, New Zealand Garrison Artillery Volunteers (NZGAV)		Auckland Garrison Artillery
Auckland Naval Artillery Volunteers (NAV)	No. 1 Company	No. 1 Company	No. 1 Company, New Zealand Garrison Artillery (NZGA)
Ponsonby NAV	No. 8 Company	No. 2 Company	No. 6 Company
Devonport Coastguard Artillery Volunteers	No. 9 Company	No. 3 Company	No. 7 Company
	New Zealand Field Artillery Volunteers (NZFAV)		Auckland Field Artillery Brigade
Auckland Artillery Volunteers	A Battery	A Battery	A Battery, NZFA
			K Battery, within months redesignated G Battery (Hamilton)
WELLINGTON	Wellington Division, NZGAV		Wellington Garrison Artillery
Nos 1 & 2 Companies, Wellington NAV	No. 4 Company	No. 1 Company	No. 3 Company
Petone NAV	No. 6 Company	No. 2 Company	No. 5 Company
		No. 3 Company	No. 9 Company
	NZFAV		Wellington Field Artillery Brigade
Wellington AV	D Battery	D Battery	D (Mountain) Battery, 1914
			J Battery (Palmerston North), 1912

Lineage	1903	1907	1911
CANTERBURY	Canterbury Division, NZGAV		Canterbury Garrison Artillery
Lyttelton NAV	No. 5 Company	No. 1 Company	No. 4 Company (Lyttelton)
N Battery, Lyttelton	No. 7 Company	No. 2 Company	
Westport Position Artillery	No. 10 Company (I Battery, FAV, 1904–07); No. 8 Company		No. 8 Company (Westport)
	NZFAV		Canterbury Field Artillery Brigade
E Battery, Christchurch	E Battery	E Battery	E Battery
H Battery, Nelson	H Battery	H Battery	H Battery
OTAGO	Otago Division, NZGAV		Otago Garrison Artillery
Dunedin NAV	No. 2 Company	No. 1 Company	No. 2 Company, Port Chalmers
Port Chalmers NAV	No. 3 Company	No. 2 Company	
		NZFAV	Otago Field Artillery Brigade
Dunedin AV	B Battery	B Battery	B Battery
			C Battery (Invercargill), formed from B Company, 8th Southland Rifles

gunners at Nelson and Westport retained their old 6-pr Nordenfelts (in six- and four-gun batteries, respectively) until 1906–07, when the batteries at the main centres were provided with a fourth 15-pr and Nelson converted from its six 6-prs to a section of two 15-prs. For now Westport retained its four 6-prs, but Babington recommended mounting guns on railway trucks to enable 'a more efficient defence' at this important coaling port. This was done at the New Zealand Railways depot at Woburn by 1909, with 12-pr quick-firing guns placed on naval-style pedestal mountings. A railway track was laid into

> ### THE FIELD ARTILLERY REVOLUTION
> A revolution in artillery technology and technique that began in the late nineteenth century soon allowed the guns to dominate tactics as never before. The replacement of gunpowder by slower-burning cordite propellant enabled longer gun barrels and greater ranges. Hydro-pneumatic recuperators to absorb recoil and run out the barrel again after each shot, first used in the French 75-mm of 1897, meant guns could remain stable in their positions and the maximum rate of fire was increased to around 25 shots per minute.
>
> At the turn of the century, British field guns were fitted only with open sights. The new quick-firing 13- and 18-prs, introduced in British regiments from 1904 to replace the breech-loading 12- and 15-prs, were not only fitted with dial sights to enable indirect fire, but also incorporated a hydro-spring recoil system and 'fixed' ammunition, with cartridge and shell in one piece. This innovation also contributed to the quick-firing revolution, though it would be abandoned for ease of ammunition handling and flexibility of charge selection in some of the larger field guns, such as the British 25-pr, developed between the wars. (For the same reasons, fixed ammunition was not a practical option for medium guns.)
>
> The importance of concealing batteries and the need for high-trajectory fire to reach over obstacles were emphasised by tactical developments in such conflicts as the South African War and the Russo-Japanese War of 1904–05. To be useful on the modern battlefield, both field guns and howitzers would need to be capable of indirect fire.

the drill shed so that the guns could be rolled out along the railway lines on either side of the rivermouth for training or in an emergency. The 12-prs were complemented by two 6-pr Nordenfelts on field carriages. In anticipation of this rearmament, in 1907 Westport's I Battery reverted to its former Garrison Artillery designation, becoming No. 8 Company, GAV.[34]

In 1911, 24 18-pr guns and eight 4.5-inch howitzers were ordered from Britain, and some of the field batteries were re-equipped as these modern weapons began to arrive in 1913. The field batteries at Auckland, Hamilton and Invercargill (the latter two created in 1911) got four 18-prs each, while those at Palmerston North (created in 1912) and Dunedin each received four 4.5-inch howitzers. Because of the capital's steep terrain, Wellington's D Battery was reconfigured as a mountain battery in 1911. It was to be armed with four 2.95-inch Vickers-Maxim mountain guns, but these had

The Westport Artillery Volunteers' quick-firing 12-pr was well and truly 'entrained'.
APG-2026-1/2-G, Alexander Turnbull Library, Wellington.

become obsolete and were returned to Britain in 1913. Their replacement with modern mountain guns was overtaken by the outbreak of war.[35]

The 18-pr gun, with its one-piece ammunition, was a very effective quick-firing anti-infantry weapon, though its full potential was not yet understood. Similarly, the 4.5-inch howitzers would come into their own at Gallipoli and on the Western Front. The field batteries, which had hitherto fired mostly in a direct-fire role over open sights, now had to apply forward observation techniques and the transmission of fire instructions to batteries by telephone. The NZFA had begun practising these techniques, but the science of indirect fire remained in its infancy when the First World War broke out.

Upgrading the Coastal Defences

The modernisation of the coastal defences started when four 12-pr Mk I quick-firing guns were ordered in 1898 and installed three years later in new positions at South Battery, Fort Cautley and Gordon Point, Fort Ballance. The former battery covered the minefield and entrance to Auckland Harbour; the latter

The former submarine-mining steamer *Janie Seddon* at Wellington, with gunners on board.
Museum of Wellington City and Sea.

served as the examination battery (see below) at Wellington. When the breech blew out of one of the Gordon Point guns in November 1904 one gunner was killed and five others were injured. By 1911 a battery established at Howlett Point, Fort Taiaroa, provided the examination battery for Otago Harbour. The garrison gunners also received new small arms when their carbines were replaced with magazine rifles in 1902–03.[36] The small submarine-mining steamer *Ellen Ballance*, which had proven unsuitable for this role in anything approaching bad weather, was redeployed to transport men and supplies to gun emplacements such as Ripapa Island and Taiaroa Head. When submarine mining was discontinued in 1907, its successors *Janie Seddon* and *Lady Roberts* were transferred to artillery service in Wellington and Auckland harbours respectively.[37]

Six-pr Nordenfelts and quick-firing 12-prs were adequate for the examination service, and the 6- and 8-inch disappearing guns, though obsolescent, were still useful for close defence (especially after 1915, when they were converted from black-powder to cordite charges). In 1904, to meet the new threat of long-range bombardment by modern naval guns, modern 6-inch Mk VII guns were ordered from Britain for New Zealand's two largest ports, and the ancient 7-inch RML guns were finally phased out everywhere. By 1906, electric order dials were being introduced to the forts to improve fire discipline, and companies were being given non-operational drill guns for preliminary training, to prevent excessive wear on the breech mechanisms of the service guns.[38] The new 6-inch guns were all installed, proofed and at operational readiness by September 1910. Two were sited at Fort Dorset, Wellington, on land purchased for the purpose, and on North Head, Auckland, overlooking the existing North Battery and covering the Rangitoto Channel. The two other main ports had to make do with their Victorian-era heavy armament.

The Defence Scheme was revised every two years from 1908, when some important changes put the coastal defences on a more warlike footing. The garrison artillery batteries at each of the four main ports were organised operationally into 'Fire Commands'. With fire control stations, examination batteries and close defence batteries linked by telephone, the RNZA and GAV companies now stood a much better chance of mounting a coordinated defence at each port. The 'Regulations [sic] of Traffic at Defended Ports in Time of War' included detailed procedures for the examination of approaching ships, with the objective of hampering 'as little as possible … entry into defended ports and the normal flow of traffic', while excluding 'vessels with hostile intentions'. It designated examination anchorages under the guns of the examination batteries and set out in full the roles of the batteries and the examination steamers. Specific craft at each port would be placed at the disposal of the 'Chief Examining Officer' – the harbourmaster. The examination batteries were to 'be always manned ready at all times to support the examination steamer, and should vessels fail to "bring to" to open fire, thus giving the alarm to the main defences'.[39] At the 'precautionary stage' the RNZA personnel were to be stationed at their assigned forts, while the GAV were to occupy their usual training camps. In the event of war Mounted Rifles units were to patrol designated beaches, while Rifle Volunteers were to defend the forts and the electric light emplacements. Field forces would be ready to repel or intercept enemy landings on the most likely beaches near each of the four major cities, supported where possible by the troops assigned to the harbour defences.

When Major-General Alexander Godley took over as GOC in December 1910, with enhanced powers and accompanied by a dozen British officers, he was generally satisfied with the coastal defences in existence or under construction. For him, the establishment of a Territorial Force (TF) was a much greater priority than further expenditure on the forts. A surprise attack on a New Zealand port was now seen as unlikely; Godley, more worried about the potential for landings elsewhere, called for 'an efficient mobile Artillery which can be sent ... anywhere round the coast'. It was impossible to provide permanent defences at 'all the innumerable ports and harbours', so the best chance of 'dealing effectively with an invader' was 'to go to meet him while he is landing or after he has landed'.[40]

From Volunteers to Territorials

In 1900 Colonel Penton had spelt out the basis for contingency planning and force structure development. As long as the Royal Navy remained intact, 'we want primarily to guard against ... an attack by a few raiding cruisers': the defended ports should be 'made safe against an enemy's cruisers, and our land Forces should be of sufficient strength to successfully cope with any raiding attacks on the ports from the land side'. Moreover, since 'the colonies [had] joined so heartily in Imperial defence' in South Africa, there should be a new focus on readiness for future expeditionary service. It would be wise, Penton suggested, 'to keep a spare store of saddlery, arms, and equipment always ready to furnish a force of mounted men for service either within or without the colony'.[41] Meanwhile, Seddon offered a New Zealand contribution to a mooted Imperial Reserve Force that would be liable for wartime service in South Africa or around the Pacific Rim, but the idea died as imperial fervour ebbed after the South African War ended.[42]

By 1909, increasing international tensions and the restructuring of the British Army to provide for an expeditionary force based on both regular and citizen soldiers, the latter trained part-time on a territorial basis, called into question the adequacy of New Zealand's Volunteer units. Would these men be competent to serve alongside British and other imperial forces? The Defence Act 1909 ended the volunteer era and instituted compulsory military training, from 1911, for all men aged between eighteen and 25. This enlarged the manpower available to the artillery, and the other corps. In February

Weapons – Field

A conventional gun, albeit powerful by nineteenth-century standards, the 15-pr had a novel method of limiting the effects of recoil: a spade hinged below the axle which dug into the ground on firing, its movement retarded by a spring in the trail. The cylinder housing this spring, and the fact that this was the last gun fitted with two seats on the axle for crewmen, also made it distinctive.

Name	Ordnance BL 15-pr
Entered NZ service	1900
Role	light horse-drawn field gun firing at a flat trajectory (16°)
Calibre	3 in
Range	6000 yds
Weight	2168 lb
Projectile	14 lb types – HE, shrapnel, star
Remarks	A high-powered weapon with a poor recoil system, this was first used by New Zealand artillery in the South African War.

Weapons – Coast Defence

The Royal Gun Factory's main 6-inch weapon first served British coast defences in 1898 and remained in service for six decades. The first arrived in New Zealand in 1904, but disagreements about where to mount them kept them in store until 1910. It was a bag charge weapon, with the propellant going into the breech after the shell.

Name	Ordnance BL 6-inch Mk VII
Entered NZ service	1910
Role	coast defence, counter-bombardment role (later, close defence)
Calibre	6 in, 45 cals
Range	11,600 yds
Weight	7-ton gun on a 9-ton Mk II central pivot and shield. (The naval P-type mounts used in the Second World War were much lighter.)
Projectile	100 lb types – common, HE, shrapnel, AP
Remarks	A high-powered weapon used until the end of the coast defences.

1910, as the transition began, the NZGAV stood at 1214 all ranks, while the NZFAV had 454 personnel. In 1911 the GAV became the New Zealand Garrison Artillery (NZGA), and its companies were redesignated to reflect their precedence in terms of lineage. The FAV became the New Zealand Field Artillery (NZFA), and its batteries were reorganised into field artillery brigades within the military districts (Auckland, Wellington, Canterbury and Otago) created by the reforms.

By 1912, under the territorial system, NZGA numbers had increased only slightly – the manning needs of the forts were finite – to an establishment of 1350; there were 1029 officers and men at the annual camps that year. The new emphasis on the Mobile Field Force had greatly increased the field artillery establishment, to 2213, though the NZFA was as yet far from fully manned: 1083 all ranks attended the annual camps.[43] The actual strength of the RNZA cadre in 1909 – 266 officers and men – had increased only to 315 by 1914.[44] The regulars were hard-pressed to carry out their multifarious duties – maintaining their technical proficiency, taking care of equipment and horses, administrative and ceremonial tasks – as well as training and overseeing the work of the territorial gunners. The RNZA was restructured to enable about one-third of its strength to form the cadre element of eight new field batteries. The rest remained in their established cadre role with the coast artillery.

The practical implementation of the new defence scheme began in January 1911 with a camp for the regular NCOs of the Permanent Staff at Tauherenikau. For the RNZA regulars the change from their traditional duties was less marked. Apart from the influx of Territorial recruits, garrison artillery training went on much as before, with the pre-existing volunteer element forming a solid core of experienced men at each battery. Most field batteries, on the other hand, had suffered greatly from a lack of realistic training, with no horse teams to allow mobile operations and very limited opportunities to undertake shoots. The stationing of a cadre of regulars and a team or teams of horses with each field battery now extended the 1901 Wellington experiment throughout the country.

Like the rest of the Territorial Force, the Field Artillery units now attended realistic annual camps, usually at racecourses or on farmland borrowed for the purpose, though training with infantry units remained

A Garrison Artillery company drills at Otago Heads on a 15-pr field gun, 1912.
c/n sheet 28a/3/a, Hocken Library, University of Otago.

infrequent. The guns and horses were prepared by the RNZA regulars and then transported, usually by train, to the designated campsite. Here, in readiness for the arrival of the Territorial Force men, the regulars set out tents, cook-houses, ablution facilities, horse lines and other necessary facilities. The new system was a great improvement on the old Volunteer camps, with their unpredictable attendance and rudimentary training.

Field training of the Territorial Force began in earnest in early 1912, when all units underwent seven-day regimental camps. Brigade camps were held the following summer, and in 1914 all-arms camps. Territorial gunners could now practise deployment and field shoots from concealed positions in cooperation with infantry manoeuvres. General Sir Ian Hamilton, Britain's Inspector-General of the Oversea Forces, who visited New Zealand in 1914, thought 'the Artillery was generally well handled' in these combined operations, though sometimes pushed forward into 'positions of undue exposure' in their opening stages.[45]

For TF and RNZA gunners alike, the usual pattern of peacetime duties was interrupted in late 1913 by a general strike during which the armed forces assisted the government. The observation in Godley's annual report that training had had to be 'practically suspended' for six weeks[46] was a considerable understatement: the military played a significant, if largely covert, role in ending the strike.[47] When Wellington's waterfront was effectively taken over by striking watersiders in late October, the government's first plan – as in the 1890 Maritime Strike – was to use unarmed artillerymen as police, allowing the regular police to control the wharves. When the Chief of the General Staff, Colonel Edward Heard (Godley was overseas), objected, he was told to raise and maintain a substantial force of special constables, using the infrastructure provided by the mounted rifles regiments.

The specials' base at the Defence Department complex at Mount Cook in Wellington was guarded by artillerymen. On 3 November an NCO in this guard was seriously injured by a metal bolt hurled from the crowd, and an officer was struck by a spent pistol bullet. The guard then broke out two machine guns on Buckle Street. The situation was saved only when the commander of the guard, Major John Hume, appealed to the strikers. Permanent officers and NCOs in plain clothes organised and trained the specials, while two entrepreneurial artillerymen opened shops to supply them with cigarettes and other comforts. The military played a similar support role in the other main centres. In Auckland, ten Permanent Staff men acted as foot special constables on the wharves.

Since 1913, New Zealand's armed forces have done their utmost to avoid being drawn into any repetition of this operation. The officers and men of the RNZA and NZFA were soon to form the core of artillery units sent overseas, joined by thousands of volunteers and conscripts. New Zealand's ability to deploy gunners and guns overseas shortly after the outbreak of war was very much a product of the preparations made in the preceding decade. In 1914, thanks to the territorial reforms, improved training and the arrival of modern guns, New Zealand's field units were at their best ever state of readiness, and the coastal companies had maintained their usual high standards.

George Richardson

George Richardson had a 'rare ability to engender [both] confidence among his superiors and loyalty from those serving under him'.[48] The first qualified instructor appointed to the Permanent Artillery, he was also the only New Zealand soldier promoted from NCO direct to captain in peacetime. Born out of wedlock in Northamptonshire in 1868, his prospects were limited when he joined the Royal Garrison Artillery in 1886. After serving in Gibraltar, he rose rapidly to staff sergeant instructor and topped the long course in gunnery at Shoeburyness. In 1891 Richardson was seconded from the Royal Artillery to help train New Zealand's permanent artillery. Promoted to master gunner (a non-commissioned rank), he initiated new training manuals, publishing *Questions & Answers in Gunnery* five years later. His artillery-related inventions 'were used to advantage throughout the colony'. He infused new life into gunnery in New Zealand, and was re-engaged several times. Colonel Francis Fox, the Commandant, thought him 'as smart as it is possible for a man to be'.

Richardson married a year after arriving in New Zealand; the couple would have six children. He was a member of the New Zealand contingent sent to the celebrations of Australian Federation in 1901. When the War Office sought his return, Nelson gunners lobbied Minister of Defence R.J. Seddon to keep him. Some, however, felt that career Royal Artillerymen should not linger too long in the colonies. The seconded imperial artillery officer G.N. (Napier) Johnston, in recommending Richardson for re-engagement in 1904, said that he 'not only has exceptional ability and capacity for work, but is still quite unspoiled, although he has been in the country for so many years'. In early 1905, however, Richardson was found to have 'identified himself too much with D Battery' during the dispute with Stokes Valley farmers.[49]

In 1907, despite having already qualified for the imperial rank of captain in tactics, fortifications and military topography, Richardson sought to requalify in all subjects in New Zealand. 'This is the proper spirit', approved the Chief of the General Staff. 'At same time, Captain Richardson can hardly sit for the artillery subjects as I will require his assistance in all matters relating to Garrison & Field Guns & Gunnery & Coast Defence when making out the problems and questions.' Clearly indispensable, Richardson gained the promotion anyway and was appointed Director of Artillery Services (later Director of Ordnance and Artillery) on top of his Chief Instructor role. He was now 'the hardest worked officer in the service'.

Captain Richardson transferred to the New Zealand Staff Corps and sat the entrance examination for the Staff College in Britain in 1911. While he was on his way to Camberley his oldest son, who was serving in the field artillery, was run over and killed by a gun carriage on the Hutt Road.[50] After completing the two-year course he replaced Colonel Alfred Robin as New Zealand's representative to the Imperial General Staff, Military Adviser to the High Commissioner and Inspector of Warlike Stores. In August 1914 Major Richardson joined the administrative staff of the Royal Naval Division. After serving in the defence of Antwerp and in France, he became the division's Assistant Adjutant and Quartermaster-General, promoted to temporary lieutenant-colonel. After serving in Gallipoli he transferred to XII Corps at Salonika in October 1915, becoming brigadier-general in December. New Zealand now 'reclaimed' him, transferring him to the NZEF in January 1916. 'Characteristically he put duty to New Zealand before his personal preference to remain in the field, where he had good prospects of advancement.'

From February 1916 Richardson again 'rendered assistance to the High Commissioner', commanded the New Zealand forces in Britain, oversaw the NZEF Administration and, from May, represented New Zealand at the War Office. In 1918 he was still 'very anxious' to get over to France on active service, but there was no one to replace him in Britain.[51] His war service saw him both mentioned in despatches and brought to the notice of the Secretary of State for War three times. He was appointed a CMG in 1915, CB in 1917 and CBE in 1919, and was awarded the Legion d'Honneur.

Richardson returned to New Zealand as Officer in Charge Administration in the Defence Department. He helped to implement military retrenchment and sat on the fledgling Air Board. Despite ill-health he presided over the Khandallah Tennis and Squash Club. He took a personal interest in the welfare of amputee ex-servicemen, and was later to be president and then patron of the Auckland RSA. His military career ended in 1923, when he was appointed Administrator of Western Samoa, a post he held until 1928. An instinctive paternalist, he misunderstood Samoan aspirations and deported adherents of the nationalist movement, the Mau.

Knighted in 1925, Sir George was elected to the Auckland City Council in 1935. He was Deputy Mayor when he died suddenly in June 1938 while planning the RSA's role in the 1940 New Zealand centenary celebrations. His coffin was borne on an 18-pr gun carriage and headed by an RNZA firing party, while North Head fired a nineteen-gun salute. Three hundred ex-servicemen and Territorials were among the 2000 people at his funeral: three VCs were among his pallbearers. That men 'ill-fitted for the ordeal ... marched in the cortege' was 'clear proof of their devotion'. One by one they 'took poppies from their coat lapels and dropped them upon the coffin'. His was a remarkable career for a man from the ranks, and his administrative thoroughness left an indelible stamp on the New Zealand Military Force.

George Campbell

George Campbell epitomised the citizen soldier on whom New Zealand relied for an efficient defence force. A keen Volunteer, he held important senior positions in both the defence services – rising to command a military district – and the civil service.[52]

Born into a settler family in Nelson in 1858 and educated at Nelson College, Campbell worked in the Public Works, Justice and Land Tax departments from 1874. A Wellington rugby representative, he was in 1884 selected to captain the first New Zealand team to tour overseas, but declined because of pressure of work. Involved in the creation of the New Zealand Rugby Football Union in 1892, he managed the first official touring team to Australia the following year. He was NZRFU president in 1893, 1903 and 1908, and a national selector in 1893 and 1894. Campbell was also one of the key figures in the leasing of Wellington's Athletic Park as a sportsground.[53]

Campbell joined the Wellington Naval Artillery Volunteers, and was voted junior lieutenant in 1887. Three years later he had moved to the Property Tax Department and in 1894 he became both Deputy Commissioner of Taxes and Lieutenant Commanding the Wellington Navals.[54] He was also involved in athletics, yachting and rowing; as President of the Star Boating Club he may have had a hand in forming its naval artillery corps in the late 1890s. Campbell 'pulled a good oar in senior crews' and was President of the New Zealand Rowing Association.

Deputy Valuer-General from 1897, Campbell rose to captain in the Naval Brigade in 1902, overseeing the administration of the Wellington and Petone companies of over 200 men, their uniforming, equipping and training in regular parades and annual encampments. By 1904, when he was appointed Valuer-General, he was undertaking staff duties in the Wellington Division of the Garrison Artillery Volunteers, for which he was

Lieutenant G.F.C. Campbell, Wellington Naval Artillery, 1889.
Defence of New Zealand Study Group. Courtesy of HMNZS Olphert (Wellington Naval Reserve).

promoted to lieutenant-colonel. In his spare time, therefore, he worked with the regular officers in the Wellington detachment of the RNZA, and his opposite number in the submarine mining volunteers, to ensure the readiness of the coast defences and their personnel to respond to any threat.

His star in the civil service continued to ascend: he became General Manager of the State Fire Insurance Department in 1908, Commissioner of Taxes two years later, and Secretary to the Treasury and Receiver-General in 1913. In the New Zealand Military Forces, he was promoted to the new position of Coast Defence Commander in March 1911, with the rank of colonel. His first task was the reorganisation of the Garrison Artillery Division from Volunteers to Territorials under the new Defence Act. He was also appointed an honorary ADC to the Governor in 1914. This role, which also lasted throughout the war, involved Campbell in ceremonial duties, liaison and providing local knowledge and influence when the Governor was in Wellington. At this time Campbell was described as 'one of the solid men' of the civil service, and a 'strict disciplinarian of the amiable type. He loathes all muddle and slovenliness, instinctively'. Schooled in Victorian values, he had 'held all through his life that a man not physically capable and fit is little likely to do the State or any private employer really good service'.[55]

The calibre of the Coast Defence Commander was tested by the mobilisation for war. In 1914 the forts were fully manned, but the subsequent strain on manpower saw them demanned by April 1915. In the absence of an incumbent Campbell was appointed to temporarily command the Wellington Military District from December 1916, and held the position until after the war.

Campbell's roles sometimes intersected with each other. He complained in 1919 when Colonel J.J. Esson of 5 Regiment was appointed Financial Adviser at General Headquarters because, as head of Treasury, he thought he should have been consulted before a senior subordinate was allowed to take on such an important additional role.

Campbell was awarded the Colonial Auxiliary Force Officer's Decoration and New Zealand Volunteer Long and Efficient Service Medal in 1909, and made a CMG in 1919. His only regret was that he had never seen active service. In 1922 he was promoted from Treasury Secretary to Auditor-General, a post he held until his death in March 1937 ended 63 years of public service.

3

Artillery Comes of Age: The First World War

The Royal New Zealand Artillery faced its first real test in August 1914, when war broke out between the British, French, Russian and Japanese empires, and those of Germany and Austria-Hungary (the 'Central Powers'). After German forces invaded Belgium in an attempt to outflank and envelop the French Army, the British government declared war, a decision enthusiastically endorsed in New Zealand and the other dominions. The outbreak of war had an immediate impact on the New Zealand artillery. Somewhere in the Pacific was the German East Asiatic Squadron, including the powerful armoured cruisers *Scharnhorst* and *Gneisenau* and three light cruisers that would be more than a match for the three ageing British P-class cruisers in New Zealand waters. Raids on New Zealand ports were feared. The garrison artillery was being mobilised when war was declared, and an NZFA battery would take part in an expedition to capture the German colony of Samoa.

Meanwhile, preparations for a much more demanding task began: the recruitment and training of an artillery brigade to accompany a New Zealand expeditionary force offered for service in France. Here, after an initial 'race for the sea' in which the key weapons on both sides were quick-firing mobile field guns based on the French 75-mm, the war would develop in ways no one anticipated. After the nearly 500-mile-long Western Front stabilised in late 1914, the next three years saw a return to siege warfare: new and heavier weaponry was introduced and increasingly elaborate strategies and tactics were devised in unsuccessful efforts to break the stalemate. Artillery dominated this battlefield as never before or since, and caused most of the millions of casualties. By 1918, the Germans and French had

15,000 heavy guns between them, while the Royal Artillery, more than half a million strong, made up a quarter of the British Army. When the New Zealand gunners eventually reached France in 1916, they became a small but valuable component in the huge machine that would finally wear down the Germans in late 1918. First, however, they had to endure an ill-starred diversion in the Mediterranean.

Manning the Coast Defences

The pre-war plans to implement the examination service and mobilise the RNZA and NZGA territorials were activated between 2 and 5 August 1914; the coast defence infantry companies were also called out. The harbourmasters were appointed as chief examination officers (CXOs), with two or three assistant XOs (usually RNZA personnel) to serve on the examination steamers and identify vessels. Auckland and Wellington used the government steamers *Lady Roberts* and *Janie Seddon* respectively, with additional steamers and crews hired as relief vessels. Vessels were also hired for the examination service in Lyttelton and Port Chalmers. The examination batteries at Fort Takapuna, Point Gordon in Wellington, Fort Jervois and Howlett Point at the entrance to Port Chalmers were manned round the clock until 15 March 1915.[1] Thereafter guns and equipment were maintained at a high state of readiness, with battery personnel available at a few hours' notice. Two 12-prs transferred from Dunedin to Fort Dorset in 1916 to provide better coverage of the harbour were never called on to serve in this role.

Some seafarers fell foul of the examination batteries early in the war. On 4 August 1914 the small coaster *Whakatu* put into Lyttelton Harbour. The skipper was 'such a belligerent type that he ignored completely the examination vessel at The Heads and came sailing on up the Harbour.... [W]hen he was just about opposite the Fort a Six Inch shell across his bows brought him to very smartly.'[2]

The batteries of heavy guns at each port were also manned immediately. '[B]eing posted to the garrison artillery at the heads was quite a thrill,' one Wellington Garrison Artillery Territorial remembered, 'because ... there was talk about [the *Scharnhorst* and *Gneisenau*] coming down to invade.' At Westport, No. 8 Company NZGA was also mobilised in the early days of the war in case local coal attracted German raiders seeking to refuel or to prevent the Royal Navy doing so.³

The pressure on the Garrison Artillery territorials soon began to tell. From November, with the German squadron known to be off the Chilean coast, only the examination batteries and the modern 6-inch Mk VII batteries at North Head and Fort Dorset were maintained at high readiness. The crews of the older guns were released from camp and the guns ceased to be fully manned, though NZGA gunners were available at short notice.⁴ By April 1915, with the German cruisers now sunk or bottled up, none of the coastal batteries was at 24-hour readiness, though small numbers of NZGA territorials remained mobilised throughout the war to maintain the guns and, if necessary, bring them into action quickly.

SAMOA

On 6 August the British government requested that New Zealand forces seize the wireless station at Apia in German Samoa.⁵ A composite force including three companies of infantry and detachments of engineers, signallers and other units was formed in Wellington for this task. It was manned mostly by personnel of specific Territorial units, whose members volunteered almost en bloc. The artillery component comprised volunteers from Wellington's D (Mountain) Battery, NZFA, made up to a strength of 100 by men from the reserve and commanded by Captain R.S. McQuarrie. By the 9th two 15-prs, two 6-pr Nordenfelts and other equipment had been loaded onto transports (two guns on each, so that if either was sunk the battery would still have pieces available).⁶ The troops embarked three days later, but the convoy's departure was delayed until the 15th, and en route it diverted to Noumea because of anxiety about the whereabouts of the East Asiatic Squadron.

The landing at Apia on 29 August was unopposed, but one section of gunners did not get ashore for some days. Having stayed aboard the *Monowai* to help unload stores and equipment, they took an unintended detour to Fiji when the transports and escorts departed in convoy. When these gunners rejoined the battery a few days later, it had emplaced its guns and pitched camp on the Apia waterfront, with a commanding field of fire over the harbour. They had hardly begun to settle into the routine of life in the tropics when the war intruded dramatically. Early on 14 September the *Scharnhorst* and *Gneisenau* were seen approaching the reef entrance to the harbour, and the occupying force turned out to repel the expected landing. The anxious gunners manning their weapons on the beach knew they would be obliterated in any exchange of fire. Fears rose as the cruisers trained their big guns on the defenders, but no shots were fired and, to the gunners' relief, the ships turned away and steamed off to the west.

The gunners' subsequent Samoan experience was uneventful, with just occasional target shoots into the lagoon – the only shells they fired in Samoa – to break the monotony. In February 1915, there were rumours of an elusive German light cruiser and merchant cruiser in the vicinity. Two Nordenfelts were dug in to defend a strongpoint centred on the wireless station, but

D Battery guns and guard party encamped on the beach at Apia, Samoa, c.1915.
PAColl-3799-17, Alexander Turnbull Library, Wellington.

nothing happened. Some of the original Samoa Expeditionary Force had already returned home when, on 3 April, the main relief draft of 360 men, mostly over age for active military service, arrived to man a much-reduced occupation force. Since the strategic situation in the Pacific had stabilised in the Allies' favour, the remnants of the original force, including the D Battery gunners, returned to New Zealand, where many promptly re-enlisted for service in Europe.

Gunners at Sea

The New Zealand Artillery provided gunners on troopships once these were armed, and two or three were assigned to the armed merchant ships that passed through areas of submarine activity. They augmented their numbers from the ship's company or troops on board. From the Fifteenth Reinforcements, for instance, Bert Stokes and two other New Zealand gunners were chosen to work the gun on HMNZT *Ulimaroa* after it left Cape Town. '[W]e were excused all other duties; we just sat by this gun. We had a practice shoot one day where all the heads of the ship came along to have a look. We threw a big oat box overboard and had a couple of shots at it.' The gun had been installed at Cape Town and came with two Royal Navy gunners. 'When we got near the Bay of Biscay everybody got a bit nervous because there were submarines supposed to be about.' Two months earlier the Thirteenth Reinforcements had acquired a 12-pr and two naval gunners at Dakar.

On the troopship *Nile* taking NZFA men from Egypt to Southampton, Gunner A.T. Stratton 'was told to take charge of the only naval gun on the ship, with another 5 chaps to help me. None of us knew anything about this gun but we soon learnt where the shells went in and where they came out. We don't shoot at moving targets with our artillery guns but this gun is on the move all the time with the dipping and rolling of the ship but I think we could have managed alright.'

From late 1917, troopships were armed in New Zealand for the voyage, and gunners detailed to their service. In mid-1918 the gunners on seven merchant ships serving New Zealand were replaced by naval personnel in Britain. Thereafter only four trans-Tasman vessels were manned by New Zealand gunners, and these were replaced by naval crews by August. The last New Zealand gunners with this role were three men manning the guns on the requisitioned minesweepers *Haranui* and *Tutanekai*, which looked for mines off Farewell Spit and North Cape in January 1919.

New Zealand gunners manning an anti-submarine gun on a troopship.
McDermott Album, 1991.1961, Kippenberger Military Archive, Army Museum Waiouru.

Not all service afloat was dull. The artillery helped to hunt for Count Felix von Luckner, the master of the German raider *Seeadler*, who escaped from internment on Motuihe Island near Auckland in December 1917 and headed out to sea on a commandeered scow, the *Moa*. Two RNZA gunners hastily mounted 6-pr quick-firing guns from North Head on the government cable steamer *Iris*, which joined 28 other vessels (three armed with machine guns) in a search of the coastline between the Three Kings Islands and East Cape.

With RNZA and Garrison Artillery Territorials as gun crew, *Iris* hunted down the escapers. Approaching the *Moa* near the Kermadec Islands, the gunners participated in the first naval action in New Zealand waters at lunchtime on 21 December, when the captain 'ordered a shot to be fired across her bows.... Owing to the ship's anchor being in the line of sight the shot was actually fired across the scow's stern. After the shot the *Moa* hoisted the German ensign, then hove to.'

Other gunners had less exciting tasks at sea. In 1918–19 government vessels, including *Tutanekai*, were armed for special missions such as escorting the Governor-General to the Pacific Islands, for which the RNZA supplied a gun and two gunners.[7]

The NZEF Artillery

New Zealand's main contribution to imperial defence was the despatch of an expeditionary force to Europe. Volunteers were sought from the Territorial Force, and others also came forward: within a week of Britain's declaration of war, 14,000 men had volunteered (some were assigned to the Samoa force). While the infantry and mounted rifles units were raised regionally and maintained a provincial identity, the artillery and other divisional units were raised on a countrywide basis, also mostly from the relevant TF units. They were assembled at Awapuni racecourse in Palmerston North. Initially it was intended that one six-gun 18-pr battery would accompany the expeditionary force, and this and the associated brigade and divisional ammunition columns were soon formed. With large numbers of men volunteering for the artillery, it was soon decided that a brigade of three batteries, each of four 18-prs and a brigade ammunition column, would form part of the Main Body of the New Zealand Expeditionary Force (NZEF). This level of contribution had been suggested by the Australian defence authorities in 1912.[8] (A battery of four 4.5-inch howitzers would be formed later and despatched with the Second Reinforcements.)[9] The men of the initial battery were allocated among the three new ones, which were quickly brought up to strength with additional volunteers, many with considerable experience. The guns were drawn from the existing TF batteries.[10] The RNZA provided some of the horses required, but many had to be purchased and trained to meet the requirements of the gun batteries and ammunition column.

The Field Artillery Brigade was placed under the command of Lieutenant-Colonel G.N. (Napier) Johnston, who had been Inspector of Artillery for just a month. The battery commanders were Majors F. Symon, RNZA (1 Battery), F.B. Sykes, RA (2 Battery) and I.T. Standish, RNZA (3 Battery). When the British accepted the offer of a howitzer battery in mid-September, an officer and a few NCOs with howitzer experience in the TF were transferred from the 18-pr batteries to help train the new unit, which assembled at Trentham under the command of Captain N.S. Falla, NZFA.

The NZEF was scheduled to leave on 25 September. The gunners of the 18-pr batteries and the Brigade Ammunition Column embarked on transports at Wellington on the 24th, but their expectations were soon dashed. Next morning they disembarked to await the arrival of a suitable escort for the troop convoy. Camped at the Lower Hutt racecourse, the gunners had another three weeks of much-needed training in moving and firing the guns. Along with the rest of the Main Body, they re-embarked on 15 October and set off next morning on their great adventure. After rendezvousing with the larger convoy of the Australian Imperial Force, the combined convoy arrived in Colombo on 15 November. One of the gunners' less pleasant shipboard tasks was carrying all the horse excrement up from the holds and dumping it over the side.[11]

As they continued across the Indian Ocean, news arrived that the Ottoman Empire (centred on modern-day Turkey) had entered the war on the side of the Central Powers. This changed the strategic picture. Instead of going directly to the Western Front, as planned, the Australasian troops would be landed in Egypt, where they could continue their training and bolster the forces available to protect the Suez Canal. After a further stopover at Aden the New Zealanders passed through the Canal and disembarked at Alexandria on 3 December. Over the following week units departed for Cairo, 150 miles away. Men led their horses down the big ramps, and slung their guns and stores up from the holds, packing them into the long troop trains that would take them to their camp on the edge of the desert at Zeitoun, near Heliopolis. The gunners began training almost immediately, while the drivers exercised the horses to restore their strength after the long sea voyage.[12]

At Zeitoun the artillery trained under its own officers. Almost at once they began comparing themselves with the British they encountered:

> [A] few young English officers used to come out with us sometimes, evidently to gain experience; most of them looked very uneasy in the saddle, and always gave one the impression that they did not quite know how much longer they would be staying in it. I am pretty sure we are just as efficient now, if not more so than we would have been under English officers. I would back our drivers any day against any of the drivers of the English Regular Batteries we have come across out here.[13]

The desert training was long and hard. 'No holiday today,' wrote one gunner on New Year's Day 1915, 'just another weary trying day in the sand with the guns – gun drill, gun drill, gun drill, from morning to night.'[14]

Though the fleshpots of Cairo appealed to many gunners, others were impressed by the ancient city's history and architecture. For most, a visit to the Pyramids was a must. Many longed for a fight. As Wes Muldoon wrote in December, 'We were all pleased yesterday when we heard the Turks were advancing on us 80,000 strong. They are a wild rabble primitively armed without a gun of any size. This will be splendid practice for our Artillery before we go to Germany.'[15]

The men were elated after an exercise on 29 January:

> We took up a covered position about 5 miles out & taking our directions from the Major on the hills a mile away we opened fire. After pumping about 20 shells in we retired & going further afield went into action again & fired our remaining shells. Of course we could not see the target at all as we were firing from cover in each case so we had to get the result on arrival back in camp. We are all in excellent mood. Report from Col Johnston 'Best shooting I have ever seen in all my experience of Artillery[']…. Our Major is an absolute marvel…. as a director of artillery he is the First & last thing. He just put a shot where ever he wanted it & just as fast as he liked. I never thought it possible for our guns to do such work. They are murderous weapons.[16]

The rumours of action proved correct – but not for the gunners. When the four New Zealand infantry battalions and a field ambulance were sent forward on 26 January to defend the Suez Canal, the Artillery stayed in camp. Australian guns would support the force. A Turkish force attempted to cross the Canal near Ismailia on 2 February, but was repulsed.[17] While this, New Zealand's first battle of the war, was going on, the New Zealand Artillery had to content themselves with inter-battery rivalry.

The gunners of 4 (Howitzer) Battery, arriving with the Second Reinforcements, had passed through the Canal only five days before the Turkish attack, their guns lashed on the deck of their transport, ready for action if needed.[18] Once ashore, these gunners joined their comrades at Zeitoun.

A shortage of 4.5-inch ammunition prevented them from undertaking live firing; the only shells on hand were the 800 rounds they had brought with them. In Egypt a Howitzer Battery Ammunition Column was formed. By now the Field Artillery Brigade had been incorporated in the New Zealand and Australian Division. This hybrid unit – it included two infantry brigades and two mounted rifles brigades – was seriously deficient in supporting units, especially artillery. Instead of the usual three artillery brigades, there was only the New Zealand brigade, and Napier Johnston found himself Commander, Royal Artillery (CRA). This division, and the Australian Division, formed the Australian and New Zealand Army Corps under the British Lieutenant-General Sir William Birdwood. In late March the ANZAC became part of the Mediterranean Expeditionary Force (MEF) commanded by General Sir Ian Hamilton.

After British and French warships failed to open the Dardanelles strait between the Mediterranean and the Black Sea on 18 March 1915, it was widely rumoured that the imperial troops in Egypt would soon be involved in a further assault on the Turkish defences along the strategic waterway. These predictions proved correct. From 9 April the New Zealand gunners began to leave camp for Alexandria, where they embarked with their horses and guns – now camouflaged for action – on four of the transports massed in the harbour. The New Zealand and Australian Division was on the move, though without its two mounted brigades, which remained in Egypt. By the 20th the New Zealanders' ships were among an imposing array of warships and the transports of the entire MEF in Mudros Harbour on the Aegean island of Lemnos.[19] Here the gunners practised unloading their guns and horses onto pontoons. Plans for the coming campaign were explained to the nervous and excited troops crammed aboard the transports. The main landing would be made by British troops at Cape Helles, on the southern tip of the Gallipoli Peninsula. At the same time the ANZAC, landed a dozen miles to the north at Gaba Tepe, would drive across the peninsula and cut the lines of communication of the Turks resisting the British landing.

GALLIPOLI

The Allied armada left Mudros for Gallipoli late on 24 April 1915. By daybreak on the 25th the New Zealand transports lay off what would become known as Anzac Cove, where the Australian Division had begun landing before dawn. The first wave of the New Zealand and Australian Division, including Johnston and his artillery headquarters, scrambled ashore under shell and sniper fire just before 10 a.m. The guns remained on board. By the end of the day only two Indian mountain batteries and a single Australian 18-pr were in action in this sector.[20]

The left section of 4 (Howitzer) Battery went ashore at Anzac Cove at 6.30 a.m. on 26 April. Within 20 minutes its two howitzers were in action. Australian horse teams had dragged them into concealed positions at the foot of what became known as Howitzer Gully. The right section landed at midday, took up positions north of the cove and was also quick to begin firing. Gunners of 3 Battery remained on board their transport, 'very much afraid that we would go back to Alexandria' because of the lack of firing positions in the tiny enclave seized on the first day.[21]

The accuracy of the howitzer battery – in its first live shoots – was greatly appreciated by the infantry, who had not managed to press forward very far in the rugged terrain before the Turks forced them back. The gunfire helped the ANZACs to cling to a ridgeline less than a mile from the beach, but want of shells caused worrying gaps in the artillery support. The guns were silenced for two hours on the 27th. Initially ammunition was short because it was difficult to supply the exposed beachhead, but when the landing failed to provide an easy victory, the Gallipoli campaign was given a low priority and starved of supplies. The operations of 4 (Howitzer) Battery, in heavy demand as the only artillery unit able to cover much of the steep ground in front of the New Zealand and Australian Division's line, suffered particularly from the general shortage of shells. The difficulty of getting supplies ashore would also result in chronic shortages of rations, particularly drinking water, so that thirst and hunger added to the miseries of life on the Anzac beachhead.

These experiences were still to come, however, when the 18-prs of 2 Battery were towed ashore at dawn on 27 April. Lacking the high trajectory of the howitzers, the 18-prs were less well suited to the confined positions at Anzac:

4 Howitzer Battery in action below Plugge's Plateau, Gallipoli, 1915.
Fenwick Collection, album 337, C54337/B12550, Auckland War Memorial Museum.

hemmed in by cliffs, they lacked enough clearance to go into action. While the right section's guns were manhandled to temporary positions near Ari Burnu, at the northern end of Anzac Cove, the others remained stranded on the beach. By the evening of 28 April the infantry had prepared a track, and the guns were hauled up Maclagan's Ridge to positions on top of Plugge's Plateau above Anzac Cove by parties of 'one hundred lusty men heaving in unison'. Ten days later they were joined by the right section. From this position 2 Battery dominated a critical section of the Turkish trenches near Quinn's Post: if they lost their tenuous position on the ridge, the Turks would destroy the enclave. The guns of 1 Battery were landed on 30 April and 1 May. After two were temporarily emplaced in an unsatisfactory position with a very restricted arc of fire, this battery was consigned to a reserve role on the beach.[22]

Located so close to the front line, the gunners were in a very uncomfortable predicament. Eight days after landing a 2 Battery gunner was:

> sitting in dugout writing. Every few minutes shells are bursting overhead & shrapnell searches the dug out hillside for human targets. We have been looking for action and at last we have got it with a vengeance. Will one ever forget this experience? Graves of our boys everywhere, marked only by a small cross with the dead men's names thereon. What with the booming of the warships, the roar of our own guns and the incessant rattle of rifle fire a fearful din is our only music, night & day.

Three days later his gun 'only fired 4 shots. Enemy's batteries hard to find. Australians shifted one of their batteries on to ridge on our right. Enemy soon spotted them & a real artillery dual [*sic*] ensued. Indian's mountain battery close to us [has] been in action off & on all day, & did good work. Indians smart gunners.'[23]

By 17 May sappers and infantrymen had constructed a track up Walker's Ridge to Russell's Top, a key position guarding the northern flank of the Anzac sector. The four guns of 1 Battery were manhandled to the summit and emplaced so they could enfilade the enemy trenches at Lone Pine and Johnston's Jolly. With these sometimes just 20 yards from ANZAC infantry, 'the ranging had to be most careful and the fuse setting most accurate'. Ammunition was carried up the gully tracks from the beach by mules burdened with boxes of four rounds on each side of their pack saddles. With the enemy lines so close, the gunners on Plugge's Plateau and Walker's Ridge dug in as best they could. Communication trenches linked the gun positions, the rear approaches and the small dugouts which the gunners 'made very comfortable and … always kept very neatly'.[24] Although the gun pits were exposed to Turkish fire, there were no better positions from which the 18-prs could command critical parts of the front and challenge the Turkish batteries. They formed part of a network of 'interlocking arcs of fire' of machine guns and artillery which provided a guarantee against the precarious Allied trench system falling like a house of cards.[25]

The 18th of May was the 'most exciting day' since the gunners had been in action:

> At four o'clock this morning enemy shelled us heavily. Was asleep in gun pit but was soon very wide awake & beat a hasty retreat to funk-holes. Schrapnel

Camouflaged New Zealand 18-pr, Gallipoli, 1915.
P01155.003, Australian War Memorial.

fairly rained on gun shield & impallment. At 10 o'clock got orders to shift our gun to our other gun pit to engage one of enemys batteries on left flank. Fired 10 shots at 6000 yards & <u>silenced enemy</u>. Enemy did not fire another shot till 7 p.m.

At 11.45 p.m. night 18th terrific outburst of rifle & machine gun fire. Continued almost unabated till breakfast time next morning (19th). Cause – enemy desperately assaulted our trenches, but slaughtered in hundreds by machine guns. Early this morning enemy's artillery shelled us with unprecedented fury. Shrapnel fell like hailstones.[26]

During this attack 'the shells of the Battery were bursting a few feet beyond the front line trenches and covering the enemy with a hail of shrapnel. ... The 18prs. fired 1,360 rounds, the Howitzer battery 143 rounds, and the Mountain Guns 1,400 rounds.' The backlash came once the Turks had been repulsed: the artillery were limited to two rounds per gun per day.[27]

Observation posts were established at the front lines, including two provided by the NZFA Brigade to direct naval gunfire, which was at times critical to the land battle, even though the high-velocity naval guns could fire only onto forward-facing slopes. Johnston initially established his Artillery HQ alongside the Divisional HQ near the beach at the northern end of Anzac Cove, but within two weeks both HQs had shifted to a new location below Plugge's Plateau.

While the ANZACs were clinging to the line inland from the beach at Anzac Cove, British and French forces had established more extensive positions at Cape Helles, but, like the Australians and New Zealanders, had been held well short of their first-day objectives. In early May General Hamilton planned a major assault to take Achi Baba, the hill commanding the Helles sector. For this attack, the New Zealand Infantry Brigade and an Australian infantry brigade were redeployed to Helles, and eventually replaced at Anzac on 12 May by the New Zealand Mounted Rifles and the Australian Light Horse, without their horses. On 3 May, 3 Battery, NZFA, which had not still disembarked at Anzac Cove for want of gun positions, was also ordered to Helles. Complete with its horses and wagons, it went ashore without incident at midnight on the 4th and was established in prepared positions on the left of the line, attached to 147 Brigade Royal Field Artillery (RFA). The battery was soon in action, supporting British units attacking Achi Baba. These assaults on entrenched positions defended by machine guns and fronted with extensive barbed-wire entanglements gained little ground at great cost. The supporting artillery lacked both strength and shells: over three days 3 Battery fired just 420 rounds.[28]

The New Zealand Infantry Brigade, which attacked in broad daylight on 8 May, suffered more than 800 casualties in gaining a few hundred yards. Next day 3 Battery shifted to positions atop cliffs at the far west of the line, from which it could fire on Turkish strongpoints. It remained in action, supporting further British assaults, after the New Zealand infantrymen were withdrawn from the line on the night of the 11th and redeployed to Anzac a week later. On 12 May the battery supported a Gurkha battalion which successfully assaulted a strategic Turkish position. On 4 June it fired almost 1000 rounds during a major operation by both British and French units. This assault was preceded by a major naval and field artillery bombardment but, despite early successes, was thrown back by heavy counter-attacks and gained only a few hundred yards. The battery supported a more successful advance on 28 June, but the tactical situation was not changed. The Turks pulled back up the slope of Achi Baba and continued their dogged resistance. On 12 and 13 July, while it was supporting yet another assault, the battery was shelled and suffered a number of casualties. It remained at Helles until 17 August, when it departed to rejoin the artillery at Anzac.

Meanwhile, the gunners at Anzac supported diversionary raids on the Turkish lines during the attacks at Helles. The most important of these actions took place on 4 June, but enemy machine-gun fire prevented the Allies from entering the captured territory. A major Turkish assault on the ANZAC lines in the early hours of 29 June was preceded by a heavy artillery bombardment. The New Zealand gunners brought down harassing fire on the troops forming up for this attack and helped to break up the enemy concentrations as they advanced. Pressing forward despite heavy casualties, the Turks reached the forward trenches in places, only to be driven back by the infantry's shellfire, suffering further casualties as they withdrew.

By midsummer the gunners at Anzac had made themselves relatively comfortable:

> We are right on the edge of a cliff and have a magnificent view of the sea. We live in … miniature caves that we have dug in the face of the cliff. The 'Marine Parade' is what a few of us have christened the narrow track that we have dug along the face of the cliff and on which most of our dwellings have their frontage…. It's the poor infantry up in the trenches that suffer.[29]

Napier Johnston, too, found his dugout 'very comfortable' except for the ever-present flies, though it got very hot in the afternoon.[30]

By now flies were everywhere. They 'bit like young scorpions and savagely attacked every patch of bare skin. Every meal was a pitched battle. With one hand the soldier fought back the black swarm that threatened to descend upon his jam and his biscuit, and with the other thrust the morsel hastily into his mouth.' Flies made sleep in daytime virtually impossible. Lice were even more loathed, crawling across skin with a 'cold, passionless persistence in quest of blood'. Men constantly scoured their clothing for them.[31]

July also brought a stronger sense of futility. 'This show gets tiresome,' Johnston noted; 'it is so slow and one feels that we ... should be in France now and not here wasting men, time and money.'[32] Late in the month the artillery was reorganised because of the anticipated arrival from New Zealand of 5 Battery and 6 (Howitzer) Battery. Johnston, promoted to colonel, took command of what was now styled the New Zealand Divisional Artillery. Brigades were formed under Symon and Sykes, both of whom were promoted to lieutenant-colonel.[33] At times some of the Indian mountain guns also came under Johnston's command.

With a stalemate at both Anzac and Helles, and the Turkish forces growing in strength, a fresh offensive was planned for early August. The ANZAC, reinforced by the British 13 Division and a brigade of 10 Division, would seize the commanding Sari Bair Range, opening the way for an advance across the peninsula to the Narrows. At the same time the British 9th Corps, of nearly five divisions, would land at Suvla Bay, some distance north of Anzac. The artillery available to support the operations at Anzac included 72 guns and howitzers. However, with ammunition still in short supply, even this modest resource could not be properly used.[34]

Elaborate planning preceded this big push. Johnston found 'Everyone very busy arranging for the big attack ...; it is an exceedingly worrying time as people get so excited, orders are constantly changed and altogether one needs the patience of a saint.' Godley in particular was 'not well and very cross in the evening and unreasonable'.[35] Preparatory bombardments began on 4 August, when New Zealand gunners fired on Turkish positions facing 1 Australian Division at Lone Pine and at other points where diversionary attacks would coincide with the assault on Sari Bair. After cutting the wire in front of Lone Pine, 1 Battery supported the successful assault by the Australians on the evening of 6 August.[36] Over the following days 1 Battery helped to repel a series of determined Turkish counter-attacks, as the Australian infantry held on desperately despite heavy losses. Life was far from easy at the gun line. All the battery's gun emplacements were so badly damaged by counter-battery fire that they had to be rebuilt, and all its weapons suffered some damage. But losses were kept to a minimum. Because the protective emplacements took the brunt of the hits, only three men were wounded.[37]

The main offensive began after nightfall on 6 August. New Zealand mounted riflemen and the Maori contingent were the first in action, seizing Turkish positions in the foothills north of Anzac.[38] This opened the way for two assault columns to advance up the valleys towards the Sari Bair heights. The New Zealand Infantry Brigade formed the main component of the right-hand column, supported by an Indian mountain battery with 10-prs. Everything depended on presenting the Turks with a fait accompli when dawn broke on the 7th. But the left-hand column became lost in the tangled gullies and never got near its objectives, Hills Q and 971. The New Zealanders, too, had fallen behind schedule. By morning they were still below the summit of Chunuk Bair, on Rhododendron Ridge. After an attempt to push onto the summit was repelled, the exhausted troops endured a long day on the slopes under shrapnel. Before dawn the Wellington Battalion under Lieutenant-Colonel William Malone moved up onto the summit, surprised to find it unoccupied. All that day, 8 August, they beat off Turkish counter-attacks. Malone was killed towards evening, probably by a 'friendly' shell. Once night fell, the survivors withdrew from the hill as men of the Wellington Mounted Rifles took their place.

The mounted riflemen, too, stood their ground for a day, but next morning Chunuk Bair was lost. A massive Turkish counter-attack overwhelmed the weak British battalions that had just taken over from the New Zealanders. As the Turks flooded down the seaward slopes of Chunuk Bair, the gunners found easy targets. This artillery fire, and resolute action by New Zealand machine-gunners on Rhododendron Ridge, halted the Turkish surge, leaving the New Zealanders holding an exposed salient on the ridge. Some of the New Zealand gunners sought to augment their fire by commandeering some British 18-prs landed at Anzac for use by 9th Corps, and two 'scratch' batteries soon had these guns in action. 'Daniell's Battery', with two British and two Australian guns, found a position to the north of the old ANZAC line from which it could fire over open sights at the Turks on Chunuk Bair.[39]

The unsuccessful offensive had cost the lives of 900 New Zealanders alone. At Anzac Cove hundreds of wounded men lay for days under Maxim gun fire awaiting medical attention. 'They periodically pick out those …

they find dead and carry them off[,] line them up in blankets and bury them in one long trench ... in some cases not too well.'[40]

This operation had involved coordinating the fire of Allied warships. Though the system of conveying information about targets to the fleet by wireless was cumbersome, the ships did sometimes manage to mount effective fire. Before the attack, at the same time each night the destroyer HMS *Colne* had illuminated with its searchlight and fired on a post captured earlier from the New Zealand Mounted Rifles. The Turks soon learned to leave at the right time, and it was recaptured with little resistance at the outset of the advance.[41]

Birdwood had the supporting fire of two cruisers, four monitors and two destroyers – a mixed blessing. Napier Johnston could call on only the cruisers HMS *Endymion* and *Bacchante* for the push up Chunuk Bair ridge. 'Their guns are old and they do their best but the shooting is not accurate enough for covering fire'. Despite this reservation, the CRA arranged for naval fire to support the left column in its attack on Hill Q on 9 August. The charge up the hill was successful, but just as the troops reached the summit and gazed east upon 'the Narrows, whose forts and mine-fields had blocked the way for the fleet ... a salvo of heavy naval shells fell among the Ghurkas. The confusion which ensued ... was yet at its height, when the enemy, rallying, charged back on to the crest' and drove them back down. As Johnston noted, 'it was said the ships guns continued the bombardment too long'; *Bacchante* had also started too late. But the problem was systemic: 'This bombardment was too quickly arranged, the G.O.C. an infantry officer doesnt realize that to concentrate the fire of so many naval and land guns requires careful thinking out and not as I had to do making all arrangments in ¾ of an hour'.[42]

At the end of the operation the Anzac perimeter had been greatly enlarged to the north and linked with that at Suvla. On 21 August an ANZAC force attacked Hill 60, a low hill near the junction between the Suvla and Anzac sectors, as part of the largest offensive launched at Gallipoli. Still dogged by ammunition shortages, the New Zealand gunners prepared to support this tactically dubious operation, but did so only belatedly because of orders to fire on Turkish positions further north. The New Zealanders again met strong resistance, and managed to seize only part of the Turkish trench system, which had been little damaged by the artillery fire. For another week they struggled unsuccessfully to dislodge the Turks from this 'abominable little hill'.[43]

No major offensives were attempted during the autumn. The Turks consolidated their positions and began preparations for a decisive attack in early 1916, receiving trainloads of Austrian heavy howitzers and German high-explosive shells.[44] Meanwhile, although the New Zealand Field Artillery was reinforced in October by 6 (Howitzer) Battery, and various British batteries arrived to add their weight to the Corps Artillery, ammunition remained scarce. The New Zealand gunners were nevertheless kept busy with calls for fire on Turkish positions and targets of opportunity behind the enemy lines. Counter-battery fire was a continuing task; this was sometimes directed by air observation, without any notable success.[45]

After a dismal demonstration by the recently arrived howitzer battery in late October – 'they took so long I left before any shooting was done' – Johnston complained that battery commanders were 'too slow in getting fire to bear on target' and resolved to send the culprits back to Alexandria.[46] This might not have been unwelcome: the gunners were adjusting to bleak winter conditions by early December, when they learned that their days on the peninsula were numbered. The authorities in London had decided to cut their losses after the new Turkish artillery did major damage to the Australian trenches at Lone Pine. The ANZACs were cheerfully told by prisoners that 'a large number of heavy guns were being placed in position to blow us into the Mediterranean'.[47]

First to go would be the units at Suvla and Anzac. The New Zealand artillery began pulling out on the night of 11 December. The guns of one section of each battery were manhandled out of their positions, pulled to the beach by horse teams and loaded onto lighters. Further guns and their crews were taken off over the following nights. Gunner Arthur Currey of Auckland was among the last to leave:

> We were to cover the retirement of the infantry, and then if possible to get away with the guns, [or] to blow them up and to get ourselves away

the best we could. ... Orders came to get rid of all ammunition possible. ... We fired most of our shells ... and were just replacing stores when a 15-pounder Turkish shell penetrated the gun pit and wounded a sergeant, corporal and gunner. That night the canteen stores we had ordered three weeks previously were brought up to the battery. Each man ... got 3 tins of sausages, 2 of tomatoes, 6 of herring, 6 of sardines, 2 of fruit, 20 packets of biscuits, beside cocoa, milk and chocolate. ... we were like balloons before we had finished. ... On the night of the 18th I was on water guard between 12 and 2am, and I saw all the stores at North Beach and at Suvla burning. It was a fine sight. It cast a gloom over all of us as we were steaming away, to think of leaving our mates on that desolate spot ...[48]

Only two New Zealand guns remained to embark for Lemnos with the last infantry units on the night of 19 December, when the evacuation at Anzac/Suvla was successfully completed. (The troops at Cape Helles followed on the night of 8–9 January 1916.) The campaign had taken the lives of more than 2700 New Zealanders, including at least 60 gunners.

For the gunners, as for all the New Zealanders, it had been a frustrating and difficult campaign – hazardous, technically demanding, hamstrung by lack of resources and physically exhausting (a third of gunner fatalities were caused by disease). Despite the inevitable occasional mistakes, relations between infantry and artillery had been strengthened. Bonds of mutual respect would now be tested in the face of the new tactics, and new horrors, unfolding on the Western Front.

Redeployment to the Western Front

By early January 1916, most of the New Zealand and Australian Division was encamped at Moascar, near Ismailia on the banks of the Suez Canal. By now many more reinforcements had arrived from New Zealand and Australia than could be absorbed into existing units, and the ANZAC needed reorganisation. The Australian units – and the New Zealand Mounted Rifles Brigade – were withdrawn from the New Zealand and Australian Division. A second infantry brigade, the New Zealand (Rifle) Brigade, had arrived in Egypt in late 1915,

Life and Death on Gallipoli

Though their diet was monotonous, the gunners were adequately fed. 'We get bread every day made down at the A.S.C. bakehouse, or rather "bake-gully", and it is very nice.' Two months later, however, this gunner's stomach had 'turned dog on me & refuses to have much to do with what I eat; consequently I am fairly weak and am feeling very home-sick & down in the dumps'.[49] The 'aggressively nourishing Army Biscuits' were especially hard to stomach.[50] The CRA endured the same diet as his men: 'One gets very tired of the food, bully beef and MaConochys [stew] ration, the lat[t]er makes me ill to even look at, it is so rich, there is nothing but stodgy food'. Only in autumn did the supplies of fresh food from Imbros become adequate. Thirst was a constant affliction, especially in summer when there was never enough water. After some promising wells dried up, the engineers built a reservoir above Anzac Cove, into which water was pumped from barges.[51]

Occasional parcels from home brought newspapers and food. A melon or a bottle of lemonade could save a bad day. Fine weather also lifted spirits: 'We had a most beautiful sunset tonight and altogether it has been a perfect day'. On his birthday, Napier Johnston enjoyed 'a nice piece of birthday cake' and a tot of rum.[52]

Soon many were suffering from influenza, colds or diarrhoea. 'My only trouble is the latter,' Johnston noted in his diary, 'and a most unpleasant one it is.'[53] Disease or wounds could mean evacuation from Anzac. 'I cannot describe the feeling of relief at getting off the Peninsula,' wrote Gunner Wes Muldoon after being evacuated during the August offensive. 'I didnt like leaving but when eventually I had to get away they put me in Hospital Ship [*Dunluce*] *Castle*. It was glorious. Fancy a nice soft bed after all the months & a dear sweet nurse to look after me, she was a brick and so was the matron. We lost 16 men coming to Malta with dysentery. It is an awful disease and doesnt leave much chance if you get it bad.'[54]

Dead mules also threatened to spread disease – 60 were killed in one day at Helles. When Turkish machine-gunners and snipers kept men off the beach at Anzac, personal hygiene suffered. In August Johnston did not wash for days. 'I havent had my clothes off for a week ... one pair of drill shorts, one shirt, one pair of puttees [leggings], one pair of boots, one under sheet.' When he next swam – at night to avoid snipers – this 'dark pleasure' was 'somewhat marred by smell of very adjacent dead men and horses and mules ... not buried deeply enough'.[55]

> Snipers were always a problem at Anzac. One 'had four shots at me today on the road', Gunner Frank Humphreys complained in October. A fortnight later 'those strays are getting a damn nuisance. ... Ive got to run the gauntlet every night now'. Work also kept Humphreys and his 4 (Howitzer) Battery colleagues alert: 'Had a night alarm tonight & was ready to fire in 3½ minutes'. On 5 December he 'went out to No. 2 [post] to mend our line & saw a terrible sight about seventeen men in a hospital blown to pieces with a 6" howitzer shell'.[56] Heavy shells were even more nerve-wracking because of the period of suspense after the 'muffled report' of a gun firing. Shells rose, seemed to hang suspended, then dropped 'with a roar which gradually changed to a diabolic, blood-curdling scream'.[57]
>
> Death became almost mundane on Gallipoli. While helping a 3 Battery mate dig his dugout on 6 June, Gunner Bert Richardson of Dannevirke was
>
>> unfortunate to stop a bullet in the side, he died within half an hour.... [A]part from being sorry that another of our mates has had to leave us, these scenes affect us but little. His wound is bound, his disc taken off, his uniform placed over him after all papers etc. have been taken out, he is then wrapped up in his blanket and pinned in. He lies just a little way off the main track along the cliff for all to see. The Minister arrives, ... we desert the guns for a few minutes and crawl along to the shallow grave dug earlier in the day by volunteers, to pay our respects.... We have to lie or sit under cover so that the enemy may not 'spot' us and let fly. We gather round the grave, his own puttees are used to lower him into his last resting place. The Chaplain speaks, all's over.[58]
>
> Time to ponder was a rare luxury. The death of Johnston's 'good friend' William Malone was 'a great blow but in the rush of events one has not much time to think over things'. Johnston had no sleep for three nights, making it 'difficult to remember details'.[59] Many found sleep deprivation one of the most difficult aspects of front-line service.

and a third was now formed from surplus reinforcements. This allowed the establishment on 1 March 1916 of a New Zealand Division, under the command of Major-General Sir Andrew Russell. Johnston's Divisional Artillery was expanded to three field brigades and a howitzer brigade. The artillery force had doubled to two brigades in 1915, and it now doubled again: the three original batteries had become fifteen. After experienced personnel were provided for each battery, all four brigades were effectively new units.

With the ignominious end of the Gallipoli campaign, the Australians and New Zealanders were at last able to continue their journey to their original destination, the Western Front, which snaked across France and Belgium from the Swiss border to the English Channel. Here the two sides faced each other from deep trench systems separated by a narrow no man's land. Artillery ruled the roost as each side bombarded the other using an increasing array of guns. Between 5 and 7 April the Divisional Artillery travelled by train to Alexandria, and thence by transport ships to Marseilles. After a two-day rail journey across France the gunners assembled at Le Havre to be equipped with guns, limbers, wagons and other equipment, and additional horses from the remount depot.

With the rest of the division, the gunners were then billeted in villages around Hazebrouck, south of Dunkirk, where there was yet another reorganisation of the artillery order of battle. The other artillery brigades received the howitzer batteries of 4 FA Brigade, which was now made up of three of the 18-pr batteries; the Howitzer Brigade Ammunition Column was replaced by a fourth section of the Divisional Ammunition Column.[60]

An additional unit was formed, the Divisional Trench Mortars, consisting of three batteries (named X, Y, Z in accordance with RFA practice, and suffixed /NZ), each of four medium mortars, and a heavy mortar battery (V/NZ Battery). In the conditions of the Western Front, medium (6-inch) trench mortars firing 60-pound bombs on high trajectories were ideally suited to the harassment of entrenched positions, wire-cutting and supporting infantry raids. These NZFA mortar batteries were in addition to the infantry mortar batteries (1, 2 and 3 Light Trench Mortar Batteries, with a fourth created later), which were each armed with eight 3.2-inch Stokes mortars firing 10-pound 11-ounce bombs. Despite their effectiveness, mortars were unpopular with the infantry in the trenches because they attracted counter-mortar fire, which also necessitated frequent shifts of position by the mortar sections and batteries.[61]

Armentières

The New Zealand Division went into the line at Armentières, near the Belgian border, in I ANZAC Corps, part of Lieutenant-General Sir Herbert

Plumer's Second Army. After advance parties spent a week with the batteries the New Zealand gunners were to relieve, the rest of the Divisional Artillery marched in from Hazebrouck. On 19 May 1916 the Divisional Artillery HQ took command of the artillery in the 6500-yard-long New Zealand sector. In a common Western Front practice that the New Zealanders never fully

6-inch Stokes mortar on the Somme, April 1918.
G13122½, Alexander Turnbull Library, Wellington.

NZEF Artillery Depots

The New Zealand Division maintained depots in Britain and France to support the huge NZEF organisation. The first Artillery Reserve Depot was opened in June 1916 as part of the New Zealand Reserve Group at the dreary Sling Camp on Salisbury Plain to provide additional training to reinforcements from New Zealand and enlistees from Britain or within the NZEF. A howitzer battery – 16 Battery NZFA – was raised at Sling in October 1916 from reinforcements and transferring mounted rifles.

In January 1917 the depot moved to Talavera Barracks, Aldershot, where it came directly under NZEF Headquarters in London. Among the first New Zealanders sent there was Gunner Bert Stokes from Wellington, who enjoyed 'the best quarters we have had since leaving the home fireside.... Three storey building, balcony at each floor, and nine rooms each holding 28 men on each flat. Every unit in the British Army is represented here.'[62] At Aldershot the depot raised four sections of gunners to enable the conversion from four- to six-gun batteries.

Between April and August 1917 the depot was based at Chadderton Camp, near Manchester. Equipment was in such short supply here that instructors drew the outline of a field gun on the ground to enable the men to do 'standing gun drill.'[63] The depot then moved to a former British Army depot, the Ewshot Barracks near Aldershot.[64] Fewer than 40 miles from London, this was a pleasant and well-appointed place to train but, as one New Zealander noted, 'with the Regular Regiments away, there is little left but the bare walls of the barracks and the stones of the parade ground. The traditions departed with the Regiments.'[65]

The Ewshot depot housed up to 700 men, twice its established strength. The gunners shared it with the New Zealand Medical Corps, but with more than 30 acres of grounds there was plenty of room. Ewshot had a library, a YMCA, sports facilities and produced its own newspaper, *Youshot*. The six-week courses included classes at an army riding school. An 'ingenious' training aid allowed practice in gun-laying and observation: 'an observation officer, operating in one hut with signallers could lay, with the aid of a map, an imaginary gun in another hut on an object in a flat model landscape, and his accuracy was tested, with the aid of mechanism, by smoke-puffs, which showed at the point indicated.'[66]

In France, Artillery Schools were maintained at Army level. Small numbers of New Zealand officers were sent to these periodically to keep abreast of the latest developments. A Divisional Artillery School established near Poperinghe in March 1918 was nipped in the bud by the German offensive later that month.[67] After so much training, most gunners were keen to get to the front. In early 1917, six days after passing his final gunnery test at the New Zealand Division depot at Étaples, south of Boulogne, Stokes found himself on a train from Calais to Steenwerck.

> At about 8pm ... most of us for the first time were within hearing of the great war. I stood in the doorway of the van and listened to the boom of the heavy gun, the crack of the 18pr and the tap of the MG. I began to realise that at last I was within earshot of the place on which the eyes of the world have been fastened for the past 2½ years.[68]

accepted – gunners prefer the known idiosyncrasies of familiar weapons – they exchanged guns with their predecessors.[69] The Divisional Artillery also had to adopt other procedures developed by the RFA in France. For major operations or 'stunts' additional RFA batteries would be placed under command of the CRA, with heavy batteries of the Royal Garrison Artillery (RGA) in support. This cooperation with other units, and with the artillery of adjacent infantry divisions, meant that doctrine, tactics and organisation were now imposed at corps and army levels. For tactical purposes, brigades and batteries were usually organised in 'groups', designated 'right' or 'left' and sometimes also 'centre', and often taking in additional batteries from other divisions as well

Building and supplying gun positions was hard work.
G13216½, Alexander Turnbull Library, Wellington (opposite).
Album 419, photo H539, Auckland War Memorial Museum (above).

as 'Army' (non-divisional) units. Falla, now a lieutenant-colonel, took charge of the Divisional Artillery Intelligence branch, which worked with the Field Survey Company to collect information on the position of German guns.

In low-lying country observation posts for counter-battery and harassing fire were hard to find. The Germans generally held somewhat higher ground, and many of the operations on this part of the Western Front sought to capture these positions.[70] Observers had to make do with whatever vantage points were available, including church steeples and factory chimneys, and balloons where necessary, to spot enemy batteries. The gunners were mostly engaged in harassment and counter-battery fire, interspersed with more elaborate concentrations of barrages to support raids or in response to SOS calls for fire to beat off enemy assaults on forward trenches. Guns were hidden behind sliding doors in factories, or under cover of hedges, walls or camouflage netting. Efforts by the New Zealanders' predecessors to brighten their surroundings by planting vegetables and flowers around gun positions were all too successful, and these plots were soon destroyed.[71]

In response to the realities of trench warfare, many techniques for massed, indirect artillery support had by now been developed. Guns constantly searched the German positions. 'For five minutes some "tender" spot would be turned into an inferno', then equally abruptly the objective would change. By late June the New Zealand batteries were firing up to 3000 shells a day, a huge number after the constraints at Gallipoli.[72] The Germans retaliated in kind. Though gunners were shelled less often than infantry, when they were the fire was often targeted and heavy. During concentrated fire sheets of flame from bursting shells spurted up everywhere, and it was impossible to distinguish the sounds of individual guns or hear anything shouted in one's ear. Coming under shellfire was terrifying. After 'noises like an express train passing at high speed through a station', there was 'a thud as the missile … buried itself in the earth just over the parapet, then the shock of the explosion, a sulphurous and phosphorous smell, and a spitting out of dust and rust'. Dead men were often unmarked, killed by concussion alone. Yet there was sometimes 'a terrific noise and dust-up for comparatively little damage'.[73] Shells landing in soft mud or water often failed to explode, and those that did 'merely threw up mud-geysers, bespattering the dug-outs with black slime'.[74] It has been estimated that 1400 shells were fired for every man killed by artillery during the war.[75]

Gunner Norman Hassell would serve throughout the war.

> It was not our first shelling that frightened us so much as the later ones three or four years afterwards. It's hard to explain … probably due to our nerves being at such a tension that the re-action inevitable in such cases did not occur until later on in the war. I could stand up to anything in the way of shell fire for the first couple of years, but the last year or so was my undoing. Every burst used to set me all quivering.[76]

Such reactions can be explained by studies of the effects of prolonged exposure to battle conditions. Few men have an inexhaustible supply of courage.[77]

The use of forward observing officers (FOOs) and observation posts (OPs) spawned yet more military abbreviations. The practice of basing a battery officer at the headquarters of each battalion, in telephone contact with his battery and brigade headquarters, dates from the early period of trench warfare. Well established by this time were SOS lines – registered zones in front of the British trenches on which defensive fire could be called down at short notice by flares and other means of signalling urgently for fire. Each battery stood a man as SOS guard against the raids that could cross no man's land in seconds. 'We stand just outside our dug-out and watch for the SOS which is two red lights and two white lights. Last night we got a false SOS. Fritz sent up our SOS colours so we opened out and gave him some iron rations for his trouble.' The SOS guard was also known as the rocket guard. 'On seeing those certain lights we are to send up the same signal for the heavy guns behind us.... The SOS lights are shot in the air through an ordinary rifle. We have the phone layed on also... [to] ring up 3rd Brigade Headquarters'. Telephone messages had to be cryptic. 'We are not to mention any names of officers'.[78]

Other innovations, such as the coordination of artillery planning at army level by the Major-General Royal Artillery of the Army (MGRA) and the use of a slow creeping barrage to lead infantry offensives forward, were first used at the Battle of the Somme in 1916.[79] The creeping barrage was a line of exploding shells that moved forward ahead of advancing infantry in 'lifts' of 25 to 100 yards. Artillery fire could destroy wire blocking the advance, mask troop movements, suppress enemy artillery fire while the objective was secured, and thwart counter-attacks. As Godley told Defence Minister James Allen, 'the heavy guns play a part in the field which one has to see to believe'. However, the overburdened infantry still had to cross a 150-yard gap.[80] Trench systems were much more elaborate than those on Gallipoli, with defence in depth provided by several parallel lines of trenches. Except when an advance was imminent, relatively few troops occupied the front line of trenches because of the danger they would be wiped out by a concentrated barrage. The risk that front-line trenches would be taken by the enemy was high; but the Germans would then be equally vulnerable to counter-attack. Unmanned trenches were also favoured positions from which to fire trench mortars, as this minimised the risk of effective retaliation.[81]

During this first deployment, Napier Johnston accompanied the New Zealand Division's CO, Major-General Russell, on a visit to 41 Division

> ### Coping with Gas
>
> Chemical warfare arrived on the Western Front on 22 April 1915, when the Germans released chlorine gas from cylinders to drift across the Allied lines at Ypres. The more deadly phosgene appeared in December, and gas shells – both lethal and tear gas – first came into use in early 1916. The Germans began using mustard gas (an oily liquid atomised by an explosive charge) in July 1917. Fatal when inhaled, mustard gas also caused severe blistering to exposed skin. The Allies responded in kind to each of these German initiatives, but always several months behind.[82]
>
> The immediate need was to protect personnel against these new weapons. The simple veil-type gas masks provided to the Allied forces on Gallipoli fortunately proved unnecessary. When the New Zealanders arrived in France in April 1916, they were issued with the 'PH' helmet, a flannel hood impregnated with phenyl-hexamine. This sticky, foul-smelling chemical offered protection against both phosgene and chlorine, but with prolonged contact it irritated and burnt the wearer's skin. The uncomfortable and unreliable PH helmet was replaced by the highly effective small box respirator in December 1916.[83]
>
> Gas was used rather sporadically during 1916. The New Zealanders were first subjected to gas shelling on the Somme on 20 September. They were shelled with phosgene the following February, at Fleurbaix, and gas shelling became an increasingly common hazard during 1917.[84] The gunners, in particular, were subjected to frequent, prolonged chemical bombardment, as both sides saw gas as well-suited to counter-battery fire. Gas discipline was tight, and the gunners became used to working in their gas masks for hours on end. Even the horses had gas helmets.

at Steenwerck to witness a shoot and discuss artillery coordination. Russell seemed heedless of danger:

> [He] took us to a place … from whence he said we could get a good view. So you could but it was only 800 yds from the enemy's lines and we were only covered by a hedge. Our batteries were bombarding a brewery supposed to be occupied by snipers, … when … quite close to us the shells began to fall, we had a lively time for some minutes, either they had spotted us from the front or from an aeroplane. … We could not run away as we would have had to cross some open ground, so we huddled into an old disused trench,

Training was as realistic as possible. At the divisional gas instruction school at Armentières in mid-1916, for example, trainees got a 'a sniff of poison gas, very nasty stuff'.[85] Another gunner described his experiences at the divisional depot at Étaples the following January: 'Had training in gas helmets. Went through a trench filled with gas, also a "tear" trench, makes your eyes water'.[86]

Tear gas continued to be used after the appearance of lethal gas shells. 'Fritz has been throwing tear gas about this afternoon[;] we have all been crying for about 4 hours,'[87] wrote Gunner Clarence Hankins in late September 1916. On another occasion, Robert Scott noted: 'A number of gas shells landed near us and we received the order "Gas Mask on". I was in charge and had to receive ... and give orders with my mask on and found it awkward doing so. However the gas proved to be lachrymatory not asphyxiating so we took our masks off. Our eyes smarted and watered but otherwise the gas does not affect one'.[88]

Batteries mounted a rotating 'gas guard' on each gun to sound the alert. The distinctive 'hollow' sound of a gas shell in flight was unmistakable, and some drivers became blasé about the dangers – 'on would go our gas masks as we galloped through'.[89] By early 1918 men no longer panicked about gas attacks: 'While I was on shift Fritz was sending over plenty of gas shells, but they were only a small shell and do practically no harm. There is very little gas in one shell'.[90]

Recreation was encouraged during spells out of the line, but precautions still had to be taken. These men lining up for a sack race in 1918 wear gas masks.
Album 419, photo H658, Auckland War Memorial Museum.

earth was thrown over us and the ground rooted up, but thank goodness none of us was injured. ... This is the last time I will go with Russell to see gun shooting.[91]

Even well behind the front line soldiers were not necessarily safe. In December 1917, four batteries and the ammunition column of 3 Brigade NZFA were shelled by a German long-range gun. 'The first four shells landed ... among the men's sleeping huts and killed and wounded fifty men. One shell landed at the end of the horse lines and killed 14 horses. ... One is never safe anywhere, we are quite six miles from the line'.[92]

THE SOMME

The New Zealand gunners were relieved from the line at Armentières on 17 August 1916 as the division prepared to move south for a renewed offensive on the Somme, where there had been enormous casualties since the beginning of July. The New Zealanders were assigned to XV Corps of Fourth Army for an assault planned for mid-September. Johnston reconnoitred the battlefield on 1 September, and five days later the first guns were moved along congested roads to positions near the village of Longueval. The New Zealand Division's objectives in the coming push were a series of German trench lines close to the nearby village of Flers.[93]

Dawn on 12 September was heralded by a heavy Allied bombardment along the whole Somme front. In the New Zealand Division's sector this was provided by 42 Divisional Artillery and 1 and 2 Brigades, NZFA; the other two brigades supported the British division to the right. The amount of artillery assistance was huge; gunners slaved over their guns day and night. With the increasing concentration of artillery along the line, especially when an offensive was planned or feared, batteries were often crammed together in a few concealed positions. One New Zealand battery on the Somme 'had eighteen 18-pounders ... about 30 yards immediately behind us and firing over our heads. At that distance the ... ear-splitting crack ... is far worse than any of the heavier guns'.[94] Gunners in such positions could add the risk of premature shell detonation to the usual hazards of counter-battery fire, gas shelling and deafness. That day the New Zealand gunners fired their first gas shells, both tear gas and lethal (mainly phosgene).[95] Instructed to use these liberally 'against all enemy positions', they were advised that gas was 'most effective for counter-battery work and for shelling villages, woods and other enclosed positions'.[96]

The gunners concentrated on planned fire programmes targeting the enemy's wire entanglements, trenches and lines of communication, and strongpoints such as machine-gun positions and observation posts. Observation officers called down concentrations by groups of batteries – 'crashes' – on anything that moved around the German lines, and heavy batteries of the RGA provided counter-battery fire.[97] A heavy bombardment began at 6 p.m. on 14 September, the evening before the attack. From 6.20 a.m. a creeping barrage, with about 100 guns supporting the New Zealand Division alone, led the infantry assault forward. Despite the intensity of the preliminary bombardment and the barrage, and the first appearance in battle of tanks ('a war machine ... which we nicknamed the caterpillar'),[98] German machine guns and artillery inflicted heavy casualties. Leaving unshelled lanes for tanks was a flawed concept: enemy machine-gunners used them to cut down the advancing troops. Nevertheless, the New Zealand infantry swept through the first line of entrenchments, and then through Flers to a new line beyond the village. Here they beat off a series of counter-attacks with the help of shelling called down by observation officers who had accompanied the advance, with linesmen rolling out the telephone lines as they went.

The gunners of 3 Brigade supporting the neighbouring British advance had a harrowing day as they moved their guns forward under heavy shelling through the shattered village of Longueval into new positions towards Flers. Each hour one battery limbered up to advance covered by the others, which then moved up in turn. Quickly into action at their new positions, the gunners maintained a heavy fire for the rest of the day, despite numerous casualties. Meanwhile the drivers hastened back to resupply ammunition, running the gauntlet of enemy shelling on each trip, while the linesmen struggled to reconnect their wires, which were repeatedly blown apart. In future battles greater effort would be made to bury wires right up to the front line before the batteries moved forward.

In the following days the other NZFA brigades also moved up to new

The old and the new: New Zealand gunners pass a British tank which (typically) appears to be disabled.
Royal New Zealand Artillery Old Comrades' Association.

positions, struggling over rapidly disintegrating roads and hampered by mud after heavy rain set in on the second evening of the battle. On the 19th it 'took a 20 horse team to get one gun thro the mud & drivers have now to go over a road that is being shelled by Fritz pretty heavy. They managed to get 2 guns up then had to turn it up on a/c of horses being done up. They arrived back covered in mud head to foot.' Next day another two guns were moved up 'over the same ground as yesterday only now it is about twice as bad. Fritz shelled the road heavily and blocked the teams. One of our corporals … went up to see if road was clear.… Was found afterwards with his horse blown to pieces & he killed alongside'.[99] Further advances were postponed while the gunners rebuilt collapsed gun pits yet maintained bombardment and observed fire. In the New Zealand gun lines, high-explosive and gas shells caused continuing casualties. The wagon lines got so much attention that some batteries moved them back.

The advance was resumed on 25 September. To retain a measure of surprise, the bombardment was not increased before the barrage moved forward. This proved fortunate, as the heavy enemy counter-bombardment fell off before the attack began. Gunners of 13 Battery made good use of two captured German

77-mm guns (and their gas shells) which, with their greater range, would be moved forward early in October to bombard enemy positions in Bapaume.[100]

Once again the infantry moved forward behind a creeping barrage. 'Our artillery was simply great', a grateful platoon commander noted.[101] A delay at the village of Gueudecourt was overcome the following day with the help of a tank and an aircraft which strafed the enemy trenches. The gunners of 3 and 4 Brigades played their part in this action. Meanwhile, 1 and 2 Brigades bombarded the next objective, the Gird Trench, which was captured on 27 September. The weather then broke again, and rain would continue to thwart the Allies throughout October.

At the end of September the gunners and horse teams struggled forward through rain and mud, often under fire, to positions around Flers. On 1 October they supported a further New Zealand advance, which again reached and held its objective, Circus Trench, and supported a British division in its attack on Eaucourt l'Abbaye. After dark some 3 Brigade batteries moved further forward along the Flers road. Delayed by shelling, the state of the road and the quagmire off it, they were still able to dig in the guns and camouflage their positions as dawn broke.[102]

When the rest of the New Zealand Division was relieved from the line on the night of 3 October, the gunners stayed behind, attached to 21 Division's artillery. They supported assaults by British infantry on 6, 12 and 18 October, but German resistance was stout and these attacks failed to reach their objectives. On the 11th the gunners executed a reverse barrage that crept backwards rather than forwards. The Germans, anticipating an assault, responded with a desperate bombardment that included their own lines. The New Zealand gunners played a full part in these actions despite coming under heavy counter-battery fire and concentrated bombardments lasting several hours.[103]

The experience of the drivers and their exhausted horses was hardly less harrowing – bringing up ammunition by wagon during the day before packing it from forward dumps to the gun positions, usually making several trips each night over congested and routinely shelled roads, and the waterlogged ground between these and the gun positions. Drivers felt for their charges: 'We are watering a[t] Fricourt now & it is a great affair[.] Thousands & thousands of horses go there & pack up in a heap outside the gate[.] it is just push through & get water where you can[.] there is no regulation [and] … the horses … get their heels torn to pieces.'[104]

By 26 October, when the New Zealand gunners were relieved by 1 Australian Divisional Artillery, they had been in the line for an exhausting 52 days and fired half a million shells. No battery was spared casualties but 3 Battery was hardest hit, losing about 80 men. Some relief was provided by men from the wagon lines, and from reinforcements from the Artillery Reserve Depot in England at the end of September, but the batteries were usually seriously under strength.[105]

Fleurbaix

The Divisional Artillery now marched north to Estaires for a brief rest before three brigades took over positions from 5 Australian Divisional Artillery at Fleurbaix on 7 and 8 November. Here they formed two groups in support of the New Zealand Division, which was already in the line with II ANZAC Corps, part of the Second Army. 2 Brigade and a trench mortar battery went to the left end of the II ANZAC Corps sector to support 'Franks' Force', a composite formation of two brigade groups cobbled together to replace a division that had been moved to the Somme. After improving their gun positions and dugouts the gunners settled down in a sector where infantry activity was mostly confined to small-scale raids. Ammunition was at first limited, and enemy counter-battery fire was very light compared with the Somme. After a snowfall in early January 1917, the weather was dry but very cold. The gunners enjoyed fraternising with the locals and visiting the many small cafés.[106]

After the New Zealand Division re-entered the line at Fleurbaix in November, the Divisional Artillery replaced the gunners of 5 Australian Division in its support. The artillery-manned trench mortars were now formed up in their batteries. The New Zealanders soon found the German trench mortars, the Minenwerfer (which they dubbed 'pineapples' or 'whizzbangs'), 'the most demoralizing weapons: perhaps it is that the bombs are shot so high into the air that they descend almost vertically, and a parapet is no protection against them, or perhaps it is the horrid coughing

Behind the Lines in France

Gunners' living conditions varied widely. Those billeted with generous locals really felt like 'Bill Massey's Tourists', but more often it was a case of 'Horses in stables our sleeping billets about a mile away in an old lousy shed'. Gunner John Heseltine, a driver in 3 Brigade, 'nearly cried' when he saw one billet – 'an old shed at the back of a farmhouse, wet, stinking manure over the boot tops. ... One look inside was enough for me. Two mules at one end and us to live at the other on lousy stinking straw'. While officers had 'white sheets and good beds, ... us boys that are fighting for our country' were 'asked to sleep in pig sties'. Sometimes there were no billets. 'Most of us drivers are not particular where we doss, underneath the wagons. ... The last three nights we have been sleeping by a fence[.] I stuck in a few sticks and put my oilsheet on the top and crept in underneath and could sleep ... through any bombardment'.[107]

'A chap can't work all night and day on the food we get', complained a gunner at Messines. 'Our baker is very sought [after:] we dont always get bread, we have to satisfy our hunger very often with dog biscuits'. Rum was issued to help maintain morale, especially on nights when the ground was 'hard as iron'. Units eventually set up their own canteens, towards which each man contributed a few francs. Here they could 'buy practically anything one wants', and get 'extra tucker' from the profits. Beer was always popular, especially on pay night. Soldiers also supplemented their rations at estaminets (café's). Cake sent from home for birthdays was usually shared with cobbers in the dugout or bivvy.[108]

Food was often stolen from civilians. 'Coming home through a Froggy's paddock, we landed a good feed of pears', wrote Heseltine, a farmer himself. Later he noticed 'several decent apple trees in the paddock we are camped [in]. There are very few left now. The first night we had a good feed. The Froggy went snaky at us..., but what did we care'. On long hot days in the saddle, drivers stopped for ten minutes each hour to rest their horses. 'One stop there was a crop of swede turnips alongside the road and our boys did bog into them. I eat one nearly the size of my head. I was hungry and we get very little tucker while on travel'.[109]

Those on cook's fatigues helped themselves to 'all the fruit about the place, strawberries, cherries and red currants are plentiful and we have some good feeds. Although looting is forbidden I do not believe in seeing good fruit go to waste'. Bigger pickings presented themselves when the Germans moved most civilians to the rear during the Allied advance in autumn 1918. At Beaudignies the artillerymen made short work of the 'abundance of vegetables' growing in the gardens.[110]

noise they make on the way down'.*¹¹¹* The Divisional Trench Mortar Officer reported on a typical engagement: 'Gaps cut in wire, dugouts blown up, body of a German ... blown into air. Retaliation: a few Minenwerfer. Casualties: Nil.'*¹¹²*

The New Zealand Division's mortars were new technology, their fuses and charges continually being improved in ordnance workshops near the front. A medium battery at Armentières had suffered four casualties when a bomb detonated before being fired. The two batteries at Fleurbaix often supported raids or special operations. The heavy battery's 152-pound shells tended to fall short. On 18 November V/NZ Battery fired a typical seven rounds, one of which fell only 20 yards beyond the front New Zealand trench. At a shoot the following month, one of five 9.45-inch rounds fell between the New Zealanders' front and support trenches. The infantry were not amused.*¹¹³* The 2-inch Stokes also suffered mechanical problems and were sent to workshops for adaptation.

The strength of the medium and heavy trench mortar batteries in early 1917 was around 161, with three officers in Headquarters, 55 all ranks in the heavy battery and between 33 and 38 in each medium battery. Twenty-two men were attached from the infantry or rifle brigades they were supporting.*¹¹⁴* To keep the batteries firing, nearby infantry units often had to form carrying parties to haul ammunition up at night.

In January 1917 there was another reorganisation of the Divisional Artillery to conform with British practice. By disbanding 4 FA Brigade and reallocating its batteries by sections, the batteries in both 1 and 3 FA Brigades were expanded from four to six guns or howitzers. Where previously a four-gun battery had two sections (left and right), each of two guns and under a section commander, it now had three (left, centre and right). 2 FA Brigade now became an 'Army' brigade, under corps command and not part of the New Zealand Divisional Artillery. Its batteries were brought to six-gun strength at the end of March, when it took in three 18-pr sections and one of 4.5-inch howitzers formed at the Reserve Depot at Aldershot. Its redesignation as 2 (Army) Brigade, NZFA, confirmed the reality of its deployment since its arrival at Fleurbaix, under first Australian and then British artillery groups.*¹¹⁵*

Meanwhile, the New Zealand Divisional Artillery continued harassment

Loading a 9.45-inch trench mortar.
Daily Mail *photo, Defence of New Zealand Study Group collection.*

programmes and observed fire to help their infantry hold the line at Fleurbaix. On 21 February, 2 Auckland Battalion and a party of sappers raided the enemy trenches. Led forward by a copybook barrage from the Divisional Artillery, an RFA brigade, and II ANZAC Corps Heavy Artillery, the raiders inflicted heavy casualties and took 43 prisoners. A week later the New Zealand gunners were relieved, their days of relative ease at an end.[116]

New Zealand Divisional Artillery HQ represented the gunners to higher command, and the Brigade Major, Captain J.M. Richmond, accompanied the CRA or Russell on visits to units. On one typical day he was 'Whisked away in the car to … somewhere near the front line and begin to walk, the General scarcely for an instant ceasing a running commentary on everything and everybody we pass. We call in at the batteries, Observation Posts and battalion headquarters, sometimes walking along roads and sometimes communications trenches. Wherever we go, the General asks questions … and, after listening to about half the answers, begins talking about something quite different.'[117] But Russell did not miss much. On 5 March, 'Napier Johnston and I went round the 11th Battery whose horses are a disgrace to the British Army.'[118] The wagon lines were inspected daily until the GOC judged them up to standard.

Messines

At the end of February 1917, 1 and 3 FA Brigades and Artillery Headquarters took up positions in the Ploegsteert Wood in western Belgium as the New Zealand Division prepared to take part in an offensive to enlarge the exposed Ypres salient, where the Germans threatened strategic ports on the coast. This attack was conceived as the first stage of a drive to the coast to cut off German U-boat bases. The opening moves were entrusted to Plumer's Second Army. The New Zealanders' immediate objective was the ridgetop village of Messines, from which the enemy could observe the British positions for miles around.[119]

Lessons had been learnt on the Somme. New tactics were developed to make the most of the increasing weight of artillery support available to the Allies, not only to assist infantry attacks, but to secure ground gained against counter-attacks and counter-bombardment. With expectations for a dramatic breakthrough having proven unrealistic, more modest objectives were now set. One limiting factor was the range of the artillery. The standard 18-pr had an effective range of 6500 yards. Emplaced 1000–2000 yards behind the front line, and required to fire at least 1000 yards in front of the furthest advance to repel counter-attacks, it could cover advances of around 3500 yards at most. Counter-battery techniques – the ability of 'spotters' to locate German batteries by triangulating the sound of the guns or the flashes from their muzzles – were constantly being refined.[120]

Elaborate preparations were necessary because of the strength and depth of the German line in this sector. Assisted by infantry working parties, the Divisional Artillery prepared 25 well-concealed and protected ('magnum opus') battery positions in Ploegsteert Wood and on and around the nearby Hill 63. Deeply buried cables connected each gun position with command posts ('control positions') behind the front. By now the organisation of supplies was:

> wonderful. Wide gauge railways carry munitions from the sea port to within a few miles of the firing line where they are transferred to a narrow light line which runs close to the guns. Oil locomotives are used on many of the light lines. One of these motors can draw 50 tons of ammunition which would require 17 motor lorries to move by road.

Tram lines ran past some battery positions, removing the need to carry forward ammunition by hand.[121]

When not deployed on working parties or resting out of the line, the gunners kept busy with counter-battery and harassing fire, and with observed fire called down to repel raiding parties. German counter-battery fire, particularly from 5.9s (as the 15-cm howitzers were known), increased in intensity as the British preparations were observed. There were casualties in the gun positions and the wagon lines, and a number of ammunition dumps were destroyed.[122]

On 22 and 23 May the Divisional Artillery units occupied their forward 'concentration areas', ready to support the advance. Together with the other units of the corps artillery they practised creeping barrages and carried out concentrations that repeatedly cut the wire in front of the German lines. From 31 May, each gun fired 150 rounds daily at German lines of communication, gun positions and supply points, with one fifteen-minute pause for aerial photography of the battlefield. When the wind was favourable, gas shells were fired. The two 18-pr brigades were each 'grouped' with RFA batteries which, along with a further RFA 'group', would provide the creeping barrage to lead the advance forward, while the corps' heavy batteries rained a standing barrage on the German positions. The howitzer batteries were also grouped in order to fire concentrations on key points. Johnston commanded 114 18-prs and 36 4.5-inch howitzers, with heavies in support.[123] 'Everywhere were guns, guns, guns. ... [The 18-prs] stood wheel to wheel in ... an endless line. In the gunpits themselves were piles of shells; at a little distance back were other piles; farther back still, but where they could be rapidly loaded on the light railway trucks, were fresh piles.'[124] In the days before the attack the medium trench mortar batteries were moved rapidly between positions along the front, firing briefly before moving on.

The opening of the offensive was apparently heard in Paris, 130 miles away. At 3.10 a.m. on 7 June, mines laid under the German lines exploded and the long-practised creeping barrage swept forward in 20 lifts over 2500 yards, with the infantry close behind. The barrage was awe-inspiring:

> Suddenly the dark dawn was rent by a thunder-clap as the mines exploded – torn by a thunder-blast of sound as the barrage opened. Fearful as was the

Sport in the NZEF

Playing sport was a popular way for New Zealand soldiers to relax. While the Third, Fourth and Fifth Reinforcements waited to embark, they competed in NZEF championships at Trentham racecourse. Infantry competed with gunners, and even the over-age men of the Samoan Relief Force, in tug-of-war, foot races and tent-pitching. Permanent staff and bandsmen had their own races.[125] During training in Egypt, inter-unit rugby matches were enthusiastically played and watched, and there were opportunities to swim in the 'pleasant and invigorating waters of Lake Timsah'.[126]

In France sport was played whenever the Division was out of the line. Boxing was popular, and perhaps cathartic, entertainment. Rugby matches were organised between sections of batteries, between batteries, with infantry, North versus South Island – anything to keep men active. On a hot day in May 1917, 3 Brigade organised a 'Marathon race in afternoon. 3.5 miles. 60 men started from each battery.' Cricket was played weekly in summer behind the lines, and in September 1917 there was a Divisional Artillery sports tournament won by 1 Battery. The Division also held horse shows linked to the gunners' field training, in which they practised 'galloping into action and out again' – even though in the line most were dismounted, manhandling guns through muddy shellholes or hauling horse teams through the mire. In the divisional horse shows six-horse teams paraded before judges for prizes such as ribbons, cash or a half-day off duty. In June 1918, 3 Brigade organised an 'unofficial, though highly successful' race meeting.[127]

Summer training also offered simple pleasures such as 'swimming and playing about [naked] in full view of the civilian population. Under abnormal conditions the most absolute conventions drop off'. In 1916 divisional aquatic sports were held in a purpose-built pool at Armentières.[128]

The New Zealand Field Artillery stirs up the dust during a driving competition.
Album 419, photo H667, Auckland War Memorial Museum.

din, yet the different parts of the great barrage could plainly be distinguished. The heavy roll of the great guns formed the dominating note, but in the heart of the long roll came the quick, stabbing bang-snap-bang of the eighteen-pounders, and the rattle of the thousands of machine guns.[129]

The Germans were temporarily stunned and resistance was slight. The New Zealand infantry advanced through the town, reaching their final objective by 8.40 a.m. 'Our barrage …was splendid', Johnston exulted, 'and all the wire was cut away'.[130] Early in the afternoon the gunners shattered a German counter-attack as it formed up. Australian units then moved up through the New Zealand positions. The artillery responded throughout the night to calls for fire into their designated SOS zones, causing casualties amongst the Australians, who had advanced further than was realised.[131]

Bodies still lay on the battlefield when Johnston inspected it next morning. Two tanks had been 'knocked out by shell fire'; he dismissed them as 'not much good'. Before the battle, Divisional HQ had reiterated the pre-eminence of the artillery over the twelve tanks that were to cooperate with the New Zealanders. 'The Assaulting Troops must clearly understand that their objective is in no way controlled by the action of the tanks but regulated solely by our Artillery barrage.'[132] The artillery groups were now reorganised and moved forward to positions south of Messines to support an attack that was to push back the German lines about 1500 yards in front of the village of La Basseville. The New Zealand infantry achieved its goals in two days, helped by a hastily arranged creeping barrage on 14 June.[133]

Since early March 2 (Army) Brigade, NZFA had been training and on operations supporting British divisions. On the day of the assault it contributed to the barrage supporting 25 Division, also part of II ANZAC Corps. The Battle of Messines was well planned and executed, and the artillery contribution went like clockwork. More than 7000 German prisoners were taken.

PASSCHENDAELE

Messines was just the preliminary to a much larger offensive which would become known as the Third Battle of Ypres. In late June the NZFA units were pulled out of the line to rest before, on 8 July, relieving Australian units in readiness for an assault on La Basseville.[134] The Divisional Ammunition Columns toiled to keep the batteries supplied while the village was shelled heavily for a week. With German counter-battery and harassment fire also heavy at times, horses and wagons were often driven at a gallop over the most hazardous sections.

A creeping barrage led the New Zealand infantry into La Basseville on 27 July, but they were soon dislodged by a counter-attack. The Divisional Artillery provided barrages when the village was taken again – and held – on the 31st. On the same day, the British launched their long-planned main offensive to the north, but from that afternoon heavy rain thwarted the artillery techniques that had been so successful at Messines. At least this offensive took some pressure off the New Zealanders at La Basseville, where the gunners traded counter-battery fire with their German counterparts. When 3 Brigade batteries fired asphyxiating gas on 10 August, the 'retaliation was fairly prompt and in kind'.[135] In early September the Divisional Artillery was relieved for a period of rest and training.

By 2 August the British assault on the Ypres salient had stalled well short of its main objective, the Geluveld–Passchendaele plateau. Further attacks were called off in the face of heavy losses, effective counter-attacks and torrential rain. Some ground was won later in August and in September, but the almost incessant rain, combined with heavy shelling which disrupted natural watercourses, turned the battlefield into a quagmire worse than the Somme. General Plumer's Second Army was now called in to replicate the 'bite and hold' operations that had been so successful at Messines. The third of these, an attack on Broodseinde and the Gravenstafel Spur, saw Godley's II ANZAC Corps and the New Zealand Division back in action.

The new operation started tragically for the New Zealand gunners. First they were ordered to inappropriate positions near Frezenberg, where their brief stay coincided with an intensive German bombardment that caused heavy casualties and loss of guns. After exchanging the remaining guns with the Australian artillery brigades that relieved them, they had to labour in the mud to construct new positions in the New Zealand sector, where a lack of cover forced the batteries together in a vulnerable space under a small hill.[136]

With the infantry assault imminent, the mortar gunners helped the ammunition column to supply the field guns with shells. In the forward areas, horse-drawn limbers sank up to their axles in mud when they left the collapsing roads. The pack mules that took ammunition on to the gun positions had to be unloaded as they got bogged down. They plodded in long strings along 'greasy shell-swept tracks, laden with ammunition for the 18-pr guns. Now and again one ... would step off the track to flounder, hopelessly bogged, in the mud and ooze.'[137]

With additional guns brought under his command, Johnston deployed ten brigades of 18-prs and 4.5-inch howitzers behind the New Zealand Division, while in support Corps Artillery provided additional firepower, including 60-prs and heavy howitzers – all covering a divisional front of only 2000 yards. In their exposed forward positions the two New Zealand brigades registered their guns before falling silent to await the infantry assault. From 6 a.m. on 4 October the New Zealand infantry brigades advanced behind a creeping barrage of five simultaneous curtains of shellfire at 200-yard intervals. The four forward barrages lifted simultaneously with the 'A' barrage (from 132 18-prs) that led the infantry forward about 1000 yards in two stages, and provided a protective barrage as they reached each objective.[138] An infantry private who took part in the assault could not:

> speak too highly of the skills of our gunners who fired that creeping barrage. The [18-prs] fired this while the heavier shelled the enemy. The creeping barrage provided a curtain of bursting shells behind which we were briefed to follow at a distance of 50 yds. We allowed it to be about a hundred yards for safetys sake. We could see only the curtain of shells ahead and that through an atmosphere of smoke and drizzle.[139]

This assault on the Gravenstafel Spur and an associated Australian advance on Broodseinde were successful. German casualties were heavy, partly because the enemy had been massing in the forward trenches for an attack when II ANZAC Corps' barrage began. The New Zealanders alone took more than 1000 prisoners. Johnston's gun line was enfiladed from its flank by a single 5.9-inch gun, but there were few casualties as the high-velocity shells buried themselves in the mud before detonating.

Passchendaele, October 1917.
PAColl-2667-014, Alexander Turnbull Library, Wellington.

Accurate registration of the guns was impossible in conditions like this.
Album 419, photo H303, Auckland War Memorial Museum.

The success of the 'bite and hold' approach depended on careful preparation over a period of weeks, the stockpiling of ammunition, and limited goals. With the final objectives well within range of batteries in positions set back from the start line, protective barrages could confound German counter-attacks with relative ease. But in the continuing rain the massive artillery support needed to achieve and consolidate advances, combined with return fire from German batteries, churned the sodden landscape into a morass of deep mud and shellholes filled with slimy, yellow water. In their sector, the New Zealand gunners and drivers struggled along the one remaining road – disintegrating and congested – to help support a British assault at Poelcappelle on 9 October. As the soldiers of 49 Division, exhausted by an all-night march to the front, staggered out of the trenches and through the mire, the timetable for the attack collapsed and the creeping barrage was abandoned in favour of a standing barrage. When this petered out, Johnston worried that a disaster was in the making. 'They are rushing this operation too quickly', he observed in his diary. 'I think there will be a great many casualties in the infantry [for want of] care and preparation'.[140]

The New Zealand Division and an Australian division were now thrown into the line, and Johnston's batteries attempted to move to new positions to support an attack scheduled for 12 October. The gunners and drivers toiled to shift the guns, but most could not be brought up through the mud. Many remained out of range of at least part of the planned advance. One gunner recalled the hopelessness of the task:

> I knew the ground around our guns as I had been there daily with ammunition and I knew how impossible it was to move the guns in time for the second attempt. Horses were useless in such mud so the guns had to be inched forward by manpower – pulled out of the muddy water in one shell hole to slide into another.[141]

With extreme effort, eight 18-prs and four 4.5-inch howitzers were manhandled forward by the end of 11 October. Like most of the guns further back, they lacked the timber platforms, built on a foundation of fascines and gravel, that were necessary on such ground. The gunners improvised as best they could, lashing any timber available to the guns, but the results were unsatisfactory. The ammunition column was also frustrated by congestion on the collapsing corduroy (tree-trunk) road, and the morass that then had to be crossed to reach the guns. One of the subsidiary horrors of this operation was the frequent need to destroy animals that became hopelessly mired; at least one mule loaded with shells sank without trace. Where mules could not get through, men carried shells on their shoulders, sometimes for several miles.

The New Zealand attack was to be supported by heavy artillery, and eight brigades (32 batteries) of 18-prs and howitzers came under Johnston's command. But when the CRA inspected the front on the morning of the 11th, he could not locate all the batteries, which were still attempting to move forward or preparing to do so. Johnston apparently told both Russell and the Corps commander, Godley, that 'they could not depend on the Artillery tomorrow'.[142] He failed to convince his seniors that his gunners' situation was impossible. While Russell recorded that Johnston was 'uneasy about the attack – says preparation inadequate', in an appalling misunderstanding of the situation the divisional commander also noted that 'The guns are all forward'.[143] The unreadiness of a single division would not, of course, have been allowed to delay such a major operation. The wider question is whether the offensive should have been continued after 9 October. Historian Gary Sheffield, who is generally sympathetic to the British commander, Field Marshal Douglas Haig, thinks not.[144]

Because of the shortage of guns in position and of ammunition at the gun line, the usual preparatory bombardments were not carried out. The inability to rehearse the creeping barrage and confusion at the scattered gun positions meant that in one sector the artillery fired on their own infantry massed for the assault:

> Through some blunder our artillery barrage opened up about two hundred yards short of the specified range and thus ... right in the midst of us. It was a truly awful time – our own men getting cut to pieces in dozens by our own guns. Immediate disorganisation followed. I heard an officer shout an order to the men to retire a short distance and wait for our barrage to lift. Some, who heard the order, did so. Others, not knowing what to do ... stayed where they

were, while others advanced towards the German positions, only to be mown down by ... deadly rifle and machine gun fire.[145]

When the barrage lifted and the infantry rushed forward, the curtain of shelling was thin, inaccurate and unreliable. With each shot, the guns lurched and buried their trails and wheels unevenly into the mud. The continuing hazard of shorts added to the misery of the infantry as, lashed by rain, they stumbled forward towards Bellevue Spur, an outcrop of Passchendaele Ridge. Here they were dismayed to find the wire entanglements in front of the German lines intact; many men were quickly cut down by machine-gun fire from the pillboxes. The feeble creeping barrage had to be abandoned in favour of a protective barrage as the surviving infantry sheltered in shellholes.[146]

This was the New Zealanders' first encounter with a new kind of impediment – "pill boxes", concrete and ferro concrete constructions, very strong and with machine guns; no [field] guns can smash them up, except with much concentrated fire, they are very small and hard to hit, ... arranged chequerwise [to] form a very stiff obstacle'.[147]

This disastrous action cost the lives of 845 New Zealanders, with 2700 wounded. Though there were few gunners among the casualties, Johnston recorded that 'To-day has been a very bad day for us':

> My opinion is that the senior generals who direct these operations are not conversant with the conditions, mud, cold, rain, no shelter, [and] the Germans are not so played out as they make out. All our attacks recently lack preparation and the whole history of the war is that when thorough preparation is not made we fail. All these pill boxes should have been heavily bombarded and the wire cut.[148]

Over the following days, 200-strong teams of the Maori Pioneer Battalion heaving on ropes laboriously moved more guns up to the positions they should have occupied on 12 October. By the 20th two-thirds of the guns were forward, and ammunition supplies were improving. When the New Zealand Division was relieved by 3 Canadian Division on 18 October, the gunners stayed on to support an attack on the 26th that took Bellevue Spur and positions around the village of Passchendaele (which was to be captured by the Canadians on 6 November). The New Zealand gunners were shelled frequently but kept up effective counter-battery and harassing fire, and concentrations to cut the German wire entanglements. The Canadian assault was supported by the usual heavy creeping and protective barrages. On 1 November the New Zealanders handed over their guns to Canadian batteries and withdrew to the wagon lines, where they suffered further casualties from shelling, and then to Wallon Cappel for much-needed rest and recuperation.[149]

Meanwhile, for most of the period since the Battle of Messines, 2 (Army) Brigade, NZFA, had been deployed near Nieuwpoort on the Belgian coast in support of British divisions. Here the gunners established protected batteries for their own guns and those of other batteries, and took part in often intensive counter-battery actions that also involved heavy guns on both sides. Brigade Headquarters was even shelled by a 17-inch coastal gun located some 10 miles away at Ostend. On 20 November the brigade was relieved by French batteries. It moved to Morbecque for rest and training before rejoining the New Zealand Divisional Artillery and replacing an Australian field brigade in support of the New Zealand Division near Ypres.[150]

POLDERHOEK

The New Zealand Division had returned to the line on 14 November, relieving a British division and initially supported by the Australian artillery brigade and two RFA 'Army' brigades, all under the command of Johnston, who established his headquarters at Chateau Segard. On 26 November the front was extended south, enabling an attack on the Polderhoek Chateau, north of Geluveld, on 3 December. An officer of 2 Infantry Brigade remembered standing beside his battalion commander in the tense minutes before the assault, both with their watches out and 'praying that the barrage would be true':

> With a great roar it came – 120 guns of all calibre concentrated on 500 yards of front supported by fifty machine guns on each flank, and batteries of trench mortars. Down the valleys on either side of us poured great screens of smoke, hiding our limited objectives from the enemy, while hundreds of gas shells

rained on his supports and batteries. Right behind the moving wall of death our first waves had gone, advancing with parade ground perfection.[151]

Supported also by the Divisional Trench Mortars, equipped for the first time with Newton 6-inch trench mortars, the infantry nevertheless suffered early casualties from shorts before being held up by strong German defences and artillery. After counter-attacks were driven off over the following days, the New Zealand units that had taken part in the assault were moved to the north after being relieved by IX Corps units on 5 December. The limited ground taken at Polderhoek was lost nine days later.

When the New Zealand line near Ypres was adjusted, 1 and 3 Brigades of the Divisional Artillery and 2 (Army) Brigade rejoined the Division at the front, relieving an Australian and two RFA brigades and digging in for the winter. Many of the gun positions and captured blockhouses used as sleeping quarters were by now in appalling condition, and had to be cleared of corpses and waterlogged ammunition, among other things. The gunners helped to provide their own comforts. 'Eight artillery chaps and two engineer chaps … started to build a YMCA hut today', a 3 Brigade gunner noted in December. In six days they 'had the floor down, walls up and rafters but cannot go on with the job until the rest of the timber comes'. General Russell opened this facility in early February 1918, after which there was almost nightly entertainment ranging from debates to pantomimes.[152]

The New Zealanders were now being reinforced largely by conscripts who, like volunteers, underwent up to ten months' training in New Zealand, England and France before seeing action. Throughout 1918, at no apparent cost to morale, conscripts would maintain the strength of the Division. It began the year by preparing strong defensive positions from which to repulse an expected German offensive. The collapse of Russian forces in the east following the 1917 Bolshevik Revolution gave the Germans a last chance for victory before large numbers of American troops arrived on the Western Front and German industry was strangled by the relentless Allied blockade.[153]

Artillery exchanges became more frequent in early 1918. Both sides fired concentrations on strongpoints and signs of movement, while German counter-battery fire from heavy batteries and high-velocity guns, and including

Relaxing in a New Zealand Field Artillery officers' club in wagon lines near Ypres, February 1918.
Album 419, photo H422, Auckland War Memorial Museum.

mixed 'shell storms' of shrapnel and gas shells (to confuse and delay the taking of precautions against gas) caused many casualties among the New Zealand gunners. They got their own back, however. In early February a German division arriving from the Eastern Front to take over the line in the New Zealand sector was greeted by a 40-minute creeping barrage from the New Zealand guns, supported by British field and heavy batteries.[154]

BACK TO THE SOMME – AND MESSINES

On 24 February 1918 the New Zealand Division was relieved from the line, along with most of 2 Brigade, NZFA; one battery remained to man four 18-prs deployed forward as anti-tank guns. 1 and 3 Brigades also remained in the line, under British divisional artillery command, until they were ordered south with the rest of the Division on 22 March, the day after the long-awaited German offensive, Operation Michael, was launched on the Somme. Here the British Fifth Army had been thinly stretched since its front was extended in October 1917 to relieve pressure on the demoralised French Army. As 60 German

Training in New Zealand

The territorial artillery units were a vital source of men for service overseas. All but one of the officers of E Battery and the Christchurch ammunition column left with Main Body – and the laggard followed with the Fourth Reinforcements.[155] Fresh intakes initially entered camp every two months. Artillery reinforcements were at first sent to the front at the rate of 7 per cent of the war establishment each month (compared with 25 per cent for infantry and mounted units). The percentage fluctuated, but for most of the war there were replacement gunners in every reinforcement contingent, and personnel constantly turned over.[156] 'Half the battery are new men', an 11 Battery gunner noted in February 1918.[157] Minister of Defence James Allen observed that service in the artillery was 'felt to be a special honour'.[158]

After signing up at the local recruitment office, men assembled at 'concentration camps' such as Tahuna Park (Dunedin), Addington Showgrounds (Christchurch) and Alexandra Park (Auckland) before going to Trentham for five weeks of basic training.

By January 1916 reinforcement drafts were being despatched every month, and Wairarapa's Featherston Camp had become the training centre for NZEF artillery recruits (and for mounted rifles and 'specialists' – machine-gunners and signallers).

After three weeks of riding, musketry drill and orderly duties, there was five weeks of gun drill. This included practising getting the guns into action quickly:

> The guns and waggons ... came in pairs, the gun to the left, a waggon to the right. At the words 'Sections Left', the guns wheeled to the front, with dancing horses. The waggons turned, too, each behind its gun. Then the guns were unlimbered, the horses with the limber ... galloping to the rear. The trail ... was seized by the gunners and swung into position to the right of the ammunition waggon, the waggon teams having been quickly unhooked and hurried to the rear. As each gun came into action, the sergeant ... leaped to the ground, and handed his horse to the wheel driver, to be taken to the rear with the others.

They fired at a hill to the east:

> By systematically searching the area, or bracket, the range is found. No.1, on No.1 gun, raises his hand to show that he has received the order [from the section commander]. His duty is to traverse the gun

NCOs training at Featherston, 1917.
Royal New Zealand Artillery Old Comrades' Association.

> – move the muzzle to either side as desired; No.2 attends to the range and the breech; No.3 fires and lays the gun; No.4 sets fuses and loads; Nos.5 and 6 are the ammunition men, crouching behind the waggon ... The whipping, stunning bang of No.1 gun broke the ... stillness .... A flare of flame ... ringed the black muzzle, blue smoke rose in a thin cloud, and the shrill cry of the shell was a diminishing note as it fled towards the white specks on the distant spur.... The voice of the fuse-setters could be heard repeating the orders loudly enough for the section commander to hear. ...

Once the battery found the range, the guns fired in quick succession. The battery commander, standing nearby, issued the orders:

> his words were repeated through a field telephone to a station behind the guns. Sometimes ... half-a-dozen runners are spaced in the short distance between the telephone and the guns, all running for dear life .... The order was; One Round Battery Fire, Fifteen Seconds. No.1 gun opened the ball. Fifteen seconds later No.2 gun's voice was heard; then No.3 spoke, then No.4. ... Now could be seen the difference between the percussion and air-bursts. The shells were bursting in pretty puffs of white smoke, apparently above the targets, but actually some distance in front of them, the shrapnel bullets released by the burst pelting forwards and down. ... The flags of the signallers on the hillside began to flutter ...[159]

Happy New Year, Fritz! New Zealand 18-pr near Westhoek, Ypres Salient, 1 January 1918.
10x8-1806-G, Alexander Turnbull Library, Wellington

divisions smashed towards Amiens between the British Third and Fifth Armies, forces were rushed from the north to stem the tide. The New Zealanders, attached to the Third Army, were ordered to close a 4-mile gap in the front between Hébuterne and Beaumont-Hamel. Thrown into battle piecemeal from 26 March, the New Zealand infantry had very little support until the Divisional Artillery reached the battlefield through a tide of refugees.[160]

The first batteries were in action near the village of Mailly-Maillet by 11 p.m. on the 27th. Johnston, based at Hédauville, was able to bring under command the New Zealand 1 and 3 Brigades, three or four RFA brigades, and two brigades and a siege battery of the RGA. Throughout the night the Divisional Ammunition Column (DAC) drivers and any gunners who could be spared toiled to bring forward thousands of shells. Initially shooting from map references, Johnston's gunners maintained harassing fire throughout the night and counter-preparation concentrations from 4 a.m. In the afternoon, concentrated fire broke up an attack by two enemy brigades before they could reach the New Zealand infantry. On 30 March the gunners provided a well-placed creeping barrage to support two New Zealand brigades in a limited advance to secure a more defensible line.[161]

By now the Allies had thwarted the initial German attack and consolidated the whole front. A further assault by ten divisions on 5 April was preceded by heavy shelling of both front and rear areas. The New Zealanders suffered a three-hour bombardment during which most of their communication wires were cut. The gunners maintained steady fire on the enemy trenches despite numerous casualties, and their counter-preparation concentrations seriously hindered the German infantry forming up for the assault. Attacks were repulsed on the left of the New Zealand line in the morning, and on the right in the afternoon. The gunners continued harassing fire over the following days, and prepared to coordinate their fire with the artillery supporting neighbouring divisions in the event of a further onslaught. In fact the German assault on the Somme had run its course, and the gunners settled down to a routine of counter-battery and harassing fire.[162]

While the other artillery brigades were in action on the Somme, 2 (Army) Brigade remained in the line at Ypres under command of 37 Divisional Artillery, and then in the Neuve Église–Ploegsteert sector under 19 Divisional Artillery. On 7 April the brigade and two RFA batteries comprising the Division's Left Group Artillery, under the New Zealand brigade commander, Lieutenant-Colonel Falla, took up positions on familiar ground below the Messines Ridge. Just two days later, a heavy German bombardment south of Armentières heralded a breakthrough to the River Lys. The guns in the 19 Division sector maintained harassing fire on the enemy trenches and rear areas, but as their southern flank became dangerously exposed the gunners prepared for a fighting withdrawal. At 2.30 a.m. on 10 April the Germans began a heavy bombardment of the trenches and rear areas with gas and high-explosive shells. Forward observers called down fire as best they could, but when German infantry appeared on the ridge overlooking the gun line, the gunners were ordered to leapfrog their batteries back to positions around Wulverghem. By 11.30 a.m. all three batteries were in action from new positions. The enemy advance through Ploegsteert Wood almost cut off 6 (Howitzer) Battery: one gun had to fire out of the back of its pit as German

Firing in the open on Germans concentrating for another attack, Somme, April 1918.
Album 419, photo H455, Auckland War Memorial Museum.

infantry surrounded the New Zealanders. It was impossible to get horse teams through because of shelling and small-arms fire, and the surviving guns were abandoned after their sights and breech-blocks had been removed.[163]

By the end of this confused day's fighting the gunners of 2 (Army) Brigade were operating independently under the brigade commander. Falla was ordered by the CRA of 25 Division, who took over the artillery in the sector during the day, to either fight or withdraw his brigade to the north-west. Falla's gunners maintained fire on Ploegsteert village and the ground east of Messines throughout the night, but the enemy advance continued. After Hill 63 fell to the enemy at 7 p.m. on the 11th, the New Zealand batteries pulled back 4000 yards towards Drânoutre. The ammunition column had already supplied shells to the new position, and the guns were soon back in action. Short of telephone wire, the FOOs reverted to using Lucas signalling lamps, and mounted orderlies maintained communication with the wagon lines. Early on the 13th, as the enemy entered Neuve Église, 2 Brigade withdrew to positions between Drânoutre and Locre. When German troops took a nearby hill the following morning, a further move became necessary. The howitzer

Kiwi ingenuity: 6-inch trench mortars adapted 'to keep contact with the enemy', 1918. G13579½, Alexander Turnbull Library, Wellington.

battery, by now supplied with replacement guns, also occupied positions near Locre. One section north-east of Drânoutre fell back on the 16th to rejoin the rest of the brigade between Westoutre and Locre. Heavy shelling necessitated another move on 18 April.[164]

On 19 April French infantry took over the sector covered by 2 Brigade, but the gunners stayed on in support for four days before withdrawing through the wagon lines for reinforcement and three days' rest. The brigade's achievement in bringing down sustained fire from each successive position despite the communications difficulties was a testament to the skills of the FOOs, the stamina of the gunners and the resourcefulness of the ammunition column in securing supplies of shells.[165]

After a brief respite, 2 Brigade returned to the line near Hazebrouck on 26 April under command of 1 Australian Division, and carried out two weeks of harassment and counter-battery fire – including possibly the first use of incendiary shells by New Zealand gunners – to drive the enemy from several strongpoints. The brigade was then ordered south to rejoin the New Zealand Division, and after a trying march along dusty roads, the tired horses, drivers and gunners took up positions behind the Purple Line, near Hébuterne, on 21 May. Here a barrage had been laid down on the 4th to cover an intended 500-yard advance on the left of the New Zealand line. This assault was preceded by three days of bombardment by heavy howitzers and accompanied by a diversionary barrage on La Signy Farm that persuaded the Germans to concentrate their defensive fire on the wrong sector. When the adjoining British division was held up, the New Zealanders had to withdraw from the ground they had taken.[166]

When the British 42 Division relieved the New Zealand Division in the line on 7 June, the gunners stayed on to continue harassment fire at night and observed fire by day. While this part of the front remained stable, each artillery brigade expended up to 1000 rounds per day. The intensity of enemy counter-battery fire fell away, but gunners and drivers were subjected to intermittent shelling; 3 Brigade, at Sailly-au-Bois, suffered mustard gas bombardment for several days.[167]

Rossignol Wood to Trescault Spur

In early July the gunners rejoined the New Zealand Division between Hébuterne and Bucquoy and helped to drive the enemy from positions in the Rossignol Wood salient. The Divisional Artillery now took in an RFA brigade and a brigade of heavy howitzers, with batteries of 60-prs in support. Heavy harassing fire was maintained around the clock, and on 15 July the gunners supported a limited advance near Hébuterne. The bombardment next day of Puisieux-au-Mont by the Divisional Artillery and the corps heavy artillery was notable for their first use of 'double crashes' – a salvo from all guns on a selected target, followed three minutes later by a second concentration within a radius of 200 yards. The enemy withdrew from Rossignol Wood on the night of 19 July, and high ground to the south was captured on the 24th. The following day a heavy bombardment thwarted a German counter-attack. New Zealand guns and howitzers – now deployed near the front line – mounted effective counter-battery fire, sometimes assisted by information from aerial observers that was passed on through brigade HQs. The Field Survey Company also assisted with calibration shoots, using the 'extremely accurate and delicately adjusted instruments' it now possessed.[168]

An Allied counter-offensive on the Marne would soon underline the failure of the German onslaught, but there was still hard fighting ahead, with new challenges for the gunners. The assault began on 6 August near Amiens. The Germans suffered heavy losses before the focus shifted north to the old Somme battlefield, where the British Third Army was preparing to attack along a 9-mile front. The New Zealand Division formed part of IV Corps. The secrecy surrounding preparations for this assault showed how much tactics had evolved. The gunners received their orders only three days before the operation. The guns were hurriedly moved forward, concealed and supplied with ammunition (450 rounds per gun) under cover of darkness. The New Zealand infantry would be supported by 1 and 2 Brigades; 3 Brigade would support 42 Division, immediately to the right. There was neither a preliminary bombardment nor ranging shots before the barrage opened at dawn on 21 August. This element of surprise allowed the infantry to reach their objectives 1000 yards east of Puisieux-au-Mont; the enemy artillery's response was unusually weak. The guns were moved forward after nightfall, and early next morning all the New Zealand batteries helped to beat back a counter-attack on 42 Division's line. Though German counter-battery and harassment fire intensified, the previous day's gains were secured.[169] A new kind of war for which the artillery had little training had begun.

The next stage of the assault, involving the Third Army and part of the Fourth Army along a 33-mile front, began on 23 August. Over the next fortnight the New Zealanders advanced about 15 miles as the crow flies, a breakneck pace by the standards of the last four years. With no time to organise creeping barrages for some assaults, artillery brigades were placed under the command of infantry brigades. Where German resistance strengthened, set-piece techniques were reintroduced: on the 27th and 28th heavy shelling of Bapaume by the Divisional Artillery culminated in a 'hurricane barrage' in which the concentrated fire of all the guns rolled slowly over the town from west to east. Flexibility was now the key. When the Germans counter-attacked with six tanks at Fremicourt on the 31st, some sections of guns were so far forward, in order to better co-operate with individual infantry battalions, that they fired on the attackers over open sights.[170]

During this period of rapid advance, the Germans still sometimes brought down counter-battery fire that caused casualties at the gun lines. As the guns were moved forward, shells were left behind to be brought up by the ammunition column. New wagon lines were usually established at the most recently vacated gun positions. Gunners and drivers laboured to keep up with the infantry and maintain fire. The gunners generally advanced in leapfrog fashion, with one or more brigades covering the advance while the others moved. Sometimes gun positions had to be established quickly to deal with points of resistance. Observation officers with the infantry were often forced to rely on visual signals as linesmen struggled to get field telephone lines back to the batteries. Each brigade now had a portable wireless set, and these were sometimes used for communication with observers. Finding enough water for the horses was another problem.

From 6 September the New Zealand Division occupied the Havrincourt and Gouzeaucourt woods. On the 9th a full-scale barrage led an assault on the Trescault Spur, but after initial successes the infantry had to dig in under a protective barrage. The New Zealanders took the spur on the 12th after undergoing some hard fighting and heavy shelling. Three days later the Division was relieved for a well-deserved rest in Corps Reserve, but as usual the gunners toiled on, under command of 5 Division, or in the case of 2 (Army) Brigade, transferred to V Corps. From the 14th they faced heavy counter-battery fire, including gas shelling, and it was a relief when 1 Brigade and most of 3 Brigade were withdrawn to the wagon lines from the 19th.[171]

THROUGH THE HINDENBURG LINE

German resistance had stiffened along the Hindenburg Line, a series of trenches prepared in depth, and on the Canal du Nord to its north. Under command of RFA units, the New Zealand Divisional Artillery supported the British 5 and 42 Divisions as a general assault on the Hindenburg Line began on 27 September. That night the Divisional Artillery came back under Johnston's command as the New Zealand Division passed through the forward positions of 42 Division in an attack coordinated with British divisions on their flanks. The New Zealanders were held up periodically while enemy machine-gun posts were neutralised. Once the objectives were taken – along with hundreds of prisoners – a brigade of each gun group brought its guns forward over country that was both heavily entrenched and broken up by shelling. When the advance was renewed on the 30th, the Allies secured a bridgehead east of the Canal de Saint Quentin and liberated the town of Crèvecœur.[172]

The next major assault, on 8 October, showed the sophistication with which the war was now being fought. Tanks helped infantry defeat a German tank attack, and aircraft gave early warning of German infantry massing to counter-attack a flanking brigade. The latter threat was nullified by New Zealand machine guns and artillery. Next day most of the New Zealand guns were brought across the canal, and with resistance now weak, the New Zealanders advanced a dozen miles with few casualties before meeting stiffer opposition on the River Selle. The New Zealand Division was relieved by 42 Division on 12 October, when the Divisional Artillery also left the line for billets in the liberated town of Beauvais.[173]

Within a week the gunners moved back to the line to support 42 Division. The New Zealand guns and five medium trench mortars took part in the barrage and concentrations fired on strategic points as the assault on the Selle began on 20 October. After the British infantry crossed the river, engineers, including a field company of New Zealand sappers, erected bridges. 2 (Army) Brigade now rejoined the Divisional Artillery after similar experiences while detached to operations with V Corps to the south, and then with XVII Corps to the north.[174]

The NZFA brigades quickly established gun positions east of the Selle and prepared for the next attack on 23 October. Heavy enemy fire had little impact on this operation, but cost the Divisional Artillery and the DAC 56 horses. The New Zealand gunners again supported 42 Division until the New Zealand Division moved through the British positions to continue the attack, when Johnston resumed command of the Divisional Artillery and attached units. By the end of the day the New Zealand infantry had completed the planned 4-mile advance, taking Beaudignies and securing bridgeheads over the Escaillon River. During the morning 2 (Army) Brigade had been brought forward in support. The gunners now settled down around Beaudignies, exchanging fire with a demoralised enemy.[175]

The fact that the fighting was not yet over was underscored by the death of Major J.M. Richmond, RNZA, on the 27th. He had sailed with the Main Body, served on Johnston's staff as Adjutant on Gallipoli, and later as Brigade Major there and in France before taking command of a battery. On the day of his death he took over one of the field brigades. Johnston judged Richmond one of New Zealand's 'most promising and certainly most brilliant Staff Officer[s]'. In a war of detailed planning, his talents were invaluable. His orders were so 'lucid and concise, they were never misunderstood and his Instructions were so well written other Divisions often copied them.'[176]

Le Quesnoy

The New Zealanders now came up against the fortress town of Le Quesnoy, which had been founded in the Middle Ages and remodelled by Marshal Vauban in the seventeenth century. When a massive British offensive opened along a 30-mile front on 4 November, the New Zealand Field Artillery was faced with one of its most technically demanding challenges. The assault on Le Quesnoy required a barrage that would move forward and encircle the town at different rates to keep pace with the flanking divisions, raining fire on the German garrison while sparing civilians. It would then move in an unbroken line towards the Forêt de Mormal, ceasing 6000 yards from the start line. Spirits were high as the barrage began at 5.30 a.m.[177]

> Suddenly the air is rent with the deafening thunder of artillery drumfire. The hour has struck! Popping of Vickers! Barking of field guns, Booming of heavies! Flashes in the greying dawn! Black smoke, red smoke, white smoke! Leaping earth, flying clods and ripping steel! A tension of muscles and the first wave is off.[178]

The barrage went off with precision despite German counter-battery fire, and the infantry soon surrounded and pushed past the town. The gunners then began moving forward, brigade by brigade, to keep pace with the infantry, which by the end of the day had moved into the Forêt de Mormal in an advance that pushed the front forward by 6 miles and captured some 2000 prisoners and 60 field guns, including whole batteries with their crews and horses. Le Quesnoy was captured by infantry with scaling ladders who surmounted the outer ramparts, encouraging the demoralised Germans to surrender. Confronted by 'wildly happy' inhabitants, the taciturn CRA 'left the place hurriedly not wishing to be embraced'.[179]

The gunners continued to leapfrog their batteries forward to support the advance. When 42 Division relieved the New Zealand Division the next evening, they were east of the Forêt de Mormal. The gunners stayed on, but problems moving the guns along tracks damaged by enemy demolitions held up the assault. By the evening of the 6th most of 2 Brigade was through, and 42 Division advanced the following morning against little resistance behind the thin barrage of this single brigade. When the other brigades were brought forward that afternoon, 2 Brigade became reserve brigade, never again to fire its guns in anger. After some harassment shooting on the 8th – the NZFA's last action of the war – 1 and 3 Brigades moved forward to Boussières, about 10 miles east of Le Quesnoy, where they were relieved in the line the following day by 42 Divisional Artillery. By now a general collapse of German arms was apparent. When the Armistice took effect on the morning of the 11th, the New Zealand Divisional Artillery and the Ammunition Column were starting a two-day march back to Quiévy to rejoin the rest of the Division.[181]

One well-educated gunner who had survived Gallipoli and the Western Front greeted the Armistice as 'Probably THE day in the world's history', but added: 'After all this time, nobody seems to realise what it means.'[182] There was 'no cheering, no demonstration'. Men had been through so much that 'this momentous intelligence was too vast in its consequences to be appreciated in a single thought'.[182]

Since 1916 the New Zealand gunners had been involved in the process of refining artillery techniques which led to the dominance of field and heavy artillery. As the stalemate in the trenches dragged on, artillery doctrine and tactics were modified to provide better co-operation with the infantry, better coordination among more artillery units, concealment of artillery massed to attack, sophisticated fire-planning for major operations, new techniques such as sound-ranging (comparing the time taken for the report of a gun to reach carefully spaced detectors)[183] and prompt concentrations in response to enemy activity. The bludgeoning preparatory bombardments of 1916 were supplemented the following year by sophisticated creeping barrages and careful limitation of infantry objectives, tactics that achieved notable success for the New Zealanders at Messines. Without well-prepared artillery support, however, the outcome could be very different – Passchendaele was tragic evidence of the cost of mounting an assault before the guns were ready. The skills of the New Zealand gunners were not restricted to static warfare: in 1918 their flexible response to the German offensive and their participation in the fast-moving Allied advance helped to bring the war to an end.

After resting at Quiévy until 28 November, the gunners marched to Germany with the Division as part of the Army of Occupation.[184] When they crossed into Belgium on 4 December the New Zealanders enjoyed generous hospitality in towns 'gaily decked with flags'. 'Flowers were thrown or wreathed round gun-barrels and the horses' necks. The very limbers were decorated.'[185] Passing through German towns was a less pleasant experience. Here they saw 'not a flag except on our own wagons, people stayed inside, doors and windows closed'. The DAC spent a 'very quiet' Christmas in Düren; 'thank God the next one will be in New Zealand'.[186]

The gunners reached their destination, Cologne, on Boxing Day. After taking up billets across the Rhine in Deutz, they enjoyed sightseeing, cultural and sporting activities. Demobilisation soon proceeded apace. The first draft left for England on 14 January, followed by weekly drafts from 28 January until 25 March. Batteries were reduced to four- and then two-gun establishments, then combined into two four-gun batteries in each brigade, with the mortar batteries disbanded. Surplus guns were returned to British depots. Apart from some mares selected for breeding, the horses were sent to England for service in the British Army or sold locally for commercial or private use, or to be butchered. On 18 March the skeletal remains of the Divisional Artillery Headquarters, the individual brigades and batteries, and the Divisional Ammunition Column were disbanded, and a week later the New Zealand Division itself ceased to exist, having been replaced in its occupation role by the British 2 Division. Most of the Divisional Artillery personnel returned to Sling Camp in England to await their return home. Behind them, on Gallipoli and in France and Belgium, they left 448 of their comrades killed in action; another 271 had succumbed to wounds, while 2353 survived them. With 135 artillerymen dead of other causes, the total casualties were 3207. In all 132 officers and 5441 other ranks had left New Zealand with the artillery (others had joined in Egypt and Britain).[187] For the gunners, as for most corps of the New Zealand Army, the Great War had demanded their greatest sacrifice.

George Napier Johnston

Born in Canada in 1868, George Napier Johnston RA began his military training in 1884. He was to have a significant role leading New Zealand's artillery, with which he served for a total of eleven years. After four years in India, in 1904 he was seconded to New Zealand as Staff Officer Artillery, declining reappointment to this position after three years because of the obstacles to promotion faced by officers on secondment; for example, no annual confidential reports on his performance were sent to the War Office.[188] His prospects may not have improved on his return to Britain: while serving with No. 39 Siege Company, RGA, in Plymouth, Major Johnston accepted another three-year posting to New Zealand, as Director of Ordnance and Artillery.[189] One of several imperial officers lent to New Zealand as it embarked on major military reform, he returned with a reputation as a 'painstaking, energetic and assiduous' man who had reformed the artillery establishment during his first sojourn.

Johnston was appointed Director of Ordnance and Inspector of Artillery in August 1911. Again his wife and child came too, this time accompanied by a nurse. One of his first problems involved the mountain guns delivered in 1912 for Wellington's D Battery, which were soon deemed obsolescent. He blamed the London High Commissioner's ageing Military Adviser, Major-General E. Harding Steward, for choosing them; Steward blamed Johnston for approving them.[190] The upshot was that Steward was forced to retire from a job he had been doing since the 1880s.

In May 1914, nine months before his term would expire, New Zealand asked for an extension to Johnston's secondment (in 1915 it would be extended again, 'for the duration'). As the NZEF was formed for service overseas, Lieutenant-Colonel Johnston was appointed to command the artillery brigade sent with the Main Body in October 1914. He led the gunners throughout their training in Egypt and – as

Commander, Royal Artillery for the New Zealand and Australian Division – the difficult eight months on Gallipoli. During exercises in Egypt Johnston got offside with Godley, the divisional commander, when he failed to move his batteries to the position ordered because he felt they could not do 'good shooting' from there. The Australian colonel John Monash saw Godley icily rebuke Johnston for this lapse of discipline.[191]

When the New Zealand Division was formed early in 1916 for service in France, Johnston was appointed CRA at the temporary rank of brigadier-general. In the many battles ahead, he would often command artillery groups far larger than its four (at most) brigades, overseeing both the artillery of neighbouring divisions and attached siege, field and horse artillery. He earned a reputation for flexibility and intelligence, using techniques such as 'leapfrogging' to keep guns firing when other CRAs could not. He stood in for the GOC as divisional commander four times. He may have been overlooked for this position because of his falling out with Godley – 'Johnston must have got some enemy at court', thought the appointee, Major-General Andrew Russell.[192] Johnston briefly headed NZEF Administration in London after the war. In November 1919 he accepted, but soon relinquished, the position of Military Adviser in London.

Johnston was appointed to the DSO and awarded the Legion d'Honneur in 1916, was made CB and CMG in 1918 and was mentioned in despatches seven times.[193] He retired in 1924 as CRA 52 (Lowland) Division, and died at Dar es Salaam, Tanganyika (now Tanzania) in 1947.

Weapons – Trench Mortars

New Zealand quickly adopted the trench mortar after its introduction in 1915. At Gallipoli, grenades and improvised 'jam-tin' bombs (fuse containers and tobacco tins were also favoured) had been hurled at the enemy using catapults or cricketing skills; the New Zealand infantry had one Japanese trench mortar.[194] The mortar did the same job over a greater range and was ideally suited to trench warfare.

New Zealand used light, medium and heavy trench mortars on the Western Front. Light (Stokes) mortars were infantry weapons; eight-strong batteries of them were formed in each infantry brigade. They were simple 'metal tube[s] into which cylindrical-shaped bombs were dropped with great rapidity and discharged at ranges of between two and three hundred yards'. They were not noted for their accuracy, and as the projectiles were visible in flight they could often be evaded.

The medium batteries (X/NZ, Y/NZ and Z/NZ), of four guns each, were manned by the New Zealand Artillery as divisional units, though the mediums were sometimes allotted to brigades. From late 1916 the medium batteries used the 'plum duff' or 'plum pudding' mortar, a spigot-based mortar with a 2-inch tube firing a large round bomb that protruded from the end of the barrel.[195] A smaller version on which reinforcements trained in New Zealand was called the 'toffee apple'. From December 1917 the mediums used a 6-inch version of the Stokes mortar, based around a conventional smooth tube design. Known as Newton mortars, these were first fired by New Zealand batteries at Polderhoek Chateau, Ypres.[196]

The heavy battery (V/NZ) of four 9.45-inch mortars (a French weapon taken into British service) fired up to ten rounds a day when in action, with each bomb capable of destroying 10 yards of trench. Taking six hours to set up, these were little used after the Battle of Messines as the fighting became more fluid. In February 1918 the heavy and medium batteries were reorganised into two six-gun Newton batteries (V and Z/NZ Batteries were disbanded). The arrival of reinforcements allowed seven guns per battery to be manned from April.[197]

Details	Light	Medium	Heavy
Name	Stokes Mk I	Newton 6-inch	Heavy Mortar Mk I 'flying pig'
Entered NZ service	1916	1917	1916
Role	wire cutting, supporting raids, eliminating strongpoints		
Calibre	3.2 in	6 in	9.45 in
Range	840 yds	1420 yds	2265 yds
Weight	103 lb	168 lb	644 lb
Projectile	10 lb 11oz	60 lb	152 lb
Remarks	The 3.2-inch Stokes remained in service with the New Zealand Army until the 1950s, even after more modern versions had been introduced. The Newton 6-inch was also issued to Divisional troops in New Zealand during the Second World War.		

Weapons – Field

The development of the 18-pr was a result of experience in the South African War. A Field Gun Committee of the RA worked with leading gun manufacturers to improve on existing designs. The result mated an Elswick (Armstrong) gun with a Vickers recoil system on a simple carriage from the Royal Gun Factory (which also supplied the sights). The Mk I was first issued to the Royal Horse Artillery in 1904 and by the First World War most field batteries in the British Empire had it. The barrel, built up by winding wire around a form, was both strong and accurate. Recoil was contained by a spring and piston, which was pulled through a constricted flow of hydraulic oil. The gun's main weaknesses were low maximum elevation (because of the pole trail) and frequent breakages in the recuperator spring, which returned the barrel to battery (its firing position) after each round. More than 10,000 of these guns were made.

In battle four men served the gun while the others brought up the ammunition. Sitting on the right of the gun, the layer for elevation worked the range-finder with his right hand, elevated the gun as necessary and operated the breech with his left. On the left of the trail the layer for line laid the gun (traversing within the 8° allowed on-carriage) and fired. The third man loaded the shells, whose fuzes the fourth man had set.

Name	Ordnance QF 18-pr Mk I
Entered NZ service	1912
Role	light horse-drawn field gun firing flat trajectory (16°)
Calibre	3.3 in
Range	6525 yds
Weight	2820 lb
Projectile	18.5 lb shrapnel, later also HE, smoke, incendiary and gas; integral with cartridge
Remarks	A versatile weapon also used as an anti-tank gun, this was well liked by gunners. It stayed in New Zealand service well into the Second World War, both in New Zealand and in the desert.

Earlier howitzers were heavy and cumbersome. Learning from the South African War, the Coventry Ordnance Works produced a versatile lightweight howitzer that was accepted by the British in 1909. Considered the best in the world in 1914, it served all imperial armies and was later supplied to Russia. It had a horizontal sliding breech block and box trail allowing high elevation. More than 3300 of these simple and robust howitzers were manufactured.

Name	Ordnance QF 4.5-inch Howitzer Mk I
Entered NZ service	1912–13
Role	light infantry support weapon firing high-angle trajectory (45°)
Calibre	4.5 in
Range	7300 yds
Weight	3010 lb
Projectile	35 lb HE, shrapnel or gas; cartridge loaded separately
Remarks	Useful for trench warfare, this howitzer remained in New Zealand service well into the Second World War.

FIELD ARTILLERY AMMUNITION

By 1914 all field artillery fired pointed-nose elongated shells with purpose-made fillings and clever fuzes. New Zealand's field guns were quick-firing guns requiring fixed (one-piece) ammunition. An 18-pr shell was propelled by a charge of around 1.5 lb of cordite or similar 'smokeless' powder in a brass cartridge case (for the 4.5-inch howitzer, this was almost 1 lb). The charge was detonated when a primer in the base of the cartridge case was struck by a firing pin in the breech mechanism after the gunner pulled the trigger.

Shrapnel. An anti-personnel shell adapted from case-shot (which discharged many small projectiles from the muzzle) by the British artillery officer Henry Shrapnel in the 1780s, it was used by New Zealand's 18-prs early in the Great War (complementing the howitzers, which fired only HE). By then it was a shell filled with 364 lead balls (around 200 in the 15-pr, 990 in the 60-pr) and a small ejecting charge. The charge opened the lightly fitted nose; momentum imparted velocity to the balls inside. The fuze was set on 'time' (rather than 'impact') – two to three seconds after leaving the muzzle if the enemy trenches were near.[198] The balls were ejected in a cone ahead of the shell and on the same trajectory, ideally from a height of about 30 feet.

HE (High Explosive). An elongated shell filled with explosive, this superseded the nineteenth-century 'common shell' as it could be fired by all types of gun against anything not armoured. It was used against defended positions and to disrupt trenches, usually with an impact fuze. Once limited quantities of HE were made available for New Zealand's 18-pr in August 1915, it began to replace shrapnel as the most common shell fired.[199]

Gas Shells. The 18-pr fired several types of gas shell, a munition strongly linked with this war. They were denoted by two-letter codes: SK (tear gas), PS (lethal tear gas), CG (phosgene), etc. Most gas shells contained only gas (in liquid form), but the German 'blue cross' had a mixture of gas and HE.[200] New Zealand used 4.5-inch howitzers to fire gas for the first time on the Somme in 1916.

Smoke. Only rather ineffective smoke shells were available in this period. A smoke barrage was fired behind which infantry advanced (in theory, unseen). The smoke, however, did not remain on the ground because, in delivering the cargo, the small bursting charge warmed the surrounding air, creating a thermal updraft. Smoke shells mostly used white phosphorus, which caused burns.

Incendiary. Shells using thermite to set fire to a combustible target, incendiaries were first used by 6 (Howitzer) Battery in April 1918 on enemy-occupied farmhouses near Messines. They were also used in barrages to mark a point or line.[201] Similar to shrapnel shells, they consisted of seven round canisters containing the incendiary mix which were propelled onto the target by a small ejecting charge.

Fuzes. These were the brass mechanisms forming the nose of a shell. By twisting the top of a time fuze the fuze setter determined how much time would elapse between firing of the charge and detonation of the shell. Two other types of impact fuzes were commonly used by New Zealand batteries. The delay or graze fuze allowed a shell to bury itself before throwing up large amounts of earth in the explosion. The instantaneous or impact fuze was usually fitted to HE shells and detonated on impact. This fuze ('No. 106') was used by New Zealand howitzer batteries from mid-1917, and by 18-prs later.[202]

Artillery Techniques in the First World War

If the fire of the guns could be controlled, they would hit their target more often. In close (and anti-tank) fighting the guns were fired using direct sights. Where the target could not be seen from the guns (indirect fire), map coordinates were used to get the shells in approximately the right spot and a forward observer informed the battery of the accuracy of its fire.

For indirect firing, the gun was aimed using the panoramic or dial sight, in conjunction with angles taken from a map. A line was drawn on the map from the gun position to the target. Then a prominent aiming point to one side, such as a large building or notable terrain feature, was selected and a line drawn from the guns to this point. The angle between these two lines was measured and applied to the dial sight, the optics in which diverged from the line of the gun barrel by the same angle.

Once the gun was manhandled around so that the line of sight was on at the aiming point, the barrel would in theory be pointing at the unseen target. The range to the target was then calculated, again using the map and a range table, which gave the elevation (in degrees) to be applied to the barrel. After the gun position officer (GPO) fired ranging shots, the forward observation officer (FOO) reported corrections (using first semaphore and later telephones with vulnerable wires laid over the intervening ground) before the battery fired for effect. Sometimes corrections were received from observers in balloons or planes, who dropped messages at the wireless stations attached to each brigade; these were telephoned to the batteries.

Battlefield surveying became important for indirect fire. In the First World War the New Zealand artillery used a Field Survey Company.[203] It would later form its own survey units.

The Barrage

A feature of the Western Front was the barrage, in which many guns combined their fire in preparation for major attacks. The New Zealand Artillery adopted the terminology associated with the different types of barrage:

Box barrage – shells exploding on three sides of a square to protect a position or isolate an enemy position.
Crash – a sudden burst of fire by all guns on a set target; also called 'shell storms'.
Double crash – as above, but ceasing for three minutes before resuming on a target near the original one.

Lifting (or creeping) barrage – to support an attack by one's own infantry, the line of exploding shells 'lifted' (advanced, usually in 100-yard increments) to a carefully planned timetable. Perfect coordination was essential – 'if it worked out well, it worked out really well'. For the infantry, there were many ways it could go disastrously wrong.[204]

Reverse barrage – occasionally used to baffle the enemy; the line of explosions started near them and 'advanced' towards the Allied lines.

Rolling barrage – the guns were divided into two groups, each laying fire down in a line of explosions which leapfrogged each other ahead of an infantry advance.

Standing barrage – shells exploding on a line to hinder enemy movement across it.

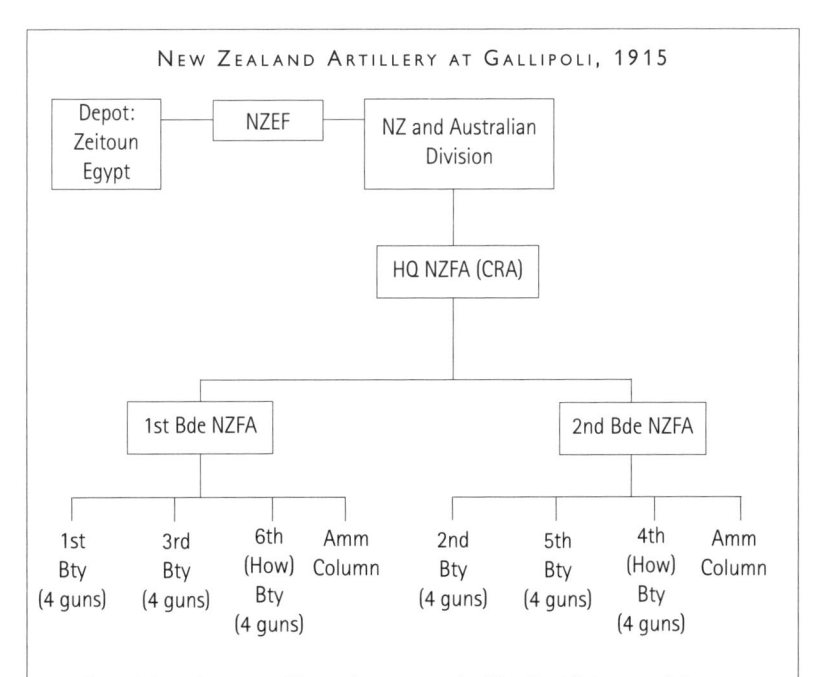

New Zealand Artillery at Gallipoli, 1915

```
Depot:          ─── NZEF ───    NZ and Australian
Zeitoun                            Division
Egypt                                 │
                                      │
                               HQ NZFA (CRA)
                                      │
                    ┌─────────────────┴─────────────────┐
                1st Bde NZFA                        2nd Bde NZFA
                    │                                   │
     ┌────┬──────┬──────┐              ┌────┬──────┬──────┐
    1st   3rd    6th    Amm           2nd   5th    4th    Amm
    Bty   Bty   (How)  Column         Bty   Bty   (How)  Column
  (4 guns)(4 guns) Bty              (4 guns)(4 guns) Bty
                (4 guns)                           (4 guns)
```

HQ 1st Bde and 1st to 3rd batteries were on the War Establishment of the Main Body, NZEF, with 4th (How) Bty following in December 1914, with the 2nd Reinforcements. HQ 2nd Arty Bde and the 5th and 6th (How) batteries were despatched from New Zealand between April and June 1915, with the 4th and 5th Reinforcements.

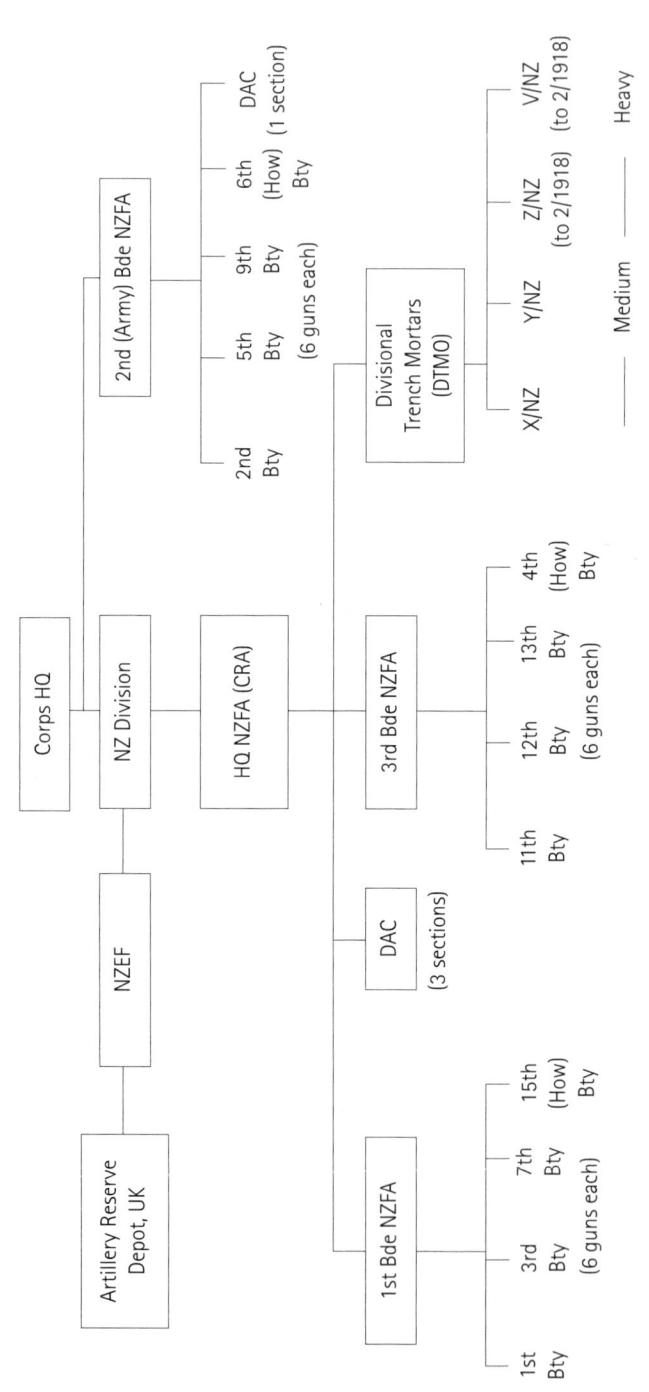

New Zealand Divisional Artillery, Western Front, 1917–18

- Artillery Reserve Depot, UK
- NZEF
  - NZ Division
    - Corps HQ
    - HQ NZFA (CRA)
      - DAC (3 sections)
      - 1st Bde NZFA
        - 1st Bty
        - 3rd Bty
        - 7th Bty
        - 15th (How) Bty
        - (6 guns each)
      - 3rd Bde NZFA
        - 11th Bty
        - 12th Bty
        - 13th Bty
        - 4th (How) Bty
        - (6 guns each)
      - 2nd (Army) Bde NZFA
        - 2nd Bty
        - 5th Bty
        - 9th Bty
        - 6th (How) Bty
        - DAC (1 section)
        - (6 guns each)
      - Divisional Trench Mortars (DTMO)
        - X/NZ
        - Y/NZ
        - Z/NZ (to 2/1918)
        - V/NZ (to 2/1918)
        - (4 guns each, 6 from 2/1918)

——— Medium ——— Heavy

HQ 4 Arty Bde (formed in 1916) was disestablished in January 1917, when its batteries (8th, 10th, 14th and 16th (How)) were redistributed by section among batteries of 1st and 2nd Bdes, bringing them up to 6-gun strength. Batteries in 2nd (Army) Bde NZFA were increased to 6-gun strength by sections raised in the UK.

4

Retrenchment and Modernisation, 1919–39

Peace soon brought with it the disestablishment of the Divisional Artillery. Less predictable was a post-war economic crisis that necessitated deep cuts in defence spending. By 1923 the Regular Force was barely 500 strong and the RNZA scarcely mustered three figures. There were no annual territorial camps for five years, and the period of compulsory training was cut from seven years to three. No cadets trained at Duntroon between 1921 and 1934. But in a world awash with surplus weaponry, ex-Great War guns were a windfall for the field artillery, even if time available for training with them was limited. New Zealand's new 'Singapore strategy' was focused on providing financial support for the great British naval base. There were just eight operational coastal defence guns, four each in Auckland and Wellington.

In the late 1920s annual camps resumed and the Territorial Force swelled to its peacetime establishment of 17,500 before the Depression abruptly reversed this progress. In the 1930s, with service voluntary and anti-militarist sentiments strong, territorial numbers fell to between a quarter and half of this figure. There were fewer than 300 regulars, and only 80 or so in the RNZA. When war threatened, a new Labour government gave priority to home defence; the coastal and anti-aircraft defences were upgraded, and a new Territorial Force Special Reserve trained more intensively to man them. Late in this decade of rapid modernisation for armies around the world, New Zealand artillerymen began replacing their horses with tractors and trucks, and experimenting with radios. But the government remained unwilling to confront the real military challenge – recruiting and training an expeditionary force for service in Europe – until war actually broke out.

Readjustment to Peace

By the end of January 1919 the Divisional Artillery no longer existed as a formation. The position of CRA, New Zealand Divisional Artillery, held by Brigadier-General Johnston, who had commanded the New Zealand Field Artillery throughout the war, was disestablished when the Division was disbanded. The Divisional Artillery units that had survived the war – three brigade headquarters, seventeen field, howitzer and trench mortar batteries and four ammunitioning sections – ceased to exist along with the NZEF.[1]

The RNZA personnel of the disbanded batteries rejoined the field and coastal artillery cadres in New Zealand, replacing the NZFA and NZGA men who had served at home during the war. The structure of the Field Artillery and the Garrison Artillery remained essentially as it had been since 1911. Lieutenant-Colonel M.M. (Murray) Gard'ner had returned from the NZEF to fill the vacant position of Inspector of Coast Defences from 23 April 1918. The following January he also succeeded Lieutenant-Colonel Alexander, NZFA, as Director of Artillery (Field), and in August he was redesignated as simply Director of Artillery. Gard'ner, who had joined the Permanent Force in 1898 and earned a first-class pass from the long course at Shoeburyness before the war, had served at Harwich and Aldershot before being posted to the NZEF in November 1915.[2]

After the Armistice annual territorial camps were suspended. Many experienced men returning from Europe were placed on the Reserve, but the future of territorial training had to be decided. The new GOC, Major-General Edward Chaytor, who had replaced Robin in December 1919, faced a budget cut of around £100,000 in 1920/21, and further cuts the following year reduced the Army's share of the Defence Estimates to around £300,000. Chaytor was forced to make major economies. The period of compulsory territorial training was cut from seven years to three (as proposed earlier by Robin), and the Regular Force was severely reduced, from 193 officers and 1535 other ranks to 100 and 401 respectively between 1920 and 1923; the RNZA's strength fell from 27 and 231 to 15 and 100.[3]

In February 1921 Chaytor rationalised the four territorial commands, based on the main centres, into three: Northern Command, with its headquarters in Auckland; Central (Palmerston North); and Southern

Exercising with 60-prs.
Graham Birch collection.

Command – the South Island – based in Christchurch. General Headquarters remained in Wellington. From 1 June 1921, territorial units were reorganised and redesignated within a brigade group structure in each new district, providing, on paper at least, for divisional mobilisation in time of emergency. For the artillery, this meant the loss of the alphabetical designations of its field batteries and of the distinction between the NZFA and NZGA. All territorial artillery personnel were now designated as NZA.[4] Further, minor redesignation of batteries in 1924 (see table opposite) would shape the artillery for the next decade.

War surplus guns – some brought out as ballast on returning troopships – re-equipped the field batteries with 18-pr Mk I or Mk II guns, and the howitzer and pack batteries got 4.5-inch and 3.7-inch howitzers respectively. With 60-pr guns and, from 1922, 6-inch howitzers available, medium batteries could now be established,[5] though instruction on the new weapons was seriously limited by the repeated suspension of annual territorial camps, except for small groups of officers and NCOs. An experiment with firing blanks from 60-prs on the parade ground in urban Mt Cook, Wellington, had a predictable outcome – 'numerous' broken windows and official censure.[6] Not until the summer of 1924–25 would batteries attend camps as complete units – and eight missed out because of a polio epidemic.[7] In the meantime, the tiny cadre of RNZA regulars was busy instructing, albeit part time, the territorial gunners who made up the establishment of each battery, maintaining the guns and other equipment, and feeding and caring for the horses assigned to each field and medium battery.

Reorganisation of Artillery Units, 1920s

Previous Designation	1921 Reorganisation*	1926 (after 1924 Redesignation)	Headquarters
	HQ 1st Artillery Brigade	HQ 1st Artillery Brigade	Auckland
A Battery, NZFA	1 (18-pr) Battery, NZA	1 Field Battery, NZA	Auckland
G Battery, NZFA	2 (18-pr) Battery, NZA	2 Field Battery, NZA	Hamilton
	3 (18-pr) Battery, NZA	3 Field Battery, NZA	Auckland
	4 (4.5-inch How) Battery, NZA	4 Field Battery, NZA	Auckland
		21 Field Battery, NZA	Onehunga
NZA Band, Auckland	NZA Band, Auckland	NZA Band, Auckland	Auckland
	(Non-brigaded units)	HQ Northern Coast Artillery Group	North Head
Nos 1 & 7 Coys, NZGA	13 (Coast) Battery, NZA	13 (Coast) Battery, NZA	North Head
	18 (6-inch How) Battery, NZA	18 Medium Battery, NZA	North Head
No. 6 Coy, NZGA	20 (3.7-inch) Battery, NZA	20 Pack Battery, NZA	North Head
	HQ 2nd Artillery Brigade	HQ 2nd Artillery Brigade	Palmerston North
D (Mountain) Battery, NZFA	5 (18-pr) Battery, NZA	5 Field Battery, NZA	Wellington
F Battery, NZFA	6 (18-pr) Battery, NZA	6 Field Battery, NZA	Napier
	7 (18-pr) Battery, NZA	7 Field Battery, NZA	Palmerston North
J Battery, NZFA	8 (4.5-inch How) Battery, NZA	8 Field Battery, NZA	Palmerston North
NZA Band, Wellington	NZA Band, Wellington		Wellington
	(Non-brigaded units)	HQ Central Coast Artillery Group	Fort Dorset
No. 3 Coy, NZGA	15 (Coast) Battery, NZA	15 (Coast) Battery, NZA	Fort Dorset
No. 5 Coy, NZGA	17 (6-inch How) Battery, NZA	17 Medium Battery, NZA	Fort Dorset & Lower Hutt
No. 9 Coy, NZGA	19 (60-pr) Battery, NZA	19 Medium Battery, NZA	Fort Dorset
	HQ 3rd Artillery Brigade	HQ 3rd Artillery Brigade	Christchurch
E Battery, NZFA	9 (18-pr) Battery, NZA	9 Field Battery, NZA	Christchurch
H Battery, NZFA	Disbanded		(Nelson)
	10 (18-pr) Battery, NZA	10 Field Battery, NZA	Christchurch
C Battery, NZFA	11 (18-pr) Battery, NZA	11 Field Battery, NZA	Invercargill
B Battery, NZFA	12 (4.5-inch How.) Bty, NZA	12 Field Battery, NZA	Dunedin
NZA Band, Dunedin	NZA Band, Dunedin	NZA Band, Dunedin (to 1935)	Dunedin
	(Non-brigaded units)	(Non-brigaded units)	
No. 2 Coy, NZGA	14 (6-inch How) Battery, NZA	14 Medium Battery, NZA	Dunedin
No. 4 Coy, NZGA	16 (3.7-inch) Battery, NZA	16 Pack Battery, NZA	Lyttelton
No. 8 Coy, NZGA	Disbanded		(Westport)

An additional 18-pr battery, 21 Field, was established at Onehunga in 1925. In August 1926, Wellington's 19 Medium Battery converted to 6-inch howitzers and its 60-prs were taken over by Auckland's 18 Medium. The light batteries, at Auckland and Lyttelton, would now be equipped for shaft-draught only; there would be no more pack drill. The Auckland and Wellington coastal and medium batteries (and the Auckland pack battery) were removed from the so-called field artillery brigades; Coast Artillery Groups were formed at these ports.[8]

THE FIJI EXPEDITION

Even before the cuts, the RNZA struggled to send a small force to Fiji in February 1920, when the Army was also committed to ceremonial duties for the forthcoming visit of the Prince of Wales. In January, Indian indentured labourers and sugar-cane farmers had struck over their wages and Sir Cecil Rodwell, the British Governor of Fiji, asked Wellington for assistance, particularly in protecting the European population should violence break out. When it became clear that Australian forces would be unavailable, the government steamer *Tutanekai* was ordered to prepare for departure at short notice, manned by regular forces. Commanded by Major Edward Puttick, NZSC, the 'Fiji Detachment' or 'Fiji Expeditionary Force' comprised mainly RNZA personnel (two officers and 50 other ranks), of whom the most senior was Lieutenant G.B. ('Ike') Parkinson.

Armed with a 12-pr, the *Tutanekai* left Auckland on 5 February. By the time it reached Suva on the 12th the situation had deteriorated, with minor riots in the Indian quarter. Armed with six Lewis guns and small arms, the detachment was deployed in reserve to support the Fijian Police and Defence Force but was not involved in any direct confrontation. Once order was restored, the colonial authorities deported the strike's leaders and increased sugar prices. The New Zealand detachment left for home on 18 April, before it became necessary to call up reservists.[9] The New Zealand government also responded positively to imperial requests to contribute expeditionary forces to Iraq in 1920 and Turkey in 1922, but these came to nothing.[10]

The Coastal Artillery Retrenched

The Washington Naval Treaty of 1922 pre-empted a post-war arms race among the three largest naval powers (Britain, the United States and Japan) and ushered in a decade of defence economies in Britain and the Dominions. Though concerned about the limitations placed on the size of the Royal Navy, William Massey's government supported the treaty, placated somewhat by the 1921 decision to build a major naval base at Singapore. By 1936 New Zealand had contributed £1 million towards the Singapore base, the lynchpin of British Pacific strategy and New Zealand defence policy between the wars.[11]

The main change to the force structure of the artillery in the 1921 restructuring was the disestablishment of the South Island coastal defences. Minor improvements had been made to the Lyttelton defences immediately after the war.[12] In 1919, Viscount Jellicoe, in New Zealand to advise the government on naval policy and harbour defences, proposed the redevelopment of fixed minefields and boom defences, supplemented by anti-submarine and minesweeping vessels, and advocated strengthening the permanent defences of Auckland, Wellington and the West Coast coalmines and ports with modern 6-inch guns. He also recommended that, in wartime, anchorages in the Bay of Islands, Queen Charlotte Sound and Stewart Island should be defended by coastal guns. Massey's government immediately agreed to support the upkeep of a cruiser lent by Britain as the

---

Artillery Cadets

Some artillery recruits came from the cadets. Many of the larger boys' schools had artillery units, particularly once cadet training came under the Defence Act. These acquired cast-off field guns from local batteries. Nelson Boys' College, for example, formed an artillery cadet corps in 1913, 38 years after establishing foot cadets. This received two 15-pr guns from H Battery, which had upgraded to 18-prs. Waitaki Boys' High (Oamaru) received German trophy guns.

Young Bert Dyson joined the Christchurch Boys' High artillery cadets because he was 'fascinated' by their 18-prs. Territorial M.A. Bull, the teacher in charge, arranged for boys to attend the annual camp at Sutton alongside

basis of the New Zealand Division of the Royal Navy that was established formally in mid-1921, but Jellicoe's proposals were too expensive, and were shelved.[13]

Instead, as the budget deficit grew, the coast defences were cut back. The garrison artillery establishments at Auckland and Wellington were reduced and the coastal defences of Dunedin and Lyttelton disestablished, saving around £16,000 per annum. Obsolete weapons were disposed of or mothballed. The old BL 6-inch and 8-inch hydro-pneumatic 'disappearing' guns and the 6-pr QF guns were decommissioned; the 8-inch shells were emptied and sold as scrap or dumped at sea, and their propellant charges destroyed or repacked for Auckland and Wellington's modern 6-inch BL Mk VII guns. The 8-inch guns were also sold as scrap, but at all four ports the 6-inch BLHP and 6-pr guns were retained in their mountings. The defences of Auckland were reduced to two 6-inch Mk VII guns and two 12-pr quick-firing guns at North Head. Wellington's operational defences were now two 6-inch Mk VII guns and two 12-prs at Fort Dorset.[14]

Field and Medium Artillery

In the early 1920s the New Zealand Artillery, like the Army generally, was in a poor state of training and readiness. After 1926, however, the resumption of annual territorial camps brought the Territorial Force close to achieving its capability. By 1929 all territorial units were at full establishment (75 per cent

> 9 Battery NZFA. This inspired Dyson to join the Territorials in Wellington, and later volunteer for 2NZEF. Major Bull also joined up, going to Greece as second in command of 5 Field and commanding 28 Battery on Crete, where he was captured.
>
> At Southland Boys' High John Masters was given a choice: librarian or sergeant in the school battery. 'I became an instant sergeant. Sergeants in those days wore absolutely beautiful gold braid stripes. We considered ourselves a very elite senior group.' There was little real training in his unit. 'We learned nothing at all about artillery; we didn't have anybody who knew anything to teach us.' He did not even see a gun before joining the Territorial Force.[15]

of wartime establishment), a strength of some 17,500 officers and other ranks, though the regular forces remained tiny, just 500 in all; 119 were RNZA.[16]

In 1926 the RNZA Detachment in each command was formally redesignated an RNZA Cadre. Their official role was 'the care and maintenance of the ordnance, equipment, animals, &c, on charge to commands, ... the receipt, issue, storage, and maintenance of gun ammunition located in commands, and ... the training and administration of Territorial Artillery'. Though these duties would not, 'as a rule', allow cadre personnel to be 'detailed for other duties and work not in connection with Artillery', the RNZA was often called upon for ceremonial and other tasks. RNZA recruits received basic and gunnery training at Fort Dorset before being posted to commands to specialise in heavy (coast) or field and pack artillery, or electric lighting, or generator engine-driving. Once a year, the whole RNZA came together for 'section and battery training on movable and coast-defence equipments'.[17]

At GHQ, Wellington, the Director of Artillery (a lieutenant-colonel) and the Staff Captain Artillery (a captain or lieutenant) were assisted by a non-commissioned establishment of two clerks and two instructors for RNZA recruits. The OC, RNZA, at Northern Command and Central Command was a major, while the pared-down Southern Command was headed by a captain or lieutenant.

The balance of the RNZA was subdivided into field cadres – at Auckland, Hamilton, Wellington, Napier, Palmerston North, Christchurch (including pack artillery functions), Dunedin and Invercargill – and coast and medium cadres at Auckland (including pack artillery functions) and Wellington. Each cadre comprised an officer (captain or lieutenant) or NCO and between three and fourteen other ranks (eighteen in the larger Coast, Medium and Pack Artillery Cadre at North Head).

The larger centres had a Quartermaster-Sergeant; a Master Gunner was responsible for maintaining the coast defence equipment in Auckland and Wellington. Each cadre had instructors responsible for training the NZA territorials, and the field cadres included up to five limber-gunners, with a fitter-farrier assigned to the larger field and pack cadres. There was an establishment of 72 horses.[18]

The regional artillery brigades were commanded by NZA lieutenant-colonels (a major in Southern Command), assisted by an RNZA adjutant (a captain or lieutenant). Each battery was commanded by an NZA major and made up entirely of territorials. The NZA camps were usually based at racecourses or showgrounds, with the local RNZA cadre overseeing the transport of horses, guns and equipment, often by train, and setting up ablution and cooking facilities before the territorials arrived for their six days in camp. Training, based on memoranda issued by the School of Artillery, Salisbury Plain, included 'equitation' (horsemanship) and parade-ground gun drill. They practised fire discipline, ranging and gun-laying and live shoots on nearby farms or public land.

In January 1923, 9 Battery held the first post-war shoot near Christchurch, in heavy rain. From 1926 annual battery practice was held at a week-long camp at Sandown station, near Sheffield. The daily routine consisted of gun drill, cleaning the camp area, guard duties and evening lectures. Concerts were given by local people and battery personnel. On Wednesday night the 'whole Battery turned out to take part in an attack. Returned at 11.30 p.m., cleaned guns, in bed at 12.30'. Next afternoon a live shoot was held. On Friday the battery returned to the range in the morning, and after lunch 'Galloped into action over a ploughed field; fired about fourteen shells; back to camp about

9 Field Battery exercising at Sandown, 1926.
J.M. Mitchell album, courtesy of John Masters.

6.30 p.m.' On Saturday there was 'cock-fighting on horses, tug-of-war, etc.,' before they caught the afternoon train back to Christchurch.[19]

Some Territorial camps were more eventful. In 1924 Napier's battery, 6 Field, was under canvas in the Esk Valley when torrential rain sent a big fresh down the river. With hills on one side and a railway embankment on the other, the water rose rapidly and flooded the camp; the gunners waded to the nearby hall. Their 18-prs and limbers were swept 100 yards, ammunition cases stuck in silt, and the piano lodged 5 feet up in a willow tree. During a 9 Battery camp at Sutton, shrapnel set fire to tussock on the range. After apparently being extinguished, the fire flared up again late at night, necessitating another 'exciting ride'. At the end of each camp men placated the landowners by scouring the range for dud rounds. 'At the same time there was a search for souvenirs.'[20]

Gard'ner described the standard at the 1924/25 camps as 'as good as could be expected under the circumstances'. Horsemanship was deficient because of the difficulty of finding horses to train with during the year (most batteries had to hire horses for their camps), and officers needed more experience in reconnaissance, ranging and giving orders at shoots; many were still 'too slow'.[21]

Men enlisted in the artillery for diverse reasons. Jim Gilberd joined in 1928 'because as a small boy I lived near the barracks in Napier, and I used to see these artillerymen with their horses exercising in a big paddock near us and I thought, that's what I want to be'. Ian Johnston and his brother were signed up by their South African War veteran father when it was announced in 1936 that a battery was to be formed in Hamilton.[22]

Some fortunate RNZA officers received training in Britain. In 1926 Captain Parkinson, the OC Harbour Defences and OC RNZA Detachment Auckland, was sent to Britain for a Gunnery Staff Course (Coast Defence and Anti-Aircraft Branch). Few gunners attended these expensive courses: only one before Parkinson, in 1924, and one later, in 1938 – 'probably because the 1924 man had retired in the meantime'.[23]

In December 1925, Colonel Frank Symon succeeded Gard'ner as Director of Artillery, a position he would hold for over a decade (from 1931 to 1935 he was also, as a temporary brigadier, Officer Commanding, Central Command).

Symon had joined the Permanent Force as a cadet in 1898, trained in England and held various appointments, mostly with garrison artillery units in New Zealand, before serving with the field artillery in Gallipoli and France. He reported steady progress in artillery training, which he attributed to 'the keenness of the officers, the knowledge and experience of the Battery Commanders, the reintroduction of Practice Instructions with the attendance of a qualified Instructor in Gunnery at camps, the better unity of effort on the part of the permanent details ... and the holding of an increased number of voluntary parades'. One serious deficiency in the training programme was the 'impossibility of carrying out [artillery] Brigade training'. As Symon explained: 'The provision of horses, the interference with business, and above all the short period of camp make it impracticable to carry out the training of more than one battery at a time.' He called for tactical exercises involving brigade and battery commanders, and where possible skeleton battery staffs.[24] Exercises with mounted rifles or infantry units were out of the question.

In the late 1920s, morale in the NZA batteries, and in the TF generally, was consistently reported to be high, even though compulsory military training (CMT) was coming under increasing criticism from the Labour Party, church and pacifist groups, who questioned both the need to maintain the basis of an expeditionary force and the efficiency of the territorials; some objected to compulsory military service on moral grounds. In the end, the Depression finished territorial training: it was suspended on 31 March 1930. In June CMT itself was suspended for a year, and formally terminated in March 1931. The Territorial Force would be maintained on a voluntary basis at a much-reduced cadre level. While the TF establishment was reduced to 9800, the numbers willing to serve initially slumped to 3589; the divisional structure was skeletal indeed. The Army's budget for 1931/32 was halved to £213,000, and the Permanent Force reduced to less than 300. The RNZA was cut to 86 personnel; two years later it would reach its nadir, 81. The field batteries at Hamilton, Napier and Invercargill were disbanded on 1 June 1931.[25]

High unemployment in the early 1930s had an unexpected impact on Territorial camps. Rather than freeing men to attend, joblessness brought a 'fear that if unemployed Territorials attended camp they might be penalized by having their registration for relief work cancelled'. On the other hand, relief workers provided cheap labour around the permanent forts.[26] Some batteries combined for their annual camps. Seven officers and 95 men of 9 and 10 Field batteries came together for a five-day camp at Sutton in January 1933. Though 'everything worked smoothly and pleasantly', the experiment was not a success. 'For some inexplicable reason, each seemed to hold the other back, particularly in the Battery staff.'[27]

In 1933, royal salutes were fired in Hagley Park for the first time since 1914. They were customary for the King's Birthday in June, and on special occasions such as a farewell for the Duke of Gloucester at Lyttelton wharves. Well-turned-out gun teams and horses took part in Anzac Day parades.

Battery nomenclature now underwent further change. In 1934 the pack batteries were redesignated light; the coast batteries heavy. In 1936 Hamilton's 2 Field Battery was reconstituted as a 60-pr Medium Battery and Auckland's 18 Medium Battery was disestablished. Napier's 6 Field Battery would be re-established in 1938, following the amalgamation of 7 Field into the other Palmerston North-based battery, 8 Field. From 1 September 1935, the headquarters of 2 Field Artillery Brigade was transferred from Palmerston North to Fort Dorset, and 2 Artillery Brigade Group was created, including 2 Field Brigade and Central Command's medium batteries. The designation Southern Artillery Brigade Group was dropped in favour of 3 Artillery Brigade Group, which included 3 Field Artillery Brigade, headquartered in Dunedin since 1929, and the light, field and medium batteries based in Christchurch. In April 1937, the coastal and newly established anti-aircraft units in Auckland and Wellington were designated as in the table below.[28]

Anti-militarist feeling in the community had grown in the aftermath of riots by unemployed men in Auckland in April 1932, when Permanent

North Head	Fort Dorset
HQ 1 Heavy Artillery Group	HQ 2 Heavy Artillery Group
13 Heavy Battery	15 Heavy Battery
HQ 1 Anti-Aircraft Group	HQ 2 Anti-Aircraft Group
18 Anti-Aircraft Battery	22 Anti-Aircraft Battery
1 Searchlight Company	2 Searchlight Company

Force and territorial personnel mounted guards at public buildings, drill halls and magazines, and ammunition and explosives factories. Attendance at territorial camps remained poor, with many employers refusing to release staff. Territorial numbers exceeded 9000 in 1935, but then declined to 7100 by 1938. Both the divisional structure and the expectation that the TF could form an expeditionary force had become unrealistic. Moreover, the Labour government elected in December 1935 gave priority to home defence, and a TF reorganisation implemented by Major-General Sir John Duigan, the new Chief of General Staff (now the senior Army position), reflected the new emphasis.[29]

From 1 September 1937 the divisional structure was replaced by what amounted to an expanded brigade group, plus 'Fortress Troops' for the local defence of Auckland, Wellington and Christchurch. The three regional commands became military districts and the number of infantry battalions and mounted rifles regiments was reduced drastically, though the existing artillery units were retained. The heavy artillery and anti-aircraft groups in Auckland and Wellington formed part of the Fortress Troops in each centre, along with an infantry battalion. (Lyttelton's fortress troops comprised an infantry battalion only.) In each district the light, field and medium batteries made up artillery brigade groups under a 'Group Commander' (a lieutenant-colonel), and formed part of the 'Field Troops', along with an infantry battalion, a mounted rifles regiment and a squadron of motorised mounted rifles, plus support services. The Director of Artillery was renamed the Commander, Royal New Zealand Artillery (CRNZA).[30]

Modernising the Coastal Defences, 1933–39

The international situation deteriorated sharply after 1932, when Japan attacked Chinese-controlled areas of Shanghai. The Western powers feared a confrontation should Japan seek to occupy more of the international city. Britain's weakness in the Far East was now starkly apparent, and the British Cabinet accepted a recommendation from its Chiefs of Staff that the 'Ten Year Rule' be abandoned: defence planning and expenditure would no longer be constrained by the comforting notion that no major war was likely within the next decade. In 1933 the Nazi Party assumed power in Germany, raising the appalling prospect of Britain having to fight major wars concurrently on opposite sides of the world.

In July of that year Major-General William Sinclair-Burgess, the GOC since 1931, initiated a review of New Zealand's defence requirements. The committee of senior officers called for a range of measures to enable the New Zealand military to fulfil its three established wartime roles: local defence, support for Britain by providing an expeditionary force and assistance with protecting imperial lines of communication. Emphasis was given to remedying the woeful state of the Permanent Air Force, to expanding the regular Army so it could provide an infantry battalion and field artillery battery to serve in India in peacetime, and to strengthening the coast defences, at a total additional cost of £500,000 per annum. Cabinet approved these recommendations on 9 October, but only some were implemented – additional regular army units for overseas service did not eventuate.[31]

Updating the coastal defences was given a priority second only to developing an effective Air Force. New coastal and AA artillery were ordered within a month of the Cabinet decision but the four 6-inch Mk XXI guns with 45° mountings, and two sections of two 3-inch anti-aircraft guns and AA searchlight units, with the necessary motor transport for the AA guns and searchlights, would have to be manufactured and could not be delivered before mid-1936.[32]

The Mark VII 6-inch guns at Auckland and Wellington, installed in 1911, were limited by their mountings to an elevation of 15° and consequently to a maximum range of 15,000 yards (compared with 21,000 yards for the Mark XXI guns on 45° mountings). They were adequate for close defence, but would be out-ranged by the guns of any cruiser standing off to bombard either the cities or their ports. In 1926, the Committee of Imperial Defence had suggested that any attack would not be greater than raids by cruisers, armed merchant cruisers or submarines. This view remained unchanged, but the revision of coastal artillery doctrine, and the availability of improved equipment, led to increased emphasis on counter-bombardment. In February 1934, sites were selected for new batteries at Red Bluff (near Castor Bay) in Auckland, and Palmer Head, south of Fort

Shoot at Fort Dorset, April 1937.
1/4-048821-G, Alexander Turnbull Library, Wellington.

Dorset in Wellington. These would complement the existing close-defence 6-inch batteries at North Head and Fort Dorset. The War Office, however, advised against Red Bluff: this was too close to Auckland city and the Devonport dockyard to protect them against bombardment from cruisers.

Assuming that a battery of heavy 9.2-inch guns was too expensive, the War Office recommended siting the 6-inch battery on Motutapu Island, so that it could engage even a heavy cruiser (of 8-inch armament) in range of Auckland or Devonport. Moreover, at an estimated £54,800, this was the least expensive option. For Wellington, the War Office recommended either a two-gun 9.2-inch battery in the hills near Karori, or two-gun batteries of 6-inch Mark XXI guns at Palmer Head and Ohariu. The 6-inch battery at Fort Dorset should be retained for close defence, but a new examination battery of 4.7-inch guns would be required at Fort Ballance.[33]

The War Office's preference for Motutapu was accepted and after discussions between Prime Minister George Forbes, Sinclair-Burgess and Sir Maurice Hankey, Secretary to the Committee of Imperial Defence, who visited New Zealand in November 1934, the Cabinet approved the purchase of a third 6-inch gun for this battery.[34] The Wellington defences posed a more difficult problem for a cash-strapped government. Hankey agreed that modern 6-inch batteries at Palmer Head and Ohariu, supplemented by aircraft, would adequately cover the bombarding areas in Cook Strait, and the 1933 'Six Year Plan' was modified. A 6-inch battery at Ohariu was included in the approved plan, but no funds were budgeted to establish it. One hundred and seventeen acres at the south end of Miramar Peninsula were acquired for the Palmer Head battery.[35]

The Military Works Section, New Zealand Engineers, had been demobilised in 1921, when the Public Works Department (PWD) was made responsible for constructing and maintaining defence buildings and works. With the redevelopment of coastal fortifications imminent, at least a planning office within GHQ was needed. After Sinclair-Burgess asked the War Office for 'a qualified officer to supervise the construction of the necessary fortifications and works', Major A.J. Edney, RE, was appointed on 9 October 1935 as Staff Officer, Fortifications and Works. The PWD remained responsible for building fortifications; mounting equipment and the repository of the guns was carried out by RNZA personnel supervised by the District Artillery Officers. The Director of Artillery, Colonel Symon, had his tenure extended for two years beyond the retiring age for his rank (55); his services were considered 'essential in the process of strengthening the harbour defences and defence against aircraft attack'. When Symon eventually retired in May 1936, he was replaced in an acting capacity by Major (temporary Lieutenant-Colonel) R.S. Park, formerly the Staff Officer, Artillery. In December 1937 Park was appointed District Artillery Officer, Central Military District, and replaced as CRNZA by Major (temporary Lieutenant-Colonel) G.B. Parkinson, formerly District Artillery Officer, Northern Military District.[36] Both men had served with the NZFA in France and Belgium from 1917.

Construction at Palmer Head was completed and the guns mounted in 1937, and the work at Motutapu was completed by September 1938. When the new installations were placed on a war footing on 4 September 1939, the newly mobilised Palmer Head garrison became 15 Heavy Battery (the existing Fort Dorset Battery becoming 14 Heavy); at Motutapu, 9 Heavy Battery

Gun crew with anti-aircraft predictor.
Royal New Zealand Artillery Old Comrades' Association.

was established. Though the guns and underground magazines were in place, additional buildings and underground accommodation for the command posts and plotting rooms would be necessary in wartime.[37]

There was concern as early as 1936 over delays in providing technical equipment because of the competing demands of the British rearmament programme. When war broke out New Zealand's new counter-bombardment batteries still lacked adequate instruments for directing fire. Palmer Head had no forward observation posts, and at both sites the equipment needed for effective fortress and battery fire control was not installed until late 1941, and the fire direction tables in 1942.[38] Until then, they managed with a manual form of battery fire control, but only during daylight hours as they had no searchlights.

THE 1938 PROGRAMME

In May 1937, with British defence manufacturers at full stretch, the War Office asked the Dominions to forecast their requirements for military stores and equipment until 1940. Later in the year New Zealand's Chiefs of Staff Committee started another review of coast defences because of the deterioration

The *New Zealand* Guns

Delays in acquiring modern armaments for coast defence were countered by a stop-gap measure: the guns from HMS *New Zealand*. Fourteen of these useful 4-inch Mk VII guns had been delivered in 1923 from the scrapped battlecruiser. They were used only in training and saluting batteries at North Head and Point Jerningham; two went to the Auckland Museum. By 1934 they were again under consideration 'to increase the strength of the inner defences of the principal ports' should 'any emergency make this course necessary'. Emplacements were started at Forts Takapuna and Dorset; by 1938 six and four respectively had been mounted. Two were mounted at Battery Point, Lyttelton, the following year. Coast gunners 'loved these guns and training on them'.[39]

Weapons – Medium

The first medium guns in service with New Zealand gunners, these were classic Great War weapons. Both were mounted on box trails and wooden wheels, and were later mechanised with pneumatic tyres.

Name	Ordnance BL 60-pr Mk I	Ordnance BL 6-inch 26-cwt
Entered NZ service	1921	1922
Role	medium gun	medium gun
Calibre	5 in	6 in
Elevation	21½°	45°
Range	12,300 yds	9500 yds
Weight	9856 lb	8144 lb
Projectile	60 lb	100 lb – shrapnel, HE, gas (for both guns)
Remarks	Used equipment shipped to New Zealand after the Great War, these guns remained in service into the Second World War.	

Weapons – Coast Defence

These had been secondary guns on HMS *New Zealand* and other battleships of its era. Wire-wound, they dispensed with the horizontal sliding breech block of earlier marks in favour of a conventional interrupted screw system. With their centre pivot mount they were well suited to the coast defence role (after a spell firing salutes), once suitable holding-down rings and bolts could be fashioned. Naval range-finders served these guns until auto-sights for them were developed during the war.

Name	Ordnance BL 4-inch Mk VII
Entered NZ service	1936
Role	coast defence – close defence and examination battery role
Calibre	4 in, 50 cals
Range	7000 yds
Weight	2.26-ton barrel plus Mk II centre pivot mount
Projectile	33 lb types – common, HE, AP
Remarks	From HMS *New Zealand*, these were transferred to New Zealand in 1923 and used from 1936 in the coast defences.

Weapons – Anti-Aircraft

The first purpose-built British AA gun was a Royal Navy project; it was later also adopted by the Army. It served throughout the First World War and was still serviceable when ordered by New Zealand in 1934 (when planes still flew relatively low and slow).

Name	Ordnance QF 3-inch 20-cwt
Entered NZ service	1936
Role	heavy mobile anti-aircraft, with 90° elevation
Calibre	3 in, 45 cals
Range	15,700-ft effective ceiling, 12,400-yd horizontal range. An earlier lighter shell (12.5 lb) gave better performance.
Weight	6000-lb gun and trailer
Projectile	16.5 lb – shrapnel, HE; rate of fire 20 rpm
Remarks	A Great War design used throughout the Second World War.

in the international situation. This found that a Japanese expedition against New Zealand remained 'highly improbable' while 'our position in Singapore is secure'.[40] An attack would still probably consist of bombardment by cruisers at most, minelaying, raids on ports or shipping by submarines or motor torpedo boats, very limited attacks by ship-based seaplanes or small landing parties, but was now more likely.

> ### Gunners on Horseback
> While its guns remained horse-drawn, the Army taught both gunners and mounted rifles to ride. Each gun, defined as a sub-section of a battery, needed a limber, two ammunition wagons, thirteen men and thirteen horses. The usual gun team had six horses, with an NCO as lead driver, a centre driver in the middle and a wheel driver behind on the left-hand mount. The sergeant commanding the gun rode separately. The other gun crew rode on the limber, and the ammunition men on the ammunition wagons.
>
> Jim Gilberd was already 'mixed up with horses' when he became a riding instructor, spending about four years at Trentham in the riding establishment that was part of the GHQ Training Depot, later Army Schools. This had about 100 acres of land, as well as several buildings that could be used for drilling in wet weather. In the 1930s the riding school was commanded by Major W.G. Stevens NZA. Every artilleryman took a full equitation course and all the regular force officers were taught to ride. The last RNZA recruits to go through the course were No. 10 Wing in 1937, but horsemanship continued to be taught into the war years.
>
> The horsed artillery performed 'drives' to show off their mounted skills. Four-gun teams with 24 horses and twelve drivers galloped into an arena and performed a few simple manoeuvres before executing a dangerous scissors movement, crossing at the centre with no gap visible. Drivers became very accomplished at this daring feat, especially after a

The 1933 plan had emphasised counter-bombardment and the establishment of basic anti-aircraft batteries at the two main ports. The four mobile AA guns ordered in 1933 arrived in 1936, with their searchlights and Leyland Terrier 6x4 towing tractors. Training in height-finding and predictor work began immediately, and heavy AA batteries were established at North Head (18 AA Battery) and Fort Dorset (22 AA Battery).[41] Attention now turned to the close defences at the main ports. Anti-motor torpedo boat (AMTB) defences – twin 6-pr quick-firing guns and additional searchlights – would be needed at North Head and Fort Dorset. The chiefs also recommended that the two-gun 9.2-inch emplacement at Karori, Wellington should go ahead rather than the 6-inch counter-bombardment battery at Ohariu, to cover areas out of range from Palmer Head.

It was now formally acknowledged that Lyttelton should be re-established as a defended port, with a counter-bombardment battery of

> collision between two teams at the Auckland military tattoo for the Duke and Duchess of York in 1927 killed a horse and hurled drivers from their saddles. The lights were extinguished, RSM Johnny Loper brought on the fresh team held in reserve for such eventualities, removed the dead animal and continued the show 'to thunderous applause'. Drives ceased in 1933 after another horse was killed and two drivers were injured while training at Trentham for a performance at Newtown Park.
>
> In the mid-1930s, Graeme Hutcheson lived in the Manawatu near two returned servicemen uncles:
>
>> When I was 15 one of them said, 'You're going into camp.' My first was Waipukurau with the 2nd Field Regiment. I became horse holder for Captain Tasker. We went to the horse lines about 4.30 in the morning, clearing away the mess, grooming, washing down the animals. The spit and polish was more on the horses than on the equipment. There is nothing more exciting or exhilarating than to watch a troop of horse-drawn artillery swinging into line abreast to come up into an action position. I went up on the first day and we took up our positions. Captain Tasker said, 'Hold my horse while I go forward and survey another position. I may be half an hour.' So I am holding onto this flighty horse, and unbeknownst to me he gave a fire order – as soon as the salvo went over the horses went mad.[42]

two 6-inch guns at Godley Head and an examination battery of two 4-inch guns at Battery Point, and two fighting lights at each. The mobile AA searchlights in Auckland and Wellington should be doubled to sections of six. There should be two searchlights at North Head (in addition to the single light already being installed) and three at Fort Dorset. Two fighting lights were already in place at Takapuna (serving the first of the 4-inch Mk VII guns installed there) and two at North Head; a fourth was needed at Fort Dorset.

The total estimated cost of these proposals was £395,675. The Karori battery, which would swallow up £215,000, was given a lower priority: work would not begin until 1940. Most pressing was the formation of Territorial Air Force squadrons at Auckland and Lyttelton (a squadron at Wellington was already authorised), followed by the close defence works at the three

Firing the 3-inch 20-cwt anti-aircraft gun, Fort Dorset.
Graham Birch collection.

ports. The committee also recommended acquiring 47 minesweeping and anti-submarine craft for the three ports, plus an examination service vessel at each to inspect suspicious vessels.[43]

The committee's paper was approved by Cabinet on 7 February 1938, for action 'as rapidly as possible', as were recommendations for the defence of Fanning Island cable station, and for the removal of restrictions on the wartime deployment of New Zealand's two designated armed merchant cruisers. Concerns remained about the cost of the 9.2-inch battery; Minister of Defence Fred Jones asked that this largest single item of defence expenditure be reconsidered by the Chiefs of Staff Committee. This noted that the Palmer Head and Fort Dorset batteries provided effective close defence for Wellington, though there was a risk of bombardment of the city and port from Palliser Bay or the vicinity of Mana Island. Given the improvements that were recommended for the 'mobile forces', particularly the Air Force, the 'risk of indirect bombardment was not sufficiently great as to warrant the additional expenditure'.[44] Once again, the cost of the 9.2-inch battery saw it deleted from planning. None of the equipment ordered in the 1938 programme had been installed when the war began.

Jumping course, Trentham, 1935.
Royal New Zealand Artillery Old Comrades' Association.

BASIC TRAINING

In the late 1930s gunners underwent basic training at Army Schools Trentham. 'No manuals of any kind' were issued to RNZA recruits in 1938, 'even though Gundrills cost only 4½d and Handbooks from 1/6 to 2/6'. Instead, recruits bought notebooks from the YMCA canteen and wrote down what they were taught. 'Manuals were few and jealously guarded'. A trainee gunner recalls doing 'IT, WT and PT' (infantry training – foot drill – weapons training – rifle, then Lewis gun – and physical training). In the third month they moved on to 'signalling with lamp and flag. And learnt how to lay telephone cables, and how to send Morse code by flag, lamp and key'. This man never saw a radio. From the fourth month they at last got to train on obsolete 18-prs.[45]

One Special Reservist remembered the RSM under whose orders he was placed on arriving at Trentham for elementary training – 'a Scotchman, a strict disciplinarian. Once you got into the way of it, it was simple. He was very straight, with an eye like an eagle. Wherever you were, he could see you. In later years I really appreciated the training that man gave us. It was drill and more drill and more drill. We were a ragtag mob when we first went there. He had us in a straight line before we were finished. We didn't cheek them.' Discipline was also fairly strict at the operational forts, 'though a lot more relaxed than at Trentham'.[46]

After basic training, mastering new techniques was largely a matter of individual study, supplemented by annual refresher courses.

Mechanising the Field Artillery

The crawler tractor used by Auckland's 18 Medium Battery was transferred to Fort Dorset in 1926 when it exchanged its 6-inch howitzers for 60-prs.[47] By 1939 Central and Southern districts each had two petrol-driven Holt 5-ton Caterpillar tractors for their medium batteries (the Hamilton-based 2 Medium Battery had to hire tractors for its annual camps). Their huge motors had to be hand-cranked:

> Noise from the motors effectively killed conversation as the exhaust system consisted … of a straight pipe. Orders could only be given provided the driver throttled back to idling speed. Needless to say no horn was fitted for a Holt could be heard a kilometre away. When moving through a built-up area the driver and his assistant invariably suffered torrents of abuse …[48]

Following the 1936 decision to mechanise the British Army, New Zealand began planning for similar action 'on mobilisation'. In March the distributors of Ford and General Motors (including Chevrolet and Bedford) trucks were asked how many short- and long-wheelbase trucks had been sold during the past year. It was estimated that an infantry brigade would require 126 short-wheelbase and 108 long-wheelbase vehicles, and a mechanised field artillery brigade 34 and 54 respectively. With 767 trucks sold in 1935, and General Motors holding 320 vehicles in knocked-down form, it would be possible to 'impress sufficient latest pattern vehicles to equip one division'. In the event of war, it would initially be easy to 'apply an impressment scheme through the firms, without approaching the individual owners'.[49]

In August 1936, options for carrying artillery pieces on trucks or trailers, or converting gun carriages to pneumatic tyres, were considered. The railway workshops made ramps and six-wheeled trucks were borrowed from the Post & Telegraph Department, plus further trucks and farm tractors from local distributors. In February 1937, guns and tractors to tow the artillery pieces into and out of position were loaded onto trucks, while limbers, fitted experimentally with truck wheels, were towed behind. There was considerable publicity about these experiments at Waiouru (where a

There was still a role for horses when this photograph was taken at Fort Dorset in the late 1930s.
Royal New Zealand Artillery Old Comrades' Association.

camp was being held for the first time on land acquired the previous year) and Sutton. While Major-General Duigan concluded that 'commercial six-wheeled lorries and tractors' were 'quite capable of dealing with light and field artillery' in the manner trialled, to the 'undying amusement of the gunners, the horses always beat the truck into action'.[50] There were further trials with Caterpillar tractors in April.

By November 1937 the Army Service Corps had established pools of two six-wheeled and four four-wheeled trucks (plus vans and motorcycles) in each military district, primarily for training purposes. Additional vehicles were hired from the P & T Department as required. Other territorial batteries were more inventive: by 1939 the guns of Christchurch's 9 Battery were 'motorised by anything that could pull it – it might be a grocery van.'[51]

A batch of 18 Martin-Parry adaptor kits from Canada would enable the conversion of 18-pr gun carriages to pneumatic tyres, and six Morris 4x4 field artillery tractors had been ordered from Britain. By 1939/40 all 18-prs and 4.5-inch howitzers would be converted to pneumatic tyres, and 6-inch howitzers to rubber-padded wheels. By the summer of 1937/38, enough guns and limbers had been converted to pneumatic tyres to enable all 18-pr batteries to attend annual camp as mechanised units. 'Instructions for MT Drivers' were issued: 'In no circumstances will a vehicle be driven at a speed exceeding 40 miles per hour, but the normal average speed for convoy work will be 25 miles per hour.' Wearing hobnailed boots while driving was prohibited.[52]

Apart from the Morris gun-tractors, and a handful of trucks available from the transport pool if not claimed by other units, motorisation relied on the impressment of commercial vehicles, mostly 4x2 trucks. By September 1938, procedures for impressment had been finalised and detailed schedules of vehicle requirements drawn up. Not until these plans were implemented after the outbreak of war were horses retired from the artillery and transferred to mounted rifle units. The last artillery horse, Barbara, lived in retirement at Waiouru until 1965.[53]

Communications

Modernisation was a theme of the late 1930s. The field artillery used radio telephones for the first time at the 1935 TF annual camps, for communication between OPs and gun positions. Manned by battery signallers, these sets weighed 100 pounds and were carried on packhorses; they had a range of no more than a mile. The dozen or so signallers in each battery were specialists. Before field telephones, they waved flags (using Morse or semaphore codes) or signal lamps by day, and lamps by night. Heliograph signalling (using mirrors that reflected sunlight) was still taught, but rarely used. Signallers rode with special saddles holding their equipment.[54]

In 1938 the RNZA practised with several Wireless Sets No. 1 at the annual field artillery refresher course at Waiouru. 'By any standards the sets were already ten years out-of-date,' Wally Ruffell recalled. 'They were far too heavy and cumbersome, and unstable in operation; to net two or more stations and keep them on net the operator was kept as busy as the proverbial one-armed paperhanger. Range on telephony was extremely limited, operators often being obliged to resort to Morse to maintain contact.' Many amateurs had more modern equipment.[55]

RNZA signallers of No. 20 Wing practise semaphore at Trentham in 1939.
Des O'Connor collection.

... but by then cumbersome field wireless sets were also in use.
Graham Birch collection.

The Territorial Force Special Reserve and Mobilisation of the Fortress Troops

As part of the 1937 reorganisation of the Army, a Territorial Force Special Reserve was established to provide 'the necessary personnel for the heavy [coastal] batteries and … the specialists required' for the fortress infantry battalions.[56] Unlike other territorials, reservists would train for three months initially, then attend ten-day annual camps during their three years of enlistment. The fortress troops could then be mobilised immediately to protect the three main ports when war broke out. (The recruitment and training of an expeditionary force, still rather unpalatable to the Labour government, was seen as less urgent.)

The first intake of Special Reservists entered camp on 21 September 1937. After a month of basic training at Narrow Neck or Fort Dorset, they did coastal artillery training with the 6-inch Mk VII and 12-pr guns, culminating in a live shoot on the former. Some trainees also received instruction on searchlights or generators. Of the 234 men in the first two drafts, 153 were posted to territorial units and 63 joined the RNZA as regulars. Subsequently the period of training was increased to six months, then reduced to five months. During the 1938 Munich crisis the Special Reservists then training in artillery at Trentham were mobilised to man the forts.[57]

In 1939, territorial officers trained with and helped to instruct the reservists. In May, with the international outlook grim, the government approved an increase in the territorial establishment, and Prime Minister Michael Savage appealed for volunteers to make up the regular establishment, fill 6000 new places in the territorials and provide another 250 special reservists for the coastal batteries. At the same time a National Military Reserve was created; this registered men aged between 20 and 35 with two years of military service, plus volunteers aged between 20 and 55, and was intended to provide the reserve for the Territorial Force. By July the Territorial Special Reserve totalled 920 men.[58]

In the same month, detailed mobilisation schemes were prepared for the fortress troops at the three main ports. For the heavy and AA batteries, these included provision for notifying RNZA officers and an NZA advance party by telephone. Serving Territorials and the Special Reservists, along with officers on the reserve list allocated to units, would be contacted by telegram, and notices would be placed in the press. War establishments and manning details were specified, as were plans for camp accommodation and messing. These plans were activated on the declaration of war shortly before midnight (New Zealand time) on 3 September; by the following evening the heavy and anti-aircraft batteries had been mobilised. Such was the state of readiness that at 7.58 a.m. on the 3rd, well before hostilities began, Wellington's 15 Heavy Battery fired two 6-inch plugged shells across the bows of the British merchantman *City of Delhi*, which had failed to heave to for the examination vessel. These shots were later claimed as the British Empire's first of a war for which New Zealand was far from ready.[59]

TRADITIONS

The daily lives of regular artillery officers were constrained by social customs derived from the British Army. For example, to speed their integration after a posting, they were required to visit the wives of fellow officers, proffering engraved calling cards. Lieutenant Leonard Thornton found this custom still operating at Fort Dorset in the late 1930s. 'The theory of the convention was good – a newcomer got to meet all the military community in short order – but it was not suitable for New Zealand, where as like as not, the wife would be caught hanging out the washing or slaving in the garden rather than receiving social calls. Like many other customs, this one died in the war.' Between social calls, young artillery officers learned how to handle their men, brushed up on their horsemanship and studied the coast defences – a subject not taught at Duntroon. One way to establish their 'presence' was to grow a 'proper military moustache'.[60]

Another tradition on its last legs in the late 1930s was the exaggerated deference expected of junior officers. Soldiers returned to Hopuhopu with one pip on their shoulders after attending the six-week OCTU course at Trentham. On his first night back in the officers' mess, one of them struck up conversation with a major, who was 'a bit upset about this'. The senior subaltern, Thornton, told the group next day: '"Don't speak to officers of field rank unless you are spoken to first. No one is interested in your views." This was to knock any conceit out of them'. Instructed to 'tighten the show up a bit', Thornton introduced an extra half-hour of physical training early each morning.[61]

Frank Symon

Frank Symon was born in 1879, joined the Permanent Force as a cadet in 1898 and was commissioned in the Engineers in 1900, when he was sent to England for a three-year course of instruction.[62] On his return Symon was posted to the Submarine Mining Electric Light Section in Auckland before taking charge in Wellington later in the year. In 1904 he was promoted to captain RNZE. Symon stayed with this corps until the war, taking various permanent force staff and instructor positions, some with the artillery. He was Adjutant and Paymaster, Adjutant Garrison Artillery Division, and in 1909 a member of the Board of Examination. After a year's training in India he returned as Instructor to D (Mountain) Battery, becoming Wellington Coast Defence Commander by 1912. He joined the NZEF on 1 September 1914 and transferred to the RNZA at the end of the year.

Major Symon was given command of 1 Battery, NZFA, one of the three original batteries formed, and sailed with his men in the Main Body, leaving behind a wife in Wellington. For the August offensive on Gallipoli, when the New Zealand artillery was expanded to two brigades, Symon was promoted to lieutenant-colonel and given command of 1 Brigade NZFA. His achievements, especially in support of the attack on Lone Pine by 1 Australian Division, and in bringing fire to bear on Chunuk Bair, earned him appointment as a CMG and a mention in despatches. By mid-1917 he had earnt a DSO and another MID. He also acted as the New Zealand Division's CRA.[63]

In June 1918, after two years on the Western Front, Symon took command of the New Zealand Field Artillery Reserve Depot at Ewshot, Hampshire. In late October he returned to France, resuming command of 1 Brigade NZFA in the juggling of officers following the death of Major J.M. Richmond. In the action at Le Quesnoy Symon commanded the Right Group of divisional artillery comprising 1 Brigade, 2 (Army) Brigade NZFA and 211 Brigade RFA.[64] He again acted as CRA New Zealand Divisional Artillery during the month in occupation around Deutz, near Cologne.

Symon returned to New Zealand and was appointed GSO1, Southern Command. From 1925 until 1936 he was Director of Artillery (with the additional job of OC Central Command 1931–5). His retirement was delayed for two years because of his role in the reorganisation of harbour and anti-aircraft defence in the mid-1930s. In his late 50s, Frank Symon, who had become a CB in 1935, retired to Eastbourne and fishing. He died in May 1956. His eldest son, Captain Bob Symon of 6 Field Regiment, had died of wounds during the Crusader campaign in December 1941.

Colonel Frank Symon (right) and Major Alan Williams (left) with a fellow officer at a 9 Field Battery camp at Kaituna, Canterbury, 1928.
J.M. Mitchell album, courtesy of John Masters.

GRAHAM PARKINSON

'Gruff and heavily built, with a sandy moustache', Graham ('Ike') Parkinson was one of several Duntroon-trained officers to command New Zealand's artillery.[65] Born in Wellington in 1896, he was sent to Australia's Royal Military College at the age of eighteen in the year war broke out. Two years later he was commissioned and joined the Royal New Zealand Artillery. He instructed recruits at Trentham for a few months before joining the New Zealand Division in France in 1917. Parkinson led the 27th New Zealand Field Artillery Reinforcements which embarked on *Maunganui* in June. In France he served with 1 Brigade NZFA as a battery second-in-command, then as Ordnance Officer, before he moved up to the senior Brigade HQ position of Adjutant, which he held until his return to New Zealand in June 1919.

As a regular force officer, Parkinson was not demobbed after the war. After a spell as Adjutant of the Wellington Division Garrison Artillery, he joined the 1920 expedition to Fiji. Parkinson then commanded Northern Command's harbour defences before becoming Staff Captain Artillery from 1927 until 1930. In 1926/27 he received training in Britain, including at the Chemical Warfare School at South Porton. Parkinson played various instructional roles until 1937, when he was appointed Commander RNZA, becoming the 'father of the pre-war RNZA'.[66]

In 1940 he was seconded to 2NZEF, sailing with the First Echelon in command of 4 Field Regiment. After performing resourcefully in the Greek campaign (for which he was made a DSO), Parkinson was earmarked for a new role. As his car approached the farewell parade in Egypt, it stopped. Ike was too overcome to face his veterans, and the parade was eventually dismissed.[67] He returned to New Zealand to lead a tank brigade being formed for service in the Middle East, but this was kept at home, then broken up after the start of the Pacific War. He was then given command of the Army Reserve (7 Brigade) based in Waiouru.

Parkinson returned to North Africa in 1943 to 'command' the phantom 6 New Zealand Division created as a deception. He took part in both the Tunisian and Italian campaigns, commanding 6 New Zealand Infantry Brigade. During the battle for Cassino in early 1944 he temporarily commanded 2 New Zealand Division after Major-General Howard Kippenberger, himself relieving for temporary corps commander Freyberg, was wounded. Though Parkinson was decorated for this service (a Bar to his DSO), his reliance on artillery and reluctance to commit his infantry during the assault on the town in March was considered to have been a mistake. Consequently, when Freyberg was later incapacitated in an air crash, Parkinson was overlooked as temporary commander, much to his anger; the job went to another gunner, the much younger Steve Weir. Parkinson returned to the gunners' fold briefly in June 1944, when he became CRA 2 New Zealand Division and Commander New Zealand

Major-General G.B. ('Ike') Parkinson.
2004.370, Kippenberger Military Archive, Army Museum Waiouru.

Artillery 2NZEF for two months before returning to lead 6 Brigade for the rest of the war.

After being appointed a CBE, Parkinson returned to New Zealand and resumed his Army career as Quartermaster-General and a member of the Army Board before becoming Military Liaison Officer in London from 1947 to 1949. He retired from the service in 1952 after three years as OC Southern Military District as CMT came into force. 'He didn't have the depth to match the Thorntons and Querees', recalled an officer who served under him, 'but he had Freyberg's approval as a commander, which says a lot.'[68] After 38 years serving his country, Ike Parkinson retired to Christchurch, where he spent a decade as secretary-treasurer of the St John Ambulance Association. He was Colonel Commandant RNZA, Southern Military District, from 1957 until 1961, and died in 1979, aged 82.

5

BATTLE REJOINED: THE SECOND DIVISIONAL ARTILLERY, 1940–41

Britain and New Zealand declared war on Germany on 3 September 1939, three days after the German invasion of Poland. Thanks to years of political procrastination and Labour's belated decision to finance home defence, the New Zealand Army was ill-prepared to deploy an expeditionary force. Nevertheless, the government immediately resolved to repeat its Great War commitment of a full infantry division to the European theatre. Once again, a New Zealand Division including Divisional Artillery would complete its training in Egypt.

The similarities between the two wars did not end there. Once again, the Divisional Artillery would unexpectedly find themselves fighting first in the Mediterranean, partly because a new combatant – this time, Italy – threatened Egypt. In 1940, as in 1915, they would be pawns in an ill-starred operation undertaken for grand-strategic reasons: a doomed attempt to defend Greece against superior German forces. In North Africa, the main Western theatre for three years after the fall of France, New Zealand gunners would play an important role in the gradual refinement of tactics and doctrine that led from the poor coordination of Crusader to the synchronised hammer blows of Alamein and beyond. Then in 1943, in a reprise of 1916, they would cross to Europe (Italy, not France) and become embroiled in a campaign of grinding attrition culminating in a rapid advance during which they mounted a series of textbook assaults against a weakened German foe.

The new war did differ from its predecessor in two significant respects. Thanks to a charter giving Major-General Bernard Freyberg some autonomy in the command of his forces, the Divisional Artillery remained with the New

Joining Up

One Auckland Territorial remembers that 'everybody wanted to get into the Expeditionary Force'. Having been called up and posted to an ack-ack battery, John Rutherfurd found manning searchlights unexciting. After two applications to transfer to the Expeditionary Force were declined, Rutherfurd's father suggested he contact Brigadier Conway, the Army's Director of Mobilisation, with whom he had played golf. 'I suppose it was a bit of cheek, but I got leave to go down to Army HQ, and asked to see him. To my surprise he was most receptive, and within two days I was on a train to Ngaruawahia, to Hopuhopu military camp, where the 6th NZ Field Regiment was just starting training – 1 February 1940.'

Others had more personal reasons. Hamiltonian 'Slim' Williams joined up because 'I wanted to be able to look the old man in the eye and say, "I was as good a soldier as you, Dad!"' His father had lost an arm in the Great War. Jim Henderson felt that it came down to 'the footy team spirit'. This was certainly true for Allan Boyd, who celebrated his 21st birthday with 'a few beers from a keg in the washhouse' with his Sydenham Rugby Club mates. When one of them joined the artillery next day, Allan cycled to Cathedral Square to sign up.[1]

Training

The recruits at Hopuhopu lived in leaky old bell tents: 'when it rained you may as well have been under the stars. Our ablutions were along horse troughs – cold water, of course. I had a cut-throat razor which wasn't any good in cold water.' The toilet facilities at night were buckets which had to be emptied in the morning. The routine 'almost gave one a feeling of sheep being mustered, with all the screaming and shouting'.

NCOs arrived to train the men. Jim Gilberd, a regular artillery sergeant since 1935, was promoted to RSM and sent to Hopuhopu. On the way he got some sound advice from the Staff Officer Artillery, Major John Joyce, who had been an NCO in 1914. 'Remember that these fellows are not regular soldiers, and they're wanting to go to the war to defend freedom and all those things. Don't indulge in a lot of the pre-war regular stuff, but if you see any serious breaches of discipline, throw the book at them.' This advice was to stand him in good stead, but not all instructors were of like mind. At Trentham Bert Dyson 'used to quiver and shake with the "Screaming Skull", quite a remarkable man; quick of eye. He soon whipped us into shape when it came to drill'.[2]

Washday at Waiouru, January 1940.
Des O'Connor collection.

Regimental Traditions

Traditions that would be associated with regiments for years began to form at Hopuhopu. When 4 Field Regiment assembled, for example, James Matheson brought his bagpipes and formed a band with two other pipers and three drummers. They played for visits by the Governor-General and Major-General Bernard Freyberg, who had been appointed to command Second New Zealand Expeditionary Force (2NZEF). Matheson also played the pipes on 26 Battery's route marches. On one occasion Captain G.J.O. Stewart's map let him down, and a two-hour march stretched out to five hours. When they finally got back to camp, someone shouted, '"Three cheers for the piper". I'm afraid that was when I collapsed and was carried off to bed'. Matheson would take to Egypt a set of pipes said to have been played during the Crimean War. These survived through Greece and Crete, being smuggled out of Greece as 'secret signalling equipment'. After being wounded in July 1942 and repatriated, Matheson played them at regimental reunions until the age of 80; in 1994 they were donated to the Army Museum. Healthy rivalries also began at Hopuhopu. The senior regiment, 4 Field, called themselves the Fighting Fourth and dubbed the latecomers the Following Fifth and Sitting Sixth.[3] They had their own epithets.

Zealand Division virtually throughout the conflict. On the other hand, Japan's decision to join the Axis powers late in 1941 brought a much more direct threat to the New Zealand homeland, which necessitated both more extensive manning of the coastal defences and the deployment in the Pacific of another New Zealand Division (including artillery) alongside a new ally, the United States. The globe-spanning contribution made by New Zealand gunners during this titanic struggle is described in the next three chapters.

THE CREATION OF THE DIVISIONAL ARTILLERY

The recently expanded 15,000-strong Territorial Force – the Army's operational units – was configured for home defence. It would fall mainly to the tiny Regular Force of around 100 officers and 500 other ranks to train and lead the overseas force. The resources available to the RNZA were extremely limited: in May 1939 the regiment comprised 17 officers and 257 other ranks. However, many of the early volunteers for the expeditionary force were not raw novices. In one of the field regiments raised, 428 of the 661 gunners had previous military experience, 342 as Territorials. While their average age was in the mid-20s, the oldest was 47.[4]

Responsibility for overseeing the huge effort of creating the Divisional Artillery fell initially to 'Ike' Parkinson, the CRNZA. On 11 December 1939 Lieutenant-Colonel A.B. Williams took over this position, allowing Parkinson to take command of 4 Field Regiment, the first artillery regiment raised for 2NZEF. (Parkinson had been commuting between Wellington and Ngaruawahia doing both jobs.)[5]

By the time Williams took the reins, the shape of the Divisional Artillery had been settled. It was significantly larger than its First World War predecessor, comprising three field regiments (each with 24 25-prs), an anti-tank regiment (48 2-prs), a light anti-aircraft regiment (initially 36 40-mm Bofors) and a survey troop. Each field regiment would be attached to the corresponding infantry brigade – 4 Field to 4 Infantry Brigade, and so on. With limited camp facilities and few RNZA regulars available to conduct training, the units were formed and trained sequentially. On 27 September the first Divisional Artillery recruits arrived at Hopuhopu. The gunners practised on 18-prs and 4.5-inch howitzers. Lacking 2-pr anti-tank guns, the anti-tank batteries made do with 18-prs on Beach platforms which could traverse rapidly through 360°. After this initial training at Hopuhopu (with the exception of 7 Light Anti-Aircraft Regiment) and live shoots at Whatawhata or Waiouru, the regiments sailed with the successive echelons of 2NZEF.

As 4 Field prepared to depart, command of the Divisional Artillery was given to the Quartermaster-General, Reginald Miles, who was promoted to brigadier on his appointment on 5 January 1940. The First Echelon of the NZEF, including 4 Field under Parkinson in the *Empress of Canada*, left Wellington next day. The voyage was a treat. Bert Dyson and a mate had a cabin with an attached lounge, and enjoyed silver room service. (Conditions for later contingents in liners that had been converted to troop transports would be more spartan. Gunner Cliff Barkle, in the Third Echelon, was 'packed in, 80 to a small mess-room, which also serves as our sleeping quarters'. The washroom/showerhouse/toilet opened directly off this.)[6] The First Echelon arrived at Port Tewfik in the Gulf of Suez on 11 February and soon settled into Maadi Camp, outside Cairo, within a dozen miles of their predecessors' base 25 years earlier.[7]

The gunners' training in Egypt was initially limited by a shortage of modern guns, but from 1 March the British provided a mixture of 18-prs and 4.5-inch howitzers. Early training with the former had its drawbacks. 'The infantry witnessed the live shoot and someone stupidly invited them to come back at the gun position, and their morale ebbed straight away. They saw wooden wheels and funny little old-fashioned guns.'[8] By April, 4 Field was able to deploy five troops in manoeuvres conducted by 4 Brigade in the desert south of Maadi, including a war game between 'Puttagonia' under the brigade commander, Brigadier Edward Puttick, and 'Milesia' under Brigadier Miles. The regiment was joined on Anzac Day by 34 Battery, 7 Anti-Tank Regiment, under Major C.S.J. Duff, which brought with it nine of its twelve 2-pr guns. This battery was manned by New Zealanders who had enlisted and trained as a unit in England. With the only 2-prs in Egypt, 34 Battery was kept busy training anti-tank gunners from Britain, Australia and India.

The Second Echelon of 2NZEF, including 5 Field Regiment under Lieutenant-Colonel K.W. Fraser, and 31 and 32 Batteries of 7 Anti-Tank Regiment under the temporary command of Major R.C. Queree, sailed from

Wellington on 2 May 1940. Because of concerns about the safety of the Red Sea route given Italy's possible entry into the war, this convoy was diverted around the Cape of Good Hope to Britain, where it arrived on the Clyde on 15 June, as France collapsed. The force encamped near Aldershot for training, but was soon reorganised into an operational formation as the danger of invasion mounted. Miles arrived from Egypt to take command of 2NZEF (UK), which approximated the strength of a brigade group. On 18 July they fought a mock battle. 'Soaked to the skin', a gunner noted in his diary. 'Bombers over during night but bombs did not wake me.... Hitler has warned Britain that he will be over this weekend, so our tactical manouvres have a more serious aspect.'[9]

Initially, only one field battery could be equipped as artillery, with 18-prs and 4.5-inch howitzers; it was dubbed G Battery. The rest of 5 Field and the anti-tank batteries served as 'infantillery'. Even small arms were not plentiful: 'We had four men to a rifle and ten men to a Bren gun,' Allan Boyd remembered. Not every man in the '5th Regitalion', as they called themselves, enjoyed the experience: 'What a joke after 9 years Artillery training', complained a troop sergeant-major. In late July, provided with 16 French 75-mm guns, 5 Field's gunners were able to revert to their true role. 'The Yanks sent over these 75s from the first war. They were 12-pounders, range 7,000 yards, 20 rounds a minute. They were bloody fabulous. They had this trail spade and when she fired she dug herself in.'[10]

In late August the anti-tank batteries finally received 2-pr guns from Woolwich Arsenal. At the same time, G Battery of 5 Field became the first New Zealand battery to get the new 25-pr Mk II gun that would be the mainstay of the field regiments in the years ahead. Over the next few months the gunners got acquainted with this 'frog-squatting' weapon, time after time scrambling into positions on and around the guns and limbers at the yell, 'Take post!' With invasion seemingly imminent, the New Zealanders were deployed to Kent. Gunners of 5 Field near Maidstone 'watched the whole goddam battle above us and we were deployed several times to the coast when the Hun were going to come over. We'd been issued with gas shells for the 25-pounder.'[11] By early November, with the immediate threat of invasion over, the gunners returned to camps near Aldershot and Guildford. New equipment was received progressively and by December, when the New Zealand force sailed for Egypt, 5 Field was fully equipped with 25-prs and worn-out Mk II Light Dragon tractors.[12]

The long passage via South Africa had its moments. The 7 Anti-Tank men left Bristol on the New Zealand Shipping Company's *Rangitiki*, along with some British units. Their RSM, Jim Gilberd, remembers an incident during the holiday season:

> We had wet canteens on the ship and the troops had had too much beer, and they were allowed to take it down, which was a mistake. There was a lot of noise, and the [English] Orderly Officer was going round with the Orderly Sergeant. He clapped his hands and said 'Disperse this rabble', and of course somebody picked up a bottle and threw it through a glass door. And that set off a minor riot. The officer was going to get the rifles out, and got the ship's police out. There was a real fight going on, and it took us two to three hours to tame it. One of [the British troops] said, 'The niggers were rioting', and one of these Maoris heard it, and they picked this bloke up and threw him down a flight of stairs. I thought he was dead. He wasn't, but that touched off another state of affairs which took us a little while to sort out.[13]

The *City of London*, carrying 5 Field, was in a convoy attacked off Spain on Christmas Day. A warrant officer on board was woken at dawn by gunfire:

> [W]ent on deck – being a WO I was not ordered between decks again.... The convoy was being attacked by something fairly big judging by the Gun flashes and the shells.... Our escorting warships were heading out towards the flashes, firing as they went.... [F]our shells straddled the Ship on our Starboard beam and then one hit her on the stern.

The convoy was ordered to scatter, and *City of London* did not rejoin the others for three days. Meanwhile, TSM A.H. Varian volunteered to man the ack-ack gun for a couple of hours to allow his mates to enjoy the roast turkey, plum duff and beer the officers were serving up. It was a rough day, and he 'got drenched every third wave. We had to tie ourselves to the gun.'

Quad gun-tractor in the desert.
Des O'Connor collection.

They had been attacked by the German heavy cruiser *Admiral Hipper*. One of the four Allied escorts that beat it off was HMS *Dunedin*, which had spent thirteen years in the New Zealand Division of the Royal Navy.[14]

Men cooped up in troopships sometimes resorted to fisticuffs to sort out their differences. 'One of my Sgts (Harry Plimmer) doubted my Authority today so we entered the "ring" with the gloves on, to settle the question', wrote Varian. His authority was restored when he administered 'a sound thrashing, proving that I haven't forgotten all my boxing training. We understand each other now, but unknown to him I'm suffering like hell with stiff joints and a bruised body'.[15] After arriving in Egypt on 16 February 1941, the Second Echelon units took up billets at Helwan, 10 miles from Maadi.

Meanwhile, 4 Field had been deployed in the defence of Egypt after Italy's entry into the war on Germany's side on 10 June 1940, which was followed by a tentative invasion from Libya. At first the New Zealand field gunners were involved in such roles as guarding airfields and digging an anti-tank trench at Garawla. In late August most of 4 Field, armed with 22 assorted guns, deployed with 4 NZ Infantry Brigade Group to the defensive 'box' (fortified area) at Baggush. One troop remained in Alexandria. In

Training on an 18-pr in the Egyptian desert.
F61435, Alexander Turnbull Library, Wellington.

Training took place outdoors — this 6 Field 4.5-inch howitzer is on manoeuvres near Helwan, January 1941.
DAF 11840¼, Alexander Turnbull Library, Wellington.

... and indoors – three scenes at the Artillery Depot, Maadi. *Bert Dyson collection.*

November four troops of this regiment were re-equipped with 25-pr Mk I guns – more commonly called the 18/25-pr – complete with quad tractors and ammunition trailers (as limbers were now known). 'Put chains on these short, high-axled quads ... and they will pull themselves out of anything', if necessary by hitching the winch-rope to 'a tree, a building, or another truck'. If this failed, a second quad could be called up to help.[16]

The deployment to Baggush provided valuable experience in desert conditions. Although the New Zealand gunners were not involved in the rout of the invading Italian Army in December 1940, 4 Field drivers and vehicles under Captain J.F.R. Sprosen supported the British advance into Libya with supply missions and by returning prisoners and captured vehicles to Egypt. In January 1941, 4 Field was transferred to Helwan Camp to join 6 Field, which was already established there. The units of 7 Anti-Tank were concentrated at Mahfouz, between Helwan and Maadi.

By this time the Third Echelon, including 6 Field Regiment and 33 Battery – the fourth battery of 7 Anti-Tank Regiment – had arrived in Egypt after an eventful voyage from New Zealand. Having left Wellington on 27 August aboard the liner *Mauretania*, at Bombay the gunners were transferred to the much smaller *Ormonde*, which was both overcrowded and filthy. The sight of meat lying on the dockside exposed to hot sunlight and the bare feet of port workers was the last straw. 'It was a very hot day and the monsoons were on, so we got back on board. When it came time to sail they found that the bridge was picketed, the engine room was picketed, and there was hell to pay.' When their complaints went unheeded, 20 gunners took over the bridge and engine room.[17] Lieutenant-Colonel C.E. ('Steve') Weir, the CO of 6 Field and Officer Commanding Troops on the ship, who sympathised with the men, convinced the activists to leave the bridge and negotiate. The *Ormonde* remained in port under arrest as the rest of the convoy sailed, but was allowed to depart eight hours later. The suspect meat was dumped overboard and no action was taken against those involved in the '*Ormonde* mutiny'.

After the convoy reached Port Tewfik on 29 September, 6 Field Regiment, 33 Anti-Tank Battery and 1 Survey Troop joined 4 Field Regiment and 32 Anti-Tank Battery at Maadi. They 'marched up a dusty track to the camp, which had been set up by Douglas McKercher. He'd been boasting to his British people what a fine body of chaps we were – and we come up the road in World War One uniforms, hot and dusty'.[18]

With the arrival of 5 Field Regiment and the two anti-tank batteries from England in February 1941, the Divisional Artillery was at last complete, with the exception of the anti-aircraft regiment, which was yet to be formed. Each field regiment consisted of two batteries, each of three troops of four 25-prs, while 7 Anti-Tank had four batteries, each of three troops of four 2-prs. The 2-prs of 34 Anti-Tank Battery were transported 'en portée' aboard 3-ton Ford and Chevrolet trucks, from which they could be fired if necessary. These trucks, with their pug-nosed Canadian military pattern cabs, were known to the New Zealand drivers as 'Blitzes' or 'puddle-jumpers'. The other batteries' 2-prs were towed.

In Egypt each regiment was given a tactical symbol to distinguish it from other divisional units (although identifying marks were removed from vehicles when they were on the move, lest spies inform the enemy).[19] For Divisional Artillery HQ units the symbol was a circle; 4 Field Regiment got a square, 5 Field a rectangle, 6 Field a pyramid and 14 Light AA a shield. All were divided horizontally into the artillery's two colours, with red above blue (36 Survey Battery would get a square divided diagonally). Vehicles used this symbol together with a code representing their gun, such as 'A1' for No. 1 gun in A Troop, usually painted on the door or side.[20] 7 Anti-Tank's black diamond came to represent the whole division, whose route was dubbed the Diamond Trail. The symbol was placed on posts along the route to be taken. For an open move, it bore a white fernleaf. 'Thousands of trucks, tanks and guns … followed it to Hell or victory.'[21] The Diamond Trail 'was a most comforting thing. Once you were on that, [you] didn't have to worry about maps'.[22]

To Greece

The Divisional Artillery did not have to wait long for its baptism of fire, which came in an unexpected place – as in 1915, a peninsula on the other side of the Mediterranean.[23] In January 1941 the British offered to help defend Greece against a possible German invasion following the defeat of an Italian attack in October 1940. On 26 February the New Zealand government agreed to the

Divisional Artillery Order of Battle, 1941

The order of battle of the Divisional Artillery, including the attached light aid detachments (LADs) of the Ordnance Corps, and the signals sections, was as follows:

Divisional Artillery Headquarters (universally known as 'Div Arty') *Brigadier R. Miles (CRA); Major R.C. Queree (Brigade Major)*			
1 Survey Troop	Captain E.T. Kensington (TC)		
4 Field Regiment	Lieutenant-Colonel G.B. Parkinson (CO)		
	25 Battery (A, B and C troops)		26 Battery (D, E, and F Troops)
	E Section, Divisional Signals		9 LAD
5 Field Regiment	Lieutenant-Colonel K.W. Fraser (CO)		
	27 Battery (A, B and C troops)		28 Battery (D, E and F Troops)
	F Section, Divisional Signals		16 LAD
6 Field Regiment	Lieutenant-Colonel C.E. Weir (CO)		
	29 Battery (A, B and C troops)		30 Battery (D, E and F Troops)
	G Section, Divisional Signals		18 LAD
7 Anti-Tank Regiment	Lieutenant-Colonel C.S.J. Duff (CO)		
	31 Battery (A, B and C troops)		32 Battery (E, F and G Troops)
	33 Battery (J, K and L troops)		34 Battery (N, O and P Troops)
	H Section, Divisional Signals		15 LAD

The by now widespread use of radio influenced soldiers' language: D, E and F Troops, for instance, were referred to as Don, Edward and Freddie.[24] The designations of the troops in 7 Anti-Tank anticipated the addition of a fourth troop to each battery.

inclusion of 2 New Zealand Division in this force, assuming, incorrectly, that the British authorities had consulted Freyberg about the operation, and that he believed it to be sound. Its hazards were soon realised, and in giving final approval on 9 March, New Zealand urged on the British 'full and immediate consideration of the means of withdrawal both on land and at sea should this course unfortunately prove to be necessary'. Doubts about the prospects of success increased at the end of March, when a German offensive in Libya saw reductions in the force committed to Greece. 'Lustre Force', under the British General Sir Henry Maitland Wilson, now comprised only 2 New Zealand Division, an Australian division and a British armoured brigade.

In early March the New Zealand Divisional Artillery shifted from Helwan and Mahfouz to Amiriya, near Alexandria, to repack its stores for the voyage. It was now made up of some 185 officers and 2500 other ranks, with 475 cars and trucks (including 108 quads), 130 motorcycles, 144 ammunition trailers, 72 field guns and 48 anti-tank guns.[25] The first unit, 4 Field Regiment, left Alexandria on 9 March, with the gunners enduring overcrowded conditions. While part of the Division was still at sea, British naval forces improved the strategic situation by defeating the Italian navy off Cape Matapan, the southernmost point of mainland Greece. This removed the main threat to the lines of communication with Egypt (and improved the prospects for a successful withdrawal should Lustre Force fail to achieve its objective).

When the force arrived at Piraeus, Greece was not yet at war with Germany. 'The German Ambassador was there, in his tweed jacket, talking impeccable English and chatting to the troops in a friendly way, and finding out all he needed to know. We knew something of security, but it was pretty lax.'[26] While the gunners camped outside Athens, Brigadier Miles and Queree, the Brigade Major, drove north to reconnoitre the as yet unformed Aliakmon Line, where the Allied force was to take up defensive positions. Vehicles and guns were repainted from desert dirty white to green and brown. 'Camouflage nets were hastily regarnished to include some green colouring, and all trucks packed ready for a trek.'[27]

Divisional Artillery Headquarters left Athens on 22 March, followed along the coast road through Molos and Thermopylae two days later by 4 Field Regiment. As the winter snows melted, 5 and 6 Field, and the portees

Lieutenant Phil Hanna's command post, high on Mt Olympus, Easter 1941.
Bert Dyson collection.

of 34 Anti-Tank Battery, took the winding scenic route across Brallos Pass. To avoid the risk of damaging their towed 2-prs, the other anti-tank batteries were transported north by train. Miles grappled with the problems posed by the size of the area allocated to the New Zealand Division. In addition to preparing a 25,000-yard front and a forward position on the Axios Plain, he made plans to defend three passes should the Aliakmon Line fall.

The gunners had barely dug in their guns and prepared observation posts when, on 6 April, German forces invaded Yugoslavia and Greece. By the end of the first day they had broken through the western end of the Metaxas Line, to the north-east of the New Zealand front, and were threatening to outflank the Greek defenders on the frontier and seize the port of Salonika. This led to an 8 April decision to pull back the Allied force – now known as W Force, after General Maitland Wilson – from the Aliakmon Line to defend the Servia and Olympus passes and the Platamon rail tunnel.

A battery each of 4 and 5 Field regiments began preparing positions at the foot of Olympus Pass. New Zealand's 4 Brigade, less 4 Field but with both 6 Field and 31 Anti-Tank Battery, took up positions in Servia Pass, supported by the 60-prs of 7 Medium Regiment, RA, and a troop of Greek 88-mm guns in an anti-tank role. Though difficult to site in the mountainous country, the guns commanded the Servia Plain and the main bridge over the Aliakmon River. On the 9th, a troop of 5 Field joined 21 Battalion in the defence of the Platamon tunnel, cut through a rock spur near the sea. The bulk of 5 Field was deployed along with 32 Anti-Tank Battery in forward positions in Olympus Pass, with 4 Field near the middle of the pass. Some of 4 Field's guns were manhandled even higher, giving them a greatly increased range with which to surprise the Germans when they advanced.[28]

As these units awaited the Germans, 5 Field's E Troop was deployed with the Divisional Cavalry as a rearguard on the Aliakmon Line. On the afternoon of 12 April the troop commander, Captain T.H. Bevan, sighted a column of German vehicles about 10 miles north of the river. When about 30 split from the main group and moved closer, these gunners had the distinction of firing the Divisional Artillery's first shells in anger, possibly achieving a hit with the second. The Germans withdrew, but further troop and vehicle movements kept the gunners busy. Next morning the enemy, now across the river and bolstered by tanks, attacked again. After firing briefly, Bevan's troop withdrew to prepared positions in Olympus Pass. This action set the pattern for the New Zealand gunners in Greece: a fighting withdrawal characterised by sharp delaying actions and a series of rapid but well-planned retreats.

After withdrawing from the Aliakmon Line, 25 Battery was dive-bombed for the first time. 'That was an interesting experience. Phil Hanna, who was GPO, put up a marvellous show: he climbed up a tree and directed the fire.'[29] One man found this 'comparative inactivity' more frightening than fighting. Having moved from a gun to a battery command post role, he thought it worse to have 'nothing to do when under fire; to have to take cover, and just wait for something to happen'.[30] The Germans dropped objects that resembled fountain pens. 'Our chaps would pick them up – "Oh, I got a German fountain pen", take the cap off and [it] blew part of the face off.'[31]

With German aircraft virtually unopposed, 6 Field's Cliff Barkle 'spent a great deal of time pressed hard into the earth'. This could be unpleasant – on one occasion the only available cover was a latrine. 'I was not too keen on … pushing my head down as far as it would go, but the "whirr" of a piece of shrapnel flying overhead soon fixed that.' Eric Young of 4 Field 'prayed for darkness. Each bomb became something very personal.' Shelter was 'ridiculously inadequate' when each crouching figure seemed the size of a haystack.*32*

On the coast, German forces reached the Platamon tunnel by the evening of 14 April. Demolition charges were fired and the track was blocked, but with less damage than intended. The troop of 5 Field gunners deployed in support of 21 Battalion knocked out a number of tanks and armoured cars. 'In about two hours the convoy turned for Katerine going faster than it came'; it was 'an Artillery man's picnic'.*33* But when the Germans attacked in earnest on the morning of the 16th, the New Zealand gunners came under heavy fire from artillery, mortars and tanks. With the defences in danger of being outflanked by alpine troops, the gunners and infantry withdrew to Tempe, at the western end of Pinios Pass. There an attempt would be made to prevent the German advance outflanking Mt Olympus and the whole Anzac Corps, as it had been renamed on the 12th.

A Fighting Withdrawal

On 10 April the Germans had opened a second front by entering Greece from Yugoslavia at the Monastir Gap. As the forces there were driven back, the Anzac Corps risked being outflanked. It was decided to withdraw to a line anchored on Thermopylae, north-west of Athens, but there was doubt whether the route south could be kept open. On 16 April most of 6 Brigade and 4 Field were withdrawn from the front at Olympus Pass to serve as a reserve and establish defensive positions near the town of Elasson, where they could in due course form a rearguard through which the forces at Servia and Olympus could withdraw. On the same day, 25 Battery of 4 Field was ordered to Kalabaka and placed under the command of 64 Medium Regiment, RA. Here, on the left flank of the Anzac Corps, it formed part of the rearguard known as 'Savige Force', built round an Australian brigade group. When the expected attack on this flank did not eventuate, Savige Force withdrew on 18 April.

The rest of the Allied force was withdrawing apace. When the German assault on Olympus Pass opened on the night of 14 April, the defences had already been depleted by the withdrawal of 4 Field; artillery cover was left to 5 Field (less one troop) and 32 Anti-Tank Battery. Heavy cloud shrouding the pass made it difficult to select the best sites for observation posts, and impossible to take crest clearance measurements. Nevertheless, when German troops advanced next morning they were held up by effective fire from 5 Field's guns. When a much heavier attack began the following day, Lieutenant-Colonel K.W. Fraser, the CO of 5 Field, set up a forward OP to bring down fire from 28 Battery on German mortars in front of 22 Battalion. He was therefore well placed to break up an unexpected tank attack with a shift of fire called down at short notice. The most serious threat to the Olympus position came from enemy infantry attempting to outflank the defences. Despite the poor visibility, the gunners of 5 Field were able to break up concentrations advancing on the 28 (Maori) Battalion to the left and 23 Battalion to the right of the pass. They fired more than 3000 25-pr shells that day – 'not a great amount by later standards, but for the type of action and under the circumstances it represented much hard work'.[34]

When 5 Brigade withdrew from the pass after nightfall the gunners maintained covering fire while leapfrogging their batteries back, often under fire themselves. Nine guns of 32 Anti-Tank Battery had to be abandoned after heroic attempts to manhandle them across the rugged terrain behind their position. Some of the anti-tankers joined 23 Battalion as infantillery and took part in a rearguard action later in the day. By the next afternoon the last units had joined the rest of the brigade south of Elasson. The overnight retreat around hairpin bends on a mountain road, without using headlights, had some hair-raising moments. 'The road in places was in shocking condition, and ... it was often difficult to see where the road turned or where the bank began.' Some vehicles 'dashed off the highway and somersaulted down the hillsides'.[35]

The experience of the gunners at Servia Pass followed a similar pattern. First the bridge over the Aliakmon was demolished and the gunners of 6 Field Regiment and 7 Medium Regiment, RA, attached to 4 Brigade, held up the German advance that had begun on 13 April. Despite counter-battery fire and air attacks, the field gunners prevented the replacement of the Aliakmon bridge and stymied attempts to move men and equipment over the river on pontoons. Surprisingly, no major ground attack developed, the Germans having decided against a frontal assault on what appeared to be a strongly held position. On the 17th misty conditions allowed the withdrawal of 6

Field and 7 Medium to begin earlier than planned. Melting snow and rain turned the gun positions into quagmires from which it was very difficult to extract the guns. Part of 31 Anti-Tank Battery was withdrawn under mortar and infantry fire, and then had to run the gauntlet around 'hellfire corner', a section of road shelled repeatedly by the enemy. The brigade and its artillery were redeployed first to Larisa or Pharsala, well to the south. 6 Brigade, with 4 Field Regiment, remained as a rearguard immediately south of Elasson. On 18 April, two troops of 34 Anti-Tank and Divisional Cavalry squadrons destroyed tanks and other vehicles in a sharp action at a crossroads north of the town, but suffered casualties. After they pulled back hastily to rejoin the main force, the Elasson bridge was demolished. This small rearguard was led by Lieutenant-Colonel Duff of 34 Battery. The 300-strong 'Duff Force' also had 'a company of infantry, some machine gunners, quite a few engineers'. Its job, recalled 7 Regiment's RSM, 'was to cover the withdrawal of the brigades to the evacuation beaches. We had some pretty hairy times because we got separated and lost. But we eventually got out.'[36]

Brigadier Miles concentrated the available artillery on the better of the two roads south from Elasson, leaving the more rugged Meneksos Pass less heavily defended but within range of the field and medium guns deployed near the other road. Miles had under his command 5 Field Regiment, 2/3 Australian Field Regiment with an attached 4.5-inch gun troop of 64 Medium Regiment, and two troops of 33 Anti-Tank Battery. As the Germans advanced, heavy and effective fire from the Australian and British gunners prevented the repair of the Elasson bridge, destroyed a number of tanks and hindered their advance through the foothills towards Meneksos Pass. The British medium troop exhausted its ammunition and was withdrawn in the late afternoon. As darkness fell, the Germans mounted a concerted attack on the Meneksos road, which was defended by 24 Battalion. Despite the best efforts of the Australian gunners, a tank assault soon reached the forward positions, but the battalion was able to slip away down the road to Tirnavos. The Australian field regiment then withdrew, along with 25 Battalion (26 Battalion had moved out in the afternoon). Portees of 33 Anti-Tank Battery brought up the rear. Guns of 27 Battery continued firing until the portees reached them, when they too joined 6 Brigade's retreat to Larisa.

The German advance through the Pinios Gorge had to be delayed sufficiently to allow both Savige Force and 6 Brigade time to retreat through Larisa. Although 21 Battalion and the troop of 5 Field guns at Tempe were reinforced with 26 Battery of 4 Field, a troop of 33 Anti-Tank Battery and three Australian 2-prs, as well as 2/2 Australian Infantry Battalion, the situation remained precarious. 4 Field's Lieutenant-Colonel Parkinson arrived to help plan the artillery defences, and the expanded force was placed under the command of the Australian Brigadier A.S. Allen.

On the 17th, German armour probed through the gorge, accompanied by infantry marching ten abreast. The New Zealand guns did terrible slaughter. 'Our shells fell among them for several hours, our machine gunners and infantry fired their weapons among them continuously.' Many became 'physically sick of killing Germans'.[37] The advance was held up, but next afternoon the four guns of 33 Anti-Tank Battery had to be abandoned in the gorge as German alpine troops advanced down the scrub-covered hillsides, though not before one gun disabled several tanks. As German armour broke out onto the plain beyond Tempe, 'Allen Force' was in danger of being overwhelmed. Attacks by Stukas increased the hazards faced by the gunners, but once again, troops and sections of guns were successfully leapfrogged back in a rolling defence that destroyed or damaged at least seven tanks. Two 25-prs had to be abandoned, but only after each had knocked out two tanks.

Allen Force's withdrawal after dark was a 'nightmare'. Men blundered along in darkness 'intermittently made as bright as day by flares – into we knew not what'.[38] It had come perilously close to being cut off, but thanks to its efforts the units retreating through Larisa were able to get clear of the town on 19 April without interference from German ground forces. Allen Force made for Volos, from where the New Zealand units rejoined their Division. For 21 Battalion and the Australian 2/2 Battalion, however, scattered in the hills around Tempe and cut off from the main retreat of Allen Force, withdrawal was more difficult and many men were captured.

Although the units withdrawn through Larisa faced repeated air attacks on their way to the New Zealand Division's new positions around Molos on the Thermopylae plain, the gunners suffered few casualties. Between Pharsala and Lamia this main artery of retreat crossed two passes. At Dhomokos Pass 31

Anti-Tank Battery was left behind when the Australian rearguard pulled out on the 19th without informing them; two guns were abandoned because the road had been made impassable. After a difficult withdrawal under fire from positions on Fourka Pass, this battery was the last unit to pass through Lamia on the road south. The gunners got to Thermopylae however they could. One man:

> arrived by himself driving a cook's truck he had salvaged from the marsh. Men dribbled in by twos and threes from Australian and Tommy trucks. Some of our trucks had a few holes in them. ... Varied was the dress we wore; some had Australian hats, tin hats, forage caps, [or] no hat at all. Tunics were torn, stained with mud or a comrade's blood; some had lost their tunics. It was a tired and ragged army which withdrew to the new line, but a cheerful one.[39]

Good humour was reinforced by opportunities to raid food dumps abandoned during the retreat.

From 19 April the New Zealand Division began to move into position at the eastward end of the new Allied line, from the coast road at Thermopylae towards Brallos Pass, where the other road through the line was held by Australian forces. For the first time the Divisional Artillery was deployed as a whole. Miles also took a number of British units under his command.[40]

Almost before the gunners had finished digging in, the capitulation of the Greek Army of the Epirus on 21 April meant that the southwestern end of the Thermopylae line was no longer defended. Threatened with encirclement, General Wilson had no choice but to begin another withdrawal. 5 Brigade withdrew through Molos on the night of the 22nd, but the artillery elements remained behind in an anti-tank role. Next day several field and medium batteries had the better of counter-battery duels despite heavy attacks by the Luftwaffe. Guns deployed primarily in an anti-tank role remained silent to conceal their positions. That night saw the major withdrawal through Molos; non-essential equipment and stores were destroyed. The Divisional Artillery Survey Troop, its work completed, withdrew to Athens. The front near Molos was now covered only by 24 and 25 Battalions, supported by most of the Divisional Artillery and an assortment of British artillery.

When the German ground attack began next morning, a last-minute decision saw the main armoured thrust directed at Thermopylae Pass. Around 6 p.m., some 20 tanks rashly advancing in single file along the road between cliffs and a swamp were hotly engaged by guns of 5 Field and 7 Anti-Tank. A 5 Field gun under Second Lieutenant H.K. Parkes not only disabled nine tanks but beat back an attack on foot by one of the tank crews. In all, up to 20 tanks were hit and a dozen destroyed. In the later stages of this ill-considered assault, Miles ordered a concentration on the road from 4 and 6 Field and 2 RHA – in effect, the Divisional Artillery's first 'murder'. The Germans were dissuaded from attempting a further attack by this route.[41] During this action, the infantry of 25 Battalion, trapped between German troops on the hills and the advancing tanks, were further hemmed in by the indirect fire brought down around the road. Some shells from the Divisional Artillery fell in the battalion's positions. Though the tank attack failed, it did help to dislodge the forward units of 25 Battalion, and with them the OP parties of 6 Field. Despite the increasing threat from German infantry, the field guns kept firing until dusk to use up their ammunition; 4 Field fired an average of 650 rounds per gun during the day.

After nightfall the positions at Thermopylae and around Molos were evacuated. The field guns and forward anti-tank guns were disabled – always an unhappy experience for gunners. They were either spiked or fired after their buffer-recuperators had been drained of oil. Breech-blocks, sights and firing mechanisms were removed. The only guns to survive the day and briefly take up rearguard positions were 34 Anti-Tank's portees, some 2-prs of 33 Battery and the British 102 Anti-Tank Battery, and six Bofors of 155 Light AA Battery, RA.

A 25 Battery sergeant described the retreat:

> 20 April – 1 a.m. pulled out in a big hurry ... just one jump ahead of the Hun.
>
> 21 April – [bombed – the nearest bomb fell only 16 paces away]
>
> 22 April – drove all night – no lights – going like blazes. last 5 trucks over the bank. it was <u>hell</u>. over [the bank] twice myself

Weapons – Field Gun

Designed to replace the 18-pr, the 25-pr combination gun/howitzer was one of the most successful pieces of artillery ever built, serving for years after the war in many armies. It was mounted in a box trail giving elevation from -5° to +40°. When it was being brought into action the gun was rolled onto a circular platform which dropped from below the box trail. It could then be rotated through 360° by lifting and swinging the trail; the layer for line had 8° of traverse on board. While it was designated a QF gun, its two-piece ammunition made it slightly slower to load than the 18-pr. The shell was rammed home first, followed by a separate cartridge case filled with three colour-coded propellant bags. Left unchanged, all three gave a normal charge (Charge 3, 6000–8000 yards). If Charge 2 was required (a reduced or three-quarter charge, for ranges of 2000–6000 yards), the blue bag was removed and the case resealed before insertion. Both blue and white bags were removed if Charge 1 was called for (leaving just a red bag in the case) for minimal ranging. Supercharge, used for AP shot or extreme ranges, came in a different sealed case and required no preparation.

Name	Ordnance QF 25-pr Mk II
Entered NZ service	1941
Role	field gun/howitzer with anti-tank abilities
Calibre	3.4 in, 27 cals
Range	13,400 yds
Weight	3968 lb
Projectile	25 lb HE, shrapnel, or 20 lb AP
Remarks	A most effective divisional field gun, this served in New Zealand until 1977.

Weapons – Anti-tank

The 2-pr was designed in the 1930s to give fast fire in all directions, hence its light shell and 360° carriage (which did not stand up well to rough roads). Mounting on trucks (en portée) improved its mobility but exposed crews to enemy fire. Though it was maligned after the war, it coped well with most German tanks until the introduction of up-armoured *Panzer* III and IV necessitated its replacement.

Name	Ordnance QF 2-pr Mk IX
Entered NZ service	1940
Role	Light anti-tank gun
Calibre (bore)	1.57 in (50 cals)
Traverse	360°
Range effective	600 yds, though gunners scored hits with it at 1800 yds
Weight	1800 lb
Projectile	2.3 lb AP
Remarks	The first dedicated anti-tank gun in New Zealand service.

> 23 April – digging gunpit all day. … [a]wake all night expecting action.
>
> 24 April – destroyed guns 2pm after tank action… longest day of my life.
>   Warned what to expect at midday
>
> 25 April – arrived Athens – such a wonderful reception[42]

Alan Jackson 'expected a cool reception' as they retreated through Athens. 'We felt that they might feel we had let them down. … But the Greeks lined the streets – men, women and children were weeping, but all cheered and clapped their hands, crying "Bravo N.Z. Come back again N.Z." … We felt like howling ourselves.'[43]

EVACUATION

The focus now was on the imminent evacuation. David Strang of 7 Anti-Tank spent Anzac Day morning 'putting a pickaxe through … tinned milk, tinned bully beef and whatever.… We were told to abandon everything. We weren't allowed to set the trucks on fire or even to run the engines; the Germans were too close. We took the pieces out of the guns, took them down to the tide, waded in as far as we could, dropped them in.'[44] By late on the 26th, the last gunners to pull out of the line had reached the embarkation beach at Rafina,

> ### Weapons – Anti-aircraft
> A Swedish design of the late 1920s, the Bofors entered British service in 1937. It sat on a light four-wheeled carriage for transport; the two axles were quickly detached for firing.
>
> | Name | Ordnance QF 40-mm, Bofors |
> |---|---|
> | Entered NZ service | c. 1941 |
> | Role | light automatic mobile anti-aircraft gun, 90° elevation |
> | Calibre | 1.57 in, 56 cals |
> | Range | 12,500 ft effective ceiling |
> | Weight | gun and 4-wheel carriage (3815 lb) |
> | Projectile | 2 lb, practical rate of fire 70 rpm |
> | Remarks | Versatile weapon, used in very large numbers by both static and mobile troops until the 1970s. |

east of Athens. That night the men of 4 and 5 Field, 64 Medium, and other gunners, left nearby Porto Rafti for Alexandria on the *Salween*, or for Crete on the *Carlisle*, *Devonshire* or *Kandahar*. Most of 6 Field and 7 Anti-Tank left Rafina for Egypt on the *Glengyle*. Around 1000 troops, including many gunners, were taken off the following night by the destroyer HMS *Havock*, which made for Crete. On the night of 29 April those still at Porto Rafti, including the Australian gunners who had served with the New Zealanders, also departed for Crete.

With the enemy so close, the embarkation was fraught. 'Some chap got drunk and was making a noise. An officer pulled his revolver out and shot him, because he was going to put the men in danger. We were told that if anybody fell off they would not be picked up. Some of the railings were down. We were going hammers, with the prop wash well above the deck line.'[45]

A large party of New Zealand reinforcements, including gunners who had not been able to reach operational units, reached Kalamata in the south of the Peloponnese peninsula, but most could not be evacuated. After spirited resistance at the dockside, the troops trapped in the port surrendered on the morning of 29 April. Many individuals or small groups were now making their way independently out of mainland Greece, and at least two parties of New Zealand gunners managed to sail to Crete.

One was a group from 6 Field's F Troop (30 Battery) under Lieutenant Charles K. Reed. Realising they were unlikely to be taken off Kalamata by ship, with 8000 soldiers waiting and the Germans near, they collected supplies and arms from abandoned vehicles and houses. Only two boats in the harbour had escaped the bombing; one was a two-masted ketch with an auxiliary motor. Two Allied ships arrived but embarked only sick and wounded, and then the British brigadier in charge surrendered to the Germans. At 4 a.m. on the 29th those left from the original party started loading the ketch with food, diesel and rifles; the untimely approach of a German patrol prevented much water being taken on. As Reed and nine F Troop gunners (plus an Australian) hid in the boat, the enemy came within 10 yards of them. That night they slipped out of the harbour, towed by two men in a dinghy. A breeze took them 25 miles south before they were becalmed. Two men then rowed across to a small village on the west side of the bay where, dodging Germans, they filled with water all the bottles, jars and paint tins they could find. Two sailors and a diesel mechanic among the original group had been captured; the others could not start the motor and their navigation was haphazard. Sailing south and east, they were hit by a storm that necessitated running repairs to the rigging. They sighted land after six days, but unfavourable winds and two more storms kept them at sea for another two days until they landed under a monastery on the westernmost point of Crete. The local villagers fed and looked after them until they were taken by truck to be reunited with their regiment at Canea. This group was lucky enough to be evacuated to Egypt before the German attack on Crete.[46]

The Greek campaign had cost the lives of 32 New Zealand gunners, five of whom died of wounds after being taken prisoner. Fifty-nine had been wounded and 204 taken prisoner, mostly at Kalamata. For the artillery, like the other corps, this campaign, undertaken for political and strategic reasons with little prospect of success, had been a difficult and disappointing baptism of fire – and their guns had to be left behind. Nevertheless, the New Zealand gunners had performed very creditably, supporting the infantry and disrupting the enemy during a rapidly moving fighting withdrawal with notable skill. In their last battle at Thermopylae Pass they demonstrated that well-coordinated divisional artillery fire could be as effective against armour as against infantry.

CRETE

The gunners who arrived on Crete expected this Greek island to be a port of call on the way to Alexandria, but many would instead find themselves fighting in its defence.[47] Some 360 men of 5 Field and 180 of 4 Field would see active service there, along with about 90 of the Anti-Tank Regiment and 80 6 Field men. All the regimental COs were in Egypt, and Miles was on Crete for only three days, as CO of the New Zealand troops, before being sent to Egypt to take command there. His role as divisional commander on Crete was assumed by Brigadier Puttick of 4 Brigade. Freyberg was placed in overall command of 'Creforce', which comprised around 30,000 British and Commonwealth and 11,000 Greek troops.

Four key points along the northern coast were the focus of the defence (and, as Freyberg knew from Ultra intelligence, of the impending German attack): the airfields at Maleme, Retimo and Heraklion, and the port at Suda Bay. The Maleme sector would be defended by the under-strength New Zealand Division, consisting of the infantry of 4 and 5 Brigades and several Greek battalions, supported by three light AA troops (two British and one Australian).

At first the New Zealand gunners on Crete entirely lacked the tools of their trade. Those for whom small arms could be found were formed into infantillery detachments alongside other non-infantrymen from the Ammunition and RMT companies. The three 'composite' battalions thus formed were grouped together as 'Oakes Force', under Major Oakes of 7 Anti-Tank, the most senior New Zealand artillery officer on Crete outside HQ. Tommy Oakes was a retired Royal Artillery officer who had been decorated in the First World War. In Jim Gilberd's view, though 'not really an experienced anti-tanker, [Oakes] was an experienced gunner'. A 'very studious man', he 'put our regiment together fairly well'.[48] From 2 May Oakes Force was deployed in defensive positions between the coast and Galatas, and began training for the anticipated paratroop assault. Many of the unarmed men on the island were withdrawn to Alexandria on 7 May. They included Divisional Artillery HQ staff, the Survey Troop, and most of those from 6 Field and 7 Anti-Tank, including Major Oakes. The armed men of 4 and 5 Field, and 200 unarmed gunners of 5 Field, remained. The 4 New Zealand Brigade position was reinforced on 10 May by the arrival from Egypt of 1 Light Troop, RA (3.7-inch howitzers).

Of the 100-odd assorted guns sent from Egypt, 49 field guns could be made serviceable; some were repaired by 16 Light Aid Detachment and allocated to the unarmed 5 Field men. Two troops of 27 Battery were restored to their rightful role with three Italian 75-mm (B Troop) and two British 3.7-inch howitzers (A Troop). Major W.D. Philp was placed in command of the battery, which was deployed to 5 Brigade near Maleme from 13 May. Three more howitzers – two Italian and one German – went to F Troop of 28 Battery and were deployed under Captain J.L. Duigan, covering Prison Valley, inland from Maleme and Galatas, in support of 4 Brigade. C Troop of 27 Battery, under Captain J.P. Snadden, received four French 75-mm guns and joined the rest of its battery in support of 5 Brigade. Each troop was supplied with from 200 to 350 rounds per gun or howitzer.[49]

The French 75s had range drums, but no sights. When the army workshops failed to remedy this, the gunners themselves solved the problem:

> The final solution was to fix a piece of wood firmly in the sight bracket, cut a groove in it to form the back sight, and stick a suitably moulded piece of chewing gum into the sight aperture in the gun shield to act as a fore sight. The barrel of the gun was lined up by means of cross threads on to a distant object and the chewing-gum fore sight then adjusted to coincide with the groove in the wood …

It would be 'primitive gunnery', with the 75s fired 'like oversized rifles'.[50] These guns were deployed to command 5 Brigade's positions around the airfield and village of Maleme.

During this calm before the German storm, officers contended with the kind of issues soldiers inevitably bring up when rations are short. On one occasion the acting QMG, gunnery officer Bert Dyson, was called out to 20 Battalion to deal with civilians' complaints that their potato crops were suddenly dying. 'The soldiers were removing the potatoes by excavating under [them] by hand and removing the tuber, taking it away to cook it and putting all the soil back.'⁵¹ On 15 May the former Oakes Force was reduced to a single Composite Battalion, under Major Lewis. This at first comprised five companies, one each from 4 and 5 Field Regiments, the RMT Company, Divisional Petrol Company and Divisional Supply Column; a company of Supply Column men was added a few days later. The Composite Battalion became part of 10 Brigade and was deployed above Prison Valley.

After days of dive-bombing and strafing, the German assault on 20 May came where and when it was expected. In the New Zealand Division's sector, it began at 8 a.m. with heavy bombing raids on the Maleme airfield. The night before, Puttick had implored Freyberg to disperse and conceal nearby AA guns, and asked that they be ordered to hold their fire during the anticipated bombing and strafing runs so as not to disclose their positions. They would then be available to deal with the low-flying troop planes and gliders at the key moment when the bombing would necessarily pause. Puttick was overruled, and the exposed AA guns were soon rendered ineffectual; the heavy AA guns were silenced after firing only one round each.⁵²

About 9.30 squadrons of Junkers 52 troop carriers appeared in the sky, some towing gliders which landed on the beach near Maleme, on the airfield itself and particularly in the undefended dry bed of the Tavronitis River to the west. The parachutists who poured from the planes were more widely dispersed. Many presented easy targets and were shot while in the air – 'rather like clay-bird shooting'.⁵³ Some fell near the gun positions or OPs, where gunners engaged them with small-arms and Bren-gun fire. Most of the Division's remaining unarmed men were soon well equipped from dead paratroopers and the capsules of arms and supplies that had been dropped with them. Snadden's C Troop claimed the field artillery's first hit of the battle: a Junkers 52 which crashed on the beach near Maleme. During the day 27 Battery's guns claimed many more victims.

Meanwhile the sole troop of 28 Battery, supporting 4 and 10 Brigades near Galatas, was also defending itself against paratroopers landing nearby. Its OP covering the 4 Brigade positions near the beach was soon overrun, as were the four guns of 1 Light Troop RA (three were disabled before the gunners were driven back). For the Composite Battalion immediately west of Galatas, the battle's first day was frustrating. They defeated paratroopers who landed near them, but misplaced caution on the part of Brigadier Howard Kippenberger at 10 Brigade's HQ prevented them from attacking vulnerable German concentrations in Prison Valley and near Galatas.

In Brigadier James Hargest's Maleme sector, this pervasive caution would have much more serious consequences. On the afternoon of the 20th, Hargest was unwilling to commit the Brigade Reserve, 23 Battalion, to a counter-attack on the airfield. When elements of Lieutenant-Colonel Les Andrew's 22 Battalion attacked alone they were driven back. That night, Andrew, with Hargest's reluctant concurrence, withdrew his battalion from a position overlooking the airfield which he mistakenly believed to be untenable. The next day, the Germans quickly flew in reinforcements, consolidating their hold on this vital objective.

For Major Philp at 27 Battery's HQ, the loss of his OP on the 20th seriously hampered fire control the following day. Nevertheless the airfield could be shelled directly by some guns, and from map references by others. Signalling from infantry units and the dust clouds thrown up by the German aircraft enabled the gunners to time their shelling to coincide with the arrival of transports. Philp himself observed from a hill near 23 Battalion's HQ, but poor communications limited the effectiveness of this effort at fire control. By the end of the day the airfield was littered with wrecked planes – mostly the work of 27 Battery's guns – but many German reinforcements had been landed safely.

Replenishing ammunition was a major challenge. Lieutenant Dyson was asked:

> to take three truckloads of ammunition to Maleme. My heart sank, because a truck was a fair target for the Luftwaffe. I took three truckloads of ammunition, three British drivers – marvellous chaps – and said, 'Look, we will not rush up the roads stirring up dust, we are going to drive very slowly, off the road. If we come to any buildings or trees casting a bit of a shadow, we will stop and take a look at the sky.' I think we stopped twice, then went to the gun positions and found Pine Snadden – bandage around his head – and unloaded the trucks. There was a lot of mayhem – presumably trying to neutralise the gunners up where the real action was. And a stray bullet set fire to one of my trucks' canvas

canopy. We put that fire out, but they must have seen a wisp of blue smoke and they really set into us. We couldn't put out any more fires. Unloading had been under way, and before you could say anything the three trucks were going up and the ammunition exploding, so we had to take cover. We crawled into a culvert and just lay there, and they realised that's where we may be and tried to come at the culvert end on. We lay there for about six hours until sundown, when all the action stopped in those days.[54]

In the early hours of 22 May, 20, 21 and 28 (Maori) Battalions counter-attacked towards Maleme airfield against strong resistance. The New Zealand gunners had no communication with the infantry, and no FOOs. Two troops shelled the airfield until they were forced to stop for want of information about the advance. During daylight 27 Battery continued to pound the airfield, destroying still more Junkers 52s, though the German airborne and alpine troops usually had time to disembark before the New Zealanders could fire. Despite serious losses of aircraft, the airborne shuttle-service was relentless and the German advantage was consolidated. By the end of the day it was clear that the counter-attack had failed and 5 Brigade risked being cut off from the rest of the Division. Early on the 23rd it was withdrawn to Platanias, halfway between Maleme and Galatas and near 10 Brigade's positions. The guns of the two troops nearest the airfield were disabled and abandoned, but two of the third troop's guns were towed out. The other survivors of 27 Battery became infantillery or Breda machine-gunners.

When the counter-attack on the airfield was planned it was to be supported by two Australian gun troops (which did not arrive), and Lieutenant-Colonel H.W. Strutt of 2/3 Australian Field Regiment was appointed temporary CRA of the New Zealand Divisional Artillery. Retaining this position after 5 Brigade's withdrawal, he was able to deploy a small, mixed artillery force in support of the Brigade's new position at Platanias. As the risk of encirclement became increasingly grave, however, 5 Brigade was withdrawn through 4 Brigade's line at Galatas.

The German attack on Galatas began in earnest on 25 May. Throughout the afternoon, the Composite Battalion was engaged in heavy fighting in a delaying action to the south of the town, and then a fighting retreat through it. The supporting troop of 28 Battery gunners, hampered by a lack of contact with FOOs and using unweighed propellant charges that made for inaccurate shooting, were mainly restricted to firing on registered targets. Although an Australian troop of 75s was able to bring down effective directed fire in support of the infantry battle, the Galatas line could not be held.

Alongside a platoon of 19 Battalion, the 4 Field infantillery platoon stood firm under Lieutenant J.P. Dill:

> At the height of the attack he went forward to the foremost spur of Pink Hill to watch the development of the assault and there he stood, scorning to take cover from the machine-gun fire which swept the area. Sergeant [N.H.R.] Hill ... tried to get him to keep down, but Dill calmly refused. Hill swore at him, exasperated, but Dill said (as he undoubtedly believed), 'If a man believes he will be hit, he will (be hit)'. There was no mock heroics here, ... only the recognition by an instinctive leader that men in a critical and desperate situation will respond to firmness in the face of danger. Enemy swarmed among the trees and thickets below and tried again and again to mount the slopes and gain this key to the southern access to Galatas.

The gunners thwarted every attack until Dill was wounded and the two platoons had to fall back.[55] The Composite and infantry battalions suffered heavy casualties, and in the retreat from Galatas the Composite Battalion ceased to exist as a unit.

Retreat

After nightfall on 25 May, as the front collapsed, the three surviving 28 Battery guns and the Australian 75s were towed out, as was the last gun of 27 Battery, which had been guarding the road from Galatas to the coast. All eventually reached a new position east of a bridge on the coast road to Canea. Next day, pinned down by constant air attacks which prevented an observation post being set up, the New Zealand gunners fired mostly from map references. That night, along with the Australian troop, they withdrew, exhausted, to a position 6 miles east of Suda Bay. On the way, the 27 Battery gun had to be abandoned when its Australian-provided tractor broke down. The following day the 28 Battery guns, now very short of ammunition, were disabled and their crews joined the withdrawal to the south coast.

28 Battery had retained some of its vehicles, but with the quads full 'many of us were compelled to ride on the guns', as Gunner James Kinder recalled. 'And they are certainly not built for comfortable riding. Down the road, one Quad went over the bank in the dark and had to be abandoned. … My own kit was on it and I lost most of my belongings. …' Kinder and three others continued on foot, attaching themselves to parties trekking over the White Mountains. Twice they awoke to find that the officer in charge of their ad hoc group had left them to flee south.

Kinder and his mates were reunited with their regiment at Sfakia:

> That night a crowd of Greeks … tried to rush the boats but were … driven off. June 1st broke and with it an order that filled us with utter horror. We were told that … word had been sent to the enemy that we had capitulated. … One Aussie blew his brains out … and the rest of us prepared for the arrival of the enemy. … [W]e were all getting weak with hunger and dysentery. … The latter was the worse of the two and many men were by now mere skeletons. We piled our arms and equipment and then destroyed any papers which might be of use to the enemy. I destroyed my diary, … which has annoyed me ever since as [the Germans] did not go through them.

These captives were soon put to work moving equipment and supplies.[56]

Luckily for the New Zealanders, the Germans were concentrating their attacks on the Australians around Retimo. The Royal Navy again performed gallantly, taking men from Heraklion as well as Sfakia. After the last evacuation on 31 May, 6500 New Zealand, Australian and British troops had to be left behind to surrender or, in some cases, take to the hills to continue the fight. The Divisional Artillery had lost 37 men in action, plus three who died of wounds, while 295 became prisoners of war. The cost of the campaign was high, but so were the losses exacted on the invaders. Different decisions at key moments might have brought victory at Maleme, and perhaps the island could have been held, albeit with great difficulty in the face of German air power. In any case, the New Zealand gunners, whether serving their motley collection of guns or fighting as infantillery, had improvised and operated effectively in the most trying circumstances. The survivors were exhausted, but also battle-hardened for their coming ordeal in the North African desert.

OPERATION CRUSADER

When the Creforce remnant arrived back in Egypt to rejoin the gunners who had gone there directly from Greece, the first priority was reorganisation and re-equipment to make up for their losses in the two ill-fated campaigns.[57] After leave and, for some, service on guard duty, the gunners returned to Maadi or Helwan and gradually received their new equipment. Freyberg ordered 'recreational training' to help restore the Division's morale; men sweated at athletics, boxing and other sports. Units were brought back to full strength with men from the Fourth Reinforcements, which had arrived in mid-May. Among them was 14 Light Anti-Aircraft Regiment, which had trained at Papakura and Hopuhopu before embarking on the *Nieuw Amsterdam*. Lieutenant-Colonel K.W.R. ('Gussie') Glasgow took command of 14 Light AA at Maadi. It now comprised 41, 42 and 43 Batteries, each of three troops of six 40-mm Bofors guns. With an establishment of 910, it was the largest unit in 2 New Zealand Division. British pressure to deploy it as a corps unit had been firmly resisted by Miles and Freyberg.

Jack Spring remembers that during the subsequent Crusader campaign they usually had three Bofors around 28 Battery. These 'did a hell of a job trying to stay alert as to what's up there – no radar! I remember a Fiesler Storch [a slow German spotter plane] flew over the back of us before Belhamed – "chugga, chugga, chugga" – and we said to the ack-ack gun, "Look, you bastards, Look!", and one of the boys had a go with the old Bren gun on a pedestal before the Bofors woke up – but they were bloody good when they got going.'[58]

The field and anti-tank regiments were also reorganised. The former would each now comprise three batteries of two four-gun troops. In 7 Anti-Tank Regiment there would be four batteries, each with three 2-pr portee troops and an 18-pr troop. The 18-prs, mounted on Beach platforms in an anti-tank role, and firing armour-piercing (AP) as well as high-explosive (HE) shells, would prove valuable. Using fixed ammunition, they could sustain a faster rate of fire than the field regiments' 25-prs which, unusually for quick-firing guns, fired two-piece rounds.

The gunners trained hard, knowing they would soon be needed in the Western Desert. The situation in North Africa had deteriorated sharply during 1941 with the arrival of the German Afrika Korps under General Erwin Rommel to bolster the faltering Italians. Rommel wasted little time launching an offensive that sent most of the Allied troops reeling back into Egypt, leaving Tobruk as a bastion in Libya. The New Zealanders now prepared to take part in a major operation designed to expel the Axis forces from Cyrenaica and relieve Tobruk. Operation Crusader, beginning on 18 November, would

2-pr anti-tank gun en portee.
DA 2279, Alexander Turnbull Library, Wellington.

Field and Anti-Tank Units, North Africa
4 Field Regiment 25 Battery: A and C Troops; 26 Battery: D and F Troops 46 Battery: B and E Troops
5 Field Regiment 27 Battery: A and B Troops; 28 Battery: D and E troops 47 Battery: C and F Troops
6 Field Regiment 29 Battery: A and B Troops; 30 Battery: E and F Troops 48 Battery: C and D Troops
7 Anti-Tank Regiment 31 Battery: A, B and C Troops (2-pr portees); D Troop (18-prs) 32 Battery: E, F and G Troops (2-pr portees); H Troop (18-prs) 33 Battery: J, K and L Troops (2-pr portees); M Troop (18-prs) 34 Battery: N, O and P Troops (2-pr portees); Q Troop (18-prs)

rudely awaken the New Zealand gunners to the realities and very different problems of desert warfare.

Crusader was a fluid and often confused dogfight.[59] The goal was to envelop the German and Italian positions on the Egypt/Libya frontier while the British armour ranged further afield to bring the enemy tanks to battle, and the Tobruk garrison broke their siege. The implementation of this plan began well enough, and after the infantry captured or encircled the frontier posts, two New Zealand brigades were ordered to move towards Tobruk. But the armoured clash did not go as expected: the British were largely defeated, though how badly was not at first realised. While the New Zealanders pressed westward, Rommel thrust south-east towards the frontier in a 'dash for the wire'. When he subsequently turned back towards Tobruk, his tanks encountered and overran 5 New Zealand Brigade; more than 700 men were captured. Further disasters for the New Zealand infantry culminated in heavy losses at Sidi Rezegh and Belhamed. But Rommel, conscious of the precarious state of his supply lines, eventually pulled back to El Agheila on the Gulf of Sirte. The Allies had secured a victory of sorts – the enemy had been driven back and Tobruk relieved – but the Axis forces had survived to fight another day.

> ### WATER IN THE DESERT
> Water supplies soon ran short during periods of action. Graham Hutcheson's experience was typical:
>
>> At one stage there was about one pint for 24 hours, which meant that cleaning teeth was about the maximum expenditure. It also meant that many stopped shaving, but then the sand got into the beard and it started to itch like the devil, and they got heat rashes, so in the finish we just had to make up little filters out of Edmonds Baking Powder tins, and we strained anything we could put through that – what came out the bottom was usable in an emergency. We were using the little heating stove – a jug with a funnel up the middle. We'd put a little can at the bottom of it, put petrol in the sand, and that created a very effective boiling situation. [This device was dubbed a 'Benghazi burner'.] I never drank tea – couldn't afford the amount of water that went into it. I used to just sip my water bottle.[60]
>
> The periodic water shortages were a real privation. In late July 1942 Bombardier John Gordon had not had 'a decent wash' for nearly a month – and that had been in the sea. 'I have washed by cloth twice with petrol'. Often there was not enough water to shave – but a can or two of beer per man was provided.[61]

For the Divisional Artillery, Operation Crusader began well. The Division had immediate success, capturing Fort Capuzzo and Sidi Azeiz. Gunners who had been through Greece and Crete were exhilarated – they were advancing for a change. Field and anti-tank units were in the vanguard of the attack, with Sidi Azeiz's Italian garrison encouraged to surrender by some 2-pr shelling. More serious action soon followed at Menastir on the 22nd, when 4 Field Regiment helped break up a counter-attack along the Via Balbia with accurate concentrations of 25-pr fire; 34 Anti-Tank Battery also chimed in. Many gunners were going into battle for the first time. When the firing started, Jim Henderson felt 'all right' until he had to cower in a slit trench under enemy fire. This literally gave him cold feet, and when the shelling stopped, 'we all had a nervous pee'. David Strang's anti-tankers were 'too busy … to think about being hit' – when they were, it came 'as an absolute surprise'.[62]

The Division's advance had cut off the advanced Italian garrisons at Sollum and Halfaya Pass from the town of Bardia to the north. Freyberg left most of 5 Brigade and the Divisional Cavalry to hold the ground taken while the rest of the Division advanced westward along the Trigh Capuzzo towards Sidi Rezegh, where part of the British 7 Armoured Division had been encircled. The nature of the terrain often made it difficult to determine the position or identity of units. On the night of 23 November, for example, part of 6 Brigade unknowingly camped near German units. When their neighbours were identified at dawn, the gunners of 6 Field Regiment and 33 Anti-Tank Battery wreaked havoc as what was later identified as the Afrika Korps headquarters scattered and fled, leaving behind invaluable code-books and radios. Pushing on to 'Point 175', east of Sidi Rezegh, 6 Brigade met determined resistance. Though the trig point was taken after concerted field and anti-tank gun support of the infantry and attached tanks, the attack faltered against German anti-tank and machine-gun fire, and the line stabilised.

Local counter-attacks periodically brought heated action for the New Zealand gunners. On 23 November a troop of 25-prs and two 2-pr portees had rushed to help a South African infantry brigade. When the South Africans were driven back through the gun line, the New Zealand gunners found themselves face to face with enemy armour. Frantic firing soon left the field guns with only smoke shells – two guns fired more than 300 shells each. The gun crews felt as if they were engaging the whole German Army. Eventually the guns pulled back, along with 26 Battalion, which had also been sent to support the South Africans. The wrecks of 24 tanks attested to the growing skill of the New Zealand artillerymen. Some had been destroyed at the very long range, for 2-prs, of 1800 yards.

Over the next five days the Divisional Artillery assisted the New Zealand infantry in a series of assaults as they pressed towards Tobruk. The immediate objectives were positions on the Sidi Rezegh escarpment. The gunners' main tasks were to neutralise enemy artillery fire and help the infantry move forward. Counter-battery fire depended on locating the enemy's guns – easier said than done in the conditions. The gunners' difficulties were compounded by enemy operations: 6 Field, for example, was shelled heavily by German guns dug in north of Belhamed. Anti-tank guns also proved a nuisance. Providing close support for advancing infantry also depends on clear observation and communications. There were problems in the early stages of the assault on Sidi Rezegh, but these had been ironed out by the 28th, when Miles oversaw an impressive display of coordinated fire control from 4 and 6 Field as infantry, divisional cavalry and armoured units overcame strongpoints between Belhamed and Sidi Rezegh. Concentrations fired on a series of objectives cleared the way for successful ground assaults and demonstrated what could be achieved with effective fire-planning and all-arms coordination. By now, elements of 4 Brigade had made contact with the Tobruk garrison, which had been able to advance to nearby Ed Duda.

Ammunition ran low during this hectic fighting, and resupply was not always assured. Each battery had 32 rounds for each 25-pr in its limber, and another 24 in the gun tractor; there were also normally three ammunition trucks, each carrying 180 rounds. And 'we made sure we had enough AP'. But

Artillery command post in the desert.
DAF 2278½, Alexander Turnbull Library, Wellington.

such quantities could be exhausted quickly. 'At Sidi Rezegh we were down to our last ten or 20 rounds until George Clifton brought more in.'[63]

German tanks came over the escarpment at Belhamed just as 46 Battery was preparing to move. Bombardier Des O'Connor remembers his crew dropping the trail and going into action. When they limbered up again:

> we went with the gun unclamped, a round of shot in the breech and a cartridge in behind it, so it was pointing at the radiator of the tractor behind us. We raced down, bumping over the desert. The ammunition limber had been pierced by a shell splinter. The tyres had Run Flats – a thick piece of rubber as well as tube, so that it would run a certain distance if it was flat. But we were running so fast – and it *was* flat – that the thing started to smoke. Fortunately we noticed, and stopped and put it out.[64]

The gunners recognised the historic nature of this first major attack against the enemy on their own territory, but understood the need for vigilant defence. While they waited to attack Belhamed on 25 November, for instance, 25 Battery, 4 Field Regiment assembled their guns in a laager formation:

> We normally point our guns outwards from the square. This night was one of the very eerie experiences of the campaign. Attack was expected, and tanks had that day penetrated our headquarters group and done considerable damage. All drivers, signallers and gunners formed a strong picket just outside the guns, for we had no infantry with us, and listening posts were set up near each gun. All night long flares were going up from Belhamed and Sidi Rezegh. It seemed strange to us that we should have to form our own 'thin red line' of rifle protection outside the gun line, but it was vitally necessary.
>
> Before dawn we were all 'standing-to' beside our guns, ready for action. Guns were laid out on zero lines. For some days we had been standing-to before dawn, … the most likely time for the wily Hun to attack. If this precaution were not taken, a dawn attack would find us either asleep or very sleepy, and therefore unable to grasp what was going on.

Two nights later 'we bedded down but left strong gun pickets on guard, our guns loaded. Close behind us were four Vickers machine guns. ... laid out on fixed enfilade lines, ... ready to do their slaughter had Jerry attacked.'[65]

Officers detailed to serve as forward observation (FO) posts were often very exposed. At this time, Bert Dyson's OP was a concrete post in a minefield, a setting that horrified Weir and Queree when they came up to inspect it. When a troop commander was controlling the guns as FOO, 'he went forward and lived with the infantry – we never saw him'. In such circumstances the gun position officer, usually a lieutenant, took charge of the gun position.[66]

The New Zealand positions in the Sidi Rezegh–Belhamed area of the Tobruk corridor were consolidated just in time to meet an onslaught from German forces returning west after their overambitious assault on the frontier from 24 November, when Rommel had surged forward with most of his armour hoping to relieve the besieged Axis positions and encircle the Eighth Army. The gunners' gallant spirit was demonstrated on the 27th, when Rommel struck 5 Brigade's headquarters at Sidi Azeiz. Gunners manning four portees, an 18-pr and three Bofors guns found themselves facing 40 tanks. The New Zealanders stuck bravely to their task as the guns were knocked out one by one:

> The No. 1 of P4, Bombardier [M.G.] Niven, directed the fire of his gun with remarkable aplomb, allowing three shots for each tank engaged and then switching to another until his gun was hit and its traversing and elevating gears wrecked. The other crews remained similarly steady in what ... all knew [was] a hopeless contest. ... The large gallery of spectators in the headquarters area ... marvelled at the parade-ground drill of the anti-tankers under such terrible fire.
>
> Niven strolled, with a deliberation thrilling and yet agonising to watch, to the other guns to lend a hand, helping the wounded aboard N4 and directing the driver to the [Advanced Dressing Station] within the perimeter. Then he brought the portée back into action with Gunner [A.D.] Hynes ... as driver. [T]he two of them ... got it back into action from a position abreast of Hargest's slit trench. The gun had had its sights shot off, the telescope smashed, and the semi-automatic firing gear [was] out of order. But with the help of a wounded gunner observing with binoculars, Niven fired seven or

eight more shots. 'I watched him load, aim, fire – load, aim, fire, time after time. ... Soon the enemy concentrated on him. His truck received a direct hit on one side, starting a fire, then another just behind the gun; a third struck the shield and shot the muzzle straight upwards where it remained pointing to the sky.' Niven then made his way to the nearest 18-pounder and stayed until it, too, was knocked out, then to a Bofors, and he joined E Troop of the 5th Field in its last agony.[67]

Indirect fire from four of 5 Field's 25-prs helped, but three of these guns were soon put out of action by fierce counter-battery fire. The surviving gun continued firing under the command of 5 Field's second in command, the parliamentarian Major A.N. Grigg, until it too eventually succumbed. Grigg was mortally wounded; he would later be recommended unsuccessfully for a posthumous VC. As one of the Bofors gunners remembered, 'the German tanks just concentrated on each of our guns, one at a time until, despite the desperate efforts of all concerned with the tanks only some two hundred yards away the Bofors on which I was, received a direct hit [which] split the barrel like a burst cigar'.[68] The survivors scrambled for cover, but the position was overwhelmed and they were soon captured, along with Hargest and the surviving members of his staff. Forty-four men had been killed and 49 wounded – most of them gunners – and 700 captured.

Sidi Rezegh

Sidi Azeiz was only the prelude to an even greater disaster. Late on 28 November the Afrika Korps surprised New Zealand infantry south-west of Sidi Rezegh, overrunning three depleted companies and capturing a portee crew. In confused fighting over the next two days the Divisional Artillery brought down concentrations on enemy forces attacking along the escarpment towards the key Point 175. At one stage, Brigadier G.H. Clifton's transport column was halted near 6 Field's positions when he spotted a German tank stalking a portee. 'I drove full speed over to the flank gun. ... "Shoot that bloody tank! It's a Jerry!" I yelled to the Number One. "Too bloody right!" he replied, and the layer started twiddling things. Before they could get a round away, the two-pounder swung quickly and hit the Panzer dead-centre at two hundred yards.'

'Advance into Libya': loading a 25-pr near Sidi Rezegh, December 1941. DA2276, Alexander Turnbull Library, Wellington.

Weir personally directed a troop of 25-prs in the destruction of three German tanks that materialised out of a cloud of dust. On another occasion he is said to have 'roared' to some of his gunners, 'Carry on! This position will be held until it's untenable!', only to be answered: 'Hell's flames! They're only a hundred and fifty yards away – when will it be untenable?'[69] At one point gunners grabbed small arms to drive the enemy out of a position near Divisional HQ. Once again, observation was difficult and units were not always identified in time to apply effective fire. Point 175 was lost after approaching enemy forces were mistaken for South Africans. There were also several friendly-fire incidents, with fire being brought down in error on the captured dressing station and possibly on a British armoured division nearby.

For 6 Brigade and 6 Field Regiment, problems of poor coordination and communication re-emerged with a vengeance on 30 November. The day began well with a concentration on Point 175 by 4 and 6 Field which scattered Italian vehicles and a regimental concentration by 6 Field saw off nearby tanks. The gunners of 6 Field fired throughout the day at enemy forces concentrating to the south-west, until an armoured assault on the 6 Brigade positions began about 4 p.m. The ammunition of 29 Battery was soon exhausted and by the time it was replenished, confusion at Divisional Headquarters had silenced 6 Field and held back from the escarpment the 18-pr troop and some of the 2-prs of 33 Anti-Tank Battery, as well as Bofors guns. For a critical period the anti-tank defence of the escarpment fell to eight 2-prs, six of 33 Battery and two of 65 Anti-Tank Battery, RA. Facing an onslaught by some 40 tanks, these guns were 'soon reduced to heaps of tangled metal, their gunners firing to the very last'.[70] Four more 2-prs were rushed up the escarpment, but these were also soon silenced. The enemy armour took hits but was undeterred, and the anti-tank gunners suffered heavy casualties. As the escarpment near the mosque at Sidi Rezegh was overrun, 24 and part of 26 Battalion were engulfed, along with the OPs of all four field regiments. When Weir was at last permitted to bring the weight of 6 Field to bear his guns did much damage, but at first also endangered captured New Zealand infantrymen.

During the night Weir moved his guns about 2 miles north towards Belhamed, out of mortar and small-arms range. He and Miles remained very concerned about the exposed position of his regiment and the scanty infantry defences on the 6 Brigade front, but were not permitted to withdraw to a better-protected position. Miles visited the corps headquarters in Tobruk, apparently to ask permission to withdraw the Division to Ed Duda. Instead he was told to await the outcome of an expected attack on Point 175 by a South African brigade. Meanwhile, the 25-prs of 4 Field successfully engaged Italian tanks and guns near Point 175, but 25 Battery came under heavy observed fire. By the time the guns were brought out of their exposed pits to take up anti-tank positions, all but two had been damaged.

6 Field's gunners were to be left exposed below Sidi Rezegh. As Weir would later put it, 'we gunners are defenceless folk and unless we have infantry protection we are liable to be shot up by small arms and as a consequence loose [*sic*] our guns'.[71] At dawn on 1 December there was uncertainty at the gun

line. Many guns were limbered in anticipation of withdrawal, and transport vehicles obscured and limited their arc of fire. A force approaching from the south was initially mistaken for the promised South African brigade. When it became apparent that it was German, the gunners frantically unlimbered their guns and positioned them for anti-tank action:

> Into our positions – scramble – load – crouching low behind the gun-shield – hard tin-opener faces and keen profiles of the tin-hats – in goes the shell, in goes the shell-case – slam the breech. … [N]o scrambling now, no ungainliness: no, we're home now. It's just a rhythm, a rhythm of arms and bodies and levers and instruments, flesh and steel, each man in his place, doing his job.[72]

By the time the attackers were identified, tanks and infantry were almost on the gun line of one of 30 Battery's troops. Two guns were destroyed after firing only a few shells; the other two fought on briefly. All four guns of another troop were quickly knocked out; the surviving crew members withdrew after removing vital parts. 'The small arms fire was heavy and vicious and to it was added mortars, field guns and tank guns. The dust and smoke was so thick that you couldn't see any more than 150 yards.'[73] A similar drama was unfolding at 47 Battery's position to the south-east. German tanks had been only 200 yards away when Weir telephoned a warning. Although some effective fire was delivered, the position was soon encircled by tanks and the guns overwhelmed by German infantry. A 48 Battery troop was also overrun. After a 29 Battery troop came under machine-gun and mortar fire, only one gun could be extricated when Weir ordered a withdrawal. The battery's other troop and a troop of 48 Battery, unable to identify targets on the smoke-covered battlefield, got all their guns out. While the surviving 48 Battery troop was sent to join 4 Brigade at Zaafran to the north, the five 29 Battery guns and three Bofors of 43 Light AA Battery headed west towards Tobruk.

As the Germans pressed forward against 18 and 20 battalions they encountered 31 Anti-Tank Battery, which soon suffered the same fate as 6 Field. A troop in front of 20 Battalion was quickly destroyed, the dedication of the gun crews epitomised by Bombardier F.S. Marshall, who continued firing until a tank crushed him and his weapon. The guns of the other two troops were overrun or disabled when continued resistance became impossible.

Both Miles and Weir were prominent on the battlefield. The former was wounded by a shell splinter, then captured when 29 Battery was overrun. The loss of the respected CRA was a serious blow. Wanting to be with his gunners in their desperate plight, and perhaps angered by the command decisions that had led to the fiasco, he walked forward to the gun line looking 'for all the world as if he were going duck shooting'. Miles' capture was mitigated to some extent by Weir's narrow escape after the last of the surviving guns had got away. He was to play an important role in rebuilding the battered Divisional Artillery.

This battle below Sidi Rezegh was the New Zealand Artillery's most tragic action: the losses to 6 Field (including 47 Battery, attached from 5 Field), the heaviest ever suffered by a New Zealand artillery unit, were 57 killed, 113 wounded and 96 taken prisoner. Of its 32 field guns, 23 were lost.[74] It was also its finest hour. A British artillery officer, Brigadier H.B. Latham, inspected the battlefield two days later: 'Practically every gun was a write-off. ... The dead were lying around each gun, each man nearly in his place and burnt out tractors and trailers ... just in rear. Here undoubtedly there had been no thought of surrender or withdrawal

46 Battery in action at Belhamed, November 1941.
Des O'Connor collection.

and all had died in the service of the guns.' Something 'quite out of the ordinary' had happened: 'a battle royal had taken place with the N.Z. guns which ended in the[ir] utter annihilation'. Latham picked up a rammer, had it inscribed and sent it to Freyberg as a memento of the action.[75] The 'Belhamed Rammer' is now one of the regiment's most treasured relics.

While this catastrophe was unfolding, the other guns of the Divisional Artillery were doing their best to disrupt the enemy's advance. 4 Field Regiment, reinforced by some of the guns pulled back from around Belhamed, shelled enemy positions in the area throughout the day. When the Germans attacked 4 Brigade in the evening, the gunners helped to blunt the advance despite suffering substantial losses, then pulled back in a pre-planned withdrawal. Several guns were destroyed by enemy fire and two others could not be extricated. The attack did not continue and the New Zealanders were able to withdraw towards the Egyptian border. By this time the Axis forces were also pulling back, though gunners near Menastir had to help repulse attacks as late as 3 December. For a few days Tobruk was again cut off, and remnants of 6 Field formed a composite field battery there. An ad hoc light anti-aircraft battery was also kept busy against German air attacks until 19 December. When the exhausted and depleted 5 Field arrived at Tobruk from Menastir with 5 Brigade, it was temporarily reformed under Major J.F.R. Sprosen, with men from all three field regiments forming five troops in two batteries. The reconstituted 5 Field, two depleted troops of 42 Light AA Battery and a troop of 1 RHA then joined 5 Brigade's advance to Gazala, the AA gunners managing to destroy four German aircraft. On the night of 16 December, the Germans and Italians withdrew from the Gazala line towards El Agheila. Over the next month the Axis positions holding out in the frontier area were mopped up; the last outpost, Bardia, fell on 17 January.

Over the festive season the gunners of 4 Field, camped at Baggush, celebrated their survival. On New Year's Eve 'it seemed as though we were in for a 5th November celebration. Rifles, mortars, Very pistols, anti-tank guns and even 25-pounders were fired at random – most of them out to sea, we hoped. The din was such that a brigade of Indians camped not far away "stood-to"', apparently thinking that 'the Huns were upon us'.[76]

Christmas dinner in North Africa.
Bert Dyson collection.

Operation Crusader ended with the Eighth Army in possession of the battlefield after suffering a series of tactical reverses, some of them disastrous. Tobruk had been relieved, but the cost had been high. The New Zealand Division's losses exceeded those in Greece and Crete combined. The Divisional Artillery lost 198 men killed and 326 wounded, while a further 223 (40 of them wounded) remained in captivity. Thirty gunners who had survived Sidi Rezegh and Belhamed lost their lives, along with 370 other Commonwealth troops, when the hospital ship *Chakdina* was torpedoed on 5 December while making for Alexandria from Tobruk.

The needless sacrifice at Belhamed was a costly lesson. The New Zealand gunners who took part in Operation Crusader showed great courage and devotion to duty, proved themselves technically proficient and inflicted much damage on the enemy. But time and again they were let down by poor intelligence, ill-conceived tactics and seriously flawed battlefield coordination that left guns firing under individual control.

The need to site the 25-prs well forward to fulfil their dual anti-tank/field artillery role had sometimes left them dangerously exposed. And while engaged with tanks they were in no position to provide close support for their infantry. As these lessons were absorbed and applied over the following year, the Divisional Artillery would be transformed from a corps of citizen soldiers into one of the most professional and operationally sophisticated elements of the Eighth Army.

> ### Painting Their Story
> In the centuries before photography, officers had to be able to make sketches in the field. The visual record of the New Zealand Wars owes much to military artists such as Major Cyprian Bridge (58th Regiment) and Lieutenant H.G. Robley (68th Durham Light Infantry); Royal Engineers officers took the lead in sketching enemy fortifications.
>
> New Zealand's first three official war artists were appointed in 1918. Among the 23 names forwarded by senior officers in response to NZEF Order 529 of 26 February seeking 'details about any artists under their command' was that of Gunner E.F. Hiscocks, then with 2 Entrenching Group. His commanding officer was happy to let him go – 'he is of no use as a soldier'. In October the NZEF's War Records Office, noting Hiscocks' 'undoubted talent', proposed to attach him to the artillery to record soldiers' 'life and work', but advised that he 'may perhaps need watching when in the proximity of Estaminets'. One of his sketches caricatures soldiers' thirst for women and alcohol. Hiscocks' posting to France was not approved.
>
> The reputation of New Zealand's gunner artists overcame this inauspicious start thanks to the commercial artist Peter McIntyre, who enlisted in 34 Anti-Tank Battery in England in 1939. He was appointed official New Zealand war artist in 1941, with the rank of captain, after the man earmarked for the job was captured in Greece. Paintings of German parachutists landing on Crete and the break-out at Minqar Qaim came to symbolise New Zealand soldiers' experience of the Second World War. Always conscious that he was producing his paintings above all for New Zealanders with family members in the services, McIntyre was effectively his own censor, 'filtering out most of the more brutal imagery associated with warfare'. His work received so much attention that on his return to New Zealand in 1946 he was able to become probably the country's only

Captain Peter McIntyre, gunner and official war artist, takes a break during Operation Crusader, December 1941. DA-02204, Alexander Turnbull Library, Wellington.

full-time painter; he was certainly the best-known. McIntyre repainted many of his works for a 1981 book, *Peter McIntyre: War Artist*, in which his adherence to the heroic tradition of military art was more explicit.[77]

In 2005 Matt Gauldie was appointed Army Artist for a term of three years. In homage to McIntyre he too was made a captain in the Royal New Zealand Artillery. During his first year in the job he painted a series depicting the return to New Zealand from France of the Unknown Warrior, and completed a twelve-week basic training course at Waiouru.

Alan Williams

Alan Williams succeeded Ike Parkinson as CRNZA in Army HQ in December 1939, and held this post for two years.[78] He had just returned from a two-year exchange with the Royal Australian Artillery and staff training in Sydney. (His opposite number in this exchange, Captain (temporary Major) F.N. Nurse, served as District Artillery Officer in Northern District and helped to plan and site Auckland's new fixed defences.)

Alan Williams' military career began in the Territorials, where he spent four and a half years in the ASC. An Auckland chemist, he was commissioned from the ranks into No. 5 Coy, NZASC, in January 1915, aged 22. He transferred to the New Zealand Field Artillery three months later and went to war as a temporary lieutenant, embarking with the Fifth Reinforcements in June. His promotion to lieutenant was confirmed the following March, and by January 1917 he was section commander, Brigade Ammunition Column. Promoted to captain, Williams was soon Section Commander Battery (in charge of two gun teams) and then Battery Captain (second-in-command), 1 Brigade. He then took charge of No. 5 Battery, 2 Army Brigade. Major Williams was one of two battery commanders wounded on 29 September 1918, when the brigade was attached to 63 Divisional Artillery, XVII Corps, for a push on the Escault Canal, south of Cambrai.[79] He was still in hospital when the war ended.

After the war Williams was appointed a DSO and mentioned in despatches. Struck off strength, he re-enrolled in the regular artillery after graduating from the GHQ School, Trentham, as a captain, RNZA. His first posting was in 1920 as FA Instructor, Wellington District and Adjutant to both D Battery and 5 Regiment. A year after marrying in 1922, he was transferred to Southern Command, where he had a variety of roles. He was Adjutant 3 Brigade NZA (1923–29) and, as major, Adjutant Southern Artillery Group (1928–29). In 1928 he also became OC RNZA Detachment in Southern Command, and he twice temporarily oversaw No. 10 Regimental District or 3 NZ Infantry Brigade. In 1937 he relinquished these posts to take up his exchange in Australia, where he attended the coast artillery short course and the command and staff course for majors. Having done well in these, he was promoted to lieutenant-colonel in April 1939 and returned to New Zealand at the end of the year.

During the early part of the war Williams was promoted to colonel, headed the Inventions Committee and went to Fiji to advise on the colony's fixed defences. After a preliminary trip in 1941, he was appointed in

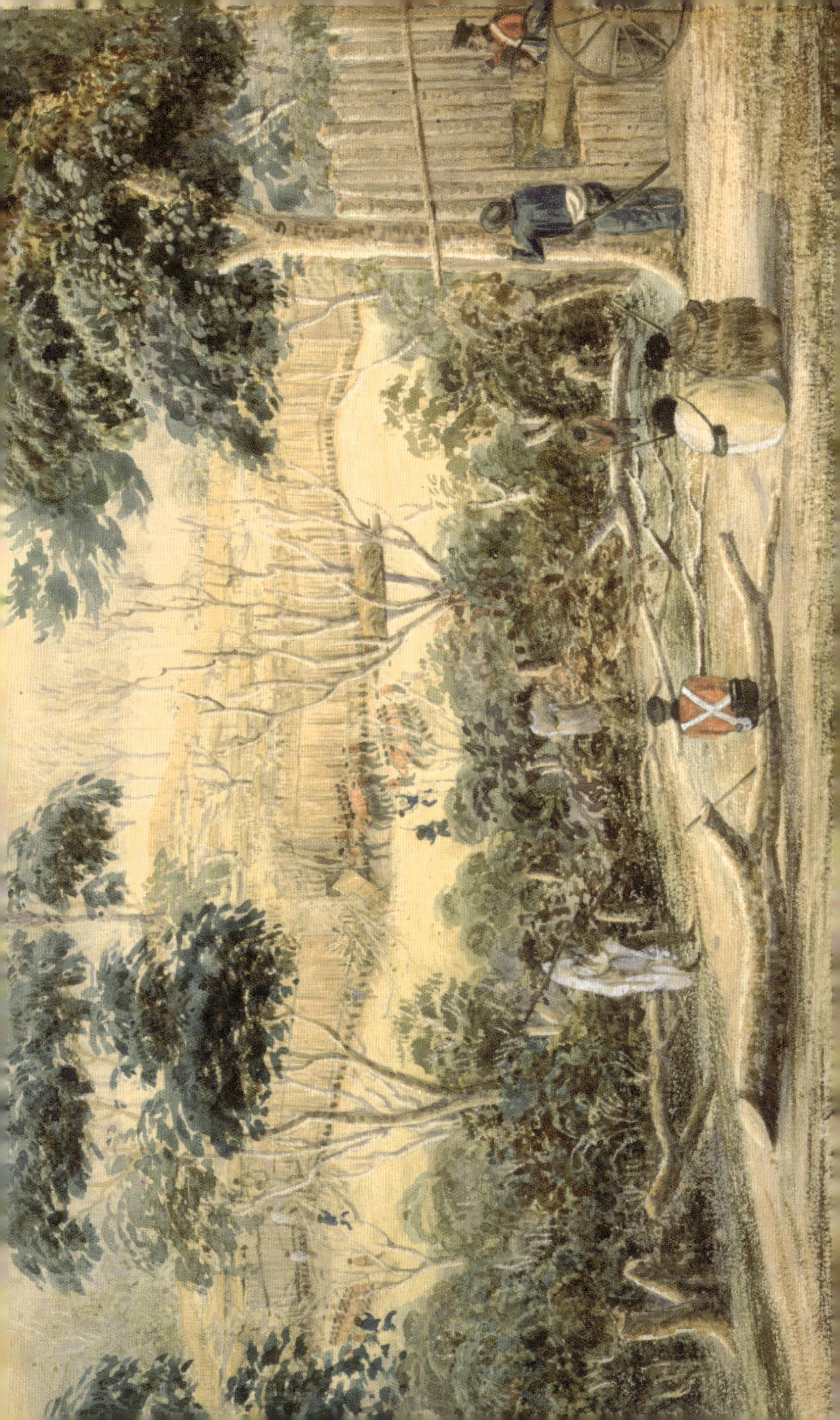

ABOVE
Artillery had to be mobile to be useful in most New Zealand Wars battles. This painting shows 6-pr Armstrong guns and Coehorn mortars at General Cameron's base at Patea, south Taranaki, 1865. Mortars were able to lob shells into low-profile modern pa that were hard to hit with field guns.
Joseph Hamley watercolour, Alexander Turnbull Library, E-047-q-050

PREVIOUS
The Northern War was a learning curve for British regiments not used to fighting sophisticated indigenous opponents. By the time of the attack on Ruapekapeka pa in January 1846, many lessons had been learnt. This painting of soldiers and Maori allies watching the final assault from the lower stockade was made by a British officer. Until battlefield photography became practicable during the American Civil War, officers were trained to sketch under fire.
Cyprian Bridge watercolour, Alexander Turnbull Library, A-079-007

The New Zealand Wars

Like the field force artillery after 1869, New Zealand's coastal defences did not fire a shot in anger. These 64-pr rifled guns were converted from elderly smoothbores. Rushed over from Sydney during the 1885 Russian war scare, they had been decommissioned by the time this tranquil scene on Auckland's Mount Victoria was painted in 1893. *Edward Payton watercolour,* Signal Station, Devonport, *Auckland Art Gallery Toi o Tamaki, 1924/3/3*

In November 1881, a decade after the New Zealand Wars ended, a 1600-strong force of Armed Constabulary and volunteer soldiers occupied Parihaka, south Taranaki. Led by the prophets Te Whiti o Rongomai and Tohu Kakahi, the 2000-strong community had been passively resisting the confiscation of land in the area for several years. A gun carriage lies abandoned in this painting by former Premier William Fox of the Armed Constabulary base at nearby Pungarehu.
William Fox watercolour, Alexander Turnbull Library, WC-024

Western Front

The First World War saw artillery duels on a previously unimaginable scale. Effective fire relied on accurate observation, which in flat country had to be made from the air or tall buildings. Pilots could report what they saw only after landing, so churches and windmills were favoured as observation posts – and key targets for enemy shellfire. This scene on the Somme was painted in 1918 by New Zealand's first official war artist.
Nugent Welch watercolour, An Artillery Outpost, Couralles Sailly Road, Archives New Zealand, AAAC 898, NCWA 413

OPPOSITE

Moving field guns in conditions such as those in Flanders in autumn 1917 was almost impossible. The Dunedin-born official Australian war artist Harold Power was renowned for his depictions of animals. This 1917 oil shows men and horses at the limits of endurance.
Harold Septimus Power, Bringing Up the Guns, Archives New Zealand, AAAC 898, NCWA Q 539

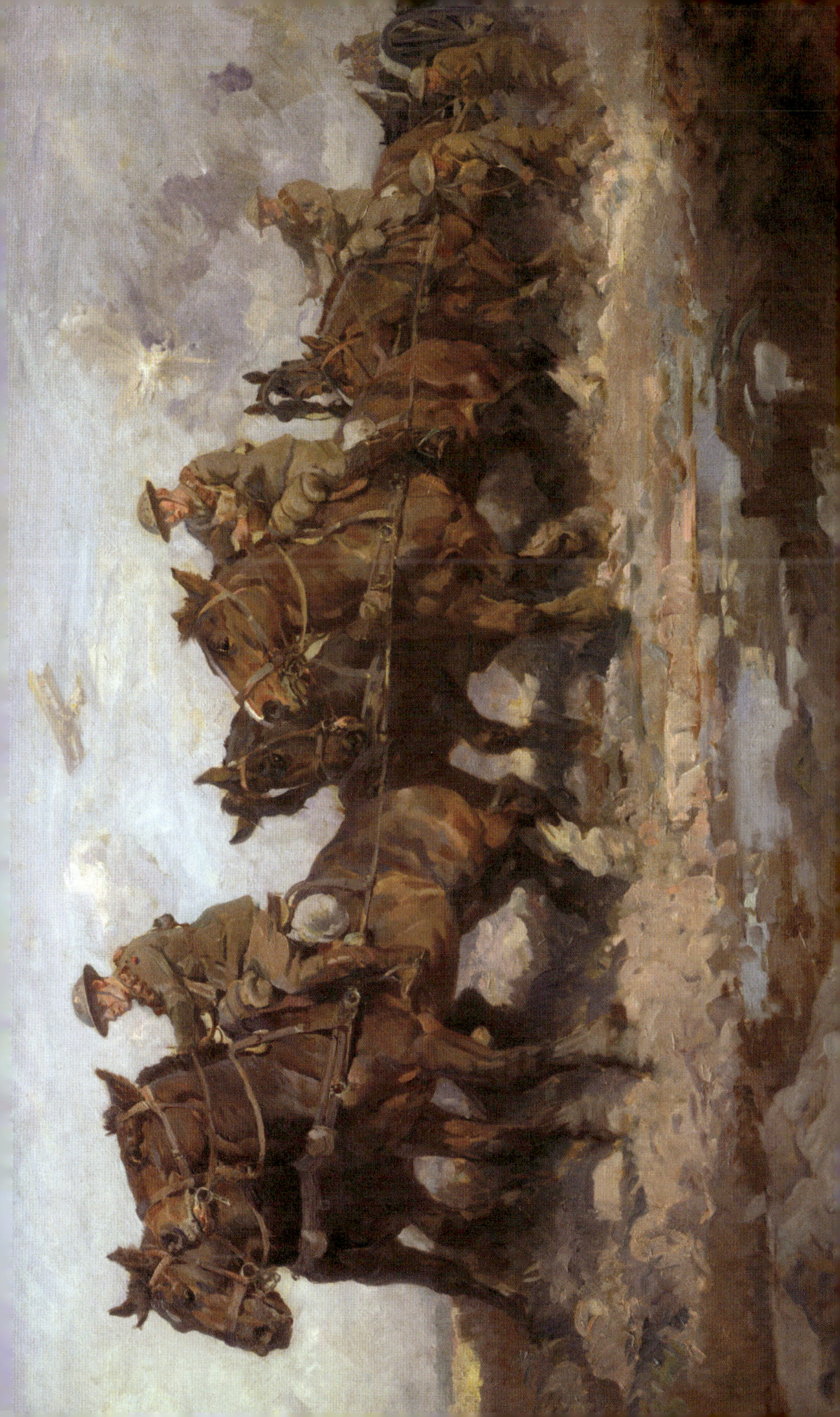

Heavy guns like this howitzer have almost totally destroyed this village on the Western Front.
Nugent Welch watercolour, Howitzer, 1918, *Archives New Zealand, AAAC 898, NCWA 422*

RIGHT
The idea that an oil painting provided the most fitting permanent image of an eminent individual survived well into the twentieth century. This 1919 portrait is of General G.S. Richardson, the wartime commander of the New Zealand forces in Britain. It is one of a series of portraits of New Zealand military leaders commissioned by the politician Robert Heaton Rhodes and Major-General Sir Andrew Russell. These paintings were later purchased by the government. The English-born artist, George Butler, had spent two decades in New Zealand before the war, and in 1918 he was appointed as an official war artist.
George Butler oil, Archives New Zealand, AAAC 898, NCWA 521

BUTLER 1919

Brigadier-General George Napier Johnston broods over a typical Western Front landscape in another portrait commissioned from Butler.
George Butler oil, Archives New Zealand, AAAC 898, NCWA 525

Greece and Crete, 1941

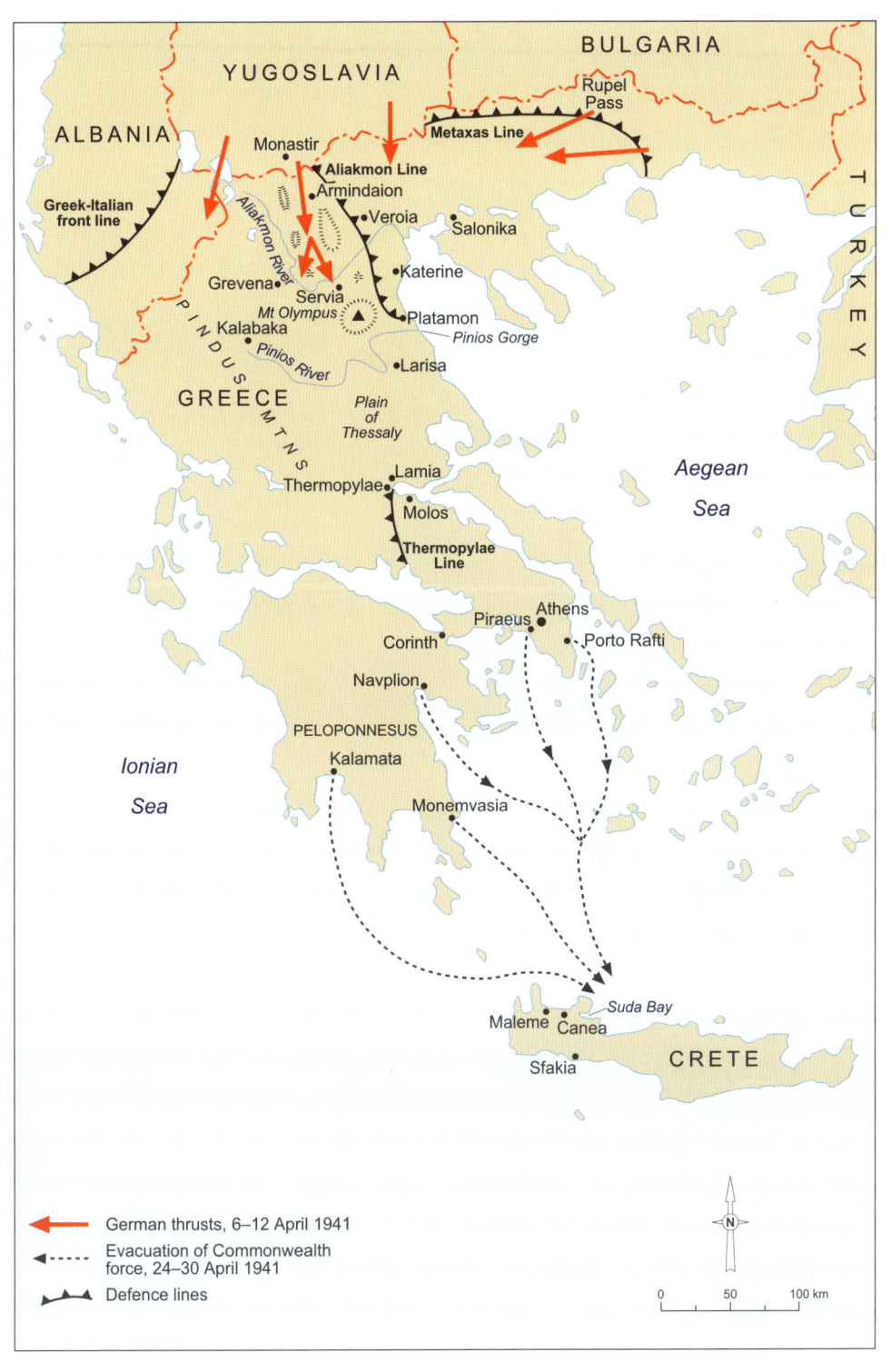

Like the rest of Lustre Force, artists moved fast in Greece. Artillery officer John Pine Snadden sketched this gun of C Troop, 5 Field Regiment, which was holding up the German advance south of Elasson, 18 April 1941.
Watercolour, Archives New Zealand, AAAC 898, NCWA Q143A

Artists were in even more danger on Crete. Lieutenant Snadden hurriedly sketched German parachutists landing at Maleme airfield on 20 May 1941 from his exposed gun position just two miles away. Snadden was wounded later in the day.
Pencil, Archives New Zealand, AAAC 898, NCWA Q148

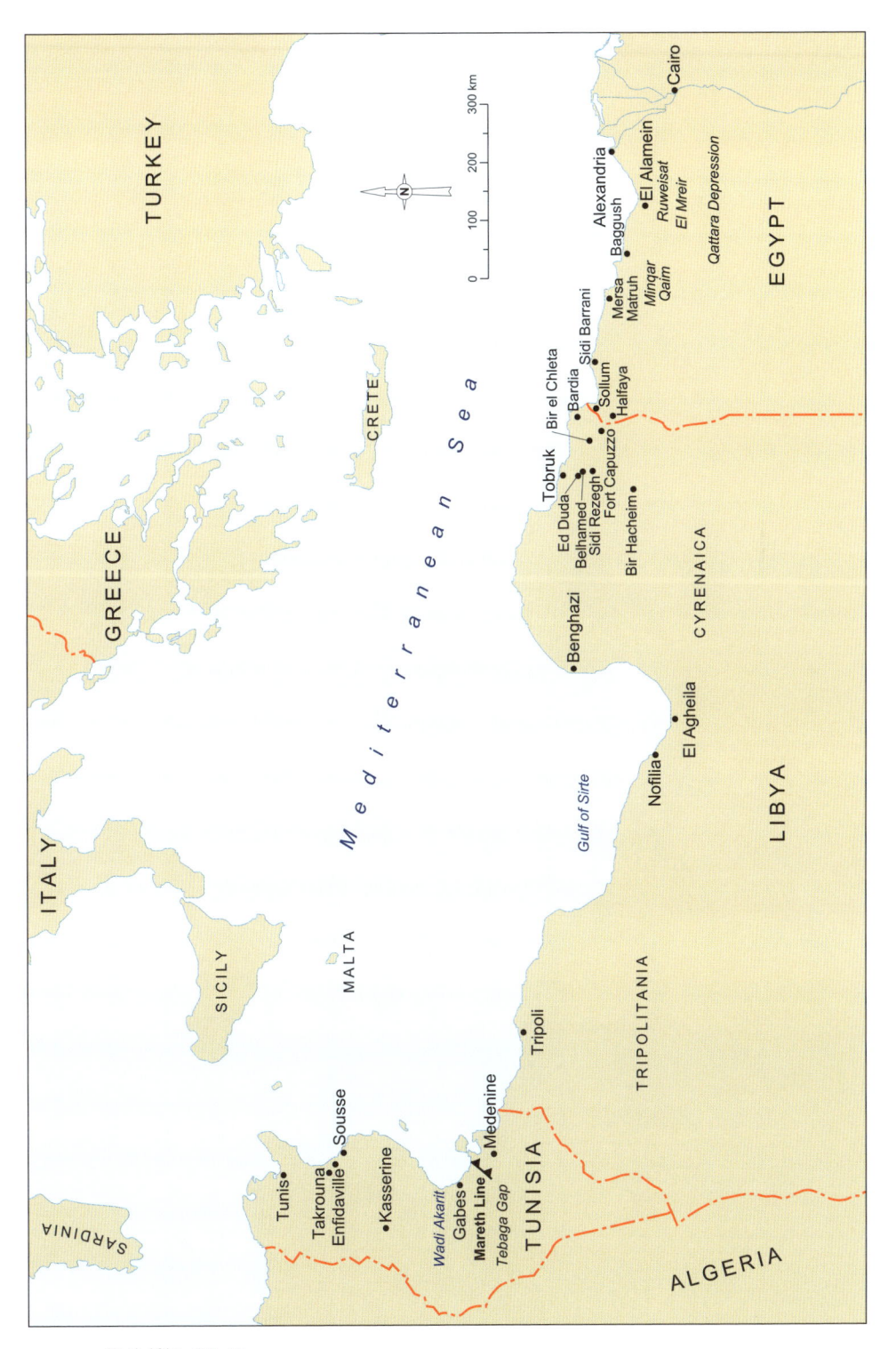

North Africa, 1941–43

Waging war in North Africa required mobility. Anti-tank guns were mounted on vehicles ('en portee') to keep up with their targets. Official war artist Peter McIntyre showed his flair for dramatic composition in this scene at Sidi Rezegh, March 1942. Oil, *Archives New Zealand, AAAC 898, NCWA 298*

OPPOSITE
Beauty can exist even in the midst of war, as this Snadden watercolour painted somewhere in North Africa shows. *Archives New Zealand, AAAC 898, NCWA Q094*

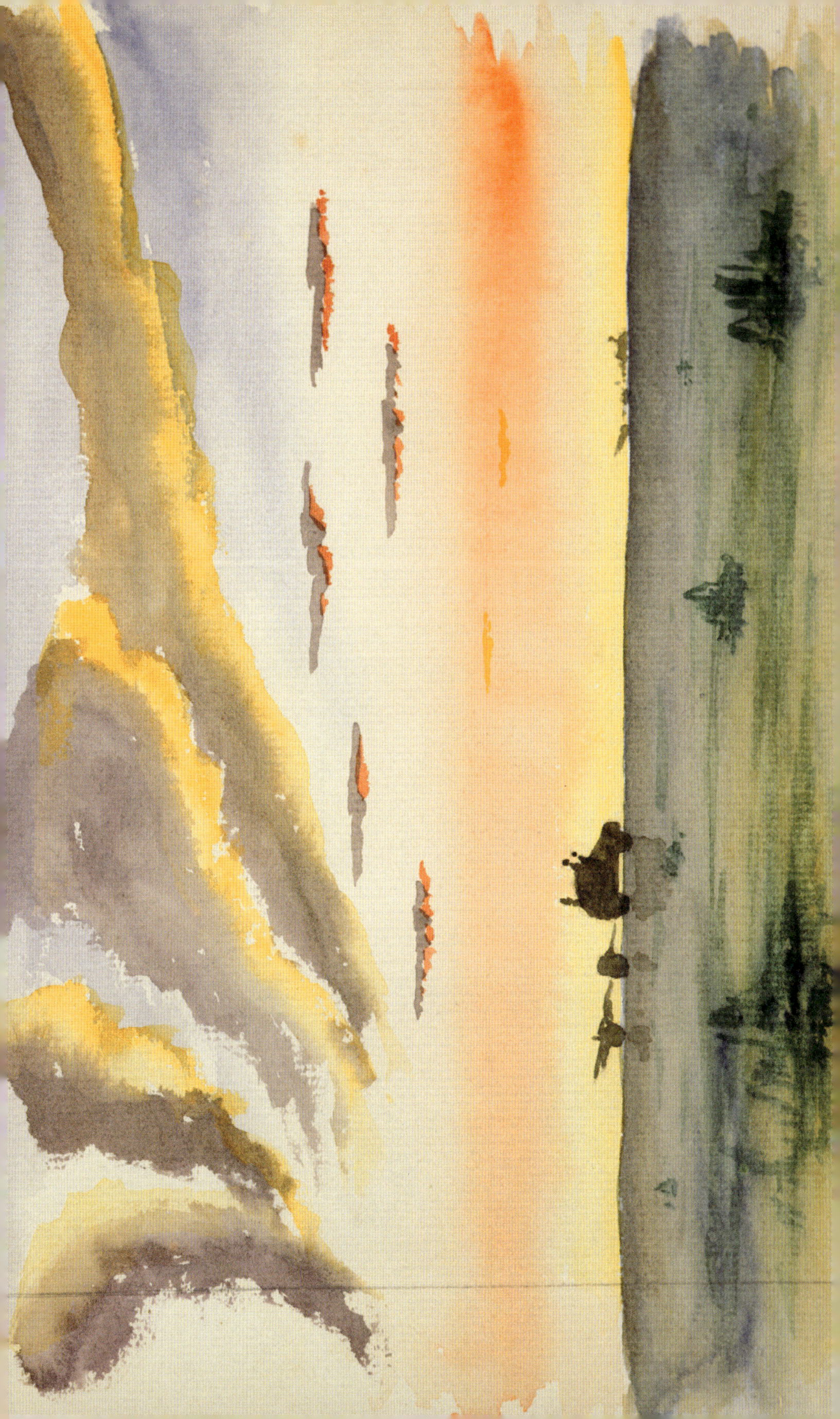

Peter McIntyre's pencil drawing, *The Gunner*, portrays the complex emotions of a man who has seen much.
Archives New Zealand, AAAC 898, NCWA 190

Accommodation in the desert was usually a tent. Gunner I. Pasmore seems at home in this 1942 watercolour by Auckland artist Jack Crippen.
Archives New Zealand, AAAC 898, NCWA 570

Italy, 1943–45

The 25-pr was the standard British field gun of the Second World War. This Peter McIntyre image shows a New Zealand gun crew in Italy, possibly near Cassino. *Archives New Zealand, AAC 898, NCWA 299*

Some 3 Division gunners obtained weapons – and much else – from their better-resourced American allies. This watercolour, 155 *Going Out*, was painted by official war artist Russell Clark.
Archives New Zealand, AAAC 898, NCWA 137

Brigadier C.S.J. Duff became CRA 3 New Zealand Division in August 1942 after distinguished service in Greece, Crete and North Africa. This oil painting is by official war artist Allan Barns-Graham.
Archives New Zealand, AAAC 898, NCWA 198

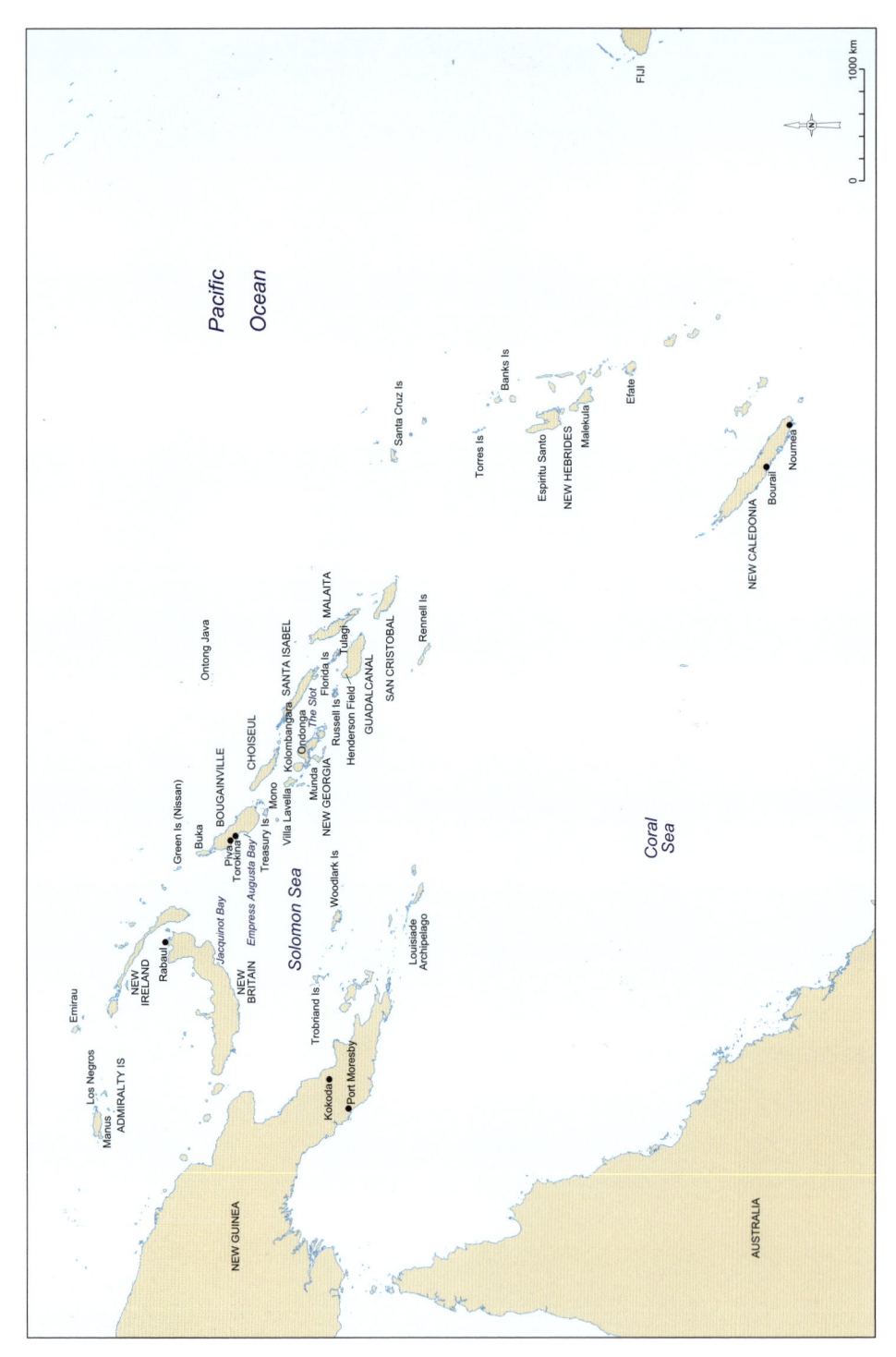

The Southwest Pacific, 1940–44

Korea, 1950–53

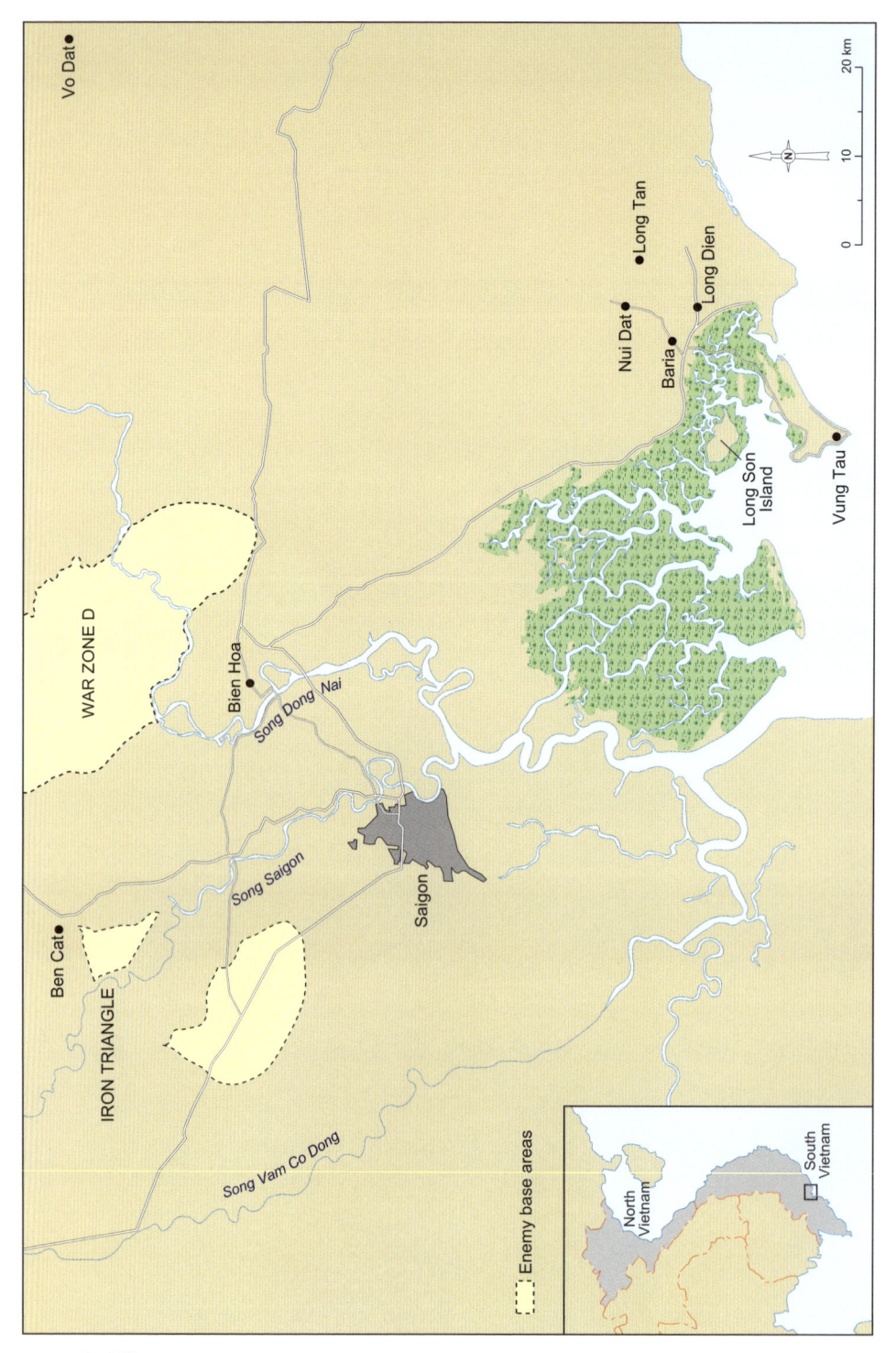

South Vietnam, 1965–71

New Zealand gunners fire M101 A1s in support of 9 Royal Australian Regiment. *Australian War Memorial, P00788.001.*

Manhandling an L5 howitzer into an M113 armoured personnel carrier was hard work under the tropical Vietnamese sun.
Roberts collection

A Mistral missile caught in flight an instant after being launched, late 1990s.
16 Field Regiment

This 105-mm light gun is about to be fired during Exercise Silver Warrior, Waiouru, November 2006.
16 Field Regiment

OPPOSITE
The first group of 16 Field Regiment gunners who served with the NATO-led Stabilisation Force in Bosnia, January to July, 1998.
16 Field Regiment

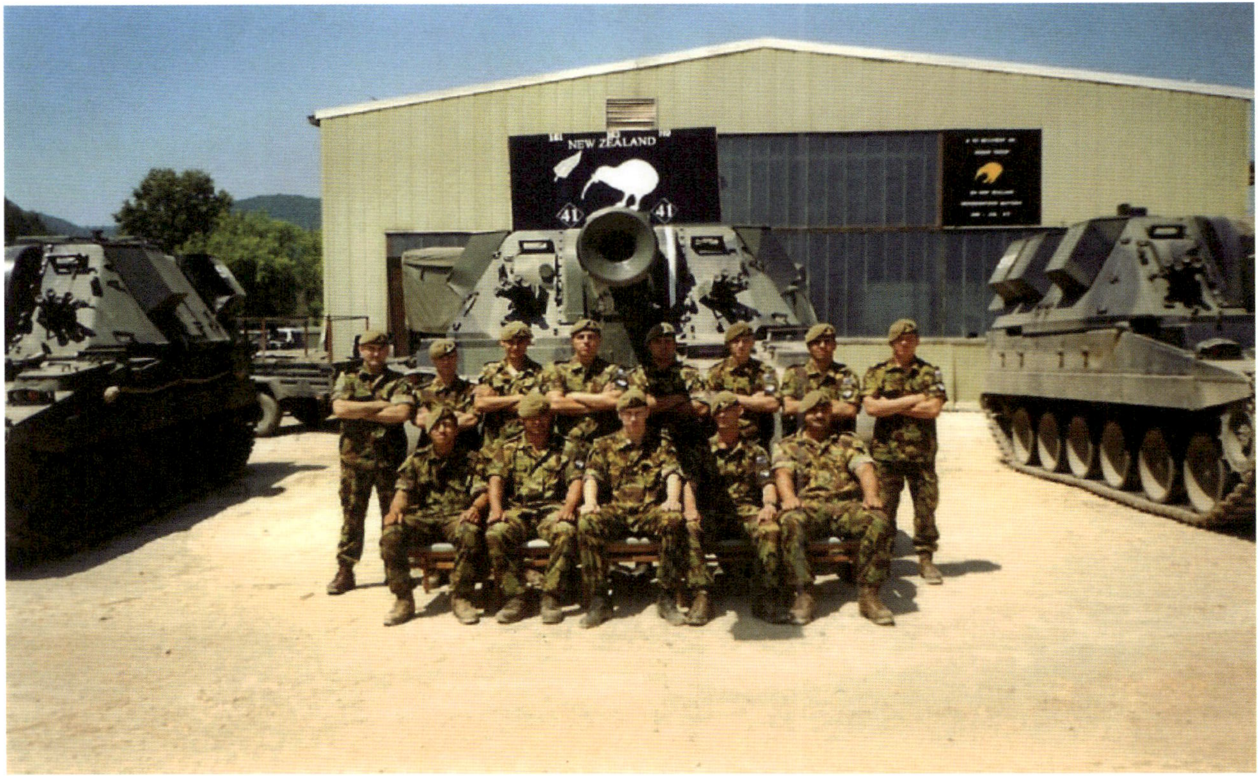
NEW ZEALAND
41
41

Queen Elizabeth II, the Captain-General, reviews the King's Troop Royal Horse Artillery in Hyde Park, London, on the occasion of their sixtieth anniversary, 26 June 2007. Behind Her Majesty is the Master Gunner St James's Park, General Sir Alex Harley KBE CB.
Ministry of Defence, UK (Army).

OPPOSITE
3 Battery patrol, East Timor.
RNZAF Official, via Air Force Museum, Christchurch

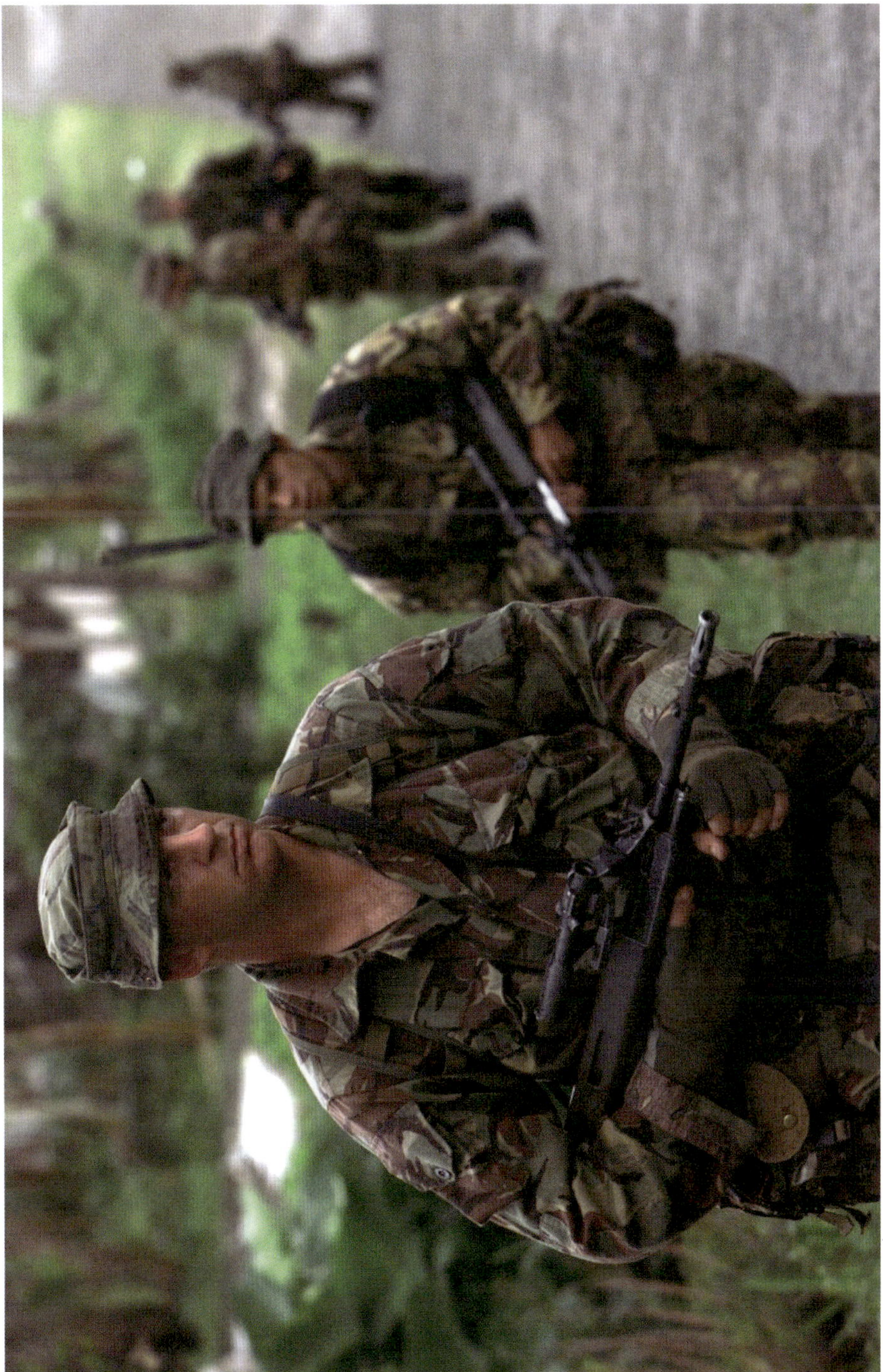

Lieutenant Sandra Weston RNZA explains an RPG-7 grenade launcher to Major Russell Croker RNZA at the Bamian range, near Kiwi Base in Afghanistan, June 2007.
16 Field Regiment

February 1942 as New Zealand Army Representative on the British Joint Staff Mission to the Far East Council in Washington. Now a temporary brigadier, Williams served in this capacity until October 1943. After a spell in Wellington Hospital he took command of Central District, and from March 1945 Northern District. He retired from this post in 1947 and died at Cambridge in 1958.

REGINALD MILES

Reginald Miles DSO and Bar, MC, ED, served with distinction in both world wars.[80] Born at Springston, Canterbury in 1892, his first military experience was as Second Lieutenant in the Rangiora High School Defence Cadets from August 1910. Leaving school for a cadetship at the Royal Military College, Duntroon, he graduated just as war broke out in 1914. Initially commissioned in the NZSC, he was soon seconded to 4 Howitzer Battery, NZFA. A forward observation officer at Gallipoli, he was wounded but returned just before the evacuation. Promoted to captain and having married in Egypt, he served on the Somme in command of 15 Howitzer Battery and won a Military Cross.[81] Moved to command 6 Howitzer Battery the following year, Captain Miles fought with his men when the Germans almost overran them in the Ploegsteert Wood in April 1918. He was wounded while attempting to extricate one of the howitzers from mud and rally nearby infantry. Recommended for a VC, he was awarded the DSO and saw out the war as Brigade Major, New Zealand Divisional Artillery.

Like other officers of the permanent force, he had a number of postings after the war. He was OC Harbour Defences Wellington in 1921, then Adjutant, 3 Brigade NZFA. Major Miles attended Staff College at Camberley (1923–26) before returning to postings in Auckland, rising to OC District and full colonel. From November 1937, he attended the Imperial Defence College and was then seconded to the War Office until May 1939. On his return to New Zealand he served briefly as General Staff Officer (Staff Duties) at Army Headquarters, then Quartermaster-General. This fitted him for the top job when the Divisional Artillery was being formed. On his arrival in Egypt by air on 1 March 1940, Brigadier Miles became Commander Royal Artillery, the standard British title for a divisional artillery commander. Two months later he was seconded to England, where from August to October he commanded the ad hoc body,

2NZEF (UK), that was formed when the Second Echelon became part of Britain's anti-invasion defences. While in Britain Miles lost his only son Reginald (killed in action on HMS *Glorious* off Norway), and, long since a widower with four daughters, remarried.

Reunited with his division in November, the 'intelligent and forceful' Miles built up the strength and morale of the artillery.[82] His leadership throughout the Greek campaign was solid, but he missed Crete owing to exhaustion and illness. During Operation Crusader he was wounded and captured when 6 Field was overrun near Belhamed on 1 December 1941. In the heat of the action he had joined his gunners carrying a rifle. After sixteen months incarcerated in Campo PG 12, near Florence, Italy, he and five other officers (all brigadiers or above, and much older than most escapees) got out through a 40-foot tunnel which had taken six months to dig.[83] Only Miles and Brigadier James Hargest reached neutral Switzerland, both receiving a Bar to their DSOs and the Greek MC (1st class).

Brigadier Reginald Miles.
2003.306, Kippenberger Military Archive, Army Museum Waiouru.

Aiming to rejoin the Allied war effort, Miles crossed Vichy France in disguise with the help of the French Resistance, and reached neutral Spain. He reported to the British consulate in Barcelona, which was preparing to get him to Gibraltar when he committed suicide. Miles was found hanged in his hotel room in Figueras on 20 October 1943.[84] He was just 50. 'Reggie Miles was an all-round gunner, interested and accomplished in every sphere of gunnery.... At all levels and in all units he was admired and respected and when he disappeared ... it was as if the Divisional Artillery had lost its father.'[85] Regarded as having died on active service, he was posthumously appointed a Commander of the Order of the British Empire in 1944.

6

Perfecting the Art: Syria to Trieste, 1942–45

At Christmas 1941, the Divisional Artillery was scarred and battered after the ordeal of Crusader. Many experienced personnel had been killed or captured, much equipment lost or damaged. As units reassembled, initially at Baggush, their depleted manpower was largely restored by reinforcements already in camp. These were now conscripts, volunteering for army service having been terminated in July 1940. Re-equipment would take longer, though it was supplemented by the salvaging of 34 damaged field guns from the battlefields.

Among the experienced personnel lost to the Divisional Artillery were not only the CRA, Miles, but also two regimental COs, Fraser of 5 Field Regiment, captured at Sidi Azeiz, and the popular Oakes of 7 Anti-Tank Regiment, killed on 30 November by German tanks on the Trigh Capuzzo. With Parkinson back in New Zealand, Weir was the obvious choice as CRA, despite his comparative youth. With his strong personality and physique, and deep booming voice, he was a commanding presence. Weir was succeeded as 6 Field Regiment's CO by his second in command, Lieutenant-Colonel 'Snow' Walter from Hamilton, and 'Gussie' Glasgow, 'that little fiery cocksparrow of a man',[1] was transferred from 14 Light Anti-Aircraft Regiment to command 5 Field. Lieutenant-Colonel Jack Carty, formerly BC of 41 Battery, took over Glasgow's old regiment, while Lieutenant-Colonel Jack Mitchell, formerly second in command of 4 Field Regiment, assumed command of 7 Anti-Tank. Lieutenant-Colonel 'Danny' Duff retained command of 4 Field.

Weir's recent experience left him in no doubt that the Divisional Artillery must lift its game to operate effectively on the modern battlefield. The

> ### A Sporting Chance
> As in the Great War, gunners needed little persuasion to play sport, and senior officers appreciated the boost to morale. In mid-1941, 36 Survey Battery played cricket against an RAF detachment at Amman in Jordan (they lost, having enjoyed strategically generous hospitality the night before). Rugby balls appeared as if by magic on one cold desert morning at the beginning of Operation Crusader. Later, some of the 'brigands' of the Syrian highlands were taught line-out drills. Wherever the Divisional Artillery paused, football fields soon appeared, constructed by pick and shovel and improvised graders towed by portees. Posts were improvised from railway sleepers or any other timber at hand; those at 4 Field's ground at Nofilia were the masts from a wrecked German ship. The sports facilities in Cairo were second to none. In the summer of 1943 there were multi-sport contests within the Division and with 6 South African Divisional Artillery (perhaps inevitably, honours in the latter were shared).
>
> Later, Italy provided better underfoot conditions than the desert. Hockey and cricket could be played in season, and horse races were fiercely contested by animals of dubious pedigree. In the last winter of the war there was a rugby tournament with the Freyberg Cup at stake. Football

opportunity to develop new techniques of fire control and coordination, and to train the many new personnel, came when most of the New Zealand Division was pulled out of the line and transferred to Syria to bolster the defence of the Middle East against a possible German invasion through the Caucasus. If the Germans did not come, the New Zealanders could readily be sent on to the new Pacific theatre. Though neither possibility was to eventuate, this sojourn was by no means wasted.

SYRIA

From late February units of the Divisional Artillery enjoyed a memorable journey to Syria; a holiday atmosphere prevailed as gunners briefly became tourists.[2] There were poignant reminders of the First World War, such as a memorial to New Zealand officers of the ANZAC Mounted Division near the Turkish border. The many ruined castles bore witness to earler conflicts. Along with the other units of their respective brigades, 4 Field took up defensive

matches against the Yugoslavs helped reduce the post-war tension in Trieste. Swimming, boating, yachting, tennis, boxing, cricket and athletics were all enjoyed during the gunners' last weeks there.[3]

Football in the desert, south of Bardia, November 1942.
Bert Dyson collection.

positions at Aleppo in the north, while 6 Field moved to the Djedeide fortress area in Lebanon's Bekaa Valley. After a frustrating time creating a fortress in the El Adem 'box', and amphibious training on the Suez Canal, 5 Field's gunners did not reach Djedeide until 23 April.

The New Zealand Division faced pressure from the Commander-in-Chief, Middle East, Field-Marshal Claude Auchinleck, to focus on operating at brigade-group level. Weir was instructed to disband the regimental HQ of 14 Light AA and incorporate its batteries into the three field regiments. He also feared for the future of 7 Anti-Tank as a unit capable of deploying its batteries in divisional orders of battle. Weir went to Freyberg with his case for divisional coordination of the guns. They were of one mind, and Syria allowed them to test the concept of the Divisional Artillery as a single operational entity.

The necessary exercises were carried out on the desert plain near Forqloss, east of the road between Aleppo and Baalbek. Starting with 6 Field and then from 24 May steadily adding other units, the techniques of divisional fire control were practised. Cross-observation between field regiments, air observation and coordination with infantry in advances managed by artillery fire-plans set the scene for the future successes of the Divisional Artillery. The terrain was 'not unlike Canterbury, burnt out. The heat was enormous. You couldn't rest on anything without leaving skin behind. Gunners didn't dare touch their guns or anything metal during the hot part of the day.' Graeme Hutcheson 'took a beer truck once to Damascus to get a load of some sort of beer with a mysterious name, which didn't improve my dysentery – but it was wet'. Opportunities to sample the local arak ('about 90% alcohol and 10% aniseed ... one of the most potent brews available') were seized.[4] As always, the soldiers made friends with local children. Those in the highlands also encountered 'wild men', recalled a 4 Field NCO. 'We had lots of robberies. They used to come in raiding parties until we tightened up our security. They had daggers in their belts.'[5]

7 Anti-Tank Regiment had received an initial supply of 6-pr guns, but it would be months before all its troops could replace their 2-prs. Some New Zealand gunners had seen this weapon at Aldershot in 1940, when it was still top-secret and code-named the 'Gibson Gun'.[6] As they became surplus to the anti-tank batteries, the 2-prs were handed over to the infantry to bolster their direct-fire capabilities. They 'still had a certain value but were rather ineffective in many cases'.[7] The 6-pr gun, on new Austin K portees, was a welcome – and overdue – response to the more versatile and heavy armour of Mk III and IV Panzers. On the negative side, a number of experienced men were sent home to stiffen the artillery of 3 New Zealand Division, being formed for service in the Pacific. There were many consequent promotions, but the new men had to be integrated into units.

MINQAR QAIM

The exercises at Forqloss were to stand the Divisional Artillery in good stead when the Division was hurriedly withdrawn from Syria in mid-June 1942.[8] Reverses inflicted on the Eighth Army in Libya by the Germans had placed Egypt and the Suez Canal in a precarious position. Once again, Tobruk was encircled (it would fall on 21 June), and the costly achievements of Crusader were negated.

Most of the New Zealand Division crossed the Suez Canal on 19 June after a headlong rush from Syria over rough roads. 'Guns towed by quads were bouncing about in spectacular fashion as they passed over bumps in the road, rising up and coming back down to earth twenty or thirty feet further on.'[9] For two days the Division was dug into positions around Mersa Matruh that were overlooked by a nearby escarpment – 'we looked on it as a sort of possum trap'.[10] They then moved 25 miles south to Minqar Qaim, where 4 and 5 Field were deployed forward with their respective brigades, and 6 Field with the Reserve Group. The anti-tank and anti-aircraft guns were distributed throughout the Division. In occupying the position at Minqar Qaim, the gunners' requirements were put first: at last Divisional HQ was learning that well-deployed and controlled guns could dominate the battlefield.

The anti-aircraft batteries were first into action, on 26 June, against a German medium bombing raid that did much damage and caused 62 casualties in the Division. The gunners claimed to have downed three Junkers 88s and would prove their effectiveness time and again over the coming days. Next morning, two troops of 30 Battery sortied forward to engage an enemy battery, tanks and troops passing to the north, but withdrew to their positions after a sharp action that knocked out a number of enemy tanks but cost the lives of five gunners. The rest of the day was memorable for artillery duels in which the New Zealand field artillery got the better of large numbers of enemy guns. Careful siting and flexibility of control meant the guns could be fired as soon as they were registered. German fire control, in contrast, was surprisingly ineffective.

During this action, another twelve 6-prs arrived and were immediately prepared for action. Within hours, the new guns, some still covered with a protective layer of grease, were firing against advancing tanks. The New Zealand Division had little difficulty holding its ground. The field and anti-tank guns dominated the battlefield, and along with determined infantry resistance and counter-attacks, the Division effectively threw back a Panzer division and supporting infantry. When 30 Battery under Major Ernie Lambourn engaged enemy tanks, there was a 'fire and leapfrog action, carried out in real horse-gunner style'. Tanks were set on fire but retreat became inevitable and the battery 'retired into divisional lines, amidst a cloud of dust and smoke'. At dusk a vehicle approached. 'As we could not see to whom it belonged nor could understand what was said we sprayed it with rifle and tommygun fire and it withdrew in a hurry.'[11]

After dark, with the New Zealand Division virtually encircled by the rapidly advancing enemy, withdrawal became an urgent priority. A ferocious infantry assault led the breakout; field guns and anti-tank portees brought up the rear and guarded the flanks. Several guns and vehicles were lost while driving through German positions during this 'spectacular and highly terrifying affair'. Only one troop of 48 Battery's 25-prs was called on to unlimber to punch a gap in the German line.

There were some lucky escapes during the breakout. 4 Field's Number 4 gun was hit, and the quad was put out of action. While some of the men scrambled onto other transport, Sergeant R.S. ('Stevie') Stevenson removed the dial sight to render his gun inoperable. In the dark this looked like a German stick grenade, and he was fired on by his comrades. 'He had to take cover. He was never captured, but eventually got out and rejoined us.'[12] The breakout succeeded and the Division, widely dispersed, made for Alamein. Minqar Qaim cost the gunners 236 casualties, including 46 killed, but astonishingly in the circumstances only 24 were captured.

Holding Actions

The Eighth Army now held a line deep inside Egypt based on a series of 'boxes' from which rather desultory sorties were made against probing enemy forces.[13] Having demonstrated the effectiveness of divisional co-ordination, the New Zealand command strongly opposed the policy of relying on boxes and mobile, independently operating 'Jock columns'.[14] However, the Division could not exclude itself from the Army's defensive plans, and elements of it took up positions at Kaponga Box, south of El Alamein.

When on 2 July the box at Deir al Shein to their north was overrun and an enemy force made for Ruweisat Ridge, two columns of New Zealand units headed for Alam Nayil to defend the ridge's eastern end. Combined under Weir's command they included, as well as infantry and cavalry units, 4 Field Regiment, a battery of 5 Field and five troops of 6-prs, with which 7 Anti-Tank was by now fully equipped. Next day Weir's gun group engaged units of the Italian Ariete Division, and when infantry units of 4 Brigade advanced they took large numbers of prisoners and captured most of the Ariete's divisional artillery, including four 25-prs which were taken over by 4 Field's gunners. The New Zealand reserve, 5 Brigade, for now including both 5 and 6 Field and anti-tank batteries, was called forward to pursue the retreating Italians. It halted near El Mreir Depression to engage in counter-battery duels with German guns to the north, then withdrew.

The gunners toiled strenuously over the following days, moving in and out of Kaponga Box as they were deployed to and from ever-changing positions towards Ruweisat. By 11 July, 4 and 5 Brigades, with 4 and 6 Field respectively, plus anti-tank batteries, were near Alam Nayil, poised for an assault on Ruweisat (5 Field was in reserve with 6 Brigade). After two days of heavy artillery action the infantry advanced towards the ridge, meeting heavier-than-expected resistance at the extreme range of the New Zealand field guns. 33 Anti-Tank Battery, advancing with the infantry, suffered heavy losses from mortar and tank fire, but 31 Battery was driven back only after inflicting losses on the German armour, at the cost of two guns. For 28 Battery:

> the next few days were a bit of bedlam. We had moved south-east from Kaponga Box ... and ... as the enemy caught up it was often hard to tell who was friend or who was the opposition. We moved in circles and ... shot completely round the clock, 360 degrees. We had been training to shoot as a division but here we were again, splitting ourselves into penny packets. ... We had many breakdowns during the march, mainly broken springs and burst tyres but our faithful LAD were there to ... get things going, while some vehicles drove a good part of the way on run-flat tyres.[15]

Meanwhile, coordination between field guns and infantry was breaking down as bypassed German units behind the lines disrupted communications, and because of attacks on the observation posts at the front. As the German counter-attack developed the field guns were moved to new positions, but many infantry units were overwhelmed. Most of the personnel of 4 Brigade were captured. The only bright spot in this disastrous battle was the heavy toll of German aircraft taken by the ack-ack gunners defending the field gun positions. The New Zealanders consolidated their position over the following

> ### HEALTH HAZARDS
> Bert Dyson lost 2 stone after contracting hepatitis A at Ruweisat Ridge. There were latrine holes everywhere, and flies moved straight from decomposing bodies to mugs of tea or food, so it was scarcely surprising that men fell ill, especially when they were dug into fixed positions for some time. Dyson's illness may have been a blessing in disguise: his replacement would be killed at Alamein. Dysentery and 'desert sores' which attracted flies were other common afflictions. Bert Hutcheson was one of many to suffer amoebic dysentery for months before it was diagnosed. Until then 'they just said it was "the runs"'. It took him years after the war to get over it.[16]

days, with the remnants of 4 Brigade withdrawing to Maadi and 6 Brigade coming forward. By 16 July the gunners of 4 and 6 Field, along with 64 Medium Regiment, RA, were firing effectively on the south of the ridge, and the enemy advance halted.

On 22 July, 6 Brigade attacked north-westwards towards El Mreir, supported by a very heavy artillery barrage from all three field regiments, 64 Medium Regiment and an RHA battery. In total nine field regiments were involved in coordinated firing as part of a wider operation, but the infantry attack was met by heavy armoured and infantry counter-attacks and bombing raids, and the assault on El Mreir faltered. Lack of armoured support and a breakdown of communication with the supporting artillery again left the infantry vulnerable; casualties were heavy and around 1000 men were captured as their positions were overrun. The anti-tankers also fared badly: eleven 6-prs were lost.

As the front stabilised in August, the field gunners conducted increasingly sophisticated counter-battery programmes. Weir took the opportunity to refine divisional control of his field regiments, which were now placed 'in direct support of' their respective brigades, under divisional (CRA) command. Artillery coordination at corps level was also improving, as were the prospects for better battle coordination. On such matters, new Eighth Army commander Lieutenant-General Bernard Montgomery agreed with Freyberg and Weir.

When the enemy advanced again on the night of 30 August, 4 Field

> ### Into – and out of – the Bag
> John Rutherfurd of F Troop, 32 Battery, was captured during the attack on El Mreir:
>
> 'At first light the Germans attacked with tanks. They quickly overran our position, and all my guns were knocked out. David Holt [commanding H Troop] and I were both wounded and taken prisoner. The German tanks came right up to us, and machine guns were firing in all directions. We had no option but to surrender, and the tank commander came past me and said, "Get going", because they marched prisoners back to the rear. We knew that if we got as far back as that we'd be kept prisoner. We were lightly wounded – Holt had a machine-gun bullet through his knee, he was pretty bloody. So we stayed in this area, even though it was very dangerous. We had a number of badly wounded with us and we popped them into slit trenches, but the shelling continued from both sides, and we were sort of caught in the middle all day. The Germans really didn't take much interest in us, they were too busy trying to keep out of trouble themselves.
>
> '[6 Brigade's Commander] Brigadier Clifton was with us and was also captured – he'd tossed his [peaked] hat away and kept up the morale of the stretcher-bearer looking after the wounded. Holt and I talked to him at the end of the day and said we were going to make a break for it, and he said, "I'll do the same". Holt said, "We'll come with you", and he said, "I'll go on my own". He realised that Holt would be a handicap. We made our way slowly because we kept running into pockets of Germans – we could hear them talking. Fortunately, although the Germans took my revolver and binoculars and things, they left me with my prismatic compass. Using the compass and the stars, we knew roughly where we should be heading. We continued until about 5 in the morning, and we were still in No Man's Land. We saw a tank which belonged to the Indian division, and we made a dash for that and they took us down to the New Zealand Division. So I was only a prisoner for one day.'[17]

supported an Indian division to the north, near Ruweisat. When it became clear that the main attack – which led to the Battle of Alam Halfa – was actually to the south of the New Zealand box, 5 Field fired heavily into Deir el Angar. The following day 14 Light AA fought against a series of Luftwaffe raids, claiming six aircraft. The New Zealand field gunners destroyed a number of tanks and vehicles in enemy columns advancing to their south. An expected assault on the

> ### CREEPY-CRAWLIES
> 'Flies were desperate for moisture, and they went for armpits or the marmalade on your dry biscuit. We'd run into the wind eating, with a swarm of flies behind us. We used Italian groundsheets which we could button together and form a sort of tent. It was terribly hot in there, but we took turns to have half an hour's relief from the flies.' With flies also attracted to desert sores:
>
>> We were issued with gloves and netting for the head, so we could play cards. Then we were issued with arsenic and we put a wick in it [to make a candle]. These flies would take one swish of this, go up, and drop – it was that quick. And just for something to do, we drew around this tent a target pattern on the ground, the inner, outer, and so on. And we used to bet on how many would be in the inner, on the outer, etcetera, after a certain period of time. The things you'd do to keep yourself amused. ....[18]
>
> Effective flycatchers were improvised from petrol tins – but there were 'always plenty of reinforcements'. The face-nets were 'hoods made of cellular material, with celluloid eye-pieces. They are very grotesque looking, but they do a good job.' Fleas, lice, mice, scorpions, lizards and asps were other hazards in North Africa.[19]

New Zealand lines did not materialise, and when the enemy offensive faltered a counter-attack southwards towards Deir El Munassib was planned to cut off their retreat. When this began on the night of 3–4 September it was supported by more than 100 25-prs of New Zealand and RA regiments, plus 7 Medium Regiment, RA, all under Weir's command. The fire of these massed guns proved highly effective, but as the infantry advanced they met stout resistance in a confusing night battle; the anti-tank batteries with the infantry also suffered losses. Though the counter-attack failed to achieve its goal, the gunners could now enjoy some well-earned leave in Cairo and Alexandria, as their units were relieved in the line by Royal Artillery regiments.

El Alamein

With the enemy now hamstrung by lack of supplies, and the Eighth Army building up reserves of men and equipment, particularly armour, preparations began for a major assault on the Axis forces.[20] Despite some resistance, Freyberg urged that the attack begin with a creeping barrage, so on 27 September the Division carried out a full-scale exercise to test the concept. Weir and his staff prepared a barrage trace and the timetabled cooperation between artillery and infantry worked well. For the first time, Bofors guns firing tracer were used to mark the brigade and divisional boundaries to be maintained during the advance.

Bofors with gun crew, El Alamein, July 1942.
DA-02575-F, Alexander Turnbull Library, Wellington.

Food in the Desert

The quantity and quality of food varied with distance from base and nearness to combat. Cheese and crackers, and tinned bully beef, were staples.[21] All Army cooks had to pass a course at Maadi, but this was no guarantee of quality fare when circumstances required improvisation. Gunners were often left to their own devices:

> In 'truck cooking', cook was the driver if the wagon lines were near the gun position. We had bully beef and M&V – meat and vegetables in a tin – a great luxury! We used to mix them up and heat it in a primus, but he couldn't heat it after dark because that showed a light. He had to stir it to stop it sticking on the bottom, and that's when the flies would go in. Cook never told us how many there were, but we always ate it after dark. They were well cooked.[22]

Food was an obsession for many in the desert. When the YMCA set up a canteen near a 25 Battery troop, the men stocked up. In the artillery, maintaining a truck larder was 'a most absorbing hobby'. Boxes – empty ammunition charge cases were favoured – were used to store 'tinned foods sent from home by thoughtful parents, together with other commodities purchased by subscription'. Such provisions supplemented desert rations of bully beef and biscuits.[23] Some gun crews clubbed together to buy treats – split peas, salmon, dates – to augment the tinned coffee and milk and cakes men were sent from New Zealand.

14 Light AA's Fritz Harris had his own technique for making breakfast from biscuits when porridge was unavailable. 'I put several packets in a sandbag and place on a board on ground and get Fin to run over them with his truck. After a time I take them and pour into a fly net', through which the crushed biscuits were strained to make a porridge substitute. On the Alamein Line, Allan Boyd breakfasted on a mixture of porridge and bacon that he remembered as 'great food'.[24]

In less harsh environments, more varied produce was often available through bargaining with locals. In Syria, Bombardier L.W. (Mac) McBeath enjoyed 'bully and prunes, onions and rice, porridge and eggs [some with chickens inside], herrings and carrots, watermelon and apricot'.[25]

In mid-October the New Zealand Division moved forward to the Alamein line; the gunners dug in and camouflaged their positions. The gun crews rehearsed the fire-plan repeatedly. Abundant supplies of ammunition were stockpiled. More than 660 rounds were brought up to each field gun's position by night, dug in and camouflaged; there was a further 720 rounds per gun at the wagon lines, and thousands more at dumps to the rear. The New Zealand Division and the attached British 9 Armoured Brigade would advance on Miteiriya Ridge. While 5 Field Regiment supported 5 Brigade on the right, 6 Field would support 6 Brigade, and 4 Field would contribute to the barrage over the whole sector before advancing in support of 9 Armoured Brigade. A battery of 7 Anti-Tank would advance with each brigade, and the fourth battery deployed with the Divisional Reserve. The Bofors gunners of 14 Light AA were positioned near the field batteries covering gaps in the minefield. All 30 Corps' field and medium guns – 480 in total – would come under the CCRA's control for the preliminary fifteen-minute counter-battery concentrations and the first stage of the barrage, up to the first 'lift', then revert to divisional control to support the infantry assault. Three troops each from 78 and 98 Field, RA, and a battery of 69 Medium would also support the advance of the New Zealand Division. Weir would have 104 field and medium guns under his command. Even so, the length of the New Zealand front (from 2500 yards to 4500 yards at the objective) made a full-scale creeping barrage throughout the advance impracticable. Instead, a series of timed concentrations would cover the advance.

At 9.40 p.m. on 23 October the stillness of the desert night was broken abruptly. The ground shook, the sky was lit up and the air reverberated with the sound of hundreds of guns; low cloud reflected the myriad flashes. This greatest Allied barrage since the Somme was an unforgettable spectacle, but those at the gun line had little time to enjoy it. The barrage gun programmes 'ran into several sheets' and required close scrutiny from the sergeants. Men laboured 'to keep up the supply of prepared shells and, at the same time, to keep the gun pits clear of empty cartridge cases and boxes. It was killing work.'[26]

The counter-battery concentrations went according to plan and met little response. After a five-minute pause, the lifting barrage and timed concentrations began. The infantry assault also went to plan, except that 23 Battalion got ahead of the barrage; three of its headquarters staff were wounded before this was rectified. Around 2.30 a.m the barrage ceased, though concentrations were fired for some time afterwards. The Division's field guns had fired an average of 630 rounds each, and most of the exhausted and undermanned gun crews took a well-earned rest, content that 'we were getting our own back'.[27]

The New Zealand advance took almost all its objectives, and the gunners of 4 Field Regiment, 31 Anti-Tank and 41 Light AA batteries now moved forward to support 9 Armoured Brigade as it attempted to break out from the new front line. The guns were moved slowly forward through the gaps in the minefields. By dawn 4 Field was dug in under Miteiriya Ridge, its OPs in armoured vehicles with the tanks, or in unarmoured vehicles following behind; the other field regiments and 69 Medium had established OPs along the ridge. The gunners deployed forward were briefly troubled by enemy infantry, but shelling of 4 Field's positions killed ten men and wounded 21. Nevertheless, from dawn on 24 October all the New Zealand field regiments hit numerous targets and supported the infantry exposed on Miteiriya Ridge. The anti-tank batteries also dug in on the ridge, though their positions too were far from ideal, and the many mines surrounding their shallow gun pits further hampered their work.

The advance of 9 Armoured Brigade was held up by strong anti-tank positions beyond Miteiriya, so a heavier armoured assault was attempted that night. Two armoured divisions and 9 Armoured Brigade moved through the minefields and beyond the New Zealand Division and the Highland Division on its right. A heavy creeping barrage was fired in front of the armour, but there was confusion as a mass of tanks and vehicles picked their way through minefields under shellfire and air attack. By morning the attack had stalled. 4 Field was kept busy with supporting fire tasks. 31 Anti-Tank Battery, operating forward with 9 Armoured Brigade, suffered heavy losses from mortar fire and shelling. The armoured attack in front of the New Zealand sector was called off, and that night 9 Armoured dug in with the New Zealand infantry while the other armoured units moved north to attempt a further advance.

The following days saw frequent and generally successful shelling of groups of enemy troops and vehicles, including tanks, in front of the New Zealand line. For the New Zealand field gunners the last major action of the 'Lightfoot' phase of the Alamein battle was a highly effective divisional creeping barrage fired by the 72 guns of all three field regiments in support of an attack by two battalions on 26 October. Once again, there were some casualties but the numbers of prisoners captured with relatively little resistance showed the impact the shelling was having on the enemy.

Next day the position was consolidated, and 5 Field's guns saw off a sortie towards Miteiriya Ridge by eighteen enemy tanks. That night the New Zealand field regiments were relieved by South African units, and with 14 Light AA Regiment and 34 Anti-Tank Battery they moved north to support 9 Australian Division. The other New Zealand units were pulled out of the line. For the New Zealand artillery, casualties in the Battle of Alamein were relatively light: the fighting on Miteiriya Ridge had killed 28 gunners and wounded 68. But their work had borne fruit. Rommel's ADC later acknowledged that the counter-attack on Miteiriya, 'which Rommel directed in person, was smashed up by our old enemies the medium bombers and the 25-pdrs'.[28] The main sector of attack now shifted to the north where, on the night of 28 October, the New Zealand guns under Weir supported an Australian attack intended to cut off enemy strongpoints. The attack faltered and was called off before the New Zealand gunners had executed much of their fire plan. When the anti-tankers of 34 Battery moved into gun pits vacated by the advancing Australians they were soon subjected to accurate shelling. Then a Scorpion mine-clearing tank accidentally drove over one of the gun pits and an Australian Bren-gun carrier mistakenly attacked another New Zealand gun crew, killing one gunner and wounding another. The anti-tankers were pulled out on 30 October but the field gunners stayed behind to back a renewed Australian advance, firing a complex series of concentrations from 10 p.m. into the early hours. This attack succeeded with the exception of a strongpoint that was shelled further during the day.

Operation Supercharge

Operation Supercharge, the next attempt at the breakout from the Alamein Line, was appropriately named.[29] The plan included a prominent role for the New Zealand Artillery and a particularly heavy concentration of field guns under Weir's command, plus three medium regiments under the Commander, Corps Medium Artillery (CCMA). The whole operation, to take place between the 9 Australian Division positions and Miteiriya, was placed under Freyberg's command. Two British brigades would carry out the initial assault; the New Zealand infantry would be reserved for the pursuit. With one 25-pr for every 20 yards of the front, Weir was able to plan both a full-scale creeping barrage over a 4000-yard front and an initial advance of 4000 yards.

The crushing barrage opened at 1.05 a.m. on 2 November. Though perhaps less impressive than that for Lightfoot, it was much more concentrated. By the time the barrage reached its final objective at 3.40 a.m., 152 Highland Brigade had advanced successfully, but on the right 151 Brigade was struggling forward through minefields, small-arms fire and shelling, leaving the New Zealanders of 34 Anti-Tank Battery exposed as they hurried forward. The armoured units had not passed through the final objective as planned but clustered hesitantly, and the second barrage was postponed until 6.15 a.m. In the meantime the British tanks and other vehicles attracted shelling from German 88-mm and field guns, endangering the New Zealand anti-tankers at the front line. The 88's muzzle velocity was so high that its targets heard 'the shell exploding, the shell coming to you, the gun firing – in that order'.[30] The New Zealanders lost some men and guns but also scored several successes against the 88s. One troop of 34 Battery had a series of collisions in the swirling dust that enveloped its advance with the armour; three of its four guns were put out of action.

The armour advanced as planned behind the second barrage, but still faced stiff opposition. Despite communication difficulties, this opposition was gradually overcome, and later in the day the gunners inflicted heavy losses on counter-attacking German tanks, enabling the infantry to achieve its objectives. In the early hours of 4 November, Weir used the three New Zealand field regiments to carry out a further creeping barrage. By the morning of the 4th it was clear that Supercharge had breached the enemy front; once their counter-attacks were driven back, Rommel's forces retreated rapidly. By noon the New Zealand Division and other elements of the Eighth Army were in hot pursuit. Command arrangements for the New Zealand Divisional Artillery were now readjusted: the field regiments were placed 'under command' rather than 'in support' of their respective brigades. Despite this decentralisation of control, Weir was still able to call up divisional concentrations if necessary, as he did on the 5th against a German gun line that then quickly withdrew.

For the gunners and the rest of the Division, pursuing the enemy along the coast road was an exhilarating experience, despite a series of clashes and some casualties. On 8 November 6 Brigade reached Mersa Matruh, where it was to rest for two weeks. The rest of the Division continued on to Sidi Barrani and Sollum, storming Halfaya Pass on the night of the 10th and opening the road through Sollum Pass two days later. By now their supply lines were overextended, and most of the Division paused at Sidi Azeiz to enjoy the satisfaction of victory and the retaking of territory familiar from earlier, unhappy battles. The enemy continued to fall back. Elements of the Eighth Army captured Benghazi on 20 November, and the Axis retreat ended only when it reached the defensive position of El Agheila.

The reinvention of divisional and corps artillery control initiated by the New Zealand Division and adopted throughout the Eighth Army was a major factor in the victory at Alamein. Weir and his gunners had proven themselves the equal of any British units and could look forward with confidence to the next stage of the campaign.

To the Shores of Tripoli

After resting and incorporating a few reinforcements into its depleted units, the Divisional Artillery set out confidently with the rest of the Division in the usual brigade formations from Sidi Azeiz west along the Trigh Capuzzo on 4 and 5 December.[31] Apart from the grim reminders of battle littering

---

36 Survey Battery

In late 1942, 36 Survey Battery returned to divisional control and was reorganised to emphasise its flash-spotting and sound-ranging roles. Since being detached from the New Zealand Division in May 1941, the battery had comprised X and Y troops, each with two sections that could operate independently. The battery barely escaped being turned into an engineers' field survey company. Assigned to surveying and map-making around the Middle East and on Cyprus, its artillery work included helping to calibrate coast defence guns in Beirut. In October 1942 the battery reassembled near Cairo and was joined by 1 Survey Troop. X Troop continued its surveying function (having also done hydrographic surveys), now using new American stereo-contouring equipment. 1 Survey Troop formed the bulk of S (Flash-Spotting) Troop; a new troop was formed as R (Sound-Ranging) Troop.

Flash-spotting used cameras in posts along the front to pinpoint the location of enemy guns through triangulation. Forwarded to the CBO (counter-bombardment officer), this data enabled rapid counter-battery fire. Sound-ranging did an analogous job using a well-dispersed line of microphones connected to the troop post; these were sometimes mistaken for landmines. An air interpretation section was retained. At the end of January, these troops (apart from R Troop) caught up with the administrative tail of the division in Tripoli, where for the first time almost all the Divisional Artillery was in one place (R Troop joined it on 26 March). The surveyors knew their craft. When an enemy map was captured at Takrouna, Captain E.L. Robinson of X Troop adjusted its grid so the CBO could 'arrange a thorough CB programme to deal with all the hostile batteries marked on it'. 36 Survey Battery, 284-strong when it crossed to Italy, would retain this organisation throughout that campaign.[32]

Men of 36 Survey Battery on a mountain track in Cyprus, May 1942.
DA 6947, Alexander Turnbull Library, Wellington.

A photographic record of the sound of enemy guns is removed from a recording machine.
DA 6469, Alexander Turnbull Library, Wellington.

Men of the Flash-Spotting Troop study a concentration board.
DA 5965, Alexander Turnbull Library, Wellington.

the landscape, the journey was uneventful. After turning inland across the desert, where they often moved as slowly as 8 miles per hour, the artillery reassembled at El Haseiat on the 9th. Two days later the Division, with 4 Light Armoured Brigade again attached, began the first of its famous 'left hook' operations to outflank and cut off the retreating enemy. After driving deep inland, crossing patches of soft sand and rocky ground, the Division turned north-west and made for the coast to the west of the rock formation known as 'Marble Arch'. The enemy was already pulling out of El Agheila, but when the New Zealanders reached Wadi Matratin after dark on 15 December, there still seemed a good chance of trapping much of the Italian/German army, including around 100 tanks. The next morning, however, with some guns under fire from German positions on higher ground and others too far away to provide much help, and with the infantry unable to hold the only position from which the coast road could be observed, the gunners could not fire effectively on the Via Balbia. Most of the enemy escaped through a large gap in the New Zealand lines. A lack of reliable maps and the confusion involved in establishing the gun lines and infantry

> ### Stonks and Lifts
>
> The sojourn at Nofilia provided an opportunity to refine the 'stonk', a technique for very rapid concentration of fire on a defined target area which was to be widely adopted by the British artillery. Divisional Artillery headquarters communicated to each battery and troop the centre of a target 1200 yards long and 300 yards wide, and the bearing of the long side. From this simple information, and using an ingenious template invented by Bombardier C.V. Gallagher of 6 Field that was superimposed on each artillery board, each gun could within seconds be provided with a bearing and range for its target within the stonk area. 'Shells coming in from many directions produced an awe-inspiring concentration of greater power than all guns firing on one point.' The stonk – initially dubbed the 'hate' – did not at first coordinate the fire of all three regiments. When the CRA went forward after an early divisional concentration, he found 'rarely more than six yards between shell holes'.[33]
>
> A standard barrage of ten lifts was developed, with its own special template also invented by Gallagher. At Nofilia opportunity was also taken to recalibrate the field guns by comparing their muzzle velocities and firing results over known ranges, and altering the range-scale indicators accordingly. The anti-tankers carried out a successful experimental shoot with HE shell using a 6-pr in indirect fire mode, but this technique would seldom be adopted in practice.

positions at night had let the Division down. This would not be the last disappointment of this kind.

On 17 December the New Zealanders again struck inland to encircle a large German rearguard at Nofilia, 40 miles west of Wadi Matratin. After long-distance shelling of the coast road and brushes with enemy tanks and artillery, positions were again taken up after dark, with the infantry dominating the ground immediately above the road. During the night, however, the enemy escaped along a track between the road and the sea. The Division now paused until the supply situation was consolidated. Some field gunners went westward briefly to cover sappers clearing mines from the road and airfield at Sultan, and a few anti-tankers remained in that forward outpost with the Divisional Cavalry, while most of the New Zealanders enjoyed a pleasant Christmas and New Year at Nofilia. Early in January, 5 Field Regiment and 32 Anti-Tank

Battery helped 5 Brigade construct an airfield south-west of Sirte. The brigade endured a series of air attacks and several casualties that were avenged to some extent when 42 Battery's ack-ack guns destroyed a number of aircraft.

Most of the Division left the Nofilia area on 9 January and headed for Tripoli. After a stuttering advance they reached Suani Ben Adem, inland from the port city, which was captured by British armoured units. During this long journey the anti-tankers and some of the field gunners experienced a number of brief and sometimes sharp actions with German rearguard units, and the ack-ack gunners had many busy days, but after each delay the enemy fell back to avoid serious losses.

Time Out in Libya and Tunisia

After the rigours of desert travel, the gunners delighted in 'green grass and trees, bright sunshine, [and] an abundance of clear water'. Near Wadi Sedada 'there must have been rain recently', an officer of 5 Field related. 'Suddenly a gunner shouted "Grass" and jumped out to roll in it, followed by a dozen or more of his friends. I would have liked to have done the same'. When his troop camped near Tripoli beside a garden that 'seemed to belong to nobody in particular', Furneaux Martyn enjoyed carrots 'by the dozen'. Sometimes produce was paid for in kind: in Tunisia, Martyn's troop swapped surplus items such as an old Italian groundsheet for eggs and 'two nice fat chickens', one of which was cooked immediately and the other kept for a while for eggs.[34]

Town leave was enjoyed in Tripoli, a city with few attractions after years of war. For 1200 gunners there was work on the docks, not entirely unwelcome because of the opportunity to supplement their rations. Unloading American foodstuffs had the most appeal: 'being only human and Kiwis at that, we did very well for ourselves regarding food and drink'. 5 Field's Colonel Glasgow had to call a regimental parade to admonish his men for loading NAAFI supplies onto marked trucks in broad daylight: 'for goodness sake use your brains – wait until it is safe and dark'. Most of 14 Light AA Regiment was deployed in the defence of the port, firing roughly 35,000 rounds; it claimed few kills but greatly diminished the effectiveness of enemy air raids. Men now had time for gambling. Officially forbidden, 'two-up was played every evening well out of sight of those in authority'. A game in which horse races were simulated by rolling a crown-and-anchor dice and cutting cards was 'sanctioned and even played by some officers', attracting such wide interest that 'on our best day we handled over forty pounds'.[35]

Near Tripoli on 4 February, 'on the flat area by our football fields and not too far away from the plonk factory we paraded in line of Troops [all guns abreast] to salute our mentor Sir Winston Churchill, "Mr Bullfinch" as he was termed to comply with security.' The British Prime Minister dubbed the Division 'the "New Zealand Ball of Fire". We were glad when all the bullshit was over. Now we received reinforcements from New Zealand, the first for over a year and glad we were to receive them. We had had so much wastage.'[36]

MEDENINE

The Divisional Artillery began exercising on 1 March, practising stonks and other concentrations, but on the same day orders came to prepare to advance to Medenine in Tunisia, and by 10 p.m. 4 Field was on the road.[37] The other artillery units soon followed, and by the 3rd the Division was digging into new positions in anticipation of a German–Italian attack from the Mareth Line, about 15 miles to the west. North of the New Zealanders, 7 Armoured and 51 Highland divisions were deployed in a line extending towards the coast. The anti-tank defences were particularly strong, with the three divisions boasting 467 6-prs. Three batteries of 7 Anti-Tank Regiment were keen to try out their much-vaunted new 'pheasant' anti-tank guns, high-velocity 17-prs mounted on 25-pr carriages, which promised much greater range and armour penetration. An RA battery of heavy 3.7-inch ack-ack guns guarding an airfield on the flank behind the New Zealand Division was also incorporated in the anti-tank defences.

The battle of Medenine was 'an artillery showpiece'.[38] It began at dawn on 6 March, when the enemy shelled forward positions. The New Zealand gunners held their fire until later in the morning, when 4 Field was called on to support 7 Armoured Division, scoring hits on three tanks. The anti-tank gunners beat off further tank attacks and the field gunners repeatedly disrupted advancing tanks and lorried infantry. In the afternoon effective counter-battery action silenced hostile batteries, including the Germans' new secret weapon, the Nebelwerfer six-barrelled rocket launcher.[39] Then one of the New Zealand OPs noticed a large force of tanks and infantry forming up to attack vital high ground at 'Point 170'. A stonk was prepared involving not only the New Zealand field regiments but also the artillery of 7 Armoured

Quick-firing anti-tank 17-pr.
Defence of New Zealand Study Group collection.

Division and the heavy ack-ack guns. When the German force reached the predicted area it was shattered with heavy losses, and the threat to Medenine was over. The day's fighting cost the enemy 52 tanks, and though most of these were lost in attacks on the British divisions, the New Zealand artillery played a key role. Unfortunately for the 17-prs' crews, these top-secret weapons were sited well back to remove any risk of capture, and they had no opportunity to fire.

The Mareth Line now provided an opportunity to attempt another 'left hook' via the Tebaga Gap and Gabes. Other formations would maintain pressure on the front of the Line to deter the enemy from turning to block the New Zealand advance. The 'New Zealand Corps' under Freyberg, including 8 Armoured Brigade and some Free French units, set out in several formations between 11 and 14 March. After a difficult journey over badly formed roads, and an attack on Divisional Artillery HQ by US Kittyhawks ('we dive for slit trenches when they show up')[40] that killed one and wounded two of the staff, the assault on the Tebaga Gap began on the 21st. The armour and infantry edged forward cautiously in the face of enemy shelling, the gunners responding according to plan.

The main attack began early on 26 March with heavy artillery concentrations in which 5 Field did not participate to conceal its forward position. British armour and artillery units also came forward. When the ground assault began, all the field and medium guns opened fire, supported by RAF fighter-bombers. By the end of the day the enemy's defences were crumbling, and early on the 27th a series of stonks fired by 4 and 6 Field helped break some stubborn resistance to the Maori Battalion. When British armour led the charge through the gap, the wrecked equipment and vehicles, and the many prisoners captured, showed that the concentrated and persistent artillery action had devastated the defences. By the next day, the rearguard formed by 5 Brigade was though the gap and on the road to Gabes with the rest of the corps. The town was occupied with little resistance from the last of the enemy units escaping west from the Mareth Line. Although the left hook had failed to encircle the Axis forces, it had undoubtedly hastened the collapse of the line and avoided some of the losses of a frontal assault.

DEALING WITH PRISONERS

One of an RSM's duties was to take charge of any prisoners captured in front of an artillery position by infantry who wanted to get on with the fighting. After taking these men back to a military police cage and handing them over, he had to return in the heat of battle to a unit that might well have moved while he was away. After 'some hairy experiences', 6 Field's RSM, Jim Gilberd, told a batch of Germans captured in Tunisia to remove their boots and walk back to the lock-up with only a few guards:

> The next minute a Honey tank comes up. Who's sitting in it but General Freyberg! He was an observant old fellow and asked what they were doing with no boots on. I told him and he said, 'Give them their boots back! Your job is to take them back to the Military Police.' The Germans put their boots on, laughing and wanting to know who he was. They knew from his red hat he was a senior officer.[41]

The New Zealand field regiments now moved north to Wadi Akarit, where they fired a lifting barrage in support of 50 Division and were among the 496 field and medium guns concentrated on the line when the attack opened early on 6 April. Indian and Gurkha units climbed steep cliffs, but at the centre of the line progress was obstructed by stout resistance, and there was much firing during the day. After nightfall the enemy melted away, and next day the columns of the New Zealand Division joined the masses of vehicles pushing forward through the battered defences onto the broad plain beyond. The following days saw numerous skirmishes with enemy rearguard units; particularly for the anti-tankers and some of the field gunners, the advance was not without its hazards. Travelling through more settled countryside also had its benefits for one troop. 'Some "Tommies" had given us a piece of mutton off a sheep they killed, so we … cooked it over a petrol sand fire for breakfast. The meat was charred on the outside, nicely cooked halfway through, nearly raw in the centre, and tasted a little of benzine, but it was still eaten with relish.' Fresh meat was 'a rare treat'.[42] On the downside, in these moister surroundings mosquitoes took over from the much-cursed flies as night fell.

Takrouna and Enfidaville

The Division halted to dig in before a strongly defended fortress on the imposing hill of Takrouna, near Enfidaville.[43] The gunners enjoyed the luxury of assistance from a sappers' bulldozer, which 'scooped out the holes in next to no time', one sweep of its blade shifting as much as men could move with shovels in an hour.[44] The New Zealand attack from hidden positions struck the hill and the country to its west with a lifting barrage at 11 p.m. on 19 April. Supporting 5 Brigade, charged with taking the hill itself, were 4 and 5 Field Regiments, 111 Field Regiment, RA, and three troops of 124 Field Regiment, RA. The allocation of guns to the 6 Brigade advance, on the right of 5 Brigade, was similarly impressive, including 6 Field, 65 Field RA and the rest of 124 Field. In addition, a series of planned concentrations was programmed for 64 and 69 Medium Regiments; 74 Field RA was available to fire concentrations on demand. Despite this firepower, the infantry advance stalled on the summit of Takrouna, and before dawn the guns of 6 Field and a battery of 5 Field withdrew from their exposed forward positions under the hill.

At daybreak Weir ordered a number of stonks to be fired on the high ground behind Takrouna, and the infantry pushed on to capture part of the summit, where the FOOs of the New Zealand regiments were soon on the scene to call down fire on enemy positions north of the hill, and on an enemy counter-attack on the summit in the afternoon. By the following morning

Takrouna was firmly in New Zealand hands and now subjected to enemy shelling, but surprisingly little counter-battery work. In response to the danger to the infantry, Weir called down a 200-gun stonk on German positions. Over the following days similar stonks were fired in support of further advances by 6 Brigade and then by 56 (London) Division, which the New Zealand field regiments supported from new positions beyond Enfidaville. The gunners could see these stonks landing on the German positions facing them on the forward slopes of the hills above. 'With the numerous bursts close together, it appeared as though a whole hillside came to life, but our view was quickly obscured by drifting smoke.'[45]

Amid the euphoria of imminent victory, some commanders took risks. At Takrouna, 46 Battery was ordered to bring a 25-pr up to the OP to do some sniping – 'the first time in artillery history; a very very funny thing to do'. With his 'muzzle pointing over the cactus hedge, we were supposed to be sniping, but fired one round of HE on supercharge'. This kicked up a lot of dust and produced a predictable reply. 'A German round came over, then copy-book stuff, ranging, and we came under sustained fire. The FOO got back into his Honey tank and yelled out to us, "Fuck off. That's an order." It was a suicidal thing to go to the OP with a gun – they always must be out of sight unless firing directly at tanks.'[46]

Most of the New Zealand Division was pulled out of the line north of Enfidaville on 1 May for a brief rest before being sent west to positions near the town of Djebibina, where 4 and 5 Field and RA units carried out counter-battery and other harassing tasks, partly in support of a French corps. From 8 May the New Zealand artillery units began to return to Enfidaville, where 6 Field had remained in support of the British 56 Division, which had already begun an advance. The infantry faltered, however, and 4 and 6 Field were soon engaged in heavy counter-battery firing. With enemy forces surrendering elsewhere on the front, and Tunis already occupied by the First Army, the end of the war in North Africa was eagerly anticipated.

Unfortunately for the New Zealand field gunners, the German batteries were determined to fire as much of their ammunition as possible before capitulating. One 4 Field gunner described 'desperation shelling by Jerry, he is heaving over all sorts'.[47] Another man who had served since Greece had to stop himself climbing out of his slit trench and running. On 11 and 12 May, 4 and 6 Field were involved in their heaviest counter-battery action of the campaign (5 Field was enjoying a rest period out of the line). Fortunately the German gunnery was inaccurate, and the enemy guns were suppressed one by one or exhausted their ammunition. At about 9.30 on the morning of 13 May, with some Germans still stubbornly refusing to surrender, 4 Field fired the last rounds of the war in North Africa. Axis resistance ended at 10 a.m. That night beer and wine was issued – 'you can imagine the celebration we had. I was one of the very few who got to bed under their own power'. Next morning there were said to be 27 sets of false teeth missing in this battery. 'You should have seen all the black eyes and battered jowls on parade.'[48]

The New Zealanders were given little time to enjoy the victory – and no parade through Tunis. Instead, the Mule Pack Company of the NZASC provided steeds for a 'donkey derby' during which thousands of pounds changed hands. On 16 May the Divisional Artillery began the 1800-mile journey back to base. After pausing at staging areas near Tripoli and Benghazi, they reached Maadi on 1 June. In Weir's hands the Divisional Artillery had become a formidable force. It ended the campaign with the greatest seniority in the Eighth Army, having been there the longest – 4 Field was the senior regiment in North Africa (and by extension, A1 Gun of 25 Battery was the senior gun).[49]

To Italy

The Division would now have time to regroup and recuperate after its exhausting campaign.[50] Many experienced men went home in the Ruapehu and Wakatipu furlough drafts. Gunners could volunteer to man the ship's guns on the voyage home – to keep themselves occupied, or to get cooler quarters (crossing the Australian Bight, these were sometimes too cool). Only one man had to be always at the gun, provided the full crew was nearby.[51]

The furloughed men were replaced from the Ninth and Tenth reinforcements (the latter included about 600 gunners). Many of the new men had served in New Zealand or in Pacific Island garrisons. The so-called 'dehydrated officers' had taken a reduction in rank to facilitate their integration into 2 Division. (With vacancies arising as furloughed officers went home, some would go through OCTU again and be recommissioned.) One man commissioned in New Zealand left for the Mediterranean as a temporary sergeant, which meant only 'a bottle of whisky a month, because they made it quite clear that I wasn't Gun Sergeant, I was just a spare number. About six weeks after I got there, they absorbed me in the ranks. I was lucky: of the 29 of us who went away, four got two stripes and the rest went down to gunners.'[52] Walter McKinnon, another such officer, saw this infusion of 'new blood' from 3 Division as crucial to 2 Division's later success in Italy, responsible 'in no small measure' for the success of the final advance to Trieste.[53] Their integration was helped by the similarities between the South Island and Italy, which was quite unlike the desert conditions the old hands were used to. Later arrivals from 3 Division would be assimilated less easily: 'we had to prove ourselves. Because we had this different kind of gunnery in the jungle, it was only natural that the fellows in Italy would wonder if we had forgotten what we ever knew.'[54]

Meanwhile, the field gunners all received new 25-prs, and there was time to calibrate the guns and train the new arrivals at the New Zealand Artillery Training Depot at Maadi, and within the various units. 'We redoubled our energies getting Artillery Training Depot into a highly specialised school', Captain J.P. Snadden recalled.

> Classrooms were to become models of efficiency. We had break-apart equipment to show the intricacies of internal combustion engines or guns. We had a signals school and a good miniature range [for practising coordinated gun-control techniques]. Draughtsmen were coopted to produce wall charts. We were combining expertise with experience. Plus all this was regular drill, gun drill and exercises in the field.[55]

August was devoted to intensive exercises in the desert, progressively at battery, regimental and divisional level; brigade exercises were then carried out.

The Artillery Training Depot at Maadi would later be known as 32 Field Regiment. 'That's where my serious training started,' a 1943 arrival remembered.[56] What had been theoretical in New Zealand was very practical at Maadi. The training regiment had two batteries, under CO Ernie Lambourn.

The instructors and gun sergeants were all experienced gunners. In the brigade exercises, gunners practised on their new 25-pr guns but dropped the old concept of desert formation. They tested the 'Meteor' data which came from meteorological stations at corps level (and was sometimes inaccurate or hours out of date). Each regiment worked with the corresponding infantry brigade. For a change, there was no shortage of ammunition.

A Tenth Reinforcements man recalled that:

> We did a route march from Cairo to Alexandria – 80 miles, not the kind of thing you forget. Then we went into the desert proper, and did our practices, and what I remember most about that was how bloody easy it was to get lost – at night, you couldn't see a bloody thing. You learnt very early in the piece where the polar star was, even if you just went out for a crap.[57]

By the time Freyberg announced that the Division was bound for Italy, this was already obvious. Italy itself was by now out of the war, but the German army had occupied the northern two-thirds of the country. The gunners were divided between troop convoys that left Alexandria for the port of Taranto on 5 and 18 October.

Across the Sangro

After being held up awaiting the bulk of its vehicles and supplies, the New Zealand Division, with other elements of the Eighth Army, began moving towards the front at the Sangro River, across the Apennines from the Naples–Rome corridor. On 14 November, 5 Field Regiment fired the Divisional Artillery's first shots in anger in the Italian campaign, and was itself shelled while some of its vehicles and guns were on the move.[58] With flooding delaying the planned crossing of the Sangro, and the German guns pulling back out of 25-pr range, counter-battery fire was left to a British medium troop under Weir's command. On the 23rd the field regiments and 3 Field Regiment, RA, supported an Indian attack on the village of Sant' Angelo, beyond the river. The gunners, engaged in counter-battery action, suffered a number of casualties.

The main assault on the Sangro came at 2.45 a.m. on 28 November. The previous evening a troop of 33 Battery 17-prs fired from concealed positions on houses and farm buildings up to 4500 yards away across the river that were likely to contain enemy OPs and machine-gun posts. The rugged terrain in this theatre necessitated modifications to well-tried artillery tactics – rather than a creeping barrage, timed concentrations of fire to support the infantry assault, and to defend pontoon and Bailey bridges erected overnight. Next day 4 Armoured Brigade advanced across the river supported by 4 Field Regiment, with three of its OPs among the vanguard in tanks, one of which was disabled when it struck a mine and shed a track. The FOOs of the other field regiments were also well forward with their respective brigades, but radio communication difficulties dogged their efforts to bring down fire at short notice. Only heroic efforts made even intermittent telephone contact possible.

Nevertheless, the advance pushed forward relentlessly, and on the 29th, after heavy firing by 5 and 6 Field and 3 Field RA, it was found that the enemy had retreated. Next day the New Zealand field regiments and the small Artillery Tactical HQ created for this phase of the campaign crossed the Bailey bridge to support an attack on the town of Castelfrentano, which fell on 2 December without resistance. Ack-ack gunners who had been defending the Bailey bridge claimed credit for downing a Focke-Wulf 190.

The enemy had fallen back to a strong defensive line. The New Zealand advance started inauspiciously on the morning of 3 December with an assault on the village of Melone. Despite a bombardment from 4 Field, the advance on the village by infantry and armour stalled. Shelling of the town of Guardiagrele, to the left of the line, and on other strongpoints, proved equally ineffective in dislodging the enemy from well-protected positions. The attack on Orsogna the same morning began promisingly and some infantry units reached the town, but after German reinforcements ran the gauntlet of shelling by a 6 Field battery along the road into the town, resistance stiffened and the New Zealanders fell back. Both the artillery and its cooperation with armour had been found wanting; the difficulties that lay ahead in Italy were becoming apparent.

The Divisional Artillery was now greatly strengthened by the addition of RA units for the next attempt on the German line. On 3 and 4 December, 111 Field and 66 Medium, both of 6 AGRA, plus 1 Air-Landing Light Regiment and a battery of 51 Heavy AA, were all placed under Weir's command. After a further attack on Melone was beaten back early on the 4th, the focus shifted to Orsogna and a planned breakout across the road leading from the town to the coast. In the meantime, the gunners of 4 and 6 Field suffered under heavy counter-battery fire, including massive 170-mm shells and airbursts fired from 88s.

After delays caused by flood damage to both bridges across the Sangro, the second attack on Orsogna began at 1 a.m. on 7 December with a massive bombardment. Despite the weight of shell that rained down, only a small part of the Sfasciata ridge north-east of the town could be held against enemy counter-attacks. Next day an air attack on an A Troop Bofors gun killed one man and wounded four. 'You can't look up. You must keep your nose down and watch where you are putting your brackets of shells. But when Stukas are coming in, you want to have a look. You feel as isolated as someone on top of a haystack.'[59] The front settled down again until 15 December, when 5 Brigade attempted to outflank Orsogna from the Sfasciata ridge, supported by a creeping barrage and timed concentrations fired by the field regiments. The attack was costly for 5 Brigade, but it managed to take and hold part of the road from Orsogna to the coast. A powerful counter-attack was repulsed with the help of a number of stonks and many direct-fire tasks called down by the OPs. Though ground had been taken, the German line remained unbreached.

The day after the field gunners supported a British attack on Arielli on 23 December, there was a further attempt to outflank Orsogna across its northern approaches, when 5 Brigade and 4 Armoured Brigade assaulted the German line. Two hundred and seventy-two field and medium guns of the British 5 Division, the New Zealand Division and 6 AGRA provided heavy artillery support. The battle saw fierce night fighting at close quarters in rugged terrain; shorts caused casualties in 21 Battalion. Though the advance failed to reach its objectives, the ground taken was held against counter-attacks.

The realities of war in the rugged Italian hills were by now all too clear. With good observation posts and often carefully prepared and well-concealed gun positions, German gunners could disrupt infantry advances, sometimes with shots just behind the advancing barrage that to the infantry seemed

Heavy going on the Sangro front, December 1943.
DA-04695-F, Alexander Turnbull Library, Wellington.

like shots fired by Allied guns. From commanding sites the German OPs could sometimes bring down heavy counter-battery fire on the Allied gun lines. However, the Sangro campaign was also noteworthy for the increasing success of the New Zealanders' flash-spotting and sound-ranging troops, the former helped by new cameras.

Through winter rain and cold, the New Zealand gunners often moved and worked in seas of mud. Given the limitations of transport on muddy roads, the New Zealanders dug in for a long stay in their current positions. On 30 December, 4 Field fired shells containing propaganda leaflets into Orsogna, and on 3 January the field regiments and 111 Field, RA, spelt out a belated 'Happy New Year Fritz' in the snow that enveloped the German lines.⁶⁰ During this period all the field regiments were engaged intermittently in harassing, predicted and directed fire, and counter-battery work. Predicted fire took advantage of accurate surveying and meteorological information to enable the guns to fire on a map reference without a FOO having to fire registration rounds that alerted the enemy. One senior officer would reflect later that this had been overdone: 'the old gunner traditions of pointing the spout in the right direction and bringing down observed fire from the gun position seemed to have been lost'.⁶¹

CASSINO: THE NEW ZEALAND CORPS ASSAULT

With the Adriatic front proving hard to crack, in mid-January the New Zealand Division was transferred west across the Apennines to join the American Fifth Army, which had stalled in its advance on the Tyrrhenian front.⁶² The Division assembled briefly at Alife for rest and recreation, including opportunity to visit the ruins of Pompeii. The Allied landing at Anzio on 23 January brought the prospect of outflanking the enemy and breaking the deadlock across the peninsula. But frontal assaults on the strong German positions on the Gustav Line, anchored by the town and peak of Cassino, could not be avoided. On 3 February another New Zealand Corps was formed, commanded by Freyberg and including the New Zealand Division and 4 Indian Division. Heavy additional artillery support from 2 AGRA included three field regiments (one self-propelled and brought under command of 4 Armoured Brigade), five medium regiments and a light AA battery, later supplemented by five American field artillery battalions and AA units.

The imposing hill of Monte Cassino, topped by a large and historic monastery, presented a formidable obstacle to the planned advance up the Liri Valley. From its heights the Germans could see not only the town of Cassino – which was still in their hands – but virtually all the Allied dispositions for miles around. The New Zealand field gunners went into position on 5 February, with their OPs on or near Monte Trocchio, just 2 miles from Cassino. The sound-ranging and flash-spotting troops also based their posts here. On the afternoon of the 6th the New Zealand field regiments opened harassing fire on roads and other targets, and two days later murders were called down in counter-battery action against Nebelwerfer positions:

As soon as they opened up we called for concentrated fire, Murders, which became a game of wits, for the Jerry would fire then shift position before we could reply. We then adopted the practice of keeping one gun laid on known positions which would fire on order as soon as the nebelwerfer was observed firing. It was a cat and mouse game. Later we developed the practice of calling for fire on all known positions whether they were firing or not, and with all guns of the Division firing at once, this caused many casualties.[63]

By now the New Zealand gunners were supporting an assault on Monte Cassino by 2 US Corps. The New Zealand Corps was reserved for the anticipated pursuit up the Liri Valley, but the American attack was repulsed. The many New Zealand and Allied guns drove back a German counter-attack. On 15 February counter-battery fire struck enemy AA positions in preparation for the heavy bombing that destroyed the hilltop monastery later that day. Indian and New Zealand formations of the New Zealand Corps undertook the next phase of the assault. After an advance by 4 Indian Division failed to reach its objectives the day after the bombing, the Maori Battalion attacked across the Rapido River on the night of 17 February. This assault was intended to secure the railway embankment and station outside the town so armoured and other units could bypass the boggy and flooded ground near the river and sweep into the Liri Valley. Though concentrations including murders were fired to support the Maori attack, with medium and US heavy guns joining in, by morning only two companies of the Maori Battalion were across the Rapido. Under heavy fire, they were threatened by a counter-attack.

The gunners had a very strenuous day firing continuously around the Maori position. They also fired many smoke shells to obscure the bridgehead from enemy observation. Firing for long periods at the rate of three rounds per minute, the guns frequently overheated. Ammunition had to be brought forward under heavy fire. The gun positions were shelled, with 25 Battery bombarded heavily but ineffectively. Despite these huge efforts, in the afternoon the Maori bridgehead was overrun by tanks and infantry, with heavy casualties; many of the infantry were captured. By the end of the day, all the field gunners were exhausted. In firing 1600 HE and 10,056 smoke shells,

25 Battery had handled more than 150 tons of ammunition. 'The gun barrels were like rusty old motorbike exhaust pipes, they'd fired so much.'[64]

The following weeks were devoted mainly to harassing tasks and counter-battery work against gun and Nebelwerfer positions. The next assault on Cassino did not begin until 15 March. Operation Dickens began with heavy aerial bombing, during which some misdirected bombs caused the hurried evacuation of a number of New Zealand gun positions; one gunner was killed. This was followed by an intense bombardment of the hill and town by all 900 guns of the Fifth Army. 6 Brigade's attack along an 800-yard front was led by a creeping barrage from 88 guns of 6 Field and other corps field and medium units, supplemented by timed concentrations and directed fire against enemy positions further back. 4 and 5 Field did their share of this work, and 4 Field also fired many smoke shells on the slopes of the hill above the town to obscure the New Zealand advance. The Allied counter-battery firing was very heavy and effective. 4 Field had found an especially good spot:

> With long, double drag ropes, twenty men on each, they had dragged these guns up 45-degree slopes, and worse, into the best gun position I have ever seen. The guns were inside the lip of the cup of the hill, whilst the enemy was away and below. It was unique. Nothing but a bomb could hit the guns; and nothing ever did.[65]

6 Brigade struggled forward, falling far behind the barrage even when its conclusion was delayed by 80 minutes. The infantry faced strong German resistance and found it very difficult to get through the rubble resulting from the bombing, which provided well-concealed positions for snipers. The ruins also initially prevented armour from helping in the town, though in later days the tanks would play their part in a grim, close-quarters battle, and 4 Armoured Brigade had a key role in the successful attack on the railway station on 17 March. Meanwhile a New Zealand battalion had taken Castle Hill below Monte Cassino, though Indian infantry were facing heavy resistance on the slopes above. All the troops were exposed to enemy observation, shelling and rocket attacks. The New Zealand field gunners were kept busy firing smoke shells on counter-battery tasks. They also attacked the Germans as they supplied

and reinforced positions at the front. In the heavy firing that continued for days many guns suffered breakages, and firing so many smoke shells also caused heavy wear on the rifling of the barrels. The gun crews were exhausted. One 30 Battery man 'was the only one on the gun position for three days. I didn't sleep, my voice had gone. And if I'd made a mistake … You just couldn't, because you were going to kill somebody [friendly].'[66]

Additional New Zealand infantry units were pushed into the town. As the attack inched forward building by building, it was difficult for the field artillery to provide indirect fire support in the confusion. When the infantry attack was halted on 23 March, part of the town remained in enemy hands. The exposed positions on Monte Cassino were evacuated, but by 26 March those immediately above Cassino and in and around the town were consolidated and handed over to units of 13 Corps. New Zealand Corps was disbanded, but the gunners' work at Cassino was not quite finished. Upper-register shoots conducted in late March, first by gunners of 4 Field and then by 5 Field, successfully engaged enemy batteries. The technique involved digging in the trail of the gun to increase its elevation. Fired at a higher trajectory, shells could reach enemy positions behind steep ridges and obscured from normal field-gun fire.

The gunners also continued their duels with the elusive Nebelwerfers, which shifted position or took cover in bunkers immediately after firing. Other counter-battery and counter-mortar tasks kept the gunners busy until 4 Field was withdrawn on 3 April to join the rest of the Division out of the line at Venafro in the Volturno Valley. 5 Field followed two nights later, but 6 Field stayed on for another two weeks before departing for Isernia, also in the Volturno Valley.

Cassino had been a frustrating and exhausting experience for the New Zealand Artillery, but their casualties were relatively light for such a hard-fought battle: 34 killed and 132 wounded, with two captured. Despite Cassino's duration, this was a toll not much greater than that suffered in the earlier fighting in the Orsogna area, where the gunners had lost 27 killed, 83 wounded and one captured.

Cassino: Supporting the Polish Assault

After the mud, endless toil, hazards and frustrations of winter at Cassino, the brief springtime respite in the Volturno was most welcome.[67] But by 10 April the first Divisional Artillery units were moving to new positions in mountainous country a few miles north-east of Cassino. Over the next few days, most of their comrades followed, crawling along steep, twisting, narrow mountain roads. To the east, 5 Field took over positions from Polish gunners, some of whom joined the New Zealanders in this area a few days later. These spots, north-west of the village of Mennella, covered the road through Cardito and into the mountains to the west. To the south-west, 4 Field replaced a British regiment guarding the roads along which the gunners travelled, North Road and 'Inferno Track'; 6 Field later covered these routes from the north. Both regiments could bring down fire on Monte Cassino.

Some of the ack-ack and anti-tank batteries were deployed with the field regiment. Anti-tankers became infantillery, with each battery fielding a platoon. Other anti-tank gunners established a heavy mortar battery, designated briefly 35, then 39 Mortar Battery.[68] This had four troops (C, G, P and L), one from each anti-tank battery, under Captain E.C.W. Nathan. Each troop was equipped with four 4.2-inch mortars taken over from the infantry for use with artillery methods of fire control and integrated into divisional fire-planning. They received their first eight mortars on 22 April, but were not ready to go into action until 20 May. A few days later, counter-mortar organisations were established under brigade counter-mortar officers – artillery officers who called down rapid fire from appropriate units (not only artillery) when hostile mortar fire was detected.

A supply dump on Inferno Track near the New Zealand positions was hit on 7 May, with spectacular consequences:

Using a director on the Cassino front.
W.E. Murphy, 2nd New Zealand Divisional Artillery.

4.2-inch mortar in action.
W.E. Murphy, 2nd New Zealand Divisional Artillery.

> A fire started on the edge of Hove Dump. It soon spread into a great conflagration. Jeeps caught fire, burning furiously until long after dark; great stores of petrol went up in vivid gushes of flame and clouds of black smoke; mingled with this was the white smoke from cannisters. Then the fire spread to the ammunition. Ton upon ton of light, medium and heavy shells, charges, cartridges, and boxes upon boxes of small arms and tracer bullets went up. Tremendous explosions rent the air. Whole boxes of shells could clearly be seen, hurtled into the air amid flame and smoke and sparks. Pieces of shells and even whole shells must have soared two thousand feet into the air, for many ... fragments fell amongst the trees we were standing under.[69]

Some New Zealand gunners were involved in sporadic counter-battery work, but their sector was relatively quiet until new offensives by both Fifth and Eighth Armies began on 11 May. To the right of the New Zealand sector, 5 Field and South African gunners supported a 'Chinese' (diversionary) attack by 2 Parachute Brigade. To the left, the guns of 4 and 6 Field, and of 2 AGRA, formed part of the artillery support for the Polish attack on Monte Cassino. They fired many murders, particularly on objectives to the west of the peak. Over the following days, these gunners were kept very busy with predicted concentrations and directed fire. Many stonks and murders were fired, some for prolonged periods and most at long range.[70]

By now the New Zealanders had murders down to a fine art. One morning Neville Mowat and an OP officer found a German camp:

> The OP Officer looked around, picked a house, and off we went upstairs. We got up onto the roof and we could see the German encampment right in front of us. They [were] all just getting out of bed, stretching like you do first thing in the morning. The OP got the [signal] going, and called for 'Murder'.
>
> You wouldn't believe it. We were just sitting there watching those shells come in. They were just like a picket fence coming down, one after another. If there was a gap so much as a body width it would be filled by another coming along behind – maybe someone had been a bit slow back at the gun-line. Someone later said they fired 75 rounds into that area – in as many seconds you might as well say. The rounds went right across the area. ... Great shooting. Poor Germans.[71]

Despite the long range, the gunners carried out many effective counter-battery and counter-mortar shoots. The action on Monte Cassino was part of a push by the Polish Corps that included attacks on hills to the north-west and an armoured assault in the Liri valley. The monastery fell to the Poles on 18 May. Over the following days further counter-battery work was required; the Germans north of the New Zealand sector apparently intended to exhaust their ammunition supplies before falling back. The last areas of resistance near Cassino were obliterated by 'William targets' – 'a procedure calling on all available guns of the Army, and concentrating at twenty minutes' notice the fire of 600 pieces'.[72]

Sora and Balsorano

The New Zealanders now advanced along the steep-sided Liri Valley towards Balsorano.[73] The infantry moved along the hills on either side, keeping contact with the artillery on the valley floor. On 2 June a stonk was fired on a target near Balsorano. 4 Field, supporting the advance on the western side of the valley, shelled the retiring enemy throughout the day. That evening the Germans fired on the vehicles of a forward OP, and next day heavy and accurate shelling from the hills caused casualties in 4 Field, including five killed in a troop that had just arrived and was not dug in. 5 Field had paused beside an olive grove, deploying the guns near the river where the ground was soft enough for slit trenches to be dug. 'We had hardly got in to position when the Germans in the hills above started shelling the 4 Field position. On the hard open ground they had many casualties.'[74]

> [One 4 Field gun crew] dropped our gun into action…, unpacked the quad, ordered it away. I looked across the river, saw great, frowning hills towering up there to the east. … At that moment, Fritz, … a mile away on the forbidding cliffs, must have been ordering line and range. … Twenty-four hours before the hills had been reported clear, but this artillery rearguard had daringly crept back (or lay hidden – we will never know). They sat up there on the arid rocks and watched the guns of the New Zealand regiments wheel in off the road. … As three of us were digging, as four of us were hoisting the camouflage net over the seven-foot poles and taut wires, Fritz ordered 'Fire.' The *pung* from the cliffs and the shrill whistle came together. Fast light shells grazed our heads and exploded in our paddock. We flung ourselves to ground, then raced to the sweet, dear ditch.[75]

While those who could returned fire from hazardous positions, frequently having to take cover, 5 and 6 Field pushed forward from the rear. Before they could dig in they too were shelled heavily, with 20 men wounded. By the next day the guns were well dug in, but it was clear that their positions were under observation. The OPs desperately sought to locate the hidden German guns and heavy mortars, while anti-tanker infantillery patrols scoured the hills with the same mission.

Enemy shelling along the road continued into the next day with many more casualties, but this did not prevent probably fruitless efforts at counter-battery fire and concentrations in support of the infantry advance. By now the location of some of the enemy batteries was becoming apparent. Counter-battery fire silenced one enemy gun position in the morning, and five more over the next 24 hours.

After Rome fell to the Fifth Army on 4 June, some of the New Zealand field gunners began withdrawing from the Liri Valley in anticipation of an advance to the west. Those who stayed fired some heavy and accurate concentrations on targets in and beyond Balsorano, supported by three medium regiments and a heavy battery of 2 AGRA. The remaining guns of 4 and 6 Field withdrew on the night of 5 June, but 5 Field continued firing. The sound of enemy demolitions next morning signalled the end of the fighting and a German retreat through Avezzano. Plans for the New Zealand Division were again changed and 'Wilder Force', including the gunners of 5 Field, who left their guns behind in the Sora Valley, moved to occupy Avezzano. Picking its way through demolitions and mines, this force entered the town on 9 June. A few days later 5 Field returned down the Liri to Arce, where it regrouped with the rest of the Divisional Artillery. During the attack up the Liri the artillery had suffered greater casualties than the infantry: thirteen killed and 128 wounded, most during the agonising four days of shelling around Sora.

Arezzo

The next few weeks brought opportunities for leave and sightseeing, including visits to Rome, before the New Zealand Division was ordered north to Lake Trasimene in Umbria on 7 July.[76] In the meantime Weir had been appointed CCRA of 10 Corps and, on 16 June, Parkinson took over as CRA in the Division. The Divisional Artillery (now some 4000 men manning 250 guns) was sent north of Cortona. Furthest forward, 39 Heavy Mortar Battery came under shell and mortar fire as it relieved a British mortar battery on 13 July. The plan for the battle involved the New Zealand field regiments, the mortar battery and an RA medium battery supporting a 6 Brigade assault on three peaks above Arezzo which it was hoped would hasten the evacuation of the ancient city.

The artillery action began on the evening of the 14th, supporting an assault on a commanding crest by a platoon of 26 Battalion. This achieved its objective but was driven off by a counter-attack, and New Zealand fire on the crest possibly caused four casualties, including two killed. This was the first of a series of accusations of short shooting during the Arezzo battle, but the casualties in these incidents may well have resulted from hostile fire, as repeated ceasefires by New Zealand batteries did not end the shelling in question. The main fire plan started at 1 a.m. on 15 July and directed fire was called down on a series of targets over the following day. Early on the 16th the field regiments supported 24 Battalion. Despite the problems created by the alleged shorts, the infantry brigades took their objectives and the enemy withdrew from Arezzo that day, before the fighting in the hills ended.

Florence

The Division now lost another group of experienced men, the Fourth Reinforcements group that departed on the Taupo furlough scheme. A 4 Field man who had been home on furlough felt the system took away 'a little of the spirit' of the Division, because men had 'one foot on the boat'. Knowing you were soon to return to a wife you had not seen for four years, and a child 'you had never seen, would you grip your bayonet with the same spirit as before?' [77]

In the Divisional Artillery, this necessitated another review of appointments. The Division was now redeployed to the west through Siena, along a rough road that cost two gun tractors, two trailers and a Bofors gun, all wrecked when they rolled down banks; two men were killed and nine wounded. The guns of 4 and 5 Field were deployed with their respective brigades, plus

---

The Anti-Tankers

During June 1944, with the likelihood of 6-pr action receding, 33 Anti-Tank Battery undertook infantry training in anticipation of a future role as infantillery. At the same time, 31 Battery took over nine M10 tank destroyers, the only armoured self-propelled guns to serve with the New Zealand Division. Sporting 3-inch guns mounted in large open turrets on Sherman chassis, these were issued to A and D troops from late June. Some officers thought the M10s invincible – 'big guns on them, belt hell out of old Jerry'. The turret, however, was slow to traverse, thinly armoured and open to the elements. Occupying it was 'blimmin' cold, miserable. On the counterweight we had a .50 Browning ready to have a go at anybody.' Training was minimal. Drivers could practise in nearby Shermans of 18 Armoured Regiment, but the gunners had to figure their new weapon out for themselves. Regular Force personnel were expected to teach their comrades.[78]

the heavy mortar battery and RA support – two medium regiments and a regiment of self-propelled 105 howitzers – with an Air OP flight attached. By 22 July the gunners were in position for the first assault on the small towns and strongpoints that barred the way across the hills to Florence.[79]

With this heavy artillery support, 5 Brigade and an armoured regiment, with an M10 troop under command, began the attack by advancing on the village of Strada, whence they were to push on to San Casciano. The attackers moved forward against strong resistance that included heavy mortar attacks and shelling, with effective counter-battery fire and close support from the M10s. The crews of the tank destroyers performed remarkably well in their first engagement, silencing opposition from a castle near Strada and helping to secure the town. The field gunners had many directed fire tasks and changed position frequently.

The Germans appreciated the strategic location of San Casciano astride the main road to Florence, and the strength of its defences necessitated a large-scale fire-plan to support an attack by 5 Brigade on Cerbaia, to the north-west, on the night of 26 July. This would include eight stonks by all the supporting field and medium guns, and a series of concentrations by the mortar battery. The attack was successful and Cerbaia was taken the following morning. The next day, 6 Brigade with 6 Field joined the action. From 1 p.m., 5 and 6 Field supported an assault by 6 Brigade and an armoured regiment across the River Pesa. At the same time 70 and 75 Medium brought down fire on targets further forward, and joined the field guns in many directed fire shoots. The infantry and armoured assault met stiff resistance that knocked out a number of New Zealand tanks.

This set the pattern for the battles on the approaches to Florence. Heavy artillery support accompanied short assaults on limited objectives. No simple breakthrough was expected as the Germans contested the advance almost every step of the way. On 29 and 30 July 6 Brigade was able to secure the town of San Michele. On the night of the 30th, an attack on La Romola opened with a creeping barrage by the New Zealand field regiments and 57 Field Regiment, RA, with concentrations fired by the two medium regiments and the SP howitzer regiment forward with the armour. Once again, heavy mortars were invaluable, especially as the Maori

M10 self-propelled anti-tank gun near Florence, August 1944.
DA 6477, Alexander Turnbull Library, Wellington.

Battalion struggled to reach its objective to the right of the town, which had quickly fallen.

The artillery support for the advance toward Florence was heavy and the work demanding, with frequent shifts of position and heavy concentrations needed to crush determined German opposition. 'Life was one long pack-up-and-move', and troops 'tended to get off the maps occasionally'. Spencer Cocks was wounded by a mortar round 'almost at the same line as the infantry. We'd already dug three gun pits and moved three times.'[80]

The advance ground forward until a major assault on the high country towards Florence began on the night of 1 August. This included three separate and rather complicated creeping barrages – one for each brigade – starting up to three and a quarter hours apart to take into account the nature of the ground. Once again several British field and medium regiments were available for heavy counter-battery concentrations. Despite some delays and confusion, all the objectives were taken. The hill of La Poggiona and high ground to the south – the last obstacles before Florence – were taken after creeping barrages supporting battalion-strength night attacks. On 3 August, enemy vehicles were shelled at long range and supporting concentrations were fired for a South African armoured division to the right. For the anti-tankers the last stages of the Florence campaign brought mixed results. A 17-pr crew destroyed a Panzer IV with a single shot on 2 August (the only tank destroyed by 7 Anti-Tank in Italy), but next day an M10 shelling a building was hit by return fire from a concealed Tiger tank and burst into flames, killing two and wounding two of the crew.

Although counter-battery work against harassing enemy guns continued until the night of 4 August, the battle had been won: Florence and most of the surrounding countryside were in Allied hands. Next day the New Zealand Division moved a few miles west to Empoli, the last German stronghold south of the River Arno. The artillery, with restricted ammunition supplies, fired small-scale concentrations in support of infantry and armoured assaults; the heavy mortars made a substantial contribution. The town was taken on the night of 11–12 August, and outposts along the riverbank were cleared over the next two days. Ammunition shortages prevented the gunners from responding appropriately to heavy German shelling and so the New Zealanders, their task complete, were relieved to be replaced by an American division on 14 and 15 August, moving out of the line to a rest area near Siena. Away from the fighting, Martyn Uren found the Arno district 'quite lovely', with its grapevines and nectarine trees, 'clucking hens, cooing doves, sheep, cattle and great-horned bullocks browsing in the fields; the hum of bees, the flight of birds, the friendly, blessed solitude of green arbours, far removed in atmosphere, yet close, in reality, to war'.[81]

THE GOTHIC LINE

For the next phase of the Italian campaign the New Zealand Division returned to the Adriatic coast.[82] At first only the field gunners went to the front, in support of 1 Canadian Corps; and they played no part in the initial assault on the Gothic Line, inland from Pesaro. On 1 September they supported a Canadian division, which achieved its objectives the following morning. The field gunners then rejoined the rest of the Divisional Artillery, moving forward again on 11 September along with 14 Light AA and 31 Anti-Tank Battery. They began firing at 6 p.m. the next day. Despite a successful Canadian attack on the Coriano Ridge, backed by the New Zealanders, German resistance was far from broken, and the gunners stayed in the line. From 14 September they backed the New Zealand 22 (Motorised) Battalion, which was attached to a Greek brigade. After moving forward to Riccione, the gunners supported attacks on Rimini airfield and San Fortunato Ridge, firing huge numbers of smoke and HE rounds over the next few days. On one day, 6 Field alone fired 13,300 rounds; more shells were fired during the assault on Rimini than in the Alamein offensive.

By the time the ridge and airfield were captured on the 20th and 21st respectively, the countryside was devastated and rain was falling heavily. Off-road movement became laborious as sodden ground at the gun positions turned into quagmires. Improvisation was called for. The Germans had concreted a Panther tank turret in the middle of the runway:

> We cracked away at that for days and couldn't do anything. And we were on the back slope of a dry river – four guns, no access behind us. So the 3-ton trucks with the ammunition came in, whizzed up the side, backed down this slope with the tailboard down, jammed on their brakes and we had 400 rounds of shells on the ground beside the gun. We had no option, we didn't have the blokes to unload them. At this stage we had our own gunner vehicles, 400 rounds in a truck. When it got intense, the ASC boys used to bring it straight to the guns, and boy, did they want it off! In theory the shells were stable enough – there were all sorts of safeguards. But we shouldn't have done it. I could probably have been court-martialled for it.[83]

The pattern was set for the winter campaign in Romagna. The Eighth Army would have to fight its way over many hills, and across many rivers on the plain below. By 23 September the New Zealand Division had crossed the Marecchia River and numerous minor watercourses and reached the Fontanaccia River. On the night of the 24th the field gunners and an attached Canadian regiment fired heavy concentrations to help 6 Brigade get across. Supporting tasks for other units crossing the river followed. The anti-tankers pushed forward with the infantry, often under heavy fire. By the 25th the three field regiments were north of Viserba, and now 4 Field pushed on to Bellaria, very close to the front, as the infantry, armour and anti-tankers moved beyond the Uso River to the Fiumicino. Here the German defences were strong, and the Division's advance stalled. Once again the field gunners engaged in fierce counter-battery duels, made difficult not only by the enemy's increasing use of armoured self-propelled guns and emplaced heavy tank turrets, but by the continuing wet weather and omnipresent mud.

One 5 Field driver remembered that the gunners 'complained that they fired their guns day and night while the drivers sat on their sterns doing nothing all day'. On one occasion the OC agreed that the two sections should change places for a while. 'Next day we drivers arrived at the guns ready for a hard day and night loading shell consigned to the enemy.'[84] This did not interrupt the standing arrangement that leave was granted to two men from each troop each day.

The campaign had been mostly quiet for the gunners of 14 Light AA Regiment. The Allied air forces dominated the skies during the day and there were few opportunities to fire Bofors guns at the rare German night-bombing attacks. On 14 September, gunners of 43 Battery claimed an unusual success when a small, fast *K-Boot* passing Rimini was stopped by shots fired over its bows, and then sunk. This was 'easy enough, and a pretty impressive sight'. The most important role now for the Bofors gunners was firing boundary traces for the many set-piece river crossings. They also re-equipped A and B troops with self-propelled Bofors, the only self-propelled guns in the division other than the anti-tankers' M10s.[85]

With Allied forces probing into the coastal foothills, the Germans made a fighting withdrawal to more easily defended positions along the Savio River. When the New Zealand Division began its next advance on 11 October, across a Bailey bridge thrown over the Fiumicino by the sappers, resistance was at first slight but increased as units moved forward. The advance was not halted for long, however; a strongpoint at Sant' Angelo was captured that night after heavy shelling. The Division pushed forward to the Pisciatello River, which 6 Brigade crossed with little opposition on the night of 18–19 October. The Division faced renewed resistance as it advanced to the banks of the Savio on the 21st. That night, the field regiments fired in support of a crossing by a Canadian division; firing on the New Zealand positions brought a sustained response from 71 tanks of the Armoured Brigade. Next day the rest of the New Zealand Division was pulled out of the line for rest and reorganisation. Concerned about the long years of war many in the Division had faced, Freyberg saw a need for recuperation – football was now the order of the day.

In reserve in Rimini, some anti-tank gunners showed their technical aptitude by modifying their guns. Q Troop of 34 Battery cut into a 17-pr carriage to lower it, and took a foot off the top of the shield for greater concealment. Though 'important Eight Army officers' were impressed, the modification would not catch on. 'Not to be beaten, 33 Battery did the same thing with a 6-pounder, with equal effect.'[86] For now the field and some of the other gunners stayed in the line, the field regiments firing concentrations to support an attack by a British division on the morning of 24 October. Now the gunners too were ordered out of the line, setting off next day to join the other units of the Division in a rest area south of Fabriano in the Apennines.

Rest and Reorganisation

Until mid-November the gunners enjoyed a respite from the pressures of the front.[87] They took leave in Rome or Florence; Fifth Reinforcements men and those who had returned from earlier drafts prepared to go home under the new policy of replacing men with more than three years' service overseas. 7 Anti-Tank Regiment was reorganised: 34 Battery, originally formed in England, was disbanded, as were the 6-pr troops in the other batteries. Each battery now had one troop of M10s and one of 17-prs, with the exception of 39 Heavy Mortar Battery, which kept its four troops and assumed the number 34. The M10 and the 17-pr ('a big boss') were retained because they were not limited to the anti-tank role; the heavy mortars had long been noted for their versatility.[88]

Allied aerial dominance had removed the need for 14 Light AA Regiment, which was disbanded. The ack-ack gunners and redundant anti-tankers remaining with the Division were either absorbed into other artillery units or became infantry in the new Divisional Cavalry Battalion. 36 Survey Battery was reduced to a small troop. Such was the weight of corps artillery, and the degree of corps coordination, that most surveying and all sound-ranging and flash-spotting were now corps responsibilities. The corps artillery structure already included numerous survey regiments.

The Division went back into the line at Forli, with the field regiments moving forward on 17 November. Divisional Artillery HQ was established in the town and the field batteries nearby. After firing concentrations in support of a British division, the gunners moved across the Cosina–Montone Canal towards Faenza. Here they had few occasions to open fire, though some concentrations were called for. Now the Division, apart from the field guns which were already in range, moved forward to relieve the British 46 Division. On the night of 14 December, 5 Brigade and armoured units mounted an attack west of Faenza. The preparations were hidden from the enemy, for whom the barrage must have come as an unwelcome surprise. An artilleryman remembered this three-hour barrage as 'one of the heaviest I have ever seen around here'. Next morning 'we moved up over the hill to a new position. I have never seen such damage done before in my life, every tree was hit and a shell-hole every 3 yards for about 3 miles.' The scene was 'awful, dead jerries are all over the place, all the houses are just about in ruins.'[89]

While the barrage swept forward, M10s covered the bridge across the Senio over which enemy reinforcements might move up. After Faenza was cut off and fell, some of the field guns were moved into its outskirts for the next major attack in the sector. A New Zealand artillery signaller was up front, in an area that was 'being shelled now and again pretty close too'. On the night of 19 December, more than 300 field and medium guns of New Zealand, Indian and British regiments mounted a creeping barrage on a wide front. 'Putting some big stuff in now attack went in tonight 9 pm big barrage 3 hours jerry is replying a bit.' This anti-tanker was just leaving his CP when:

> jerry put down one stonk which caught us fair and square. I got a hell of a fright we hopped into the jeep and went like hell and got caught again. I hopped in the ditch up to my knees in water the shelling was heavy. I ran over the road into another ditch then into a slitty one of Ted's. ... My nerves were very bad.[90]

By now, massed artillery support was the rule even for attacks at brigade-group level. Although the Germans reacted strongly with mortar and shellfire, and Nebelwerfer bombardments, 6 Brigade and a Gurkha brigade achieved their objectives. An intelligence summary captured from the German 278 Division acknowledged the effectiveness of the artillery tactics they faced: 'The New Zealanders have learned … to work forward under heavy artillery support close up behind their barrage, and in this way take their opponents off guard without suffering heavy losses themselves'.[91]

Not all rounds were fired with lethal intent. At Farinella, for instance, 'A small pamphlet war was indulged in, the Germans starting it and then a shell postal service began'.[92] Most guns had a 'cargo round' capable of disgorging leaflets over enemy lines. The 25-pr's 'Propaganda' shell was a smoke shell in which the smoke canisters had been replaced by leaflets. A tiny expelling charge opened the round, and the passing air did the rest.

It was clear that the Senio Line was strongly established. The front stabilised, and for the gunners Christmas and the following two months were surprisingly quiet, apart from some sniping by the 17-prs, and harassing and counter-battery concentrations by the field guns. The Tongariro draft left the Division, to be replaced by reinforcements from the disbanded 3 Division, its role in the South Pacific having ended in early 1944.

In early March 1945, Polish units relieved the New Zealand gunners as the Division again left the line and returned to Fabriano. Here they trained for an assault on the Senio River and subsequent actions. It was hoped that once the Senio Line was broken the advance would be rapid, and the anti-tankers looked forward to joining the cavalry, armour and infantry in the pursuit. Demonstration shoots by the field gunners helped to dispel the rumours of shorts that had dogged them throughout the Italian campaign. Queree and his staff took the opportunity to develop procedures for the rapid repositioning of the field regiments – wherever possible Queree himself would study the ground from an Air OP Auster – and to reduce delays in calling down fire.

6-pr anti-tank gun in northern Italy, January 1945.
DA8050, Alexander Turnbull Library, Wellington.

OPERATION BUCKLAND

The New Zealand Division and an Indian division were 5 Corps' contribution to Operation Buckland, the Eighth Army's assault on the Senio Line on 9 April 1945.[93] The gunners were recalled to positions north-west of Faenza in early April. While infantry and some gunners cleared the last pockets of resistance from the near stopbank, most of the gunners held their fire to conceal their positions. The New Zealand fire plan for the Senio crossing in its sector – the most complex and detailed ever prepared – went off like clockwork.

Softening up for the assault began about 1.50 p.m., when 500 heavy bombers pounded the German lines. At 3.20 p.m around 1300 guns opened up. Under Queree's command for the 3000-yard wide barrage in the New Zealand sector were the three New Zealand and three British field regiments, plus two medium regiments. In addition, a self-propelled field regiment and a heavy AA battery would carry out counter-mortar concentrations, while the medium and heavy guns of 2 AGRA would fire linear concentrations and murders against batteries. The New Zealand and a British heavy mortar battery would fire similar concentrations on defensive positions close to the river. The New Zealand heavy mortars

> ### CHRISTMAS IN ITALY
> Over winter the gunners had opportunities for time off. On Christmas Eve 1944, 34 Battery's Lance-Corporal McMahon took leave in Taranto. 'Had a pretty good time in all the shops then sneaked back home to camp and went on the piss on some good vino. ... Got drunk ... pretty bad.' Next morning he enjoyed the contents of parcels from home. By Boxing Day he was 'taking it easy' but 'may have a bit more to drink tonight'. A few days later McMahon lost his Africa Star while drunk: 'What a bugger.' He also did 'a bit of looting' and met 'a couple of lovely girls' who 'used to take me around to their house' for 'a wonderful time'. When orders to move arrived, the young women were 'unhappy'.[94] In static situations like these, batteries roofed their gun pits. 6 Field's were 'quite elaborate shelters' with brick floors; beams and heavy tarpaulins kept the snow out. In Carreto in March 1945, men enjoyed 'wine, eggs and macaroni meals' provided by the locals whose houses they were living in.[95]

had spent nearly two weeks training for this assault in the hills above Fabriano.

The fire-plan involved five 'dragnet' barrages of up to eight lifts from the far stopbank forward, as if covering an infantry assault. Then each barrage switched back to the start briefly to hit the defensive positions along the stopbank. This made 'a hell of a roar'. After a ten-minute pause while fighter-bombers strafed and bombed the far bank, followed by harassing artillery fire on the defensive positions, the dragnet was repeated. Smoke was fired after the fifth barrage. Then flame-throwing tanks scorched the far bank before the final barrage started at 7.20 pm. This stood for ten minutes while the infantry stormed almost unopposed across the river in small assault boats. For the New Zealanders this involved two battalions each of 5 and 6 Brigades. Then the final barrage lifted forward and the infantry followed. With the defences devastated, the infantry assault was particularly successful in the New Zealand sector and engineers soon bridged the river. 4 Armoured Brigade crossed in the early hours of 10 April, and the M10s and 17-prs by 6 a.m. Other artillery units followed during the day, including 4 Field in support of the armoured brigade:

The banks of the river were black and burned where the big flame throwers had been at work. [T]he river was not very wide the water was low. We went on slowly past dugouts and holes all the houses here are demolished … and the ground is a mass of shell and bomb holes, a few dead are lying around.[96]

A New Zealand M10 layer remembered 'the stench of burning bodies'.[97]

From the Senio to Trieste

The anticipated war of movement had begun, and the advance pushed forward to the Santerno River.[98] On the morning of 11 April, 5 and 6 Field crossed the Senio and established new positions to support the attack on the Santerno, where it was feared the Germans might set up another strong defensive line. In fact the New Zealand infantry easily established a bridgehead, which the field and medium guns protected against a strong counter-attack while the sappers bridged the wide river. Despite the pace of the advance and difficulties of radio communication over crowded airwaves – mitigated by some enormous efforts to maintain telephone lines – the gunners continued their work. The Allies held the bridgehead and next day Queree ordered a quick barrage ('Kettle') by four field regiments. This dislodged the defenders of Massa Lombarda, north of the New Zealanders' crossing point, and further fire was called down on the retreating enemy. A second quick barrage, 'Doormat', led the infantry into the village in the small hours of 13 April.

Later that day five field and two medium regiments under Queree moved through the bottleneck of the Santerno bridge to new positions. Early the next morning, another quick barrage ('Foxy') led infantry across the Sillaro River. On the main line of advance, the New Zealand Division faced increasing opposition as German reserves were thrown in from other parts of the front. Freyberg now called for 'Operation Spaniel'. This began at 9 p.m on 15 April with a substantial barrage arranged at short notice from numerous regiments only recently dug into their positions, and including full counter-battery and counter-mortar programmes. The success of the almost three-hour barrage, along a 3000-yard front, was testimony to the skill of the New Zealand, British and Polish gunners involved, and not least to the professionalism of Queree and Divisional Artillery HQ. But resistance had by no means evaporated, and as the infantry pushed forward the German artillery again made itself felt.

A programme prepared for the crossing of the Gaiana Canal was cancelled late on 17 April. The next night saw a barrage even heavier than 'Spaniel', complemented by heavy counter-battery programmes. This devastated the strong defences close to the canal and the infantry were able to clear the far bank. The Germans were still able to bring artillery and Nebelwerfer fire to bear, and retreated only slowly over the following two days. A quick barrage at regimental strength, called for at very short notice and delivered by 5 Field, helped some of the infantry crossing the Idice on 20 April before several regiments fired a more substantial barrage from midnight to assist the advance. Directed fire support was still needed, and the gunners remained busy.

After crossing the Reno River without need of a barrage, the Division reached the Po on 24 April. That night, 5 Brigade crossed this river in an amphibious assault supported by the last division-sized artillery programme fired by New Zealand gunners. The crossing encountered very little resistance, and over the next two days most of the Divisional Artillery followed. The gunners continued to fire on the retreating enemy, but organised German resistance had ended, and after the New Zealand Division crossed the Adige most raced along the road to Padua, which was liberated early on 28 April. Later that morning, guns of 4 Field had to be hurriedly dug in outside the town to reply vigorously to some desultory German shelling. By a cruel stroke of luck, a 25-pr suffered a premature which killed a nearby gunner.

The advance continued apace, and it is claimed that Major 'Huck' Sawyers of 5 Field was the first Allied soldier to enter Venice, at 1.50 p.m. on 29 April. The following day, while units were being ferried across the Piave River, 5 Brigade positions came under counter-attack. Two batteries fired for almost two hours to beat off the enemy. With surrendered Germans filling the roads, however, such last-ditch stands were the exception as the Division raced towards Trieste. At Prosecco on 2 May, a British cavalry unit, the 12th Lancers, advancing with the New Zealanders, was held up by shelling and small-arms fire. Shells called down by 4 Field's second-in-command, Major C.K. Reed, persuaded these Germans to surrender after 20 minutes. On other occasions the deployment of field guns was sufficient inducement to throw in the towel. The Germans by now had

Trieste tryst: a 6 Field gunner practises his Italian.
DA-09365-F, Alexander Turnbull Library, Wellington.

a healthy respect for the New Zealand field regiments which, in the last month of the war, fired 222,443 shells.

When the New Zealanders reached Trieste late on 2 May, some entered the town and others camped outside. That day the German forces in Italy surrendered to the Allies, and a few days later the gunners celebrated Victory in Europe (VE) Day. But the New Zealanders could not yet let down their guard. The Italian claim to Trieste was disputed by Marshal Tito's communist Yugoslav partisans, with whom the Division shared an uneasy occupation of the city. While the Divisional Artillery prepared fire plans, field batteries registered Yugoslav gun positions. The stand-off ended without bloodshed in mid-June, when Tito's forces withdrew from Trieste.

The end of the war in Europe brought a change in attitude. Now the problem was to keep idle hands occupied, and while training continued considerable effort went into establishing rest and recreation facilities. A Divisional Artillery Holiday Centre was established adjacent to Divisional Artillery HQ. The Hotel Miramare was commandeered and staffed with chefs, stewards, dance bands and other employees of the shipping line Lloyd Triestino, which had its headquarters in Trieste. Batteries were rotated through this enticing facility at five-day intervals.

At the end of July the Division returned south to Lake Trasimene, where the goalposts were still standing from their sojourn a year earlier. After the Eighth Reinforcements men departed on 5 August, the Division gradually ceased to exist, with men going home in the order in which they had arrived. Lack of shipping prolonged the process, but during December and January the much-reduced artillery regiments were disbanded.[99] Meanwhile, with some shuffling of personnel, and after a few days planning for a deployment to Burma that became unnecessary when Japan surrendered, 9 Brigade became Jayforce, New Zealand's contribution to the British Commonwealth Occupation Force in Japan.

Conclusion

The effectiveness of the doctrine and techniques of the Second New Zealand Divisional Artillery were recognised by friend and foe alike. The official British history of artillery developments during the war concluded that 'In the hands of practised and skilful exponents, such as the 2nd New Zealand Division, there seemed little that the barrage could not do. It was in fact their normal method of artillery support. ... The results achieved speak for themselves.'[100]

But this was only part of the Divisional Artillery's achievement. In the stonk and the murder, the New Zealanders had powerful techniques of predicted fire available at short notice, and the importance of their application at many decisive moments – Medenine is a fine example – should not be underestimated. Nor should the roles of Freyberg and Weir in fighting for and extending the application of the doctrines of divisional unity and corps coordination. The scale of the concentrations and barrages in Italy, with close coordination between the organic artillery of each division and massive corps artillery support, was a far cry from the 'penny-packeting' of the early days in North Africa. At the OPs, the gun and wagon lines, the regimental HQs and battery command posts, the skills developed over years of often intense activity ensured that the gunners could apply the most complicated fire-plans with a confidence born of hard experience.

Divisional Artillery Headquarters relax in the grounds of the Miramare hotel, Trieste, May 1945. *2000.572, Kippenberger Military Archive, Army Museum Waiouru.*

The headquarters of the Divisional Artillery was judged by Lieutenant-General Sir Leonard Thornton to have been the most efficient of the Division's 'second-tier command organisations'. He attributed this to a combination of factors. First, there were in effect only three CRAs – Miles, Weir and Queree – throughout the war. 'Div Arty' was also usually an uncluttered area, with few subordinate units attached. And gunner staff had to be unusually competent, both in 'normal' control procedures and in the technical skills needed to manage the fire control of many guns.[101] Freyberg gave 'the whole set up of the Div Arty' much of the credit for there being relatively few casualties in the Division during the advance from the Senio.[102]

The skills of the Second Divisional Artillery's gunners, officers and men alike, would provide a solid basis for the maintenance of artillery capabilities in the New Zealand Army in the years ahead. The price of its achievements had been high. The Divisional Artillery lost 652 men killed in action or from wounds. More than 2000 were wounded and 678 taken prisoner, of whom 32 died in captivity.

Writing Their History

By 1942 the Army had appointed unit historians: Sergeants R.J. Larkin (4 Field), W.J. Fisk (5 Field) and James Johnson (6 Field); W.E. ('Spud') Murphy had had this role in 7 Anti-Tank Regiment since March. Following a 2NZEF directive in July 1944, a historian of the Divisional Artillery was sought.[103] Earlier in the year, 2NZEF's Official Archivist had asked that Sergeant Martyn Uren, a law student before the war, be transferred to Army HQ in Wellington to assist him. Uren's self-published gunner's account *Kiwi Saga* must have brought him to notice, but he was deemed too fit not to fight.[104] Instead, in September 1944, Murphy was appointed Divisional Artillery Historian.[105] With the exception of the Sangro and Orsogna fronts, when he was severely injured, Murphy saw every major battlefield 'either just before, at the time, or soon afterwards'. After the war he continued to work on the history, first at Army Headquarters in Wellington, then from 1947 as an employee of the War History Branch of the Department of Internal Affairs.[106]

By 1946 six volumes were planned: the overall volume plus one for each regiment (with 36 Survey Battery and 14 AA Regiment combined).[107] A NZA Unit History Committee set about locating narrators and authors, to whom they channelled personal accounts, diaries and photos. *Evening Post* journalist Neville Webber (4 Field) and Captain John Fullarton of New Plymouth (6 Field) were contracted.[108] Problems soon arose: difficulties accessing material, especially for non-Wellingtonians; completing the narratives; disagreements within the gunner community over the subject matter. Then, in 1950, with government expenditure constrained,[109] Cabinet decided to publish a single 160,000-word volume, which was offered to Fullarton, who had served in the artillery from 1939 before becoming a journalist and sub-editor for the *Taranaki Daily News* and writing three novels.[110] Fullarton's earlier work on 6 Field was said to be 'well above the usual run', despite having 'evoked much criticism from "originals" of the regiment'.[111] The other authors' contracts (now including separate books on 7 and 14 regiments) were cancelled. Fullarton foresaw 'a lot of people with sub-unit patriotism being dissatisfied with the space accorded their doings'.[112] But with little of the work he submitted actually devoted to the artillery, his contract was terminated in early 1952.

Reeling from this latest setback, the War History Branch concentrated on its other books. At their many reunions gunners loudly criticised the delay in writing their story. A complaint from 4 Field's Regimental Association reached the Minister of Internal Affairs. They were all the more galled because the regimental narratives had been largely completed, and the Third Division Histories Committee had published its unofficial artillery account in 1948.[113] By 1954 Murphy was once again earmarked for the job, but commitments to other volumes delayed him. He resumed work on the artillery in 1961, but was soon appointed to a university lectureship. Murphy submitted his last chapters in February 1966, and later that year the 2 New Zealand Divisional Artillery history was finally published.

Ray Queree

Born in 1909, Raymond Queree spent five years in the Christchurch Boys' High cadets.[114] He won a cadetship at the Royal Military College, Sandhurst, in 1927, and was commissioned into the New Zealand Staff Corps after two years of study. He was attached to the British Army for a year before returning to New Zealand in 1931 with his wife and family. Queree taught at Trentham and transferred in this role to the RNZA in 1935. He moved to Fort Dorset the following year and in 1937 became Adjutant 1 Artillery Brigade and Field Cadre Auckland before attending the School of Artillery in Sydney.

Two years later Captain Queree returned to Britain for a Field Gunnery Staff Course, but after only two months he was seconded to 2NZEF and came back to New Zealand. After commanding 5 Field Regiment at Ngaruawahia, he embarked with the Second Echelon as second-in-command of 7 Anti-Tank Regiment. In November 1940 he became Brigade Major and GSO2 at New Zealand Divisional Artillery Headquarters, and headed for Egypt. He was wounded on 27 May 1941, the only Divisional Artillery HQ casualty on Crete. From June 1942 Lieutenant-Colonel Queree commanded 4 Field and the Maadi-based training regiment (32 Field) before returning to the Division in September as GSO1, building up the efficiency of the division 'with an almost puritanical zeal'. After a War Staff Course in 1943, he again briefly commanded 5 Field.

He then held a corps position, Brigadier General Staff, before replacing Steve Weir as CRA in August 1944, becoming probably the only CRA to take the field for the Divisional Artillery rugby team. His war service earned him three mentions in despatches, an OBE and CBE. He was made a DSO for overseeing the overwhelming artillery barrages that characterised the advance from the Senio River crossing to Trieste. The citation said that 'he maintained constant personal touch with forward troops and commanders. His reconnaissances were carried out often under heavy fire and in areas not cleared of the enemy.'

Queree was a technical gunner, 'highly professional, uncompromising, a strong disciplinarian and a master of detail'.[115] His men held him in high regard. One newcomer remembered arriving in Italy and reporting to Brigadier Queree, then CRA, for the first time. 'As I said my name, and Queree was writing it down, a Five-Five gun went off outside the window.... It is the measure of these guys, that that man didn't lift his head, didn't say anything – what an outfit!'[116] Queree was tough yet fair; he would forgive an honest mistake once – but not twice.[117] Dubbed 'Sabre-tooth', he 'combined a very agile mind with a unique mental robustness. He didn't suffer fools gladly and was prepared to be very direct' when necessary.[118] Those who served on his staff revered him and felt that his achievements in overcoming the logistical problems of the last weeks of the war never received the recognition they deserved.[119]

Ray Queree.
2004.375, Kippenberger Military Archive, Army Museum Waiouru.

After the war Queree returned to training as GSO1 at the Staff College, Camberley. A brilliant administrator, he was to be 'one of the architects of the post-1945 Army'. He returned to New Zealand as Quartermaster-General and had a seat on the Army Board (1948–54). He attended the Imperial Defence College in 1950, helped to form K Force – the first New Zealand expeditionary force to leave with its heavy equipment – commanded Central Military District (1953–54), and was Adjutant General (1954–60). He was also Vice Chief of General Staff (1956–60) and then headed the New Zealand Army Liaison Staff in London until his retirement in 1964. Ray Queree was Director of Civil Defence from 1965 to 1970, using his management and planning skills during a period marked by the *Wahine* storm and the Inangahua earthquake. Colonel Commandant of the RNZA from 1968 until 1970, he died in 1975.

Steve Weir

A natural leader, Steve Weir epitomised the New Zealand artilleryman's self-image – gruff but effective.[120] Weir 'stood nearly six feet tall, but ... carried the physique of a nuggety fighter, quick in movement, with the shoulders and voice of a bull'.[121] He was also noted for his 'direct gaze and immaculate moustache'.

Born near Dunedin in October 1904, the young Weir was christened Cyril but always known as 'Steve'. After three years in the Otago Boys' High School cadets he joined the Territorials, spending time in the saddle with 5 Otago Hussars and then 6 Manawatu Mounted Rifles from 1922 before joining the regular army three years later. He went to London on a cadetship to train at the Royal Military Academy, Woolwich. Not academically inclined, he needed extra tuition in mathematics and science before gaining his commission in the RNZA in 1927. After attachment to various RA units and further courses in Britain, Weir returned to New Zealand in 1929 and had various posts in all three commands, including the ASC. He served in Napier for five months in 1931 after the devastating Hawke's Bay earthquake.

The outbreak of war saw him miss the Staff College course he was due to attend at Camberley. Instead he was appointed to command and train 25 Battery, 4 New Zealand Field Regiment, on its formation at Hopuhopu camp. 'To his great disgust and disappointment he was withheld from the First Echelon ... to act as CO of the nucleus of the 7th Anti Tank Regiment, and again he was to be disappointed, for, just prior to their sailing, he was appointed CO of the 6th NZ Field Regiment upon that unit's formation.' By now a lieutenant-colonel, he sailed with 6 Field, which he led throughout the ordeals of Greece and Crete. His 'forceful training methods, firm precepts and defined principles' ensured 'the success of the regiment as

Steve Weir with the Belhamed rammer.
PAColl-6407-90, Alexander Turnbull Library, Wellington.

a fighting unit. He possessed unlimited drive and vigour and spared neither himself nor his men in his efforts to obtain a high standard of field gunnery and physical fitness.'[122] Despite his abilities, however, he knew little about the technical side of artillery.[123]

In the fighting in North Africa later in 1941, Weir showed his preference for leading from the front. At Belhamed 'he visited each troop on foot in the heat of action, and upon returning to his headquarters, found his own vehicles and staff either shot up or dispersed'. After seeing his three batteries withdraw safely, he was almost the last man on the battlefield. Discovering an abandoned vehicle ('a blitz buggy, two sizes too small for him'), he drove it out, 'to the great delight of 48 Battery, who by this time had written him off'.[124]

Weir's time as CRA from December 1941 to June 1944 helped him to refine techniques developed by Miles which enabled centralised control of the Divisional Artillery. Towards the end of this period he was also Corps CRA directing the artillery of 10 Corps, then commanded the New Zealand Division for six weeks after Freyberg was injured. Later in the year he became the only Dominion officer to command a British Army division during the war when he was appointed GOC 46 Division. Though it 'wondered for a while what had struck it',[125] Weir led this division until 1946, controversially forcing the repatriation of Russians – not all ex-POWs – from Austria.[126] His war service was recognised with the DSO in 1941 (for Operation Crusader) and Bar a year later (after El Alamein), and a CBE and CB by 1945. The Americans and Greeks also decorated him, and he was mentioned in despatches six times.

Weir's drinking companions could attest to his loutish side. On one occasion, after shouting his officers a fine meal in a Cairo restaurant, he suddenly decided to 'wreck this joint'. As the party threw chairs and a table down to the courtyard, the owner and his servants remonstrated with them. Weir said, '"Gentlemen, follow me", and went to the entrance, which was guarded by a couple of red-caps

[Military Policemen] who said, "No-one is to pass." Steven simply said, "I am General Weir, these are my officers, make way", the red-caps fell back and we moved out.'[127]

After illness and a year or so back in New Zealand from 1948 commanding Southern Military District, Weir attended the Imperial Defence College, whose students were generally being groomed for higher office. He became Quartermaster-General in 1951 after experience at the War Office. From 1955 until 1960, as both Chief of General Staff and GOC of the New Zealand Division, he oversaw the shift in focus from a potential return to the Middle East to actual service in South-east Asia. In 1960, 'to the dismay of the service Chiefs of Staff', who saw their advisory role being usurped, Weir was appointed Military Adviser to the government within the Prime Minister's Department, focusing on 'military matters with external affairs implications'. In October 1961 he became ambassador to Thailand (later cross-accredited to South Vietnam and Laos) and New Zealand's representative to the South-East Asia Treaty Organisation, which was based in Bangkok. Weir retired from the Army, relinquishing his appointments as Honorary Colonel, New Zealand Scottish Regiment, RNZAC, and Colonel Commandant, New Zealand Special Air Squadron.

As ambassador, Weir favoured New Zealand playing a military role in the developing Vietnam War. Once troops were committed, he visited them regularly and was always well received by 161 Battery, which named one of its Fire Support Bases after him.[128] When Weir retired to Tauranga in 1967, former gunner colleagues formed a guard of honour to welcome him. In 1960, when members of the Canterbury branch of the regimental association had toasted both his KBE and the 'regularising of a nickname that will always be associated with 6th Field', his health was drunk 'with such keenness that the proposer scarce had time to complete his eulogies'.[129] He died in September 1969, not yet 65.

Weapons – Anti-tank

New Zealand used the three main British anti-tank guns during the war. The advent of heavier tanks necessitated larger guns than the 2-prs: the 6-pr in 1941 and then the 17-pr in 1942. These both limited their traverse and had slit trails for quicker deployment, but when necessary later in the war they could also provide HE in indirect fire.

Name	Ordnance QF 6-pr Mk IV	Ordnance QF 17-pr Mk 1
Entered NZ service	1942	1943
Role	Light anti-tank gun	Heavy Anti-tank gun
Calibre (bore)	2.24 in	3 in
Calibres	45	55
Traverse	90	60
Range effective	1000 yds	1310 yds
Weight	2515 lb	4614 lb
Projectile	6.3 lb AP	17 lb AP
Remarks	For these purpose-designed armour-piercing guns the maximum range was academic: most could fire out to several thousand yards, but at long ranges armour penetration was virtually zero; range scales and sights were set to effective ranges.	

Weapons – Mortar Artillery

The 4.2-inch mortar was taken into the New Zealand artillery in Italy at the time of Cassino, and remained in service after the war in an infantry support role.

Name	4.2-in Mortar Mk II
Entered NZ service	1944
Role	fire support
Calibre	4.2 in
Range	1050–4100 yds
Weight	837 lb mobile, 257 lb static baseplate
Projectile	20 lb – HE
Remarks	mounted on a 2-wheel trailer

Weapons – Self-Propelled Guns

The only armoured self-propelled gun used in New Zealand service was an American gun on an American tank chassis. This high-velocity 15-pr had been a coast defence and then an anti-aircraft gun for four decades before being standardised as the M5 anti-tank gun in 1941. In 1942 it was mated in an open-topped turret with the chassis of the diesel M4A2 Medium Tank (known as the Sherman III by New Zealand users). As the M10, it was called Wolverine in British use. The turret was thinly armoured and slow to traverse. By the time it was issued to New Zealand the ammunition had been improved and the 3-inch gun had significant advantages over the 40-cal 75-mm tank gun of the Sherman III (which Kiwis felt was a match for any German tank).[130] While firing shells only 1.2 mm wider, it had 2.3 times the chamber capacity. The extra propellant produced almost twice the muzzle energy for long-range hitting power.[131]

Name	M10 Gun Motor Carriage, 'Wolverine'
Entered NZ service	1944
Role	self-propelled anti-tank and fire support gun
Calibre	3 in, 50 cals
Range	16,100 ft AP – 14,780 yds HE
Weight, Vehicle	29.47 tons
Vehicle specs	30 mph, 200-mile range, 7.5-ft trench, 2-ft step. Crew 5.
Projectile	15.4 lb. AP, HE, APC, Smoke. 54 rounds carried (6 ready)
Remarks	This successful open-topped gun mount with 19° elevation was based on a diesel M4A2 tank carriage.

Tactical Developments

The **'Murder'**, first known as 'Method A', was 'a defensive fire method that concentrated all 72 [field] guns of the Divisional Artillery' on a single pre-selected point.[132]

> Once the enemy appeared in its vicinity, all ... a forward observer had to do was send the ground co-ordinates (or nickname) of the target prefixed by the word Murder. All batteries of the division within range would then immediately engage the target using all their guns, without the usual preliminary adjusting rounds from a single barrel. Up to 360 rounds could be brought down on the target within about two minutes.

Rapidly implemented divisional concentrations of fire had previously been trialled by Brigadier H.J. Parham RA at the School of Artillery in England. Parham had realised their potential value against concealed tanks during the May 1940 Blitzkrieg. Radio communication made them feasible; shortcutting the usual chain of command made them practicable.

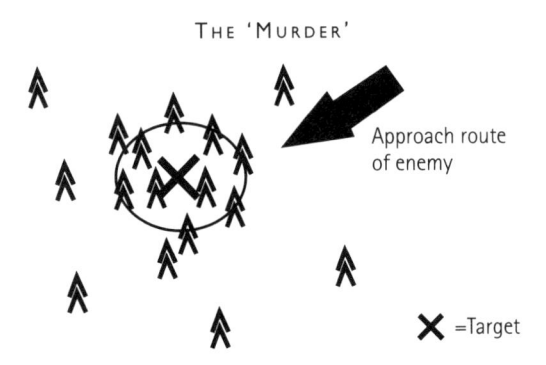

THE 'MURDER'

Approach route of enemy

✗ =Target

The 'Stonk', originally the 'hate', was the 'other (and best known) innovation whose development began in Syria, and which was later extensively used in North Africa and Italy'. Though similar to the murder, its target was 'a rectangular area of 1200 x 600 yards (later reduced to a 600 or 525 yards frontage) identified by its centre point and vertical axis, rather than a single converging point'. This achieved 'roughly even' coverage of 'the entire beaten zone whereas the centre of the murder caught the full impact of the fire, with the effect diminishing ... towards the periphery'. The Divisional Artillery 'could put down 504 rounds in about three minutes with shattering effect, particularly on soft transport or infantry in the open'. Weir and Brigadier H.M. Stanford (CCRA XIII Corps) came up with the name during the build-up to El Alamein. '"Stonk" was adopted and initiated into 2nd NZ Div as a fire drill about early August 1942.'

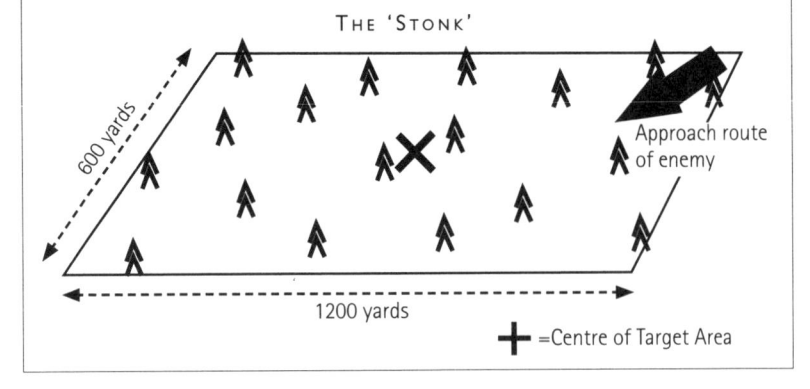

THE 'STONK'

600 yards

Approach route of enemy

1200 yards

✚ =Centre of Target Area

7

PACIFIC THEATRE AND HOME DEFENCE, 1939–45

Though the defences of New Zealand's main harbours were on high alert from 1939, their significance grew enormously after the Japanese attacks on Pearl Harbor and South-east Asia on 7 December 1941. Particularly after the fall of Singapore in February 1942, massive efforts were made to defend New Zealand against a large-scale invasion as well as cruiser or air raids. Meanwhile, garrison gunners in far-flung Pacific outposts were participating in the coordinated Allied defence of the South Pacific, though they would not be called upon to fire in anger. The gunners of 3 New Zealand Division, which was raised to serve alongside American forces in the south-west Pacific, would make their most important contributions during three successful amphibious landings in the Solomon Islands in 1943–44.

FORTRESS NEW ZEALAND

On 25 March 1942, the Chiefs of Staff, relying on a report produced the previous October by Major-General Sir Guy Williams, who had been brought to New Zealand to assess the home defences, identified three likely sites for a Japanese amphibious assault: the Bay of Islands, Marlborough Sounds and Akaroa Harbour.[1] The home defence force, mainly Territorial Force (with which the National Military Reserve was amalgamated in February 1942) and Home Guard, provided fortress and area troops at Auckland, Wellington and Lyttelton; each of the three military districts had a field force based on divisional formations. The Chiefs of Staff called for expanded garrison forces and an increase to five field divisions. The latter requirement was met, in effect, when two US divisions arrived in New Zealand from June 1942 to train for service in the Pacific. By then the most acute threat to New Zealand had passed; the Japanese plan to cut off Australasia from the United States had been foiled at the Battle of the Coral Sea in May, and the overall strategic situation had turned against Japan with the American victory at the Battle of Midway (4–6 June). But defensive preparations continued: coastal and anti-aircraft artillery, in particular, kept expanding until mid-1943. Then there was an even more rapid contraction, beginning with the field forces. By early 1944 only a few skeletal coastal and AA units remained ready for action at short notice.

The Coastal Defences

For the coastal and (particularly) the anti-aircraft defences, it was a case of too much too late: few of the emergency measures planned in late 1941 would be ready until late 1942. Meanwhile, the coastal defences completed after the outbreak of war in Europe provided some protection for the three main ports. After the coastal gunners were mobilised on 3 September 1939, the RNZA and (mainly) TF gunners had settled down to a routine based on high readiness. The examination batteries faced frequent alerts, checking that unidentified vessels were not hostile.[2] They were manned around the clock, in three watches, which meant a day on, a day off, then half a day's leave. Of the new emplacements, the counter-bombardment battery at Motutapu

---

Coast Artillery Duties

Many RNZA men shunned the coast artillery because of the difficulty of the work. Everything was a potential target until proven innocent and the duties were technically complex, with officers and NCOs needing some mathematical knowledge. Instead of reading maps with simple Northings and Eastings coordinates, the Coast Artillery used a Block-Square-Point system, a grid of diminishing squares with the largest termed blocks and the smallest – 25 yards by 25 – points.

Personnel fed information into a mechanical computer which calculated the position of the target when the next round landed. If they came under counter-bombardment fire, 'the bloke at Table Fire Direction' took control. 'When you are actually observing, you can have three or four

was fully operational a few weeks after war was declared, and Palmer Head was ready by March 1940. Interim measures were called for at Godley Head, and two 60-pr medium guns were in place at Taylor Battery by 9 September 1939, to be replaced a year later by 6-inch Mk VII guns on naval mountings as a further interim measure until the new two-gun 6-inch Mk 24 counter-bombardment battery became operational in early 1942.

Godley Head's interim 6-inch guns came from Admiralty stocks. Two more provided for a new battery at Castor Bay in Auckland were emplaced and proofed by July 1941. By February 1941 the two 6-inch Mk VII guns from North Head were in place on Whangaparaoa Peninsula, where a full-scale counter-bombardment emplacement was constructed with the usual underground magazine and plotting facilities, linked to the Auckland Fortress Fire Command. Though limited in elevation, they were far enough from Auckland to play a counter-bombardment role.

As the Admiralty made more naval guns available, a new 6-inch battery was established at Fort Opau on Wellington's west coast; these guns were proofed by February 1942. Another obsolete 6-inch HP BL gun was brought back into service at Taiaroa Battery in January 1941, with more success than at Fort Jervois. The following January two 6-inch Mk VII guns on naval mountings were installed at the new Rerewahine Battery at Taiaroa Head to defend Port Chalmers. One of these was resited at the original Taiaroa Battery in early 1944 to replace the 6-inch

> salvoes in the air at the same time, and you as a "Tech-Ack" need to know when they hit the water, because the rounds are falling with a different correction on. You might have three or four corrections in the air at the same time. Sitting beside the BC, you say that's round 3, shot 3, which means he might have two other brackets still on the way.'
>
> Most coast gunners were either too young or too old to go overseas, or had health problems. A battery sergeant recalled of the first group that 'if they're not getting into trouble there's something wrong with them. It was monotonous, and they had money to get drunk.' Keith Mills, the battery commander at Takapuna, despatched his troublemakers to Castor Bay, Flagstaff or Moturoa – and then became battery commander at the latter two sites![3]

HP gun in the close defence and examination roles. Two ex-naval 6-inch guns were mounted at St Kilda (Tomahawk Battery) by October 1942, but this battery did not become operational. After the Bay of Islands, judged at greatest risk of amphibious assault, was declared a Fortress Area in June 1942, two-gun 6-inch batteries were mounted on Moturoa Island and at Russell.

Shore-defence radar sets which arrived from Australia in August 1942 provided early warning and assisted with fire control at the counter-bombardment batteries at Whangaparaoa, Motutapu, and Palmer and Godley Heads.[4] Additional sets, manufactured in New Zealand or imported from Britain, were installed at Rerewahine, the close defence batteries, and OPs on Tiritiri Matangi (off Whangaparaoa) and Sinclair Head, Wellington. These radar stations had a secondary role: providing early warning of air raids. To the gunners the first radar 'contraptions' installed in the coastal batteries (in huts which rotated along with the antenna mast) 'looked like Gypsy caravans'.[5]

The major ports also had examination batteries capable of bolstering the close defences of the ports; since 1938 drafts of Special Reservists had been trained to man these. The 4-inch naval guns from HMS *New Zealand* provided the armament for the examination batteries at Auckland, Wellington and Lyttelton. They were supplemented by light machine guns, which had primarily an AA role but could also cover areas of water hidden from the main guns across which fishing boats sometimes attempted to sneak. Emplacements for Lyttelton's examination battery, which would guard the inner harbour from Battery Point, were ready by mid-1939, and its two guns (from the Point Jerningham saluting battery) were proofed three days after the declaration of war. Small civilian vessels were still somewhat casual about examination procedures and a tragic accident occurred here on 12 October, when an examination gun fired a round of solid shot to warn the fishing boat *Dolphin*, which had failed to halt. The shot accidentally hit the boat, killing crewman Fred Brasell, the only fatality caused by the coast defences during the war.[6]

The examination battery at Narrow Neck was increased to six guns in 1940, but the next year pairs of guns were shifted to North Head and Tonga. In 1942 its strength was partially restored by the addition of a third 4-inch gun. With these weapons in high demand for close defence purposes, two were salvaged from outside the Auckland War Memorial Museum and refurbished for deployment at North Head and Narrow Neck.[7] Two of Fort Dorset's 4-inch guns were shifted to Gordon Point, but in Wellington, as at the other major ports, they were complemented in the examination role by the 6-inch close-defence guns covering the same water. There was no dedicated examination battery at Otago Harbour: the anchorage outside the harbour was covered by the Taiaroa and Rerewahine guns.

To fire accurately at visible targets the 4-inch guns of the examination batteries needed autosights – telescope range-finders linked to the barrel of the gun so that range information could be converted into an elevation adjustment. The Auckland Technical Development Committee, a branch of the Department of Scientific and Industrial Research, developed and manufactured sights that were installed on all ten operational 4-inch guns by November 1942. Similar sights were also developed for the 6-inch naval guns emplaced at the minor ports and in Fiji.[8]

Examination batteries were served by coast artillery searchlights (CASL, later called defence electric lights – DEL). The searchlight sections were manned by gunners, supplemented from early 1943 by Home Guardsmen and Women's Auxiliary Army Corps volunteers (WAACs). At each major port, a sentry beam or beams illuminated the harbour entrance and examination anchorage at night, while other lights swept over the surrounding area. The DEL sections also provided the 'fighting lights' for the examination and close

---

Women Join the Artillery

In December 1942 the first WAACs entered camp in the fortress commands to take over much of the 'technical assistance' work in the fire command posts, observation posts and plotting rooms of the batteries defending the major ports, and in the associated radar installations. They would later play an increasing role in operating searchlights, and staffed the 'directors' of the two 6-pr twin AMTB installations. In battery observation posts and plotting rooms, WAACs operated all the instruments. As Captain John Horrocks observed, 'where the work calls for quick movement, the women have gone through their course in a much shorter time than men'. Horrocks got his first battery command at Whangaparaoa. 'I had a detachment of WAACs out there, and the sergeant in charge was my elder sister. So I had her under my command; she was only 22'.[9]

Twin 6-pr coast defence guns.
PAColl-4161-01-020-77-41, Alexander Turnbull Library, Wellington.

defence batteries, which were concealed until the guns were ready to fire. Much of the DEL equipment was of First World War vintage, but it was progressively updated. Searchlights were provided at the four major ports and the Bay of Islands.

Anti-motor torpedo boat defences were increasingly integrated into the close defences of the major ports. At first, this role had to be filled by ancient 12-pr and 6-pr quick-firers already installed or resited at North Head, Bastion Point and on the harbour side of Rangitoto Island in Auckland; at Fort Dorset and Fort Ballance in Wellington; and from 1941, at Harrington Point Battery at the entrance to Otago Harbour. In 1942, a range of 2-pr anti-tank guns, 18-pr field guns on Beach platforms, and Bofors and machine guns were hurriedly pressed into service to supplement these batteries. In May 1943 two US 75-mm guns were installed at Fort Gordon in Wellington. By February 1944, 6-pr guns in two twin mountings – the definitive AMTB equipment, ordered in March 1938 – had at last arrived and been installed at Bastion Point and Fort Ballance.

From June 1942 beach defence batteries protected beaches in the fortress areas that were particularly suitable for amphibious assault, and supplemented the AMTB defences. Armed with 18-prs on Beach platforms and an assortment of Italian guns captured in North Africa, and manned by TF and

Home Guard gunners, these batteries were based at Waitangi, Takapuna, Fort Ballance, Dunedin and Port Chalmers (one battery), and (briefly) Timaru. When all the pieces were in place – guns and booms, patrols and detection devices – a port became 'a very very locked cupboard'.[10]

When invasion seemed possible, the number of ports deemed to require close defence was greatly increased and they were hurriedly given 6-inch howitzers or 60-pr guns. In February and March 1942 approval was given to build more conventional coastal defences for a number of ports, anchorages or potential landing sites – 'minor ports'. The Ministry of Works or contractors built the emplacements; the gunners did the rest. At some of these relatively inaccessible spots, hauling the heavy guns and mountings from barges to the gun sites, and mounting them without using heavy machinery, required both gunners' traditional skills and a good deal of ingenuity.

Guns destined for Whangaroa and the Bay of Islands went by train from Auckland to Opua, where George Milne and his Repository Squad colleagues 'had a bit of fun [because] they couldn't put the engine and gun on the wharf at the same time – too heavy. So they had to get some trucks and back the gun and mounting onto the wharf, and a crane lifted them across to the barge.' The civil contractors had left a ring of bolts protruding from the emplacement. 'First we put the mounting in, got that bolted down. It took us about ten days for the whole lot.' The Repository Squad left the proofing to the battery personnel, who were 'virtually waiting for us to instal these jolly things. Everything was put in in a bit of a rush.'[11]

Whangaroa's 6-inch gun came from the armed merchant cruiser *Monowai*, and an incident in late 1941 gave the coast gunners a sobering insight into its power. '*Monowai* had a big bang that killed [four] people when it was firing. Someone was a bit quick on the [lever breech mechanism] and just blew it, blew everybody back'.[12]

Once the range-finding and other equipment became available and the guns could be proofed, their crews settled down to a routine of regular training and watchfulness, characterised by informality and considerable boredom, particularly at more isolated sites.[13] After numerous changes of plan, the guns eventually emplaced were either 6-inch Mk VII guns on P.III naval mounts or 5-inch US Mk VIII 51-cal naval guns (in unique cases, a 4.7-inch QF

MK IX naval gun and US 155-mm guns). Some of the gun sites were shared with Bofors guns for local anti-aircraft defence. Most were put on a care and maintenance basis in September or October 1943; all were disarmed and abandoned a year later.

Proposals for 9.2-inch counter-bombardment batteries at Auckland, Wellington and Lyttelton had been put forward since 1934, but rejected or deferred on grounds of expense. Wartime concerns about bombardment by cruisers with 8-inch guns spurred efforts to establish such batteries. Lyttelton was dropped as a possible site in May 1943, when work was well under way at the others: Whangaparaoa, Waiheke Island and Wrights Hill, Wellington. All were originally conceived as three-gun batteries, but the third gun was

---

Far North Coasties

Life was slow at Whangaroa:

> It was a great place to be posted. There was always someone in the OP, and someone to relieve them. In the afternoons, everyone else went fishing or swimming. We stood-to at first light. When we could see Stevenson Island we were allowed to take it easy. When the tide was on the make, at first light, kingfish used to be had very easily.

One of the battery would go in to Kaeo 'to get our rations, and they'd stop at the police station, the matron's, the hotel, the hospital, the sergeants' mess and officers' mess – we'd that much kingfish you couldn't get round it'. There were flounder and shellfish, and oysters on the rocks. 'We did get into trouble once. We used half a plug of explosive to get some bait. The fishing inspector sailed around the corner and caught one of the "kingies" floating belly up.' After delivering a lecture, he presented the men with a bait net.[14]

The usual tedium was occasionally interrupted. On 12 July 1942, D Section of 68 Heavy Battery on Great Barrier Island was 'advised by the 2nd Waikato Battalion that an enemy aircraft carrier was in the vicinity. Weather very bad, visibility ver[y] limited.'[15] On 4 August there was a reported 'sighting of submarine 1900 hours by launch "Nancy Bell" inside KAWAU ISLAND. Followed [by it] for five minutes. Warn infantry posts.'[16] Such alarms kept the coastal gunners on tenterhooks until they were disproved by a naval or air patrol. Removing boats from prohibited areas, and investigating mysterious beacons and noises, also cost time and nerves.

9.2-inch gun being mounted at Wrights Hill.
RNZAF Official, via Air Force Museum, Christchurch.

Weapons – Anti-Aircraft

A successful design by Vickers-Armstrong, the 3.7-inch anti-aircraft gun was manufactured between 1937 and 1945. Special rifling allowed for great accuracy to a high altitude. They were powerful weapons, with a muzzle velocity of more than a kilometre per second. Each battery had a predictor and height and range-finder that fed aiming information to dials on the guns. The shell had a proximity fuse with a killing range of about 25 yards.

Name	Ordnance QF 3.7-inch Anti-Aircraft
Entered NZ service	1942
Role	heavy anti-aircraft (and, for some, coast defence), 80° elevation
Calibre	3.7 in, 50 cals
Range	32,000 ft effective ceiling, 20,600 yds horizontal range
Weight	20,541 lb gun and 4-wheeled trailer; 23,100 lb static
Projectile	28 lb – shrapnel, HE; rate of fire 10 rpm
Remarks	The mobile version was Mk III, the static Mk II. Used in field AA and coast defences (with both mobile and static mountings in the coast defence role), it was in service until the 1960s.

cancelled in January 1944. Only one gun, at Whangaparaoa, was proofed before the war ended.

By mid-1942, the fortress commands in each military district included the heavy batteries and beach defence batteries (plus two to four TF battalions of infantry and related units). Though the coastal batteries had been manned at full readiness since September 1939, and Fortress Area HQs were established for Auckland, Wellington, Lyttelton and Dunedin in November 1940 and manned at weekends from March 1941, the other TF Fortress Troops were not called out until after Pearl Harbor. The fifth fortress, in the Bay of Islands, was created in June 1942.

In the defensive 'area commands' outside the fortress areas (simply 'fortresses' from June 1942), infantry companies and mounted rifles squadrons, supported by Home Guard units, protected strategic points, including the heavy batteries of the 'minor ports'. As the coast defences expanded the three coastal regiments – 9 Heavy in Auckland, 10 Heavy in Wellington and 11

Weapons – Coast Defence

Small numbers of two later versions of the ubiquitous British 6-inch Mk VII gun served in New Zealand's coast defences. The Mk XXI had originally been made for Chile's coast defences in the First World War. The Mk XXIV was a late 1930s version that became the standard.

Name	Ordnance BL 6-inch	
	Mk XXI	Mk XXIV
Entered NZ service	1937	1941
Role	coast defence; 45° counter-bombardment role	
Calibre	6 in, 50 cals	6 in, 50 cals
Muzzle velocity	2550 fps	2890 fps
Range	20,000 yds	21,700 yds
Weight	8.7-ton barrel	7.5-ton barrel
Projectile	100 lb HE, AP	100 lb HE, AP
Remarks	These effective weapons were in use until the abolition of the coast defence arm.	

Heavy in Lyttelton – created in July 1940 to take over the existing heavy batteries in the three fortress areas found themselves responsible for many more widely dispersed batteries. From July 1942 the coastal defence guns and beach defence batteries outside the three fortresses were placed operationally under the local fortress or area commanders, but remained administratively attached to the coastal regiments based in Auckland, Wellington and Lyttelton. Dunedin also briefly had a heavy regiment of coast defence artillery: 13 Heavy Regiment was formed in May 1943 but dissolved seven months later.

In the fortress areas the gun batteries, which usually overlapped in their coverage of the harbour approaches, were run from a fire command post to which all the battery command posts were linked. Though the fortress and area HQs were disbanded from June 1944, some very limited close defences were maintained at high readiness to assist in defence against submarines, the only remaining credible threat. The examination service ceased to operate and the use of sentry beams was discontinued. In August 1945, with the end of the Pacific War, the last few active guns in Auckland and Wellington, whose crews had been reduced in June, were put on a care and maintenance basis, and the heavy regiments ceased to be operational.

At its peak, coast defence employed many personnel. On 22 July 1942 a typical unit, 9 Heavy Regiment, NZA, had 1402 men and women on its books. A quarter of them were at North Head, in the RHQ (109), attached signals (fifteen) or 61 Battery (258, manning the 12-pr and 4-inch guns). There were 291 on Motutapu and Rangitoto islands and in FOPs on Waiheke and Tiritiri Matangi. The rest were scattered in the five batteries (140–170 in each) and sections covering harbours from Great Barrier to Manukau Head and Bastion Point to Whangaroa. Ten men were attached to the naval training 'stone ship' HMNZS *Tamaki*, whose two little naval 4-inch guns were earmarked for emergency defence.[17] Northern District had 2673 static anti-aircraft troops in two regiments and several detached batteries. Numbers grew into 1943 – 9 Coast Regiment swelled to nearly 2000 – before New Zealand's manpower crisis saw them decline.[18]

Anti-Aircraft Artillery

New Zealand's four heavy anti-aircraft guns (3-inch, 20-cwt) and their

> ### Alarms and Excursions in Wellington
> Tensions reached their highest pitch in mid-1942. Before dawn on 28 May, Wellington's Signals Officer reported from Beacon Hill that a ship had 'tried to rush the beam with out asking for a pilot or reporting to watch tower. The vessel proved to be the "Cape Alara", a yank. After going into a series of flat-spins, the army and harbour board made her wait until day break. Then the fun started'. When the examination steamer *Janie Seddon* intercepted the vessel near Steeple Rock, the 'jolly old yank' hoisted two incorrect signals in succession. The two vessels were 'half way to Somes Island' by the time the *Cape Alara* hoisted the correct signal. It was lucky not to have been fired on.
>
> On 2 June, the day after the Japanese submarine attack in Sydney Harbour, the posts went on alert again:
>
>> About 2120 hrs ... Gnr Parris rushed into the place puffing like a steam-engine [Beacon Hill is a long steep climb above Fort Dorset], and in a real 'flattie'. After staggering around the Sig. Station blindly, for about two minutes, he commenced hunting for his web-gear. Pulling everything down, tripping over everything, and in a real 'spin'. 'A' Watch remained on duty, calmly reported the Alarm to [the examination steamer], changed to R/T, and carried on everything in their usual efficient manner.
>
> The post contained a wireless operator, lamp operator, telescope operator, telephonist and shore telephonist/ALO.
>
> Three weeks later, another alert sounded at Wellington's forts and the signal station:

associated searchlights were deployed on 4 September 1939, two each on the Mt Victorias in Wellington and Auckland.[20] Skeleton crews manned the guns round the clock, with the full crews available at short notice. For a year from mid-1941 Auckland's guns were augmented by three naval 3-inch AA guns sited at Kauri Point; machine-gun posts had supplemented the AA defences since May 1940. In December 1941, all four HAA guns went to Fiji with B Force, along with the only four Bofors guns on hand. Thus at the moment of greatest danger, New Zealand was without AA protection, apart from Lewis and Bren machine guns. Requests to the British authorities from September 1941 for AA guns and searchlights were answered in part. By June 1942, 68

> Bells clang, lights flash, phones ring and the hooter fails to work at approx 0755. ... Our dear old Futurist [a requisitioned trawler patrolling for the Navy] located a submarine and JK [the signal station's call sign] once more goes efficiently into action. [Almost immediately] our personel were on the spot and 3 balls were flying from the starboard yardarm. However the port was soon open again and our balls were dropped. About 1 hr after the alarm was sounded the yankee fleet [left harbour] to do a spot of patrolling. At the time of writing [1335 hrs] sub is as yet unlocated and the alarm is still on.
>
> Later the signal station was told that *Futurist* 'not only located the Sub but sighted it on the surface. When the sub in turn sighted the Futurist she crashed dived' and got away. This may have been one of the submarines which had raided Sydney.
>
> The men manning the defences attached to Fort Dorset also watched the last American division depart in November 1943. They were not sorry to see it go:
>
> > Today ... we witnessed a sight that gladens the heart of any NZer as 22 ships full to the bulwarks of Uncle Sam's over-sexed, over confident, over dressed, over payed and under nourished degenerate nephews left our shores ... we hope – never to return. No doubt the young women of the country viewed the proceedings with feelings ... in a direct contrast to those displayed by us.[19]

3.7-inch guns with nine searchlights, and 134 Bofors, had arrived. At the end of the year the total available for home defence had reached 104 HAA, 51 searchlights and 158 Bofors.

The ack-ack equipment was well chosen, according to a post-war chief instructor. The Bofors was 'a very good gun; the 3.7-inch was a beautiful gun'.[21] With the guns came a number of high-tech instruments – notably predictors and height-finders – needed because of the complexity of anti-aircraft fire. The predictor, manned by about eight people, was a 'very clever instrument'. Three layers followed the aircraft visually, giving bearings, adjusting dials for height and other factors. It predicted the future position of the aircraft and relayed this information to dials at the guns, where the gun layer had merely to match the pointers and fire. 'There were four girls on the predictor, and we had to wait for it to be balanced. They called out "On balance", the guns called out "On balance". It was a bugger of a job trying to get the predictor balanced.'[22]

On one occasion Ponsonby's 69 HAA Battery thought they had locked onto a Japanese plane with their Mk II ground-locating radar:

> much to everybody's amazement. So we got in touch with the HQ of 15th Ack-Ack Regiment, at Epsom Teachers' College. The Operations Officer consulted somebody and said, 'No, no, for Christ's sake don't fire.' So we didn't, but we knew the Japanese plane was there. I later asked him why we didn't fire. He said the shell would have taken the roofs off the houses. They also didn't want to disclose the positions of the guns.

They had practice shoots at drogues towed by Air Force planes, Oxfords or obsolete Vildebeestes. Once the flak got too close to the pilot, who complained to the battery safety officer, 'I'm towing this bloody thing, not pushing it.' Not every ack-ack gunner had faith in New Zealand's air defence: 'I don't think we would have hit anything; our training wasn't good enough. We were quick and the equipment was OK, but it was all playing games.'[23]

A major building programme began in mid-1942. As guns arrived they were dispersed to batteries and sited in concrete emplacements constructed by the Army Engineers or the Public Works Department (PWD), or placed on mobile mountings in virtually unprepared positions. The emplacements for the heavy guns were of standard designs based on troops of four guns, and including command posts and director stations, some later supplemented by radar installations. (Initially, only two guns could be made available at each emplacement.) The fixed heavy AA sites were confined to the fortress areas of Auckland (twelve sites), Wellington (six), Lyttelton and Dunedin (one each). Heavy anti-aircraft emplacements built to cover Nelson's bomber airfield were in the end armed only with Bofors. Centralised AA fire command posts were established in the Auckland and Wellington fortress areas. These heavy AA defences were supplemented by Bofors guns.

From late 1942 heavy AA batteries began to receive ground-locating (GL) radar sets from Britain. These were used to supplement the Air Force's early-warning radar system, but mainly to provide fire-control data to the mechanical predictors. Thirteen HAA batteries in New Zealand were eventually equipped with GL installations; others were sent to New Zealand units in Fiji, Tonga and Norfolk Island, and three went to New Caledonia with 3 Division. In New Zealand, the radar units were staffed mainly by WAACs, who soon impressed with their competence, as Auckland's Major Martin Blampied recalled: 'although the prospect was viewed initially with some alarm, a few months' experience with our woman gunners on predictor height-finder and radar cabin soon convinced us of their superiority in operating these delicate aids to accurate gunfire'.[24]

In March 1943 the many AA guns allocated to airfield defence were withdrawn, except for Bofors guns to be manned by Air Force personnel at Waipapakauri, Whenuapai, Hobsonville, Nelson and Blenheim. This released 72 mobile 3.7-inch guns and 96 Bofors for deployment overseas. Bofors at the minor coastal defence sites were handed over to the coastal gunners. The unlikelihood of air attack had already curtailed the development of numerous planned AA sites and units. The South Island AA defences were placed on a care and maintenance basis in April 1943, and most static AA units were demobilised by June.

With such a tremendous build-up of the anti-aircraft defences – each port's ack-ack battery expanded to a regiment and then to a brigade, seemingly overnight – outside help was needed. Ack-ack officers well versed in such defence since the Battle of Britain were borrowed from 'Home' and given charge of Auckland's 15 AA Brigade, Wellington's 16 AA Brigade and 17 AA Brigade (which trained the 3 Division AA and coast gunners).[25] Colonel W. Rowbotham RA, who arrived late in 1942 to command 15 AA Brigade, brought with him fifteen officer and warrant officer instructors (and his terrier, which accompanied him to shoots). 'Some of the warrant officers were inclined to correct mistakes with their swagger sticks and on more than one occasion a women predictor gunner was rapped over the knuckles for not operating the dials properly.' Colonel Elliott NZA, commanding the heavy AA regiment, 'told the instructor that if it happened again he would be put aboard the next boat for England. Coming from the stark conditions of an

The School of Artillery

A School of Artillery had been established at Fort Dorset in mid-1940 to train coastal and anti-aircraft gunners; field artillery training continued at Trentham.[26] In April 1942 the school's branches were amalgamated in Wellington, with HQ and anti-aircraft taking over the former Karitane hospital buildings, together with nearby Melrose Park three months later. Pressure on these facilities (including from the hospital, which wanted to reoccupy the buildings) led it to move again in stages from mid-1943 to a camp at Plimmerton recently vacated by the US Marines.[27] By now the school was commanded by Jim Dunn, formerly the legal officer for *New Zealand Truth*. At its peak ten buildings and 300 huts occupied the site. A gun park

Training on a 3.7-inch anti-aircraft gun at the School of Artillery, Melrose Park, Wellington. *Graham Birch collection.*

English gun-site where there was no favour shown to man or women, the instructor was startled, but he soon got into our ways.'[28]

Field Forces

Many TF gunners served in the field force, manning light, field and medium batteries.[29] In March 1940 the NZA field artillery structure was reorganised and redesignated, the 'artillery brigade groups' in each district becoming 'field regiments' and the four-gun 'batteries' troops within batteries. This more

> with covered shelters protected the field guns from the sea air. Les Wright recalled that the guns were 'far better looked after than the personnel of the battery'.[30] Here gunners were taught to drive Bren carriers, one of the OP vehicles of the day. They fired across Karehana Bay into rocks on the northern point, land under the mana of Lady Miria Pomare, from whom permission was sought for each shoot. Notices telling fishing boats to avoid the harbour during these shoots were posted in a shop run by the local harbourmaster; one illiterate old-timer was sometimes caught out.[31]
>
> The trainee gunners were deployed to Porirua and Pauatahanui, and to a depot battery in the Upper Forks area near Levin. They familiarised gunners of 2 Marine Division with 25-prs when it was thought the Americans might be equipped with these weapons from Australia. The school also conducted research for 3 Division. For instance, it evaluated and developed a range table for a captured Japanese field gun.
>
> The field artillery wing of the school had four 25-pr guns complete with quads. Gunners underwent a three-week course. 'The whole camp was basic', one instructor recalls. 'I lived in a two-man hut. The mess was three or four four-man huts put together. There was only one regular and, except for the Battery Commander, the staff were inexperienced.' As well as teaching basic gunnery, the school trained sergeants who were upgrading their mobilised Territorial batteries from 18- to 25-prs. Men could be posted from this course to the Training Battery at Trentham, under Battery Commander Doug Green and his offsider Needham – 'both returned servicemen, experienced. They'd been wounded, and this was their return to duty.'[32] Some then got further training at Maadi, or went to units in 3 Division. Others stayed in New Zealand to stiffen the artillery units retained for homeland defence. The School of Artillery was disbanded in February 1944.

closely resembled the structure of the 2 Division field regiments sent to the Middle East. Each TF field regiment consisted of two field batteries, each of three four-gun troops, though initially not all could be formed or fully manned. Two troops of each battery were to be armed with 18-prs, and the third with either 4.5- or 3.7-inch howitzers. The former medium batteries were removed from their respective district commands to form 8 Medium Regiment, headquartered in Auckland and with batteries based there and in Wellington, each of two troops armed either with 60-prs or 6-inch howitzers.

In late 1940 a reserve unit, 12 Field Regiment, was formed from National Military Reserve gunners; this would eventually evolve into a 3 Division regiment. From 1941 all the field regiments received 25-prs.

The officers and NCOs of the field and medium regiments were called out on a limited basis in June 1941, and plans to expand the field artillery into a two-brigade divisional structure for each military district were in place by late in the year. After Pearl Harbor a sequence of orders called out the Territorial Force and the National Military Reserve, with full mobilisation, including 12 Field Regiment, on 10 January 1942. There was further reorganisation to establish the units necessary to flesh out the divisional formations and area commands, including new AA, heavy, field and anti-tank batteries. In the meantime, batteries from the existing regiments provided each brigade group with field artillery support.

The fully mobilised territorial units were manned largely by gunners who were too young to be sent overseas. When he was called up, Ray Munro of Wairoa chose the artillery because he thought it would have a better survival rate than the infantry. With several hundred others he trained at Borthwicks' Wairarapa freezing works, where 12 Field was forming its three batteries. Three infantry battalions and engineers were also gathering, all part of 7 Brigade, the Army Reserve. It was very wet; they lived in tents and enjoyed weekend leave once in eight weeks. These boys mingled with men in their 40s, some of them gnarled veterans from the Pacific. They were not happy days: 'We had worse conditions in Greytown than in Italy'. They trained hard with their full complement of 25-prs, going to Linton and Waiouru for live shoots.[33] On his 21st birthday Munro was summoned to the OC's office and, after cursory congratulations, told he would be leaving by train that afternoon for Trentham and the Eleventh Reinforcement draft heading overseas.[34]

Further attempts at reorganisation were hampered by lack of equipment. In June 1942 the field forces in each military district were formally designated as 1, 4 and 5 divisions. These provided a total of seven mobile brigade groups concentrated near potential invasion sites. Each division included an Artillery HQ, two field regiments of three batteries each (with the third batteries yet to be formed), the remnants of a medium battery (many of the medium guns

New Zealand gunners manning a 4.7-inch gun, Suva Battery, 1940.
Royal New Zealand Artillery Old Comrades' Association.

and gunners had gone to the heavy batteries to bolster the coastal defences), a heavy and two light AA batteries (existing as yet only on paper) and two anti-tank batteries armed with obsolete 2-prs that could probably handle any Japanese tanks likely to be encountered. In theory, this provided each infantry brigade group with support from a field regiment, anti-tank battery and LAA battery. In reality, many units could not be formed for lack of manpower or were under strength, and would remain so until the Territorial field force was demobilised in July 1943.

Home Guard Gunners

The first Home Guard artillery unit was raised in Dunedin in mid-1941, but with no guns available its men were transferred to the local beach defence battery a year later.[35] Many Home Guardsmen served in such batteries. From December 1942 they also manned two-gun sections or troops of field guns attached to 27 Home Guard battalions. They were armed with 65-mm Italian guns, or 18-pr guns or 4.5-inch howitzers made available as the TF rearmed with 25-prs. Along with the rest of the Home Guard, these units were stood down on a reserve basis from June 1943 and formally disbanded in January 1944. In early 1943, Home Guardsmen supplemented the TF gunners

> ### Preparations for Chemical Warfare
> Large quantities of mustard gas in 25-pr shells and 4.2-inch mortar bombs were imported into New Zealand from late 1942 or early 1943. These weapons were stockpiled by the Army 'as a reserve for the use of our forces in the Pacific and for the forces mobilised for the defence of [New Zealand]'.[36] The use of this arsenal was subject to rules similar to those adopted by the British authorities. It was to be used only in retaliation to chemical attack and after reference by the New Zealand Chiefs of Staff to the War Cabinet, which would make the decision, 'very possibly after reference to the United Kingdom Government, as to whether or not gas will be employed in retaliation.'[37] The need for more flexible arrangements to provide for retaliatory chemical warfare by New Zealand forces in the South-west Pacific, in concert with the US forces under whose command they served, was raised in New Zealand in early 1943 but fortunately not put to the test.[38] New Zealand's arsenal of chemical weapons was dumped offshore soon after the war.[39]

manning searchlights at the major ports. They usually provided three-quarters of the crews of the coast defence batteries at the minor ports.

Island Garrisons

On 30 August 1939 an infantry platoon with two light machine-gun sections was despatched to defend the strategic cable station at Fanning Island, part of the British colony of the Gilbert and Ellice Islands. This remote station had been damaged by a German raid at the beginning of the Great War. In March 1941 this first expeditionary force of the war was supplemented by the 30-man 45 Battery, which was to defend the main entrance to the lagoon. This initially had only a single 3.7-inch howitzer, replaced in May by an old 6-inch gun on a naval mounting received from Australia. The defence of Fanning Island was handed over to American forces in May 1942.[40]

Closer to home, during the late 1930s the government had developed plans for New Zealand's role in the defence of Fiji, its 'immediate outpost in the Pacific'.[41] In October 1939 two RNZA instructors were despatched to mount two ancient naval 3-prs, on which Fijian gunners were trained. To deter German raiders, two dummy coastal guns had been emplaced overlooking Suva Harbour by late September, and in December two ex-Admiralty 4.7-inch guns sent from Auckland were mounted on Mission Hill on Suva's peninsula. In March these were supplemented by searchlights, and the guns were proofed when a small RNZA detachment ('Suva Battery') arrived to man them. In July local territorials were trained for this work.

Meanwhile, more substantive plans were made for the defence of Fiji. Units of the planned 'B Force' began training in September 1940 and started to arrive in the colony on 1 November. Commanded by Brigadier W.H. Cunningham, B Force was built around 8 Infantry Brigade and included Fijian as well as New Zealand units. Its artillery component was 35 Field Battery, NZA, plus the Suva Battery. Plans for the defence of Fiji were centred on two areas, around Suva and between Lautoka and Momi on the west of Viti Levu. The field battery, armed with six 18-prs on Beach platforms, deployed in three two-gun sections, two at Momi covering the Navula Passage in Nadi Bay, the other at Lami overlooking Suva Harbour.

After a visit by the CRNZA, Colonel A.B. Williams, in December 1940, two 6-inch Mk VII guns originally intended for Godley Head replaced the 4.7-inch guns on Mission Hill. Williams decided to resite the latter at Dalaimbilo ('Bilo'), also covering the approaches to Suva. In October 1941, 1 Heavy Regiment, Fiji Artillery, was created with three batteries, armed with the guns at Mission Hill and Bilo (A and B Batteries, respectively) and at Momi (C Battery). The regiment included gunners seconded from the RNZA and NZA.

Work on the projected counter-bombardment battery on Suva's Flagstaff Hill, a few hundred yards north of the original Suva Battery, began in October 1941. Its three 6-inch guns on modern 45° mountings were proofed by July 1942. A further two-gun 6-inch battery, on naval mountings, was emplaced at Vuda, at the north end of Nadi Bay, in the first half of 1942. 1 Heavy Regiment, Fiji Artillery, now consisted of 1 Heavy Battery (Flagstaff Battery, 6-inch 45°), 2 Heavy Battery (Bilo, 4.7-inch guns), and the three batteries with 6-inch guns on naval mountings: 3 (Momi), 4 (Suva, Mission Hill) and 5 (Vuda) batteries. With the exception of the Flagstaff Hill counter-bombardment battery, all were handed over to US units in August 1942.

After the first 6-inch guns became operational at Momi, all three sections of 35 Field Battery were deployed around Suva. When the battery was later expanded and reorganised into five troops, two were deployed in the Nadi area and three around Suva. The battery had an odd combination of 25- and 18-pr guns and 3.7- and 4.5-inch howitzers – an odd combination. In early 1942 the NZA presence in Fiji was further expanded with the deployment of a medium battery of two 6-inch howitzers and two 60-pr guns near Vuda in the west, and four American 155-mm guns at Esivo and Momi. As B Force expanded to two brigades, the field artillery element was increased to two oversized batteries, one based around Nadi and the other at Suva.

The four heavy AA guns in New Zealand when the war broke out were sent to Fiji in December 1941, along with four Bofors guns, and 27 Mixed AA Battery was formed. Its equipment was updated in June 1942 when the 3-inch were replaced by more modern 3.7-inch guns. Two anti-tank troops formed in February 1942 were armed with US 37-mm anti-tank guns. One was deployed with 8 Brigade, the other with 14 Brigade. Their role included contributing to anti-submarine and beach defences.

In early 1942 the Pacific war edged closer to the Fiji garrison. On 14 January the examination battery at Momi fired a shell across the bows of the troopship *Rangatira*, which was carrying 37 Battalion, when it failed to respond to a signal demanding identification.[42] Eleven days after the fall of Singapore on 15 February, a New Zealand gunner wrote home that this 'was a bit of shock to some of the boys. … In fact I thought it was going to be our turn next. … However we have the "Yanks" here now and they have some very good equipment … and some warships which, combined with ours and allied warships, make a formidable sea force.' A month later, however, 'Things don't look too bright. … The general opinion seems to be that we will be attacked here very soon.' His fears were not misplaced: until they were defeated in the Coral Sea and at Midway the Japanese did plan to capture Fiji. Meanwhile, military censorship irked some: 'one chap is complaining very loudly because the censor has done him out of a whole page of one letter. Several of them have windows cut out. … One boy had the name of a camp cut out from his letter … there is so much that one cannot mention.'[43]

From May 1942 this 'Pacific Section, 2 NZEF', now 10,000 strong, was known as 3 New Zealand Division.[44] In July American forces took over responsibility for the defence of Fiji and most of the New Zealand personnel went home, though many of the gunners stayed on to serve the Fijian coast defence guns.

Life in Fiji was not onerous. The Momi Battery men had their own launch and also enjoyed occasional unauthorised trips on naval vessels patrolling the Navula Passage. On one occasion, a few men were taken to an offshore island for a day's fishing and swimming. Their return was delayed when the patrol boat was unexpectedly called to Lautoka; when it eventually dropped them back on the mainland late at night, they had to clamber ashore in front of an American position. 'We floundered through the mangrove swamp and mud, disturbing all sorts of splashy nasties in the process, until we eventually came to some barbed wire. We squeezed through this, with much cursing and discomfort, when suddenly we were surrounded by US marines in full battle kit with levelled, loaded carbines.' Some choice Kiwi language 'made them realise we were not a small Japanese commando invasion force coming ashore'. The Americans fed them and drove them back to their camp.[45]

Elsewhere on New Zealand's northern approaches, a small Tongan Defence Force had been established with New Zealand help in 1939.[46] After Pearl Harbor, two 18-pr guns were despatched with New Zealand gun crews who trained Tongans to man them. By March 1942 two 4-inch guns from Fort Takapuna were covering entrances through the reef, manned by composite Tongan and New Zealand units. By this time Tonga was under US control, but New Zealand forces remained. New Zealand again accepted primary responsibility for the defence of Tonga in early 1943: 16 Brigade Group, formed for the purpose, had five artillery batteries with New Zealand officers and Tongan gunners. These units manned the old 18-prs, the 4-inch guns, three installations of two 6-inch guns set up by the Americans, and HAA and LAA batteries. As the threat of attack abated, the 4-inch guns were returned to New Zealand in early 1944. By this time 16 Brigade Group had been disbanded, and in February responsibility for the island group reverted to US Fiji Command.

Amphibious Gunners

As the Americans began to push back the Japanese in the south-west Pacific, the government decided to send the Fiji force to support them.[47] The

> ### Sport in the Tropics
> While training in New Zealand, 3 Division's many sporting gunners had kept their hands in, especially at rugby.[48] Like their counterparts in the desert, they were not to be put off by the stifling heat and other trivial inconveniences they experienced in the Pacific. When the artillery arrived in New Caledonia, no sports grounds were available, so all ranks took up deck tennis. This soon gave way to cricket, baseball (US instructors were very helpful) and then rugby (29 Light AA Regiment made the final of an eight-team competition for the Barrowclough Cup). New Zealanders also took part in American-organised boxing and wrestling matches in Nouméa, and – with marked lack of success – played soccer against Royal Navy personnel. There were divisional sports in May 1943, then in June and July the only two meetings of the 14th Brigade Northern Racing Club at Népoui – 'a magnificent show with all the trimmings of stands, lawn, birdcage, saddling paddock and tote, and real horses of doubtful vintage and variable speed' supplied by a local French colonist.

establishment of 3 New Zealand Division for this deployment began in August 1942, when Divisional Headquarters, including Divisional Artillery Headquarters, was established at Manurewa under Major-General H.E. Barrowclough.[49] Appointed as CRA was Brigadier C.S.J. Duff, who had wide experience in artillery methods and operations and had served in Greece, Crete and North Africa. In an arrangement unique in the British Commonwealth, Duff was provided with two staffs, each with its own brigade major: one for field and anti-tank units, the other for coastal and anti-aircraft artillery. Also unusually, 3 Divisional Artillery would include coastal and heavy AA units as well as field and anti-tank elements. This would enable it both to support amphibious actions by field forces and to defend base positions against air raids, naval bombardment or amphibious assault. On 5 October, artillery HQ shifted briefly to Papakura Camp before moving to Tirau for exercises.

The gunners of 35 and 37 batteries, back from Fiji, formed the core of 17 Field Regiment, established in early September under Lieutenant-Colonel H.W.D. Blake. On 15 October the regiment's third battery, 12 Battery, the former National Military Reserve battery, joined the rest of the regiment at Tirau, and in December calibration shoots were carried out at Rerewhakaaitu, near Mount Tarawera. With resources stretched, each battery comprised two

> At Necal, 144 Battery constructed a swimming pool, to which VADs and WAACs were lured 'to disport themselves'. At 'an afternoon carnival ... the female form divine was exhibited to whet the appetite and add glamour to the scene. They joined with a will but nobody remembers much about the serious side of the day'.[50] Twelve events were contested at an athletics meeting.
>
> Once the Division moved north, deck tennis regained its popularity, as did canoeing, yachting (local canoes were converted, with tents jury-rigged as spinnakers), swimming – many landlubbers were taught to swim, or at least flounder briefly – and water polo. Volleyball, rugby, boxing and tug-of-war enlivened garrison duty in the Treasuries. An axemen's carnival on Nissan gave a chance to display skills honed while clearing gun sites in the jungle. Inter-unit competition was given an even greater edge by the large amounts invested with battery bookmakers.

rather than the usual three troops of four 25-pr guns. 29 Light AA Regiment had assembled at Pauatahanui in August with a core of AA-trained gunners from the Territorials; it was brought up to strength by other recruits. 17 AA Brigade was established to train the coastal and ack-ack units. By the end of September, with all its sub-units established, the regiment comprised four batteries – 207, 208, 209 and 214 – each of three troops of four 40-mm Bofors guns. Like its counterpart, it was the largest unit in 3 Division: at its peak it would have 180 officers and 3500 men, only 10 per cent fewer than 2 Divisional Artillery.[51]

One troop each from 207 and 208 Light AA batteries was sent to Norfolk Island in early October as elements of 215 Composite Battery; they would later rejoin their respective batteries in New Caledonia. The Norfolk Island force was truly 'composite': it also included single troops of 3.7-inch heavy AA guns and 25-pr field guns, and a heavy battery of four 155-mm coastal guns.[52]

Two regiments of 3 Divisional Artillery never fired a shot in anger. Its heavy AA component consisted of the three batteries – 202, 203 and 204 – of 28 Heavy AA Regiment. Each had two troops of four 3.7-inch heavy AA guns (204 Battery contained only one troop). Like the light ack-ack gunners they trained north of Wellington, at Pauatahanui and Judgeford. The Division would also boast a coastal element: 32 Heavy Regiment was formed at Pauatahanui on 14 September and redesignated 33 Regiment in October. Its 150 Battery was manned from coastal and other artillery units around New Zealand, while RHQ and 151 and 152 batteries comprised mostly coastal gunners who had returned from Fiji. (The regiment was commanded by Lieutenant-Colonel B. Wicksteed, who also had Fijian experience.) Armed with four 155-mm guns, 152 Battery embarked for Norfolk Island on 10 October to begin its separate existence as part of N Force, and henceforth the regiment would consist of only two batteries, whose service would be confined to Nouméa, New Caledonia.

When the organisation of the Divisional Artillery was finalised in early September 1942, a number of units took formal shape, manned mostly by men who had been in camp at Papakura since August and already had some indication of their intended role. The anti-tank troops returned from Fiji now formed the basis of 53 and 54 Anti-Tank batteries, which received their official designations at the beginning of September at Papakura, where they had been training on 2-pr anti-tank guns. The following April, while in New Caledonia, these batteries would receive replacement 6-prs. A curious component of the Divisional Artillery was 144 Independent Battery, made up mostly of men from a medium troop and one of the field troops from Fiji, but armed with 3.7-inch light or 'pack' howitzers, modified with pneumatic tyres. This unit was under the direct control of the CRA and independent of the field regiments. The Division also included 4 Survey Troop and the usual allocation of light aid detachments and signals sections.

After initial fears that 3 Division might have to be rushed to Guadalcanal to help the Marines who were fighting doggedly for possession of the island, it was wisely decided that it would replace American forces defending New Caledonia, where its personnel could undertake further training.[53] After advance parties departed for Nouméa on 28 October, the artillery followed in two main groups: 28 Heavy AA (two batteries), 29 Light AA and 33 Heavy regiments left Wellington on 5 November on the US Army Transport *Maui*, and on 29 December, 17 Field and the independent and anti-tank batteries left Auckland on the *West Point*.

On arrival in New Caledonia, the artillery units soon fanned out to their new homes. The 6-inch coastal guns of 150 Heavy Battery were emplaced on Île Nou, off Nouméa, while the 155-mm guns of 151 Heavy Battery were sited on Point Tere at Naia, 30 miles from Nouméa and covering its approaches. Two of the heavy AA units were deployed to defend airfields to the north – 202 Battery at Plaine des Gaiacs, near Népoui, and 203 Battery at Oua Tom, midway between Nouméa and Népoui, then at Tontouta from May 1943 – while the single troop of 204 Battery was incorporated into the coastal defences on Île Nou. Of the light AA batteries, 207 went to Plaine des Gaiacs and 208 to Oua Tom before also shifting to Tontouta. 214 Battery was based at Népoui in a mobile role, and when it arrived in December, 209 Battery, which had trained after the rest of the regiment, was based at the Taom River, also in a mobile role. When the men of 215 Battery rejoined the regiment from Norfolk Island in April 1943 (replaced by the newly raised 218 Light AA Battery), the four batteries on New Caledonia were reorganised from three four-gun to four three-gun troops.

The Independent Battery and 53 Anti-Tank Battery settled in at Néméara, while 54 Anti-Tank Battery went to Népoui. Of the field gunners, 35 Battery went to Taom, while 12 and 37 batteries encamped near Népoui. With the artillery units either in static positions effectively as composite heavy/light AA or coastal/heavy AA units, or spread between two (from January to June 1943, three) field brigades, operational command arrangements bore little resemblance to the administrative structure in the formal order of battle.

The artillery arrived from New Zealand in mid-summer. 'Boy, was it hot! Mosquitos, ants, acclimatising was difficult'. Black widow spiders which liked to lurk in the latrines were a particular hazard. This experience in combating heat and insects proved invaluable when they moved later to the even hotter Solomons.[54] Men stripped off more the further north they went. By Guadalcanal, 'formal attire was a pair of underpants'.[55] Minimal attire was encouraged by the propensity for scorpions and centipedes to hide in the folds of clothing. But men had to wear long trousers and shirts at night (and take Atebrin tablets) to avoid contracting malaria from mosquito bites. Even for a visit by the Governor-General, Sir Cyril Newall, to the Division's base on New Caledonia, dress was varied and informal. An artilleryman based at Dumbéa found that he could tolerate the 'terrific' heat, and the red dust 'which covered everything in a crimson mantle' could be washed off in a nearby river – but dysentery was 'a horse of another colour'.[56] The humidity 'forced us to design an oven powered by car batteries in which we could put our very cumbersome and heavy radios'.[57] This ingenious treatment was also applied to gunsights.

When the Divisional Artillery first went to New Caledonia it included only one field regiment, though plans were made for the usual three. The second to be formed was 38 Field, which began training at Papakura in early April 1943. Initially commanded by Lieutenant-Colonel G.R. (later Sir Guy) Powles, this regiment comprised 49, 50 and 52 batteries. After hurried and incomplete training, its units left piecemeal for Bouloupari in New Caledonia over a period of two months from late May. During this time the regiment lost some of its men to the RNZAF but recouped its numbers when 37 Field Regiment, which had also begun training, was disbanded because manpower shortages required that 3 Division be reduced to two brigades.[58]

The sojourn on New Caledonia was generally pleasant, with much fraternising with French colonists and opportunities to get to know the ever-generous American units with whom the AA and heavies worked closely. Interaction with the Kanak people was minimal, and understanding probably even less. 'Kanaka soldiers were on duty guarding a city building' in Nouméa, a Petone property overseer serving with 29 Light AA Regiment remembered. 'They were short and stocky with muscular build and very proud of themselves. They threw us a salute at every opportunity. We acknowledged with a careless wave of the hand, one finger extended.'[59]

The field and related units undertook amphibious exercises, and in June 1943 a divisional exercise was conducted at Moindou. In July, with the Division preparing to go into battle in the Solomon Islands and the safety of New Caledonia now assured, 33 Heavy Regiment and 28 Heavy AA Regiment were disbanded. Some of their personnel joined the Artillery Wing of the Base Training Depot to form the Artillery Training Depot, based at Néméara, 10 miles from Bourail. The other units of the Divisional Artillery formed elements of 8 and 14 brigades as the Division made its way to the Solomons in late August and early September. For the remaining units, training continued relentlessly. 'After a few weeks of hard work and broken sleep the strain began

Training for amphibious warfare: loading a Bofors of 29 Light AA Regiment onto a landing craft near Nouméa, New Caledonia.
PA1-q-302, WH154, Alexander Turnbull Library, Wellington.

to tell. Spirits dropped ... and trifles were magnified out of all proportion. Posts [at which the light ack-ack manned their guns] became short of men through sickness caused by the long hours and the ... American tinned food.'

Alerts increased the tension:

> We were feeling the need of a spell and a few nights of unbroken sleep when some bright person on the coast 'saw' a submarine land a party of Japs. Double picquets were put on immediately. Rifles were carried through the bush. Working parties had to have their rifles at hand in case of attack. The stillness of the night would be shattered as a trigger-happy picquet blazed away ... [W]e saw nothing but shadows and our own fears.[60]

The Divisional Artillery was deployed with the two brigades of 3 Division, its field batteries and anti-tank troops transported with one of the three infantry battalions of each brigade. 14 Brigade Group left Nouméa on 17 August, with

17 Field Regiment, 53 Anti-Tank Battery and 207 Light AA Battery, in the transports *President Adams*, *President Hayes* and *President Jackson*. Divisional Headquarters, including Divisional Artillery HQ, and the divisional troops including 208 and 209 Light AA batteries and 144 Independent Battery, departed on 24 August in two more humble transport ships. After the return of the 'President' ships, 8 Brigade, including 38 Field Regiment, 54 Anti-Tank and 214 Light AA batteries, embarked on 4 September. All three convoys paused at Éfaté in the New Hebrides for amphibious exercises before continuing to Guadalcanal. 'On hitting the beach the ramps were dropped. We poured out on to the sand and made a dash for the trees. After the imaginary enemy had been disposed of to everyone's satisfaction we were allowed to wallow in the briny.'[61] Boxing, Dorothy Lamour movies and drinks with the British Consul also helped to pass the time.

During the voyage to Guadalcanal, a Japanese 'submarine fired two long-range torpedoes clear through the convoy', 144 Independent Battery's chronicler wrote from the 'Listing [*Hunter*] Liggett' (or 'bloody Altmarck', as they called their troopship). 'Amazingly, both tin fish scored near misses.'[62] Safely ashore, 'we trained hammering guns into landing crafts', a 3 Division gunner remembered. Each small LCVP ('landing craft, vehicles and personnel', or 'Higgins Boat') could carry two 25-prs (or limbers) and 30 to 40 fully-equipped men. The batteries repeated the drill for disembarking from transports, scaling down nets slung over the sides. 'There was more than a degree of urgency going up it, three fellows at a time. It was an experience we didn't enjoy.'[63]

While making camp on Guadalcanal, inland from Point Cruz and Lunga Point, the Division prepared to face air raids for the first time. The night bombing attacks which came, however, were on airfields and shipping some miles away and out of range of the New Zealand Light AA guns. The Kiwi gunners were fascinated spectators as American heavy AA units and night fighters went into action. The uneven beat of the Japanese plane engines led to the nickname 'Washing Machine Charlie'. As air-raid sirens sounded, 'lights were doused and we fell over each other in the rush for our foxholes', from which they 'watched the flak bursting in the sky in little black fluffs'. When enemy planes 'crashed to earth in flames … we cheered ourselves hoarse'.[64]

There were more amphibious exercises in the form of landings on nearby Florida Island, and Divisional Artillery units took turns practising loading and unloading for beach assaults, and familiarising themselves with the various US amphibious vessels that would carry them into battle.

The light ack-ack camped on Bloody Ridge. Their jungle training included route marches:

> ... in enervating heat. With packs and rifles we climbed up and down steep hills till we came to a 'nice bit of jungle'. We pushed our way through heavy undergrowth and tripped over hidden roots; crossed and recrossed twisting creeks. ... The sun didn't penetrate the bush but we trudged through the murky gloom in a lather of sweat. When we finally emerged into bright sunlight our clothes were as wet as if they had just been lifted from the wash-tub. We dropped wearily to the ground and steamed out in the blazing sun. After a ten-minute spell we plunged into heavier jungle. A native track ... led through a native village. As we filed through ... the chief stalked to the far end of the compound and stood with outstretched arm. Very dignified and very unapproachable, he had 'shown us the door' in no uncertain manner.[65]

144 Battery camped near a sawmill:

> [T]he rain gave us an excuse to try out our new pup tents (U.S. pattern). These tents ... are a sort of 'gable lean to'. Each man carries one side (they dome together on the ridge) one pole and four pegs. Pitched in a few minutes, they allow two men to sleep sardine pattern (head to tail). Quite excellent though, and as near waterproof as anything can be in these tropic downpours.[66]

Other American equipment was also superior. Whereas the small hand shovels provided by the PWD routinely broke, the Americans had well-made entrenching tools for digging foxholes. The New Zealanders were grateful too for their PXs, which provided 'top-line cigarettes, cotton underwear – perfect for the tropics. We had woollen underwear, which was terrible. They had camouflaged shirts, jackets and trousers – not shorts in the Solomons because of the mosquitos – and jungle hats. Everything they had was 100 per cent.'[67]

One American felt that the war could be won by putting 'you Kiwis on one island with all the Japanese and in a week the war would be over for you'd have all their equipment'.[68]

Mingling with the Americans also gave the New Zealand gunners opportunities to discuss intelligence reports on the Japanese defences they would encounter. Major Powles of 144 Battery shared information after a trip to Munda in New Georgia. On nearby Kolombangara Island:

> The Japs must certainly have worked. On the beach, practically on the waterline, are roomy dugouts with a weapon slot facing seawards, and a roofing composed of at least three thicknesses of cocoanut logs, with about three feet of coral on top of that. ... [T]heir strength is shown by a 155mm crater on top of one of these defense posts. The ... shelter is intact. ... The evacuation of Vila must have been a last minute show, guns everywhere with only the sighting apparatus removed. ... At one point, obvious by the shell craters as a target, was a really well made dummy of coconut logs, hollowed out ... It was reported that coincident with the firing of the gun half a mile away, and effectively screened, the Japs set off powder at the dummy to draw ... the American fire.[69]

Vella Lavella

The interlude at Guadalcanal was brief for 14 Brigade and its artillery. On 16 September the first units embarked for the thickly forested island of Vella Lavella, 250 miles to the north-west, to mop up the remaining Japanese opposition (US troops had landed the previous month). For this operation the brigade assembled three self-contained combat teams, each based on an infantry battalion and with a battery of 17 Field Regiment and a troop each of 207 Light AA Battery and 53 Anti-Tank Battery, plus headquarters elements including a light AA troop. An advance party had already reconnoitred bivouac areas, and the main landing took place on the beaches of Barakoma, Maravari and Uzamba, in the American-controlled south of the island. An air attack hastened unloading but was driven off by Allied fighters without doing damage. The heavy bush and deep mud that hindered movement was a foretaste of the difficulties awaiting the gunners on this fiercely contested island.

6-prs of 53 Anti-Tank Battery up to their axles in mud on Vella Lavella.
PA1-q-302, WH198(B), pic. 285, Alexander Turnbull Library, Wellington.

Barrowclough assumed command of all US as well as New Zealand forces on Vella Lavella. With the 30 Battalion Combat Team in reserve near Divisional Headquarters in the south, a pincer movement was executed on the Japanese stronghold, which was defended by perhaps 600 to 800 men. The combat teams landed on 21 September, at Matu Soroto and at Boro on Doveli Cove. Once a radius of 2000 yards around these bases had been secured, on 25 September infantry patrols pushed along the coast through dense bush to ensure a safe landing for the rest of each combat team, a process repeated several times in the western sector. At the first landing in each sector, field guns were manhandled ashore and emplaced with great difficulty in the jungle to cover the infantry patrols. There was opposition from Japanese positions well hidden in the dense jungle, but infantry assaults and artillery fire from the field guns gradually drove the enemy back. The stiffest resistance was encountered at the bottleneck of 'machine-gun gully'.

By 6 October the combat teams had converged in an area between Warambari and Marquana bays to which the Japanese had fallen back. That night the two field batteries were tied in on a common grid and put under regimental control. Firing on the Japanese positions was called off for fear of revealing the gun positions to enemy aircraft and destroyers. During the night most of the surviving Japanese escaped to these warships on barges. Perhaps 200 to 300 Japanese were killed in this operation; around 600 escaped. 14 Brigade lost 32 killed or died of wounds (15 in 29 Light AA Regiment on 1 October), and 32 wounded.

The ack-ack troops were deployed with the combat teams as far forward as the advanced bases; one of the gun crews shot down a dive-bomber. The light AA gunners suffered the only artillery losses of the Vella Lavella operation. On 1 October, as 209 Battery moved forward by sea to reinforce the air defences, a direct hit on an LST (landing ship, tanks) killed a gun sergeant and his crew, wounded others and set the craft on fire. Earlier, one of the battery's guns on another LST in the convoy had brought down an attacking aircraft. The same day 207 Battery, already ashore, claimed a probable kill. After the ground action concluded, the AA crews maintained their role in the defence of the island against air raids that persisted until the end of the year.

For the field gunners this was a strenuous operation, manhandling guns ashore, hacking tracks to gun positions on beaches or headlands and clearing arcs of fire in dense jungle. The cover also hindered conventional means of observation, including air; the FOOs had to move forward with the infantry to within 25 to 50 yards of shellbursts to redirect fire onto a well-concealed enemy. Communication problems added to the difficulties, as moisture had damaged radio sets; in the final stages of the operation, field telephone networks were used. The anti-tank gunners found that in this theatre their role became beach defence. Their guns covered the bays at the advanced bases, and one troop moved forward with the infantry to fulfil this role at Tambama.

For the first – but by no means the last – time, New Zealand gunners had to apply artillery techniques in jungle. It was very difficult to see – 'a metre in and you could be lost', Second Lieutenant John Foote of 38 Field Regiment remembered:

The FOOs from our regiment with the advancing infantry would call for target registration. This is where gunnery in the jungle is totally different from gunnery in the desert ... It is so difficult to observe the fall of shot that we ranged with smoke shells to register targets. Then we would register those on what we called our Artillery Board – a gridded board, really a plan of where we were, with a map on it, so we then knew what range and bearing our guns needed to fire. We registered each one – it would be given a number so that if supporting fire was called for during the night, it was a simple matter.[70]

Barrages were not fired here, but individual targets were pinpointed. Even the training on New Caledonia now seemed inappropriate: because of the density of the jungle, FOOs 'didn't know where their shots were landing'. The somewhat unnerving solution was to direct the fire at themselves, while sheltering behind a tree.[71] Reinforcements took this technique to Italy, and it would later be used in Korea.

The Treasuries

The next stage in the Division's contribution to the Allies' island-hopping strategy was the capture of the Treasury Islands, Mono and Stirling, a necessary preliminary to a US landing at Empress Augusta Bay on Bougainville to the north. 'On the Shortlands thirty miles away were 15,000 Japs. Fifteen miles further on, Bougainville was garrisoned with 45,000 Japs. A heavy counter-attack was expected.'[72] The larger island, Mono, is steep and rugged, while the smaller island to the south, Stirling, is low-lying. It provided sites from which the field guns of 38 Field Regiment could cover the operations on Mono from static positions. Under the overall command of the First Marine Amphibious Group, Brigadier R.A. Row of 8 Brigade commanded the land forces, including approximately 2000 Americans, allocated to the assault. Lieutenant-Colonel Walter McKinnon of 29 Light AA Regiment also took command of an American coast artillery (anti-aircraft) regiment with 16 90-mm and 32 37-mm guns, plus 20 searchlights. 29 and 36 Battalions would land on Mono, on beaches coded Orange just west of Falamai village, and 34 Battalion on Stirling's Purple beaches. Reconnaissance parties from the light AA batteries went with this first wave, the guns following about an hour later.

The slower landing craft left Guadalcanal from 23 October and the fast APDs (converted destroyers) on the 26th. On the following day the invasion force rendezvoused off Blanche Harbour, between Mono and Stirling islands, under cover of Allied fighters. After softening-up fire from the destroyers and LCI ('landing craft, infantry') gunboats, the first wave trans-shipped to landing craft and went ashore near the Japanese HQ at Falamai, on the southern side of Mono, at 6.26 a.m., in the New Zealand Army's first opposed landing since Gallipoli. Japanese machine guns fired at the landing craft as they rounded the westernmost point of Stirling Island on the approach to the two landing zones.[73] Bofors guns of 208 and 214 Light AA batteries were at the ready.

> The destroyers in the van plummeted shell after shell into the jungle, but we could see no signs of damage. There was nothing to concentrate on. It was a case of firing indiscriminately into the jungle and trusting to luck that some damage would be done. If it did nothing else it kept the Japs quiet until we landed. With its guns firing into the bush our barge crept in between two islands to be met by a stream of tracer ...[74]

The Japanese were easily driven back from the beach, but they soon regrouped to bring down machine-gun, shell and mortar fire on the successive waves of the first echelon's assault.

The forward parties of 29 Light AA regimental HQ, and of 208 and 214 batteries, along with the field FOO parties, got ashore on Orange-1 beach ten minutes after the first wave before coming under a hail of small-arms fire from Japanese bunkers bypassed in the initial advance. The two reconnaissance parties of 208 Battery took on the first post. Gunner Michael Compton, who later received the Military Medal, 'worked around to the rear of the fox-hole where he shot and killed two Japanese. He kept the entrance blocked until the post was cleared by a bayonet party.'[75] Another strong Japanese bunker continued to resist, and it took a resourceful American 'Seebee' (construction battalion engineer) with a bulldozer to neutralise the last machine-gun post, which had opened fire as the heavy LSTs lowered their ramps an hour after the initial assault. John Foote of 49 Battery saw it happen:

> When the drawbridge was lowered the first piece of equipment out was a bulldozer, and the driver's prime task [was] to be up the beach, and he actually buried the Japanese machine-gun posts and the trench. He used the blade for protection. We were all cheering because they were very troublesome.[76]

Shelling and mortar attacks caused numerous casualties on the beach, and at times seriously hindered the unloading of the LSTs, briefly setting fire to two of them. The Japanese had a 75-mm field gun and two mortars covering Falamai village, and camps on either side of Orange Beach.[77]

> Bombs fell that night and [ack-ack] gun crews went into action. There were no searchlights and targets were hard to see. Guns on the beach were strafed when they began to fire at sound. A bomb dropped alongside a gun and the crew were hurled to the ground from the concussion.[78]

Enemy mortar and shellfire also damaged or destroyed equipment, including a 25-pr, a Bofors gun and an American 90-mm AA gun, along with large amounts of ammunition. LST399 took a direct hit as the guns of 208 Battery were preparing to unload in the wake of 29 Battalion, killing Sergeant L.J. Rickard and five men of F Troop. A hit on 214 Battery's LST485 wounded several gunners as it came in after 36 Battalion. By midday infantry units scouring the hillsides had overrun all the enemy positions troubling the beach, and the beachhead was secure:

> The guns couldn't be dug in because we were right on the beach – it was hardly a beach: coral, stones and boulders. Our first few days and nights were spent supporting the infantry, who by this time were able to locate and destroy both the Japanese camps. The Jap force which was there – they weren't large, 300 to 400 men – because they'd been pushed away from their own food sources, they were obviously fairly keen to get back and have something to eat after nightfall, and it was then that our registration of targets around the perimeter of Falamai would be useful. The Japanese were very adept at living off the land, raw fish and all that.[79]

This 208 Light Anti-Aircraft Battery gun was credited with the only Japanese plane shot down on Mono Island. *PAColl 5547-031, Alexander Turnbull Library, Wellington.*

The two 38 Field batteries set up headquarters on Stirling Island once all their guns had arrived (about 1 November). They camped near an airfield that was being built hurriedly of compacted white coral by US construction battalions. This 'was easily seen by Japanese planes, even at night, making life even more uncomfortable' for those nearby. Even after the island was officially cleared, 'the odd remaining Jap soldier (the last one being sighted by a 50th Battery patrol near Laifa Point as late as 10 March) and the ever present possibility of a Japanese counterattack' kept the men on their toes. When they were not patrolling or conducting the occasional live shoot, 'most of the time was spent as "navvies" for the Americans, unloading fuel drums from beached barges and rolling them up coconut logs on Wilson Island'.[80]

While the landing at Falamai was under way, a 200-strong force based on a company of 34 Battalion, with attachments including an American radar

One of the 38 Field Regiment guns covering the entrance to Blanche Harbour, Mono Island, 1944.
1/2-044736-F, Alexander Turnbull Library, Wellington.

unit (to cover the Shortland Islands and give early warning of any attack) was landing at Soanotalu to the north. 'Loganforce' under Major G.W. Logan landed without opposition and established a perimeter. US Navy Seebees began building a road for the vital radar equipment, which arrived by barge the following day and was operating a day later. Loganforce encountered its first opposition on the 29th, when Japanese began arriving from Falamai. That night the field guns on Stirling Island, 6 miles to the south, registered on targets outside the perimeter, lobbing shells over the peak of the island. Over the following days Loganforce was reinforced in the face of increasing pressure from Japanese concentrating in the area, culminating in a desperate assault on the night of 1 November that was destroyed in fierce close-quarters fighting. By the next night, organised resistance on Mono had ceased. Groups of Japanese remained hidden in the jungle and in caves on the northern coast, from where some attempted to escape on rafts. On 12 November, after some sharp encounters with these stragglers, the island was declared clear of the enemy, and 14 Brigade settled down to its role as garrison force. Two hundred and twenty-three Japanese were confirmed dead; the Allies had lost 52 killed.

Included in the first echelon of the assault were 208 and 214 AA troops and 49 Field Battery. While 208 Light AA Battery was deployed to defend the beach at Falamai, most of the guns of 214 Battery were ferried to positions on Stirling, and on Watson and Wilson islands in Blanche Harbour. 208 Battery scored a kill on the second night of the invasion, and all troops were soon linked to a radar warning system.

While the headquarters units of 38 Field Regiment were delivered by LCI directly to Stirling Island, the field guns of 49 Field Battery had to be landed by LST at Falamai for trans-shipment to Stirling. From here they could cover all of Mono Island, directed not only by 49 Battery's own OP parties but also by two FOOs from 50 Battery, and one from 52 Battery. Another 52 Battery observer registered shoots against targets on the eastern end of Mono from an aircraft based on New Georgia, while on one occasion a 49 Battery observer on a barge offshore called down fire on a possible mountain gun position. Subsequent echelons of the assault included 50 Battery, which landed on 1 November, and 52 Battery on the 6th. The field guns on Stirling Island were based in static positions; some had to relocate once US construction units began work on the airfield. This was a tempting target for the Japanese: on the night of 12–13 January, during three separate air raids, 214 Battery fired 2200 rounds and 208 Battery 1600.

As resistance on Mono was subdued, the field batteries increasingly concentrated on the coastal defence role they had also planned for in this unusual operation. One troop of 54 Anti-Tank Battery had gone ashore on the first morning to cover Blanche Harbour against a landing-craft attack. The other troops were deployed to the Treasuries somewhat later, also in beach defence roles. There was not much to do: 'we might have had a few practice shoots,' one 54th gunner recalled.[81] One troop was in place by 2 November, covering Blanche Harbour from Stirling Island; on the 7th a further troop arrived to take up positions covering the beaches at Soanotalu and Malsi on the north coast. As they settled into a garrison role it became important to keep busy.[82] On reconnaissance they visited native villages bearing gifts of beads, but otherwise had little contact with the locals. After months in camp, tentmates had become family, with the older married men – some of them over age – having a stabilising influence on their younger comrades. Losing a mate could be devastating.

The landings on the Treasuries had been costly for 3 Divisional Artillery. On 27 October alone, 29 Light AA Regiment lost nine killed and 34 wounded, 38 Field two dead and five wounded. The names of these casualties were read out to gunners back in Guadalcanal and posted on battery notice boards, a sobering prelude to their landing on Nissan Island.[83]

Nissan Island

While the 8 Brigade gunners got used to an occupation role in the Treasuries, the Division planned its third, and as it turned out final, amphibious operation: an assault on the Green Island atoll group, usually known by the name of the largest island, Nissan, which surrounded most of a large lagoon. Its conquest would both cut off the supply route to the Japanese forces fighting on in Bougainville and provide a base for air attacks on their stronghold at Rabaul, on New Britain to the north. Under Barrowclough's command, the assault would involve 14 Brigade and attached divisional units, including 144 Independent Battery and the tank squadron, plus US units. It was preceded by audacious exploratory raids on 10 and 30–31 January that established the feasibility of the main landing – and of the development of naval and air bases – on this little-known island group. The first was carried out in secret by US PT (patrol torpedo) boats. The second involved a full day's stay on the atoll by a company of 330 New Zealanders who protected US and New Zealand specialists while they assessed it.

These raiders had exercised on Guadalcanal in mid-December:

> The 'Commandos' [from 30 Battalion] under Sgt. Roy Anderson had a realistic manoeuvre. They were to 'take' a ridge under cover of a smoke screen to be laid down by the guns [of 144 Battery]. There was a mis-understanding and Roy and his merry men were right up on the first screen when an unexpected shell came whistling up to … keep them company. They really 'bit the dust' … and

stoutly maintain that one shell burst but 20 yds from them. Probably good, if unintentional, training.[84]

When they returned to the gun positions, the party was 'not silent' about this experience.[85]

The main assault began at first light on 15 February. Several waves of landing craft got the force ashore, and perimeters were established before any resistance appeared. The artillery element, under Duff's command, included most of the units involved in the Vella Lavella operation: 17 Field Regiment, two troops of 53 Anti-Tank Battery, two batteries of 29 Light AA Regiment and, this time, the pack howitzers and crews of 144 Independent Battery, plus 4 Survey Troop. Once again the anti-aircraft defences were strengthened by a US battalion. On the first day 44 field and AA guns, plus ten radar sets, were landed, and by 11 a.m. field and AA guns were ready for action. Landings were made on both sides of the inner lagoon: 30 Battalion landed on Blue Beach at the Pokonian plantation in the west, 37 and 35 Battalions on Red and Green beaches respectively at Tangalan plantation on the eastern shore. Gunners went in as infantillery, those on Blue Beach comprising a quarter of the storming party. 'This high proportion of gunners in a party of shock troops may have been a tribute to the fighting qualities of artillery personnel, but it was hardly appreciated at the time.'[86] Observation parties landed from the batteries to assist the assaults, their guns following once the beaches were clear.

144 Independent Battery, in its first action, had trans-shipped B Troop's guns to Barahun Island, from where they destroyed Japanese barges at Sirot Island, one of the smaller islands surrounding the lagoon, and fired southwards to support the Pokonian landings. Later a 'barrage put down on Sirot Is. by the Bty landed in the wrong place but the accomodating Infantry changed their plans on the spot to suit the situation. We're not sure what the Inf. think of us but have an idea that the sun doesn't shine from anywhere in our area.'[87]

Next day it became clear that most of the small Japanese garrison had withdrawn to this heavily forested island: an assault was mounted after a barrage by 144 Independent Battery. A sharp infantry action cost a number of New Zealand casualties before the island was cleared. On the 20th the remnants of the Nissan garrison were found hiding in the bush on the southern end of the atoll, and killed in action almost to a man. The survivors were accounted for the next day. Three days later another small group of Japanese was found on an island in the lagoon inside the atoll of Pinipel, just north of the main Green Islands. After refusing to surrender they were killed in a brief struggle, and the islands were secured. Allied forces and supplies poured in as they became a major base for operations against Rabaul and Japanese positions on nearby New Ireland.

In April 1944, 207 and 208 AA batteries returned to New Caledonia, en route for New Zealand, and were replaced by 209 and 214 batteries from the Treasuries. In March, with pressures on manpower at home, 3 Division had been reduced in size. The last artillery units to leave the Solomons were Divisional Artillery HQ, which arrived in New Caledonia on 21 June 1944, and 214 Light AA Battery (6 July). By now the remaining units of the Divisional Artillery were encamped with the Training Depot in Néméara Valley. Most were disbanded and had returned to New Zealand by August, and 3 Division officially ceased to exist in October. Many of its personnel were sent to reinforce 2 Division in Italy.

The 'Coconut Bombers'[88] drifting home after almost two years in the Pacific, received 'no public welcome, parades or acknowledgement'. Men returned to their families in varying states of health. One Geraldine homecoming party turned 'fairly sombre' when the guest of honour arrived yellow from anti-malarial Atebrin tablets – and thin from the undiagnosed malaria they had failed to prevent. 'Aunty Bid' had 'a cry in the pantry', and 'a dozen beer was enough for the whole family'.[89]

Conclusion

By the time the last 3 Division gunners came home, the Pacific War had moved far away and home defence had been virtually discontinued. Those engaged in home defence, garrison duty in the Pacific and amphibious assaults on Japanese-held islands had had disparate experiences. At home, coastal, anti-aircraft and field artillery units had reached by far their greatest scale and highest state of readiness in a very short time. Though many of the defensive measures were begun too late for the period of greatest peril, there can be no doubting the

These New Zealand anti-tank guns have just been unloaded on Nissan Island.
PA1-q-303, WH528, pic. 635, Alexander Turnbull Library, Wellington.

seriousness of the preparations and training, or the frustration that some felt at being kept at home. The garrison gunners in Pacific outposts played an important role in the coordinated Allied defence of the South Pacific, though fortunately they too were never called upon to fire in anger. The amphibious actions of the 3 Division gunners in the Solomons are a unique part of the story of the New Zealand Artillery. Though not well known except by those who took part, all these deployments were fine examples of the transformation of citizens into fully trained, professional artillerymen.

Charles Duff

Charles ('Danny') Duff was one of many senior New Zealand gunners to attend both Christchurch Boys' High and Duntroon. He became 'a stern disciplinarian' who was 'able to unbend at the right moment'.[90] After starting his military career in the school cadets and the shooting eight, he became a staff cadet in 1917 and entered the Royal Military College. Lieutenant Duff was appointed to the New Zealand Staff Corps in December 1920. His training continued at the GHQ School at Trentham, where he qualified on Vickers and Lewis guns. He later passed more exams and was promoted to captain.

Duff's first postings were as adjutant to the infantry in Christchurch and Nelson/Marlborough/West Coast regiments; he transferred to the RNZA in 1923. After moving to its Wellington Detachment, Duff was Staff Captain Artillery at GHQ from 1925 and became Adjutant Coast Artillery Northern Command the following year. In 1933 he did the Gunnery Staff Course at Larkhill School of Artillery, followed by a field survey course. Duff returned as Assistant Staff Officer Artillery in 1935 before being appointed OC Fort Dorset and Central Command's chief gunnery instructor. He had further training in the Staff College at Quetta, India, from 1937, and when war broke out he was attending the Staff College, Camberley.

Major Duff was seconded to 2NZEF and given command of the expatriate anti-tank battery being formed at Aldershot. (This was to become 34 Battery, the 'Pommy Battery' of 7 Anti-Tank Regiment, which served with distinction until it was reconstituted as a mortar unit in 1944.) He sailed with 34 Battery to Egypt but then returned to Britain, becoming Brigade Major with the Divisional Artillery before leading 7 Anti-Tank in Greece. After a spell at Artillery Training Depot, Duff took command of 4 Field, asserting his authority by 'placing the whole Regt under CB. Confined to unit lines – for generally dirty and untidy area ... and that includes officers'.[91] Duff's élan during the Crusader campaign earned him appointment as a DSO. On 1 December he:

> displayed a high degree of personal coolness and gallantry in controlling his batteries from an exposed command position under heavy fire and exercising excellent judgement in breaking off close action in accordance with his orders and reassembling his batteries. Wherever the fighting was hardest, this gallant officer was to be found, inspiring all ranks of his Field Regiment by his personal example of courage and of determination.[92]

Charles Duff returned to New Zealand in June 1942 to take command of the artillery in 1 New Zealand Division, put together to defend Northland. General Harold Barrowclough then selected him for 3 Division, which was being formed for service in the Pacific. Duff's wife of sixteen years, Florence, who was rejoining him in New Zealand, was lost at sea when the *Port Hunter* was torpedoed on 11 July 1942 in the Atlantic. Less than a month later, Duff took charge of the 3 Division gunners assembling at Manurewa. Brigadier Duff served as CRA for 3 Division from November 1942 until August 1944; he was the most senior gunner in the theatre. Duff then returned to the RNZA as a lieutenant-colonel. He was mentioned in despatches twice.

Duff was AQMG at Army HQ until December 1945, when he was posted to Melbourne as Director Joint Plans; he headed the New Zealand Joint Services Liaison Office in Melbourne for eighteen months from July 1947. After retiring from the Army in May 1949, he worked for the Main Highways Board in Wellington. Charles Duff died in 1972.

George Salt

'Coasties' remember the legendary George Salt as the backbone of their cadre. 'Salty' rose from gunner to major in the coast artillery. Highly respected by all, he had a great sense of humour and could turn his hand to anything. When Fort Takapuna's guns were relocated, it was he who recovered and restored to operational condition the two pieces that had long been outside the Auckland Museum.

> He was a soldier's soldier, but never fired a shot in anger. He was so good in his instructing and his gunnery that he served here, went to Fiji and served again here, having missed active service. Once a gunner, always a gunner.[93]

Harold George Salt was born at Lyttelton on 4 February 1903, the son of Lieutenant Jasper Salt, NZASC, who had served in South Africa and would be a defence administration during the First World War. Before being attested in 1921, he was in 97 Company Senior Cadets and the Featherston Camp Trumpet Band. He had also worked as a farmhand and in a garage at Pigeon Bay on Banks Peninsula. His first experience of service was foreshortened by cuts to the permanent force: he was discharged after only six months. Working long days for low pay, he applied successfully for a vacancy in the

Military Forces in 1923. He served first in Wellington, as a driver based at Alexandra Barracks, but transferred to Auckland the following year. Lacking formal education, Salt failed the staff sergeant's promotion examination twice, the second time (1938) when acting in the rank.

On the outbreak of war Sergeant-Major Salt was Adjutant, 1 Heavy Group. He was intimately involved in the installation of batteries on Motutapu Island and at Takapuna. He transferred to 2NZEF in May 1941, and entered camp the following month as a lieutenant/quartermaster. His knowledge of and skill in mounting heavy ordnance were in demand, given the hurried work to rearm the main ports and establish new coast batteries in smaller ports. By now he had installed or relocated guns of three different calibres at Whangaparaoa, Castor Bay, North Head and Rangitoto Island. He had proved himself adept at barging heavy equipment in bad weather and installing guns in exposed places without the benefit of heavy equipment.

With the 5-inch high-velocity 60-pr medium gun still a useful weapon, Salt attempted to give it more application for coast defence. He converted the old 8-inch coast defence 'disappearing' mount recently dismantled from North Head's North Battery to take the 60-pr Mk III on a local-pattern mechanised undercarriage. Dispensing with the gun-raising feature, he gave the 60-pr 360° traverse 'from the handwheel that is part of the equipment – better than traversing by trail'. Two rounds fired in proof trials late in 1941 showed the mounting to be steady. Putting the idea into service was delayed by Salt's call to 2NZEF; the Army had more coastal guns to mount in Fiji.[94]

George Salt as Battery Commander, 64 Battery, 9 Coast Regiment, Whangaparaoa, 1943.
Courtesy of Frank Whiting.

Salt served with B Force in Fiji from January to September 1942. He mounted a pair of naval guns at Vuda in the west, and three 6-inch guns on Suva's Flagstaff Battery. Returning to 9 Heavy Regiment as quartermaster, he helped on the installations at a number of minor ports. Captain Salt commanded 64 Heavy Battery (the old 6-inch guns at Whangaparaoa he had previously moved from North Head) for seven months from April 1943 before taking command of the whole regiment as a temporary major in November 1944. Before the war was out he was made an MBE, and he got a Meritorious Service Medal in 1946.

George Salt was always one of the men. The regiment's Master Gunner, asked by a visiting dignitary how he knew as much as he did, replied – in Salt's hearing – that if he made a mistake the Regimental OC 'would use his boot on my bum'.[95] With his eyesight deteriorating – a particular problem when he was taking bomb-disposal courses – Salt relinquished command of 9 Coast Regiment in 1947. After working on the 9.2-inch batteries and Godley Head's third gun, he retired three years later as 'one of [the] leading experts of the time in Coast Artillery Installations'.[96]

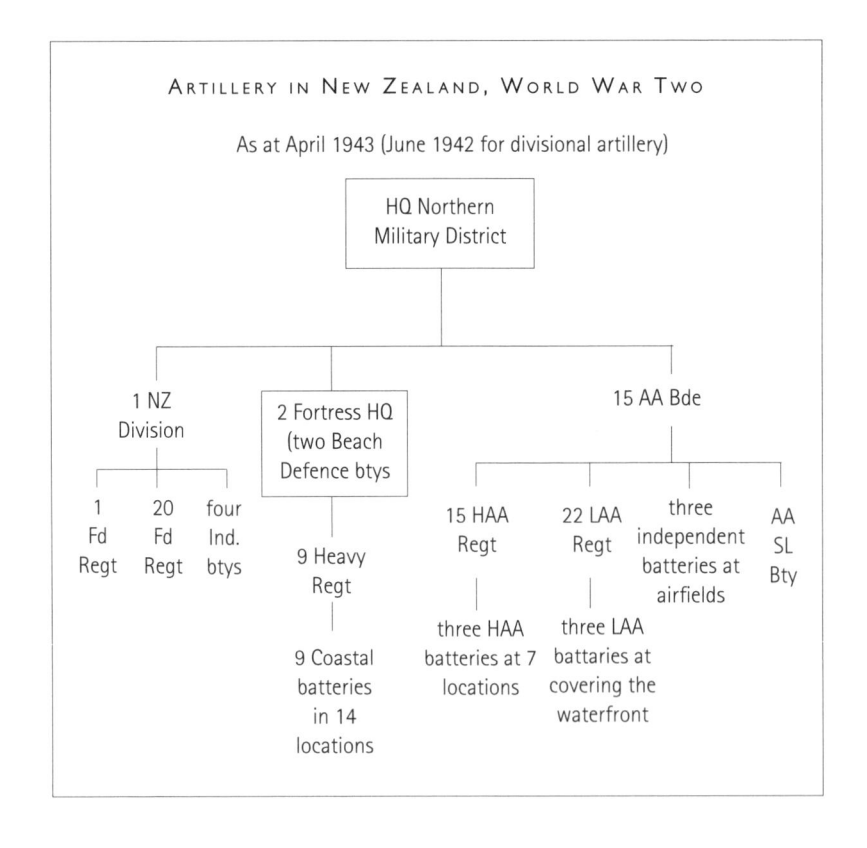

Artillery in New Zealand, World War Two

As at April 1943 (June 1942 for divisional artillery)

- HQ Northern Military District
  - 1 NZ Division
    - 1 Fd Regt
    - 20 Fd Regt
    - four Ind. btys
  - 2 Fortress HQ (two Beach Defence btys
    - 9 Heavy Regt
    - 9 Coastal batteries in 14 locations
  - 15 AA Bde
    - 15 HAA Regt
      - three HAA batteries at 7 locations
    - 22 LAA Regt
      - three LAA batteries at covering the waterfront
    - three independent batteries at airfields
    - AA SL Bty

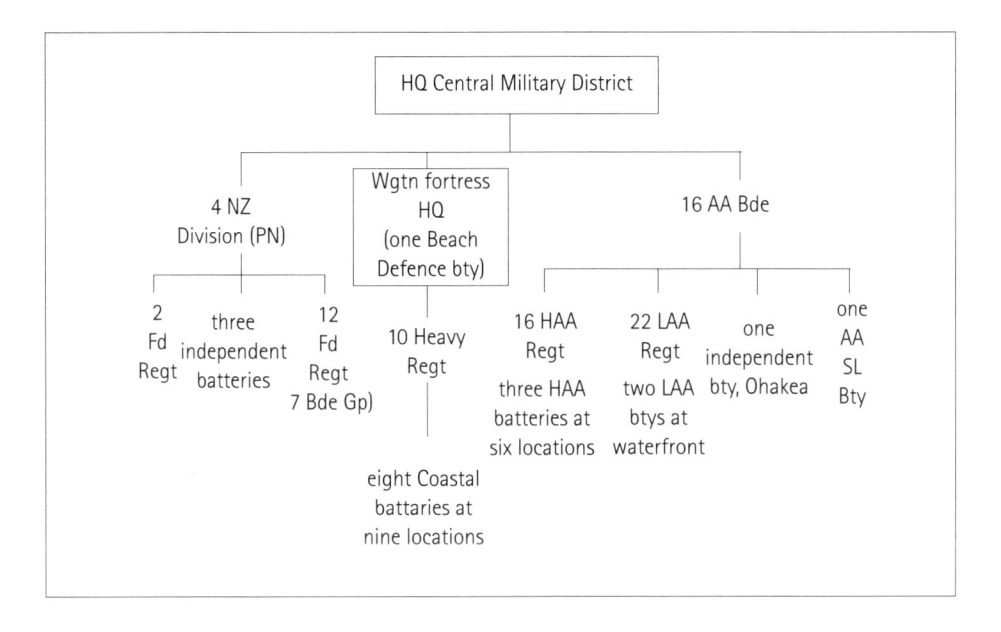

Pacific Theatre and Home Defence, 1939–45

HQ Central Military District

- **4 NZ Division (PN)**
  - 2 Fd Regt
  - three independent batteries
  - 12 Fd Regt (7 Bde Gp)
- **Wgtn fortress HQ (one Beach Defence bty)**
  - 10 Heavy Regt
    - eight Coastal batteries at nine locations
- **16 AA Bde**
  - 16 HAA Regt — three HAA batteries at six locations
  - 22 LAA Regt — two LAA btys at waterfront
  - one independent bty, Ohakea
  - one AA SL Bty

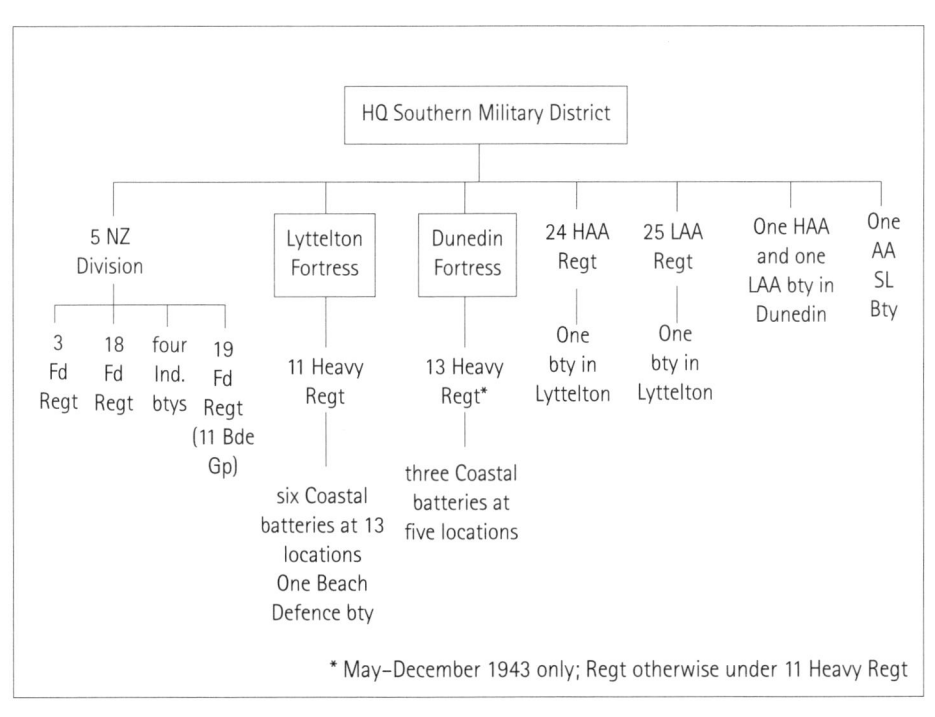

HQ Southern Military District

- **5 NZ Division**
  - 3 Fd Regt
  - 18 Fd Regt
  - four Ind. btys
  - 19 Fd Regt (11 Bde Gp)
- **Lyttelton Fortress**
  - 11 Heavy Regt
    - six Coastal batteries at 13 locations
    - One Beach Defence bty
- **Dunedin Fortress**
  - 13 Heavy Regt*
    - three Coastal batteries at five locations
- **24 HAA Regt**
  - One bty in Lyttelton
- **25 LAA Regt**
  - One bty in Lyttelton
- **One HAA and one LAA bty in Dunedin**
- **One AA SL Bty**

* May–December 1943 only; Regt otherwise under 11 Heavy Regt

3 New Zealand Division Artillery Units and Coast Defense in Pacific

As at April 1943

Artillery Training Depot — **HQ 3 Divisional Artillery** (1942–44)

Under HQ 3 Divisional Artillery:

- **29 Light AA Regt**
  - 207 LAA Bty
  - 208 LAA Bty
  - 209 LAA Bty
  - 214 LAA Bty
  - 215 LAA Bty
  - X Sec Sigs
  - Workshops (40mm LAA)

- **28 Heavy AA Regt***
  - 202 HAA Bty
  - 203 HAA Bty
  - 204 HAA Bty
  - Sig Sec
  - Workshops (3.7n HAA)

- **17 Field Regt**
  - 12 Fd Bty
  - 35 Fd Bty
  - 37 Fd Bty
  - E Sec Sigs
  - 20 LAD
  - (25 pr)

- **37 Field Regt** (M2 only)*

- **38 Field Regt**
  - 49 Fd Bty
  - 50 Fd Bty
  - 52 Fd Bty
  - Sig Sec
  - 42 LAD
  - (25 pr)

- **144 Ind. Bty** (3.7 in How)

- **53 A-TK Bty** (6pr)

- **54 A-TK Bty** (6pr)

- **4 Survey Tp**

33 Heavy Regt*
- 150 Hy Bty (6in)
- 151 Hy Bty (155mm)
- 152 Hy Bty (155mm)
- Sig Sec

* Disbanded 1943

8

COLD AND HOT WARS, 1946–72

After the Second World War, as for the First, New Zealand gunners helped to occupy the territory of a defeated enemy – this time, a single battery had a lengthy sojourn in Japan. When this ended, attention turned to the problems of maintaining in peacetime the basis for the artillery component of the Middle East expeditionary force that would once again be New Zealand's contribution to any future war. The next enemy was expected to be the Soviet Union, but when the Cold War did catch fire, it was in East Asia, and New Zealand sent not a full division but a specially enlisted field regiment. This performed well in conditions often more reminiscent of the First than the Second World War.

Over the next two decades, New Zealand defence planners and politicians wrestled with the problem of making an effective and affordable contribution to the defence of the West. In the mid-1950s, with New Zealand now a member of the ANZUS alliance with the United States and Australia, planning for a Middle East division was replaced by plans for 'forward defence' in South-east Asia, which soon materialised as an infantry regiment sent to Malaya. New Zealand's next war, in Vietnam, would also be its most contentious. In 1965, an artillery battery was the ideal contribution to this conflict: it was likely to both suffer fewer casualties and provide less graphic media coverage than an infantry force (though infantry companies were sent later in response to continued American pressure).

How best to prepare for this sort of commitment remained debatable. The civilian component of New Zealand's armed forces was sometimes volunteer, sometimes conscript; the Regular Force, which grew to its largest ever peacetime levels, initially focused on training these civilians, but later concentrated on its own overseas deployment. Throughout this period, artillery remained the core of the regular army, and from 1955 to 1978 the Chief of the General Staff was usually a gunner.

JAYFORCE

New Zealand's contribution to the 35,000-strong British Commonwealth Occupation Force sent to Japan after its surrender in August 1945 was dubbed Jayforce.[1] The Labour government wished to underline New Zealand's strong commitment to maintaining post-war global and regional security, and to strengthen ties with Britain: these had weakened after the fall of Singapore, which had necessitated reliance on the United States. Counting later relief drafts, some 12,000 New Zealand men and women would eventually serve in the 4400-strong Jayforce. They included a group of gunners making up a reconstituted 25 Field Battery, augmented by about 25 Regular Force gunners drafted from the Tenth and later Reinforcements sent to the Middle East.

The battery trained in Italy at Lake Trasimene and then near Siena under Major Jack Spring before joining the rest of Jayforce in Florence. The guns and transport were then moved to Naples, from where the gunners sailed for Japan on 21 February 1946. Because of uncertainty about the extent of Japanese acceptance of the occupation, no chances were taken. 'Weapons to meet any emergency were provided for and included 25 pdr Guns, 6 pdr Anti Tank Guns, MMG's and PIAT Mortars.'[2] Stores were low: some clothing supplies were inadequate and little ammunition was taken – but 'somehow we acquired a piano', one gunner remembers. 'Rather than have it locked down below decks I arranged with the captain to have it hoisted aboard and tied to a deck crane with a tarpaulin cover.' Music helped the six-week voyage pass more quickly.[3]

Under Spring's command, 25 Field Battery settled into former Japanese army barracks in Yamaguchi, the prefecture at the south-western tip of the main island of Honshu for which Jayforce became responsible in March 1946. This facility had a workshop and recreation facilities, but, like Japanese infrastructure in general, was in dire need of maintenance. The initially basic rations were supplemented by supplies left by departing US Marines. By April the men were suffering from malnutrition, the result of poor diet and hard work, including digging drains, and worsened by the after-effects of a measles epidemic that had struck on the voyage out. The poor quality of the food provoked a 'strike' for which 80 25 Field men were sentenced to fourteen days' packdrill (an hour each day). Maintaining morale was to be a continuing problem in Japan.

This occupation was anything but an artilleryman's event.

> We had one live shoot. In the 25 square miles of territory in our care we had to take an inventory of everything, and we found this artillery range which we could use. It was part of another kind of boredom. We had to make sure our guns were cared for, but also how to occupy the men. Stagnation takes place very easily.[4]

25 Battery parades through Yamaguchi, Japan, May 1946. *Graham Birch collection.*

They were not issued with much ammunition – 'it was clear we were never going to have to deploy the guns on operation.'[5] 25 Field became effectively an infantry unit, sharing in duties such as picketing and searching for black-market operators and military equipment. It also provided personnel for a ceremonial guard battalion that from October 1946 was periodically deployed to Tokyo for a month to six weeks at a time.

Japan provided some culture shocks for the gunners. Women wheeled wheelbarrows filled with concrete for road work, and defecated in public.[6] The Japanese were 'zonked', a 25 Field officer remembered. 'There was no resistance, absolutely nothing. We couldn't talk to them because of the language and a stupid non-fraternisation rule.'[7] Relations began badly with rumours that the New Zealanders were cannibals. Even after these were allayed, 'the people were very shy & disappeared at our approach'. As time passed, however, tensions eased and men visited private homes. After one visit, R. Buchan enthused that 'Tea was tremendous!' despite his farcical attempts to eat with chopsticks.[8] Some studied, went sightseeing or to the races. Many formed relationships with local women. Inter-unit sport and the associated drinking became major preoccupations; drunkenness was common.

One gunner died in an accidental shooting before the Italy draft men went home at last in mid-1946. Among them was Lieutenant G.D. Speight, a future High Court judge. A volunteer relief draft maintained 25 Field's presence in Yamaguchi. Its personnel included J. Lindsay Smith, who was to rise to brigadier in the regular army and then spend nearly a decade as Director of the New Zealand Security Intelligence Service. 25 Field, the unit with the least real soldiering to do, was the first component of Jayforce to be disbanded, on 22 May 1947.

Towards Compulsory Military Training

With the exception of Jayforce, New Zealand's armed forces had virtually completed their post-war demobilisation by the end of 1946. While the RNZA regulars concentrated on training the relief drafts for 25 Battery, the Territorial Force (TF) artillery was left in limbo by the disestablishment of the wartime home defence units. In March 1946, the number of serving Regular Force (RF) officers and other ranks in all corps, 127 and 400 respectively, was below establishments which remained at pre-war levels. Recruitment of regulars recommenced in April 1947, two months after greatly increased establishments (359 officers and 3377 other ranks) were announced; the initial source of recruits was Jayforce. In early 1947 the corps structure of the Army was substantially revised. For the artillery this involved removing the somewhat invidious distinction between the regular RNZA and the territorial NZA. Henceforth all would be RNZA, and when the regiment was redesignated the Royal Regiment of New Zealand Artillery on 10 April 1958, this abbreviation was retained.[9]

With the Cold War intensifying as the Soviet Union installed client regimes in Eastern Europe, the TF was revived in February 1948 with the appointment and training of officers, all of whom were 2NZEF veterans. NCOs were soon enlisted, and skeleton territorial units were established in October to provide a full-scale divisional field force. For the artillery this meant the establishment of three field regiments (1, 2 and 3 Field), effectively the successors of the pre-war regional artillery 'brigades', along with 4 Medium Regiment, 5 Anti-Tank Regiment and 6 Light Anti-Aircraft Regiment. Although a 'serious invasion of New Zealand' was now seen as very unlikely, the possibility that an unspecified 'combination of Asiatic powers' might blockade the country to prevent it contributing to a wider war ensured a continuing role for coastal and AA defences.[10] The wartime coastal units, which had survived on paper (9, 10 and 11 Coast regiments), were revived, and three composite AA regiments (13, 14 and 15), were established, with rather tenuous lineage links to wartime units bearing the same numerical designations.

As relations between the Western powers and the Soviet Union continued to deteriorate, and particularly with the Berlin crisis of 1948, plans were developed for New Zealand again to commit a division to the Middle East in the event of war. To make a useful contribution to resisting a Soviet advance into the region, though, a New Zealand expeditionary force would have to arrive much more quickly than it did in either of the world wars. As a result, the post-war Army was structured for deployment as an expeditionary force, and under the New Zealand Army Act 1950, which superseded the Defence Act 1909, territorials could be deemed 'liable for continuous service within and outside New Zealand' in 'a state of war or other like emergency'. Experience had shown that a deployable division could not be maintained through reliance on volunteers and, after consultation with the British authorities and a referendum on 3 August 1949, the Labour government reintroduced compulsory military training (CMT) through the Military Training Act 1949.[11]

For the duration of CMT, teaching trainees would be a heavy commitment for the understrength RF, which was responsible for both basic and corps instruction during each intake's initial period of training. The volunteer TF was also stretched to provide the necessary ongoing refresher training. As a result, the number of intakes varied between four and three per annum, and the total annual training required of CMT personnel over three years was reduced from 60 to 51 days in 1956 to allow RF and volunteer TF personnel

Colonel Commandant

The title of Colonel Commandant, RNZA, originated in the appointment of the first Colonel of the Royal Artillery, Albert Borgard, in 1727. In the New Zealand Army, Colonel Commandants of corps are retired senior officers, normally aged under 65. Appointed at their previous rank after a process of consultation 'through corps channels', they have no powers of command or administrative responsibilities. Serving terms of approximately four years, their main roles are to foster esprit de corps, promote community interest in the regiment and advise senior serving officers (especially the regimental colonel) on regimental matters, including customs, history, dress and memorials. They maintain close liaison with allied corps in other Commonwealth armies and with the Captain-General or Colonel-in-Chief, play a role in visits by distinguished guests and other ceremonies, send traditional loyal greetings to the monarch, and give advice on the administration of regimental charities and other funds. The Colonel Commandant is 'the father of the Regiment' and oversees its general well-being.

The RNZA's first Colonel Commandants were appointed with effect from 1 January 1949. Until 1964 each military district had its own Colonel Commandant (with two initially for Southern Military District). Lieutenant-Colonel C.L. Walter's purview was extended from Northern Military District to the whole of the North Island in October 1964, and in December 1965 he became the first Colonel Commandant of the whole RNZA.*12* In the subsequent four decades nine other retired gunner officers have held this position.

Captain-General

The Captain-General has precedence over all other officers of the Royal Artillery, and therefore of the RNZA. From the fifteenth century the title denoted the army's effective head. Until 1855 a Master-General of the Ordnance was responsible for the artillery, engineers, fortifications and supplies. After the abolition of the Board of Ordnance, the Commander-in-Chief of the British Army, the second Duke of Cambridge, was appointed as the Royal Artillery's Colonel-in-Chief in 1861. Earl Roberts, a former commander-in-chief of the British Army, was made Colonel-in-Chief of the RNZA and NZA in 1911. Renamed Captain-General, this role for both the RA and the RNZA has more recently been held by the reigning monarch. The duties of the position are now essentially ceremonial and social.

time for their own training, professional development and other duties. On top of their other responsibilities, the regulars also trained men of the Fiji Military Forces in coastal gunnery.

REVIVAL OF THE COAST AND ANTI-AIRCRAFT DEFENCES

New Zealand's coast and anti-aircraft defences had been effectively mothballed from 1944, with armaments removed from the minor ports and the installations in the fortress areas placed on a care and maintenance (C&M) basis. In March 1946 the Chiefs of Staff Committee decided that the defences at Auckland and Wellington should be maintained in an operational condition but with only a small regular peacetime garrison. The first of the 9.2-inch guns at Whangaparaoa had been proofed in March 1945 and further shoots by both guns of this battery were carried out in late 1946, when the fire control instrumentation was fully installed and operational. It was 'beautiful' to be able to 'see the shells disappearing', an RF officer recalled.[13] In February 1947, with no direct threat to New Zealand foreseeable, all coastal installations were again put into care and maintenance with the exception of the 9.2-inch battery at Whangaparaoa, which became the

9.2-inch gun, Whangaparaoa, 1945.
Department of Conservation, Auckland.

Gunners at Sea

From the 1880s the artillery hired launches or used their own cutters to reach batteries inaccessible by land, such as Ripapa Island and Taiaroa Head.[14] *Ellen Ballance* briefly played this role after being superseded as a minelaying steamer at the turn of the century by *Janie Seddon* (at Wellington) and *Lady Roberts* (Auckland). When submarine mining ended in 1907, these vessels were transferred to the RNZA. They were often hired out to other government departments, but served as examination steamers during the First World War (and, in the case of *Janie Seddon*, the Second, by when it had been transferred to the Navy). The Electric Light Section provided most of *Janie Seddon*'s crew.[15]

Bombardier and *Lance Bombardier* at Torpedo Bay Wharf, North Head, Devonport, in the 1950s.
Dan Foley collection.

In the mid-1930s the RNZA planned to build a launch that could tow targets for coastal battery practice. Instead, in 1938 a 64-foot RAF-type rescue craft capable of 38 knots was ordered from Britain. Based at Hobsonville and later Wellington, this was shared with the RNZAF. During the war Auckland's 9 Coast Regiment acquired the small launches *Gunner* and *Nissan*. In 1946 a former harbour defence motor launch was converted to tow targets and carry personnel and stores to Motutapu and Waiheke islands. Renamed *Bombardier*, this 72-footer remained in service until 1959, making several voyages to Wellington to tow targets. In 1948 *Gunner* was replaced by a converted towboat, *Lady Roberts II*, which was in return replaced in 1955 by a converted pleasure launch which alternated in name between *Lance Bombardier* and *Sapper*. After the demise of the coastal artillery this last Army launch carried stores to Motutapu Island and served the Engineer Corps until 1961.

Weapons – Coast Defence

The 9.2-inch gun was the archetypal British coastal gun from the 1880s until the 1950s. The updated mark installed in New Zealand had an Asbury breech mechanism. The ammunition was brought up from the magazine about 40 feet below on a chain hoist. The shells were stored in the emplacement in recesses or ready-round shelves. The gun mounting had a mini-hoist for raising the shells from the lower level, and a rigid-chain rammer for loading them. The charge bags were delivered by hoist but loaded by hand. The gun layers received information on bearing and elevation, and the size of charge to be used (super, full, three-quarters or half), from dials driven by the instruments in the plotting rooms, which converted data from observation posts (and radar).

Name	Ordnance BL 9.2-inch Land Service Mk XV, Mk IX Mount
Entered NZ service	1945–48
Role	counter-bombardment role, with 35° mounting
Calibre	9.2 in (234 mm), 46.7 cals
Range	36,700 yards (20.8 miles, or 33.6 km)
Weight	28-ton barrel on 105-ton mount with gun house
Projectile	380 lb (172 kg) – HE and AP, with one or two charge bags (each 53.5 lb)
Remarks	Six of these last and largest New Zealand coast defence weapons were installed.

> ### Weapons – Medium Guns
>
> The New Zealand Army's post-war general support artillery weapon had been developed by Britain in the 1930s to replace Great War-vintage 6-inch guns and howitzers. The design entered British service in 1941. It had a split trail and two distinctive hydropneumatic balancing cylinders projecting vertically on either side of the barrel. RA batteries with this gun supported 2 NZ Division in the Second World War. A regiment (later a battery) of them served in New Zealand until 1986, when their irreplaceable obturation pads (which prevented the escape of gases to the rear when the propellant was ignited) had become too worn.[16]
>
> | Name | Ordnance BL 5.5-inch Mk III |
> |---|---|
> | Entered NZ Service | 1951 |
> | Role | medium wheeled gun |
> | Calibre | 5.5 in (140 mm), 30 cals |
> | Range | 18,000 yds (16,460 m) |
> | Weight | 12,870 lb (5850 kg) |
> | Projectile | 80 lb (36.3 kg) or 100lb (45.4 kg) |
> | Remarks | A useful weapon, with 45° elevation and 60° on-board traverse. |

focus for RNZA coastal training. Work continued on the similar batteries at Waiheke and Wrights Hill, but these too were placed on C&M immediately after being proofed in late 1947. Stocks of both heavy and light anti-aircraft guns were maintained, with plans for their deployment at the four main ports if necessary. Only with the introduction of CMT was coastal and AA artillery resuscitated on anything like an operational basis. The last years of the coastal and AA artillery in the 1950s would also be their peacetime heyday in New Zealand, even though the gunners viewed their equipment as 'pretty ancient stuff'.[17]

From 1950 the coast batteries at Auckland, Wellington and Lyttelton were raised to a high standard of peacetime readiness under 9, 10 and 11 Coast regiments respectively. Training focused on the modern 6-inch batteries at Motutapu, Palmer Head and Godley Head, and on the examination batteries at Castor Bay, Fort Dorset and Battery Point, all of which were rearmed in the

ARTILLERY IN NEW ZEALAND, 1956

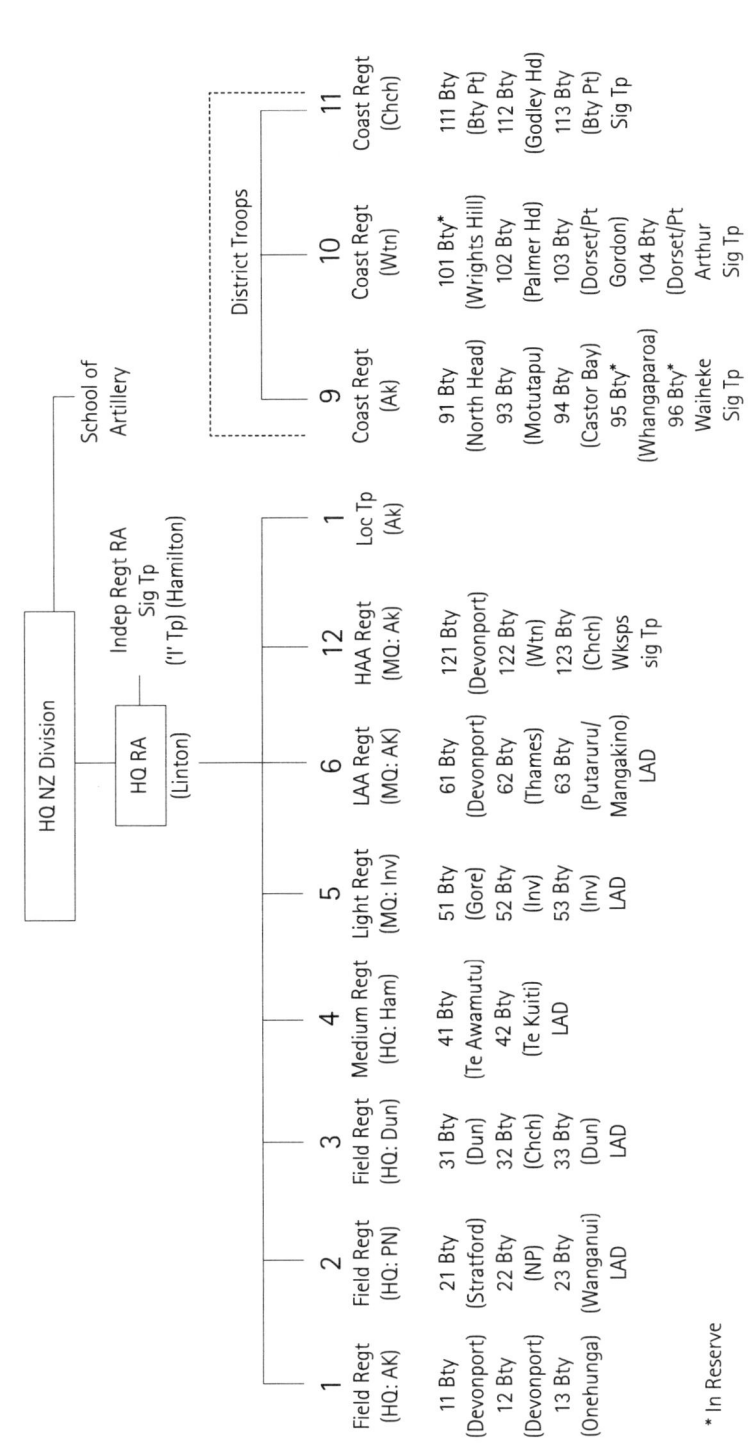

```
                                    HQ NZ Division
                                          |
                                          |—— School of Artillery
                                          |
                                        HQ RA ———— Indep Regt RA Sig Tp
                                      (Linton)         ('I' Tp) (Hamilton)
```

1	2	3	4	5	6	12	1
Field Regt (HQ: AK)	Field Regt (HQ: PN)	Field Regt (HQ: Dun)	Medium Regt (HQ: Ham)	Light Regt (MQ: Inv)	LAA Regt (MQ: AK)	HAA Regt (MQ: Ak)	Loc Tp (Ak)
11 Bty (Devonport)	21 Bty (Stratford)	31 Bty (Dun)	41 Bty (Te Awamutu)	51 Bty (Gore)	61 Bty (Devonport)	121 Bty (Devonport)	
12 Bty (Devonport)	22 Bty (NP)	32 Bty (Chch)	42 Bty (Te Kuiti) LAD	52 Bty (Inv)	62 Bty (Thames)	122 Bty (Wtn)	
13 Bty (Onehunga)	23 Bty (Wanganui) LAD	33 Bty (Dun) LAD		53 Bty (Inv) LAD	63 Bty (Putaruru/ Mangakino) LAD	123 Bty (Chch) Wksps sig Tp	

District Troops

9	10	11
Coast Regt (Ak)	Coast Regt (Wtn)	Coast Regt (Chch)
91 Bty (North Head)	101 Bty* (Wrights Hill)	111 Bty (Bty Pt)
93 Bty (Motutapu)	102 Bty (Palmer Hd)	112 Bty (Godley Hd)
94 Bty (Castor Bay)	103 Bty (Dorset/Pt Gordon)	113 Bty (Bty Pt) Sig Tp
95 Bty* (Whangaparoa)	104 Bty (Dorset/Pt Arthur) Sig Tp	
96 Bty* Waiheke Sig Tp		

* In Reserve

early 1950s with 3.7-inch heavy AA guns in a combined examination and close defence role. A gunner who trained on them regarded these as 'a magnificent weapon in the coast role' and was surprised that they had never been used in the field.[18] Training on mobile 6-prs rounded out the experience of the TF coastal gunners. Occasional 9.2-inch shoots were carried out at Whangaparaoa until this installation was put into care and maintenance in July 1953.

The field regiments also reached a pinnacle of peacetime readiness during the 1950s. They were modelled closely on their 2 Division predecessors, with the same three-battery (six-troop) organisation and with each regiment fielding 24 of the familiar 25-pr Mk II guns. The batteries were numbered after each regiment: thus 3 Field had 31, 32 and 33 Batteries (in Dunedin, Christchurch and Invercargill respectively).[19] The medium regiment (4 Medium) was made up of two batteries (41 in Hamilton and 42 in Te Kuiti), each of two four-gun troops which had the old 6-inch howitzers until they were re-equipped with modern, albeit used, 5.5-inch Mk III guns from 1951. In January 1953, two muzzle prematures, fortunately without casualties, led to the immediate withdrawal from service of the 6-inch howitzers. A troop of 25-prs briefly filled the gap until 4 Medium was brought up to its full strength of 16 5.5-inch guns by the end of the year.[20]

5 Anti-Tank Regiment, established in 'skeletal form', would have consisted of three batteries (each of two troops of four 17-prs), headquartered in Invercargill.[21] The intention was to train men here and equip them overseas, where 'we would have 17 prs thrown at us'.[22] But in mid-1949 it was decided to discontinue training on the 17-prs with a view to converting the regiment to self-propelled 25-prs, and to add a fourth battery of four troops armed with the 4.2-inch heavy mortars that had been adopted by 7 Anti-Tank Regiment in Italy.

In the event 5 Anti-Tank Regiment was disestablished on 1 June 1950, the day that an independent 1 Heavy Mortar Battery, based in Tauranga, was established.[23] The 17-prs intended for the latter were never acquired,[24] and the dedicated anti-tank role was left to infantry anti-tank platoons equipped with the obsolescent 6-pr gun, supplemented by 18 BAT 120-mm recoilless rifles and rocket-launching 'bazookas'.[25] Two years later, 5 Anti-Tank Regiment was belatedly replaced in the artillery order of battle by 5 Light Regiment, headquartered in Petone.[26] This unit absorbed the personnel of the existing heavy mortar battery and was configured around three batteries (51 in Putaruru, 52 in Gisborne, 53 still in Invercargill)[27] of three troops, each with four 4.2-inch heavy mortars.

The junior unit in the divisional artillery structure of the 1950s was the Locating Battery, based at North Head. It comprised two troops – sound-ranging and radar – and had a survey troop attached to it for administrative convenience.[28] The division was somewhat weak in light anti-aircraft defence, with 6 Light AA Regiment made up of three batteries (at Devonport, Stratford and Dunedin). Each had only two – instead of the standard British three – six-gun Bofors troops.

Of much greater concern was the time taken to build up the CMT-based Army to operational strength.[29] It was 1956 before the 33,000-man establishment of 3NZEF's augmented division was filled; the original intention of deployment in theatre within 90 days would remain unrealistic. By now many of the battery locations had changed, as regiments were concentrated to

Staff of the School of Artillery, Waiouru, 1983.
Mike Subritzky collection.

The Post-War School of Artillery

Army Schools are responsible for establishing tactical and training doctrines and standards, and, in particular, the training of officers and NCOs, and instructor and basic training of regular soldiers. The School of Artillery was re-established at Trentham in 1948, but moved almost at once to Waiouru because of the unrivalled scope there for live firing, manoeuvres and cooperation with other arms and schools. Initially it taught anti-tank and field artillery subjects under its first Chief Instructor, Captain J.G. Gilberd. It was equipped with 6-pr and 17-pr anti-tank guns, a troop of 25-prs, and sections of 6-inch howitzers and 4.2-inch mortars. The first three-week course began just nine days after the transfer from Trentham.[30]

The anti-tank guns were soon disposed of, and the howitzers replaced by 5.5-inch guns. In 1950 the School was integrated with the other Army Schools to facilitate the cooperation with other arms that is an essential aspect of the training of gunners. Lectures and demonstrations were shared with other schools and services. The RNZAF's light AA batteries trained at the School of Artillery from 1952 until they were abolished in 1961, after the cancellation of CMT.

In the early 1970s the School provided training for surveyors, instructors, technical assistants, signallers, limber gunners, radar operators, and in mortar location. Instruction was given on the 105-mm pack howitzer, the 25-pr gun/howitzer and the 5.5-inch gun. Other courses were available by correspondence from the School of Artillery at Larkhill in Britain. Painstakingly stripped-down guns and ammunition were used for teaching purposes, and a miniature range was employed to impart observation of fire skills. An indoor gunpark was also provided. By the mid-1980s the School of Artillery's Field and Locating Branches were between them conducting around 20 courses each year for about 150 students.[31]

Becoming a Gunner

Recruits joined the artillery in the 1950s with few illusions. Invercargill bank clerk John Masters decided to volunteer so as to complete his CMT service as quickly as possible. He was posted to 33 Battery, 3 Field (then equipped with 4.2-inch mortars). Masters thinks he was:

> a pretty useless gunner. There was no room to be a Battery Clerk – those cushy jobs had all been filled. I was the junior fellow on the junior gun in the junior troop of the junior

battery in the New Zealand field artillery – I could only go up. It taught me an awful lot about men, but didn't make me anything of a gunner.

The need for employment or a bolthole were other motivations for joining up. When his mother was widowed, Masters took a job in a freezing works to support her, but soon 'felt the need to escape'. The 'naive, green, raw-boned' youth was not technically inclined. This later Chief Instructor 'in those days couldn't spell "Chief Instructor"'.

Quite a few men who joined as gunners were eventually commissioned. Jim Gilberd of Napier, an instructor at Burnham, was an RSM throughout the Second World War. He was commissioned in 1945, aged 35, in a batch of sixteen pre-war RSMs. 'They couldn't find any red ink on us so they flung us into Trentham for a high-pressure officers' course', despite the prevailing view that lengthy service in the ranks could give men 'fixed ideas about certain things. Officers are supposed to have a broader mind – but we served a purpose.'

While some regular officer recruits went to Australia to attend the Royal Military College, Duntroon and (from 1956) the Officer Cadet School, Portsea, others joined up under a scheme which involved a year's training at the Army School, Trentham, followed by a year at university. Commissioned as acting second lieutenants, they then went through the Officer Cadet Training Unit (OCTU) at Waiouru.

One such recruit, Clyde Stewart, began his first all-arms instructors' course in April 1952, and was then posted to the training battery at Waiouru. The following year he went to university, but 'failed abysmally, because I had got engaged'. He went back to the Training Depot as a Second Lieutenant until the university results came out. 'One day they said to me, "The Army has said you've got to go."' Stewart decided to join the regular force as an acting bombardier and 'found that the guys treated me pretty well. It was good to return to the ranks. It was the best bursary.' After going on courses he went through another OCTU to get commissioned, ending up about three months behind his original colleagues in seniority.[32]

make better use of RF personnel or facilities. For example, 5 Light Regiment's HQ moved from Petone to Invercargill (with a battery in Gore), and 63 Light Anti-Aircraft Battery from Dunedin to Putaruru.[33] By this time the RNZAF had established two light AA batteries for station defence, 51 and 52 squadrons. Each was equipped with 12 ex-Army Bofors, organised in two troop-sized flights.[34]

In 1956 Britain decided to disestablish its coastal artillery defences on the grounds that they would be useless against nuclear attack. New Zealand's Chiefs of Staff initially felt that they were still a 'comparatively cheap deterrent' against Soviet attack but the National government's 1957 Defence Review accepted the British argument, and TF coast training was immediately discontinued.[35] The approximately 1000 personnel of the three regiments were discharged from further CMT obligations. The coast artillery had quietly died. A small cadre of regulars was retained, but some of the coastal guns and most other equipment were soon dismounted and put into storage, and all the fixed gun installations had been dismantled and sold for scrap by the early 1960s. The three regiments survived on paper until 1967, each in its final years at an actual

5.5-inch guns towed by Matador gun tractors, Tihoi, early 1950s.
John Valintine collection.

strength of a single warrant officer, the District Gunner, whose duties mainly involved taking care of the mobile 3.7-inch guns allocated for emergency harbour defences.

Territorial Camps and Training

In May 1950 the first draft of eighteen-year-old males began their fourteen weeks of compulsory training before being posted to territorial units for three years of part-time service of 20 days, including two weeks in camp, each year. The CMT drafts enabled field artillery units to be manned at full (in some cases, over) strength. Each regiment's adjutant, RSM and RQMS were regulars. Officers who had served with 2NZEF were encouraged to serve in the TF, and in the early years of CMT, almost all officers above lieutenant were war veterans. Given these factors, the regiments of the 1950s were the most proficient in the history of the TF artillery, and the same could be said for other corps. Basic and corps training took place at Waiouru, Linton or Burnham, but it was the annual regimental camps, usually held at Tihoi, Waiouru, Tekapo or Sutton, that brought the TF artillery units to life.

Training in the 1950s was not always easy. At out-of-the-way Tihoi, near Lake Taupo, for instance, there were only enough washing and toilet facilities for one unit. When the gunners deployed in full regiments of three batteries, they had to improvise. Camps were tented. 'We'd follow the Auckland Regiment [1 Field],' remembers Colin Stanbridge, a lieutenant in the Wellington-based 2 Field Regiment, 'or heavy ack-ack might come in before or after us. Generally from early January to April, all units would have gone through it, for two weeks each, with two or three days on either end for preparation and clean-up.' 'Tihoi was not a pleasant place – very dry in summer. The dust could well be over the top of your boots.' Another TF officer recalls that the 'tracks in the area were almost non-existent, which extended we young, very inexperienced officers in our map reading'.[36]

Batteries concentrated for training from wherever they were based. 1 Field Regiment, for instance, had two batteries based at Narrow Neck and one at Onehunga. The Second World War quads left from the North Shore. 'We had to take the vehicle ferry across the Waitemata, and you weren't very popular when you turned up with six guns and six gun tractors, because nobody else could use the ferry.' After calling at Northern District Ordnance Depot and the Vehicle Depot at Sylvia Park, they started the seven-hour drive to Tihoi. Here they spent the first week brushing up on their skills and the second in battery exercises. On the final days the CRA would inspect them. Batteries competed for the CRA Shield, which was 'usually won by Harry Honnor of 3 Field.'[37]

Competition between units was intense, with fair play sometimes sacrificed. The sound-ranging troop maintained the Second World War practice of placing four microphones in the ground, precisely surveyed and linked by cables to a central post, so that incoming shells could be tracked and their source located. On one annual exercise at Tihoi, the Sound Locating Troop 'had two very competitive sound-ranging sections' which 'did all sorts of awkward things to each other', such as cutting sections of wire. After A Section spent a morning trying to reinstate their wire, they retaliated that night by switching B Section's wires so that the firing appeared to be coming from the wrong direction.[38]

Coastal training also had its share of incidents. One of the participants recalls an officers' course at 10 Coast Regiment at Wrights Hill in 1947–48, on which commissioned officers worked the guns, magazines, engines,

---

AIRBORNE GUNNERS

In 1945 an abortive attempt had been made to set up an Air Observation Post (AOP) Flight in 2 New Zealand Division. After the war the Army and the Air Force debated whether to use Air Force pilots for ground liaison or train artillerymen to fly. They chose the latter because it was felt that Air Force pilots did not fully understand what went on below them. From 1947 young artillery officers were selected for courses at Wigram. The initial aim 'was to form an AOP Flight so that the artillery could spot, the Army [could] use them for communications, carry their commanders around, [and] infantry people do their recces for patrols'. 1 AOP Flight appeared on the order of battle of the Divisional Artillery until 1961, but though pilots were trained, the unit was never raised.[39]

'The Air Force didn't count us a very high priority,' one AOP pilot trainee recalled. 'We trained alongside their 18 year olds. We were all 20 plus. It

radar and fire control instruments, doing everything except actually fire:

> The turret of the 9.2 is hydraulic – everything is under pressure – and all the electrics and oil pipes were inside the turret, unprotected. The shell would come up on the hoist from the emplacement floor and flop onto a tray that would move over to behind the breech. It was rammed by a large arm which was like a very large bicycle chain. And then the cartridge was put in by hand. What kept it balanced on the hoist was a knob about the size of my thumb. And the lever that released this little knob was very sensitive. The instruction we had said, 'No matter what you do, don't touch the shell release lever.'
>
> Jack Pountney – one of the short-course fellows who'd done terms as a gunner – flipped the lever before there was a tray under the shell. The shell [weighing 380 pounds] fell on the turret floor, sheared the first oil pipe it came across, and we had 1200 pounds of oil pressure going around the turret. The nearest way to turn it off was down in the engine room, which we got to by telephone. It took some little time for the engineer down there to turn off the power, by which time we had a few gallons of oil in the turret. And when it was turned off Master Gunner Stan Cashmore said, 'Well, Mr Pountney, you did that – you clean it up.'[40] That was the last course on the 9.2.[41]

---

wasn't hard to look better than the Air Force boys, except that they were quicker.'[42] Air OP pilots had to pass the same test as transport aircrew, including flying at just 50 feet above Lake Ellesmere. Also training in Harvards, Army pilots notched up 200 to 300 hours in the air. Basic flying training was followed by field exercises in which two Auster J/5 spotter planes usually flew together. The gunners practised landing on farm paddocks and radioing fire instructions to regimental command posts. On one exercise, Ray Andrews and Chris Brown of No. 5 AOP Course failed to clear a line of trees while climbing out of a valley. The second plane, with students John Masters and Barry Hardy, radioed Wigram Operations, waited the regulation 30 minutes and began search and rescue procedures. They eventually found the plane upside down 20 feet up a tree. The pilots were shaken but unhurt. All four men flew again the same day to revive their confidence.[43]

On 9 August 1963, the New Zealand Army Air Corps (NZAAC) was established, with three staff and three Austers. The Director of Artillery was now also designated Director of Army Aviation.[44] This development reflected the Army's appreciation of the growing importance of helicopters, not only in AOP, reconnaissance and liaison roles, but also for transport and even airborne assault. As the Army began helicopter flying training, using a civilian contractor, it remained unclear where helicopters would fit within the New Zealand armed forces. In May 1965, No. 3 (Battlefield Support) Squadron, RNZAF, was formed, and its first Bell UH-1D Iroquois and Bell Sioux helicopters were delivered over the following year.[45] The ground crew and most of the pilots were RNZAF personnel, but RNZA and other Army flyers, as well as Navy pilots, were attached.[46]

16 FIELD REGIMENT IN KOREA

As the first CMT gunners were familiarising themselves with their role, an unexpected task arose for the RNZA.[47] In the early morning darkness of 25 June 1950, forces of the Soviet-backed Democratic People's Republic of Korea (DPRK, 'North Korea') invaded the Republic of Korea (ROK, 'South Korea') in a bid to forcibly reunify the country and extend communist control over the whole peninsula, which had been effectively partitioned along the 38th parallel in 1948. ROK forces fell back in disarray, and within three days the southern capital, Seoul, had fallen. At the instigation of the United States, the United Nations Security Council called on member countries to assist South Korea. The retreat continued, and by early August American and ROK forces were confined to a small pocket based on the port of Pusan.

New Zealand's first response was to despatch two RNZN frigates to the Korean theatre. As the situation on the ground deteriorated, further assistance was called for, and on 26 July the New Zealand government agreed to provide an 1100-strong ground force. This deployment was seen as something of a distraction from the Army's main purpose, preparing 3NZEF for deployment to the Middle East in the event of a global war with the Soviet Union. Thus the New Zealand Army's contribution to Korea – dubbed Kayforce – was specially recruited for the purpose, with a new artillery unit, 16 Field Regiment, created as the core of the New Zealand force. 16 Field lives on as the Army's artillery component half a century later. Though the New Zealand tradition of transforming citizens into soldiers in wartime was to be perpetuated, 483 of the 1056 men who departed with the main body of Kayforce had previous service in the New Zealand Army, and another 280 had experience in the other services or other Commonwealth forces.

Colin Stanbridge saw an advertisement for service in Korea. 'The only alternative they gave you was guns, unless you were a specialist or signaller.' After completing a conversion course at Linton and Waiouru, he became a captain. 'Of 25 of us, all but three passed.' Many had been in Jayforce, and the senior officers were 2NZEF veterans.[48] Others had been 'just waiting for the day we could go to war', according to a man whose father and uncles had served in the Second World War.[49]

After basic training at Papakura, Linton and Burnham, Kayforce was concentrated in early October for corps training at Waiouru, where its HQ had been established on 13 September under Brigadier Ronald Park. Lieutenant-Colonel John Moodie, a territorial with wartime experience in 2 Divisional Artillery, was appointed to command 16 Field Regiment. His second in command, Major Richard Webb, and four other officers were regulars, as were a few NCOs and men, but most of the RF gunners were prevented from serving in Korea by the demands of training CMT territorials and Kayforce replacements. Some of the recruits were selected for an OCTU course, or for a conversion course if they had previously been commissioned in the other services, but Moodie would later claim that only 16 per cent of these officers had actually seen a field gun in action. With time for technical training at a premium, command post and signalling skills still left much to be desired when the regiment was visited by the CGS, Major-General Keith Stewart, on its final exercise. Fortunately, operational conditions in Korea would allow time for further training.[50]

The main body of Kayforce embarked in the passenger liner *Ormonde* (of Second World War infamy) at Wellington on 10 December 1950. Their vehicles and equipment, including 34 25-prs, of which 24 would be required at any one time, were already on their way in a freighter. This was the first time a New Zealand expeditionary force had taken its own heavy equipment with it. During a two-day stopover in Brisbane, the gunners marched through the city. 'They had a beer drought on in Brisbane. The pubs had restricted opening hours – but they opened them for us.'[51] After another stopover in Manila, and keeping submarine watch in the South China Sea, the *Ormonde* docked in Pusan on 30 December.[52] An advance party including Brigadier Park had set up a base in the city and organised the unloading of the vehicles and equipment that had arrived a few days earlier.

After the heat and humidity of Manila, the Korean cold was:

> quite a traumatic change. People didn't realise what we were going into. Brigadier Park said we'd be issued with three pairs of underwear – well, you couldn't get your battledress on over three pairs of underwear, or even two. Even two or three months in Waiouru hadn't really prepared us for it. That wind comes down the peninsula from Siberia.[53]

By now the UN situation in Korea was again rather desperate. General Douglas MacArthur, the theatre commander, had achieved spectacular success with the amphibious assault on Inch'on, on 15 September, which saw the North Koreans in the south outflanked and routed. But as the UN forces pushed deep into North Korea towards the Yalu River border with China, Chinese forces intervened. Mass assaults by these 'Chinese People's Volunteers' (actually People's Liberation Army formations) in late October soon drove the now disorganised UN forces back over the 38th parallel; Seoul fell for the second time on 3 January. A UN defeat seemed a real possibility.

The New Zealand force's journey to Miryang from 13 January was marred by 16 Field's first fatal casualties when a warrant officer and gunner who had been assisting stragglers were ambushed after dark by guerrillas. One was wounded, then beaten to death; the other was captured, then apparently wounded while attempting to escape, and died from loss of blood during the night. The same night, two gunners were wounded when their vehicle was machine-gunned. The regiment spent five days at Miryang calibrating its 25-prs; Park's reservations about its readiness for operations had to be set aside because of the desperate combat situation. By 21 January Kayforce was camped at Naegon-ni, near the front, where they joined 27 British Commonwealth Brigade, under command of the US 24 Infantry Division, part of IX Corps.

Next day 16 Field relieved an American artillery battalion at the gun line to form an integral part of 27 Brigade: the infantry welcomed the regiment's familiarity with British fire support doctrine and procedures. The three batteries, while remaining under command of the regimental and brigade HQs, were assigned to support the three infantry battalions, and as usual the BCs were attached to the battalion HQs. 161 (nicknamed 'Peter') Battery was deployed to support the Middlesex Battalion, 162 ('Queen') Battery to the Argyll and Sutherland Highlanders, and 163 ('Roger') Battery to 3 Royal Australian Regiment. Defensive fire targets were registered on 23 January, and the following evening 163 Battery fired 16 Field's first shots in anger when it drove off a small enemy party which had fired on the Australian positions, beginning a long association with the Royal Australian Artillery (RAR) in Korea. 'There was a very strong bond of friendship between the Australians and New Zealanders', a 162 Battery gunner recalled. 'Far more so than in WWII when the two forces were seldom in close proximity.' But this bond 'didn't show on the surface' – 'the abuse hurled at passing Australian trucks was comprehensive and quite unprintable, and they gave us as good as they got or better'.[54]

The next few days were quiet. The Chinese advance had stalled, and UN forces were regrouping for a counter-offensive, Operation Thunderbolt. When 27 Brigade was pulled out of the line at the end of January, 16 Field remained under command of a US formation (24 Division). On 30 January the regiment moved forward to new positions at Ich'on and began harassment fire on suspected Chinese positions as 24 Division advanced against strong resistance. This required guns to be fired regularly, often at night, 'one round every few minutes. The man on picket, 2 hours, is by himself and puts the round away on written instructions stating the time, elevation (range) and switch [traverse].'[55] Twice fire was called down at short notice, and the regiment also fired three regimental targets ('Mikes', in Korean War parlance).

The regimental HQ controlled the standard three batteries. Sometimes FOOs would request more fire support than was available. A former assistant adjutant recalled that:

Battery Life in Korea

The Korean climate was one of extremes. The New Zealanders experienced the cold first. One gunner remembered 'having about four sleeping bags and still being cold'. Water or beer was frozen hard in the morning.[56] Cold weather also made the guns difficult to handle: 'the grease is so stiff and the traversing and elevating gear and the sights are always getting stuck and it makes us pretty slow to get on to a target'. After Christmas 1952 the temperature dropped to minus 5°F. 'George Gillespie's hand stuck to the gun's brake lever and it tore the skin off his palm. I made a note – must use gloves.'

Summer clothing was issued around May – green singlets, shorts and trousers, and bush shirts, topped off with a tropical hat. 'The nights are cold, but we have got sleeping bags and two blankets, so we are always warm.' Some men had to sleep in their clothes each night in case the gun had to fire at short notice. As it got hotter they swam in the rivers, to wash more than to frolic. By May mosquitoes were a nuisance. Anti-malarial paludrine pills were issued, and men were told to cover up at night and sleep under nets. At the end of September winter sleeping bags were issued. By now 'the blankets weren't enough, even sleeping fully dressed. There were two bags, an inner and an outer, and a rubber bag for the whole lot to fit into.' Winter clothing included greatcoats, windproof jackets and trousers, heavy woollen jumpers and leather-covered mittens.

On arrival at a new position, a battery's first task was to dig its guns in:

> It is surprising what six or seven men can do with shovels in a few days. We moved tons ... of earth and filled several hundred empty ammo boxes. That made [the gun pits] more steady and solid for building. ... We lined the walls with boxes so that the blast of the gun didn't crumble them. After one wet night the floor of the pit got very muddy in spite of a good drain, so we got a load of metal from the river.
>
> After the pit came the ammunition bay, big enough to store five or six hundred rounds. ... We dug into the wall of the gun pit, then lined the place with boxes and roofed it with logs, sandbags and pieces of old tarpaulin.
>
> [Then] we turned our attention to our personal comfort. That meant digging and more digging and we ended up with a nice little hutchee built on to one end of the tent, lined with a double row of ammo boxes and roofed again with logs, half-filled sandbags and a tarpaulin. With the Yankee stove (going all night), my Coleman lamp, a packing case for a table and boxes for chairs, we made the place look quite homely.

Typical Korean winter quarters: Gunner Phil Hansen (left) and Lance-Bombardier Hori Chesnutt, December 1951. K-0625-F, Alexander Turnbull Library, Wellington.

> Each gun crew had a petrol stove and a tent with room for kitbags and lilos brought from home, or perhaps camp stretchers. Some stoves were 'borrowed from the Yanks, though they probably don't know about it'.
>
> Daily routines were important. 'The last man on picket [overnight] lights the stove and puts on a tin of washing water at about 5.30 so there is always some hot water'. Two hours later he went to the cookhouse to get breakfast for the whole gun crew – typically this was toast, fried eggs and a billy of tea.[57]
>
> Playing sport helped pass the time, especially once the front had stabilised. Inter-unit rugby and cricket contests were keenly fought out on rough grounds close to the guns. Sometimes matches had to be abandoned when fire orders came through. Athletics, softball and boxing were also popular, and gunners tried their hands at ice hockey on a rink created by the Canadians on the frozen Imjin.[58]

When they were calling for regimental fire here, here and here, you had to allocate portions to each of those targets. If they were calling for a regiment, perhaps I'd have to put a battery on it, and then I beefed up the number of rounds. 'Mike target! Mike target! Mike target!', they used to scream, and everybody was on their feet.

The 16 Field gunners soon mastered their art, benefiting from having experienced men in key roles. 'Training a gunner is relatively straightforward. You teach him how to open the breech block and shove a shell in and point the thing the right way. It is the technical people who are critical, and they were pretty good.'[59]

On 4 February, after moving forward to new positions, the gunners had a busy and anxious day firing defensive fire tasks to support two US battalions which were falling back before a determined Chinese counteroffensive. But when the regiment was ordered out of the line at the end of the day it was not retreating, as some thought – the line had by then stabilised. It rejoined 27 Brigade, based near Yoju, east of Ich'on, to form part of the corps reserve.

A major Chinese offensive launched on 12 February broke through the UN line and captured Hoengsong. With Chip'yong-ni under serious threat, 27 Brigade and 6 ROK Division were transferred to X Corps to help close the breach. Crossing the Han River at dawn on the 14th, 27 Brigade, now attached to 2 US Division, pushed forward to reopen the road to Chip'yong-ni, where American units were in danger of encirclement. The Middlesex Battalion and 3RAR, supported by 161 and 163 batteries respectively, retook hills commanding a vital junction at Chuam-ni, where the British battalion faced a fierce counter-attack in the early morning of 15 February. The New Zealand gunners sent down defensive fire in front of the Middlesex positions, causing heavy casualties among the Chinese, who still reached the position of one company before being thrown back. Further fire was called down from the forward OPs, one of which had nearly been overrun at the peak of the assault. Two days of heavy firing followed as the battle for control of the road junction continued. Then, once Chip'yong-ni had been relieved by American forces, the Chinese fell back. Their offensive had run its course, and 16 Field's batteries were moved forward and dug in near Chuam-ni.

After a brief lull the UN forces launched Operation Killer to encircle a Chinese salient that almost reached Chech-on, east of Chuam-ni, and drive the front back across the 38th parallel. From 21 February, 16 Field Regiment supported the advance of the Argyll and Sutherland Highlanders and a Canadian light infantry battalion that had joined 27 Brigade. While 163 Battery covered the advance, the other batteries moved forward to Sangsok, so close to the front line that the Middlesex Battalion was called on to protect the gun line. During five days when the Commonwealth advance stalled in front of two well-defended hills, fire tasks by 16 Field culminated in ten Mike concentrations before 3RAR took Hill 614, leading to the Chinese evacuation of Hill 419. As on many occasions in Korea, the number of bodies littering the battlefield were testament to both Chinese tenacity and the effectiveness of the UN artillery. While the brigade moved forward, the gunners were kept busy with concentrations on the next two objectives, hills that were secured by the infantry on 2 March, and with harassing fire on Chinese units and targets including supply dumps, some of this fire being directed by air observation.

The next stage of the advance, Operation Ripper, opened in the Commonwealth sector with heavy softening-up fire on 6 March. The following day was strenuous for the gunners, whose heavy concentrations led the attack by Canadian and Australian infantry on strong defensive positions on two strategic hills (532 and 410) north of Sangsok. In this action 163 Battery alone fired more than 2300 shells in support of the Australians, who took Hill 410 late on the first day. By dawn the Chinese had not only evacuated the brigade's other objective but fallen back along the whole IX Corps front. The 16 Field drivers and their Commonwealth brigade counterparts now had to negotiate a mountain pass on a single-lane road that was tortuous even by contemporary Korean standards, before the guns were dug into new positions to support an advance by the Middlesex and Argyll battalions, which, although led forward by artillery concentrations, was in fact unopposed.

After the rest of 27 Brigade was pulled back into the reserve on 13 March, 16 Field was placed under command of 1 US Cavalry Division for the virtually unopposed attack on the town of Hongch'on on the 15th. The next day,

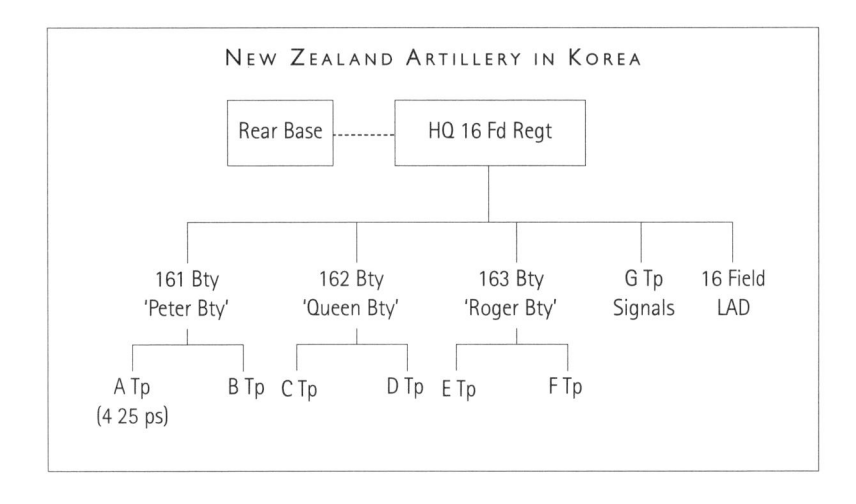

```
                    NEW ZEALAND ARTILLERY IN KOREA

              Rear Base --------- HQ 16 Fd Regt
                    ┌──────────┬──────────┬──────────┬──────────┐
                 161 Bty    162 Bty    163 Bty     G Tp      16 Field
                'Peter Bty' 'Queen Bty' 'Roger Bty' Signals    LAD
                   ┌─┐      ┌─┐        ┌─┐
                 A Tp  B Tp C Tp   D Tp E Tp    F Tp
                (4 25 ps)
```

Chinese forces, fearing encirclement, abandoned Seoul. As 1 Cavalry Division met increased opposition in its advance beyond the Hongch'on River, 16 Field and US artillery units were kept busy supporting the US infantry assault on high ground north of the river until the Chinese withdrew from their positions on the 18th.

After a brief attachment to a US Marine regiment, 16 Field rejoined 27 Brigade for the next stage of the advance, north along the valley of the Chojong River to 'Line Benton', 5 miles south of the 38th parallel. The gunners, leapfrogging their batteries forward as usual in such circumstances, engaged targets on several occasions, but encountered very little opposition. Now 27 Brigade was moved east to the valley of the Kap'yong River, where from 3 April it took part in Operation Rugged, the advance to Line Kansas, north of the 38th parallel, followed by Operation Dauntless, the push to Line Utah, 3 miles further north. These advances at times faced stiff resistance, and 16 Field's gunners had some very busy days in the next fortnight as they were called on repeatedly to suppress enemy positions or break up counter-attacks. From the 10th, when 162 Battery moved forward to new positions, it provided most of the regiment's fire support, complemented by fire from the 155-mm howitzers of an American medium battery. The other batteries of 16 Field were too far from the action to shell the enemy without using super-charge until the end of the operation, when 161 Battery moved forward to positions just south of the parallel.

On 17 April, soon after the Commonwealth Brigade infantry consolidated on Line Utah, they were relieved by an ROK regiment, and the long-serving British elements of 27 Brigade prepared to leave Korea. The batteries of 16 Field remained in their positions in the valley of the Kap'yong River just south of the 38th parallel, and the gunners relaxed as the front remained quiet – indeed, suspiciously quiet.

The Battle of Kap'yong

Whenever the Chinese broke contact and pulled back from the front, it was a sign that they were regrouping for another major assault.[60] On 21 April, 16 Field, still deployed in the Kap'yong valley, supported the advance of 6 ROK Division, initially against light resistance, from Line Utah to a new defensive position, Line Wyoming. When the South Koreans' advance put them out of range of the New Zealand guns, which could go no further up the rugged valley, US artillery units were moved up other valleys in support, while 16 Field was ordered to rejoin the Commonwealth Brigade in reserve near the village of Kap'yong. This move had yet to be made, however, when the South Koreans were overwhelmed by a Chinese attack on 22 April, part of the massive Phase Five offensive unleashed that day. Panic set in at the front, and as the night wore on the scale of the resulting 'bug out' became increasingly apparent to the New Zealand gunners as South Korean troops fled through their positions. The regiment began to pull out before dawn on 23 April, and was digging in near the village of Naech'on when it was ordered forward again to support South Korean units now thought to be regrouping on Line Kansas. 162 Battery remained behind to cover the other two batteries as they moved forward to Kwanam-ni, about 3 miles south of the positions they had left that morning.

While the rest of the Commonwealth Brigade took up defensive positions near Naech'on and Chuktun-ni, a few miles north of Kap'yong, the Middlesex Battalion went forward to protect the gunners in their hazardous advanced position. By early evening it was clear that the front had collapsed. The Middlesex men and the gunners prepared to move out at short notice to

New Zealand gunners in action in the Kap'yong valley, April 1951.
J. Fitzpatrick collection.

avoid being outflanked. The two batteries fired an intensive sustained barrage without the benefit of FOOs to use up ammunition that would otherwise have to be jettisoned to take the infantry. While this was under way the final evidence of the ROK collapse reached the gun line as hundreds of soldiers ran down the road through the gun positions. The gunners progressively shortened the range of their barrage and prepared to shoot over open sights. When the order came to withdraw, the vehicles of three troops carried out the men of the Middlesex Battalion, with one troop covering the others until it too limbered up for the difficult night-time journey back to Naech'on along a road clogged with fleeing South Koreans.

The whole regiment now deployed with 27 Brigade in support of 3RAR and 2 Battalion, Princess Patricia's Canadian Light Infantry. An American artillery battalion was also deployed in support of the brigade as it awaited the Chinese onslaught. From 10 p.m. the Chinese struck at 3RAR and an American tank platoon deployed with them. Unable to communicate by radio and with no ground lines laid, the FOOs could not call down close defensive fire. The New Zealand guns therefore kept busy with fire patterns on the approaches to the Australian positions, which it seemed might be encircled. In the small hours of the following morning, as the Chinese infiltrated between the Canadian and Australian positions and came ever closer to the gun line,

16 Field began to pull back to new positions near Chungch'on-ni, as did two of the three batteries of the American artillery battalion, leaving 163 Battery and one American battery to support the Australians. One of 163 Battery's troops maintained fire in support of the Australians, under increasing pressure, until its ammunition was exhausted and it too withdrew. Although inadequate communications prevented artillery support when a further Chinese assault against the Australians began at 4 a.m., by dawn the guns, surveyed into position on a regimental grid, were able to provide much more effective assistance. Fire – including very effective VT (variable time-fused) air-burst shells from the American 105s – was brought down by one of the New Zealand FOOs and an Australian company commander. The gunners came into their own, shelling movements on the approaches to the Australian positions and beating off wave after wave of Chinese assaulting the hilltop, while the New Zealand Transport Platoon struggled to bring up supplies of ammunition from the rapidly dwindling stocks behind the lines.

That afternoon the Australians pulled back to new positions behind the Middlesex Battalion under cover of an artillery barrage including smoke shells, which obscured their movements. The barrage followed close behind the Australians and inflicted heavy casualties on the advancing Chinese. By now the American 5 Cavalry Regiment had arrived to bolster the line, and with them came 61 Field Artillery Battalion and a battery of 8-inch howitzers. A radio net set up by 16 Field Regiment, with New Zealand officers stationed with the American batteries, coordinated the fire of 56 guns and howitzers.

The enemy now focused on the Canadian positions but encountered effective gun, howitzer and American mortar fire as they advanced. The gunners fired without respite throughout the night of 24–25 April, with Chinese infiltrators at times very close to the gun positions. At one point, a Canadian company commander called down fire on his own position when it was overrun. As the Canadians lay in their foxholes, the New Zealand concentration shattered that phase of the assault and enabled the Canadians to drive the enemy back. The Chinese pulled back during the day and the road to the Canadian position, which had been encircled during the night, was reopened. The Australians and Canadians, with 16 Field and the American gunners in support, had blunted the Chinese offensive in this sector, and the guns had proven extremely effective in dealing with massed infantry assaults. The battlefield was covered with Chinese dead. Seventy-one bodies were found on the banks of the Kap'yong River at one point where a concentration had been brought down during the assault on the Canadians. Six months later, 16 Field Regiment was awarded a South Korean Presidential Unit Citation for having 'operated its guns ceaselessly and efficiently and played an important part in the holding of the position'.[61]

At midnight on 25 April 27 Brigade was relieved by 28 British Commonwealth Brigade, but 16 Field remained to augment the fire support for a planned American advance. At noon next day, however, this was called off. Chinese successes to the west meant that the forward position of IX Corps would become untenable, and the corps was ordered back to new positions just north of Seoul. 28 Brigade pulled back to secure a road junction vital to the retreat of the rest of the forward elements of IX Corps, and then further south to cover the crossing of the Pukhan River before moving to a reserve area. After a brief move forward to cover the remnant of 6 ROK Division, which had now regrouped to some extent, and an American division, on 1 May, 28 Brigade was deployed near Tokso-ri as part of the new 'No Name Line', north-east of Seoul on the wide Han River.

The next stage of the Chinese offensive began to the east on 16 May. Though there was no major assault in IX Corps' sector, the New Zealand gunners supported an American counter-attack against Chinese units that had overrun its forward positions. With the Chinese advance to the east halted by 20 May, three corps on the west of the front were ordered forward to threaten enemy supply lines. This involved 28 Brigade in a slow advance along mined roads north of the Han River, against pockets of Chinese resistance. Tenacious Chinese defence of a strategic hill on 22 May called for heavy shelling in support of a determined but unsuccessful assault by a British regiment, the King's Own Scottish Borderers. By the next morning, however, the Chinese had abandoned the hill. An armoured attack on Ch'unch'on, to the north of Kap'yong, had precipitated a disorderly Chinese retreat, and the UN forces advanced to Line Wyoming.

In the meantime 28 Brigade and the New Zealanders had redeployed to the west to join the other two Commonwealth brigades in I Corps. In this sector only a small advance took place, to establish a bridgehead north of the Imjin ('swift-flowing with a lovely metal bottom and clear bluish water, it could easily be the Waimak[ariri] in Canterbury'),[62] and this faced little serious opposition. The New Zealanders were, however, called on for supporting fire tasks for Commonwealth patrols cleaning out pockets of resistance. By mid-June the Chinese had broken contact again and the gunners settled down near the Imjin to sweat out the summer, enjoy opportunities for recreation, and endure refresher training, while awaiting developments at a higher level. Armistice talks opened at Kaesong on 10 July, but made very slow progress.

On 28 July the growing Commonwealth presence in Korea, now making up three brigades, was brought together as 1 Commonwealth Division under the British Major-General A.J.H. Cassels. 16 Field formed part of the Divisional Artillery, along with Canadian and British field regiments, a light battery and an AA battery. Under the CRA, Brigadier W.G.H. Pike, they now trained to fire divisional concentrations. Kayforce's base was shifted to Hiro Camp, near Kure in Japan, with only a small forward base remaining at Pusan. A Reinforcement Training Unit was established at Hiro, where the Commonwealth Artillery Training Centre (formerly Gunner Training Element) was also based.

The Second Reinforcements arrived from New Zealand on 31 July. The much larger Expansion Draft of 579 officers and men (most were to expand Kayforce's transport element from platoon to company size, plus some additional signalmen and RNZEME ordnance craftsmen) arrived in Japan by air in late August and early September after an eventful journey during which their troopship, the *Wahine*, ran aground in Indonesian waters. After being rescued the men returned to Darwin while arrangements were made for them to be flown to Japan.

Subsequent 'reinforcements' were essentially replacement drafts. The original members of Kayforce had signed on for the duration, but after an unexpected stalemate developed on the battlefield Cabinet agreed in October to replace them after 18 to 24 months' service. Less than one-seventh of the original force re-enlisted for another twelve months: few were willing to endure another Korean winter. There was inevitably some loss of efficiency while new men got up to speed, and, with their chance for promotion now blocked, battle-hardened volunteers resented the increased numbers of regular NCOs without combat experience.

Meanwhile, between July and September the New Zealand gunners in position south of the Imjin River covered patrols and raids by 28 Brigade to its north, where contacts with Chinese units sometimes necessitated heavy supporting fire programmes. Operation Minden, a more substantial advance by 25 and 29 brigades in early September to occupy territory north of the river, encountered little resistance, and 16 Field moved forward to the former front line on the Imjin.

At about this time the gunners brought their guns up to Mk III standard by screwing baffles onto the muzzle and a counterweight onto the breech to keep the barrel balanced. This 'muzzle brake' deflected some of the blast to the sides, counteracting or braking the recoil. This was good for the gun but not for the crews, who suffered more noise and concussion than when all the blast had gone forward. 'Hence the photographs of us covering at least one ear, if it was practical.' With the help of a troop artificer ('tiffy'), gun crews periodically took their charges out of action in the gun pit to paint them and service the recoil cylinders. Such was the care lavished on guns that some referred to them as if they were ships – as 'she' or 'her'.[63]

OPERATION COMMANDO

The relative quiet in the I Corps area contrasted with events further east, where X Corps and I ROK Corps were fighting hard for strategic high ground above a valley known as the Punchbowl.[64] In early October, however, there was an advance in the I Corps sector to better defensive positions at Line Jamestown, 6 miles north of the Imjin. The Commonwealth Division's role in Operation Commando was to take a series of strategic hills. 28 Brigade and the Canadian brigade would advance on successive days so that each could be supported by the whole Divisional Artillery. On 2 October, 16 Field crossed the Imjin to positions near the Paehak Reservoir. After a series of harassing fire tasks that night, the regiment joined in the divisional fire-plan, which opened up at 5.30 a.m. Previously the New Zealand gunners had fired regimental concentrations, but never a fire-plan supporting an advance along the lines of the North African and Italian campaigns of the Second World War.

Command post, Korea.
Graham Birch collection.

After a series of devastating barrages, 28 Brigade's objectives were secured, though enemy resistance on some objectives was determined and Commonwealth units sustained numerous casualties. The rolling barrages, supplemented by effective observed fire called down by the FOOs with the infantry, caused heavy losses before the Chinese survivors fled the field. At 11 a.m. on 4 October, the Divisional Artillery switched its fire to support the Canadian assault, which, with its flank secure, rolled forward with less resistance. When 28 Brigade recommenced its assault, however, it faced some of the hardest fighting of the operation. Heavy fire-plans led Australian and British troops towards the next hills, where one objective was subjected to a two-hour concentration before the Australian infantry went in. The Northumberland Fusiliers faced the greatest difficulties in their assault on Hill 217. After gaining a precarious foothold on the summit they were forced to withdraw, short of ammunition, under artillery protection.

Next morning the Chinese repelled a further assault despite support from the entire Divisional Artillery, and when the Australians took a nearby feature, the Hinge, on the morning of the 7th, they were subjected to a very heavy artillery bombardment followed by a concerted infantry counter-attack. After some anxious moments, the New Zealand FOO with the Australians was able to call down regimental Mike concentrations, which were quickly upgraded to divisional concentrations, known as 'Uncles'. This devastating fire took a heavy toll on the Chinese, few of whom managed to get to the Australian positions, where they were dealt with by the infantry. By 5 a.m. the attack had petered out, and the Chinese were later found to have withdrawn not only from the Hinge but also from Hill 217. As the Division consolidated its defensive positions on Line Jamestown, the gunners enjoyed a well-earned respite. During Commando the New Zealanders had fired more than 37,000 shells, including the first of the carefully rationed VT shells available to them. Once again the Transport Platoon had laboured mightily to keep the guns supplied with ammunition, which they brought forward directly to the gun line.

The appearance of heavy Chinese artillery support for their infantry heralded a new phase of the war. Counter-battery arrangements had to be improvised, with some successes, during the fighting. Steps were taken to remedy the lack of a locating battery or counter-battery staff at Divisional Artillery Headquarters. As October wore on, the Commonwealth gunners were kept busy with harassing tasks and defensive fire-plans, and increasingly with counter-battery work, while awaiting the anticipated Chinese counter-offensive. This started on 4 November with heavy fire along the ridge between Hill 217 and the Hinge (on Hill 317). When a massed enemy infantry assault began in the afternoon, 16 Field fired a series of urgent Mike concentrations. The attack was broken up, then finally driven off by the Borderers defending the position.

The next assault was more successful. The telephone line between the FOO and 16 Field had been cut by enemy shelling and radio contact was also lost, greatly impeding the gunners' ability to bring down supporting fire as the infantry fought desperately at close quarters on the ridge. After forcing the Borderers back from their positions, the Chinese attacked Hill 217 and the ridge linking it with the Hinge. Despite heavy concentrations by the Divisional Artillery, including fire called down on the Borderers' own positions for 20 minutes, the Chinese drove the defenders back;

further concentrations were needed to cover them while they dug into new positions. On the first day of this assault the New Zealand gunners not only fired their highest 24-hour total of shells in Korea – more than 10,000 – but also came under counter-battery fire for the first time, mercifully with little damage.

As the Chinese paused next day, the Borderers were protected by a divisional fire-plan on Hill 317, supplemented by air strikes. Further concentrations took a heavy toll on Chinese digging in or moving forward, but there were more attacks on a number of the strategic hills of Line Jamestown over the next few days, and Commonwealth forces made tactical withdrawals from two hills to more easily defended features. As the Chinese offensive continued the gunners were kept very busy repelling massed attacks and bombarding the positions already taken. Hundreds of Chinese were killed in some of these assaults, but the fighting was also costly for some Commonwealth units.

On 22 November, with fighting continuing along the line, 28 Brigade was relieved by American units and moved 9 miles south as the Commonwealth Division's front was shortened to the north-west and extended by a lesser distance to the south-east, beyond the Samichon River. In its new positions 16 Field was soon engaged in counter-battery exchanges with the Chinese, and on 27 November a shell hit an ammunition truck, wounding two gunners, one of whom later died. With peace negotiations continuing at Panmunjom, the UN command ordered a 30-day ceasefire on 27 November, but soon abandoned this in favour of retaliation against the Chinese batteries. The front settled down to a pattern of harassing and counter-battery fire from both sides; there were no further ground advances. Defences were strengthened, with the Chinese in particular establishing deeply entrenched positions.

THE STATIC WAR

In February 1952, Lieutenant-Colonel Moodie relinquished command of the regiment, rightly satisfied with the high standards it had reached under his leadership.[65] He was replaced by Lieutenant-Colonel R.M. Paterson, a Regular Force veteran who, while no less exacting in his demand for professionalism, had a more relaxed personality. Paterson soon bridged the gulf between regimental headquarters and the batteries.

By now it was clear that any future UN advance would be prohibitively costly. With the line stalemated, the gunners settled into semi-permanent positions. One British staff officer referred to the 'Great Wall of Chinograph' because of the amount of drawing done on artillery boards. 'It very much became an artillery war. Once we'd stabilised, we moved the gun positions very infrequently – we'd dug in, and really there was nowhere to go. You'd only be changing location with other field regiments. It was a pretty boring existence, really.'[66] While Chinese firepower continued to be strengthened, the UN artillery maintained their advantages in technique, numbers of guns and, particularly, quantities of ammunition. Although the Chinese could mount troubling harassing and counter-battery concentrations, their inability to bring down concentrated fire on new targets at short notice hindered their effectiveness. A trench-line understanding with the enemy developed: 'unless it was an important target coming up, our guns virtually went out of action for a couple of hours a day', a 163 Battery radio operator remembered. Their opponents did the same. 'If they weren't getting disturbed in the siesta, they weren't going to disturb ours!'[67]

Chinese fire was usually localised and some personal duels developed, such as one between a 163 Battery OP officer based on a hill with 3RAR and a well-hidden mortar:

> As the crow flies I wouldn't have been more than 100 to 150 yards from the Chinese. They'd got a mortar a couple of hundred yards further back, and every night he had a go at us. Every night I tried to get him. Every night he fooled me. I called up troop fire for that purpose. There was no point in having more than a section of two guns – it was only to make him put his head down. I never did get them.[68]

Dug into widely spaced, deep and sandbagged positions concealed by ridges, and shifted between several prepared pits in the light of intelligence or enemy activity, the New Zealand guns were generally safe from fire, though seemingly random artillery and mortar attacks caused casualties at the gun lines, where

A 163 Battery gun crew relaxes after a busy night, July 1952.
16 Field Regiment.

about 60 shells fell during 1952. Added to this ever-present danger were the hazards of disease and the old minefields behind the front. Prematures also continued to unnerve the men. When a sergeant of C Troop, 162 Battery died of a fever, 'gloom settled over the mess. Damn this country.'[69] One consolation of a static war was the opportunity to improve living conditions, and a variety of 'hutchies' sprang up among the usual tents. Improvised petrol burners eased the bleakness of the winters.

Busy with harassing and observed fire on enemy positions, and covering the patrols that ventured at night into the wide no man's land between the lines, the gunners also had to be ready for the occasional localised assaults with which the Chinese probed the UN positions. Targets were registered on all the approaches to the Commonwealth lines so that fire could be brought down rapidly. The FOOs in their dugouts constantly scanned the enemy lines for signs of movement. High levels of readiness were maintained around the clock.

On 5 April 1952 the Chinese attacked positions held by the Borderers after a heavy bombardment. They were driven back thanks to a devastating series of regimental and divisional concentrations, with the New Zealanders contributing 4500 shells to the defensive fire tasks. On the night of 22–23

The Gunners

Maori Gunners

About 15 per cent of those who served in Kayforce were Maori (who then comprised 6 per cent of New Zealand's total population).[70] The proportion rose as the war dragged on – Maori were almost a quarter of the men sent to Korea in the year to March 1953. The Korean War was a watershed for Maori participation in the New Zealand Army. In both world wars, most

Gunners take a smoko break in Korea, December 1952.
16 Field Regiment.

October a battalion-strength assault was made on the Canadians holding Hill 355, and the gunners were again busy. The enemy reached their objective but were driven back by a counter-attack. A month later an attack on a Black Watch company on the Hook was broken by a divisional concentration of airburst shells, achieved by the 'time on target' technique that took account of the distance of gun troops from the target and ensured that all shells reached it simultaneously. The enemy were upon the British position when they were devastated by this concentration; in a strenuous night the gunners drove back this and subsequent assaults.

Stealthy night attacks on the Chinese lines, which sometimes captured prisoners for interrogation, usually required pre-arranged fire-plans to be called

> Maori had served in separate units – the Pioneer Battalion and 28 Battalion – with others pepperpotted through 'Pakeha' units. In Korea, the official emphasis on integration was offset by the higher profile for Maori made inevitable by their increased numbers.
>
> Though at first there were no Maori units as such, some groups of Maori were allowed to serve together. The 'South Island Battery', 163, had several guns manned mainly by Maori, with whanau members serving together. As personnel came and went, such arrangements continued to evolve: by 1953, 162 Battery had an all-Maori gun detachment. Formal discipline was backed up by the arrival that year of a Maori chaplain who proved a 'godsend' in keeping order. There were haka competitions, and a concert party gave performances. By the time 'Blackie' Burns, the popular commander of 16 Field Regiment, was farewelled with a haka in March 1954, the Maori element of the force was conspicuous. Warrant Officer Carlyle Waaka had been appointed RSM.
>
> Maori would make up nearly a quarter of the infantry battalion in Malaya in 1958, and perhaps half of the troops sent to Vietnam, where their generally amicable relations with their Pakeha comrades fascinated American soldiers. There were Maori–Pakeha tensions when some Maori adopted Black American mannerisms and fashions.[71] In the early 1990s the New Zealand Army assumed the identity of Ngati Tumatauenga, 'one tribe' with a duty to protect all the peoples of Aotearoa. Cultural practices such as poroporoaki (farewells) for overseas deployments are now routine, and an Army Marae was established at Waiouru in 1994.[72]

down as the raiders extricated themselves. When a raid by the Royal Fusiliers was ambushed with numerous casualties on 26 October, 16 Field Regiment, in the direct support role, fired more than 5000 rounds as the party struggled back to the Commonwealth line. In January 1953, 16 Field, bolstered by a Canadian and a British battery, supported a daylight South Korean attack in the sector to the right of the Commonwealth line.

Between these periodic crises and some major pre-planned harassing barrages, the daily routine of the gunners included lower-intensity harassing fire, usually with one or two guns from each troop moving to forward positions each night to fire a programme of 100 rounds per gun (200 from January 1953) before returning to the defensive gun line by dawn. The Chinese bunkers along the line were virtually impervious to 25-pr fire. 'Some of them were made by tunnelling through a ridge and they just wheeled up their guns, poked them out on our side, fired a few rounds, and then pulled them back into the tunnels again. They were practically impossible to get at, either by our planes or our guns.'[73] US 8-inch howitzers and 155-mm gun-howitzers were made available to support the Commonwealth regiments from January 1952. In March 1953 a British medium regiment joined the Division for this role, and to add its weight to the field artillery in repelling Chinese assaults. On 15 April 1952 16 Field moved to the left of the Commonwealth line with 28 Brigade, becoming the reserve regiment. In this role they were no longer called on to deliver observed fire but continued to contribute to the other tasks of the Divisional Artillery. In October they moved again, but except for one battery were soon back in the positions they had occupied over the summer, where most would remain until the following July. Although positions behind the front were prepared in case of a further massive Chinese assault, this precaution proved unnecessary. Such an assault would have been extremely costly in the face of the UN's artillery predominance. Nevertheless, particular attention was paid to the defence of the strategic positions at each end of the Commonwealth front, the Hook and Hill 355.

When the Commonwealth Division was relieved by a US division at the end of January 1953, three field regiments, including 16 Field, stayed on in support. The first task of 16 Field's new commander, Lieutenant-Colonel John ('Blackie') Burns, who had been a battery commander in Italy, was therefore to develop a good working relationship with his American counterpart. The British practice of using troop commanders as FOOs able to order fire from OPs – rather than relying on requests from more junior officers – impressed the Americans with the speed of response that could be achieved. This proved invaluable on a number of occasions, extricating American patrols isolated in no man's land and breaking up Chinese attacks on the nights of 19 February and 2 March, and in the early hours of 17 March. The latter two attacks, against positions on Hill 355, were substantial assaults during which the forward elements reached defensive positions but were then isolated from support by prompt heavy fire brought down by the New Zealand FOOs, one of whom remembers firing 'a regimental stonk along the valley. We counted

57 bodies. Goodness how many more the Chinese had taken away.'[74]

The Commmonwealth Division returned to its former positions in early April, and 16 Field resumed its connection with 28 Brigade. After a lull in the fighting when the armistice negotiations showed promise, the gunners were soon busy again with a heavy programme of bombardments and supporting fire as Commonwealth patrols reasserted a presence in no man's land. Another Chinese assault was broken up on 1 May, and next night 16 Field helped the Canadian brigade beat off an attack on its positions. The last major assault on the Commonwealth forces came on 28 May, when 29 Brigade positions on the Hook were threatened. Pre-arranged regimental and divisional concentrations brought down on the approaches shattered four Chinese attacks: the New Zealanders contributed about 4500 shells.

By 25 June, the third anniversary of the initial North Korean attack, when 16 Field fired its 750,000th shell of the campaign – more than any other Commonwealth Division field regiment – the front was relatively quiet as the peace talks moved fitfully towards a conclusion. Despite the progress in the negotiations, in July the Chinese attempted a number of major advances, perhaps seeking to gain territory to justify an adjustment to the demarcation line proposed in the draft armistice agreement. A major assault on 13 July pushed back six South Korean divisions before being halted with American help. On the night of 24 July an assault on US Marine positions on Hill 119 to the left of the Commonwealth Division was accompanied by large-scale diversionary attacks on Hill 111 on the divisional boundary, and on Hill 121 held by 2RAR. The gunners had a hectic night firing sustained concentrations in support of the Marines and the Australians. Though the Chinese initially penetrated the forward defences on Hill 111, all the attacks failed with very heavy losses.

When the next night the Chinese made a further assault on the Marine positions, the defensive fire included corps as well as divisional concentrations. The New Zealanders contributed 5700 rounds, almost half of them the deadly VT shells. Once again the attack was driven back, with Chinese dead numbering in the thousands. Less threatening attacks were fought off in the Marines' sector on the night of 26 July. Next morning the armistice agreement was finally signed. It did not take effect until 10 p.m. and the New Zealand gunners engaged in counter-battery tasks until evening. Seventeen members of 16 Field Regiment had been killed in action or died of wounds in Korea; another nine died in accidents or of disease. Raised and trained from scratch, like its 2NZEF predecessors, the regiment had proven the equal of any artillery unit in the campaign. However, after the Fifth Phase Offensive of April/May 1951 the Chinese had recognised that competently handled artillery made the mass frontal assaults they favoured impossibly costly. The Commonwealth Division's 25-prs were much less effective against the well dug-in troops they confronted for most of the remainder of the war, during which the New Zealanders' role became primarily one of harassment.

After the armistice both sides pulled back from the demarcation line to create the demilitarised zone specified in the agreement. New positions along Line Kansas were prepared with much back-breaking labour by 16 Field Regiment as part of precautions against the possibility of a resumption in hostilities. The gunners settled into a camp on the north bank of the Imjin River which they transformed into a comfortable regimental home complete with a market garden. An impressive rugby field, 'Freyberg Park', doubled as a landing pad for the helicopters of Marines in search of relaxation and refreshment. Practice deployments to the defensive positions, cross-country marches and range shooting also helped to pass the time, but the continued discipline rankled with some. Long-serving men began to return to New Zealand, replaced by continuing reinforcement drafts. In a very successful experiment during 1954, British national service gunners were attached to 16 Field to maintain its strength.[75] The popular Burns departed in March 1954, his Jeep towed out of the camp by gunners to the accompaniment of a haka. His replacement as commander of 16 Field was Lieutenant-Colonel John Pountney.

With reductions in Commonwealth forces in Korea, 16 Field became non-operational on 5 October 1954. The men went home the following month, travelling on the troopship *New Australia* from Pusan to Brisbane or Sydney, where some marched in a welcome-home parade. They flew on to New Zealand after socialising so enthusiastically that some had to be taken on a route march to sober up before boarding the aircraft. The last elements of Kayforce did not leave Korea until 1957.

Refocusing on South-east Asia

After the Korean War, with growing fears of Sino-Soviet designs on South-east Asia and the reality of communist insurgency in the region, New Zealand reoriented its security policy away from planning for a role in the Middle East. Following the signing of the Manila Pact in 1954, the government agreed at a Commonwealth Prime Ministers' Conference in February 1955 that in the event of war 3NZEF would be deployed to South-east Asia. Later that year 28 Commonwealth Brigade was reconstituted in Malaya as part of the Commonwealth Far East Strategic Reserve, to which New Zealand agreed to contribute units. The brigade was active during the latter years of the Malayan Emergency in containing local Chinese communist guerillas, who were not finally suppressed until 1960. New Zealand initially contributed an SAS squadron. Once the residual commitment to Korea ended a regular infantry battalion, 1 Battalion New Zealand Regiment, was formed and deployed to Malaya. This began a gradual shift in emphasis away from territorial units toward the expansion of the regular Army, boosted with short-service special enlistments to an establishment of 4500.[76] The structure of the artillery was at first unaffected by this development, but the shift to sending regular units overseas would be applied in the deployment of a field battery to South Vietnam in the 1960s.

The 1957 Defence Review took a more realistic approach to the mobilisation of the New Zealand Division. A Combat Brigade Group would be deployed initially. Units including 2 Field Regiment and single batteries of 5 Light and 6 Light Anti-Aircraft regiments were allocated to this brigade group with the intention that they be maintained at a strength 20 per cent over establishment; other units of the division would be allowed to fall somewhat below establishment. This decision and other changes to the CMT scheme were soon overtaken by the election of a Labour government in November 1957. CMT would now be abolished as soon as recent conscripts had fulfilled their residual annual training obligations. The 1958 Defence Review foreshadowed a transformation of the Army to enable it quickly to deploy a regular infantry brigade overseas.[77] This policy required the establishment of a second regular infantry battalion and an artillery field regiment (though not the light

National servicemen on parade at Waiouru.
16 Field Regiment.

anti-aircraft and heavy mortar elements that had been envisaged for the Combat Brigade Group).

In August 1958 16 Field Regiment was re-established, with 161 Battery based at Papakura and 163 Battery at Burnham; activation of 162 Battery was deferred. The regiment was manned on a virtually skeleton basis pending recruitment for the enlarged Regular Force: in August 1959, only about

150 all ranks were available to its two active batteries. The regiment's 25-prs were supplemented by 4.2-inch mobile base-plate mortars which provided a lightweight option for rapid overseas deployment; about a third of gunnery training was on these weapons.[78] The existing territorial regiments – field, light and AA – were maintained while the last CMT gunners finished their training, but their long-term prospects in an all-volunteer force were gloomy.

In the event, the return of a National government in 1960 was followed by the reintroduction of a selective version of territorial conscription (National Service) based on an annual ballot of 18- to 21-year-old males (later restricted to 21-year-olds) to provide 2000 trainees per annum, with the balance of the TF made up of volunteers. Territorials were still thought to have a vital role overseas, as either reinforcements or 'follow-up forces'. The new scheme would involve fourteen weeks' full-time training for each territorial soldier, whether volunteer or National Serviceman, followed by 20 days a year for three years, including attendance at an annual camp. The divisional force structure was clearly unsustainable and in 1961, in anticipation of the implementation of National Service the following year, the TF order of battle was drastically revised to provide three 'reduced brigade groups' or a 'light division'.

The TF artillery took the heaviest cuts: its light, medium and two anti-aircraft regiments were disbanded. Three field regiments remained, each with a regimental HQ, attached light aid detachment and signals section, and three batteries:[79]

1 Field Regiment: 11 (Field) Battery; 12 (Field) Battery; 4 (Medium) Battery.
2 Field Regiment: 21 (Field) Battery; 22 (Field) Battery; 23 (Field) Battery.
3 Field Regiment: 31 (Field) Battery; 32 (Field) Battery; 5 (Light) Battery.

The field and medium batteries were reduced to two troops, each of three 25-pr or 5.5-inch guns, in line with recently introduced British practice. The light battery was equipped with the 4.2-inch mortars. The regular regiment, 16 Field, likewise saw its two undermanned batteries reduced to the new six-gun standard, and 163 Battery was relocated to Waiouru in March 1961 to support the School of Artillery. 16 Field's regimental HQ now absorbed the old Headquarters Battery, while 162 Battery was deleted from the regimental structure.

16 Field Regiment gunners take over from the Irish Guards at Buckingham Palace, November 1964. *Graham Birch collection.*

The writing had been on the wall for the AA batteries even before the 1961 Defence Review. In September 1954, 15 Composite Anti-Aircraft Regiment was disbanded, leaving only a single independent unit (151 Anti-Aircraft Battery) in its place. This battery and the other two composite regiments (13 and 14) were disestablished in April 1956 in an acknowledgment that gun-based home AA defence was unrealistic in an age of strategic bombing and nuclear weapons. A new unit, 16 Heavy Anti-Aircraft Regiment, of three batteries each of two troops of four 3.7-inch guns, was formed to provide tactical AA defence for 3NZEF's base and area of operations. Without re-equipment with missiles that were deemed too expensive, however, the new regiment could not serve effectively in its intended role, and it was axed in 1961. The Bofors guns of 6 Light AA Regiment were also obsolete, particularly without modern radar directors, but Sir Stephen Weir, now the government's Military Adviser, advocated keeping at least one battery to maintain basic skills. Instead, the regiment was disbanded in 1961 along with its Heavy AA counterpart, and the RNZA lost its role in anti-aircraft defence, though 1 Light AA Battery survived on paper for some years.

At this time 16 Field prepared for possible service in Fiji, where there was recurring industrial and ethnic unrest. The gunners trained in riot control and anti-insurgency operations, and practised loading equipment for deployment by frigates or RNZAF Sunderlands. Instead, the regiment enjoyed its first peacetime foray overseas when in March 1962 it went to Australia on Exercise Tasman 1. Forming a single New Zealand battery, the members of 161 and 163 batteries began a long tradition of exchanges and links with the Australian gunners of 4 Field Regiment by training with them at Wacol, near Brisbane, and conducting live firing exercises at Tin Can Bay.[80]

Two years later, 84 16 Field gunners, along with 16 RNZEME personnel from 16 Field's LAD and a contingent of RNZAC, travelled to Britain under the command of Major Spencer Cocks for Exercise Powderhorn. For the gunners this involved a week's training at the School of Artillery at Larkhill – 'firing in two days more than our annual allocation of ammunition in New Zealand'[81] – and four days at the home of the Royal Artillery, Woolwich. When the New Zealand gunners also stood guard at Buckingham Palace, the Tower of London and the Bank of England, it was said to be the first time an artillery unit had guarded all three landmarks.[82]

Further restructuring of the field force in 1963–64 saw yet another major reorganisation of artillery units. With the notion of an all-regular brigade group forgotten, and the concept of a 'light division' already seen to be unrealistic, planning for overseas operations was now based on the deployment of a mixed regular and territorial 'combat brigade group' (1 Brigade) supported by a 'combat reserve brigade group' (3 Brigade).

For the RNZA, this meant losing a number of units in a pragmatic response to the manpower available. 16 Field Regiment would now consist of the regular 161 Battery and two TF units, 11 and 22 batteries, from the disestablished 1 and 2 Field Regiments respectively. Along with 4 Medium Battery, now designated an 'independent battery' and equipped with 4.2-inch mortars as well as 5.5-inch guns, 16 Field was assigned to 1 Brigade. The South Island-based 3 Field Regiment was reduced to two field batteries (31 and 32), equipped with surplus 4.2-inch mortars in addition to 25-prs when

5 Light Battery was disbanded. This all-territorial regiment was assigned to 3 Brigade.[83]

The RNZA had to make do with guns of Second World War vintage until the arrival in 1962 of 24 Italian OTO-Melara 105-mm pack howitzers, designated L5 in British and Commonwealth service.[84] While the 25-pr remained an effective gun, it was long out of production. Crucially, the 105-mm shell had become the standard weapon for NATO and Commonwealth close support artillery units, and 25-prs might well pose logistical difficulties in operations with allied formations. The L5 seemed well suited to jungle operations in South-east Asia; it could be dismantled into eleven pieces for off-road transport, and its all-up weight was only 1290 kilograms (compared with 2030 kilograms for the US M1A1 105-mm howitzer). In 1963, 18 L5s were allocated to 16 Field; the other six went to the School of Artillery. The other RNZA units had to make do with their vintage 25-pr and 5.5-inch guns, and the 4.2-inch mortars.

From 1962 to 1965, New Zealand and other Commonwealth forces were involved in the Borneo border war that was named for Indonesia President Sukarno's policy of 'Confrontation'. While no New Zealand artillery units fought in this conflict, artillerymen saw action with 1RNZIR, as they had during the Malayan Emergency.[85] At least four RNZA Air OP pilots flew in the Borneo bush war from 1963.[86] Among them was Lieutenant Ray Andrews, who had got his wings three years earlier and was unofficially lent to the British Army Air Corps as a pilot in 656 Light Aircraft Squadron. He was attached to 7 Reconnaissance Flight, which flew for 28 Commonwealth Brigade, 17 Gurkha Division.[87]

Another New Zealand gunner to serve in Borneo was Captain John Masters. Having been commissioned in the Territorial Force and then the RNZA, he went to Malaya with 1RNZIR as an acting company commander. Seconded to the Royal Artillery (in exchange for a British Army officer lent to New Zealand as Chief Instructor) to train their gunners in infantry and jungle work, Masters went first to 45 Medium Battery RA. 'I'd spent a lot of time in the jungle. I was tanned and fit; these Poms were white to the point of being blue. So I'd take them out and train them in all levels, still not knowing much about gunnery.' After six months the regiments rotated, and Masters spent a month learning gunnery with 104 Battery RAA before going to Borneo. Here he commanded a troop in 29 (Corunna) Battery, 4 Light Regiment RA, seeing action as a FOO with 2/2 Gurkhas, 2 Paras and 3RAR. In one firefight in September 1965 he was cut off in the jungle and carried a wounded Gurkha CSM for a day and a half, earning an immediate Military Cross. The experience of surveying and firing in 200-foot-high rainforest, so dense and dank that clothes rotted, prepared Masters well for a later tour in Vietnam. These were 'platoon commanders' wars'. Masters went back to Britain with the regiment in 1966 to take part in the Royal Artillery's 250th anniversary celebrations, leading his troop in the parade at the Horse Guards.[88]

161 BATTERY IN VIETNAM

A new task for the RNZA arose in the mid-1960s. Indo-China's French colonial rulers had departed during the previous decade after losing a protracted war against indigenous resistance. As the communist leader Ho Chi Minh consolidated his power north of the 17th parallel and sought to reunify the country, the United States marshalled support for the new Republic of Vietnam (South Vietnam) against Viet Cong guerillas and eventually large-scale intervention by the North Vietnamese Army (NVA). New Zealand's initial assistance to South Vietnam was a civilian surgical team established in Qui Nhon in 1963, followed the next year by a small detachment of non-combatant Army engineers. As the US stepped up its military involvement, it sought combat forces from its regional allies. New Zealand responded in May 1965 by announcing a limited contribution: a field artillery battery.[89]

The decision to deploy artillery no doubt reflected the experience of Korea and an expectation that casualties could be kept low. Moreover, it did not detract from New Zealand's obligations in Malaysia, although two infantry companies and an SAS troop would join 161 Battery in Vietnam over the following two years. And though it would inevitably come under the operational control of larger allied forces, 'an artillery unit is not involved in the day-to-day melée with the infantry. They can at least stand back a little bit from the battle and have some independent role. There can be some tactical control of their involvement.'[90] As in Korea, these personnel would all 'volunteer' for this service, but in Vietnam they would be regular soldiers rather than volunteers

Vietnam-bound men of 161 Battery listen to an address by Governor-General Sir Bernard Fergusson, at Waiouru, June 1965.
EP/1965/2099/6-F, Alexander Turnbull Library, Wellington.

enlisted for an ad hoc expeditionary force. In a new development for the RNZA, an existing regular battery was readied for deployment. The Duntroon- and Larkhill-trained Kayforce veteran Don Kenning was brought in as battery commander (BC) with six weeks to get it into shape.

Although 161 Battery was configured as a six-gun battery, albeit undermanned, a misunderstanding of the structure of the field batteries already in action in South Vietnam led to a decision to deploy only four guns. 'The planners said the Americans had a four-gun battery. They did a recce and got it wrong.'[91] Once in theatre, the battery used its spare gun to field a five-gun battery on numerous occasions, until instructed from Wellington to discontinue this practice – for financial reasons, and because it was outside the parameters of the Cabinet decision.[92] 'They were quite angry about it.' Renaming the fifth gun his 'training gun', Kenning continued using it, despite occasional queries. 'Personalities aside, the Australians probably would have taken me with three guns. Technically it doesn't matter: it is the number of shells on the ground.'[93] In March 1966, 161 Battery was formally expanded to the standard six-gun structure and establishment for the sake of uniformity with other allied units.

Transferring volunteers from other units to 161 Battery brought it to its initial combat strength of 86, plus 13 first force reinforcements; 44 of these personnel were from 16 Field Regiment at Papakura.[94] A 161 Battery Depot was established at Papakura to train and periodically replace the personnel in theatre, a process that was to continue for seven years. A total of 870 all ranks would serve on tours of duty that were initially nine months for married and eighteen months for single men, later twelve months for all.[95]

As in Korea, the New Zealand gunners would fight mainly within a Commonwealth – in this case, an Anzac – formation, but would also be frequently required to work closely with US units. The effectiveness of the battery would rest partly on its familiarity with British command and fire control procedures that were also second nature to Australian gunners and infantrymen. The decision was made to retain the British practice of posting the BC with the infantry battalion HQ and authorising FOOs to order fire from their positions with the infantry companies (and not merely request fire – the US system). The effectiveness of the British system would be of particular value in 161 Battery's most critical engagement, at Long Tan in August 1966. It was an additional challenge to coordinate operations with American batteries and air observers accustomed to quite different means of fire control. The New Zealanders used US procedures when firing American guns.

The battery's Italian L5 pack howitzers were air-portable by the ubiquitous UH-1 Iroquois ('Huey') helicopters, whereas the American M101A1 105-mm howitzers could not be moved by helicopter until the introduction of the heavy-lift Chinook. The L5 could also be transported inside an M113 armoured personnel carrier. 'The L5 was a very good gun, providing the operational commanders understood them', in the view of one New Zealand officer. They were particularly effective at ranges of around 5000 metres.[96] But the L5 proved insufficiently robust in operation, particularly for sustained long-range shooting on full charge, and in March 1967 the battery was re-equipped with six M101A1s – known mistakenly as M2A2 in New Zealand service in Vietnam[97] – that were borrowed and later leased from the Australian Army. These guns were not only more rugged but had a range (11,270 metres)

> ### Weapons – Field Howitzers
>
> The Italian Mle-56 Pack Howitzer was the first post-1945 design used by New Zealand artillery. Light enough to be carried by helicopter, it could fire the same ammunition as the American M101A1, a design dating from the 1920s, which was adopted during the Vietnam War. Both had a seven-man crew and could fire five rounds per minute. The ammunition was semi-fixed: the shell was fitted to the brass cartridge case immediately before loading, after the charge had been adjusted. For a full charge all seven bags were left in the cartridge, while for reduced charges some bags came out (to be disposed of by burning). Later in their life the L5s were restricted to firing Charge 5 (five bags) or less.
>
> | Name | Howitzer 105-mm M101A1 | Howitzer 105-mm L5 Pack |
> | --- | --- | --- |
> | Entered NZ service | 1967 | 1963 |
> | Role | howitzer | howitzer with anti-tank ability |
> | Elevation | 66° | 65° |
> | Calibre | 4.1 in (105 mm), 22 cals | 4.1 in (105 mm), 14 cals |
> | Range | 12,030 yds (11,000 m) | 11,150 yds (10,200 m) |
> | Weight | 4967 lb (2258 kg) | 2838 lb (1290 kg) |
> | Projectile | 33 lb (15 kg) – HE, HEAT, HEP, smoke, etc. | Same ammunition, plus AP |
> | Remarks | Leased from Australia during Vietnam War. 1977 purchase brought number in New Zealand to 20. | Clever Italian profile-lowering carriage – but the guns 'wore out quickly'.[98] Known as L5 in New Zealand, which bought 24. |

about 700 metres beyond that of the L5, meaning that fewer changes of gun position were required.

The battery travelled to South Vietnam in July 1965 in the RNZAF's new C-130H Hercules transports – the first time a New Zealand artillery unit with its guns and vehicles was deployed to a combat theatre solely by aircraft. Within 24 hours of leaving New Zealand, the first gun was ready to fire.[99] The flights involved 1 a.m. departures from Whenuapai to enable both refuelling at Port Moresby and arrival in Vietnam during daylight hours. But with public opinion sharply divided over the war, it seemed to some gunners that they left 'in the middle of the night, like thieves.'[100] On arrival the gunners were initially based near Bien Hoa airbase, about 20 miles north-east of Saigon, and deployed in support of 1 Royal Australian Regiment (1RAR) and under the command of the US 3/319 Artillery Battalion, part of the US 173 Airborne Brigade. It was soon found that 161 Battery's 1950s-vintage British radios provided inadequate range for the FOOs and were incompatible with those used by 173 Airborne and 1RAR. Within a month the New Zealand gunners obtained a full range of new sets from US Army sources, one of many such gifts that filled gaps in 161 Battery's equipment and supplemented its supplies. By now Australia had decided to reinforce 1RAR with an artillery battery, complicating the anticipated affiliation between 161 Battery and the Australian infantry.[101]

The New Zealanders soon learned to put up with an environment dominated alternately by heat and dust and heavy rain and mud, irritants more easily tolerated when the battery was operating from the relative comfort of its main bases. The first month at Bien Hoa was spent setting up base and acclimatising, while the FOO parties patrolled with 1RAR. On 18 August the battery undertook its first operation away from base when the guns deployed to a rice paddy near the Dong Nai River in support of an ARVN infantry battalion. Although normally in direct support of 1RAR, 161 Battery functioned as an integral part of 3/319 US Field Artillery Battalion, and took part in all ten of 173 Airborne's brigade-level operations between September 1965 and May 1966. While moving to the first operation on 14 September, the battery suffered its first casualties when a Land Rover ran over a mine on the road to Ben Cat; two men were killed. This five-day operation introduced the battery to US search and destroy tactics and involved 'saturation patrolling and rapid movement of guns by Landrover, M113 APC and Iroquois helicopter'. The brigade returned to the Ben Cat sector between 8 and 14 October to mount a 'spoiling operation' in the Iron Triangle, a Viet Cong (VC) stronghold. This 'fast-moving operation resulted in a number of VC being killed and numerous jungle camps destroyed.'[102] The gunners also witnessed their first B-52 carpet-bombing strike, about 3000 yards from the forward positions.

In early November 1965 the gunners participated in Operation Hump in support of 1 RAR. In a massive assault involving 150 helicopters, the battery and the other units involved were airlifted from Bien Hoa to an area near the Dong Nai River in War Zone D, a long-standing Viet Cong training area. The force landed unopposed, but minor infantry clashes over the next two days were followed on the afternoon of 7 November by a major assault on an American infantry battalion. Then A Company of 1 RAR was ambushed by a larger Viet Cong force. Captain Bruce Murphy, 161 Battery's FOO with A Company, called down the full firepower of 3/319 Field Artillery Battalion to hold the enemy for three hours. A reverse barrage covered the Australian withdrawal, with the American and New Zealand gunners also firing on grid targets in case of a simultaneous VC retreat. The following day 161 Battery was called on to support the US 1/503 Infantry Battalion in a battle which 'raged all day until the VC broke at dusk'. It had been 'a busy two days for the guns'.[103]

Operation New Life provided another novel experience for the New Zealand gunners. This began on 21 November with an airlift of the entire 173 Airborne Brigade over the 35 miles from Bien Hoa to Vo Dat. 161 Battery was allocated four C-130 Hercules, which landed about 30 seconds apart, with the battery emplaning teams reducing the lashings on vehicles and guns just before landing, and leaving the aircraft as soon as they came to a very rapid halt. The aim of this operation was to prevent the rice harvest in the La Nga valley falling into Viet Cong hands, and to bring the valley back under government control. On 18 December, 173 Airborne was moved to Operation Smash in the Courtenay Rubber Plantation and Hat Dich areas, where it appeared the Viet Cong was building up for an attack on Baria. There was a major contact on 18 December, 'but the VC chose to break rather than fight, so it was back to Bien Hoa for Christmas'.[104]

New Year's Day 1966 saw 173 Brigade deployed to the Plain of Reeds, in the Mekong Delta near the Cambodian border. Operation Marauder was marred for 161 Battery by a friendly fire incident on 3 January, when two rounds of eight fired landed among the GIs of C Company, 2/503 Regiment, killing three and wounding seven. 'One of their FOs brought the rounds in, gave the orders,' recalled Kenning, who put the drop-shorts down to 'damp powder, cold tube or climatic conditions'.[105] After a number of firefights on the Plain of Reeds, the brigade moved to the Hobo Woods on the 8th to take part in the largest US operation in Vietnam to date, Operation Crimp – an attempt to destroy the headquarters of the Viet Cong Military Region 4 (MR4), the area around Saigon. In this action, 1RAR, 'after a few hours of running fight, found it had landed almost on top of the MR4 headquarters', a maze of tunnels that was part of the vast Cu Chi network. On this operation 1 RAR was supported by an Australian battery (105 Field), with 161 Battery's Captain Graham Birch and his FO party attached to A Company, 1 RAR. The area 'was laced with booby traps and harassed by VC popping up unexpectedly out of manholes and taking shots at opportunity targets by day and by night'. Birch had 'a chilling few days with little sleep'.[106] When the MR4 headquarters was taken, a vast quantity of documents containing valuable information on Viet Cong structure and planning was found.

173 Airborne now returned to War Zone D for Operations Roundhouse and Silver City. The New Zealand gunners' final operation with 173 Brigade, Operation Hardihood in May 1966, involved a road journey to Phuoc Tuy province and clearance of the Nui Dat base, about 45 miles south-east of Saigon. The New Zealanders farewelled both 173 Brigade and 1RAR, which was returning to Australia after its tour of duty. At Nui Dat, the guns were always manned, with a daytime patrol 1000 yards outside the fence and a night-time listening post. With their living area near the perimeter wire, some felt that '80% of the Battery ... take life under the rubber [trees] far too casually'. The command post was 'fully operational with a duty crew and the cooks produced three good meals a day'. Nui Dat, the base camp for 4000 men, was like a village, boasting a shop, rubbish collectors, a barber, film shows, a wet canteen open for one and a half hours each day, and 'a workshop that not only repairs weapons and equipment, but also makes all those things that make life pleasant like showers, barbecues and a supply of electric power from some fairly temperamental generators'. The only drawbacks were the limited scope for social activities – and the snakes. The former problem was countered with periodic rest and recreation leave in lavish facilities at the nearby seaside town of Vung Tau, where copious supplies of alcohol sometimes imperilled trans-Tasman relations.[107]

From June 1966, 161 Battery and six Australian field regiments in succession supported at different times all nine RAR battalions that served with 1 Australian Task Force, eventually a brigade-strength unit. For six years the New Zealand gunners would be based at Nui Dat, but with much of their time spent on short-term deployments – anywhere between a day and a month – in improvised positions or well-prepared fire-support bases (FSBs), mostly within Phuoc Tuy province. The battery would undertake a wide range of operations, including the application of many prepared fire-plans on known or suspected enemy positions and transit routes – the so-called harassment and interdiction (H and I) missions – as well as observed fire in support of infantry patrols or to repel enemy assaults, and occasionally direct fire to protect firebases from attacking VC or NVA troops. At times single guns were deployed covertly in 'pistol shoots' to surprise and confuse the enemy.

THE BATTLE OF LONG TAN

The New Zealanders' most significant action in Vietnam took place on 18 August 1966 at the rubber plantation of Long Tan, about 3 miles east of Nui Dat.[108] The battery was then commanded by Major Harry Honnor, a Duntroon graduate who had served in Korea. Viet Cong mortars had bombarded the base at Nui Dat in the early hours of 17 August, rousing men who had enjoyed 'quite a few beers' a few hours earlier.[109] Although this attack was broken up by a regimental fire-plan, it appeared that the enemy were assembling for an assault on the base. On the 18th, D Company of 6RAR was involved in a sweep through Long Tan when it came under heavy small-arms and mortar fire from main-force Viet Cong units. The Australians were forced back, with several killed. The FOO with D Company, Captain Maurice Stanley, RNZA, quickly called down fire from 161 Battery, and then the whole of the reinforced 1 Field Regiment, including 103 and 105 batteries, RAA, with the US A Battery, 2/35 Howitzer Battalion (155-mm self-propelled) attached. Lieutenant Barry Dreyer RNZA was attached to this American unit first as liaison officer then, somewhat unusually, as its executive officer, in charge of firing the guns. His presence greatly assisted the coordination of fire control with the Anzac regiment, where Honnor was managing the artillery battle.[110]

The living quarters at Nui Dat were tents, c.1967.
PAColl-1728-27-2, Alexander Turnbull Library, Wellington.

In his dangerous forward position Stanley peered through the heavy monsoon rain that swept a battlefield frequently illuminated by spectacular lightning flashes, and was able to bring down heavy regimental fire with shattering effect. Seemingly the calmest man in company HQ, he worked out fire orders as if on an exercise, walking the artillery in from all sides to less than 100 yards from his position.[111] New Zealand gunner Murray Broomhall, who along with radio operator Willie Walker was in the FO party, began to grasp 'how serious things were. I was hearing snatches of conversations as I moved about and I realised ... we were surrounded. As well as the obvious concentration of VC, that were hitting the front two platoons, we had confirmed reports of a group of 40 to 50 moving around ... to cut us off.' The bombardment the night before was the first shots Broomhall had heard in anger.[112] Despite the closeness of the enemy, no friendly casualties were caused by the shellfire. In two and a half hours, 161 Battery's guns fired more than 180 shells each, with all available hands – cooks, clerks, drivers, the visiting commander of New Zealand's V Force – keeping the guns supplied with ammunition. Stanley's regular radio operator sprang naked from his sickbed to help. Men cut themselves and lost fingernails tearing the wrappings off cylinders and opening the tin cans containing the fuses. Two were knocked over when lightning struck nearby.[113]

The rubber trees triggered the fuses of many of the shells, turning them into devastating air-burst rounds; the trees were stripped of foliage or blown apart. Together with the small-arms fire of the embattled D Company, the gunners broke up repeated enemy assaults until two more companies of 6 RAR and an APC troop arrived. The Viet Cong then withdrew under continued harassing fire. Next day nearly 250 enemy dead were found on or near the battlefield. Stories of the 'awesome' havoc wreaked by the 'New Zealand orchestra' spread among Viet Cong fighters.[114]

After Long Tan, 161 Battery settled down to a routine of base maintenance work and mobile operations, including harassment and interdiction shoots. Because 1ATF consisted of only two infantry battalions but three field batteries at this time, the battery was at times placed in 'general support' (GS) rather than 'direct support' of a battalion. It was in the former role on 6 February 1967, deployed to FSB Lance in support of Operation Tamborine, that the battery tragically fired short into a 6RAR position, killing four and wounding thirteen Australian soldiers from the ill-starred D Company. One New Zealand gunner experienced an 'enormous sense of grief' on hearing of the death of the Australian CSM Jack Kirby, whom he knew from Long Tan. Dying in friendly fire was 'an enormous irony given the way he had walked and stood up amongst the most devastating fire and not been scratched'.[115] The subsequent Australian court of inquiry determined that this sad episode was 'entirely due to an error on the battery's part' – a mechanical fault in the command post plotter.[116] This was the second time shorts from 161 Battery had fallen into Australian positions. The first was on 25 July 1966 in Operation Hobart, during the repulse of a VC attack in which 161 Battery provided effective fire support very close to Australian positions, when a laying error at the gun line resulted in the wounding of four Australians. The respect between the New Zealand gunners and the Australian infantrymen was such that these incidents were accepted without notable rancour. Such accidents are 'sadly a fact of war when risk tolerances are minimised'. The rate of friendly-fire deaths was undoubtedly much higher in earlier conflicts.[117]

After these incidents the margin of error applied to FO shoots was increased from 400 to 1000 yards for the first round – 'then you walked it back towards your position'.[118] The Tamborine tragedy also 'totally changed' the nature of training back home, with more ammunition fired from full six-gun batteries.[119] The next battery 'captain', Temporary Major Clyde Stewart, was put through a refresher course 'because we had had the accident in Vietnam'. School of Artillery fifteen-week courses now became a prerequisite for officers appointed to the active service battery. A very

The number two gun at Nui Dat, still firing the morning after the Battle of Long Tan, August 1966. Note how far the trail has buried itself into the ground.
Dick Wilson collection.

> ### Fire Support Bases
> Deployment to fire support bases became a routine matter. A battery reconnaissance party went in with the assault group which secured the area:
>
>> The recce party would do a technical layout of the gun position. We'd fix the battery centre, make the reference to where we were, get the command post ready, make sure the signals were working, work out a defence plan. The guns would go in over a two-hour period and then start firing. The observers would be forward with the infantry. We very rarely saw the FO. Very rarely did we have infantry protecting us once we were in action. Sometimes if we got some trouble on our perimeter the Australians would send in a rifle platoon to help protect the guns, but it was most unusual. We were rarely in position more than two or three days. Then off again, deploy in the afternoon, secure by nightfall, work for a couple of days. By about the second night there might be some probes on our perimeter, and on the third day we were gone. After Tet they started to have very significant fire bases that were there for a long time.[120]
>
> At these longer-term bases, the first few days were spent 'filling sandbags to build a protective wall around the gun. It would normally take about 5,000 sandbags to properly prepare a gun-pit. You could then add about another 1000 ... for the sleeping bays and slit trenches and then there were the barbed wire entanglements'. The reddish laterite soil was 'a bloody curse when it was dry and another bloody curse when it got wet'. Maintaining the guns had a high priority. 'We would clean and oil it to a standard that would have made any gunnery instructor proud. ... You could go to bed at night after firing and cover the gun up with the usual muzzle and breech covers but in the morning there would be nothing but rust on all the bare metal parts'. This had to be removed and replaced by a protective coating of oil.[121]

highly qualified British Assistant Instructor Gunnery, Lieutenant David ('Spike') Hughes, 'a stickler for protocol in the command post', was sent to 161 Battery as GPO.[122] These measures did not prevent another friendly-fire incident on 22 July 1970, when an inexperienced commander of an Australian reinforcement unit incorrectly plotted his position and brought down on his platoon fire that killed two men and wounded four.[123]

There was much rivalry between the field batteries in the Anzac taskforce. The last BC noted that:

> one of the ways of competing was to be first to report, 'Ready'. We were accused of cheating. Two or three times that was tested by 161 actually firing when calling ready, and we always did. There was never a moment I wasn't comfortable with the New Zealand response. Whenever a regimental target was called, the first battery to report 'Ready to fire' got the job of adjusting rounds. I have no knowledge of 161 ever being beaten by an Australian battery.[124]

Though their reputation for efficiency was deserved, men from 'Kiwi Battery' were not above bending the rules to trump their Australian colleagues. On one occasion in 1966, the regiment deployed to a derelict French fort:

> We'd been there before – flat paddy fields all round. We were the last battery to go in, towing the guns by Land Rover. The orders told us where we were going to be. So we snuck down beforehand – about five of us with a few armed guys – and we got our position ready, put steel pickets in the ground. We did all the survey unbeknown to the Australians, and when we deployed we had our first gun ready in about 45 seconds. All the Australians were standing there watching us, and RHQ and the Adjutant were watching, and we said, 'We're ready' before any of the Australians did. They came over to have a look, and by the time they got across we had three guns ready to fire. The Australians didn't have any, and they never found out how we did it.[125]

The quality of the American artillery with which 161 Battery also still worked could vary enormously, as some units suffered from the low morale and indiscipline that became endemic in the largely conscripted US forces. 'Their worst was awful and their best [notably the Marine gunners] better than anything we'd ever see.'[126] The New Zealand battery was not without its own problems of indiscipline, but these were generally confined to off-duty hours. Some tension with Australians – and with New Zealand officers – had been discernible when 161 Battery was attached to the

ATF in mid-1966. 'Setting up the new base camp [at Nui Dat] was like another living hell, the morale was at breaking point, we fought amongst ourselves, the Aussies we hated so we had a few run ins with them.'[127]

161 Battery was maintained in theatre by a 'trickle' system of replacing small groups of personnel periodically (a dozen or so a month), so that the battery was always made up mostly of experienced men. In contrast, the Australians replaced whole batteries, which were 'green as grass' initially. 161 Battery was relied on during the changeover.[128] In late April 1967, it was designated GS battery for 7 RAR when this joined 1 ATF. For the first time the battery deployed its newly borrowed M101A1s by air, slung under twin-rotor Chinook helicopters. By now it was developing a firebase at an outpost near Nui Dat named The Horseshoe, where it would be based for 55 days, firing numerous H and I shoots, and to which it would return a number of times.

THE TET OFFENSIVE AND LATER OPERATIONS

At the time of the major Viet Cong/NVA 'Tet Offensive', which began during the lunar New Year holiday at the end of January 1968 with simultaneous attacks on many cities and towns, 161 Battery was deployed at Nui Dat in support of 3 RAR.[129] On the night of 31 January the battery responded to a mortar attack on the 1 ATF base with counter-mortar fire. Next morning it fired heavily in support of 3 RAR as the Australian infantry drove VC units from the nearby provincial capital of Baria in heavy street fighting that saw both men in the New Zealand FOO party wounded when the APC in which they were travelling was hit by a rocket-propelled grenade. That night a record 572 illumination rounds were fired above Route 23, which was being used by the enemy.

The gunners had to work hard between 3 and 6 February, with elements of 3RAR involved in intensive action to drive VC units out of the village of Long Dien. In the following days 161 Battery was deployed on mobile operations to harass VC and NVA units that were retreating in the face of superior firepower. In late February, while deployed at FSB Andersen on a major enemy communications route, the battery helped to drive off three attacks, one of which reached the perimeter wire of the firebase. Though the

NVA forces were eventually routed, the Western media saw the Tet Offensive as an indication that the war was far from over, and might be unwinnable. This had a decisive impact on public opinion in the US and elsewhere.

After several largely uneventful deployments in March and April, the battery was deployed on 12 May to positions near FSB Coral, an intended ATF base in an area where US forces were involved in heavy fighting. That night, before the Australians had prepared wire entanglements or completed other defences, a battalion-strength NVA attack overran the positions of 1RAR and 102 Battery RAA, causing heavy casualties and the temporary abandonment of two guns before being driven back by the infantry with the help of 102 Battery and supporting fire from 161 Battery at its nearby, better prepared position. Next day the New Zealand battery moved 300 yards to another newly prepared position, FSB Coogee, from which two days later they were heavily engaged in repelling another assault on FSB Coral. By the time the battery was redeployed into FSB Coral the position had been developed into a major ATF base. Here the New Zealand battery joined 102 Battery RAA and an American self-propelled medium battery.

A second major firebase, Balmoral, had been set up to draw enemy attacks, and when the NVA obliged by assaulting both this 3RAR position and FSB Coral in the early hours of 26 May, the heavy regimental artillery fire that was called down, along with tank, mortar and machine-gun fire, drove them back with heavy losses. A repeat assault two nights later was also repelled. On 6 June FSB Coral, having served its purpose, was abandoned and 161 Battery returned to Nui Dat.

Another important deployment in August 1968 saw the battery and an American medium battery fire more than 12,000 rounds from FSB Avenger in support of Operation Platypus. This pattern of frequent redeployment to various firebases in support of search and destroy operations by 1 ATF continued for the battery's remaining three years of service in Vietnam. The New Zealand gunners sometimes had to build firebases from scratch, and they became expert at constructing strongly defended positions. From October 1968 161 Battery's howitzers were increasingly deployed in three-gun sections ('right' and 'left') and assistant gun position officers (AGPOs) were appointed.

Unfortunately, on 16 February 1970, with half the battery deployed at FSB Pat and the other section at Nui Dat, none of the New Zealand guns was within range to support C Company of 8 RAR in a fierce encounter with the enemy. A New Zealand FOO, Lieutenant Angus Rivers, called down effective fire from the rest of the regiment as well as naval gunfire support, a role he repeated twice over the following month. In an unusual deployment in April 1970, a single L5 was sent to Long Son Island in the Mekong Delta for two weeks to destroy rocket-launching positions. Another innovation was the use of TPC 25 radars by FO parties at Nui Dat and The Horseshoe from August 1970 for observation and to call down fire on bodies of enemy troops moving at night.

The experience gained in Vietnam was beginning to have an effect at home. Vietnam service created vacancies in New Zealand, and also highlighted a lack of qualified senior instructors for the School of Artillery at Waiouru. Major John Allen RA had been brought out as Chief Instructor in late 1965, but a suitable New Zealand officer needed to be trained to replace him at the end of his term. Captain John Masters was then in England, still seconded to the British Army. 'The cheapest and quickest way to get an Instructor Gunnery was to send me to Larkhill, so they sent me 13 miles across Salisbury Plain to the School of Artillery.' Masters found the Larkhill course 'wide-ranging' and 'leading-edge'.

When he took over at the School of Artillery, Masters had not served with the battery in Vietnam, though he had been there on a three-month familiarisation tour. 'I really had to be very careful before I pronounced on some of the principles and practices. I knew one thing, but Graham Birch had seen something else work in practice. We had to decide between the two of us.' The Chief Instructor had enormous influence:

> Blokes like Geoff Hitchings, Tom Martin and John Horsford were gunners, but too senior to be involved in the regimental side – they were all in staff or command jobs. I would have to – almost on a one-to-one basis – take them through fire orders, fire planning, and artillery operational procedures, and then say, 'Yes, you can go and be battery commander.'

Men lacking the necessary technical skills or aptitude had to be turned down.[130]

In its final months in Vietnam the battery continued the existing pattern of long periods at Nui Dat, firing frequently in support of infantry patrols, punctuated by short-term deployment, usually in sections, to firebases to support designated operations or carry out H and I tasks. With the US decision to withdraw from Vietnam and the 'Vietnamisation' of the defence of South Vietnam, the ATF was wound down in early 1971. On 1 May, 161 Battery fired its final shoot and returned its leased howitzers to the Australians. It left Vietnam on 8 May and landed at Whenuapai three days later. The contentious nature of the involvement in Vietnam was highlighted by the battery's homecoming parade up Queen Street on 12 May. Though most onlookers were supportive, protesters disrupted the band, one subsequently taking legal action against Masters for behaving in an 'offensive or disorderly manner'. The case was thrown out as 'misconceived', with costs awarded to the defendant.[131]

While opponents of the war made headlines, others had quietly backed the battery. Betty May of Levin became 'Battery Mother', a relationship that has been maintained. She wrote regularly, sending poetry to her 'treasured soldiers', and her portrait hangs in the offices of 161 Battery.[132] The Waikato town of Raglan also adopted the battery during the Vietnam War. The relationship started with the Raglan Fire Brigade and was linked to the Raglan Club by RSA members. 'They made contact with individual soldiers. The battery encouraged soldiers to write back.' Local man Doug Arter was the prime mover. After the battery's return to Papakura, Masters arranged for it to visit Raglan for a weekend. 'We went with guns and vehicles shining and had a full battery parade' down the main street. Sir Leslie Munro, the local MP, took the salute. 'We went inside the club, met all the dignitaries. We played rugby against them that afternoon, snooker, darts, and there was a large amount of drinking. They made us so welcome.' After Masters noted that the fire brigade used the Raglan coat of arms, Arter wrote to Lord Raglan asking if this could be applied to the battery. Though that proved impossible, elements of it could be used, including a panther breathing fire. The 'Rampant Panther' went on the guns from August 1972.[133]

Vietnam had meant action for the gunners after more than a decade of peace. This was significant even for those who had fought before. Neither his service in Borneo nor his stint as Director of Artillery was the highlight of John Masters' career: 'commanding New Zealand troops in action in Vietnam was better'.[134] 161 Battery was on active service for nearly six years, the longest stint ever of any New Zealand army unit. It provided close artillery support to units of all the allied forces engaged other than the South Koreans, occupying 73 firebases and carrying out 21,138 fire missions, 665 in direct support of troops engaged with the enemy. Its overall ammunition bill was nearly $8 million.[135] Four of its members were killed in action; another committed suicide.

In a frustrating war with no defined front line, and with artillery often penny-packeted in small-scale operations, the gunners of 161 Battery proved themselves the equal of any with whom they worked. Unlike their Second World War predecessors, they were not subjected to air or armoured attack, or even counter-bombardment on the scale encountered in Korea, but the security of the gun line was often threatened by infiltration. One gunner who had been to Korea was 'more frightened' in Vietnam, 'where we were moving in jungle, and you didn't know where they were or who they were. One night we were fired on from all round.'[136] The Battery won two citations for its Vietnam service. The US Army Chief of Staff's Unit Meritorious Service was awarded to 173 Airborne Brigade, including 161 Battery and its members who served with the brigade. All members of the battery who went to Vietnam received the Republic of Vietnam Presidential Citation. The active service experience gained by many regular artillery officers and other ranks would serve the RNZA well over the next two decades.

Some Vietnam veterans, however, found themselves suffering long-term consequences. Many had resented the extent of the opposition to New Zealand's involvement in this most internally divisive of overseas wars – feelings that were only compounded by the communist victory in 1975. Some have suffered health problems that may have been caused by exposure to herbicides such as 'Agent Orange' that were used routinely to provide clear fields of fire around bases and elsewhere. Discontent that this has not been officially acknowledged – or adequately compensated for – is stronger in families with children who were born with or subsequently developed major health problems. New Zealand veterans as a group received $750,000 when a class action against American chemical companies was settled out of court in 1984. The money was disbursed through a trust.[137]

While 161 Battery was in Vietnam, the National Service Scheme and volunteers sustained the TF batteries in New Zealand. In April 1971 these were redesignated to provide a link with the nineteenth-century volunteer batteries with which they were associated geographically, if not by direct lineage. The two territorial batteries of 16 Field Regiment became 11(A) and 22(D), 3 Field's batteries 31(B) and 32(E), and the independent medium battery 4(G).[138] A decline in the annual total of TF volunteers on strength (all corps) from 3675 to 1433 between 1963 and 1972 was offset by an increase in the National Service intake from 2000 to 3000 per annum between 1964 and 1966, when the TF reached its target strength of 10,000 (it would exceed 11,000 thereafter).

A month after the election of a Labour government in late 1972, however, National Service was abolished; all obligations of National Servicemen were deemed to be fulfilled with effect from 31 December. Despite the prospect of much-reduced TF manpower under an all-volunteer scheme, all the existing RNZA batteries were retained, though it was obvious that they were likely to train at strengths well below establishment and would lose the capability to deploy overseas as established units.[139] This reinforced the importance of 161 Battery as the RNZA's only potentially operational unit, a development that reflected the wider trend towards reliance on the Regular Force and the effective abandonment of the New Zealand tradition of the citizen soldier.

Walter McKinnon

Walter Sneddon McKinnon was one of the few artillery officers in 3 NZ Division to rise to post-war prominence in the New Zealand Army.[140] Born in July 1910, he spent four years in the Otago Boys' High School cadets before attending the University of Otago, from which he graduated with a science degree. (When his eldest son started his Compulsory Military Training in 1957, he was put in the artillery on the basis that 'if your old man could do maths, so can you'.)[141]

Walter McKinnon's formal military career began inauspiciously: after he had received some training, his application for a commission in the Staff Corps was rejected in December 1935 because of 'lack of fitness'. Succeeding at the second attempt, he was taken on by the RNZA on twelve months' probation in March 1936 as commander of the Ordnance Workshops in Auckland, to which was added OC Coast Cadre and Adjutant Northern Coast Group in 1937. He studied at the Australian School of Artillery in 1937. Within a year he went to Britain for a Gunnery Staff Course, specialising in radio direction-finding and fire control.

Captain McKinnon returned to New Zealand after the war began, touring districts to inspect the fixed defences (a role he performed later in Fiji and Tonga). He also worked with the new technology of radio direction finding (radar), overseeing equipment purchases in Australia in 1941. During 1942 he rose through staff positions in Army HQ: GSO2 in transport training and Senior Staff Officer Artillery. Seeking front-line experience, he was promoted to lieutenant-colonel and given command of 28 Heavy Anti-Aircraft Regiment, 3 Division, with which he sailed in November for New Caledonia. On its break-up in mid-1943 he took over 29 Light AA Regiment. Walter McKinnon commanded all the anti-aircraft forces engaged in the landing on the Treasury Islands. He was mentioned in despatches, and received an OBE in 1947.[142]

Walter McKinnon.
2004.380, Kippenberger Military Archive, Army Museum Waiouru.

Like many other 3 Division officers, McKinnon accepted a drop in rank (to major) to see action in Europe. In June 1944 he transferred to 2NZEF UK to undertake a Staff Course at Camberley; in January 1945 he went to 2NZEF Middle East, becoming second-in-command of 4 and then 6 Field Regiments in the last months of the war. He felt that the ex-3 Division artillerymen contributed as much to 2 Division as they learned from it. McKinnon was Chief Administrator with J Force until July 1946. In 1948 he studied at the Joint Service College, becoming Assistant Adjutant-General on his return to New Zealand. Colonel McKinnon was then CRA, NZ Division (1951–54) and commanded Southern District (1953) before spending three years leading the New Zealand Joint Service Mission in Washington from 1954. After a period of ill-health he commanded Northern District, and was Adjutant-General and Third Member of the Army Board (1958–64).

In 1964 Brigadier McKinnon became Quartermaster-General. He was appointed Chief of General Staff in April 1965, just as pressure fell on New Zealand to commit troops to Vietnam. 'His firm advocacy of the proposition that New Zealand must pay the fees required of its membership of the ANZUS "club" helped persuade a reluctant government to contribute an artillery battery'. He was made a CB in 1966 and retired a year later.

McKinnon always enjoyed contact with ex-soldiers. In the 1950s he encouraged US Marines to revisit New Zealand, and in 1964 he became Patron of the 3 Division Association. A man to whom other soldiers could relate, he also made a contribution beyond the armed forces, including terms as Chairman of the New Zealand Broadcasting Commission (1970–75) and a Taupo borough councillor (1977–80). He died in 1998, having seen the eldest of his five children, Don, become Deputy Prime Minister.

LEONARD THORNTON

Leonard Whitmore ('Bill') Thornton, one of a generation of 'brilliant' and 'handsome' young artillery officers, rose meteorically during the war and remained a charismatic leader into the 1970s.[143] He has been described as the 'father of post-war defence' and New Zealand's 'most prominent soldier' since the Second World War.

Born in 1916, Thornton began his military career in the Christchurch Boys' High School artillery cadets. Attracted by the chance to travel to obtain a free tertiary education, he excelled at Duntroon (1934–37), winning the King's Medal. Any cockiness he may have had when he

A youthful Brigadier Leonard Thornton.
2002.203/1, Kippenberger Military Archive, Army Museum Waiouru.

entered was transformed into gentle authority. Commissioned into the RNZA, Lieutenant Thornton received further instruction in coast artillery in Australia before being posted to Wellington to train gunners. At Fort Dorset the 'tall young officer ... always seemed to be striding about the place'.[144]

Captain Thornton was transferred to 2NZEF, leaving with 5 Field Regiment in the Second Echelon. Transferred to 4 Field as second in command of 25 Battery, he served through the Greek campaign. Major Thornton gained command of 43 Anti-Aircraft Battery in May 1941. In February 1942 he became Brigade Major 6 NZ Infantry Brigade, before returning to the gunners as second-in-command of 4 Field in September. He was then GSO II, 2 NZ Division, working closely with Freyberg, until mid-1943, when, aged 26, he was promoted to lieutenant-colonel and given command of 5 Field Regiment. From December he was briefly GSO I at Divisional HQ before returning to 5 Field.

His skills at divisional level saw him pulled out of the line in Italy several more times, and promoted to temporary colonel, before he was furloughed with the Kaikoura draft. He was made a military OBE in 1944 and twice mentioned in despatches. On his return to Europe in June 1945, he was appointed CRA, succeeding Ray Queree. Commanding a divisional artillery of 3000 men was an exceptional achievement for a 28-year-old: he was New Zealand's youngest brigadier. He held the post for six months while the regiments were disbanded. Thornton went to Japan with Jayforce and became Senior British Liaison Officer in the Tokyo sub-area. In July 1946 'Gunner Bill' came home to a posting as GSO1 for Operations and Intelligence at Army Headquarters.

Thornton was appointed to the Army Board, became Deputy Chief of General Staff and worked on the introduction of Compulsory Military Training in 1950. He became CRA, NZ Division in 1951 before attending the Imperial Defence College in 1952 and then heading the New Zealand

Joint Services Liaison Staff in London until 1954. Thornton returned to New Zealand to the top jobs available to a capable senior officer — Quartermaster-General (1955–56), Adjutant-General (1956–58) — before being appointed to the SEATO Planning Office at Bangkok (1958–59). He was made a CBE (1957) and a military CB (1962). Thornton replaced Steve Weir as Chief of General Staff in 1960. During four and a half years in this post he refocused the Army's role from deploying a territorial-based infantry division to putting a brigade group with a mix of regulars, volunteers and conscripts in the field.

Thornton became the second Chief of Defence Staff in 1965, and for the next six years he applied his reforming zeal to the overall defence structure. He was promoted to KBE in 1967. Like Weir before him, Thornton became New Zealand's ambassador to South Vietnam and Cambodia (1972–74). He returned to New Zealand to oversee the disciplining of doctors and chair the Alcoholic Liquor Advisory Council until 1983. He also fronted television documentaries on New Zealand's military history and spoke out on defence issues. This 'military godfather' was rebuked by Prime Minister David Lange, who called him a 'geriatric general' after he criticised the government for its anti-nuclear and ANZUS policies. Thornton was President of the Army Association from 1976, and a member of the trust that brought the Army Museum to Waiouru. He died in 1999.

Stan Catchpole

Stanley Frederick Catchpole was the most significant Territorial Force gunner. Born in Huntly in 1916, he was head prefect and a member of the First XV at Mount Albert Grammar School. When war broke out he was working as a salesman and had five years' experience in the Territorial Force. After volunteering immediately, he was posted to 2NZEF in January 1940. By the time he departed with the Fourth Reinforcements at the end of the year, Catchpole was married. He served initially in 5 Field Regiment, being awarded a Military Cross in 1943 for gallantry at Takrouna as a FOO for 28 Battery. He was also mentioned in despatches. From November 1944 he was Brigade Major NZ Divisional Artillery, in which capacity he signed the Operation Order for the crossing of the Senio, 'by far the most complicated of the NZA operation orders of the Second World War', with a record 29 appendices.[145]

After the war Stan Catchpole owned and operated a Four Square store until 1967. He was also active in Civil Defence and was Auckland Area Scout

Commissioner for fifteen years. A keen territorial gunner, he was Battery Commander and then Commander of 1 Field Regiment, and CRA, NZ Division from 1957 – the year he was appointed an OBE (Military) – until 1964. From 1964 to 1968 he was Associate Member of the Army Board representing the Territorial Force. Catchpole was made a CBE (Military) in 1966. He was Colonel Commandant of the RNZA from 1970 to 1975, and died in Auckland in July 1983.

Lieutenant-Colonel Stan Catchpole leads a march-past on Gunners' Day, 1955.
New Zealand Defence Force.

9

Towards a New Role, 1972–2006

The Vietnam War marked the beginning of the end of New Zealand's Cold War policy of forward defence in Asia.[1] The United States' withdrawal from South Vietnam and Britain's disengagement east of Suez undermined the framework of New Zealand's defence presence in South-east Asia; the American rapprochement with China removed much of the perceived threat. Australia withdrew its troops from Singapore in 1973, but New Zealand kept forces there until 1989. The abolition of National Service in 1972 removed the Territorial Force's guaranteed annual intake of 2000 men. While the Territorial batteries suffered initially, the effect on the artillery was limited because by the 1990s it was reduced to a single regiment. As the focus of defence changed to the Pacific, the Army honed its ability to deploy a small force to low-level conflicts at short notice.[2] With no role for medium artillery, this was disestablished, but air defence returned. At the end of the century, with just two Regular Force batteries, the Territorial field batteries were disestablished in favour of nesting indirect fire support within the infantry battalion group. The latter, with armour, artillery and engineering sub-elements, became the focus of a 'One Army' concept. With doubts about the role of artillery in 'ready reaction' operations, the Royal Regiment of New Zealand Artillery ended its first century struggling to remain the focal point for the country's artillerymen and fire support.

After Vietnam
Following the withdrawal from Vietnam, 16 Field Regiment replaced the reinforcement unit 161 Battery Depot with a short-lived Training Cadre

within Regimental Headquarters. In 1975 the RNZA's Director adjusted establishments to bring them into line with Australian regiments (even though 3 Field had one less battery). In both countries regiments sported 33 officers; New Zealand had three fewer majors and captains, but three more subalterns. On the other hand, one of the Australian OP officers was a lieutenant, whereas the RNZA posted captains. Vietnam had shown that 'as a lieutenant the officer has insufficient experience to act as an artillery adviser to another corps and insufficient rank to press an argument'. When these changes were implemented, the RNZA's strength rose by eight to 922.[3]

A year after leaving Vietnam, the guns of 161 Battery returned to South-east Asia as part of the Australian, New Zealand and United Kingdom (ANZUK) Force created under the Five Power Defence Arrangements (FPDA) between Malaysia, Singapore, Britain, Australia and New Zealand that came into effect in November 1971. The artillery component was 28 ANZUK Field Regiment, on paper three L5 batteries of which two (one each from the RA and RAA) were permanently stationed in Singapore; New Zealand would provide the third when it was needed. The CO was British, the second in command Australian. 161 Battery had spent six weeks in Singapore in 1972.[4] In addition to live shoots and practising movement by air, the battery conducted an unusual amphibious exercise off the east coast of Malaya. Barry Dreyer remembers a deployment in assault boats with a squadron of Australian engineers:

> There were two engineer boats at the front and two at the back, and then our sixteen boats. And one of these Australian engineers came out of the queue and drove up the line and got in front, and created this wake. I could see that in one of the boats the water had started to come over the front ramp, and of course – pretty heavily loaded – it started to go down by the bow. I could see the gun barrel go 'plop' and the carriage go 'plop'. I am sure that I am the only BC who lost a gun in the South China Sea. We found every bit of it in the water, except the firing lock.[5]

Despite this incident, the deployment showed New Zealand's willingness to fulfil its commitment to forward defence. Though the New Zealand Force South East Asia that replaced the ANZUK Force in January 1974 had no

Members of 31(B) Battery enjoy a cuppa after a fire mission during their annual camp, Mt White, 1975. *16 Field Regiment.*

artillery component, RNZA personnel have exercised with Singaporean forces since 1975, and FPDA forces have trained in New Zealand.[6] 161 Battery also exercised in Fiji in 1974, practising deployment by air.[7]

The end of National Service signalled the demise of large citizen soldier-based units, with the army focusing instead on small ready-to-go units of regulars. The Territorial batteries continued as training units but struggled to attract volunteers in a changed social climate. Even the usually strong 3 Field Regiment dwindled 'to the point of being impracticable'.[8] The Dunedin battery had a one-gun detachment in Invercargill, where interest remained high. When recruiting picked up, 3 Field asked unsuccessfully in 1977 to reform its third battery there.[9] Instead, the gun was withdrawn in 1979 when Dunedin's 31(B) Battery moved from Central Battery to Kensington Army Hall.[10]

These batteries were equipped with the old 25-prs, whose days were numbered once Britain and Australia stopped using them in the early 1970s. 3

> ### LOCATING TROOP
> Locating Troop's role was surveying, meteorology, locating enemy artillery and mortars, and artillery intelligence. It had two mortar locating radars, and mobile and static meteorological radars.[11] With the old sound-ranging equipment in storage, the Director sought to purchase a new generation of gear in about 1972.[12] Assistant Chief of Defence Staff Ron Hassett felt obliged to defer action for two years so as 'not to be seen as a gunner' by other elements of the army. In the interim the cost nearly doubled, and no purchase was made.[13]
>
> Instead, a new radar designed for locating and surveying was obtained. An early anti-aircraft radar system, No. 3 Mk VII, had been converted to mortar location in the 1960s. It identified the parabolic path of enemy bombs, enabling the mortar's position to be determined. This cumbersome system required manual calculations, but it worked. The new radar, EMI's Cymbeline, introduced in 1976, was able to give a plot within 20 to 30 seconds.[14] With the coordinates of its own position fed in, it observed the fire of enemy mortars or howitzers up to 20 kilometres away.[15] It calculated the enemy position and displayed the coordinates, which were either relayed verbally to the gun command post or used by the locating officer to direct the guns. 'He could actually fire the battery' from the radar position.[16] The meteorological section mobile radar provided artillery meteorological data in the field, and the static system provided data three times daily to the Meteorological Office in Wellington.[17]

Field had the last shoot on 21 January 1977, and this most significant weapon ever used by New Zealand artillery was officially struck off after a parade in Christchurch on 12 September. Sixteen M101A1 105-mm howitzers were purchased as training guns, supplementing the four already on hand. 32(E) and 31(B) batteries converted to these in February 1978, while the northern batteries continued with the L5.[18]

READY REACTION ARTILLERY
The 1978 Defence Review led to the creation of three Task Force Regions (TFRs) and the first steps towards a Ready Reaction Force (RRF) and a Framework Force (later called the Integrated Expansion Force or IEF). The RRF would be an all-arms infantry battalion group, with small supporting elements of artillery, armour and engineers. The artillery component was

to be deployable by air at 'short notice' (fourteen days) to low- and mid-intensity limited war operations (later termed 'short-warning conflicts'). 161 Battery had tried parachuting their guns, but did not adopt this technique; they would be delivered by C130.[19] The IEF would expand the RRF to a brigade group, with the RNZA deploying a full field regiment (two more batteries). This too would be available at short notice (later defined as six months).[20]

This restructuring required a reorganisation of the artillery, and on 2 July 1979, 161 Battery was designated as the RRF's artillery component. The regular component of 32(E) Battery, now under 3TFR, became its reinforcing unit (later called Training Troop) and moved from Addington Camp to Burnham, effectively splitting the battery in two.[21] 22(D) Battery was detached from 16 Field to nest under 2TFR as an independent unit. 16 Field (reporting to 1TFR) now comprised HQ Battery, 161 Battery and 11(A) Battery, and was to incorporate Hamilton's 4(G) Medium Battery.

In the divisional artillery, a medium regiment provided supporting fire, particularly counter-bombardment and fire at ranges beyond the reach of field guns.[22] After the Defence Review proposed phasing out medium guns in favour of expanding the field artillery, successive 4(G) Medium Battery commanders tried to prevent this.[23] Citing the administrative advantages of autonomy and their value in supporting the region's two infantry battalions, they lobbied to remain an independent unit of 1 TFR. The battery's seven guns were another string to its bow.[24] Still 'in fairly good shape', they would have up to another decade of life 'with some mothering'.[25] The 1550 rounds on hand represented seven years' stock for practice firing. The battery also enjoyed good TF attendance and a close relationship with Hamilton city – qualities which had 'regressed' when the battery last lost its independent status (in 1962).[26] The lobbying succeeded: 4(G) Medium was permitted to remain independent and self-accounting for the life of its guns.[27]

In advocating both the Ready Reaction Force and Task Force Regions, the Defence Review allowed for confusion between support and operational units. Each TFR was required to support its two battalions with artillery. Wellington's 2TFR had regained 22(D) Battery but this was seen as inadequate,

Life in the RNZA

Consistent with its motto, a career in the regular artillery involved moving a lot. John Rout shifted fifteen times in under 30 years, including four stints at the School of Artillery and three with 161 Battery.[28] An RNZA major and his family faced change after three years in an Auckland staff job, during which they had bought a house in Takapuna:

> I went home to my wife and said, 'I've got good news and bad news.' The good news was that I had been promoted to temporary lieutenant-colonel. We jumped around celebrating that for a while. Then she asked me the bad news. The bad news was that I had been posted to Waiouru – starting on Monday.[29]

During the equal employment opportunities revolution of the 1980s, more women joined the TF, and a higher proportion opted for the artillery. Initially they were designated by the suffix (W) and encouraged into roles for which they were thought to be suited – 'radar and stuff like that' – because 'they were better with their hands, finer detail, doing drawings ...' Those who joined 4(G) Medium Battery were enthusiastic but lacked the necessary physical strength.[30] In 1982 there was a novel occurrence: a marriage between two 16 Field gunners. This couple was of equal rank, but the bride in a similar 3 Field union three years later, Sergeant W. Gatt, was senior to the groom, so they would be known on formal occasions as 'Sergeant and Mr Montgomery'.

The place of women in the artillery is still argued: 163 Battery narrowly lost a debate with 161 Battery on the subject in 1998, 'despite a spirited, yet

so the Director investigated raising a field regiment in 1980 and a Tactical Artillery HQ the following year. The regiment, 2 Field, would also run Fort Dorset, where 22(D) Battery was based, by raising a regimental and battery headquarters; a second field battery (23) would 'not be raised in peace'. Land Force Command feared that this would 'spread too thinly' the Army's artillery resources;[31] Brigadier I.H. Burrows described the establishment as 'an empire'. The proposal was also criticised for not having 'justified the need for another regiment vis-a-vis other Army priorities', particularly in terms of RRF roles.[32] Nevertheless 2 Field Regiment was informally reformed in 1982. It participated in Command Post exercises and first paraded in April 1983. The 'Arty Tac cell' held its first training weekend in May but was quietly

politically-dubious, performance'. Women have excelled in the light artillery, Lieutenant Hayley May commanding a contingent in Bosnia-Herzegovina. Women having demonstrated their ability to meet a wide variety of challenges, restrictions on their service in combat roles in the artillery (and other corps) were lifted from early 2000. In mid-2005, 14 per cent of Regular Army personnel were women, the lowest proportion of the three services. Full gender integration remains a distant prospect.[33]

The changing face of the artillery – women taking part in Exercise Hauraki Gulf.
RNZAF Official, via Air Force Museum, Christchurch.

disestablished after the annual camp the following year, along with 2TFR.[34]

The 1983 Defence Review not only led to the formal establishment of the Ready Reaction Force the following year, but also involved a rethinking of army structure. The RNZA's role was defined as providing 'such fire supremacy in the battle area that the enemy can neither interfere with our operations nor effectively develop his own'. As well as 161 Battery, the RRF would now include one or two air defence sections and a surveillance function.[35] 1 Locating Troop acquired two new sections, Surveillance and RPV (although remotely piloted vehicles were unlikely to be purchased before 1990), and was later reattached to 16 Field Regiment in Papakura. In 1990 the 'electric gunners' would be absorbed into 16 Field as Surveillance Troop HQ

Battery.³⁶ Meanwhile, 16 Field also reincorporated 22(D) Battery and finally ended the independence of both 4(G) Medium and the RNZA Band.³⁷ 4(G) Medium still had a future because a fourth battery was deemed essential for the Integrated Expansion Force (this was confirmed in 1986, when a second regular battery was mooted).³⁸ The RNZA's establishment now rose to 1079, of whom 791 were in 16 Field and 234 were regulars.³⁹

Medium and Light Artillery

After surviving the 1979 reorganisation, the medium gun had soon faced another test. The 40-year-old 5.5-inch was being phased out in allied armies, and in 1983 Australia began receiving replacement howitzers. When New Zealand's Defence Review recommended the retention of the medium role, the RNZA expected to follow suit.⁴⁰ In 1985 formal establishment charts for 4(G) Medium Battery showed eight towed 155-mms; one even specified the M198.⁴¹ The Army instead negotiated for the Austrian Noricum GHN-45, and the Defence Council approved the $18.9 million purchase in October 1985.⁴²

But its chairman, Labour Defence Minister Frank O'Flynn, did not agree. Rather than use his ministerial veto, he took the matter to Cabinet, which deferred the purchase until a post-ANZUS rupture Defence Committee of Inquiry chaired by the retired diplomat Frank Corner had reported.⁴³ Departmental sources told the *Evening Post* that Cabinet objected to the M198 because 'it appeared too offensive and, because of its size, too obtrusive'.⁴⁴ When the 1987 Defence Review rejected the Army's 'requirement to serve as part of a larger force in some distant conflict', there was no longer a role for medium artillery in New Zealand.⁴⁵

While the issue was being debated, 4(G) Medium familiarised themselves with 105-mm howitzers, first firing the L5 in late 1986. The 5.5-inch gun had been fired for the last time on 16 February.⁴⁶ The battery continued to train with it, floating one across the Waikato River in November (with 1 Field Squadron).

The 1987 Defence Review confirmed the continuing need for mobile light artillery. The 24 L5 pack-howitzers still in service, however, had become a 'major hindrance' because of their 'worn parts and lack of spares'.⁴⁷ They could

Territorial Force gunners about to cross the Waikato River in assault barges.
RNZAF Official, via Air Force Museum, Christchurch.

no longer fire to their full range. New Zealand had been seeking a new airmobile piece for years, having sent a trials officer when Australia assessed the new British L118 Light Gun against the M101A1 and a new US 105-mm in 1969. The light gun performed well, but neither country bought it immediately because its long-range projectile was yet to be developed. After Britain adopted it the Director RNZA, Don Kenning, visited in 1972 to reassess it. Improved Abbott ammunition had increased its range to 17.2 kilometres but was so expensive that his British hosts quipped that they should give the gun to clients – 'we'd make our money on the ammunition'.[48] Then a two-barrel concept able to use much cheaper US M1 ammunition was developed.[49] All light guns thereafter came in two configurations, which took two to four hours to change: the L118 fired the Abbott round, the L119 M1 rounds (up to 11.5 kilometres). In 1981 Australia bought six and a licence to manufacture another 105.[50] New Zealand ordered 24 of these cheaper Australian guns in May 1986 for $1.09 million each. Because Australian manufacturing would not begin in time to meet New Zealand's urgent delivery target for the RRF battery, Australia purchased eight more guns from Britain for New Zealand, which got its first two in March 1987.[51]

An RNZA Project Officer, Captain A.A. Mitchell, was among the critics of this 'impetuous' purchase. Two of the first six guns received had a 'nitrogen leak in the recoil system'. This persisted into the first official shoot on 21 October, and other defects were soon being reported.[52] New Zealand soon negated the gun's air-portability by its choice of tractor. The U1300L Unimog initially allocated was upgraded (in the RRF battery) to the much larger U1700L, which could carry more ammunition. No New Zealand helicopter could lift the U1700L (or the gun, without breaking it in two), and even the C130 Hercules could carry only one gun-and-tractor combination at a time, making 'rapid' deployment 'extremely extended'. Spares were bought for only eight guns. All the guns were grounded in April 1988 because of a stub-axle fault.[53] The last ones were received in December 1989.[54] While the problems were corrected, a 1991 audit concluded that the project had been both rushed and undermanaged.

The RRF's efficiency of movement had been tested in March 1984 by the ten-day Exercise Northern Safari, during which 161 Battery flew its guns off the deck of HMAS *Tobruk* onto a fire-support base on Great Barrier Island.[55] This exercise revealed that headquarters failed to understand the difficulty of moving the guns in mountainous terrain – one senior officer suggested that they be manhandled. This was dangerous even in tattoos (one man broke three fingers at a 1976 Western Springs pageant),[56] and quite unrealistic for moving long distances in rough conditions. Once this issue was sorted out the battery contributed, without actually firing, to a BC's fire-plan that also involved the infantry's mortars, the guns of HMNZS *Waikato* and two Skyhawks.[57] The ready reaction artillery was further tested in 1985 in the 'somewhat frustrating' Exercise Herekino Safari, when the RRF attempted to deploy to Kaitaia airfield. 'The guns arrived in quick succession: then waited for eight hours before the ammunition and survey equipment arrived. A staff Snafu.'[58] At this time the RRF was no more than 'a planning structure into which elements from Army units can be placed as circumstances require'.[59]

These exercises showed 161 Battery's strength to be inadequate for the

ARTILLERY BANDS

Bands have long been part of military life, providing entertainment as well as keeping marching soldiers in step.[60] Nearer the battlefield, beating drums and martial music raised spirits and demoralised the enemy. Trumpeters and buglers helped to control movement during battle, while other band members carried stretchers.[61] Bugles were used for calls common to all arms, trumpets for those peculiar to the mounted arms. In barracks, the duty trumpeter also sounded routine calls.

The 58th Regiment brought the first military band to New Zealand in 1845 when it came to fight in the Northern War, and Bugler William Allen died heroically in the action at Boulcott's Farm the following year. Many of its members took their discharge in Auckland, and in 1860 some joined the new Auckland Volunteer Rifles Band, which within a few years became the Auckland Artillery Band. By 1885, the volunteer corps' nine bands throughout the colony had a total of 207 members.[62] They provided music for social occasions and embodied the prestige of the unit in splendid uniforms. Dunedin's artillery band is reputed to have played the first public performance of 'God Defend New Zealand' in 1876.[63]

Long-lived military bands usually went through several metamorphoses. For example, the Southern Military District Artillery Band, a component of 3 Field Regiment from 1949 to 1964, began life as Dunedin's Caledonian Band before being linked to volunteer units from 1878, and becoming part of 4 Otago Regiment in 1911. The creation of the Territorial Force brought unit bands under closer central control; they were limited to 25 members of military age. The Otago Artillery band was national B Grade champion in 1925, as was Wellington's in 1934. The number of army bands was cut to seven in 1964, when Dunedin's reverted to civilian status.[64]

Auckland's Artillery Band was thwarted in its desire to serve overseas in the Great War; instead, it played at patriotic events and marched departing troops down Queen Street, duties which may have helped it win several national quickstep titles in the 1920s. From January 1941 it spent three and a half months at Waiouru training camp, where it was 'gradually welded into a fine musical and military combination, its ability to perform intricate evolutions on the parade ground being a star attraction for the troops'.[65] The bandsmen trained as stretcher bearers and received rifle training. A year later they were mobilised 'for the duration' (in the event, until October 1944), attached first to 1 Field Regiment at Hopuhopu camp and then to the Northern Military School at Narrow Neck.

The RNZA Band plays the national anthems at a Davis Cup tennis tie, Stanley St, Auckland.
RNZAF Official, via Air Force Museum, Christchurch.

In the post-war years the now Territorial-based RNZA band entertained rugby crowds and royalty, and performed at military tattoos. Under the direction of Bandmaster Captain J.G. Sinton, it was national C Grade champion in 1979. By the mid-1980s, still based in Auckland, it was administered by 16 Field Regiment. In the late 1990s it practised in its own facilities at Panmure under Bandmaster WO1 John Knowles and was administered by the Auckland Northland Regiment. However, on Gunners' Day 2003, RNZA Colonel Commandant Brigadier Ray Andrews was able to announce that 'after a short period away from the fold, the RNZA Band (the oldest unit in the RNZA) was back under RNZA control'.[66] It celebrated its 140th anniversary in 2004 as New Zealand's longest continuously existing band.[67] The RNZA Band still plays an indispensable role on ceremonial occasions and contributes strongly to the regiment's relationship with the wider community.

RRF. Despite being a six-gun unit, it was 'at a manpower level less than that which deployed operationally [to Vietnam] in 1965 with only four guns'. The BC explained that while he had removed personnel from the gun line, he still had 'trained BC & OP parties' and 'trained and manned CP teams'.[68]

INTERNATIONAL EXERCISES AND NUCLEAR FALLOUT

Exercises with the United States, Australia and the other Five Power Defence Arrangements nations helped the RNZA to maintain its efficiency and exposed soldiers to conditions they would not otherwise encounter, such as the heat of the Australian outback. New Zealand trained in divisional Kangaroo-series exercises in Queensland between 1974 and 1979, and Tasman Links in the 1980s.[69] The RNZA's reputation for 'timeliness, sense of urgency and professionalism' was somewhat dented at the end of a Suman Warrior (Five Power Defence Arrangements) exercise in 1996 when a gunner arrived at RAAF Base Amberley in a taxi direct from a party, with no money for his fare and having left his kit in barracks. Fortunately other passengers spotted him driving onto the tarmac and he managed to board the plane home. Conversely, 103 Battery RAA had earlier let its side down by not leaving the Linton barracks 'in acceptable order'.[70]

At an ANZUS meeting in Honolulu in 1972 the New Zealand delegation were treated as equal partners – 'which of course we were not, but it did mean that we developed a very close relationship with the US forces'. With the American army lacking adequate training areas in the Pacific, 'we were able to negotiate reciprocal training visits whereby US Army units came down to Waiouru and we sent officers and technical units to Hawaii'. Thus began an exchange scheme that 'gave the NZ Army the opportunity to see first hand and train on the latest American equipment'.[71]

The annual technical exchange – dubbed Tropic Lightning, 25 Infantry Division's nickname – alternated between artillery and signallers. Gunners learned the intricacies of the American M114 155-mm howitzer ('the pig') at Oahu's Pohakuloa firing area. Though this provided a rare opportunity to train in a divisional context, 'the shooting was very clinical, from concrete gun platforms'.[72] The RNZA also enjoyed regular individual exchanges, with officers attending air defence training courses at Fort Sill, Oklahoma.

Tropic Lightning exposed New Zealanders to another dimension of warfare. Brigadier Ray Andrews, Commander 2TFR, took over a brigade headquarters for an exercise with an American general tasked with command in Korea:

> If we would make a contribution we would be up to speed – with anything. General Wolf was briefing his brigade commanders – he was sitting down, pretty relaxed, pointing to the map with his feet. He said, 'Now, Ray, you take the right flank. Don't go any further west than this area. Use these two routes, split your forces any way you like. I think there is going to be a threat from over here, so I am going to nuke here, here, here and there.' I was amazed.[73]

The new Labour government's introduction in 1985 of a nuclear-free policy to which the United States objected saw New Zealand effectively excluded from the ANZUS alliance. The American ambassador brought the Land Force Commander in Auckland the news. '"You guys are the ones who are going to be carrying the burden because there won't be any more exchange programmes, any more exercises".' Tropic Lightning ceased, and New Zealanders attending Canada's National Defense College no longer visited the United States' underground strategic command centre, 'Dr Strangelove's headquarters'. The number of RNZA personnel posted overseas on exchanges or courses fell from 24 in 1980 to 11 in 1987.[74]

Though exercises with Australia continued, some American material provided to Australia was stamped 'Not For Dissemination to NZ'.[75] But the Royal Artillery continued its Long Look exchanges, and those who thought the American response too severe backed New Zealand. When the head of the Defence Liaison staff in London was called in by the British Defence Secretary, George Younger, he wondered if New Zealanders were to be denied access to courses because the Americans objected to sharing classified material. Instead, Younger described his experience as a twenty-year-old English National Serviceman 'sitting on a hillside in Korea, and then suddenly over the other hill comes the whole of the Chinese army'. His platoon would have been

> ### THE DIRECTORATE
> The Directorate RNZA was the small team at Army Headquarters headed by the senior artillery staff officer who was responsible to the Chief of General Staff for all technical and professional matters pertaining to artillery. Under various titles, the Director RNZA dated back to Tudor Boddham's appointment as Staff Officer (Artillery and Engineers) in 1885. From 1966 the Director (DRNZA) was also the Director of the Army Air Corps. In its maturity the Directorate comprised three or four officers who advised the CGS on technical and professional matters, planned appointments and oversaw career development, sponsored equipment purchases (involving hundreds of items ranging from guns and radars to binoculars and command post equipments), conducted corps conferences at home and represented the Army overseas at standardisation conferences and on working groups, and helped to manage the domestic affairs of the regiment.[76]
>
> As part of a general retrenchment in 1989, Chief of Defence Force John Mace asked that the Army General Staff be cut markedly in size. The knife fell on many arms and service directorates. Lieutenant-Colonel Mike Pearce was the last Director RNZA, his oversight functions being reallocated in 1990.[77] The Regimental Colonel was subsequently to provide advice on a less formalised basis.

overrun had it not been for the presence nearby of Captain H.G. Menzies and his sergeant, who brought down fire from 16 Field Regiment that halted the Chinese attack. Thanks in large measure to this kind of personal debt to New Zealand servicemen, 'the British were very good to us'.[78]

READY REACTION?

Regular artillerymen have had a counter-terrorism role since the 1970s. When activated by the codeword 'Saraband', 161 Battery's task was to secure the outer cordon in a situation such as a hostage-taking, allowing the SAS or the Police's Internal Security Assault Team to resolve the crisis inside an inner cordon. In 1988 it participated in a counter-insurgency exercise in which the Mount Smart stadium was occupied by terrorists. On another occasion they acted as passengers on a 'hijacked' plane at Mangere airport. 'Internal Security training was hated by everyone.'[79]

The Fiji coup of May 1987 both confirmed the validity of refocusing on the Southwest Pacific and highlighted dissatisfaction with the RNZA's ready reaction role. When an Air New Zealand airliner was hijacked at Nadi airport on 19 May as a protest against the coup, and there was rioting in Suva, 161 Battery was mobilised to provide 'personnel in support of evacuation of NZ nationals from Fiji', according to its official diary. Australia had mobilised naval and special forces to rescue its nationals; HMNZS *Wellington* was already in Suva.[80] Under one contingency, Operation Fargo, sub-units of 161 Battery would secure the airports at Nadi and Nausori and retrieve New Zealand's High Commissioner from Suva.[81] 'At one stage a 30-man platoon was on two hours notice to move.' The regimental CO, Lieutenant-Colonel Barry Dreyer, 'had soldiers sitting at Whenuapai inside a Hercules with the engines running. We were armed to the teeth.' The flight was cancelled less than an hour before take-off after the hijacker was overpowered by cabin crew. Although men slept in platoon groupings on the battery's premises for another fortnight, the force was never sent. Many officers expressed concern over their intended role; the DRNZA, Lieutenant-Colonel David Lough, later claimed to have resigned because of it.[82]

Just how would an artillery battery quell political upheaval on a Pacific island? After exercises tested the RNZA in low-level conflict scenarios, one commentator thought it 'most unlikely' that there would be a role for artillery in the RRF. 'In practice the artillery weapons could become valuable monuments, requiring continuous protection, rather than the providers of fire support.'[83] The force's ability to deploy speedily and then be backed up was tested in Exercise Golden Fleece in 1989. This largest joint-force exercise in 20 years showed that 'low-intensity conflict' was an ill-defined concept; any such conflict might well grow.

The search for solutions coincided with the return of the New Zealand battalion from Singapore to Linton Camp. The artillery was officially defined as an RRF Support Unit, and along with other such units 161 Battery moved to Linton in October 1991. The RRF was renamed the Army Ready Reaction Unit (ARRU), and 161 Battery ceased to be under command of 16 Field Regiment. The Gulf War provided the impetus for this change. One option for New Zealand participation had been the deployment of 161 Battery, which moved to Waiouru and intensified its training until the government decided to send only a medical detachment and C130s.⁸⁴ This experience, together with the major ARRU Exercise Ivanhoe 91, led to the time for deployment being doubled to a more realistic 28 days.

Having detached 161 Battery to Linton, 16 Field left Papakura in December 1991 to allow the base to close. 16 Field Regimental Headquarters, HQ Battery and the workshops moved to Mount Wellington Barracks, then within a year to Waiouru.⁸⁵ The second regular battery, 163, was re-formed at Waiouru in 1993 (affiliated to 2/1 Battalion RNZIR) to strengthen the regiment's ability to deploy the IEF. The batteries adopted a two-troop format and had their first regular regimental shoot.⁸⁶ The rump of 16 Field (minus 163 Battery) moved to Linton in November 1997, and 163 Battery followed in December 2001 as part of a rationalisation of bases, leaving the RNZA concentrated at Linton (HQ 16 Field, its two batteries and workshops) and Waiouru (the School).⁸⁷

Equipment

By the mid-1990s, overseas exercises such as Kiwi Tamasek in Singapore were the official measure of the artillery's capacity.⁸⁸ Singapore's artillery began reciprocal training with New Zealand in 1997, having previously fired in Thailand, Taiwan and the Philippines. The annual Thunder Warrior exercises with this well-equipped modern artillery force partially replaced exercises with the Americans, providing an outward focus and sharpening skills.

A premature detonation in one of the Singaporeans' new 155-mm howitzers at Waiouru soon injected a dose of reality. While the RNZA was officially merely an 'interested party', the incident left its mark. 'Of the 14 men there, I was one of three left standing,' RSM Paul Galloway recalled. This was the first time the Singaporeans had deployed their guns at Waiouru; 23 Battalion brought six 52-calibre FH2000 howitzers, locally developed modern weapons. When they set up at Robinson's Pond on 9 March 1997, each gun was accompanied by a New Zealand detachment. This was an extended-range shoot, with standard ammunition used for correction purposes. A defect in a Chinese-made fuse caused a shell containing 6 kilograms of high explosive to detonate while being rammed and before the breech was closed, killing two Singaporean gunners and wounding eleven. Galloway had fired the previous round, which 'did what it was supposed to do'. Standing ten paces behind the gun, the New Zealand Liaison Officer, Sergeant Mike Smith, was also injured. Beside him was Lieutenant Leroy Forrester, whom the Singaporeans decorated for preventing further mayhem by moving away propellant charges.[89] These were not the first fatalities during this exercise, and safety procedures were checked.[90] New Zealand's were not found wanting – the last premature detonation here had been in the late 1950s.[91]

In serving the big Singapore howitzers, New Zealand gunners 'prove their skill and gain valuable experience on a different weapon system'. The Singapore regiment subsequently increased its firing here, leaving eighteen guns behind between shoots. An APU version was seen in 1999, and six of the Primus tracked self-propelled version were used for the first time in the 2004 exercise.[92]

A premature in a light gun in Australia in 2002 also had implications for New Zealand. With the gun firing on full charge, there was a loud bang, flash and cloud of smoke. The barrel soared 10 metres into the air and the breech sheared off, landing near ammunition. The cause was faulty ammunition: New Zealand and Australia buy theirs from similar sources. There have also been incidents with the light gun in New Zealand. During Exercise Sunny Coast in 1992, part of a copper driving band came off in a barrel. The next round stripped all the lands of the rifling and cracked the barrel. 'There was a real danger of the gun actually coming to pieces.'[93]

In recent years the light gun has had less range than the 25-pr. The short-range barrels firing M1 rounds were used for training, and the L118 configuration firing long-range Abbott ammunition for operational deployments. Each year the regiment changed barrels for an L118 Abbott shoot, sometimes on charge super for maximum range. When these began in 1993, gunners sarcastically noted the 'great privilege of holding an Abbott round.' By then Britain had stopped developing this round, and Australia abandoned proposals to manufacture it, concentrating on the M1. The New Zealand regiment held its last L118 shoot on 17 June 1999, when 163 Battery fired the country's remaining L118 ammunition – more than 2000 Abbott rounds, including 800 on charge super, compared with the usual daily limit of ten. The L118 barrels then went into storage until 2002, when all but eight

Captain Brian Frances uses a Vanguard artillery computer, watched by a representative of Marine-Air Systems Ltd, 1990.
EP 1990-4056-11 Alexander Turnbull Library, Wellington.

were destroyed long before reaching their 20,000-round life expectancy. The regiment was incredulous at being left without long-range capacity until a long-range version of the M1 round (range 18,000 metres) could be adopted.[94]

In 1990 the six Field Artillery Computer Equipments (FACE) were replaced after 20 years in service.[95] They had superseded the old plotting methods by allowing rapid calculation of firing data modified by weather information. FACE could control up to three eight-gun batteries, amazing old-time gunners. Small for the time, it nevertheless occupied the back of a long-wheelbase Land Rover, leaving room, with careful arrangement, for two operators. It was also tested in helicopter deployment – by 'putting it on its side and taking the wheels off' – but proved insufficiently rugged to withstand a ride in an M548 tracked truck. FACE soon gave 'constant trouble' by storing corruptions, and from 1982 the Directorate collaborated with a local company, MAS (which had developed a mortar computer), to replace the already aged machines. By the late 1980s the slowness of progress was demoralising for both staff officers and gunners.[96]

A much smaller computer, Vanguard, was introduced in 1991.[97] Unlike FACE, its calculations can be relayed directly to the guns, where the gun sergeants have small display units. In 1998 six command post Unimog trucks were modified to carry Vanguard in the field.[98] Recent developments such as GPS devices and laser range-finders have made the GPO's task easier.[99] In other respects, however, New Zealand has failed to keep up with advances in artillery equipment.

AIR DEFENCE

After New Zealand's anti-aircraft artillery was abolished in 1961, the artillery periodically considered its return.[100] In 1982 the Director complained of 'a trend to diminish and/or discard some of our Artillery capabilities', including 'Air Defence' (AD), as it was now called. AD was duly revived, for the RRF, by the 1983 Defence Review, with a project team set up in the Directorate office. Periodic development and acquisition studies always foundered on grounds of cost. By 1996/97 the requirement was defined as Very Low Level Air Defence in 'short-warning conflicts', and an AD Troop became a deployment output for 16 Field.[101] At first considerations of inter-operability with the Australians favoured the RBS70 'beam-rider' system, but by the mid-1990s this was both outdated and too expensive.[102] The Ministry of Defence preferred the newer American Stinger 'fire-and-forget' missile, but New Zealand was denied access to this because it remained officially a 'friend', not an 'ally'. But as the ABCA (America, Britain, Canada and Australia – and New Zealand in association with Australia) Quadripartite Working Group on Air Defence required inter-operability among partners, New Zealand's AD unit was expected to be able to cooperate with an Australian battery at short notice.[103]

The next choice, the French Mistral, was much cheaper: a dozen launchers could be acquired for the price of five RBS70s. The missile, with warhead and solid-fuel rocket, comes pre-packed in a tube which is fitted to the firing post alongside optical target-acquisition equipment. Seated on the post, the operator activates the gyroscope and infrared detector head, and fires when a target is sighted. Both post and missile are man-portable. An order for twelve Mistral launcher posts and 23 missiles was placed once French nuclear testing at Moruroa had ended.

The Mistral arrived in 1997, and an air defence sub-unit, G Troop 43 Air Defence Battery (Light), was formally established within 16 Field Regiment in October 1998.[104] This has five firing parties; seven firing posts remain in storage. A second troop is planned when TF air defence training begins; both will then become mixed TF/RF units. The unit was named with a sense of tradition: the original 43 Battery fought with 2 Division from 1941 to 1944, and 16 Field invited former 'bird gunners' to G Troop's formation parade.[105] The troop exercised for the first time in 1998 on Exercise Brimstone at Waiouru, in which the RNZAF participated. The first live firing took place on 18 November. VIPs assembled at the RNZAF Air Weapons Range, South Kaipara Head, for the occasion, during which five remote-controlled Banshee target planes worth $40,000 each were brought down by missiles costing $250,000 each. Officers have attended air defence courses in Britain, Australia and Singapore. Most instruction takes place on a computer-based simulator, but this has proved unreliable.[106]

The original order did not cover the Alerting and Cueing Radar, which incorporates an IFF (Identification Friend or Foe) feature without which friendly aircraft are vulnerable, as well as enabling fire at night and in low visibility. After attempts to piggyback on an Australian purchase fell through, the radar was received by 16 Field Regiment in October 2006.[107]

Gunners as Peacekeepers

Peacekeeping duties have become an increasingly important role for the New Zealand armed forces over the last half-century, as the United Nations has sought military personnel from member states to observe or maintain order in post-conflict situations. A gunner's training can be of use for such duties.

Major Peter Willis was sent to the Middle East in 1956 as an observer with the United Nations Truce Supervision Organisation:

> The Israelis objected to the Military Observers saying they fired the rounds which killed a lot of people in Gaza, so I brought back a tail fin of a mortar. Alan Smith [another New Zealand officer] and I sat down with maps and a few bits and pieces, and we worked out the fall of shot. With triangulation we figured out where the mortars were – in a kibbutz. The Israelis were a bit nonplussed.[108]

Gunnery skills can help observers detect strengths and weaknesses in the forces being monitored. In Angola in 1992–93, for example, an RNZA observer saw government artillery 'firing off maps using a scale of 1:250,000 – a map the air force would use – and no meteorological data. They were so inaccurate.' A decade later, observers on the Golan Heights could anticipate trouble from the positioning of artillery and other equipment. At one point they were so convinced that Israel was about to reinvade south Lebanon that they ran a sweepstake on when H-hour would be. Two tank divisions had moved up to the border, along with a gun-locating radar that was used to adjust long-range artillery.[109]

From August 1994, the RNZA sent personnel to Bosnia-Herzegovina to serve with the United Nations in Operation Radian. Lieutenant-Colonel Graeme Williams, a gunner, headed the New Zealand Contingent, UNPROFOR, while others had roles such as liaison officer in the combat element, Kiwi Company. The RNZA also sent a dozen NCOs to drive its armoured personnel carriers.[110] The Forward Air Control (FAC) unit sent in 1995 was an RNZA sub-unit. This Tactical Air Control Party, a five-man team under Captain Shay Bassett, directed close air support by NATO jets from their base in a school at Maglaj, which came under Bosnian Serb shellfire. During one attack, a tank round passed through the room in which Captain Kevin Scott was working.[111] The RNZA prepared other soldiers for this deployment by simulating battlefield conditions. During Exercise Kiwi III, for instance, two guns of '161 (Serbian) Battery brought the fire in close'.[112] The RNZA used Bosnia to upskill its forward air controllers, some of whom notched up

100 controls. In New Zealand they trained with the RNZAF until the air combat wing was dissolved. Calling in jets requires rapid decision-making. FACs can qualify overseas, but they cannot stay up to speed in New Zealand. 'The regiment recognised it as a loss.'[113]

During the transition of authority from the UN to NATO, fifteen New Zealand officers were deployed as members of the Implementation Force. They were commanded by Lieutenant-Colonel Matt Beattie, the CO of 16 Field Regiment, who worked as a military adviser to the Organisation for Security and Cooperation in Europe, and later in 'G5' (Civil Affairs) in the Allied Rapid Reaction Corps Headquarters. New Zealand defence thinking was that gunners might be well suited to such work in trouble spots closer to home.

In 1997, with the situation in Bosnia still very tense, the NATO-led Stabilisation Force (SFOR) made another call on New Zealand and in 1998 16 Field Regiment sent 35 personnel to SFOR(G) in two waves.[114] They manned British medium guns – the first time since Vietnam that RNZA soldiers had been sent overseas to man guns operationally. Three detachments, each of nine men, converted to the massive AS90 155-mm self-propelled gun, gaining valuable experience on six-month tours. The AS90 was a 'useful deterrent' to unfriendly locals.[115] The first SFOR(G) gunners – three members of a Warrior APC-based FO party – served with 159 Battery, 26 Regiment, at Glamoc sawmill. The second deployment served with B Battery, 1 Regiment RHA. Training on and serving the equipment of other forces enables the army to deploy soldiers without having to deploy equipment. In 2004, ten artillery personnel were attached to the Stabilisation Force for six months as a liaison and observation team in the edgy Bosnian Serb town of Mrkonji Grad.[116]

East Timor

In 1999 New Zealand committed itself to assisting East Timor's transition to independence from Indonesia. With pro-Indonesian militias terrorising the populace, New Zealand agreed to contribute a battalion-sized unit to the Australian-led and UN-sanctioned International Force East Timor. This was replaced in 2000 by another infantry-based unit (NZ BATT2), now serving under the auspices of the UN Transition Administration in East Timor.

The Defence Force faced problems finding sufficient personnel for the next relief unit. It decided to form NZ BATT3 largely from 16 Field Regiment, supplemented by armoured and 1RNZIR personnel.[117] Most of the regular gunners participated in this six-month tour, which was to have unexpected consequences for both training and the RNZA's relationship with the TF.

A few gunners with specific skills had already served in East Timor, four with BATT2 to experience combat conditions. Warrant Officer Rob McLean was there when Private Leonard Manning died. 'The rules of engagement changed overnight. If the militiamen were armed, or had their weapons slung, or were carrying grenades, you could shoot them. Previously we had to issue a verbal warning, and then fire a warning shot, and then only if they were in an aggressive position.'[118]

On 7 September 2000, a month before BATT3's deployment, UN aid workers were slaughtered in Indonesian West Timor. As the gunners prepared to leave New Zealand for East Timor, they learned of fifteen-strong parties of armed militiamen in the New Zealand sector; two men had been shot by BATT2. McLean believes that these were former Indonesian special forces personnel. Ambushes, called blocks for political reasons, were set up. Just before BATT2 was relieved, patrols sighted eighteen militiamen returning to West Timor along a riverbed. SAS trackers followed them, calling down illumination mortar rounds in an attempt to head them into a block. About 60 rounds were fired on this, the only time indirect fire support was provided.[119]

For BATT3 the regiment formed two companies, 161 and 163, under battery commanders Majors Nick Gillard and Shay Bassett; Captain Matt Boggs was the Battalion Adjutant. A Combat Services Support Company and a Fire Support Troop backed them up. BATT3 inherited both the area of operations of its predecessors ('AO Canterbury') and the same sub-units – a company each of Fijians and Nepalese, and an Irish platoon (attached to 161 Company). The New Zealand battalion served with an Australian battalion in the 'hottest' sector, HQ Sector West. More than 50 of its 700 soldiers were women, many of them in combat roles.[120]

BATT3's tour began with a change-of-command parade on 12 November 2000. During its first week 86 refugees were repatriated to three villages in the area, which now had a threat assessment of 'low'. The following week

95 refugees came home, along with six ex-militiamen. A suspected militia sighting turned out to be a hunter wearing an Indonesian Army uniform. In the event, inter-community flare-ups and theft were BATT3's biggest worries. Even the anniversary of the 1975 declaration of independence from Portugal – the prelude to annexation by Indonesia – did not produce the predicted volatile crowds.[121]

BATT3, commanded by Lieutenant-Colonel David Gawn, was an infantry structure infused with a gunner culture. Not only were the two companies named after batteries; the RSM was a gunner, Warrant Officer 'Bo' Ngata, who designed the battalion's emblem and flag and composed its haka.[122] 163 Company commemorated St Barbara, the patron saint of artillerymen, on 4 December, receiving greetings from former gunners.[123] The RNZA's Colonel Commandant, Brigadier Ray Andrews, visited BATT3 in April 2001, just before it handed over to BATT4. 16 Field organised a welcome-home medal parade. While the tour was less eventful than BATT2's, it was not without incident. The accidental drowning of Private 'Popeye' Atkins on 14 March hit members of 161 Company hard. As New Zealand soldiers in East Timor lacked access to alcohol, there were far fewer disciplinary problems than had occurred in Vietnam, for example.[124]

Embodying BATT3 interfered with the regiment's primary job: artillery training ceased for a year around the time of the deployment. 'It was a conscious decision by government to take the risk and not be artillery-capable.' A residual company trained, but not as gunners. The CGS wasn't willing to attempt a second rotation from the units comprising BATT3. The regiment was up to speed again within a year of its return, and there were also the positive outcomes common to other peacekeeping tours by gunners, including the dozen who served in Rhodesia in 1979 and a half-dozen sent to Solomon Islands in July 2003. Operational deployments provided experience. 'It took me 20 years to get one,' observed a Timor veteran. Most found it professionally rewarding, and exciting, to be doing what they were trained to do.[125]

Service in East Timor also identified personnel unable to meet expectations. 'The biggest fear for most military people is that they won't cope with fear, and it is quite a relief to realise that you can still operate under even very fearful conditions.' As always, a few proved unable to meet this challenge.[126]

> ### The RNZA's Community Role
> New Zealand's armed forces routinely carry out a range of activities to support other government agencies and the wider community. Regular Force units, especially those stationed in major centres, have sometimes been used as cheap labour. When 161 Battery was based at Papakura it was often called out to disasters and police manhunts, or to run institutions during industrial disputes. The gunners took over Auckland's Oakley hospital when psychiatric nurses went on strike; their charges included psychotic killers. One evening after lock-up a head-count found a patient missing, and a ladder underneath his second-storey window. After the police were informed it was realised that, as a 'trusty' who was allowed out, he had used the ladder to let himself back *in* after nipping down to the dairy. The artillery has run prisons, including Waikeria, Mount Eden and Manawatu, on several occasions. At the two latter locations the regiment stepped in during a fifteen-day prison officers' strike in September 1996, duty that was marred by the suicide of a Manawatu inmate.[127]
>
> 161 Battery was called out to a civil defence emergency in Te Aroha in February 1985. The Operations Officer arrived at 5 p.m. to find the local civil defence team knocking off for the day. 'The civil engineer had done a quick assessment of the dam above Te Aroha and said it could go at any time, and there would be something like seconds before a wall of water hit the town. So we had to have a sentry up there to tell us.' While the battery patrolled the evacuated town, one man sat in a Land Rover with the engine running in case the dam burst.[128]

The Last Territorial Gunner?

At the end of the century the Territorial Force batteries were abolished, leaving the RNZA comprising only the regular two-battery regiment at Linton. This changed a fundamental aspect of New Zealand's artillery make-up. Citizen gunners had provided the bulk of the manpower for active service, and the traditions associated with this 140-year link were not easily severed. Within a couple of years, the TF artillery would gain a reprieve.

Under a programme called TF Regionalisation, the TF batteries were disestablished in 1999, and (with one exception) their personnel 'infantryised' in battalion groups with an all-arms approach to combat. TF numbers fell from 5627 in 1990 to 2986 in 2000 (and 1888 by 2005).[129]

> 161 Battery has also assisted the civil power. It laid barbed wire at rugby grounds during the 1981 Springbok tour. It had helped police to prepare by acting as protesters in riot squad training at Papakura, 'attempting to obstruct the passage of a "springbok bus" and a "football crowd"'.[130] During the 1985 *Rainbow Warrior* affair, the Prime Minister feared a French raid to rescue or 'remove the embarrassment' of having two army officers in prison, convicted of manslaughter and arson. One of the pair, Captain Dominique Prieur, was moved from Mount Eden to Ardmore Detention Barracks in the dead of night while the gunners helped to guard the perimeter. 'It was very secret, but when we got there at 5 a.m. all the press cameras were there.'[131]
>
> The RNZA remains conscious of its place in society, and its ceremonies are community occasions. Gunners attend Anzac Day gatherings, provide funeral parties and march in Freedom of the City parades. On Gunners' Day, 26 May, RNZA members fire the dawn gun and drink coffee spliced with rum. They also raise money for charities such as the Cystic Fibrosis Association, towing an L5 howitzer on foot in Auckland's Round the Bays fun run.[132] Every gunner becomes familiar with Tchaikovsky's '1812 Overture', which is played frequently at tattoos and pageants.[133] The band is the public face of the Army at events such as rugby matches and Christmas parades. Members have attended shoots of another kind as extras in film and television productions.[134] The RNZA erects tents for community events, and assisted at both the 1974 and 1990 Commonwealth Games. Gunners have eradicated noxious animals on Stewart Island and served as aircraft loaders in Antarctica.[135]

At one annual camp 22 Battery fielded just twenty people, compared with around 75 in the 1970s. 3 Field's regimental HQ had been disbanded in 1990.[136] Its two batteries continued to independently train TF gunners, but falling numbers often necessitated amalgamation on exercise. In Exercise Southern Union in 1991, for example, 32(E) Battery mustered only 30 personnel, less than half its establishment.[137] The ranks of 11(A) Battery were boosted by a few TF personnel when the Army Air Corps, based at Hobsonville alongside 3 Squadron RNZAF, ceased to exist in July 1995.[138] 4(G) Medium's declining number of TF members led first to it teaming with 11(A) Battery on exercises, then to a marriage with the Auckland unit as 162 Battery in 1998, giving TF gunners a greater role in the regiment.*¹³⁹* This merger was very successful, with 22(D) Battery providing forward observer parties.

Poor TF performance had implications for the regular batteries, which could meet the regiment's requirement for initial deployment but would not be able to sustain this. Low TF numbers would also prevent the field regiment augmenting an initial deployment with two additional TF batteries as part of the Expanded Brigade Group.*¹⁴⁰* By the late 1990s the TF batteries had shown they were not up to the task.

Tradition had obstructed their reform. Links to antecedent batteries had been strengthened retrospectively in 1971 through a change of nomenclature. 'Everybody was saying you can't cut 31 Battery or 32 Battery – they'd been around 140 years.' Now TF Regionalisation began consolidation within regional boundaries, with all elements coming under the command of a TF regiment.*¹⁴¹* The aim was to blur the distinction between TF and RF, making the regular units 'centres of excellence' and training TF members to fill positions within previously full-time units. In this 'One Army', all new soldiers enjoyed the same combined-arms training. The first course for Auckland-Northland Regiment recruits took place on 30 July 1999.*¹⁴²*

Of the six TF regiments, only Auckland's would have an artillery role. Overturning the short-lived 162 Battery union, 11(A) and 4(G) Battery were merged as the Indirect Fire Support (IFS) Company for 3 Auckland-Northland Regiment.*¹⁴³* While the gunner RSM's title changed to Company Sergeant-Major, other trappings of a battery, such as the title 'gunner', remained. The guns (as a four-gun section) would now operate alongside a four-mortar section manned by existing battalion personnel. Battalion Groups were divided into three elements: combat (the infantry and armoured elements), Combat Support (including fire support, engineering and signals) and HQ (Administration Company). Auckland-Northland's IFS Company exercised for the first time in Exercise Baseline early in 1999, along with the reformed Mortar Platoon. They also fired at the last L118 shoot in June.*¹⁴⁴* Many TF gunners decided to leave, while some stayed reluctantly. Those dedicated to the artillery felt a loss of identity: they identified with the regiment, not as infantry. 'The camaraderie wasn't there,' recalls a warrant officer who experienced both environments. 'There was a division between us at first, the green berets [infantry] and sand berets [gunners]. But now we're all green berets.'[145]

Without TF batteries, the regiment could no longer provide three batteries for the IEF expanded brigade. With 22(D) Battery gone, gunners had to be sent from Linton to man Wellington's saluting battery. (Infantry units filled this role elsewhere.)[146] The South Island lost all connection with artillery. After being reduced to a troop, Dunedin's 31(B) Battery was disbanded on 12 June 1999, its personnel going to 4 Otago and Southland Battalion Group. In Christchurch, 32(E) Battery personnel formed an OP Troop attached to 2 Battalion Group.[147] 32(E) paraded as a battery for the last time in Hagley Park on 7 June 1999 to fire a 21-gun salute to Queen Elizabeth II, the Captain-General of the RNZA.[148] Low numbers blighted even this occasion: one of the four howitzers had to be manned by 'retired' gunners.[149]

The Territorial Force enjoyed an unexpected benefit from the peacekeeping mission in East Timor. On the surface, TF training suffered because of the drain on personnel,[150] but their value as a reserve was highlighted. TF members comprised 15 per cent of BATT3, and their willingness to serve overseas even at the cost of their jobs was salutary. The Timor experience also confirmed that the TF could sustain field deployments through multiple rotations.[151]

The next CGS, Major-General Jerry Mateparae, allowed Auckland-Northland Regiment's IFS Company to rename itself 11/4 Battery to retain a sense of identity for the two TF units, each of which contributed a troop. It also reaffiliated itself with 16 Field Regiment, while remaining under command of Auckland-Northland Battalion Group. Recruiting recovered, with 11/4 Battery numbers nearly doubling in 2003. As part of this reprieve, the remnants of 22(D) Battery returned to gunnery. Initially a reconnaissance troop was attached to the Wellington Company of 7 Wellington-Hawke's Bay Battalion Group. By June 2003 the company was training Mistral Detachment members, thereby providing the TF input to 43 Air Defence Battery.[152]

In early 2006, the TF element of the RNZA fired as an identifiable entity for the first time in the new millennium when 11/4 Battery joined 161 and 163 batteries on Titan 6, an eight-day regimental live-fire exercise at Waiouru.[153]

John ('Blackie') Burns.
2004.394, Kippenberger Military Archive, Army Museum Waiouru.

'BLACKIE' BURNS
Despite suffering from 'shyness and diffidence' as a young man,[154] John ('Blackie') Burns rose to the rank of brigadier and earned immense respect from his fellow gunners. Born in 1917, he had four years with St Patrick's College Cadets, Wellington. In 1936 he attended Duntroon, where he acquired his nickname, and then the Short Coast Artillery Course in Sydney. Commissioned in the Staff Corps, Burns's first positions were Adjutant 1 Heavy Group and instructing at Fort Dorset. He then joined 2NZEF, sailing with the Sixth Reinforcements in 1941. After getting some field artillery experience as a troop commander, Burns attended the Middle East Junior Staff School.[155] He was taken prisoner with 30 Battery of 6 Field near El Alamein on 5 July 1942. Escaping after several attempts, he took refuge in the Vatican City until the Allies liberated Rome. Made an MBE for this exploit, Burns immediately returned to the division.

After the war in Europe ended while he was home on leave, he was posted to coast artillery jobs and became GSO2 Army HQ. He attended various courses, including the British Military College of Science's Technical Staff Course at Shrivenham (1948–49). Promoted to major, he trained reinforcements for Kayforce before himself embarking for Korea early in 1953. He commanded 16 Field during the hard fighting that preceded the Armistice in July, and was admitted to the DSO. Returning in 1954 to the post of DRNZA, he relinquished this in 1959 to become Director of Cadets and from 1961 CO Army Schools (and commandant of Waiouru Camp). This fitted him for the post of Deputy Head of the New Zealand Defence Liaison Staff London, which he took up in 1964. He later commanded Home Command, retiring as New Zealand's then longest-serving soldier in 1972 after modernising the Army's welfare services. He was Colonel Commandant of the RNZA from 1975 until 1981 and remained actively involved in the RNZA history project until his death in January 2003.

Ron Hassett.
New Zealand Defence Force.

RON HASSETT

Ronald Hassett was 'a well-built lad of good physique and excellent character'.[156] He also had a good mind, and was soon recognised as officer material. Born in 1923, he grew up in the Wellington suburb of Mount Cook. After four years in the St Patrick's College Cadets he went to Duntroon in February 1941, graduating from a course shortened to two years by the war. After missing out on his chosen corps, the engineers, he drew straws with two colleagues for branches of the artillery – no one fancied anti-aircraft. Hassett lost, and was appointed to the school's anti-aircraft wing in 1943. Later in the year he left with the Eleventh Reinforcements, serving in the training regiment at Maadi before joining 5 Field in Italy in April 1944. Promoted to captain, he joined HQ 2 Div Arty in November as GSO3 Ops. He was chosen as the first commander of an Air OP Flight proposed for the Division early in 1945, but its formation was suspended as the war ended. Instead he was posted to Senior Staff College Middle East. After seven months with Rear HQ 2NZEF at Caserta, and appointments in London, he came home in 1947.

Hassett rejoined the RNZA and learned to fly in the first Army wings course at Wigram. He was soon posted back to London as Secretary of the

New Zealand Joint Services Liaison Staff. Two years later Major Hassett went to Larkhill as the second New Zealander to attend the Long Gunnery Staff Course. He came home in 1952 to be Chief Instructor at the School of Artillery before joining Kayforce as second in command of 16 Field Regiment. During his six months in a 'brutal' climate he relieved as regimental CO and even disarmed a 'berserk and irrational' soldier. He was mentioned in despatches.

Hassett returned to New Zealand, married and resumed his Chief Instructor role, in which he excelled at the 'cut and thrust' of exchanges with the Chief Instructors of other Schools.[157] A move to Linton in 1955 as Brigade Major Divisional Artillery allowed him to celebrate the birth of his son with sixteen rounds fired from 4 Medium Regiment's guns. He transferred to Army HQ in Wellington before being posted to 28 Commonwealth Brigade, Malaya, and then to the Australian Staff College.

Made an MBE, Lieutenant-Colonel Hassett returned to Wellington. As Director of Equipment, and Deputy Quartermaster-General from 1966, he helped prepare the Army for Vietnam. After a year as Deputy Chief of General Staff in 1970, Hassett was sent to the Royal College of Defence Studies (the renamed Imperial Defence College). As Assistant Chief of Defence Staff (Policy), he represented New Zealand at the ANZUS restart meeting in Honolulu in 1972. Hassett became Deputy Chief of Defence Staff in 1974 and two years later was made Chief of the General Staff (together with a spell as Aide-de-Camp to the Queen). In a period of budget cuts and reduced overseas commitments, his leadership qualities proved invaluable.

Hassett saw his biggest achievements as creating HQ Land Force, ending the Army's division into Field Force and Home Command, and setting up the office of Sergeant-Major of the Army as a conduit for communication with other ranks. He also reintroduced the lemon-squeezer hat for ceremonial purposes, and was the driving force behind the establishment of the Queen Elizabeth II Army Memorial Museum at Waiouru. Made a CBE in 1970, General Hassett earned appointment as a CB on his retirement in November 1978 as the last of the 'gunner generals'.

In retirement he set up a business in Kuala Lumpur promoting New Zealand exports. He was among the group of former defence chiefs who trenchantly criticised the Labour government's defence policies in the 1980s, and were in turn denigrated by Prime Minister Lange as 'geriatric generals'. Ron Hassett was Colonel Commandant of the RNZA from 1989 until 1994, and headed the Executive Management Committee of the Army Memorial Museum from 1992 to 1996. He died in August 2004.

Weapons – Field Gun

The development of a 105-mm light field gun to replace the 1956-vintage Italian pack howitzer of the same calibre began in the mid-1960s. It was accepted for British service in 1971, and by New Zealand in 1986. For firing it sits on its own turntable, like the 25-pr. The barrel is swung around and clamped to the trail for travelling. Eighteen of the 24 guns ordered by New Zealand were manufactured in Australia.

Name	Ordnance QF 105mm Light L118
Entered NZ service	1987
Role	field gun/howitzer (70° elevation)
Calibre	105 mm (4.1"), 30 cals
Range	15,000 m (16,400 yds)
Weight	1860 kg (4100 lb)
Projectile	15.8 kg (34.7 lb) – HE, HESH, smoke, shrapnel
Remarks	Traverse 11° on board, or 360° on the firing platform. The only gun still in service with the RNZA.

Weapons – Missiles

This man-portable air defence system intercepts enemy planes by detecting their infrared radiation. The two-stage solid-fuelled rocket has a speed of 1492 knots. A laser proximity fuse detonates it near the target. This was the first anti-aircraft system to enter New Zealand artillery service since the last of the 3.7-inch guns and 40-mm Bofors guns were mothballed in 1961.

Name	Mistral
Entered NZ service	1997
Role	anti-aircraft
Diameter	90 mm
Length	1.8 m
System weight	18 kg, plus 24 kg post
Range	5 km (4 km vs helicopters)
Warhead	3 kg HE with 3000 pellets
Remarks	All-weather and IFF radar purchased subsequently.

Conclusion

New Zealand's gunners have often felt both 'a sense of grim satisfaction that they had saved their infantry from danger' and a 'sorrowful awareness ... of what it must have been like at the receiving end'.[158] They have, as ever, a dual function in the twenty-first century: maintaining their efficiency and honing their craft in their primary role, and undertaking the non-gunnery duties required of all soldiers.

In the Army's current strategic plan, 'Army 2005', the RNZA's task is to provide fire support.[159] The fire support disciplines required of a modern army include long-range precision strike, round-the-clock surveillance and target acquisition, command and control of offensive fire, ground-based air defence and expertise in control of the battle space. Developments in equipment and systems suggest that the artillery of the future will require higher mobility. The indirect fire control system will be networked and digitised, and integrated into the overall command, control, communication, intelligence and logistic system.

In moving away from medium artillery, New Zealand diverged from an international consensus as to the value of the longer-range and more lethal 155-mm rounds. Most recent advances have occurred in this calibre. The RNZA's current guns have an operational life to 2012 but, given the Army's record on new purchases, are likely to remain in service well beyond that year.[160] Fire-plans for exercises with ABCA or FPDA forces now routinely combine artillery, mortars, armour and aircraft.[161] Other ABCA armies are considering new platform and delivery systems: wheeled and self-propelled medium guns, mortars, and lightweight rockets with much greater ranges than conventional artillery. In any event, some form of fire support will be necessary for as long as men, and women, go into battle.

Since at least the first Gulf War, the potential value of gunners in collective military actions has been apparent. After the 2001 terrorist attacks on the United States, such policing actions were stepped up. New Zealand has twice been invited to participate in conventional ground conflicts. The first request was accepted: small SAS parties were sent to Afghanistan in 2001. In 2003, sappers were deployed to Iraq after conventional fighting there ended. Gunners have filled key positions in the New Zealand-led Provincial

Reconstruction Team established in Afghanistan's Bamian province in 2003[162] to help create a more secure environment. In 2007, more than 120 Field Regiment gunners served in Bamian in two six-month deployments, patrolling for up to four weeks at a time from remote forward operating bases.

In its first century the RNZA was the élite corps of the New Zealand Army. For two decades the Chiefs of General Staff came almost exclusively from the artillery, whose officers dominated the regular force. With about 350 personnel in a 6300-strong Army, today's RNZA is a third of its 1985 size, and a shadow of its heyday strength. 16 Field has 260 personnel, there are around 50 TF gunners, and the rest are in non-gunnery appointments.[163] A deprioritising of the artillery's role over the last 30 years has seen a loss of capability; New Zealand's technical standing in comparison to similar arms overseas has slipped. But the RNZA has never lowered its standards.

Since 1902 more than 20,000 New Zealand artillery personnel have served overseas, and many more have been volunteers, territorials or conscripts within New Zealand.[164] Eight members of one family have served in the artillery, as have many fathers and sons.[165] The artillery has always been a powerful 'tribe within a tribe'; its members have always been proud to be gunners.

Notes

Introduction

1. This brief historical survey is derived mainly from D. Chandler (ed.), *The Oxford Illustrated History of the British Army*, Oxford University Press, Oxford/New York, 1994; J. Norris, *Artillery: A History*, Sutton Publishing, Stroud, 2000.
2. R. Holmes, *Acts of War: The Behaviour of Men in Battle*, revised edn, Cassell, London, 2003, pp. 297–98.
3. The title 'Royal Regiment of Artillery' was conferred in 1722. The Royal Horse Artillery, whose drivers were trained soldiers, was formed in 1793. A military Corps of Drivers was created the following year and abolished three decades later; thereafter drivers were also gunners. K. Brookes, *Battle Thunder: The Story of Britain's Artillery*, Osprey Publishing, Reading, 1973, pp. 31, 53, 89. (Gunners' Day, 26 May, derives from the formation by George I of the first regular artillery unit in Britain in 1716.)
4. J.B.A. Bailey, *Field Artillery and Firepower*, Military Press, Oxford, 1989, p. 118.
5. Granted to the Royal Regiment of Artillery by King William IV in 1833. Brookes, *Battle Thunder*, p. 90.

Chapter 1

1. This section is based especially on A. Salmond, *Two Worlds: First Meetings Between Maori and Europeans, 1642–1772*, Viking, Auckland, 1991; T.W. Bentley, 'Tribal Guns, Tribal Gunners: A Study of Acculturation by Maori of European Military Technology during the New Zealand Inter-tribal Musket Wars', MPhil. thesis, University of Waikato, 1997.
2. This section is based especially on Bentley, 'Tribal Guns, Tribal Gunners'; R.D. Crosby, *The Musket Wars: A History of Inter-Iwi Conflict*, Reed, Auckland, 1999.
3. J.S. Polack, *Manners and Customs of the New Zealanders…*, James Madden & Co., London, 1840, reprinted Capper Press, Christchurch, 1976, pp. 68, 86.
4. I. Wards, *The Shadow of the Land: A Study of British Policy and Racial Conflict in New Zealand, 1832–1852*, Department of Internal Affairs, Wellington, 1968, pp. 79, 233–34.
5. For the Northern War, see especially J. Belich, *The New Zealand Wars and the Victorian Interpretation of Racial Conflict*, Auckland University Press, Auckland, 1986, pp. 29–70; Wards, *Shadow of the Land*.
6. Lieutenant Wilmot RA, son of the Governor of Van Diemen's Land, assisted by two Peninsular War veterans, commanded a miscellany of Auckland militia and sailors with no experience of land-based sieges. See T. Ryan, 'Spies, Engineers and Artillerymen', *Forts and Works*, no. 6, Dec 1998, p. 4.
7. R. Hattaway, *Reminiscences of the Northern War*, 1899, quoted in M. Barthorp, *To Face the Daring Maoris: Soldiers' Impressions of the First Maori War, 1845–47*, Hodder & Stoughton, London et al., 1979, p. 95.
8. W.T. Power, *Sketches in New Zealand, with Pen and Pencil*, 1849, reprinted Capper Press, Christchurch, 1974, pp. 23, 38.
9. The main source for this box is Barthorp, *To Face the Daring Maoris*.
10. The Coehorn (also spelt 'Cohorn') was a 'stubby bronze tube mounted on a heavy wooden base plate' (I. McGibbon (ed.), *The Oxford Companion to New Zealand Military History*, Oxford University Press, Auckland, 2000, p. 336). Used in European sieges since the seventeenth century and light enough to be carried easily in the field, it fired an 8½-pound shell at a high angle over a shortish distance which varied with the amount of powder in the charge.

11. Quoted in J. Cowan, *The New Zealand Wars: A History of the Maori Campaigns and the Pioneering Period*, 1922–23, republished Government Printer, Wellington, 1983, vol. 1, p. 87.
12. No Royal Artillery units were stationed in Australia until 1856: C. Winter, 'The Origins of Australian Defence: The Royal Artillery in Australia and New Zealand, 1845 to 1870', *Army Journal*, Feb 1973, p. 38.
13. A 30-strong detachment apparently took seventeen months to reach New Zealand in 1854–5 (when their first ship sank they spent four months stranded on St Helena before returning to England): L. Barber, G. Clayton & J. Tonkin-Covell (eds), *Sergeant, Sinner, Saint, and Spy: The Taranaki War Diary of Sergeant William Marjouram, R.A.*, Random Century, Auckland, 1990, p. 5.
14. T. Ryan, 'Sieges, Sappers and Gunners', *Forts and Works*, no. 7, Jun 1999, p. 16.
15. Apr 1858 entries in Barber, Clayton & Tonkin-Covell (eds), *Sergeant, Sinner, Saint, and Spy*, p. 10.
16. The main source for this section is Belich, *NZ Wars*, pp. 73–116.
17. Cowan, *NZ Wars*, vol. 1, p. 188.
18. Ryan, 'Sieges, Sappers and Gunners', p. 17. 'Brigade' and 'battery' had replaced 'battalion' and 'company' respectively in RA terminology in 1859: Winter, 'Origins of Australian Defence', p. 38.
19. The new weapons were said to deliver more accurate fire at a range of 2 miles than smooth-bore guns did at half a mile. Nevertheless, the British Army reverted to muzzle-loading artillery from 1870 until the 1890s, partly on the grounds of expense.
20. For the Waikato War, see Belich, *NZ Wars*, pp. 119–76.
21. C Field Battery, 4 Brigade Royal Artillery, became 94 (New Zealand) Battery RA and is now 94 (New Zealand) Headquarters Battery, 4 Regiment RA. See 'The Battle of Rangiriri: The Application of Artillery in the New Zealand Land Wars', Royal New Zealand Artillery Old Comrades' Association website, http://www.riv.co.nz/rnza/hist/rang/index.htm, accessed 9 Aug 2005; A.F. Pickard, 'Remarks on the Operations of the Royal Artillery During the Campaigns in New Zealand, in 1861, and 1863–1864', *Minutes of the Royal Artillery Institution*, [1865,] reprinted in *The Volunteers*, vol. 10, no. 2, Sep 1983, pp. 63–65; Winter, 'Origins of Australian Defence', pp. 38–39.
22. Ryan, 'Sieges, Sappers and Gunners', p. 18. The first such tests had been conducted by Royal Engineers at Chatham in 1847: Ryan, 'Spies, Engineers and Artillerymen', pp. 4–5.
23. Lieutenant Arthur Frederick Pickard 'traversed the parapets under heavy defender cross-fire to provide water for the wounded [including his mortally wounded commander, Captain Mercer], and Assistant Surgeon William Temple provided medical aid'. 'The Battle of Rangiriri', RNZAOCA website, http://www.riv.co.nz/rnza/hist/rang/index.htm, accessed 10 Nov 2006.
24. Lieutenant-General Cameron to Secretary of State for War, 4 Mar 1864, *Supplement to the London Gazette*, 13 May 1864, reprinted in *The Volunteers*, vol. 15, no. 2, Jun 1989, p. 69.
25. For Gate Pa, see Belich, *NZ Wars*, pp. 178–88; M. Wright, *Two Peoples, One Land: The New Zealand Wars*, Reed, Auckland, 2006, pp. 141–50.
26. C. Pugsley, 'Walking the Taranaki Wars: Cameron's West Coast Campaign and the Battle of Nukumaru, 24–25 January 1865', *New Zealand Defence Quarterly*, no. 28, Autumn 2000, p. 28.
27. F.J.W. Gascoyne, *Soldiering in New Zealand, being Reminiscences of a Veteran*, T.J.S. Guilford, London, 1916, facsimile edn, Kiwi Publishers, Christchurch, 1999, p. 107.
28. Cowan, *NZ Wars*, vol. 1, pp. 321–5; vol. 2, pp. 109, 111, 126–7, 277.
29. T. Ryan and B. Parham, *The Colonial New Zealand Wars*, Grantham House, Wellington, 1986, p. 135.
30. Cowan, *NZ Wars*, vol. 2, p. 257.
31. Belich, *NZ Wars*, pp. 268, 271; Cowan, *NZ Wars*, vol. 2, p. 291.
32. The main sources for the material on New Zealand's nineteenth-century coastal defences are I. McGibbon, *The Path to Gallipoli: Defending New Zealand, 1840–1915*, GP Books, Wellington, 1991; P. Cooke, *Defending New Zealand: Ramparts on the Sea, 1840s–1950s*, Defence of New Zealand Study Group, Wellington, 2000, pp. 9–132.
33. These were the guns that had bombarded Meremere from Whangamarino Redoubt in 1863: W.L. Ruffell, 'The Royal Regiment of New Zealand Artillery (Regular Force): A Short History', *The Volunteers*, vol. 9, no. 1, Jun 1982, p. 31.
34. The *Daily Southern Cross* panicked Aucklanders by 'reporting' that many prominent citizens were being held hostage on a Russian cruiser which had put a prize crew aboard a British warship in the Waitemata. Its editor hoped to provoke debate on the defence of the colony. See McGibbon, *Path to Gallipoli*, pp. 27–28.
35. Annual reports, 'Volunteer Force of New Zealand', *AJHR*, 1880, H-10A, pp. 4, 13; 1881, H-23, p. 1.
36. 'Defences of New Zealand', *AJHR*, 1880, A-4, pp. 6–8, 23–28.
37. 'Cautley, Colonel Henry', in McGibbon (ed.), *Oxford Companion*, p. 80.

38. Annual reports on Constabulary Force and New Zealand Forces, *AJHR*, 1885, H-4, p. 1; 1886, H-13, pp. 1, 4, 7, H-18, p. 7.
39. The major sources for New Zealand's artillery volunteers are J.A.B. Crawford, 'The Role and Structure of the New Zealand Volunteer Force, 1885–1910', MA thesis, University of Canterbury, 1986; G. Clayton, 'Defence Not Defiance: The Shaping of New Zealand's Volunteer Force', PhD thesis, University of Waikato, 1990.
40. Minute Book, Auckland Volunteer Rifle Company, reproduced in *Official History of the Band of the Royal Regiment of New Zealand Artillery, Northern Military District*, Auckland Artillery Band Association, Auckland, 1964; Cooke, *Defending NZ*, pp. 138, 143; P. Dennerley, 'New Zealand's First Naval Volunteers', *The Volunteers*, vol. 11, no. 2, 1984, pp. 5–8; P. Dennerley, 'Naval Artillery in Nelson', *The Volunteers*, vol. 12, no. 2, 1985, pp. 11–12; R. Chapman, 'The Lyttelton Volunteer Artillery: A Brief History', *Forts and Works*, no. 1, Nov 1996, p. 12. Questions of seniority among corps are complicated by reorganisations in 1862 and 1866 during which existing units lapsed.
41. 'Second Report of the Civil Service Commissioners', *AJHR*, 1866, D-7A, pp. 22–23.
42. 'Reports of the Inspection of Certain Volunteer Corps in New Zealand', *AJHR*, 1868, D-4; G.C. Bliss, *Gunners' Story: A Short History of the Artillery Volunteers of Christchurch, 1867–1967*, Canterbury Artillery Officers' Mess, Christchurch, 1970, pp. 7, 10; Chapman, 'Lyttelton Volunteer Artillery', p. 13.
43. R.A. Chapman, 'A Brief History of the Lyttelton Artillery Volunteers', *The Volunteers*, vol. 13, no. 3, 1987, pp. 85, 90, 92; Annual reports on Volunteers, *AJHR*, 1871, G-5B, p. 15, table H; 1878, H-20; 1881, H-23, p. 2; 1886, H-13, p. 5.
44. Annual reports, *AJHR*, 1870, D-8A, p. 3; 1871, G-5B, p. 8.
45. Annual reports, *AJHR*, 1873, H-24A, p. 2; 1874, H-24, pp. 5–6; 1878, H-20; K.C. McDonald (ed. G. McLean), *Oamaru 1878: A Colonial Town*, Waitaki District Council, Oamaru, 2006, pp. 139–40.
46. Bliss, *Gunners' Story*, pp. 23, 24.
47. The guns of the Royal Artillery and its imperial offshoots are assumed to be their colours.
48. 'Annual Report on Volunteer Force', *AJHR*, 1879, Session II, H-15A. The batteries were designated as follows: A Auckland, B and L Dunedin, C and E Canterbury, D Wellington, F Napier, G and K Invercargill, H Nelson, I Oamaru, J Poverty Bay.
49. M.H.S. Stevens, 'New Zealand Defence Forces and Defence Administration, 1870–1900', MA thesis, Victoria University of Wellington, 1977, pp. 55–57; Chapman, 'Lyttelton Artillery Volunteers', p. 87; H. Slater, *Fifty Years of Volunteering: The Army of Regulations*, Whitcombe & Tombs, Christchurch, 1910, pp. 98–99.
50. 'Defence Forces of New Zealand', *AJHR*, 1900, H-19, p. 7.
51. Chapman, 'Lyttelton Artillery Volunteers', p. 93.
52. 'New Zealand Volunteer Force', *AJHR*, 1874, H-24, p. 1; Chapman, 'Lyttelton Artillery Volunteers', pp. 82–86.
53. 'Report on the Oamaru Encampment', *AJHR*, 1886, H-12; *Lyttelton Times*, 31 Mar 1891, quoted in Crawford, 'Role and Structure', p. 28.
54. Chapman, 'Lyttelton Artillery Volunteers', p. 84; Bliss, *Gunners' Story*, pp. 8 (quote), 10, 18, 22.
55. Bliss, *Gunners' Story*, pp. 13, 35–36.
56. Chapman, 'Lyttelton Artillery Volunteers', p. 90; Bliss, *Gunners' Story*, p. 21; McDonald, *Oamaru 1878*, p. 78.
57. E Battery's Surgeon was Sunnyside's Medical Superintendent: Bliss, *Gunners' Story*, pp. 21–22, 33, 34. *New Zealand Times*, 26 Mar 1886, quoted in S. Butterworth, *Petone: A History*, Petone Borough Council, Petone, 1988, p. 116.
58. Slater, *Fifty Years of Volunteering*, pp. 54, 61, 87; *Evening Post*, 26 Nov 1919; Butterworth, *Petone*, pp. 89, 116; M.J.G. Smart and A.P. Bates, *The Wanganui Story*, Wanganui Newspapers, Wanganui, 1972, p. 169; B.H. Bull, *The Years Between: Greytown Borough Centennial 1878–1978*, Roydhouse Publishing for Greytown Borough Council, Carterton, 1986, p. 25.
59. See Crawford, 'Role and Structure', pp. 47–52.
60. For an overview of the invasion of Parihaka, see D. Scott, *Ask That Mountain: The Story of Parihaka*, Reed/Southern Cross, Auckland, reprinted 1994.
61. The Nelson Naval Artillery was a new unit, the Naval Brigade having recently been disbanded because of 'mutinous conduct': Crawford, 'Role and Structure', p. 86.
62. Annual report on New Zealand Constabulary, *AJHR*, 1882, H-14, p. 3.
63. A. Ward, 'Documenting Maori History: The Arrest of Te Kooti Rikirangi Te Turuki, 1889', *New Zealand Journal of History*, vol. 14, no. 1, 1980, p. 38.
64. See Cowan, *NZ Wars*, vol. 2, pp. 499, 501.
65. Reports on Volunteer Force, *AJHR*, 1882, H-10; H-22, p. 1.
66. 'Annual Report on Volunteer Force', *AJHR*, 1883, H-17, pp. 1–3.
67. Annual Reports, *AJHR*, 1885, H-4A, p. 2; 1886, H-13, p. 2; 1887, Session I, H-12, p. 3.
68. Gascoyne, *Soldiering in NZ*, p. 132.

69. 'Defences of the Colony', *AJHR*, 1887, Session II, A-7, p. 1.
70. 'Report on the New Zealand Forces', *AJHR*, 1888, H-5, pp. 1, 3.
71. 'Report on the Military Forces and Defences of New Zealand', *AJHR*, 1890, H-10, pp. 2–3, 5.
72. J. Crawford, 'Overt and Covert Military Involvement in the 1890 Maritime Strike and 1913 Waterfront Strike in New Zealand', *Labour History*, no. 60, May 1991, pp. 69–70.
73. See McGibbon, *Path to Gallipoli*, pp. 74–80.
74. 'Report on the New Zealand Permanent and Volunteer Forces', part 1, *AJHR*, 1893, H-9, p. 38.
75. *AJHR*, 1893, H-9, pp. 12, 21, 26, 34, 35; H-9B, p. 8.
76. *AJHR*, 1893, H-9, p. 49; McGibbon, *Path to Gallipoli*, p. 93; Bliss, *Gunners' Story*, p. 30.
77. Crawford, 'Role and Structure', pp. 169, 172, 175; *The Cyclopedia of New Zealand*, Cyclopedia Company, Christchurch, vol. 3, 1903, pp. 976–7; vol. 6, 1908, p. 324.
78. 'Defences and Defence Forces of New Zealand', *AJHR*, H-19, 1895, p. 1; 1896, p. 5; McGibbon (ed.), *Oxford Companion*, p. 40.
79. *AJHR*, 1893, H-9, p. 5; 1898, H-19, p. 2.
80. Crawford, 'Role and Structure', pp. 164–65 (quote).
81. McGibbon, *Path to Gallipoli*, p. 87.
82. 'Defence Forces of New Zealand', *AJHR*, 1898, H-19, p. 1.
83. *AJHR*, 1901, pp. 3, 5, 6.
84. *Navy and Army Illustrated*, 1899–1900, cited in J.T. Gill, 'History of the New Zealand Army', typescript, NZ Defence Force Library, pp. 55–56.
85. Based on D. Veart, 'Design Pioneer or Liar of the Century: The Life of Lt Col Tudor Boddam', *Forts and Works*, no. 14, Jul 2002, pp. 11–15.
86. *AJHR*, 1886, H-13, p. 4.
87. *AJHR*, 1888, H-30, p. 12.
88. Based on F.J.W. Gascoyne, *Soldiering in New Zealand, being Reminiscences of a Veteran*, T.J.S. Guilford, London, 1916, facsimile edn, Kiwi Publishers, Christchurch, 1999.
89. E.C. Richards (ed.), *Diary of E.R. Chudleigh, 1862–1921, Chatham Islands*, Simpson & Williams, Christchurch, 1950, p. 395.

Chapter 2

1. The main sources for this section are D.O.W. Hall, *The New Zealanders in South Africa, 1899–1902*, War History Branch, Wellington, 1949; John Crawford with Ellen Ellis, *To Fight for the Empire: An Illustrated History of New Zealand and the South African War, 1899–1902*, Reed, Auckland, 1999.
2. C. Pugsley, *The ANZAC Experience: New Zealand, Australia and Empire in the First World War*, Reed, Auckland, 2004, pp. 41–43.
3. *AJHR*, 1900, H-6, p. 5 (nominal roll).
4. Ibid., H-6I, p. 1; H-6K, pp. 4–7.
5. A New Zealander [S.E. Hawdon], *New Zealanders and the Boer War, or Soldiers from the Land of the Moa*, Gordon & Gotch, Christchurch, n.d., p. 58.
6. N. Taylor, 'Saddle Up! The Story of Saddler Sergeant William (G.F.W.) Taylor, 5th and 8th New Zealand Contingents NZMR', *The Volunteers*, vol. 25, no. 2, pp. 92–101.
7. Battery Squadron Report, AD 34, 3/8009, Archives New Zealand.
8. Ibid.
9. Battery memorial, Albert Park, Auckland; Roll of Honour in Crawford, *To Fight for the Empire*, pp. 99–107.
10. T. Pakenham, *The Boer War*, Weidenfeld & Nicolson, London, 1979, pp. 345–46, 457.
11. *New Zealand Gazette* (*NZG*), 4/1903, 15 Jan 1903, p. 102; General Order (GO) 37/1903, 23 Jan 1903. Approval for the title Royal New Zealand Engineers was sent in October 1902 (Secretary of State for Colonies to Governor NZ, 15 Oct 1902, *AJHR*, 1903, A-2, p. 42). The title Royal New Zealand Artillery had been requested by the New Zealand government the previous year, a few days after the end of a royal visit by the Duke and Duchess of Cornwall in which the military had played a prominent ceremonial role (Ranfurly to Secretary of State for Colonies, 2 Jul 1901, *AJHR*, 1902, A-1, p. 14). Approval was sent in October 1901 (Chamberlain to Governor NZ, 24 Oct 1901, *AJHR*, 1902, A-2, p. 63).
12. I. McGibbon, *Kiwi Sappers: The Corps of Royal New Zealand Engineers' Century of Service*, Reed, Auckland, 2002, pp. 30, 60.

13. See W.L. Ruffell, 'The New Zealand Permanent Force', Royal New Zealand Artillery Old Comrades' Association website, http://www.riv.co.nz/rnza/hist/pf/pf4.htm#rnza, accessed 9 Aug 2005.
14. *AJHR*, 1902, H-19, p. 1, and subsequent Annual Reports; I. McGibbon, *The Path to Gallipoli: Defending New Zealand, 1840–1915*, GP Books, Wellington, 1991, pp. 196–97.
15. *AJHR*, H-19, 1903, pp. 3–4; 1904, p. 3.
16. GO 28/1903. The companies (excluding the Westport unit) were formed into divisions, one at each main port, as follows: Auckland Division 1, 8 and 9 companies; Wellington Division 4 and 6 companies; Lyttelton Division 5 and 7 companies; Dunedin Division 2 and 3 companies.
17. *The Cyclopedia of New Zealand*, vol. 2, Cyclopedia Company, Christchurch, 1902, pp. 163–64.
18. GO 25/1903, effective 18 Dec 1902.
19. GO 28/1903 (12 Jan 1903), effective 19 Dec 1902.
20. GO 27/1903 (12 Jan 1903), effective 19 Dec 1902.
21. *AJHR*, 1904, H-19, p. 2.
22. *AJHR*, 1903, H-19, p. 4.
23. As recounted in Parliament by George Fowlds, MP for Grey Lynn, *NZPD*, 4 Nov 1903, vol. 127, pp. 323, 333; 8 Aug 1905, vol. 133, p. 479.
24. *AJHR*, 1905, H-19, p. 7.
25. *Otago Daily Times*, 28 May 1903; Master Gunner George Richardson to Artillery Staff Officer, 24 February 1905, on Richardson's Personal File, D 1/314/2, NZ Defence Force.
26. *AJHR*, 1905, H-19, p. 3.
27. *AJHR*, H-19, 1901, p. 4; 1906, p. 5.
28. G.C. Bliss, *Gunners' Story: A Short History of the Artillery Volunteers of Christchurch, 1867–1967*, Canterbury Artillery Officers' Mess, Christchurch, 1970, pp. 51–2; *AJHR*, 1905, H-19, p.3.
29. The conditions for the two challenge shields and the examination results for each company are set out in *AJHR*, 1906, H-19, pp. 12–21. See also S. Butterworth, *Petone: A History*, Petone Borough Council, Petone, 1988, p. 116.
30. *AJHR*, 1910, H-19, p.3.
31. See J.A.B. Crawford, 'The Role and Structure of the New Zealand Volunteer Force', MA thesis, University of Canterbury, 1986, pp. 226–27. The standard of training and readiness of the various corps are evaluated in the Annual Reports of the Commandant (from 1907, of the Council of Defence) reproduced as *AJHR*, H-19.
32. From P. Cooke, *Defending New Zealand: Ramparts on the Sea, 1840–1950s*, Defence of New Zealand Study Group, Wellington, 2000, p. 199.
33. GO 27/1903 (effective 19 Dec 1902).
34. *AJHR*, H-19, 1900, p. 4; 1901, pp. 4, 10; 1904, p. 3; 1906, p. 1; Cooke, *Defending NZ*, pp. 183–85, 199.
35. *AJHR*, H-19, 1913–14; Cooke, *Defending NZ*, p. 200. The rejected mountain guns were subsequently sold to Turkey and, according to Australia's official historian, C.E.W. Bean, deployed against the ANZACs on Gallipoli in 1915. See P. Cooke, 'The Poor Cousin: New Zealand's Home Defence in World War One', paper to 'Zealandia's Great War' conference, 10 Nov 2003, pp. 6–9.
36. Cooke, *Defending NZ*, pp. 55, 102–103, 116–17, 835; also Sir W.J. Steward, *NZPD*, 8 Aug 1905, vol. 133, p. 481 (re Fort Ballance accident); *AJHR*, 1903, H-19, p. 4.
37. R.J. McDougall, *New Zealand Naval Vessels*, GP Books, Wellington, 1989, pp. 163–64.
38. *AJHR*, 1906, H-19, p. 7.
39. 'Defence Scheme of New Zealand', Part III, Auckland District, p. 22.
40. *AJHR*, 1911, H-19, p. 2.
41. *AJHR*, 1900, H-19, pp. 1–2.
42. McGibbon, *Path to Gallipoli*, pp. 131–35.
43. *AJHR*, H-19, 1910, p. 2; 1912, pp. 13–14.
44. *AJHR*, H-19 (figures included each year). See Cooke, *Defending NZ*, p. 174, for data on RNZA strength between 1909 and 1939.
45. *AJHR*, 1914, H-19A, p. 23.
46. Ibid., H-19, p. 4.
47. This account relies on J. Crawford, 'Overt and Covert Military Involvement in the 1890 Maritime Strike and 1913 Waterfront Strike in New Zealand', *Labour History*, no. 60, May 1991', pp. 66–83.
48. This biography is based on I. McGibbon, 'Richardson, George Spafford 1868–1938', *The Dictionary of New Zealand*

Biography, vol. 3, Auckland University Press/Department of Internal Affairs, Wellington/Auckland, 1996, pp. 429–31; Richardson's Personal File, D 1/314/2, NZ Defence Force; Obituaries, *Evening Post*, 14 Jun; *Dominion*, 15 Jun 1938.
49. Richardson to ASO, 24 Feb; OC District to ASO, 6 Apr 1905, both on Richardson's Personal File.
50. Two other sons were also in the artillery, Lieutenant Hugh Richardson in 6 Field Regiment and Captain Guy Richardson in 4 Battery. Hugh would be killed in action while Guy died at the age of 35, four years after being wounded twice.
51. A.H. Russell to Sir James Allen, 3 Apr 1918, Allen Papers, J 1/9, Archives New Zealand (thanks to John Crawford).
52. This biography is based on G.H. Scholefield (ed.), *A Dictionary of New Zealand Biography*, Department of Internal Affairs, Wellington, 1940, vol. 1, p. 134; Obituary, *Dominion*, 4 Mar 1937.
53. For Campbell's rugby career, see T. Donoghue, *Athletic Park: A Lost Football Ground*, Tim Donoghue Publications, Wellington, 1999, pp. 3–6, 18; R.H. Chester & N.A.C. McMillan, *The Encyclopedia of New Zealand Rugby*, Moa Publications, Auckland, 1981, pp. 223, 249.
54. *The Cyclopedia of New Zealand*, vol. 1, Cyclopedia Company, Wellington, 1897, p. 133.
55. *New Zealand Free Lance*, 14 Dec 1912, cited in M. McKinnon, *Treasury: The New Zealand Treasury, 1840–2000*, Auckland University Press, Auckland, 2003, p. 99.

Chapter 3
1. P. Cooke, *Defending New Zealand: Ramparts On the Sea, 1840–1950s*, Defence of New Zealand Study Group, Wellington, 2000, pp. 185, 189.
2. Alfred Evenden, MS-Papers 91-264, Alexander Turnbull Library (ATL), p. 14.
3. Bert Stokes, interviewed by N. Boyack and J. Tolerton, *In the Shadow of War: New Zealand Soldiers Talk About World War One and Their Lives*, Penguin, Auckland, 1990, p. 223; Cooke, *Defending NZ*, p. 183.
4. Cooke, *Defending NZ*, p. 193.
5. This section is based on S.J. Smith, *The Samoan (N.Z.) Expeditionary Force, 1914–15*, Ferguson & Osborn, Wellington, 1924.
6. Logan to Governor, 2 Sep 1914, *AJHR*, 1915, H-19C.
7. Stokes, in Boyack & Tolerton, *In the Shadow of War*, p. 226; E.E.P. Wix, memoir, p. 49, MS-Papers-2214, ATL; A.T. Stratton, MS-Papers-3823, ATL, p. 2; Roll 92, NZEF Rolls; [A.W. Brainsby, (ed.)], *Pirate Von Luckner and the Cruise of the 'Seeadler'*, Geddis & Blomfield, Auckland, 1919; Gunner Harry L. Dixon, diary entry for 21 Dec 1917, reproduced in 'The Search for Von Luckner', *The Volunteers*, vol. 5, no. 5, Feb 1978, p. 17.
8. I. McGibbon, *The Path to Gallipoli: Defending New Zealand, 1840–1915*, GP Books, Wellington, 1991, p. 240.
9. J.R. Byrne, *New Zealand Artillery in the Field 1914–18*, Whitcombe & Tombs, Auckland et al., 1922, p. 4.
10. *AJHR*, 1912, Session II, H-19, p. 6.
11. Byrne, *NZ Artillery*, p. 12; P. Norman, *A Silent Soldier: The Story of Edward Gilbert Norman*, Bowstring Press, Greytown, 2000, p. 21.
12. F. Waite, *The New Zealanders at Gallipoli*, Whitcombe & Tombs, Auckland et al., 1919, pp. 14–31; Byrne, *NZ Artillery*, pp. 15–17.
13. Gunner Eric Burnett to father, 12 Jul 1915, MS-Papers-2091-1, ATL.
14. John W. Muldoon, diary entry, 1 Jan 1915, MS-Papers-4309, ATL.
15. Muldoon diary, 21 Dec 1914. Wes Muldoon was the uncle of future Prime Minister Sir Robert Muldoon. See B. Gustafson, *His Way: A Biography of Robert Muldoon*, Auckland University Press, Auckland, 2000, pp. 17–18.
16. Muldoon diary, 29 Jan 1915.
17. Waite, *New Zealanders at Gallipoli*, p. 47.
18. Byrne, *NZ Artillery*, pp. 19–20.
19. Ibid., p. 22; Waite, *New Zealanders at Gallipoli*, pp. 64–73.
20. Waite, *New Zealanders at Gallipoli*, pp. 74–85; Byrne, *NZ Artillery*, pp. 25–26.
21. Gunner Eric Burnett to father, 6 Jun 1915, MS-Papers-2091-1, ATL.
22. Byrne, *NZ Artillery*, pp. 28–30.
23. George Francis Armstrong, diary entries, 5, 8 May 1915, MSX-4176, ATL.
24. H.C.M. Norris, 'Lecture on the History of the 2nd Battery', 22 Oct 1936, typescript provided by E.J. Valintine.
25. T. Kinloch, *Echoes of Gallipoli in the Words of New Zealand's Mounted Riflemen*, Exisle Publishing, Auckland, 2005, pp. 127–28.
26. Armstrong diary, 18, 19 May 1915.
27. Byrne, *NZ Artillery*, pp. 38, 46.

28. Ibid., pp. 61–66.
29. Gunner Eric Burnett to father, 6 Jun, 12 Jul 1915. MS-Papers-2091-1, ATL. Burnett was from Napier, which has a more salubrious Marine Parade.
30. Diaries of Brigadier-General G.N. Johnston, 01/12/1, Imperial War Museum, London (courtesy John Crawford), entries for 4 Jul, 13 Aug 1915.
31. O.E. Burton, *The Silent Division: New Zealanders at the Front, 1914–1919*, Angus & Robertson, Sydney, 1935, pp. 82–83.
32. Johnston diary, 1, 3 Jul 1915.
33. Symon commanded 1 Brigade (1 and 3 Field Batteries and 6 (Howitzer) Battery), and Sykes 2 Brigade (2 and 5 Field Batteries and 4 (Howitzer) Battery): Byrne, *NZ Artillery*, p. 60.
34. Ibid., pp. 67–71.
35. Johnston diary, 3, 4 Aug 1915.
36. Byrne, *NZ Artillery*, pp. 71–74.
37. 'Historical Records and War Diary, 1 Battery, NZFA', [Maj C. McGilp, Diary], 6, 7 Aug 1915, MS-1172, ATL.
38. A Native Contingent initially raised for garrison duty had been sent to Gallipoli in July. Its members dug trenches and performed other labouring duties as well as fighting the Turks. A. Gould, 'Maori and the First World War', in I. McGibbon (ed.), *The Oxford Companion to New Zealand Military History*, Oxford University Press, Auckland, 2000, p. 297.
39. Byrne, *NZ Artillery*, pp. 75–85.
40. Johnston diary, 12 Aug 1915.
41. Byrne, *NZ Artillery*, pp. 32, 78–79.
42. Ibid., pp. 70–1, 84; Johnston diary, 9, 10 Aug 1915.
43. Byrne, *NZ Artillery*, pp. 86–89.
44. Kinloch, *Echoes of Gallipoli*, p. 260.
45. Byrne, NZ Artillery, pp. 90–94.
46. Johnston diary, 26 Oct 1915.
47. Waite, *Gallipoli*, p. 276.
48. Gunner Arthur Henning Currey, account published in C. Townsend, *Gallipoli 1915: Tribute to Those Who Were There*, author, Paeroa, 1999.
49. Gunner Eric Burnett to father, 12 Jul 1915; to parents, 9 Sep 1915, MS-Papers-2091-1, ATL.
50. O.E. Burton, *The New Zealand Division*, Clark & Matheson, Auckland, 1936, p. 19.
51. J. Millen, *Salute to Service: A History of the Royal New Zealand Corps of Transport and its Predecessors 1860–1996*, Victoria University Press, Wellington, 1997, pp. 79–80, 83.
52. Johnston diary, 3 Jul, 2, 14 Aug, 25 Oct 1915.
53. Ibid., 3 Jul 1915.
54. Muldoon diary, page 'Written in Malta'.
55. Johnston diary, 13, 14 Aug 1915.
56. Gunner Frank Humphreys, diary, MS-Papers-1623, ATL, entries for 31 Oct, 3, 15 Nov, 5 Dec 1915.
57. Burton, *NZ Division*, p. 47.
58. Gunner Robert Wait, NZFA, diary entry, 6 Jun 1915, cited in C. Pugsley, *Gallipoli: The New Zealand Story*, Hodder & Stoughton, Auckland, 1984, p. 200.
59. Johnston diary, 8, 10, 13 Aug 1915.
60. Byrne, *NZ Artillery*, pp. 100, 103–106.
61. Ibid., p. 119.
62. Bertram Oliver Stokes, MS-Papers-4888-1, ATL, diary entry, 11 Jan 1917.
63. John Eric Beveridge, in Boyack and Tolerton, *In the Shadow of War*, p. 158.
64. Byrne, *NZ Artillery*, p. 303.
65. C.H. Weston, *Three Years With the New Zealanders*, Skeffington, London, c.1919, pp. 134–35.
66. Army HQ, 'NZEF – Its Provison and Maintenance', Wellington, 1919, p. 7; H.T.B. Drew, 'The New Zealand Camps in England', in Drew (ed.), *The War Effort of New Zealand*, Whitcombe & Tombs, Auckland et al., 1923, p. 257.
67. Byrne, *NZ Artillery*, p. 216.
68. Stokes diary, 29 Jan, 4 Feb 1917.
69. Byrne, *NZ Artillery*, pp. 106–107.
70. Ibid., p. 113.

71. H. Stewart, *The New Zealand Division: A Popular History Based on Official Records, 1916–1919*, Whitcombe & Tombs, Auckland et al., 1921, p. 25.
72. Burton, *Silent Division*, p. 150.
73. C. Malthus, letter 11 Jun 1916, in his *Armentières and the Somme*, Reed, Auckland, 2002, pp. 54, 77.
74. A. Aitken, *Gallipoli to the Somme: Recollections of a New Zealand Infantryman*, Oxford University Press, London, 1963, p. 74.
75. J.T. MacCurdy, *The Structure of Morale*, cited in R. Holmes, *Acts of War: The Behaviour of Men in Battle*, Weidenfeld & Nicolson, London, 2003 edn, p. 170.
76. Gunner Norman Hassell, 'Memories of France', MS-Papers-2295, ATL.
77. Holmes, *Acts of War*, pp. 213–15.
78. Byrne, *NZ Artillery*, p. 113; John C. Heseltine, MSX-4337, ATL, diary entries, 29 Dec 1917, 24, 29 Jan 1918.
79. S.W.H. Rawlins, 'A History of the Development of the British Artillery in France, 1914–1918', typescript compiled from records of the MGRA at GHQ, designated 'UNOFFICIAL. For Private Reference Only', n.d., pp. 100–101, Stagg Collection, Kippenberger Archive.
80. C. Pugsley, *The ANZAC Experience: New Zealand, Australia and Empire in the First World War*, Reed, Auckland, 2004, pp. 175–76, 183; Godley to Allen, 15 Jul 1916, J. Allen Papers, M1/15, in Millen, *Salute to Service*, p. 109.
81. Stewart, *NZ Division*, pp. 28–29.
82. For an overview, see 'Weapons of War: Poison Gas', www.firstworldwar.com/weaponry/gas.htm, accessed 18 Jul 2002; also R. Harris and J. Paxman, *A Higher Form of Killing: The Secret Story of Gas and Germ Warfare*, Chatto and Windus, London, 1982, pp. 16–19.
83. A.D. Carbery, *The New Zealand Medical Service in the Great War, 1914–1918*, Whitcombe & Tombs, Auckland, 1924, pp. 119, 254.
84. See Carbery, p. 254.
85. Robert H. Scott, MS-Papers-1649, ATL, diary entry, 25 Jul 1916.
86. Stokes diary, 27 Jan 1917.
87. Hankins diary, 28 Sep 1916.
88. Scott diary, 15 Apr 1917.
89. A.T. Stratton, memoir, p. 2, MS-Papers-3823, ATL.
90. Heseltine diary, 14 Aug, 28 Dec 1917, 30 Jan 1918.
91. Johnston diary, 7 Jun 1916.
92. Heseltine diary, 10 Dec 1917.
93. Byrne, *NZ Artillery*, pp. 121, 128.
94. Gunner Clarence Hankins, diary entry, 27 Sep 1916, MS-Papers-1439, ATL.
95. Byrne, *NZ Artillery*, p. 129.
96. NZ General Staff, 'Notes for the Employment of Gas Shells', 23 Aug 1916, WA 20, 3/6/63, Archives NZ, cited in O. Wilkes, *A History of New Zealand Chemical Warfare, 1845–1945*, Working Paper no. 4, Centre for Peace Studies, University of Auckland, 1993, p. 19.
97. Byrne, *NZ Artillery*, p. 129.
98. Scott diary, 14 Sep 1916.
99. Hankins diary, 19, 20 Sep 1916.
100. Byrne, *NZ Artillery*, pp. 137–38.
101. Diary of Lieutenant Wilfred Fitchett, 26 Sep 1916, reproduced in S. and R. Fitchett, *New Zealand's Sons Awake to Glory!*, authors, Christchurch, 2000, p. 108.
102. Byrne, *NZ Artillery*, pp. 139–42.
103. Ibid., pp. 142–47.
104. Hankins diary, 27 Sep 1916.
105. Byrne, *NZ Artillery*, pp. 148–51.
106. Byrne, *NZ Artillery*, pp. 152–56.
107. Heseltine diary, 22 Apr, 14, 16 May [actually Jun] 1917.
108. Ibid., 24 Jan, 21 Feb, 23 Mar, 16, 18, 21–22 Jun, 4 Sep, 9 Dec 1917.
109. Ibid., 19 Jul, 8, 10 Sep 1917.
110. Scott diary, 22 Jun 1916; Byrne, *NZ Artillery*, p. 281.
111. Weston, *Three Years With the New Zealanders*, p. 119. Minenwerfer threw mines – 'huge canisters with a thin metal case

and a great weight of high explosive, which burst with a terrific rending report to make holes ten feet deep and fifteen feet or more across'. Their fuse-lights arced across the sky for up to five seconds before impact. Aitken, *Gallipoli to the Somme*, pp. 78, 93.

112. War Diary of Divisional Trench Mortar Officer, 12 Nov 1916, Fleurbaix, WA 105/1, Archives NZ. 92 rounds had been fired.
113. Ibid., 18 Nov, 11 Dec 1916.
114. Nominal Roll, Divisional Trench Mortar Officer, WA 105/2, Archives NZ.
115. Army HQ, 'NZEF – Its Provison and Maintenance', Wellington, 1919; Byrne, *NZ Artillery*, p. 157.
116. Byrne, *NZ Artillery*, pp. 159–60.
117. James M. Richmond, letter to aunt, 14 Dec 1916, 77-173-21/1, ATL.
118. Russell diary, 5 Mar 1917, quoted in Pugsley, *ANZAC Experience*, p. 213.
119. Byrne, *NZ Artillery*, pp. 160–61.
120. Pugsley, *ANZAC Experience*, pp. 183–85.
121. Scott diary, 1, 11 Jun 1917.
122. Byrne, *NZ Artillery*, pp. 162–65.
123. Ibid., pp. 166–68.
124. Burton, *Silent Division*, p. 195.
125. 'Official Programme of NZEF Championship Meeting, Trentham, Saturday 30 January 1915', Papers of Farrier Sergeant Reg. J. Hancock, MS-Papers-2323, ATL.
126. Byrne, *NZ Artillery*, p. 102.
127. Heseltine diary, 24 Feb, 2, 13 May 1917; Byrne, *NZ Artillery*, pp. 164, 183, 232.
128. Burton, *Silent Division*, p. 198; Stewart, *NZ Division*, p. 34.
129. Burton, *NZ Division*, p. 78.
130. Johnston diary, 8 Jun 1917.
131. Byrne, *NZ Artillery*, pp. 169–70; McGibbon (ed.), *Oxford Companion*, p. 185.
132. Johnston diary, 8 Jun 1917; Item 17 in Order No. 86 to 3 NZ Rifle Brigade, 4 Jun 1917, for attack on Messines–Wytschaete Ridge, in W. Fergusson Hogg, MS Papers 1102-1, ATL.
133. Byrne, *NZ Artillery*, p. 177.
134. Ibid., p. 179.
135. Ibid., pp. 166, 182.
136. Ibid., pp. 185–86.
137. I.N. Ingham diary, published as *Anzac Diary: A Nonentity in Khaki*, Treharne Publishers, Christchurch, n.d., p. 48.
138. Byrne, *NZ Artillery*, pp. 186–88.
139. Private Athol Stretton, 'Passchendaele As I Saw It: The Storming of the Abraham Heights, October 4th 1917', *The Volunteers*, vol. 7, no. 4, Mar 1981, p. 16.
140. Johnston diary, 10 Oct 1917.
141. 'Experiences of Gunner Alfred Thomas Stratton, 35467', quoted in G. Harper, *Massacre at Passchendaele: The New Zealand Story*, HarperCollins, Auckland, 2000, p. 63.
142. Johnston diary, 11 Oct 1917.
143. Russell diary, 11 Oct 1917, quoted in Harper, *Massacre at Passchendaele*, p. 62.
144. G. Sheffield, *Forgotten Victory: The First World War – Myths and Realities*, Headline Book Publishing, London, 2001, pp. 178–80.
145. Leonard Hart, letter to family, 19 Oct 1917, quoted in Phillips, Boyack and Malone (eds), *The Great Adventure*, p. 145.
146. Byrne, *NZ Artillery*, pp. 193–95.
147. Johnston diary, 12 Oct 1917.
148. Ibid. Johnston continued in this vein the following day: 'Exhausted men struggling through mire cannot compete against men in ferro concrete boxes with machine guns waiting for them'.
149. Byrne, *NZ Artillery*, pp. 196–99.
150. Ibid., pp. 200, 202–204.
151. R. Norman Geary, diary, 3 Dec 1917, in Phillips, Boyack and Malone (eds), *The Great Adventure*, p. 105.
152. Heseltine diary, 14–21 Dec 1917; Byrne, *NZ Artillery*, p. 209.
153. Pugsley, *ANZAC Experience*, p. 163; Byrne, *NZ Artillery*, pp. 209–210.
154. Byrne, *NZ Artillery*, pp. 212–14.

155. Christchurch *Press*, 11 Nov 1967.
156. Army HQ, 'NZEF, Its Provision and Maintenance', 1919, p. 6.
157. Heseltine diary, 25 Feb 1918.
158. *New Zealand Parliamentary Debates*, vol. 181, 19 Oct 1917, p. 271.
159. W. Lawson, *Featherston Military Training Camp: Being a Record of its Wonderful Growth and Daily Operation – Soldiers in the Making*, Brett Publishing, Auckland, 1917, pp. 59–67.
160. Byrne, *NZ Artillery*, pp. 216–21.
161. Ibid., pp. 222–24.
162. Ibid., pp. 225–27.
163. Ibid., pp. 237–41.
164. Ibid., pp. 241–46.
165. Ibid., pp. 246–48.
166. Ibid., pp. 228–29, 248–49.
167. Ibid., pp. 229–30.
168. Ibid., pp. 231–36.
169. Ibid., pp. 250–5; Pugsley, *ANZAC Experience*, p. 270.
170. Ibid., pp. 255–64.
171. Ibid., pp. 267–72.
172. Ibid., pp. 272–73.
173. Pugsley, *ANZAC Experience*, p. 295; Byrne, *NZ Artillery*, pp. 275–77.
174. Ibid., pp. 277–78.
175. Ibid., pp. 279–81.
176. Ibid., p. 282; Johnston diary, 28 Oct 1918.
177. Byrne, *NZ Artillery*, pp. 289–91.
178. Ingham diary, 5 Nov 1918, in *Anzac Diary*, p. 132.
179. Byrne, *NZ Artillery*, pp. 291–93; Johnston diary, 5 Nov 1918.
180. Byrne, *NZ Artillery*, pp. 293–95.
181. J.D. Hutchison, diary entry, 11 Nov 1918, MS-Papers 4172, ATL.
182. Byrne, *NZ Artillery*, pp. 295–96.
183. Ernest Marsden, Professor of Physics at Victoria University College, who had enlisted in January 1916 and been posted to the Divisional Signals Company, was involved in the development of sound-ranging techniques in 1917 while on secondment to the Royal Engineers. McGibbon (ed.), *Oxford Companion*, p. 312.
184. Byrne, *NZ Artillery*, p. 304.
185. Burton, *Silent Division*, p. 313.
186. Lieutenant-Colonel J.P.E. Veale, DAC, NZFA, diary entries, 20, 25 Dec 1918, Manuscript 1999-1631, Kippenberger Archive, Waiouru,
187. Byrne, *NZ Artillery*, pp. 302, 306–308.
188. This biography is based on Johnston's Personal File, Base Records, NZ Defence Force; R. Grover, 'Johnston, George Napier', in I. McGibbon (ed.), *The Oxford Companion to New Zealand Military History*, Oxford University Press, Auckland, 2000, p. 260; A. Taylor (ed.), *The New Zealand Roll of Honour: New Zealanders Who Have Served Their Country In Peace and War, 150 Years, 1845–1995*, Alister Taylor, Auckland, 1998.
189. J.S. Bolton, *A History of the Royal New Zealand Army Ordnance Corps*, The Corps, Wellington, 1992.
190. Draft, Commanding Officer NZ Military Forces to Minister of Defence, May 1912, in file 'Mountain Battery – Correspondence Re', AD 1, 57/5/1, Archives NZ.
191. F. Glen, *Bowler of Gallipoli: Witness to the Anzac Legend*, Army History Unit, Canberra, 2004, pp. 20–21.
192. A.H. Russell to Sir James Allen, 3 Apr 1918, Allen Papers, J 1/9, Archives NZ (thanks to John Crawford).
193. W. McDonald, *Honours and Awards to the New Zealand Expeditionary Force in the Great War 1914–18*, Helen McDonald, Napier, 2001, p. 164.
194. T. Kinloch, *Echoes of Gallipoli in the Words of New Zealand's Mounted Riflemen*, Exisle Publishing, Auckland, 2005, p. 170; C.H. Weston, *Three Years With the New Zealanders*, Skeffington, London, c.1919, p. 47.
195. H. Stewart, *The New Zealand Division, 1916–1919: A Popular History Based on Official Records*, Whitcombe & Tombs, Auckland et al., 1921, p. 329; W.E.L. Napier, *With the Trench Mortars in France*, Alpe Bros, Auckland, 1923, pp. 94–95; J.R. Byrne, *New Zealand Artillery in the Field 1914–18*, Whitcombe & Tombs, Auckland et al., 1922, p. 119; W.L. Ruffell,

'The Mortar', RNZAOCA website, http://www.riv.co.nz/rnza/hist/mortar/ndx.htm, accessed 17 Jun 2005.
196. Byrne, *NZ Artillery*, p. 205.
197. Entries for late 1916 and early 1918, War Diary, Divisional Trench Mortar Officer, WA 105/1, Archives NZ.
198. N.E. Hassell, MS-Papers-2295, Alexander Turnbull Library.
199. Byrne, *NZ Artillery*, p. 301.
200. Ibid., pp. 230, 301.
201. Ibid., p. 248.
202. Ibid., pp. 301–302.
203. Ibid., p. 235.
204. C. Malthus, *Armentières and the Somme*, Reed, Auckland, 2002, p. 96.

CHAPTER 4

1. J.R. Byrne, *New Zealand Artillery in the Field 1914–18*, Whitcombe & Tombs, Auckland et al., 1922, pp. 307–308; GO 84/1922; Annual Report, *AJHR*, 1920, H-19, p. 2.
2. M.M. Gard'ner, Personal File, NZ Defence Force.
3. *AJHR*, 1923, H-19, p. 2. The figures are for 30 June in each year. See also W.D. McIntyre, *New Zealand Prepares for War: Defence Policy, 1919–39*, University of Canterbury Press, Christchurch, 1988, pp. 46–51.
4. GO 93/1921, 307/1921.
5. AD 1, 57/265, Archives NZ; see also P. Cooke, *Defending New Zealand: Ramparts On the Sea, 1840–1950s*, Defence of New Zealand Study Group, Wellington, 2000, pp. 200, 233.
6. [P. Cooke,] '"Headquarters, NZ Military Forces": The Military Home at Mt Cook', *Forts and Works*, no. 20, Jan 2006, pp. 5, 7. The judgement of those involved may have been impaired – it was St Barbara's Day.
7. M.M. Gard'ner, Memorandum on Artillery Training, 1924–25, 16 Oct 1925, AD 1, 210/7/5, Archives NZ.
8. GO 303/1926; Army Lists.
9. I.C. McGibbon, 'New Zealand's Military Policing Activities in the South Pacific, 1919–30', typescript, Ministry for Culture and Heritage, Wellington.
10. See McIntyre, *NZ Prepares for War*, pp. 71–75.
11. See I.C. McGibbon, *Blue-Water Rationale: The Naval Defence of New Zealand, 1914–1942*, Government Printer, Wellington, 1981; also W.D. McIntyre, *The Rise and Fall of the Singapore Naval Base, 1919–1942*, Macmillan, London, 1979.
12. The 6-pr guns from Fort Jervois, Ripapa Island, were relocated to Battery Point, the better to control the harbour entrance. It was similarly proposed to shift one of Fort Jervois's 6-inch BLHP guns to Battery Point, but this plan was overtaken by events. See Cooke, *Defending NZ*, p. 233.
13. Vol. 1 of Jellicoe's report of 30 October 1919 was published as 'Naval Mission to the Dominion of New Zealand', *AJHR*, 1919, A-4. The subsidiary recommendations regarding coastal defences contained information on the weaknesses of existing coastal defences and were not published. They are contained in vol. 2 of Jellicoe's report, one of two secret volumes. See N 10/3, Archives NZ; also I. MacGibbon, 'The Constitutional Implications of Lord Jellicoe's Influence on New Zealand Naval Policy, 1919–1930', *New Zealand Journal of History*, vol. 6, no. 1, Apr 1972, pp. 57–80; McGibbon, *Blue-Water Rationale*, pp. 35–65.
14. See report by Brigadier G.S.R. Richardson, 22 Feb 1922, AD 10, 16/24, Archives NZ; also W.L. Ruffell, 'Defences of Auckland, Part 1: North Head (continued)', *The Volunteers*, Sep 1983, vol. 10, no. 2, p. 53. The scrap merchant who purchased the Auckland guns failed to complete their removal, and one 8-inch BLHP gun survives. See also Cooke, *Defending NZ*, pp. 232–23.
15. Richard (Bert) Dyson, interviewed 7 Dec 2000; John Masters, interviewed 1 Oct 2000; Christchurch *Press*, 19 May 1934.
16. Annual Reports, *AJHR*, H-19.
17. 'Royal NZ Artillery: Reorganization' (effective 15 Aug 1926), GO 301/1926.
18. 'Royal NZ Artillery: Reorganization'.
19. G.C. Bliss, *Gunners' Story: A Short History of the Artillery Volunteers of Christchurch, 1867–1967*, Canterbury Artillery Officers' Mess, Christchurch, 1970, pp. 66–69, including extracts from diary of Sergeant Ray Collins.
20. *Press*, 11 Nov 1967.
21. Gard'ner, Memorandum on Artillery Training.
22. Jim Gilberd, interviewed 20 Sep 1999; Ian T.Y. Johnston, interviewed 17 Oct 2000.

23. Director of Artillery to Captain G.B. Parkinson, 4 Mar 1927, in Parkinson's Personal File, DA 1/743, NZ Defence Force; W.L. Ruffell, 'The New Zealand Permanent Force', Royal New Zealand Artillery Old Comrades' Association website, http://www.riv.co.nz/rnza/hist/pf/pf5.htm#moi, accessed 20 Dec 2005.
24. Symon, Personal File, NZ Defence Force; 'Report on Artillery Training, 1927–28', AD 1, 210/7/5, Archives NZ.
25. Army Lists; Annual Reports, *AJHR*, H-19.
26. In 1938 Fort Dorset still employed about 40 men under No. 13 Scheme, with a civil foreman. They presented a 'sad picture', according to Lieutenant Leonard Thornton, RNZA. He and the other unmarried officers (who had to set up their own mess) acquired the services of two of them as cook and waiter by augmenting their 'miserable' wages. Thornton, '"Marking Time": A Personal Memoir', c.1988, p. 30.
27. Bliss, *Gunners' Story*, pp. 69, 72.
28. GO 271/1935, 39/1936, 93/1937; New Zealand Army Order (NZAO) 184/1938.
29. McIntyre, *NZ Prepares for War*, pp. 126–27, 174–77.
30. 'Reorganization of New Zealand Military Forces', GO 296/1937, Oct 1937; Army List, Feb 1938; *New Zealand Gazette*, 13 Aug 1936, p. 1585, 13 Jan 1938, p. 17.
31. McIntyre, *NZ Prepares for War*, pp. 129–31; Sinclair-Burgess to Cobbe, 2 Nov 1933, AD 11, 11/14, Archives NZ.
32. Sinclair-Burgess to War Office, London, 27 Jun 1933; Sinclair-Burgess to Cobbe, 2 Nov 1933; PM to High Commissioner, 7 Nov 1933; CIGS London to GOC, NZMF, 25 Jan 1934, AD 11, 11/14.
33. A.E. Widdows, War Office, to Sinclair-Burgess, GOC, NZMF, 4 & 16 Oct 1934, AD 11, 11/14. The changing British views and New Zealand's response are set out in 'Correspondence re. Coast Defence for New Zealand', Nov 1934, AD 11, 11/14.
34. Widdows to Sinclair-Burgess, 16 Oct 1934; H. Turner (Under-Secretary of Defence) to Cobbe, 13 Feb 1935, with Cabinet approval 15 Feb 1935, AD 11, 11/14. The estimated cost of the additional gun with its Mk V mounting was £12,250. On 21 February the High Commissioner was instructed to order it.
35. Sinclair-Burgess to Hankey, and file note, 23 Nov 1934; NZ Periodical Letter to CIGS, London, 17 Jun 1935, AD 11, 11/14; *New Zealand Gazette*, 4 Jul 1935, pp. 1829–30.
36. Sinclair-Burgess to Lieutenant-General Sir J.R.E. Charles, Master-General of the Ordnance, War Office, 21 Feb 1934, AD 11, 11/14; *AJHR*, 1936, H-19, p. 1; Sinclair-Burgess to Minister of Defence, 30 Mar 1936, Symon, Personal File; NZAO 46/1938, 145/1938, 109/1939.
37. See 'Official War History of the Public Works Department' (war narrative), vol. 3, pp. 476–77, 498–99, Archives NZ.
38. *AJHR*, 1936, H-19, p. 3; Fort Record Book, Palmer Head, Section A, pt 2, pp. 1–3, AD 88/3, Archives NZ.
39. Under-Secretary of Defence to Minister, Nov 1934, 'Guns 4-inch Coast Defence,' AD 1, 257/6/1, Archives NZ; M. Hursthouse, *Vintage Doctor: Fifty Years of Laughter and Tears*, Shoal Bay Press, Christchurch, 2001, p. 37.
40. A. Widdows, War Office, circular to Dominion governments, 4 May 1937; Chiefs of Staff Committee, 'The Defence of Ports at Home and Abroad: New Zealand Ports', 5 Oct 1937, p. 2, AD 11, 11/14/1.
41. *AJHR*, 1936, H-19, p. 2. Captain W.G. Gentry, NZSC, who was already in Britain undergoing training, attended an anti-aircraft searchlight duties course at Biggin Hill in November–December 1935: GO 85/1936.
42. Jim Gilberd, interviewed 20 Sep 1999; J.G. Gilberd, 'Boot and Saddle', http://www.riv.co.nz/rnza/hist/boot.htm, accessed 6 Jun 2005; J.G. Gilberd, 'Gunners and Horses', typescript, Napier, 1991, pp. 20–21; Graeme Hutcheson, interviewed 28 Aug 2001.
43. Chiefs of Staff Committee, 'The Defence of Ports at Home and Abroad: New Zealand Ports', COS/4, 5 Oct 1937, AD 11, 11/14/1.
44. Cabinet Minute, 7 Feb 1938; PM to High Commissioner, 21 Mar 1938; Lieutenant-Colonel W.G. Stevens (Secretary, Organisation for National Security) to Chief of General Staff, 21 Apr 1938; COS Committee to ONS, 19 May 1938 (COS/10), AD 11, 11/14/1.
45. Ruffell, 'NZ Permanent Force' and 'Army Schools, Trentham, Jan–Jun 1938', typescript; Bill Powrie, interviewed 18 Nov 1999.
46. George Milne, interviewed 19 Nov 1999. The RSM was Warrant Officer George McCulloch, a former Grenadier Guardsman who, on the parade ground, whipped into shape generations of trainees who knew him as 'the Screaming Skull'. McCulloch retired in the early 1950s with the rank of major.
47. GO 303/1926.
48. Ruffell, 'NZ Permanent Force'.
49. G.H. Clifton (Secretary, National Supply Committee, NZ Committee of Imperial Defence) to QMG, 2 Mar & 10 Jun 1936, AD 11, 15/14.

50. *AJHR*, 1937, H-19, p. 4; Ruffell, 'NZ Permanent Force'; Gilberd and Ruffell interviews.
51. George Smith, interviewed 9 Oct 2000.
52. Minister of Defence to Minister of Finance, 24 Nov 1937, AD 11, 15/14; Special GO 296/1937; *AJHR*, 1938, H-19, p. 4; NZAO 347/1937.
53. Clifton to CGS, 16 Sep 1939, AD 11, 15/14; Gilberd, 'Boot and Saddle'. Barbara, the patron saint of Artillerymen, is celebrated in a feast on 4 December.
54. Bliss, *Gunners' Story*, pp. 73–74; Gilberd, 'Gunners and Horses', pp. 18–19.
55. Ruffell, 'NZ Permanent Force'.
56. Special GO 296/1937.
57. W.L. Ruffell, 'The Territorial Force Special Reserve, 1937', typescript, c. 1995; *AJHR*, H-19, 1938, p. 7, 1939, p. 15; Milne interview.
58. McIntyre, *NZ Prepares for War*, p. 235; Duigan to Army Board, 3 Jul 1939, AD 1, 209/3/13; AD 1, 210/7/9, Archives NZ.
59. See, for example, 'Artillery Mobilisation Scheme for Home Defence, Fort Dorset', Jul 1939, AD 89/2, Archives NZ; Cooke, *Defending NZ*, p. 377.
60. Thornton, '"Marking Time"', pp. 27, 29.
61. Richard (Bert) Dyson, interviewed 14 Aug 2000.
62. This biography is based on Symon's Personal File, Base Records, NZ Defence Force.
63. W. McDonald, *Honours and Awards to the New Zealand Expeditionary Force in the Great War 1914–18*, Helen McDonald, Napier, 2001, p. 310.
64. J.R. Byrne, *New Zealand Artillery in the Field 1914–18*, Whitcombe & Tombs, Auckland et al., 1922, pp. 230, 282, 290.
65. This biography is based on Parkinson's Personal File, Base Records, NZ Defence Force; and entries in I. McGibbon (ed.), *The Oxford Companion to New Zealand Military History*, Oxford University Press, Auckland, 2000, p. 412; A. Taylor (ed.), *The New Zealand Roll of Honour: New Zealanders Who Have Served Their Country In Peace and War, 150 Years, 1845–1995*, Alister Taylor, Auckland, 1998; G.C. Petersen (ed.), *Who's Who in New Zealand*, 10th edn, A.H. & A.W. Reed, Wellington et al., 1971.
66. Sir Leonard Thornton, 'HQ Divisional Artillery', Royal New Zealand Artillery Old Comrades' Association website, http://www.riv.co.nz/rnza/rf/ww2/hq2.htm, accessed 23 Nov 2005.
67. James Matheson, 'Piper at War', 1994, typescript, 16th Field Regiment RNZA History Collection, Linton, p. 6.
68. Ian Diggle, interviewed 26 Oct 2000.

Chapter 5

1. John Rutherfurd, interviewed 29 May 2001; Martyn Thompson, *Our War: The Grim Digs – New Zealand Soldiers in North Africa, 1940–1943*, Penguin, Auckland, 2005, pp. 12, 15, 17.
2. Allan Boyd, interviewed 27 Oct 2000; Jim Gilberd, interviewed 20 Sep 1999; Thompson, *Our War*, pp. 21, 23. The 'Screaming Skull' was Warrant Officer George McCulloch.
3. J.R. Matheson, 'Piper at War', typescript, 1994, 16th Field Regiment RNZA History Collection, Linton; F. Martyn, *Tripoli and Beyond*, Collins, Auckland, 1944, p. 126.
4. W.E. Murphy, *2nd New Zealand Divisional Artillery*, Department of Internal Affairs, Wellington, 1966, pp. 12–13.
5. Richard (Bert) Dyson, interviewed 14 Aug 2000.
6. Thompson, *Our War*, pp. 25, 29.
7. By 1941 Maadi was a prefabricated town with sporting and welfare facilities: I. McGibbon (ed.), *The Oxford Companion to New Zealand Military History*, Oxford University Press, Auckland, 2000, pp. 38–39.
8. Dyson interview.
9. A.H. Varian, diary, 18, 19 Jul 1940, 5th Field Regiment Association collection.
10. Boyd interview; Varian diary, 4 Jul 1940; Jack Spring, interviewed 18 Aug 2000.
11. Spring interview.
12. 'History of 6th Field Regt NZA', Waikato Branch, 6th Field Regimental Association, c. 1975, MS-Papers-6109-3, Alexander Turnbull Library (ATL).
13. Gilberd interview.
14. Varian diary, 25 Dec 1940; S.W. Roskill, *The War at Sea 1939–45*, HMSO, London, 1956, vol. 1, p. 291; R.J. McDougall, *New Zealand Naval Vessels*, GP Books, Wellington, 1989.
15. Varian diary, 31 Dec 1940.

NOTES

16. M. Uren, *Diamond Trails of Italy*, Collins, Auckland, 1945, p. 152.
17. Ian Johnston, interviewed 17 Oct 2000.
18. Dyson interview. The First World War uniforms were soon replaced by battledress – a waist-length khaki jacket with many pockets and baggy trousers secured at the ankle with gaiters.
19. See John Burns' account of the division's race to Egypt in June 1942: *Life is a Twisted Path: A Time of Imprisonment, Escape, Evasion and Final Refuge*, Santa Maria dell'Anima, Rome, c. 2002, p. 18.
20. Each vehicle also sported a unit serial number at the front. This was a square, divided horizontally with red above blue, bearing a trail number representing the unit. See J. Plowman and M. Thomas, *4th New Zealand Armoured Brigade in Italy*, J. Plowman, Christchurch, c. 2000.
21. Uren, *Diamond Trails*, p. 213. This was not the only printed account to use the word: in 1945 the New Zealand Army Board published *The Diamond Track: From Egypt to Tunisia with the Second New Zealand Division, 1942–1943*; 16 Field Regiment's magazine is entitled *Black Diamond*.
22. Ian Diggle, interviewed 26 Oct 2000.
23. This section and the next are based on Murphy, *2nd NZ Divisional Artillery*, pp. 24–73. See also W.G. McClymont, *To Greece*, Department of Internal Affairs, Wellington, 1959.
24. A contemporary example is given by Martyn Uren in *Kiwi Saga: Memoirs of a New Zealand Artilleryman*, Collins, Auckland, 1943, p. 105. Other troops were known by the British phonetic codes: Ace, Beer, Charlie, George, Harry, Ink, Johnnie, King, London, Monkey, Nuts, Orange and Pip. See 26/GS Publications 742/Signals Training (All Arms), Pamphlet No. 1, *Signalling Codes*, 1942.
25. Murphy, *2nd NZ Divisional Artillery*, p. 23.
26. Dyson interview.
27. Uren, *Kiwi Saga*, p. 83.
28. Slim Williams, quoted in Thompson, *Our War*, p. 53.
29. Dyson interview.
30. Uren, *Kiwi Saga*, p. 70.
31. Gilberd interview.
32. Quoted in Thompson, *Our War*, pp. 55, 59.
33. Alan Jackson, 'Diary of Greece', 15 Apr 1941, in M. Subritzky (ed.), *Kiwi Gunners in War and Peace*, Kiwiana Publishing, Tauranga, 2004, pp. 180–81.
34. Murphy, *2nd NZ Divisional Artillery*, p. 43.
35. N.H. Brewer, letter, 7 Jul 1941, quoted in his *The Soldier Tourist: A Personal Acount of World War II*, Reed, Auckland, 1999, p. 112.
36. Gilberd interview.
37. Uren, *Kiwi Saga*, p. 101.
38. Ibid., p. 108.
39. Ibid., p. 115.
40. The remainder of this section is based on Murphy, *2nd NZ Divisional Artillery*, pp. 74–101.
41. In a 'murder' the whole Divisional Artillery concentrated its fire on a single point. See the box on 'Tactical Developments', pp. 307–308.
42. James Pickett, diary entries, 23–26 Apr 1941, MS-Papers-4146, ATL.
43. Jackson, diary entry 25 Apr 1941, in Subritzky (ed.), *Kiwi Gunners*, pp. 184–85.
44. Quoted in Thompson, *Our War*, p. 60.
45. Dyson interview.
46. G.M. Craigie, 'How I Got Away from Greece', MS-Papers-4165-1, ATL. See also Murphy, *2nd NZ Divisional Artillery*, p. 100.
47. This section is based on Murphy, *2nd NZ Divisional Artillery*, pp. 102–66. See also D. Davin, *Crete*, Department of Internal Affairs, Wellington, 1953.
48. Gilberd interview.
49. Davin, *Crete*, p. 64.
50. Murphy, *2nd NZ Divisional Artillery*, pp. 112–13.
51. Dyson interview.
52. This argument was overheard by Lieutenant Bert Dyson. See M. Hutching (ed.), *'A Unique Sort of Battle': New Zealanders Remember Crete*, HarperCollins, Auckland, 2001, pp. 52–53.

53. Jackson, diary entry 6 Jun 1941, in Subritzky (ed.), *Kiwi Gunners*, p. 200.
54. Dyson interview; and see Murphy, *2nd NZ Divisional Artillery*, p. 135.
55. Murphy, *2nd NZ Divisional Artillery*, pp. 150–51. Dill died of his wounds eight days later.
56. James Kinder, account written in captivity, pp. 61, 67, MS-Papers-1622, ATL.
57. This section is based on Murphy, *2nd NZ Divisional Artillery*, pp. 167–84.
58. Spring interview.
59. This account of Operation Crusader is based on Murphy, *2nd NZ Divisional Artillery*, pp. 185–296. See also his *The Relief of Tobruk*, Department of Internal Affairs, Wellington, 1961.
60. Graeme Hutcheson, interviewed 28 Aug 2001.
61. Gordon, 'Memoirs', diary entries 1, 10, 23 Jul 1942.
62. Quoted in Thompson, *Our War*, pp. 210–11, 213.
63. Spring interview.
64. Des P. O'Connor, interviewed 19 Nov 1999.
65. Uren, *Kiwi Saga*, pp. 158, 168, 171.
66. Dyson and Diggle interviews.
67. Murphy, *2nd NZ Divisional Artillery*, pp. 241–43, quoting Brigadier J. Hargest, *Farewell Campo 12*, Michael Joseph, London, 1945. Niven, a 28-year-old farmer, later escaped from captivity in Italy.
68. D.J.M. Alexander, 'Another Man's War', typescript, 1992, p. 17.
69. G. Clifton, *The Happy Hunted*, Cassell, London, 1952, pp. 146, 147.
70. Murphy, *2nd NZ Divisional Artillery*, p. 263.
71. Weir to Colonel Sandy Thomas, 12 Dec 1941, letter courtesy Brigadier John Burns.
72. J. Henderson, *Gunner Inglorious*, Whitcombe & Tombs, Christchurch, 1974, p. 25.
73. Weir to Thomas, 12 Dec 1941.
74. Brigadier John Burns, notes on draft ch.
75. Quoted in 'Epic Battle By New Zealand Gunners Recalled at Annual Reunion', *Waikato Times*, clipping, n.d., c.1975.
76. Uren, *Kiwi Saga*, p. 185.
77. T. Martin, *New Zealand Images of War*, Dunmore Press, Palmerston North, 1990, esp. pp. 34–36, 51, 53–54, 59; W. Feeney, 'McIntyre, Peter, 1910–1995', *DNZB*, vol. 5, pp. 316–17; P. McIntyre, *Peter McIntyre: War Artist*, A.H. & A.W. Reed, Wellington etc., 1981.
78. This biography is based on Williams' Personal File, Base Records, NZ Defence Force.
79. J.R. Byrne, *New Zealand Artillery in the Field 1914–18*, Whitcombe & Tombs, Auckland et al., 1922, p. 286.
80. This biography is based on Miles' Personal File, Base Records, NZ Defence Force; G.J. Clayton, 'Miles, Reginald 1892–1943', *Dictionary of New Zealand Biography*, vol. 5, Auckland University Press/Department of Internal Affairs, Auckland/Wellington, 2000, p. 348; 'Miles, Brigadier Reginald', in I. McGibbon (ed.), *The Oxford Companion to New Zealand Military History*, Oxford University Press, Auckland, 2000, p. 319.
81. W. McDonald, *Honours and Awards to the New Zealand Expeditionary Force in the Great War 1914–18*, Helen McDonald, Napier, 2001, p. 218.
82. Sir Leonard Thornton, 'HQ Divisional Artillery', Royal New Zealand Artillery Old Comrades' Association website, http://www.riv.co.nz/rnza/rf/ww2/hq2.htm, accessed 23 Nov 2005.
83. W.W. Mason, *Prisoners of War*, Department of Internal Affairs, Wellington, 1954, p. 213.
84. Some writers have questioned the circumstances of Miles' death. See M. Avery, 'The Mystery About Brigadier General Reginald Miles', *Historical Review*, vol. 49, no. 1, May 2001, pp. 16–21.
85. W.E. Murphy, *2nd New Zealand Divisional Artillery*, Department of Internal Affairs, Wellington, 1966, p. 296.

Chapter 6

1. J.P. Snadden, 'One Up the Spout: A Gunner's Story', typescript, c.1990, p. 148, Acc 1996:437, Kippenberger Archive, Army Museum, Waiouru, p. 148.
2. This section is based on W.E. Murphy, *2nd New Zealand Divisional Artillery*, Department of Internal Affairs, Wellington, 1966, pp. 297–311. See also J.L. Scoullar, *Battle for Egypt: The Summer of 1942*, Department of Internal Affairs, Wellington, 1955.
3. Murphy, *2nd NZ Divisional Artillery*, pp. 187, 424, 447–48, 515, 551, 607, 669, 734; R. Kay, *Italy, Volume II: From Cassino to Trieste*, Department of Internal Affairs, Wellington, 1967, pp. 559, 570.
4. Graeme Hutcheson, interviewed 28 Aug 2001; 'Memoirs of a Kiwi Soldier during the Second World War: Extracts from

the diary of L.W. (Mac) McBeath', 17 Apr 1942, http://www.bakedbean.co.nz/LWMcB/lwmcbeath.htm, accessed 20 Dec 2005.
5. Des P. O'Connor, interviewed 19 Nov 1999.
6. Jack Spring, interviewed 18 Aug 2000.
7. Hutcheson interview.
8. This section is based on Murphy, *2nd NZ Divisional Artillery*, pp. 312–32.
9. N.H. Brewer, *The Soldier Tourist: A Personal Acount of World War II*, Reed, Auckland, 1999, p. 143.
10. Snadden, 'One Up the Spout', p. 146.
11. Ibid., p. 147.
12. O'Connor interview.
13. This section is based on Murphy, *2nd NZ Divisional Artillery*, pp. 333–71.
14. These were named for their originator, Brigadier J.C. Campbell, RHA. See K. Brookes, *Battle Thunder: The Story of Britain's Artillery*, Osprey Publishing, Reading, 1973, p. 180.
15. Snadden, 'One Up the Spout', pp. 148–49.
16. M. Thompson, *Our War: The Grim Digs – New Zealand Soldiers in North Africa 1940–1943*, Penguin, Auckland, 2005, p. 188; Hutcheson interview.
17. John Rutherfurd, interviewed 29 May 2001.
18. O'Connor interview.
19. Bdr J.J. Gordon, 'Memoirs of World War II, October 1939–November 1943', diary entry, 5 Aug 1942; Thompson, *Our War*, pp. 184, 189; H. Paton, *Private Paton's Pictures: Behind the Lines with Kiwi Soldiers in North Africa 1941–1943*, Penguin, Auckland, 2003, pp. 7, 37.
20. This section is based on Murphy, *2nd NZ Divisional Artillery*, pp. 372–97. See also R. Walker, *Alam Halfa and Alamein*, Department of Internal Affairs, Wellington, 1967.
21. Paton, *Private Paton's Pictures*, p. 7.
22. O'Connor interview.
23. M. Uren, *Kiwi Saga: Memoirs of a New Zealand Artilleryman*, Collins, Auckland, 1943, p. 151.
24. Thompson, *Our War*, pp. 181, 182, 185.
25. McBeath diary, 18 Jul 1942.
26. Uren, *Kiwi Saga*, p. 279.
27. Allan Boyd, quoted in Thompson, *Our War*, p. 115.
28. H.W. Schmidt, *With Rommel in the Desert*, Albatross Publishing, Durban, 1950, p. 205.
29. This section is based on Murphy, *2nd NZ Divisional Artillery*, pp. 398–422.
30. Richard (Bert) Dyson, interviewed 14 Aug 2000.
31. This section is based on Murphy, *2nd NZ Divisional Artillery*, pp. 437–67. See also W.G. Stevens, *Bardia to Enfidaville*, Department of Internal Affairs, Wellington, 1962.
32. Murphy, *2nd NZ Divisional Artillery*, pp. 423–36, 462, 484, 504n, 520.
33. Snadden, 'One Up the Spout', p. 158; Murphy, *2nd NZ Divisional Artillery*, p. 476.
34. Brewer, *Soldier Tourist*, p. 157; Snadden, 'One Up the Spout', p. 175; F. Martyn, *Tripoli and Beyond*, Collins, Auckland, 1944, pp. 20, 103–104.
35. Martyn, *Tripoli and Beyond*, pp. 17–18, 21; Gunner Alex Young, quoted in Thompson, *Our War*, p. 199.
36. Snadden, 'One Up the Spout', p. 179.
37. This section is based on Murphy, *2nd NZ Divisional Artillery*, pp. 468–97.
38. Snadden, 'One Up the Spout', p. 179.
39. On launching its salvo of rockets the Nebelwerfer emitted a streak of flame and a plume of blue smoke. It was therefore easily spotted in the open, but counter-battery work against it was challenging, especially in the Italian mountains.
40. Clunie ('Fritz') Harris, diary entry, 24 Mar 1943, in Thompson, *Our War*, p. 144.
41. Jim Gilberd, interviewed 20 Sep 1999.
42. Martyn, *Tripoli and Beyond*, pp. 95–96.
43. This section is based on Murphy, *2nd NZ Divisional Artillery*, pp. 497–514.
44. Martyn, *Tripoli and Beyond*, p. 131.
45. Ibid., pp. 138–39.
46. O'Connor interview.
47. J. MacGibbon (ed.), *Struan's War*, Ngaio Press, Wellington, 2001, p. 137.

48. Thompson, *Our War*, pp. 151, 217, 221.
49. Murphy, *2nd NZ Divisional Artillery*, p. 512.
50. This section and the next are based on ibid., pp. 515–49. See also N.C. Phillips, *Italy, Volume I: The Sangro to Cassino*, Department of Internal Affairs, Wellington, 1957.
51. Martyn, *Tripoli and Beyond*, pp. 194, 199.
52. Spencer Cocks, interviewed 20 Nov 1999.
53. Walter McKinnon, Obituary in *3 NZ Division Assn Inc* newsletter no. 33, 1998.
54. John Foote, interviewed 22 Mar 2001.
55. Snadden, 'One Up the Spout', pp. 204–205.
56. Les Wright, interviewed 25 Oct 2001.
57. Horrocks interview.
58. Murphy, *2nd NZ Divisional Artillery*, p. 523.
59. Hutcheson interview.
60. This piece of fire commander's artifice could be read only from the air. See *Roads to Rome: With the Second New Zealand Division from Maadi to Florence*, Army Board, Wellington, 1946, p. 19.
61. Snadden, 'One Up the Spout', p. 240.
62. This section is based on Murphy, *2nd NZ Divisional Artillery*, pp. 550–80.
63. Snadden, 'One Up the Spout', pp. 225–26.
64. Dyson interview.
65. M. Uren, *Diamond Trails of Italy*, Collins, Auckland, 1945 p. 54.
66. George Smith, interviewed 9 Oct 2000.
67. This section is based on Murphy, *2nd NZ Divisional Artillery*, pp. 581–592.
68. See ibid., pp. 590–92; R.D. Munro, *39/34 Heavy Mortar Battery, 7 NZ Anti-Tank Regiment, 2 NZEF in Italy, 1944–45*, author, Upper Hutt, 1990. The designation was changed because number 35 had been allocated to a battery in New Zealand (this was never actually formed).
69. Uren, *Diamond Trails*, p. 60.
70. In April 1944, Divisional Artillery HQ tried to alter the terminology applied to standard concentrations to bring it into line with that used by other formations. The 'murder' (firing on a point) remained unchanged, but they wanted the term 'stonk' applied to the former Divisional Artillery Method 'B' (firing at a linear target 600 yards long). The former stonk, firing at a target 1200 by 300 yards, was renamed 'rumpus', but this change did not stick. See Murphy, *2nd NZ Divisional Artillery*, p. 587, n. 8. The 'Chinese barrage' returned later in the Italian campaign. Unlike in the First World War, the term denoted a feint 'to provoke the enemy into wasteful response': ibid., p. 685.
71. Mowat, in Subritzky (ed.), *Kiwi Gunners*, p. 230.
72. Brookes, *Battle Thunder*, p. 189.
73. This section is based on Murphy, *2nd NZ Divisional Artillery*, pp. 593–606. See also Kay, *Cassino to Trieste*.
74. Snadden, 'One Up the Spout', pp. 239–40.
75. Uren, *Diamond Trails*, p. 79.
76. This section is based on Murphy, *2nd NZ Divisional Artillery*, pp. 607–637.
77. Uren, *Diamond Trails*, pp. 103–104.
78. Alan Petrie, interviewed 15 Jan 1999. For a short history of the M10s in New Zealand Artillery service, see J. Plowman and M. Thomas, *4th New Zealand Armoured Brigade in Italy*, J. Plowman, Christchurch, c. 2000, pp. 31–32; J. Plowman, *Rampant Dragons: New Zealanders in Armour in World War II*, Kiwi Armour, Christchurch, c. 2002, ch. 8.
79. This section is based on Murphy, *2nd NZ Divisional Artillery*, pp. 619–37.
80. Uren, *Diamond Trails*, p. 109; Cocks interview.
81. Uren, *Diamond Trails*, p. 119.
82. This section is based on Murphy, *2nd NZ Divisional Artillery*, pp. 638–63.
83. Smith interview.
84. Brewer, *Soldier Tourist*, p. 192.
85. Cocks interview; Murphy, *2nd NZ Divisional Artillery*, p. 641.
86. Murphy, *2nd NZ Divisional Artillery*, p. 661.
87. This section is based on ibid., pp. 664–87.
88. The 17-pr-armed M10c, called Achilles in British service, arrived in January 1945: Petrie interview.
89. M. McMahon, diary entries 15 & 16 Dec 1944, Acc No.1999.105.2, Kippenberger Archive.

NOTES

90. Ibid., 18, 19, 20 Dec 1944.
91. Quoted by P. Singleton-Gates, *General Lord Freyberg VC: An Unofficial Biography*, Michael Joseph, London, 1963, p. 294.
92. 'History of 6th Field Regt NZA', Waikato Branch 6th Field Regimental Association, c.1975, p. 139, MS-Papers-6109-3, ATL.
93. This section is based on Murphy, *2nd NZ Divisional Artillery*, pp. 688–703.
94. McMahon diary, entries late Dec 1944, 1 Jan, Mar 1945.
95. 'History of 6th Field Regt NZA', p. 137.
96. McMahon diary, narrative for 1945.
97. Petrie interview.
98. This section is based on Murphy, *2nd NZ Divisional Artillery*, pp. 703–733.
99. Ibid., pp. 735–38.
100. A.L. Pemberton, *The Development of Artillery Tactics and Equipment*, War Office, London, 1950, p. 279.
101. Sir Leonard Thornton, 'HQ Divisional Artillery', Royal New Zealand Artillery Old Comrades' Association website, http://www.riv.co.nz/rnza/rf/ww2/hq2.htm, accessed 23 Nov 2005.
102. GOC's papers, cited in Murphy, *2nd NZ Divisional Artillery*, p. 550.
103. On 10 July 1944, W.G. Stevens, Officer in Charge Administration, 2NZEF, instructed units to gather material for unit histories: 5th Field Regt History, IA 1, 181/7/12, Archives NZ.
104. Uren, *Diamond Trails*, p. 138.
105. 2nd NZ Divisional Artillery History, IA 1, 181/7/10, pt 1, Archives NZ.
106. Murphy, *2nd NZ Divisional Artillery*, page facing p. 796.
107. 14th AA Regimental History, IA 1, 181/7/15, Archives NZ.
108. 4th Field Regimental History, IA 1, 181/7/11; 6th Field Regimental History, IA 1, 181/7/13, Archives NZ.
109. Associate Editor, NZ War Histories, to Neville Webber, 14 Jun 1950, IA 1, 181/7/11.
110. Fullarton wrote *Troop Target* 'mostly between October 1942 and January 1943 on the march from Alamein to Tripoli, scribbled in dust storms behind the doubtful protection of a "bivvy" tent; during march halts, often under shell-fire, sandwiched between fire orders, and corrected after dusk by the dim light of a truck lamp.' It is a 'record' of the trials of a New Zealand field artillery troop, A Troop (manned by fictional characters), in Greece, Crete and North Africa. Fullarton himself started with anti-tank guns but over the period covered in this novel served with 29 Battery, 6 Field, as Command Post Officer (see Murphy, *2nd NZ Divisional Artillery*, p. 452, n. 19).
111. Associate Editor, NZ War Histories to John Fullarton, 21 Mar 1950, IA 1, 181/7/13, Archives NZ.
112. John Fullarton to Associate Editor, 17 Mar 1951, IA 1, 181/7/10, Archives NZ.
113. *The Gunners: An Intimate Record of Units of the 3rd New Zealand Divisional Artillery in the Pacific from 1940 until 1945*, A.H. & A.W. Reed for the Third Division Histories Committee, Wellington, 1948. Eleven authors under Major John Warrington wrote chapters on individual regiments and batteries. All thirteen Third Division 'unofficial narratives' were edited by Oliver Gillespie.
114. This biography is based on 'Queree, Brigadier Raymond Candlish', in I. McGibbon (ed.), *The Oxford Companion to New Zealand Military History*, Oxford University Press, Auckland, 2000, p. 437; and G. Cox, *The Race for Trieste*, William Kimber, London, 1977, pp. 37–38.
115. Sir Leonard Thornton, 'HQ Divisional Artillery', Royal New Zealand Artillery Old Comrades' Association website, http://www.riv.co.nz/rnza/rf/ww2/hq2.htm, accessed 23 Nov 2005.
116. Ian Diggle, interviewed 26 Oct 2000.
117. Les Wright, interviewed 25 Oct 2001.
118. F. Rennie, *Regular Soldier: A Life in the New Zealand Army*, Endeavour Press, Auckland, 1986, pp. 237–38.
119. Ron Hassett, comments on draft, n.d.
120. This biography is based on Weir's Personal File, Base Records, NZ Defence Force; T. Rowe, *Steve Weir: New Zealand's Master Gunner*, Occasional Paper No. 4, Military Studies Institute, New Zealand Army, Upper Hutt, 2004; J.A.B. Crawford, 'Weir, Stephen Cyril Ettrick 1904–1969', *The Dictionary of New Zealand Biography*, vol. 5, Auckland University Press/Department of Internal Affairs, Auckland/Wellington, 2000, pp. 549–50; G. Harper, 'Weir, Major-General Sir Stephen Cyril Ettrick', in McGibbon (ed.), *Oxford Companion*, p. 598.
121. Pen Portrait, Lieutenant-Colonel C.E. Weir, DSO, WAII, 1, DA 406/397, Archives NZ.
122. Pen Portrait.
123. Stuart Norrie, interviewed 21 Mar 2001.
124. Pen Portrait; J.H. Fullarton, quoted in 'Epic Battle By New Zealand Gunners Recalled at Annual Reunion', clipping from

Waikato Times, c.1975.
125. W.E. Murphy, *2nd New Zealand Divisional Artillery*, Department of Internal Affairs, Wellington, 1966, p. 665, n. 1.
126. As General Mort Stirling, Weir is the main character in Natasha Templeton's 1994 novel *Firebird* (Hodder & Stoughton, London), in which this is a central episode.
127. John Snadden, interviewed by John Crawford, 22 Jul 1997.
128. S.D. Newman, *Vietnam Gunners: 161 Battery RNZA, South Vietnam, 1965–71*, Moana Press, Tauranga, 1988, pp. 48 (map), 59.
129. Secretary, Canterbury Branch, 6th Field Regiment Association, to Major-General Sir Steve Weir, 15 Mar 1960, Personal File. Weir changed his first name to Steven by deed poll in 1960: Rowe, *Steve Weir*, p. 5.
130. M. Uren, *Kiwi Saga*, Collins, Cairo, 1943, p. 286.
131. R.P. Hunnicutt, *Sherman: A History of US Medium Tanks*, Presidio, California, 1978.
132. This box is based on Rowe, *Steve Weir*.

CHAPTER 7

1. This and the next section rely on P. Cooke, *Defending New Zealand: Ramparts on the Sea, 1840–1950s*, Defence of New Zealand Study Group, Wellington, 2000, especially pp. 239–304, 463–508.
2. Ibid., pp. 375–84.
3. Bill Powrie, interviewed 18 Nov 1999.
4. Cooke, *Defending NZ*, pp. 663–72.
5. John Horrocks, interviewed 27 Oct 2000. Horrocks, who was to become a general, was then based at Motutapu, the first battery to receive a radar set.
6. For more on this incident, see Cooke, *Defending NZ*, pp. 377–79.
7. These were not the only guns retrieved from the Auckland Museum. Its 18-pr field gun exhibit accompanied 35 Battery's deployment to Fiji in November 1940: B. Pasley, '35th Battery, NZA', typescript, Jun 1984.
8. Cooke, *Defending NZ*, pp. 684–85.
9. *Christchurch Star-Sun*, Jan 1943, quoted in D.A. Buckley, *Godley Head and Battery Point: A History of Coastal Defence During World War II*, Ministry of Defence, Christchurch, 1984, Appendix D, p. 5; Horrocks interview.
10. Horrocks interview.
11. George Milne, interviewed 19 Nov 1999.
12. Powrie interview.
13. For first-hand accounts of the experiences of the Public Works Department staff, contractors and gunners at the emplacements in the Marlborough Sounds, see K. Neal and N. Leov, *The Price of Vigilance: The Building of the Gun Emplacements in the Marlborough Sounds, 1942*, authors, Nelson, 1999.
14. Powrie interview.
15. 'Monthly Report of Security and Intelligence from Officer-in-Charge, 'D' Sect. 68th Battery', 18 Jul 1942, in War Diary, 9th Hy Regt, WAII Z 205/1/-, Archives NZ.
16. Ibid., entry for 4 Aug 1942. The 'submarine' was later thought to have been a rock. Ibid., 1 Sep 1942.
17. Location Statement, Northern Fortress Area, 9th Heavy Regt NZA War Diary.
18. A.A. Wright, '9th Coast Regiment Royal NZ Artillery', typescript, 1952, ch. IV, p. 2, MS 80-077, ATL.
19. Entries for 28 May, 2 & 20 Jun 1942, 1 Nov 1943, Signals Officer Diary, Fort Dorset. These informal diaries were donated to the Defence Library, Wellington, in 2003 by former Gunner Henry ('Granny') Parris. The departing 'yanks' were the 2nd Division, US Marine Corps.
20. This section is based on Cooke, *Defending NZ*, pp. 544–70.
21. Bill McAllum, interviewed 28 Aug 2001.
22. Spencer Cox, interviewed 20 Nov 1999.
23. Peter Willis, interviewed 21 Mar 2001.
24. M. Blampied, 'The Story of our Ack-Ack: World War 2 Air Defence of Auckland', RNZAOCA website (first published *NZ Herald*, 1964), www.riv.co.nz/rnza/hist/auck.htm, accessed 7 Mar 2005.
25. Wellington's 16 AA Brigade was commanded by Colonel E.l'E. Davies RA. Colonel V.A. Young RA commanded 17 AA Brigade training 3 Division artillery units. Several of the brigade majors were also British loan officers. See *The Gunners: An Intimate Record of Units of the 3rd New Zealand Divisional Artillery in the Pacific from 1940 until 1945*, A.H. & A.W. Reed for Third Division Histories Committee, Wellington, 1948, pp. 23–25; W. Fraser, *Defending Wellington's Sky*, author, Wellington [1992], p. 29.

26. *The Army Schools Centennial Journal, 1885–1985*, Government Printer, Wellington, 1985, p. 47.
27. F.G. Grattan, *Official War History of the Public Works Department*, The Department, Wellington, 1948, p. 589.
28. Blampied, 'Story of Our Ack-Ack'.
29. This section is based on Cooke, *Defending NZ*, pp. 305–70.
30. Les Wright, interviewed 25 Oct 2001.
31. Local resident Murray Henderson, interviewed 18 Jun 2003.
32. Wright interview.
33. The first stage of a camp at Waiouru – an ideal site for artillery firing and tank maneouvres – had been built in the second half of 1940. Work on a major camp at Linton, near Palmerston North, began in February 1942. I. McGibbon (ed.), *The Oxford Companion to New Zealand Military History*, Oxford University Press, Auckland, 2000, pp. 38–9.
34. R.D. Munro, pers comm, 27 May 2003. Munro joined 7 Anti-Tank Regiment in Italy.
35. This section is based on Cooke, *Defending NZ*, pp. 598–612.
36. AD 1, 203/317, quoted in Wilkes, *History of New Zealand Chemical Warfare*, p. 53.
37. Secret Schedule No. 4 of the Minutes of the 108th Meeting of the Chiefs of Staff Committee, Wellington, 21 Jan 1943, EA 1, W1784, 80/6/1, quoted in Wilkes, p. 45.
38. See Wilkes, p. 46.
39. See Wilkes, p. 55.
40. O.A. Gillespie, *The Pacific*, Department of Internal Affairs, Wellington, 1952, pp. 288–91; Cooke, *Defending NZ*, pp. 785–87.
41. This section is based on *The Gunners*, pp. 9–21; Gillespie, *The Pacific*, pp. 19–56; Cooke, *Defending NZ*, pp. 787–97.
42. F. Rennie, *Regular Soldier: A Life in the New Zealand Army*, Endeavour Press, Auckland, 1986, pp. 32–33.
43. Charles Fraser, letters to aunt, MS-Papers-2269-5, ATL.
44. This title was never gazetted; the force remained legally 'Pacific Section, 2NZEF': Gillespie, *The Pacific*, p. 72.
45. M. Hursthouse, *Vintage Doctor: Fifty Years of Laughter and Tears*, Shoal Bay Press, Christchurch, 2001, pp. 51–52.
46. Gillespie, *The Pacific*, pp. 292–300; Cooke, *Defending NZ*, pp. 803–806.
47. The remainder of this chapter relies mainly on *The Gunners* and Gillespie, *The Pacific*.
48. This box relies on *The Gunners*, passim.
49. See Gillespie, *The Pacific*, pp. 71–77.
50. 'The Unofficial History of the 144 (Ind) Battery (Commenced at Guadalcanal 11/10/43)', pp. 9–10, Guy Richardson Powles Collection, 96-208-1, ATL.
51. *The Gunners*, p. 26. 2 NZ Divisional Artillery had a strength of 4070 when it crossed to Italy in October 1943: W.E. Murphy, *2nd New Zealand Divisional Artillery*, Department of Internal Affairs, Wellington, 1966, p. 520.
52. Cooke, *Defending NZ*, pp. 807–808.
53. Ibid., pp. 800–803.
54. Milne interview; Rennie, *Regular Soldier*, pp. 38–39.
55. M. Lysaght, 'Going Back', typescript, 1996, p. 11.
56. F. Cooze, *Kiwis in the Pacific*, A.H. & A.W. Reed, Wellington, 1944, p. 15.
57. John Foote, interviewed 22 Mar 2001.
58. Ibid., pp. 152–76.
59. Cooze, *Kiwis in the Pacific*, p. 16.
60. *The Gunners*, p. 20.
61. Ibid., p. 31.
62. 'Unofficial History of the 144 (Ind) Battery', p. 2.
63. Foote interview.
64. Cooze, *Kiwis in the Pacific*, p. 34.
65. Ibid., p. 35.
66. 'Unofficial History of the 144 (Ind) Battery', p. 5.
67. Foote interview.
68. *The Gunners*, p. 86.
69. 'Unofficial History of the 144 (Ind) Battery', pp. 5–6.
70. Foote interview.
71. Wright interview. Les Wright took this method from the School of Artillery to Italy.
72. Cooze, *Kiwis in the Pacific*, p. 39.

73. J. Rentz, *Bougainville and the Northern Solomons*, USMC Operational Narrative, 1948, Map 23: Treasury Island Assault, 27 Oct 1943, facing p. 96.
74. Cooze, *Kiwis in the Pacific*, p. 37.
75. Citation for Military Medal, *The Gunners*, p. 290.
76. Foote interview.
77. Rentz, *Bougainville and the Northern Solomons*, Map 23. A 37-mm anti-tank gun captured in the Treasuries is now in the Auckland War Memorial Museum.
78. Cooze, *Kiwis in the Pacific*, p. 38.
79. Foote interview.
80. M. Lysaght, 'Going Back', p. 15; Andrew Lysaght, interviewed 13 Jun 2003.
81. Milne interview.
82. Foote interview.
83. *The Gunners*, pp. 287–9; 'Unofficial History of the 144 (Ind) Battery', p. 8.
84. 'Unofficial History of 144 (Ind) Battery', p. 11, entry for 15 Dec 1943.
85. *The Gunners*, p. 191.
86. Ibid., p. 194.
87. 'Unofficial History of 144 (Ind) Battery', entry for 11 Feb 1944.
88. The whole campaign was characterised by the c-word. For instance, Herbert Priday's 1945 account of 'the defence of the island bases of the South Pacific' was titled *The War from Coconut Square* (A.H. & A.W. Reed, Wellington).
89. Lysaght, 'Going Back'; Lysaght interview.
90. *The Gunners: An Intimate Record of Units of the 3rd New Zealand Divisional Artillery in the Pacific from 1940 until 1945*, A.H. & A.W. Reed for Third Division Histories Committee, Wellington, 1948, p. 32.
91. A.H. Varian, diary entry, 2 Sep 1941, 5th Field Regimental Association collection.
92. Citation quoted in A. Taylor (ed.), *The New Zealand Roll of Honour: New Zealanders Who Have Served Their Country In Peace and War, 150 Years, 1845–1995*, Alister Taylor, Auckland, 1998, p. 341.
93. John Horrocks, interviewed 27 Oct 2000.
94. '60pr Guns for Coast Defence', AD 11, 5/27, Archives NZ.
95. Bill Powrie, interviewed 18 Nov 1999.
96. 'The George Salt Trumpet', NZ Permanent Force Old Comrades' Association, n.d. The trumpet was donated to the old gunners after Salt's retirement.

Chapter 8

1. This section is based on L. Brocklebank, *Jayforce: New Zealand and the Military Occupation of Japan 1945–48*, Oxford University Press, Auckland, 1997.
2. D.L. Fyfe, quoted in Brocklebank, *Jayforce*, p. 37.
3. John Foote, interviewed 22 Mar 2001.
4. Ibid.
5. Ian Diggle, interviewed 26 Oct 2000.
6. See the reminiscences of Jayforce gunner Wally Ruffell: http://www.riv.co.nz/rnza/tales/wlr1.htm, accessed 4 Aug 2005.
7. Diggle interview.
8. Diaries cited in Brocklebank, *Jayforce*, pp. 101, 117.
9. D.M. Fenton, *A False Sense of Security: The Force Structure of the New Zealand Army 1946–1978*, Centre for Strategic Studies, Wellington, 1998, pp. 6–7.
10. For the last decade of the coastal defences, see P. Cooke, *Defending New Zealand: Ramparts on the Sea 1840–1950s*, Defence of New Zealand Study Group, Wellington, 2000, pp. 817–23.
11. Fenton, *False Sense of Security*, p. 10. CMT was suspended during the waterfront dispute of 1951, when Army personnel replaced many striking workers.
12. *New Zealand Gazette*, no. 4, 27 Jan 1949, p. 115; no. 21, 14 Apr 1966, pp. 628–29.
13. Diggle interview.
14. Based on R.J. McDougall, *New Zealand Naval Vessels*, GP Books, Wellington, 1989, pp. 92, 125–29, 163–69.
15. A.J. Baigent, 'Coast Artillery Defences', transcript of 1959 radio broadcast, http://www.riv.co.nz/rnza/hist/baigent1.htm, accessed 31 May 2005.
16. Paul Galloway, interviewed 2 Jul 2003.

17. Bill McAllum, interviewed 28 Aug 2001.
18. Clyde Stewart, interviewed 16 Oct 2000.
19. *16 Fd Regt RNZA: Some Aspects of Regimental History,* The Regiment, Papakura, 1976, p. 57.
20. John Valintine to David Green, pers. comm., 14 Oct 2003.
21. John Masters, interviewed 4 Jul 2003.
22. Director Training to DCGS, 20 Oct [1949], AD 209/1/90, quoted in Fenton, *False Sense of Security,* p. 16.
23. Fenton, *False Sense of Security,* p. 17.
24. New Zealand's 17-prs were probably on loan from Australia, which had these in service until 1962.
25. The M40A1 106-mm recoilless rifle was adopted in 1961 to replace the 120-mm, which was used by Territorial units until ammunition for it ran out. New Zealand acquired the Carl Gustav M2 anti-armour rocket launcher in 1965; this was augmented by the medium-range Javelin in 2006. *Army News,* no. 219, 11 Apr 2000; Fenton, *False Sense of Security,* p. 53; http://www.defence.govt.nz/acquisitions-tenders/current-acquisition-projects/medium-range.html, accessed 15 Mar 2006.
26. Fenton, *False Sense of Security,* p. 49.
27. 'Cadre PEs – Artillery Units', Appx A to Div 19.3, 4 Nov 1954, AD 79/5/19, Establishments: RNZA, Archives NZ.
28. CGS, 20 Nov 1987, DEF 1920/210, 'Establishments and Inspections: Army Establishments: 16 Field Regiment, RNZA', NZ Defence Force.
29. Fenton, *False Sense of Security,* p. 41.
30. I. McGibbon (ed.) *The Oxford Companion to New Zealand Military History,* Oxford University Press, Auckland, 2000, p. 41; *The Army Schools Centennial Journal, 1885–1985,* Government Printer, Wellington, 1985, especially pp. 47–9; 'The School of Artillery', typescript.
31. *Army Schools Centennial Journal,* p. 48.
32. Interviews with John Masters (1 Oct 2000), Jim Gilberd (20 Sep 1999), Clyde Stewart (16 Oct 2000).
33. 'Peace Order of Battle. PE – Recommendations RNZA Cadre Staffs', May 1956, AD 79/5/19; Don Kenning, interviewed 3 Jul 2003.
34. P. Napier, 'The Forgotten Squadrons: The RNZAF Light Anti-Aircraft Squadrons', *Forts and Works,* no. 12, Oct 2001, pp. 9–11.
35. Fenton, *False Sense of Security,* pp. 45–47.
36. Colin Stanbridge, interviewed 23 Mar 2001; Alan Busfield, interviewed 25 Mar 2001, 7 Jul 2003; Valintine to Green, pers. comm., 14 Oct 2003.
37. Stanbridge interview.
38. Busfield interviews.
39. Graham Birch to John Valintine, pers. comm., 18 Apr 2004.
40. Despite this mishap, J.A. Pountney MBE would command 16 Field Regiment in Korea and become Director of Artillery.
41. Les Wright, interviewed 25 Oct 2000.
42. Ray Andrews, interviewed 13 Jul 2003.
43. John Masters, interviewed 1 Oct 2000, 27 Aug 2001; Andrews interview.
44. 'Army Air Corps Deactivated', *Army News,* no. 110, 12 Jun 1995.
45. Fenton, *False Sense of Security,* p. 153.
46. *Gunfire,* vol. 4, no. 4, Apr 1983; vol. 7, no. 1, Sep 1985.
47. This section is based on I. McGibbon, *New Zealand and the Korean War, Volume II: Combat Operations,* Oxford University Press, Melbourne, 1996, pp. 41–107.
48. Stanbridge interview.
49. Gunner Laurie Stack, quoted in T. Stewart, 'I'm No Bloody Hero', text for 50th anniversary exhibition.
50. R. Porter, 'With 16 Field Regiment Royal NZ Artillery in Korea', *Duty First* (NSW branch, RAR Assn), vol. 1, no. 3, Jun 1992, p. 43.
51. Stanbridge interview.
52. Porter, 'With 16 Field Regiment', p. 45.
53. Stanbridge interview.
54. W. Poulton, *K Force in Korea: A Soldier's Life in the 16th New Zealand Field Regiment,* author, Woodville, 2004, pp. 21–23.
55. Ibid., pp. 15–16.
56. Ibid., pp. 14–15, 17–18, 27–29, 62, 75, 78.

57. Ibid.
58. McGibbon, *NZ and the Korean War*, pp. 299–301.
59. Kenning interview.
60. This section is based on McGibbon, *NZ and the Korean War*, pp. 108–154, 191–204.
61. Ibid., p. 378.
62. Wilfred Poulton, letter, Apr 1952, quoted in his *K Force in Korea*, p. 19.
63. Ibid., pp. 56, 64.
64. This section is based on McGibbon, *NZ and the Korean War*, pp. 205–232.
65. This section is based on ibid., pp. 235–66, 329–59.
66. Stanbridge interview.
67. Stack, quoted in Stewart, 'I'm No Bloody Hero'.
68. Stanbridge interview.
69. Poulton, diary entry 27 Dec 1952, quoted in *K Force in Korea*, p. 78.
70. Box based on McGibbon, *NZ and the Korean War*, especially pp. 295–96.
71. D. Challinor, *Grey Ghosts: New Zealand Vietnam Vets Talk About Their War*, Hodder Moa Beckett, Auckland, 1998, pp. 71–73.
72. http://www.army.mil.nz/?CHANNEL=ABOUT+NZ+ARMY&PAGE=Army+Marae, accessed 16 Jun 2005.
73. Poulton, diary entry 27 Dec 1952, quoted in *K Force in Korea*, p. 27.
74. Vern Duley, interviewed 17 Aug 2000.
75. R. Porter, '16 Field Regiment RNZA in Korea, Part III: Towards the End', *Duty First*, vol. 1, no. 8, Jun 1995, p. 51; Major D.A. Mannering, pers. comm., Nov 2005.
76. Fenton, *False Sense of Security*, pp. 38–40.
77. Ibid., pp. 67–68.
78. Birch to Valintine, 18 Apr 2004.
79. Fenton, *False Sense of Security*, pp. 102–108.
80. Green Folder of captioned photographs, 16 Field Regiment Headquarters, Linton.
81. Birch to Valintine, 18 Apr 2004.
82. *16 Fd Regt*, pp. 67–68.
83. Fenton, *False Sense of Security*, pp. 121–22.
84. Ibid., p. 129.
85. 24 RNZA men are listed in 1RNZIR's nominal roll (May 1964–Oct 1965) reproduced in R. Gurr, *Voices From a Border War: A History of 1 Royal New Zealand Infantry Regiment, 1963 to 1965,* the author, Melbourne, 1995.
86. Ray Andrews and Chris Brown, followed by Roger Pearce and Walter Steward. See C. Pugsley, *From Emergency to Confrontation: The New Zealand Armed Forces in Malaya and Borneo 1949–1966,* Oxford University Press, Melbourne, 2003, pp. 184, 223.
87. Andrews interview.
88. Masters interview.
89. This section is based on S.D. Newman, *Vietnam Gunners: 161 Battery, South Vietnam, 1965–71,* Moana Press, Tauranga, 1988, pp. 21–53. This work was commissioned by the regiment and used its archives and gunners' accounts. Lieutenant-Colonel Conrad Flinkenberg prepared the material on the first three battery commanders.
90. Sir Leonard Thornton, interviewed by Pat Craddock, quoted in C.L. Nelson, *Long Time Passing: New Zealand Memories of the Vietnam War,* National Radio, Wellington, 1990, p. 23.
91. Kenning interview. Another account has it that Prime Minister Keith Holyoake had seen a four-gun American battery in action, and would not accept that it had two guns out of action at the time: R. Hassett, 'Once Upon a Time', unpublished memoir, 2003, p. 142.
92. B. Breen, *First to Fight: Australian Diggers, NZ Kiwis and US Paratroopers in Vietnam, 1965–66,* Allen & Unwin, Sydney/Wellington, 1988, p. 251.
93. Kenning interview.
94. *The New Zealand Army in Vietnam 1964–1972: A Report on the Chief of General Staff's Exercise, 1972,* Ministry of Defence, Wellington, 1973, p. 64.
95. The Battery Commanders were, in order of service: Majors Don Kenning, Harry Honnor, Tom Martin, Geoff Hitchings, John Horsford, Ray Andrews and John Masters.
96. Barry Dreyer, interviewed 24 Mar 2001.

97. Fenton, *False Sense of Security*, p. 176.
98. Don Kenning, interviewed 3 Jul 2003.
99. Graham Birch to John Valintine, pers. comm., Jan 2004.
100. Kenning interview.
101. *NZ Army in Vietnam*, p. 17.
102. Birch to Valintine, Jan 2004.
103. Ibid.
104. Ibid.
105. C. Flinkenberg, 'Major Kenning's Battery', typescript, 1968, p. 19; Breen, *First to Fight*, p. 173; Kenning interview.
106. Birch to Valintine, Jan 2004.
107. C.W. Brown, 'Some Notes on Vietnam', in M. Subritzky (ed.), *The Vietnam Scrapbook: The Second Anzac Adventure*, Three Feathers Publishing, Papakura, 1995, p. 111; Lance-Corporal J.T. Lissette, RNZE, letter, Oct 1966, quoted in I. McGibbon, *Kiwi Sappers: The Corps of Royal New Zealand Engineers' Century of Service*, Reed, Auckland, 2002, p. 140.
108. In addition to Newman, *Vietnam Gunners*, pp. 54–68, see L. McAulay, *The Battle of Long Tan*, Hutchinson of Australia, Melbourne, 1986; and B. Grandin, *The Battle of Long Tan as Told by the Commanders to Bob Grandin*, Allen & Unwin, Crows Nest NSW, 2004.
109. Murray Broomhall, in Subritzky (ed.), *Vietnam Scrapbook*, p. 210.
110. Dreyer interview.
111. R.L. Rencher, quoted in McAulay, *Battle of Long Tan*, p. 71.
112. Broomhall, in Subritzky (ed.), *Vietnam Scrapbook*, pp. 211, 212.
113. J. Millen, *Salute to Service: A History of the Royal New Zealand Corps of Transport and its Predecessors 1860–1996*, Victoria University Press, Wellington, 1997, p. 386; unsourced newspaper article in Subritzky (ed.), *Vietnam Scrapbook*, pp. 149–50.
114. Long Tan has become legendary in Australian military history. Forty years later, in winter 2006, 16 Field Regiment gunners stripped to the waist in pouring rain at Linton to recreate the battle for a History Channel documentary. *Army News*, no. 358, 11 Jul 2006. For Viet Cong accounts, see http://bulletin.ninemsn.com.au/bulletin/site/articleIDs/81241BD2EFF6A64BCA2571C4000CC51C, accessed 23 Aug 2006.
115. Broomhall, in Subritzky (ed.), *Vietnam Scrapbook,* p. 214.
116. C. Flinkenberg, 'Draft – Major Honnor's Battery', typescript, n.d., p. 20.
117. Birch to Valintine, Jan 2004. On one estimate 75,000 French soldiers were killed by their own artillery during the First World War: R. Holmes, *Acts of War: The Behaviour of Men in Battle,* revised edn, Cassell, London, 2003, p. 189.
118. Andrews interview.
119. Dreyer interview.
120. Ibid.
121. P. Duggan, 'What Have They Done to the Rain?', typescript, 2000, pp. 18, 41–42.
122. Stewart interview.
123. John Rout, interviewed 15 Jul 2003.
124. Masters interview.
125. Dreyer interview.
126. Masters interview.
127. Bill Subritzky, in his *Vietnam Scrapbook*, p. 143.
128. Dreyer interview.
129. This section is based on Newman, *Vietnam Gunners*, pp. 68–116.
130. Masters interview.
131. Ibid.
132. As Betty May Browne, she published her poetry as *With Our Boys in Vietnam,* Cloudy Bay, Blenheim, 1996.
133. M. Subritzky, 'The 161 Battery Panther', *Commonwealth Heraldry Bulletin*, no. 21, 1995; Masters interview. Masters got into trouble for making this application through unconventional channels.
134. Masters interview.
135. *NZ Army in Vietnam*, p. 38.
136. Kenning interview.
137. McGibbon (ed.), *Oxford Companion*, pp. 1–2. The 1999 *Inquiry into the Health Status of Children of Vietnam and Operation Grapple Veterans* (Department of the Prime Minister and Cabinet, Wellington) found little evidence for any

link between veterans' exposure to 'defoliants, herbicides and pesticides' in South Vietnam and the health of their children (p. 21). However, in October 2004, the Health Select Committee of the House of Representatives recommended that the government 'accept that New Zealand's Vietnam veterans were exposed to a toxic environment', monitor the international research into the long-term health effects of this exposure, and 'ensure all children of New Zealand Vietnam veterans are entitled to reimbursement of additional costs associated with medical treatment for any condition listed as being related to dioxin exposure': *Summary of Recommendations, Inquiry into the Exposure of New Zealand Defence Personnel to Agent Orange and other Defoliant Chemicals during the Vietnam War and any Health Effects of That Exposure, and Transcripts of Evidence*, Health Committee, House of Representatives, Wellington, 2004, p. 5. The government soon accepted the first recommendation, and in mid-2005 Prime Minister Helen Clark announced a process of 'consultation with Vietnam veterans to hear issues, and suggestions for the resolution of them, and to ensure that veterans are receiving their health care ... and other entitlements'. When this process had concluded she would apologise formally to Vietnam veterans for the failure of previous governments to recognise their exposure to a toxic environment. 'PM Address: RNZ RSA National Council Meeting', 11 Jul 2005, http://www.scoop.co.nz/stories/PA0507/S00236.htm, accessed 22 Dec 2005.
138. R.J. Pearce, DRNZA, to President, Auckland Artillery Officers Mess, 1 Feb 1991 (courtesy Colin West).
139. Fenton, *False Sense of Security*, pp. 155–62.
140. This biography is based on McGibbon (ed.), *Oxford Companion*, p. 287; obituary, *3 NZ Division Assn Newsletter*, no. 33, 1998.
141. Don McKinnon and Malcolm McKinnon, pers. comm., 29 Jun 2003.
142. *The Gunners*, A.H. & A.W. Reed for Third Divisional Histories Committee, Wellington, 1948, pp. 110, 121, 134.
143. This biography is derived from Thornton's Personal File, Base Records, NZ Defence Force; his unpublished '"Marking Time": A Personal Memoir', c.1988; *Oxford Companion to New Zealand Military History*, p. 531; and obituaries in *Sunday Star-Times*, 13 Jun, and *Evening Post*, 17 Jun 1999.
144. F. Rennie, *Regular Soldier: A Life in the New Zealand Army*, Endeavour Press, Auckland, 1986, p. 21.
145. Personal File, Base Records, NZ Defence Force; A. Taylor (ed.), *The New Zealand Roll of Honour: New Zealanders Who Have Served their Country in Peace and War, 150 Years, 1845–1995*, Alister Taylor, Auckland, 1998, p. 238; W.E. Murphy, *2nd New Zealand Divisional Artillery*, Department of Internal Affairs, Wellington, 1966, p. 697.

CHAPTER 9

1. For an overview of New Zealand's strategic situation, see these entries in McGibbon (ed.), *Oxford Companion*: McGibbon, 'ANZAM', 'Five Power Defence Arrangements', 'Forward Defence'; D. Dickens, 'SEATO'; C. Pugsley, 'Malayan Emergency'; R. Rabel, 'Vietnam War'; J. Subritzky, 'Confrontation'.
2. P. Jennings, *Exercise Golden Fleece and the New Zealand Military: Lessons and Limitations*, Working Paper no.187, Strategic and Defence Studies Centre, Australian National University, Canberra, 1989, p. 18, n. 5.
3. CGS to Army GS, 6 Aug 1971, 'Establishment: Home and Operational Commands: Army Field Force. 16 Field'; DRNZA, 'Rewrite of RNZA Field Force Establishments', 29 Apr 1975, 'Establishment: Home and Operational Commands: Army Field Force. 16 Field', both DEF 107/6/1/5; DEF 107/6/1/6, 4 Medium Battery RNZA, HQ NZ Defence Force.
4. Ray Andrews, interviewed 13 Jul 2003. Twenty-seven of the 66 men who went to Singapore had not served in Vietnam: Conrad Flinkenberg, pers. comm., 9 Jul 2003. The RAA battery, 106 Field, was withdrawn in 1974 and disbanded. The British battery, 1 Light Battery, RA ('The Blazers'), was withdrawn in 1975.
5. Barry Dreyer, interviewed 24 Mar 2001.
6. Unit History 161 Battery, diary entry 2 Sep–2 Oct 1976. The Five Power Defence Arrangements of the early 1970s saw Britain, Australia, New Zealand, Malaysia and Singapore commit themselves to military cooperation: 'ANZ UK', Vertical File, NZ Defence Force Library.
7. C. Rayward, *The Distinguished History of 3rd Field Regiment, Royal New Zealand Artillery, 1940–1990*, The Regiment, Christchurch, 1990, pp. 72–73; Photos of the Tropic Moon exercise, n.d., 'NZ Army – Manoeuvres', Vertical File, NZ Defence Force Library. This was the only other occasion the RNZA took its own guns on exercise.
8. DRNZA, 'Rewrite of RNZA Field Force Establishments', 29 Apr 1975, 'Establishment: Home and Operational Commands: Army Field Force. 16 Field.' DEF 107/6/1/5, HQ NZ Defence Force.
9. '3 Field Regiment', http://www.riv.co.nz/rnza/units/3fd/index.htm, accessed 13 Jun 2003; John Rout, interviewed 15 Jul 2003; HQ 3 Field to FF Comd, 23 May 1977, File 77/2/8, 'Organisation – RNZA', NZ Defence Force.
10. Rayward, *Distinguished History of 3rd Field*, p. 78.
11. Special instruments were used to accurately measure distances and angles, and find north: *The Gunners Handbook: An Introduction to the Regiment*, Royal Regiment of New Zealand Artillery, c. 1986, pp. 36–37.

12. The artillery formed sound-ranging command post groups in exercises as late as 1981 (Exercise Triad 81). See *Gunfire*, vol. 2, no. 2, Feb 1981, p. 2.
13. Don Kenning, interviewed 3 Jul 2003. Australia bought new sound-ranging equipment in 1986. Hassett, the last gunner general, was also careful in 1976 not to appear to favour his corps when appointing the first Sergeant-Major of the Army, who 'could not be a gunner'. See R. Hassett, 'Once Upon a Time', unpublished memoir, 2003, p. 177.
14. Annual Report, Ministry of Defence, *AJHR*, 1976, H-19; *Jane's Weapon Systems*, 1970/71 edn.
15. Cymbeline can detect 81-mm bombs 14 kilometres away, 120-mm bombs at 20 kilometres: *Gunners Handbook*, p. 33. By the end of the century the remaining unit was thought to be 'of little operational value', being 'probably not compatible with equipment operated by likely allies': J. Rolfe, *The Armed Forces of New Zealand*, Allen & Unwin, St Leonards, NSW, 1999, p. 130.
16. Rout interview; *Army News*, no. 172, 31 Mar 1998.
17. 'Charter of the Meteorological Section of 1 Locating Troop, Waiouru', 13 Jul 1978, File 77/2/8. The meteorological station, which plotted data for live firings, was handed over to the New Zealand Meteorological Service when the troop was reattached to 16 Field Regiment at Papakura in 1987.
18. M. Subritzky, 'The Last Regimental Shoot with the 25-Pr in NZ', http://www.riv.co.nz/rnza/tales/last25.htm, accessed 13 Jun 2003; Annual Reports, Ministry of Defence, *AJHR*, H-19, 1977, 1978; D. M. Fenton, *A False Sense of Security: The Force Structure of the New Zealand Army 1946–1978*, Centre for Strategic Studies, Wellington, 1998, p. 177. A dozen of 3 Field's M101A1s remained operational into the 1990s after being sent to the US for an overhaul.
19. The trials were conducted by Captain Angus Rivers near Raglan in the early 1970s, but a mooted Pegasus Troop of RNZA parachutists was never formed.
20. Jennings, *Exercise Golden Fleece*, p. 2; Mike Baker, interviewed 21 Jul 2003; 'Output Class D9, Contingent Military Capability to provide Field Indirect Fire Support for Land Forces.' *Departmental Forecast Report*, 1 Jul 1996 to 30 Jun 1997, Ministry of Defence, Wellington, 1997; see also *The Shape of New Zealand Defence: A White Paper*, Ministry of Defence, Wellington, 1997.
21. HQ 3TF to Army GS, 4 Dec 1986, LF 1910/1/1, 'General Administration, Organisation, Management: Reorganisation: RNZA', NZ Defence Force; Col Horsford, Army GS, RNZA Reorganisation, 20 June 1979, File 77/2/8; Rayward, *Distinguished History of 3rd Field*, pp. 77–8. The battery divided its guns between the RF and TF sub-units.
22. Controller of Establishment & Inspections, Establishment No. 05-1214 4th (G) Medium Battery RNZA, 19 Jun 1979, LF 1920/214, NZ Defence Force.
23. Handwritten notes, '4 Mdm Battery, 12 March 1980', DEF 107/6/1/214, Establishments: Army: 4th Medium Battery, RNZA. The outspokenness of its officers reflected the battery's independence under 1 Brigade since being reduced from a regiment two decades earlier. Col J. Horsford to Maj-Gen Poananga, 4 May 1979, 'Status of Command: 4(G) Medium Battery', DEF 107/6/1/214, NZ Defence Force.
24. Major Vercoe and his successor Major Horsford took part in this lobbying: Maj Vercoe BC 4 Medium to HQ 1 Brigade, 2 Apr 1979, File 77/2/8. In the mid-1980s nine 5.5-inch guns remained in service; the other two were at the School and with 32(E) Battery: *Gunners Handbook*, p. 31.
25. DEME to Co-ordinator, 4 May 1979; Co-ordinator to Army GS, n.d., File 77/2/8.
26. Maj Vercoe BC 4 Medium to HQ 1 Brigade, 2 & 4 Apr 1979, File 77/2/8. Its strength in 1979 was seven TF officers and 96 TF ORs, with one and six cadre regulars respectively
27. Co-ordinator to Army GS, 5 Jun 1979, File 77/2/8.
28. Rout interview.
29. John Masters, interviewed 27 Aug 2001. Masters was to spend two years in Waiouru in the Territorial Force Depot.
30. Former serving officer quoted in C. Burton, *Report of the Gender Integration Audit of the New Zealand Defence Force, October 1998*, New Zealand Defence Force/New Zealand Human Rights Commission, Wellington, 1998, p. 172; Rout interview.
31. The Tactical Artillery HQ exercised control at brigade level. HQ 2 TFR to NZ LF, '2 TFR Arty Tac HQ', 2 Nov 1981; DRNZA, 'Proposal to Raise a Field Regt to Support 2TFR', 18 Aug 1980, both LF 1920/1/1, 'General Administration, Organisation, Management Establishments: RNZA', NZ Defence Force.
32. Brig I.H. Burrows to Col OT, '2 TFR Arty Hac HQ', 16 Nov 1981; Col R.K. Rutherford, Col Ops/Trg to Army GS, 19 Dec 80, both LF 1920/1/1, NZ Defence Force.
33. *Gunfire*, vol 3, no.7, Oct/Nov 1982, p.3; vol. 7, no.1, Sep 1985, p. 8; Unit History of 163 Battery, diary entry 7–9 Aug 1998; *Black Diamond*, 1998/99, p. 12; E. Cox, 'Women in the Armed Forces', *Oxford Companion*, pp. 620–4; New Zealand Defence Force website, http://www.nzdf.mil.nz/at-a-glance/personnel-composition.htm, accessed 20 Dec 2005.

34. *Gunfire*, vol. 4, no. 4, Apr 1983, p.2.
35. Maj-Gen Williams, CGS, 'Corps Restructure Instruction – RNZA', 12 Sep 1984; Col Aldridge response to Draft RNZA Corps Restructure, 9 Aug 1984, both LF 1910/1/1. The establishment changes for these new troops, which took effect on 31 March 1986, finally removed the sound-ranging function. Maj Heard to SO2, 10 Oct [1986], 'RNZA Restructure proposal', LF 1910/1/1.
36. *Gunfire*, vol. 2, no. 4, May 1981, p.1; AGS to CGS, 26 Mar 1985, 'Army Restructure, RNZA Establishments', on file Establishment & Inspections: Corps Establishments: RNZ Artillery, DEF 1920/5/1, NZ Defence Force; Unit History of HQ Battery, 16 Field, diary entry 10 Jun 1991.
37. If the Bandmaster was a TF Warrant Officer he was styled 'Bandmaster'; if he held an honorary commission he was 'Director of Music': 'Establishment & Inspections: Army: Band of Royal Regt of NZ Artillery, DEF 1920/213.
38. Cmdr LF to Army GS, 'RNZA Restructure proposal', 7 Nov 1986, LF 1910/1/1. This had reverted to three batteries by the 1990s.
39. AGS to CGS, 26 Mar 1985, 'Army Restructure, RNZA Establishments', DEF 1920/5/1, NZ Defence Force.
40. *1983 Defence Review*, p. 30. Australia purchased 36 American M198 155-mms in 1981: Horner, *The Gunners*, p. 508. The DRNZA envisaged buying 'light and medium guns': *Gunfire*, vol. 4, no. 10, Oct 1983.
41. For example, 'Establishment Amendment, 16 Field RNZA', 29 Mar 1985, DEF 1920/210, NZ Defence Force; Brig McIver for CGS, 'Proposed Structure, Annex B to RNZA Restructure proposal', 9 Sep 1986, LF 1910/1/1.
42. *Evening Post*, 27 Jan 1987.
43. *The Defence Question: A Discussion Paper*, Government Printer, Wellington, 1985; *Defence and Security – What New Zealanders Want: Report of the Committee of Inquiry*, Wellington, the committee, 1986; *Defence of New Zealand: A Review of Defence Policy*, Government Printer, Wellington, 1987.
44. See *Press*, 24 Jan 1986. The *Evening Post* had reported this criticism the previous week in an article which also covered a public spat between the Minister and his CGS, Major-General John Mace, over sending officers to the National Defense College, Canada.
45. *Defence of New Zealand*, 1987, p. 35. The 1987 Defence Review did not specifically mention medium guns, allowing the DRNZA to express hope as late as November that 155-mm guns (in fact, M198s from Australia) would be purchased.
46. Unit History, 4(G) Medium Battery, diary entries 7–8 Sep, 8 Nov 1985, 21–23 Nov 1986; *Gunfire*, vol. 7, no. 2, 1986, p. 2.
47. *Gunners Handbook*, p. 30; Unit History 161 Battery, diary entry 11–28 Sep 1987.
48. Dreyer and Kenning interviews.
49. This ammunition cost $200 a round, compared with $1250 for the Abbott rounds: A. Mitchell, 'The Close Support Weapon System for the RRF to the Year 2005', *NZ Army Journal*, no. 8, Jul 1989. It is now about one-quarter the price of HE: Baker interview. All the self-propelled guns in British and American use since the Second World War have been given clerical names.
50. The Australians named it the Hamel, after their artillery battle in the town in May 1918. See Horner, *The Gunners*, pp. 169, 509.
51. NZ Army News Release, 'New Field Gun for Army', 10 May 1986; 'Report on 105mm Light Gun Replacement', Evaluation Report No.26, Assessment & Audit Division, Ministry of Defence, 30 Apr 1992, pp. ii, iv; *Dominion*, 6 Mar 1987.
52. The first light gun shoot was called Exercise Virgin Guns. *Dominion*, 6 Mar 1987; Unit History 161 Battery, diary entries 7–28 Sep, 20–29 Oct 1987.
53. Mitchell, 'Close Support Weapon System'; 'Report on 105mm Light Gun Replacement', p. 28; Unit History 161 Battery, diary entry 11–15 Jan 1988.
54. As the new guns were issued units handed in their L5s; two remain operational with 161 Battery.
55. This was not the first time gunners had exercised on 'the Barrier'. In December 1959, 121 Battery 12 HAA Regiment exercised there with HMNZS *Endeavour*, HMNZS *Royalist* and the HDML *Mako*: Alan Busfield, interviewed 25 Mar 2001. 161 Battery exercised on Great Barrier in 1962: Graham Birch, pers. comm., 14 Nov 2005.
56. They were 'trying to replace the barrel, slipper and muzzle brake, total of 554lb, onto the upper recoil when the three pieces slipped and the lot landed, muzzle brake first, onto Gnr Rattray's hand. This soldier must be commended for his … courage in carrying on regardless, and finishing the gun's reassembly before passing out.' Unit History 161 Battery, 26 Mar 1976.
57. Unit History 161 Battery, diary entries 18–26 Mar 1984. During the exercise the battery also attempted to save 140 stranded pilot whales.
58. AGS to CGS, 26 Mar 1985, 'Army Restructure, RNZA Establishments', DEF 1920/5/1; Unit History 161 Battery, diary entry 17–23 Apr 1985.

59. Jennings, *Exercise Golden Fleece*, p. 9.
60. The main sources for this box are 'Bands', in McGibbon (ed.), *Oxford Companion*, pp. 51–52; [H.F. Batley,] *Official History of the Band of the Royal Regiment of New Zealand Artillery, Northern Military District*, Auckland Artillery Band Association, Auckland, 1964; S.P. Newcomb, *Challenging Brass: 100 Years of Brass Band Contests in New Zealand, 1880–1980*, Powerbrass Music, Takapuna, 1980.
61. R. Holmes, *Acts of War: The Behaviour of Men in Battle*, 2003 edn, Weidenfeld & Nicolson, London, pp. 163–64.
62. Figures from Annual Reports, in P. Cooke, *Defending New Zealand: Ramparts on the Sea, 1840–1950s*, Defence of NewZealand Study Group, Wellington, 2000, pp. 151–52.
63. W.S. Broughton, 'Bracken, Thomas 1843–1898', *The Dictionary of New Zealand Biography, Volume Two, 1870–1900*, Bridget Williams Books/Department of Internal Affairs, Wellington, 1993, p. 53.
64. G.A. Mains, 'Orion Military Band of Dunedin (Inc)', *The Volunteers*, vol. 4, no. 4, Dec 1976, pp. 9–13.
65. Batley, *Official History*, p. 98.
66. *Gunners Handbook*, p. 22; '16th Field Regiment', http://members.tripod.com/hitchnz/index.html, accessed 21 Dec 1999; *NZPFOCA Newsletter*, no. 118, Jun 2003, http://www.riv.co.nz/rnza/news/nl118.htm, accessed 1 Jun 2005.
67. Graham Birch, pers. comm., 14 Nov 2005.
68. Maj-Gen Williams, CGS, 'Corps Restructure Instruction – RNZA', 12 Sep 1984; Brig McIver for CGS, 9 Sep 1986; Maj Heard to SO2, 10 Oct [1986], 'RNZA Restructure proposal', all LF 1910/1/1, NZ Defence Force.
69. D. Horner, *The Gunners: A History of Australian Artillery*, Allen & Unwin, St Leonards, NSW, 1995, pp. 503, 517.
70. Unit History 161 Battery, diary entries 16 Mar 1992, 15–28 Oct 1996, 12–31 Jan 1998. The New Zealand gunner was confined to barracks for eighteen days and fined $100.
71. Hassett, 'Once Upon a Time', p. 165.
72. Baker interview.
73. Andrews interview. An Australian brigadier also participated in this exercise.
74. Andrews interview.
75. Baker interview.
76. G.D. Birch, 'The Directorate RNZA', Dec 2003, http://www.riv.co.nz/rnza/units/dir1.htm, accessed 14 Jun 2005.
77. Mike Pearce, pers. comm., 28 Nov 2003.
78. Andrews interview. Andrews had previously received US information via contacts in NATO.
79. Unit History 161 Battery, diary entries 10 Feb, 10–14 Apr 1988; Mike Subritzky, pers. comm., 14 Jul 2003.
80. The Australian response is discussed in Jennings, *Exercise Golden Fleece*, p. 12.
81. Mike Subritzky, pers. comm., 26 Jul 2003.
82. Unit History 161 Battery, diary entry for 20 May 1987; S. Evans, articles in *Dominion*, 18, 19, 20, 21 May 1992; R. Harman, 'Duel of the Davids: The Standoff of 19 May', *New Zealand Defence Quarterly*, no. 22, Spring 1998, pp. 17–19; Barry Dreyer, interviewed 24 Mar 2001.
83. G.A. Todd, 'The Role of the Royal NZ Artillery Within the Ready Reaction Force', *Commandant's Papers*, RNZAF Command & Staff College, 1988, pp. 1, 4.
84. Appendix 1, 'The New Zealand Defence Force,' *The Defence of New Zealand: A Policy Paper*, Ministry of Defence, 1991; Unit History of 161 Battery, diary entries 15, 16, 30 Oct 1991. At Linton the battery stayed in Wellington Lines, the 1RNZIR base, until moving to the former Engineers' headquarters, the White House, a decade later: Unit History 161 Battery, diary entry 1–3 Dec 1993; Baker interview.
85. Willie August, interviewed 2 Jul 2003; Unit History of HQ Battery 16 Field, diary entry 13 Dec 1991. Mount Wellington Barracks closed in mid-1998, when the Logistics units still there moved to Arch Hill: *Army News*, no. 184, 15 Sep 1998.
86. 163 Battery was welcomed on 4 December 1993, in the presence of South Korea's president. The troops were numbered as in Korea, A and B (161 Battery) and E and F (163 Battery): Allan Kinsella, interviewed 3 Jul 2003. See Unit History 161 Battery, diary entry 24–30 Mar 1994, for the regimental shoot.
87. *Army News*, no. 167, 16 Dec 1997; no. 258, 11 Dec 2001.
88. 'Output Class D9, Contingent Military Capability to provide Field Indirect Fire Support for Land Forces', *Departmental Forecast Report*, 1 Jul 1996 to 30 Jun 1997.
89. Paul Galloway, interviewed 2 Jul 2003; *Army News*, no. 169, 17 Feb 1998; no. 216, 29 Feb 2000; Unit History of 161 Battery, diary entry 17 Jul 1997. Forrester earned the SAF Medal for Distinguished Act. WO1 Brett Rigden and WO2 Paul Galloway also received awards, and six other New Zealand artillerymen got letters of commendation from the Singaporean CGS: *Army News*, no. 157, 22 Jul 1997.

90. One Singaporean soldier had died and three had been injured when their Land Rover rolled in February. *Jane's Intelligence Weekly and Jane's Sentinel Pointer*, Jun 1997.
91. Annual Report, NZ Army, *AJHR*, 1959, H-19, p. 10. This 25-pr premature killed two and wounded two TF gunners in a 2 Field Regiment shoot at Waiouru.
92. Unit History 163 Battery, diary entry 20 Jan 1999; *Army News*, no. 192, 2 Feb 1999; Baker interview. These were the first self-propelled howitzers ever seen in New Zealand: *Dominion Post*, 28 Jan 2004.
93. Baker interview; Unit History 161 Battery, 12–22 Oct 1992. Lands are the raised parts of the rifling inside a gun barrel, between the grooves.
94. Unit History 161 Battery, diary entry 20 Jan 1993; Horner, *The Gunners*, p. 509; R.A. Wood, 'Exercise Firebird: 163 Battery Fires the Last Light Gun L118 Round', *Black Diamond*, 1998/99; *Army News*, no. 205, 3 Aug 1999; Baker interview.
95. DRNZA, 18 Aug 1980, LF 1920/1/1. When FACE was introduced, the old tables and slide rules for calculating firing data were renamed MACE – Manual Artillery Computation Equipment.
96. *Brassey's Artillery of the World*, 1977; Rout interview; Unit History 161 Battery, diary entries 21 & 23 Jan, 24 Feb 1976; Graham Birch, notes on draft, 22 Sep 2003; Marine Air Systems website, www.masnz.co.nz/products, accessed 1 Aug 2003; *Gunfire*, Nov 1987, p. 2.
97. Unit History 161 Battery, diary entry 17–21 Sep 1990; Unit History, 32(E) Battery, diary entry 27 Oct 1990; *Dominion*, 15 Aug 1991.
98. *Army News*, no. 175, 12 May 1998.
99. 163 Battery trained with the GPS in 1998: *Army News*, no. 181, 4 Aug 1998. For command post computers, see Unit History, 3 Field, diary entry 16–17 Jul 1988; Gun Laying Positioning Equipment, *Army News*, no. 161, 16 Sep 1997; a radar jammer simulator, Unit History of HQ Battery, 16 Field, diary entry 30 Aug 1990.
100. In the early 1970s, the DRNZA costed a replacement, the M167 Vulcan air defence system, at $56 million. This was a modern radar-controlled 20-mm Gatling gun, firing at 1000–3000rpm, twinned with a missile system: Kenning interview.
101. *Gunfire*, vol.3, no.1 [early 1982,] p.1; vol.[5] no. 3, Mar 1984, p. 1; no. 4, Apr 1984, p.1; 'Output Class D8, Contingent Military Capability to Provide Air Defence for Land Forces', *Departmental Forecast Report*, 1 Jul 1996–30 Jun 1997.
102. *Gunners Handbook*, p. 38; *Cannonball*, Journal of the Royal Australian Artillery Historical Company, no. 51, Jun 2003. 111 Air Defence Battery (Light), RAA, had used it successfully in the 1991 Gulf War. An RBS70 troop from the same battery participated in the 2003 Gulf War.
103. 'Tests Delay Army Missile', *Dominion*, 15 Dec 1995; *Army News*, no. 175, 12 May 1998. The ABCA programme, formalised in 1949, commits the armed forces of the United States, Britain, Canada and Australia to maintaining the levels of cooperation, inter-operability and standardisation achieved during the Second World War. New Zealand became an associate member through Australia in 1965. See http://www.army.mil.nz/default.asp?CHANNEL=ABOUT+NZ+ARMY&PAGE=ABCA+Programme
104. *Black Diamond*, 1998/9, p. 42. For administrative purposes G Troop is part of Headquarters Battery: Unit History 161 Battery, diary entry 31 Oct 1998.
105. Baker interview; Kendall Peacock, interviewed 3 Jul 2003.
106. *Black Diamond*, 1998/99, pp. 42, 44; *Army News*, no. 167, 16 Dec 1997; no. 189, 24 Nov 1998.
107. *Army News*, no. 310, 8 Jun 2004; no. 365, 17 Oct 2006.
108. J. Crawford, *In the Field for Peace: New Zealand's Contribution to International Peace-Support Operations, 1950–1995*, New Zealand Defence Force, Wellington, 1996, p. 16; *Army News*, no. 257, 20 Nov 2001; Peter Willis, interviewed 21 Mar 2001.
109. Baker interview.
110. Unit History HQ Battery, 16 Field, RNZA, entry for 30 May 1994; Rob McLean, interviewed 14 Jul 2003.
111. Crawford, *In the Field for Peace*, p. 64.
112. Unit History 161 Battery, diary entry 14–20 Aug 1995. They were training for Operation Radian III, the second rotation of Kiwi Company.
113. The combat and training squadrons, 2, 14 and 75 Squadrons RNZAF, had their final parade at Ohakea on 13 December 2001: *RSA Review*, Feb 2002; Baker interview.
114. *Army News*, 28 Oct 1997. SFOR(G) took fifteen gunners in January, and SFOR(G)2 twenty in June. Unit History 163 Battery, diary entry 27 May 1998; Lt Hayley May, 'SFOR(G)2', *Black Diamond*, 1998/9, p. 12.
115. Unit History of 163 Battery, diary entry 1 Jan 1998; *Army News*, no. 174, 28 Apr 1998.

116. 'SFORGII Deployment Map July–Dec 1998', 16 Field HQ; May, 'SFOR(G)2'; *Army News*, no. 188, 10 Nov 1998; no. 321, 9 Nov 2004; Baker interview.
117. J. Crawford and G. Harper, *Operation East Timor: The New Zealand Defence Force in East Timor, 1999–2001*, Reed, Auckland, 2001; *Army News*, no. 227, 1 Aug 2000.
118. McLean interview. McLean was the Operations Duty Officer in HQ Section West, Suai. Manning was the only New Zealander to die in combat in East Timor.
119. *Evening Post*, 8 Sep 2000; *Army News*, no. 232, 10 Oct 2000; McLean interview.
120. *Army News*, no. 227, 1 Aug 2000; Unit History, Key Appointments for the Month of October 2000; McLean interview. There were two other HQs, Central and East, with all three reporting to HQ Peacekeeping Force (PKF) in Dili. Lieutenant-Colonel Rob Hitchings, a former CO of 16 Field, served as Chief of Staff, HQ Sector West: *Cook Strait News*, 18 Sep 2000. See also Crawford and Harper, *Operation East Timor*, p. 144.
121. Security Brief 019, and diary entries 13 Nov–3 Dec 2000, 'NZ BATTIII History', n.d., no author, 16 Field Regiment, Linton.
122. *Army News*, no. 235, 21 Nov 2000. BATT3's emblem was the tarakona, a winged dragon said by Maori to protect those on dangerous journeys. Armed with a tongue and a taiaha, it was reminiscent of 161 Battery's Rampant Panther (armed with belching flames) and 163 Battery's phoenix.
123. 'NZ BATTIII History', diary entry for 4–11 Dec 2000. This says Gunners' Day was celebrated by 'over 300 Artillery soldiers serving with BATT3', but the actual number was probably lower.
124. *Army News*, no. 240, 27 Mar 2001; Galloway interview.
125. Baker and McLean interviews; *Evening Post*, 13 Oct 2000.
126. Baker interview.
127. Dreyer and Baker interviews.
128. Unit History 161 Battery, diary entry 17–25 Feb 1985; Baker and Galloway interviews.
129. 1990 figure (excluding the TF Reserve) from 'Territorial Force Statistics, 1980–94', in NZ Army Territorial VF, Defence Force Library; 2000 figure from Mark Burton, Minister of Defence, answer to Question no. 5880 in the House, 6 Apr 2000; 2005 figure from NZDF website, http://www.nzdf.mil.nz/at-a-glance/personnel-composition.htm, accessed 9 Dec 2005.
130. Unit History 161 Battery, diary entry 10 Jun 1981.
131. Andrews and Galloway interviews.
132. Unit History 161 Battery, diary entry 13 Oct 1991; *Gunfire*, vol. 3, no. 3, Jun 1982, p.2. The 11(A) Battery personnel covered the 10-kilometre course in 45 minutes. The gun weighs 1.2 tonnes.
133. An L5 caught fire at Western Springs in 1976 because the 1-lb blank round had been over-'pepped' (boosted for effect with oil-soaked newspaper). Mike Subritzky, pers. comm., 14 Jul 2003.
134. Including *Under the Mountain* and *Start Runner*: Unit History 161 Battery, diary entries 30 Apr 1981, 18 Apr 1990.
135. Unit History 161 Battery, diary entry 13–17 Sep 1993: three gunners were among twenty New Zealanders working as Aircraft Loaders for VXE6 Squadron, US Navy Air Devrons, on the ice runway of Williams Field. This occurred first in 1973. Subritzky, pers. comm., 14 Jul 2003.
136. Baker interview; Unit History 22(D) Battery, entry Feb 1977; Unit History 32(E) Battery, diary entry 1–3 Jun 1990.
137. When 31(B) and 32(E) Batteries combined for Exercises Southern Union (Nov 1991) and Modetrain (Feb 1992), they formed '163 Battery' (before that RF battery re-formed in its own right). See Unit History 31(B), Feb 1992; 32(E) Battery, 8–10 Nov 1991.
138. 'Army Air Corps Deactivated', *Army News*, no. 110, 12 Jun 1995. The New Zealand Army Air Corps mustered twelve at its final parade.
139. *Army News*, no. 188, 10 Nov 1998.
140. Appendix 1, 'The New Zealand Defence Force', *The Defence of New Zealand*, 1991.
141. Baker interview; *Army News*, no. 217, 14 Mar 2000.
142. '250 infantry, artillery, engineer, logistic, signals and medical soldiers, RF and TF, came together at Whangaparaoa for … combined arms training.' *Army News*, no. 206, 17 Aug 1999.
143. *Army News*, no. 217, 14 Mar 2000. The six regiments, each fielding a numbered battalion group, were centred on Auckland (3rd Battalion Group), Tauranga (6th), Napier (7th), Wanganui (5th), Burnham (2nd) and Dunedin (4th). 1st and 2nd/1st Battalion Groups, RNZIR, the regular force infantry battalions, are based at Linton and Burnham respectively. Other Battalion Groups had RSMs with different specialities appointed, e.g. 5th Wellington West Coast engineering, 6th Hauraki armoured.

144. *Army News*, no. 196, 30 Mar 1999; no. 205, 3 Aug 1999. Ironically, the 'regionalised' IFS gunners mingled with their 22(D) Battery colleagues at this last L118 shoot.
145. Dave Williams, interviewed 17 Jul 2003. Corps affiliations have traditionally been denoted by beret colour. In 2002 the Army adopted the green beret for all corps except the SAS (which retains the donkey brown beret of its British mother unit), to lessen parochial corps loyalties.
146. *Army News*, no. 199, 11 May 1999. 4 Otago and Southland Battalion Group fired the 1999 Anzac Day salute in Mosgiel.
147. '16 Field Regiment, RNZA: A Short History', http://www.riv.co.nz/rnza/units/16fd/16fdhist.htm, accessed 13 Jun 2003.
148. The rank of Captain-General lasted for only twenty years after 1716, but it was revived by King George VI in 1950 as an honorary higher office for the thirteen Commonwealth units making up the Royal Regiment of Artillery, including those in New Zealand, Australia and Canada.
149. *Army News*, no. 202, 22 Jun 1999.
150. Warrant Officer Dave Williams felt that there were 'too many guys going off to Timor for there to be enough for this reorganisation' and the necessary training: Williams interview.
151. Crawford and Harper, *Operation East Timor*, p. 144; S. Hoadley, 'Lessons From New Zealand's Engagement with East Timor, 1999–2003', *New Zealand International Review*, vol. 28, no. 3, May/Jun 2003.
152. *Army News*, no. 291, 15 Jul 2003.
153. *Army News*, no. 349, 7 Mar 2006.
154. Lt-Col Goss to NMD, 14 Jun 1939, Burns' Personal File, Base Records, NZ Defence Force.
155. J. Burns, *Life is a Twisted Path: A Time of Imprisonment, Escape, Evasion and Final Refuge...*, Santa Maria dell'Anima, Rome, c.2002, p. 15.
156. Medical Boarding Report, 1940, on Hassett's Personal File, Base Records, NZ Defence Force. The other sources for this biography are his unpublished 2003 memoir, 'Once Upon a Time'; the biographical entry in *The Oxford Companion to New Zealand Military History*, Oxford University Press, Auckland, 2000, pp. 215–16; and the obituary in *Dominion Post*, 19 Aug 2004.
157. F. Rennie, *Regular Soldier: A Life in the New Zealand Army*, Endeavour Press, Auckland, 1986, p. 129.
158. W.E. Murphy, *2nd New Zealand Divisional Artillery*, Department of Internal Affairs, Wellington, 1966, p. 633.
159. This falls within Strategic Goal 2: Combat Excellence, Strategy 1 of which is: 'Optimise Army capabilities to effectively and efficiently conduct land operations through appropriate structures, training, doctrine and culture'; Strategy 2 is: 'Modernise Army capabilities on a continuous and sustainable basis.' The Army's mission is 'to provide world-class operationally focused land forces that are led, trained and equipped to win.' New Zealand Army Strategic Plan, NZ Defence Force, 2005, http://www.army.mil.nz/?CHANNEL=PUBLICATIONS&PAGE=Strategic+Plan+%2D+Foreword
160. Baker interview. *The 1997 White Paper: The Shape of New Zealand Defence*, for instance, projected no replacement for them by 2017.
161. One example is Exercise Black Diamond, Unit History 161 Battery, diary entry 5 May 1996.
162. *Army News*, no. 348, 21 Feb 2006.
163. New Zealand Defence Force, 'Personnel Composition', www.nzdf.mil.nz/at-a-glance/personnel-composition.html, accessed 9 Dec 2005; Baker interview. The non-gunnery personnel are called Extra Regimental Appointments.
164. This is derived from: 5573 in the First World War (J. R. Byrne, *New Zealand Artillery in the Field 1914–18*, Whitcombe & Tombs, Auckland et al., 1922, p. 302), 13,000 in the Second World War (CGS to Sec Internal Affairs, 6 Aug 1962, IA1, 181/7/10, ANZ), at least 1000 in Korea (I. McGibbon, *New Zealand and the Korean War, Volume II, Combat Operations*, Oxford University Press, Auckland, 1996, p. 380), and more than 750 in Vietnam ('Flinkenberg List', Vietnam Services Association, p. 29).
165. Former gunner Mike Subritzky cites his father, a son, two cousins and three brothers. Pers. comm., 1 Aug 2003.

Bibliography

Unpublished Sources

Brooker, L.F., 'NZ Army Historical Records, Vol I Volunteer & Territorial Units, Part I 1800–1937', typescript, n.d.

Civilian Narratives, various, WA-II 21/..., Archives NZ

Cooke, P., 'The Poor Cousin: New Zealand's Home Defence in World War One', paper to 'Zealandia's Great War' conference, 10 Nov 2003

Fort Record Books, various coast defence batteries, AD 88, Archives NZ

Fraser, W., '20th Century Military Wellington. A History of the Capitals Defences 1907–1970, Part I: Fort Dorset', typescript, n.d.

Gilberd, J.G., 'Gunners and Horses', typescript, Napier, 1991

Gill, J.T., 'History of the New Zealand Army', typescript, New Zealand Defence Force Library

'History of 6th Field Regiment NZA', Waikato Branch, 6th Field Regimental Association, c. 1975, MS-Papers-6109-3, ATL

McGibbon, I.C., 'New Zealand's Military Policing Activities in the South Pacific, 1919–30', typescript, Ministry for Culture and Heritage, Wellington

Manuals, Handbooks and Instructions, various, NZ Army, 1873–

Nankivell, J.H., 'A Brief History of the NZ Military Forces 1840–1940', typescript, 1940

Newman, S., '3rd Field Regiment, RNZA: During World War Two', typescript, [1983]

Norris, H.C.M., 'Lecture on the History of the 2nd Battery', typescript, 22 Oct 1936

'NZEF: Its Provision and Maintenance', New Zealand Army, Wellington, 1919

Rawlins, S.W.H., 'A History of the Development of the British Artillery in France, 1914–1918', typescript compiled from records of the Major-General RA at GHQ, n.d. [inter-war], Stagg collection, Kippenberger Archive, Army Museum

'Scheme of Defence for the Fortress of Wellington', ABFK, W4052, Box 3, Archives NZ

Signals Officer Diary, Fort Dorset, 1941–43, NZ Defence Force Library, Wellington

Unit Diaries, various artillery units, DA series (North Africa and Italy) and DA-Z series (New Zealand and Pacific), Archives NZ

Unit Histories: 31(B) Battery, 32(E) Battery, 161 Battery, 163 Battery, HQ Battery

War Diary of Divisional Trench Mortar Officer, WA105/1, Archives NZ

Wright, A.A., '9th Coast Regiment, Royal NZ Artillery', typescript, 1952, 80-077, ATL

Personal Diaries, Memoirs and Correspondence

[held at Alexander Turnbull Library, Wellington, unless otherwise stated]

Alexander, D.J.M., 'Another Man's War', typescript, 1992

Anstice, Bert, letters, MS-Papers-5535-01

Armstrong, George Francis, diary, MSX-4176

Burnett, Eric, letters, MS-Papers-2091-1

Craigie, George M., 'How I Got Away from Greece', MS-Papers-4165-1

Duggan, Pat, 'What Have They Done to the Rain?', typescript, 2000

Evenden, Alfred, MS-Papers-91-264

Fraser, Charles, letters, MS-Papers-2269-5

Gordon, J.J., 'Memoirs of World War II, October 1939–November 1943', diary, edited 1996

Hancock, Reg. J., MS-Papers-2323

Hankins, Clarence, diary, MS-Papers-1439

Hassell, Norman, memoir, MS-Papers-2295

Hassett, R., 'Once Upon a Time', memoir, 2003

Heseltine, John C., diaries, MSX-4337

Hogg, W. Fergusson, MS-Papers-1102

Humphreys, Frank, diary, MS-Papers-1623

Hutchison, J.D., transcripts of diaries, MS-Papers-4172

Johnston, G.N., diary, Imperial War Museum, London, 01/12/1

Kinder, James, memoir, MS-Papers-1622

Lysaght, M., 'Going Back', family history, 1996

McBeath, L.W., 'Memoirs of a Kiwi Soldier during the Second World War: Extracts from the diary of L.W. (Mac) McBeath', http://www.bakedbean.co.nz/LWMcB/lwmcbeath.htm, accessed 20 Dec 2005

[McGilp, C.] 'Historical Records and War Diary, 1 Battery, NZFA', MS-1172

McMahon, M., diary, Acc. 1999:105.2, Kippenberger Archive, Army Museum

Matheson, James R., 'Piper At War', typescript, 1994, 16 Field Regiment RNZA History Collection, Linton

Muldoon, John W., diaries, MS-Papers-4309

Pickett, James, diary, MS-Papers-4146

Richmond, James M., letters, 77-173-21

Scott, Robert H., diaries, MS-Papers-1649

Snadden, John P., 'One Up the Spout: A Gunner's Story', typescript, c. 1990, Acc. 1996:437, Kippenberger Archive, Army Museum

Stokes, Bertram Oliver, diary, MS-Papers-4888-1

Stratton, A., memoir, MS-Papers-3823

'The Unofficial History of the 144 (Ind) Battery', Guy Richardson Powles Collection, 96-208-1

Thornton, L.W., '"Marking Time": A Personal Memoir', c.1988

Varian, A.H., diary, 5th Field Regiment Association Collection

Veale, J.P.E., diary, MS 1999-1631, Kippenberger Archive, Army Museum, Waiouru

Wix, Ernest Ebenezer Portal, memoir, MS-Papers-2214

Interviews

[conducted by Alan Henderson unless otherwise stated]

Andrews, Ray, Auckland, 13 Jul 2003 (Peter Cooke)

August, Willie, Linton, 2 Jul 2003 (Peter Cooke)

Baker, Mike, Linton, 21 Jul 2003 (Peter Cooke)

Bell, Ian D., Christchurch, 10 Oct 2000

Bell, R.G. (Geoff), Christchurch, 10 Oct 2000, 27 Aug 2001

Birch, Graham, Tauranga, 20 Oct 2003 (Peter Cooke)

Boyd, Allan, Auckland, 27 Oct 2000

Busfield, Alan, Auckland, 25 Mar 2001, 7 Jul 2003 (Peter Cooke)

Cocks, H. Spencer, Auckland, 20 Nov 1999

Crawley, Matt, Tauranga, 14 Aug & 16 Oct 2000

Diggle, Ian, Auckland, 26 Oct 2000

Dreyer, Barry, Howick, 24 Mar 2001

Duggan, Pat, Christchurch, 13 Oct 2000

Duley, Vern, Papakura, 17 Aug 2000

Dyson, Richard H. (Bert), Tauranga, 14 Aug & 7 Dec 2000 (Megan Hutching)

Foote, John, North Shore, 22 Mar 2001

Galloway, Paul, Linton, 2 Jul 2003 (Peter Cooke)

Gilberd, Jim G., Napier, 20 Sep 1999

Harrop, Barney, North Shore, 19 Aug 2000

Henderson, Murray, telephone, 18 Jun 2003 (Peter Cooke)

Hill, S.F. (Tiny), Christchurch, 11 Oct 2000

Horrocks, John B., Auckland, 27 Oct 2000

Hutcheson, Graeme, Christchurch, 28 Aug 2001

Johnston, Ian T.Y., Hamilton, 17 Oct 2000

Kenning, Don, Palmerston North, 3 Jul 2003 (Peter Cooke)

Kinsella, Allan, Linton, 3 Jul 2003 (Peter Cooke)

Lane, R.K. (Dick), Christchurch, 12 Oct 2000

Lysaght, Andrew, telephone, 13 Jun 2003 (Peter Cooke)

McCallum, W.B.F. (Bill), Christchurch, 28 Aug 2001

McLean, Rob, Auckland, 14 Jul 2003 (Peter Cooke)

Masters, John, Christchurch, 11 Oct 2000, 27 Aug 2001

Milne, George, Auckland, 19 Nov 1999

Norrie, Stuart, Auckland, 21 Mar 2001

O'Connor, Des P., North Shore, 19 Nov 1999

O'Connor, J.B. (Brian), Christchurch, 12 Oct 2000

Peacock, Kendall, Linton, 3 Jul 2003 (Peter Cooke)

Powrie, Bill, Greenhithe, 18 Nov 1999

Ross, Jim, Whenuapai, 17 Nov 2000

Rout, John, Auckland, 15 Jul 2003 (Peter Cooke)

Ruffell, Wally, North Shore, 17 & 18 Nov 1999

Rutherfurd, John, Auckland, 29 May 2001

Simpson, Derek, Auckland, 29 May 2001

Smith, George, Christchurch, 9 Oct 2000

Snadden, John, 22 Jul 1997 (John Crawford)

Spring, Jack, Auckland, 18 Aug 2000

Stack, L.L. (Laurie), Christchurch, 12 Oct 2000

Stanbridge, Colin, North Shore, 23 Mar 2001

Stewart, Clyde, Tauranga, 16 Oct 2000

Valintine, John, Hamilton, 15 Aug 2000

Williams, Dave, telephone, 17 Jul 2003 (Peter Cooke)

Willis, Peter, Auckland, 21 Mar 2001

Wright, Les, Auckland, 25 Oct 2000

THESES

Bentley, T.W., 'Tribal Guns, Tribal Gunners: A Study of Acculturation by Maori of European Military Technology During the New Zealand Inter-tribal Musket Wars', MPhil thesis, University of Waikato, 1997

Clayton, G., 'Defence Not Defiance: The Shaping of New Zealand's Volunteer Force', PhD thesis, University of Waikato, 1990

Crawford, J.A.B., 'The Role and Structure of the New Zealand Volunteer Force 1885–1910', MA thesis, University of Canterbury, 1986

Fox, A.P., 'Silent Sentinels: The War Trophies of the First New Zealand Expeditionary Force in War and Peace', BA(Hons) essay, University of Otago, 1987

Mitchell, J., 'The Disappearing Guns of Auckland: The History and Archaeology of the Forts of Auckland Harbour 1885–1925', PhD thesis, University of Auckland, 1995

Stevens, M.H.S., 'New Zealand Defence Forces and Defence Administration, 1870–1900', MA thesis, Victoria University of Wellington, 1977

Taylor, R.J., 'British Logistics in the New Zealand Wars', PhD thesis, Massey University, 2004

Books and Pamphlets

16 Fd Regt RNZA: Some Aspects of Regimental History, The Regiment, Papakura, 1976

31 (B) Battery Royal New Zealand Artillery: A History of Proud Lineage, The First 125 Years 1863–1988, For Home, Country And Empire Stand By Your Guns, The Battery, Dunedin, 1988

120th Anniversary Celebrations, Band of the Royal Regiment NZ Artillery, 1864–1984, Auckland, 1984

Aitken, A., *Gallipoli to the Somme: Recollections of a New Zealand Infantryman*, Oxford University Press, London, 1963

Bailey, J.B.A., *Field Artillery and Firepower*, Military Press, Oxford, 1989

Barber, L., G. Clayton and J. Tonkin-Covell (eds), *Sergeant, Sinner, Saint, and Spy: The Taranaki War Diary of Sergeant William Marjouram, R.A.*, Random Century, Auckland, 1990

Barratt, G., *Russophobia in New Zealand 1838–1908*, Dunmore Press, Palmerston North, 1981

Barthorp, M., *To Face the Daring Maoris: Soldiers' Impressions of the First Maori War, 1845–47*, Hodder & Stoughton, London et al., 1979

Batley, H.F., *From Reveille To Lights Out: A Short, Incomplete, Somewhat Boring And Wandering Account of Members of the Artillery Band's Days in Camp During World War II*, author, Auckland, 1996

[Batley, H.F.] *Official History of the Band of the Royal Regiment of New Zealand Artillery, Northern Military District*, Auckland Artillery Band Association, Auckland, 1964

Begg, R.C., and P.H. Liddle (eds), *For Five Shillings A Day: Experiencing War, 1939–45*, HarperCollins, London, 2000

Belich, J., *The New Zealand Wars and the Victorian Interpretation of Racial Conflict*, Auckland University Press, Auckland, 1986

Bliss, G.C., *Gunners' Story: A Short History of the Artillery Volunteers of Christchurch, 1867–1967*, Canterbury Artillery Officers' Mess, Christchurch, 1970

Blythe, J., *Soldiering On: A Soldier's War in North Africa and Italy*, Hutchinson, London/Auckland, 1989

Boyack, N., and J. Tolerton, *In the Shadow of War: New Zealand Soldiers Talk About World War One and Their Lives*, Penguin, Auckland, 1990

Breen, B., *First to Fight: Australian Diggers, NZ Kiwis and US Paratroopers in Vietnam, 1965–66*, Allen & Unwin, Sydney, 1988

Brewer, N.H., *The Soldier Tourist: A Personal Account of World War II*, Reed, Auckland, 1999

Brocklebank, L., *Jayforce: New Zealand and the Military Occupation of Japan 1945–48*, Oxford University Press, Auckland, 1997

Brookes, K., *Battle Thunder: The Story of Britain's Artillery*, Osprey Publishing, Reading, 1973

Buckley, D.A. (ed.), *Godley Head and Battery Point: A History of Coastal Defence During World War II*, Ministry of Defence, Christchurch, 1984

Burns, J., *Life is a Twisted Path: A Time of Imprisonment, Escape, Evasion and Final Refuge...*, Santa Maria dell'Anima, Rome, c.2002

Burton, C., *Report of the Gender Integration Audit of the New Zealand Defence Force, October 1998*, New Zealand Defence Force/ New Zealand Human Rights Commission, Wellington, 1998

Burton, O.E., *The New Zealand Division*, Clark & Matheson, Auckland, 1936

Burton, O.E., *The Silent Division: New Zealanders at the Front, 1914–1919*, Angus & Robertson, Sydney, 1935

Byrne, J.R., *New Zealand Artillery in the Field 1914–18*, Whitcombe & Tombs, Auckland et al., 1922

Bibliography

Carbery, A.D., *The New Zealand Medical Service in the Great War, 1914–1918: Based on Official Documents*, Whitcombe & Tombs, Auckland, 1924

Challinor, D., *Grey Ghosts: New Zealand Vietnam Vets Talk About their War*, Hodder Moa Beckett, Auckland, 1998

Chamberlain, P., and T. Gander, *Anti-Tank Weapons*, Macdonald & Jane's, London, 1974

Chamberlain, P., and T. Gander, *Heavy Artillery*, Macdonald & Jane's, London, 1975

Chamberlain, P., and T. Gander, *Infantry, Mountain and Airborne Guns*, Macdonald & Jane's, London, 1975

Chamberlain, P., and T. Gander, *Light and Medium Field Artillery*, Macdonald & Jane's, London, 1975

Chandler, D. (ed.), *The Oxford Illustrated History of the British Army*, Oxford University Press, Oxford/New York, 1994

Chant, C., *Artillery: Over 300 of the World's Finest Artillery Pieces from 1914 to the Present Day*, Silverdale Books, Leicester, 2005

Clayton, J.C., *The New Zealand Army: A History from the 1840's to the 1990's*, New Zealand Army, Wellington, 1990

Clifton, G., *The Happy Hunted*, Cassell, London, 1952

Cooke, P., *Defending New Zealand: Ramparts on the Sea 1840–1950s*, 2 vols, Defence of New Zealand Study Group, Wellington, 2000

Cooze, F., *Kiwis in the Pacific*, A.H. & A.W. Reed, Wellington, c. 1944

Corbett, D.A., *The Regimental Badges of New Zealand: An Illustrated History of the Badges and Insignia Worn by the New Zealand Army*, Ray Richards, Auckland, 1980

Corbett, P., *World War II Defences at Stony Batter (Waiheke Island) and Whangaparaoa: 9.2-inch Counter-bombardment Batteries A-1 and A-2*, Department of Conservation, Auckland, 1996

Cowan, J., *The New Zealand Wars: A History of the Maori Campaigns and the Pioneering Period*, 2 vols, reprinted Government Printer, Wellington, 1983

Cox, G., *The Race for Trieste*, William Kimber, London, 1977

Crawford, J., *In the Field for Peace: New Zealand's Contribution to International Peace-Support Operations, 1950–1995*, New Zealand Defence Force, Wellington, 1996

Crawford, J., and G. Harper, *Operation East Timor: The New Zealand Defence Force in East Timor, 1999–2001*, Reed, Auckland, 2001

Crawford, J., with E. Ellis, *To Fight for the Empire: An Illustrated History of New Zealand and the South African War, 1899–1902*, Reed, Auckland, 1999

Crosby, R.D., *The Musket Wars: A History of Inter-Iwi Conflict*, Reed, Auckland, 1999

Dennistoun-Wood, C., *The Naval Volunteers in New Zealand*, 1991

Dial Sights: Sketches of the NZFA by an Artillery Digger, New Zealand War Records, London, 1919

Drew, H.T.B. (ed.), *The War Effort of New Zealand*, Whitcombe & Tombs, Auckland et al., 1923

Fenton, D.M., *A False Sense of Security: The Force Structure of the New Zealand Army 1946–1978*, Centre for Strategic Studies, Wellington, 1998

Fifty Years On, A Time to Remember: Historical Record of the 14th NZ Light Anti-Aircraft Regiment..., 1941–1945, 14th NZ LAA Regimental Association, Levin, 1991

Foss, C.F., *Artillery of the World*, Ian Allan, London, 1974 and 1976 edns

Fraser, W., *Defending Wellington's Sky: A Short History of the Capital's Anti-Aircraft Units 1937–1958*, Acton, Fraser & Associates, Wellington, 1992

Fullford, R.K., *We Stood and Waited: Sydney's Anti-Ship Defences, 1939–1945*, Royal Australian Artillery Historical Society, Manly, 1994

Gander, T., and P. Chamberlain, *Small Arms, Artillery and Special Weapons of the Third Reich*, Macdonald & Jane's, London, 1978

Gascoyne, F.J.W., *Soldiering in New Zealand, Being Reminiscences of a Veteran*, 1916, facsimile edn, Kiwi Publishers, Christchurch, 1999

Gillespie, O.A., *The Pacific*, Department of Internal Affairs, Wellington, 1952

Grandin, B., *The Battle of Long Tan as Told by the Commanders to Bob Grandin*, Allen & Unwin, Crows Nest NSW, 2004

Grattan, F.G., *Official War History of the Public Works Department*, The Department, Wellington, 1948

Halberstadt, H., *The World's Great Artillery from the Middle Ages to the Present Day*, Grange Books, Rochester, 2002

Hall, D.O.W., *The New Zealanders in South Africa 1899–1902*, Department of Internal Affairs, Wellington, 1949

Harper, G., *Massacre at Passchendaele: The New Zealand Story*, HarperCollins, Auckland, 2000

Henderson, J., *Gunner Inglorious*, H.H. Tombs, Wellington, 1945

Hogg, I.V., *A History of Artillery*, Hamlyn, London, 1974

Hogg, I.V., *Allied Artillery of World War One*, Crowood, Marlborough, 1998

Hogg, I.V., *An Illustrated Encyclopedia of Artillery*, Stanley Paul, London, 1987

Hogg, I.V., *British and American Artillery of World War 2*, Arms & Armour, London, 1978

Hogg, I.V., *The Illustrated History of Ammunition*, New Burlington, London, 1985

Hogg, I.V., and J. Batchelor, *Naval Gun*, Blandford, Poole, 1978

Hogg, I.V., and L.F. Thurston, *British Artillery Weapons and Ammunition, 1914–1918*, Allan, London, 1972

Holmes, R., *Acts of War: The Behaviour of Men in Battle*, revised edn, Cassell, London, 2003

Horner, D.M., *The Gunners: A History of Australian Artillery*, Allen & Unwin, St Leonards NSW, 1995

Howlett, R.A., *The History of the Fiji Military Forces, 1939–1945*, Crown Agents for the Colonies, London, 1948

Hunnicutt, R.D., *Sherman: A History of American Medium Tanks*, Presidio Press, California, 1978/94

Hursthouse, M., *Vintage Doctor: Fifty Years of Laughter and Tears*, Shoal Bay Press, Christchurch, 2001

Hutching, M. (ed.), *'A Unique Sort of Battle': New Zealanders Remember Crete*, HarperCollins, Auckland, 2001

Ingham, I.N., *Anzac Diary: A Nonentity in Khaki*, Treharne Publishers, Christchurch, 1987

Jennings, P., *Exercise Golden Fleece and the New Zealand Military: Lessons and Limitations*, Australian National University, Canberra, 1989

Laws, M.E.S. (compiler), *Battery Records of the Royal Artillery, 1859–1877*, Royal Artillery Institute, London, 1970

Lawson, W., *Featherston Military Training Camp*, Brett, Auckland, 1917

McAulay, L., *The Battle of Long Tan*, Hutchinson of Australia, Melbourne, 1986

MacGibbon, J. (ed.), *Struan's War*, Ngaio Press, Wellington, 2001

McDonald, K.C. (ed. G. McLean), *Oamaru 1878: A Colonial Town*, Waitaki District Council, Oamaru, 2006

McDonald, W., *Honours and Awards to the New Zealamd Expeditionary Force in the Great War 1914–18*, Helen McDonald, Napier, 2001

McDougall, R.J., *New Zealand Naval Vessels*, GP Books, Wellington, 1989

McGibbon, I., *Blue-Water Rationale: The Naval Defence of New Zealand, 1914–1942*, Department of Internal Affairs, Wellington, 1981

McGibbon, I., *Kiwi Sappers: The Corps of Royal New Zealand Engineers' Century of Service*, Reed, Auckland, 2002

McGibbon, I., *New Zealand and the Korean War, Volume II: Combat Operations*, Oxford University Press, Auckland, 1996

McGibbon, I., *The Path to Gallipoli: Defending New Zealand 1840–1915*, GP Books, Wellington, 1991

McGibbon, I. (ed.), *The Oxford Companion to New Zealand Military History*, Oxford University Press, Auckland, 2000

McIntyre, W.D., *New Zealand Prepares for War: Defence Policy, 1919–39*, University of Canterbury Press, Christchurch, 1988

McLintock, A.H. (ed.), *An Encyclopaedia of New Zealand*, 3 vols, Government Printer, Wellington, 1966

Martin, T., *New Zealand Images of War*, Dunmore Press, Palmerston North, 1990

Martyn, F., *Tripoli and Beyond*, Collins, Auckland, 1944

Mason, H.B., *Memoirs of a Gunner Bandsman, 1907–1932*, author, Orpington, c.1978

Millen, J., *Salute to Service: A History of the Royal New Zealand Corps of Transport and its Predecessors 1860–1996*, Victoria University Press, Wellington, 1997

Munro, R.D., *4th NZ Field Regiment – 2NZEF, 1939–46*, author, Upper Hutt, 1992

Munro, R.D., *5th NZ Field Regiment – 2NZEF, 1940–46*, author, Upper Hutt, 1992

Munro, R.D., *6th NZ Field Regiment – 2NZEF, 1939–45*, author, Upper Hutt, 1990

Munro, R.D., *7th NZ Anti-Tank Regiment – 2NZEF, 1939–46*, author, Upper Hutt, 1992

Munro, R.D., *14th NZ Light Ack-Ack Regiment – 2NZEF, 1941–45*, author, Upper Hutt

Munro, R.D., *39/34 Heavy Mortar Battery, 7 N.Z. Anti-Tank Regiment, 2 N.Z.E.F. in Italy, 1944–45*, author, Upper Hutt, 1990

Munro, R.D., *Artillery Surveyors – 2NZEF, 1940–45*, author, Upper Hutt, 1994

Murphy, W.E., *2nd New Zealand Divisional Artillery*, Department of Internal Affairs, Wellington, 1966

Murphy, W.E., *Point 175: The Battle of Sunday of the Dead*, Department of Internal Affairs, Wellington, 1954

Napier, W.E.L., *With the Trench Mortars in France*, Alpe Bros, Auckland, 1923

Neal, K., and N. Leov, *The Price of Vigilance: The Building of the Gun Emplacements in the Marlborough Sounds, 1942*, authors, Nelson, 1999

Nelson, C.L., *Long Time Passing: New Zealand Memories of the Vietnam War*, National Radio, Wellington, 1990

Newman, S.D., *Vietnam Gunners: 161 Battery RNZA, South Vietnam, 1965–71*, Moana Press, Tauranga, 1988

New Zealand Field Artillery: B Battery, 1863–1913, John McIndoe, Dunedin, 1913

Norris, J., *Artillery: A History*, Sutton Publishing, Stroud, Gloucestershire, 2000

Official History of the Band of the Royal Regiment of New Zealand Artillery, Northern Military District, Auckland Artillery Band Association, Auckland, 1964

Pakenham, T., *The Boer War*, Weidenfeld & Nicolson, London, 1979

Paton, H., *Private Paton's Pictures: Behind the Lines with Kiwi Soldiers in North Africa 1941–1943*, Penguin, Auckland, 2003

Pemberton, A.L., *The Development of Artillery Tactics and Equipment*, War Office, London, 1950

Phillips, J., N. Boyack & E.P. Malone (eds), *The Great Adventure: New Zealand Soldiers Describe the First World War*, Allen & Unwin/Port Nicholson Press, Wellington, 1988

Plowman, J., *Rampant Dragons: New Zealanders in Armour in WWII*, Kiwi Armour, Christchurch, c.2002

Plowman, J., and M. Thomas, *4th New Zealand Armoured Brigade in Italy*, J. Plowman, Christchurch, c.2000

Polack, J.S., *Manners and Customs of the New Zealanders...*, James Madden & Co., London, 1840, reprinted Capper Press, Christchurch, 1976

Poulton, W., *K Force in Korea: A Soldier's Life in the 16th New Zealand Field Regiment*, author, Woodville, 2004

Powles, C.G., *The New Zealanders in Sinai and Palestine*, Whitcombe & Tombs, Auckland et al., 1922

Priday, H., *The War from Coconut Square: The Story of the Defence of the Island Bases of the South Pacific*, A.H. & A.W. Reed, Wellington, 1945

Pugh, S., *Fighting Vehicles and Weapons of the Modern British Army*, MacDonald, London, 1962

Pugsley, C., *From Emergency to Confrontation: The New Zealand Armed Forces in Malaya and Borneo 1949–1966*, Oxford University Press, Melbourne, 2003

Pugsley, C., *Gallipoli: The New Zealand Story*, Hodder & Stoughton, Auckland, 1984

Pugsley, C., *The ANZAC Experience: New Zealand, Australia and the Empire in the First World War*, Reed, Auckland, 2004

Rayward, C., *The Distinguished History of 3rd Field Regiment, Royal New Zealand Artillery, 1940–1990*, The Regiment, Christchurch, 1990

Rennie, F., *Regular Soldier: A Life in the New Zealand Army*, Endeavour Press, Auckland, 1986

Rolfe, J., *The Armed Forces of New Zealand*, Allen & Unwin, St Leonards, NSW, 1999

Rowe, T., *Steve Weir: New Zealand's Master Gunner*, Occasional Paper no. 4, Military Studies Institute, New Zealand Army, Upper Hutt, 2004

Ryan, T., and B. Parham, *The Colonial New Zealand Wars*, Grantham House, Wellington, 1986

Salmond, Anne, *Two Worlds: First Meetings Between Maori and Europeans 1642–1772*, Viking, Auckland, 1991

Scholefield, G.H. (ed.), *A Dictionary of New Zealand Biography*, Department of Internal Affairs, Wellington, 1940

Scott, D., *Ask That Mountain: The Story of Parihaka*, Heinemann/Southern Cross, Auckland, 1987

Seacoast Artillery Weapons, TM 4-210, US War Department, 1944

Sheffield, G., *Forgotten Victory: The First World War – Myths and Realities*, Headline Book Publishing, London, 2001

Slater, H., *Fifty Years of Volunteering: The Army of Regulations*, Whitcombe & Tombs, Christchurch, 1910

Smith, E.H., *Guns Against Tanks: L Troop, 33rd Battery, 7th New Zealand Anti-Tank Regiment in Libya, 23 November 1941*, Department of Internal Affairs, Wellington, 1948

Smith, S.J., *The Samoa (N.Z.) Expeditionary Force, 1914–15*, Ferguson & Osborn, Wellington, 1924

Stanley, J.H. (ed.), *World War I Diaries of Cyril Gordon Haultain 1916–1919: A Waikato Dairy Farmer Goes to the Great War*, R.D. & J.C. Stanley, Matamata, 2002

Stewart, H., *The New Zealand Division, 1916–1919: A Popular History Based on Official Records*, Whitcombe & Tombs, Auckland et al., 1921

Subritzky, M. (ed.), *Kiwi Gunners in War and Peace*, Kiwiana Publishing, Tauranga, 2004

Subritzky, M. (ed.), *The Vietnam Scrapbook: 'The Second ANZAC Adventure'*, Three Feathers, Papakura, 1995

Summary of Recommendations, Inquiry into the Exposure of New Zealand Defence Personnel to Agent Orange and other Defoliant

Chemicals during the Vietnam War and any Health Effects of That Exposure, and Transcripts of Evidence, Health Committee, House of Representatives, Wellington, 2004

Taylor, A. (ed.), *The New Zealand Roll of Honour: New Zealanders Who Have Served Their Country In Peace and War, 150 Years, 1845–1995*, Alister Taylor, Auckland, 1998

Taylor, N.M., *The New Zealand People at War: The Home Front*, 2 vols, Department of Internal Affairs, Wellington, 1986

Taylor, R., *Tribe of the War God: Ngati Tumatauenga*, Heritage New Zealand, Napier, 1996

The Army Schools Centennial Journal, 1885–1985, Government Printer, Wellington, 1985

The Dictionary of New Zealand Biography, Department of Internal Affairs et al, Wellington, 5 vols, 1990–2000

The Gunners: An Intimate Record of Units of the 3rd New Zealand Divisional Artillery in the Pacific from 1940 until 1945, A.H. & A.W. Reed for Third Division Histories Committee, Wellington, 1948

The Gunners Handbook: An Introduction to the Regiment, Royal Regiment of New Zealand Artillery (updated periodically)

The New Zealand Army in Vietnam 1964–1972: A Report on the Chief of General Staff's Exercise, 1972, Ministry of Defence, Wellington, 1973

Thompson, M., *Our War: The Grim Digs – New Zealand Soldiers in North Africa 1940–1943*, Penguin, Auckland, 2005

Todd, G.A., *The Role of the Royal New Zealand Artillery Within the Ready Reaction Force*, Commandant's Paper, NZAF Command & Staff College, 1988

Uren, M., *Diamond Trails of Italy*, Collins, Auckland, 1945

Uren, M., *Kiwi Saga*, Collins, Cairo, 1943

Waite, F., *The New Zealanders at Gallipoli*, Whitcombe & Tombs, Auckland et al., 1919

Wards, I., *The Shadow of the Land: A Study of British Policy and Racial Conflict in New Zealand, 1832–1852*, Department of Internal Affairs, Wellington, 1968

Waters, S.D., *The Royal New Zealand Navy*, Department of Internal Affairs, Wellington, 1956

Weston, C.H., *Three Years With the New Zealanders*, Skeffington, London, c.1919

Weston, D., *Memories: South Vietnam, 1968–1969*, author, Upper Hutt, 1998

Who's Who in New Zealand, various publishers, 1908–78 edns

Wilkes, O., *A History of New Zealand Chemical Warfare, 1845–1945*, Working Paper No. 4, Centre for Peace Studies, University of Auckland, 1993

Wright, M., *Two Peoples, One Land: The New Zealand Wars*, Reed, Auckland, 2006

Articles

Crawford, J., 'Overt and Covert Military Involvement in the 1890 Maritime Strike and 1913 Waterfront Strike in New Zealand', *Labour History*, no. 60, May 1991

Gates, J.M., 'James Belich and the Modern Maori Pa: Revisionist History Revised', *War and Society*, vol. 19, no. 2, Oct 2001

Hoadley, S., 'Lessons from New Zealand's Engagement with East Timor, 1999–2003', *New Zealand International Review*, vol. 28, no. 3, May/Jun 2003

Mitchell, A., 'The Close Support Weapon System for the Ready Reaction Force to the Year 2005', *New Zealand Army Journal*, no. 8, Jul 1989

Porter, R., '16 Field Regiment in Korea, Part III: Towards the End', *Duty First*, Jun 1995

Porter, R., 'With 16 Field Regiment Royal NZ Artillery in Korea 1950–51', *Duty First*, Jun 1992

Springer, R., 'Rangihaeata's Cannon', *Journal of the Whanganui Historical Society*, vol. 22, no. 2, Nov 1991; also at http://www.riv.co.nz/rnza/hist/rangi.htm

Subritzky, M., 'The 161 Battery Panther', *Commonwealth Heraldry Bulletin*, no. 21, 1995

Turner, P., 'The Royal Artillery in New Zealand', *Journal of the Victorian Military Historical Society*, no. 46, Dec 1986

Winter, C., 'The Origins of Australian Defence: The Royal Artillery in Australia and New Zealand, 1845 to 1870', *Army Journal*, Feb 1973

Witana, R.G., 'Role of the Royal New Zealand Artillery in Low Level Operations', *New Zealand Army Journal*, no. 13, Dec 1991

BIBLIOGRAPHY

SERIALS

Army News

Black Diamond, 16 Field Regiment, RRNZA

Flak, 22 Light Anti-Aircraft Regiment, Auckland (bi-weekly from Mar 1943)

Forts & Works, Defence of New Zealand Study Group, Wellington

Gunfire, RRNZA newsletter

Jane's Armour and Artillery

Journal of the Coast Defence Study Group (US)

Journal of the Ordnance Society (UK)

Navy and Army Illustrated (UK), 1890–1900s

New Zealand Antique Arms Gazette

New Zealand Defence Quarterly, 1993–2000

Newsletter of the Coast Defence Study Group (US)

Newsletter of the Ordnance Society (UK)

The Volunteers, 1973–

WEBSITE

Royal New Zealand Artillery Old Comrades' Association,
    http://www.riv.co.nz/rnza/index.htm

Index

1 Australian Task Force 416, 418, 422
1 Battalion New Zealand Regiment 403
1 Commonwealth Division 391, 395, 400–2
1 Royal Australian Regiment 413–5, 423
1 Cavalry Division (US) 385
1/503 Infantry Battalion (US) 414
2 Auckland Battalion 121
2 Battalion, Canadian Light Infantry 385
2 Parachute Brigade (UK) 280
2 Royal Australian Regiment 401
2 Waikato Battalion 316
2/3 Australian Field Regiment 208
2/35 Howitzer Battalion (US) 416
2/503 Regiment (US) 414
3 Field Regiment RA 272
3 Royal Australian Regiment 381, 384–5, 388, 396, 422–3
3/319 Field Artillery Battalion (US) 413–4
4 Armoured Brigade 272–3, 277, 290, 294
4 Brigade RA 23–4
4 Indian Division 275
4 Light Armoured Brigade 261
4 New Zealand Brigade 193–4, 197, 204, 207, 217–8, 220, 234, 236, 248–50
5 Cavalry Regiment (US) 389
5 New Zealand Brigade 207, 210, 217, 220, 225, 227, 230, 236, 249, 255, 263, 266, 273, 285, 291, 294, 296
6 Battalion RA 22
6 New Zealand Brigade 188, 206, 208–9, 227, 232–3, 249–50, 255, 267, 277, 285, 288–9, 292, 294
6 Royal Australian Regiment 416, 418
7 Armoured Division 264
7 Battalion RA 22, 24
7 Medium Regiment RA 204, 207–8, 252
7 New Zealand Brigade 326

7 Royal Australian Regiment 422
8 Armoured Brigade 265
8 Brigade 329–30, 336, 338, 343
8 Medium Regiment 325
8 Royal Australian Regiment 424
9 Armoured Brigade 255–6
9 Australian Division 257
9 New Zealand Brigade 298
10 New Zealand Brigade 218–20
14 Brigade 330, 332, 336–7, 340, 342, 348–9
16 Brigade Group 331
18 Battalion 234
19 Battalion 221
20 ANZUK Field Regiment 434
20 Battalion 220, 234
21 Battalion 205–6, 209, 220, 273
21 Division 117
22 Battalion 207, 219
22 (Motorised) Battalion 288
23 Battalion 207, 219, 255, 449
24 Battalion 208, 210, 233, 284
24 Infantry Division (US) 381
25 Battalion 208, 210–1
26 Battalion 208, 227, 233, 283
28 (Maori) Battalion 207, 220, 266, 276, 286, 399
29 Battalion 343, 345
30 Battalion 341, 349–50
33 Regiment RA 25
34 Battalion 343, 346
35 Battalion 350
36 Battalion 343, 345
36 Regiment RA 24
37 Battalion 330, 350
41 Division (UK) 111

INDEX

42 Division (UK)   114, 142–4
50 Division (UK)   266
51 Highland Division   264
56 Division (UK)   268
61 Field Artillery Battalion (US)   389
64 Medium Regiment RA   206, 208, 214, 250, 267
65 Field Regiment RA   267
69 Medium Regiment RA   255–6, 267
74 Field Regiment RA   267
78 Field Regiment RA   255
98 Field Regiment RA   255
111 Field Regiment RA   267, 274
124 Field Regiment RA   267
147 Brigade RFA   96
173 Airborne Brigade (US)   413–5, 426
211 Brigade RFA   186

A

Abbott ammunition   441, 450
ABCA Quadripartite Working Group   452, 466
ablution facilities   76, 165, 191
Achi Baba   96–7
Addington Racecourse & Showgrounds   66, 135, 437
Aden   89
Adige River   296
Admiral Hipper   197
aerial observation, New Zealand   376–8
Afghanistan   466–7
Africa   4, 14, 56, 58, 73, 190, 196, 224, 268–9, 298, 314, 332
Afrika Korps   224, 227, 231
Agent Orange   427
AGRA   272–3, 275, 280, 283, 293
air defences   320–3, 342, 365, 368, 370–1, 374, 406, 452–3
air transport   412
Akaroa Harbour   309
Alamein Line   254
Alam Halfa   251
Alam Nayil   248–9, 251
Albert Park   41, 471
alcohol   119, 191, 196, 226, 238, 246, 269, 351, 380, 382, 415, 416, 457
Aldershot   107, 120, 158, 195, 246, 353
Aleppo   245
Alerting and Cueing Radar   453
Alexandra (Pirongia)   55
Alexandra Barracks   355
Alexandra Park   135

Aliakmon Line   203–5, 207
Alife   275
Allen, Hon James, Minister of Defence   135
Allen, William (bugler)   443
Allen Force   209
Alligator, HMS   18
Amberley, RAF Base   445
Amiens   137, 142
Amiriya   203
Amman   244
ammunition   12, 15, 19, 24, 29, 30, 47, 65, 69, 71, 88, 91–2, 94, 98, 100–2, 115, 117–8, 120, 122–3, 127, 129–31, 133, 135, 142, 151–3, 164, 166, 169, 200, 203, 208, 211, 219–20, 224, 228–9, 233, 255, 268–9, 276–7, 280–1, 287–8, 360–1, 388–9, 393–6, 412, 441–2, 449–50
ammunition columns   88, 105, 135, 137, 144, 240
amphibious exercises   245, 296, 309, 312, 314, 332, 336–9, 343, 349, 351–2, 380, 434
AMTB (anti-motor torpedo boat) defences   176, 314
anchorages, strategic   72, 162, 313, 315
Anderson, Sgt Roy   349
Andrew, Lt-Col Les   219
Andrews, Brig. Ray   377, 408, 446, 457
Angola   454
Antarctica   459
anti-malarial pills   335, 351, 382
anti-motor torpedo boat defences   176, 314
Anzac Cove   92–3, 96, 99, 103, 341
Anzacs   91–4, 96–105, 118, 121, 125–7, 168, 194, 206, 213, 244, 411, 416, 421
Anzio   275
ANZUK Force   434
ANZUS   359, 429, 431, 445–6
Apennines   271, 275, 290
Apia   84, **85**
Arce   283
Arezzo   283–4
Argyle Battalion   385
Ari Burnu   93
Arielli   273
Ariete Division   248–9
Armed Constabulary   25–6, 28, **32**, 33, 44, 46, 55
Armentières   105–6, 108–14, 120, 124, 138
Army Ready Reaction Unit   448–9
Army Reserve (7 Brigade)   188
Army Schools   176, 179, 372–3, 462
Army Service Corps   181

509

Arno River 287
ARRU (Army Ready Reaction Unit) 448–9
Arter, Doug 425
Artillery Depot **199**
Artillery School 61
Artillery Tactical Headquarters 272
artillery techniques 154–5
Artillery Training Depot 270, 336, 358
'Arty Tac Cell' 438
Asia 82, 84, 309, 359, 363, 403, 408, 433–4
assault barges 441
assistant gun position officers (AGPOs) 423
Athens 203, 206, 210, 213–4
Auchinleck, Fd Mshl Claude 245
Auckland 2, 26–8, 31, 33–4, 36, 38–9, 41–2, 45–7, 49, 55, 62–3, 66–7, 69–72, 75, 77, 83, 101, 121, 135, 157–8, 160–4, 166, 168–71, 177, 180, 241, 309, 311–6, 318–20, 322–3, 325, 329, 334, 355, 365–6, 368, 375, 443–4, 446
Auckland Artillery Band 42, 443
Auckland Garrison 67
Auckland Volunteer Coastguard 26, 33
Auckland Volunteer Rifle Company 33
Auster aircraft 292, 377–8
Australia 13, 80, 102, 194, 240, 312, 325, 328, 359, 373, 407, 412–3, 415, 428, 430, 433–5, 440–2, 445–6, 448, 450, 452–3, 465
Australian Light Horse 96
Australian Staff College 464
Australian Task Force 418, 422–3, 425
Austria 304
Avezzano 283
Awapuni Racecourse 88
Axios Plain 204

B

Baalbek 245
Babington, Maj. Gen. James 63, 65–6, 68
Bacchante, HMS 100
Baggush 197, 200, 236, 243
bagpipes 192
Bailey bridges 272, 289
Balsorano 281–3
Bamian 467
bands 41, **42**, 47, 192, 425, 440, 443, **444**, 459
Bangkok 305, 431
Bapaume 117, 142
Barahun Island 350

Barakoma 340
Barbara (last artillery horse) 182, 457
Bardia 227, 236, **245**
Baria 414, 422
Barkle, Gnr Cliff 194, 205
barrages 60, 111, 115, 121, 123, 125–7, 130–2, 141–6, 153–4, 250, 253, 255–6, 258, 262, 268, 273, 277, 281, 291–6, 298, 301, 307–8, 343, 350, 388–9, 393, 399
 creeping 13, 59, 111, 115, 117, 123, 125–7, 129–31, 134, 138, 142, 147, 253, 255–6, 258, 272–3, 277, 285–6, 291
 diversionary 141
 'dragnet' 294
 hurricane 142
 lifting 255, 266–7
 protective 127, 132, 143
 reverse 117, 414
 rolling 393
 standing 129
 types 154–5
Barrett, Dicky 19
Barrowclough, Maj. Gen. H.E. 332, 341, 349, 354
Bassett, Capt. Shay 454, 456
Bastion Point 47, 314, 319
Battery Point 174
Bay of Islands 17–22, 162, 309, 312, 314, 315, 318
Beacon Hill 320
Beattie, Lt-Col Matt 455–6
Beaudignies 119, 144–5
Beaumont-Hamel 137
Beauvais 144
Beira 58
Beirut 259
Bekaa Valley 245
Belgium 82, 105, 122, 147–8, 172
Belhamed 223, 225, 228–9, 233, **235**, 236–7, 242, 303–4
Bellaria 288
Bellevue Spur 131
Benghazi 226, 259, 269
Berlin 363
Bevan, Capt. T.H. 205
Bien Hoa Airbase 413–4
Birch, Capt. Graham 415
Birdwood, Lt. Gen. Sir William 91, 100
Blampied, Maj. Martin 323, 424
Blanche Harbour 344, 347–8
Blenheim 323
Bloemfontein 58

Boddam, Lt-Col Edmond Meyer Tudor 54
Boer War *see* South African War
Boggs, Capt. Matt 456
Bombardier **366**
Borgard, Albert 364
Borneo 408–9, 426
Boro 341
Bosnia–Herzegovina 439, 454–5
Bougainville 343, 349
Boulcott's Farm 443
Boulogne 107
Bouloupari 336
Bourail 336
Boussières 146
Boyd, Allan 191, 195, 254
Brallos Pass 204, 210
Brasell, Fred 312
Bridge, Maj. Cyprian 238
Brisbane 380, 402, 407
Bristol 196
Britain 27–30, 33, 51, 69, 70, 72, 76, 79, 86, 88, 107, 148, 162, 166, 169–70, 181, 187, 190, 194–5, 301, 303, 312, 323, 349, 353, 360, 367–8, 372, 374, 407, 409, 428, 433–5, 441–2, 450, 452–3
British Commonwealth Brigade 381, 387, 390
British Commonwealth Occupation Force 360
Britomart Point 27
Broodseinde 127
Broomhall, Murray 417
Brown, Chris 377
Bucquoy 141
Buffelshoek 59
buglers 443
Bulawayo 58
Bull, Major 163
Buller, Gen. Sir Redvers 59, 60
Burma 298
Burnham Camp 373, 375, 379, 404, 437
Burns, Brig. John (Blackie) 400, 402, **462**
Burrows, Brig. I.H. 438

C
cadets 162–3
Cairo 89, 90, 194, 244, 252, 259, 271, 304
Calais 107
calibration shoots 142, 332
Camberley Staff College 78, 241, 302–3, 353, 429
Cambrai 240

Cameron, Gen. Duncan 21, 24–5
Campbell, George **80**, 81
camps **32**, 39, **40**, **44**, **52**, **57**, **62**, 72, 75, **76**, 84, 89–90, 135, 157–8, **165**, 167–8, 177, 180, 294, 324, 332, 345, 375, 422, 439, 459
Canada 56, 148, 181, 446, 452
Canal de Saint Quentin 144
Canal du Nord 143
Canberra 61
Canea 215, 221
canister shot 17
Canterbury 34–5, 39, 41, 75, 187, 241, 246, 391
Cape Alara 320
Cape Helles 91, 96–8, 102, 103
Cape Matapan 203
Cape Town 57, 59, 86, 91, 96, 102, 195, 203
capitation funding 37, 41, 50, 53
captain-general 364
Cardito 279
Carlisle 214
Carreto 294
carriage guns 17
Carrington, Gen. Sir Frederick 11, 58–9
carronades 18–9, 22
Carty, Lt-Col Jack 243
Caserta 463
Cashmore, Mtr Gnr Stan 377
Cassels, Maj. Gen. A.J.H. 391
Cassino 188, 275–81
Castor Bay 311, 355, 368–9
Castries 17
casualties 20, 24–5, 96–7, 99, 102, 114–6, 118, 120–1, 123, 125–7, 129, 131–4, 138, 143–4, 148, 208–9, 215, 221–2, 231, 233, 235, 237, 247–8, 250, 256–8, 263, 271, 273, 276, 278, 282–3, 299, 301, 342, 345, 349–50, 359, 370, 380, 384, 389, 393, 396, 399, 402, 417–8
Catchpole, Lt-Col Stanley **431**, 432
Cautley, Col Henry 32–3, 70
ceremonial roles 459
Chadderton Camp 107
Chakdina 237
Chateau Segard 132
Chatham Islands 19, 55
Chaytor, Maj. Gen. Edward 158
Chech-on 385
chemical warfare 13, 20, 112–5, 188, 328
Chesnutt, Lce-Bdr Hori **383**

Chile 84, 318
China 2, 380, 433–4
Chip'yong-ni 384
Chojong River 386
Christchurch 33, 37–8, 40–1, 44, 47, 66, 68, 135, 159, 164–6, 168–9, 181, 189, 317, 353, 370, 436, 439, 441, 444, 461
Chuam-ni 384–5
Chuktun-ni 387
Ch'unch'on 390
Chungch'on-ni 389
Chunuk Bair 99, 100, 186
Churchill, Sir Winston 264
Chute, Gen. Trevor 25
City of London 196
Civil Defence 432, 458
Clendon, James 18
Clifton, Brig. G.H. 229, 231, 251
Cloudy Bay 19
Coast Defence Commander 81
coastal defence weapons 29–31, 74, 174–5, 307, 318, 367
coastal defences 8, 12, 14, 27, 39, 45, 49, **53**, 56, 60–1, 70–3, 77, 83–4, 132, 157, 162–4, 168–78, 184, 193, 289, 307, 309–13, **314**, 315–6, 318–21, 327–8, 330, 348, 351, 363, 365–8, 370–2, 374–6
Cocks, Maj. Spencer 286, 407
Colne, HMS 100
Cologne 147, 186
Colombo 89
colonel commandant 364
Colonial Defence Force 25
Combat Brigade Group 403
Commander of the New Zealand Forces 63
Commander Royal Artillery **55**, 158
communications 182, **183**, 184
community roles 458–9
Composite Battalion 218, 220–1
compulsory military training 73, 167, 362–3, 375, 403, 407, 428, 430
computers **451**, 452
Congreve rockets 11, 20
conscripts 12–3, 77, 133, 243, 360, 403, 431, 467
Conway, Brig. 191
Cook, James 17
cordite 12, 69, 71, 152
Coriano Ridge 288
Cortona 283
Cosina–Montone Canal 291

counter-battery techniques 13, 98, 101, 109, 114–5, 117–8, 122–3, 126, 132–3, 138, 140–3, 145, 207, 210, 227, 231, 249–50, 255, 264, 268–9, 271, 273–8, 280–2, 285–7, 289, 292, 295–6, 394–6, 402
counter-bombardment 116, 122, 170, 173, 176, 310–2, 316, 329, 426, 437
counter-terrorism 15, 447, 466
Creforce 216, 223
Crete 163, 192, 214–23, 226, 237–8, 301
Crèvecœur 144
Crimean War 27, 29, 33, 192
Cu Chi tunnel network 415
Cunningham, Brig. W.H. 329
Curaçoa, HMS 40
Currey, Gnr Arthur 101
Cymbeline radar 436
Cyprus 259, **260**
Cyrenaica 224

D

Dakar 86
Dalaimbilo 329
Damascus 246
Daniell's Battery 99
Dardanelles 91
Darwin 391
Defence Act
   1886 13, 45
   1909 73, 363
Defence Committee of Inquiry 1986 440
defence reviews
   1880 28
   1887 46
   1933 170
   1941 307
   1957 374, 403
   1958 403
   1961 405–6
   1978 436–7
   1983 439–40, 452
   1987 440
Defence Scheme 1908 72
Deir al Shein 248
Deir el Angar 251
Deir El Munassib 252
Delhi 185
demobilisation 147, 362
Depression years 157, 167

INDEX

Despard, Col. Henry 20
Deutz 147, 186
Devonport 62, 171, **366**, 369, 371
Dhomokos Pass 209
Diamond Trail 201
Director of Army Aviation 378
Director of Artillery 158
Director RNZA 447
directors 65, **279**, 313, 322, 406
Divisional Ammunition Column 146–7, 155
Divisional Artillery School 107
Divisional Cavalry 227
Divisional Petrol Company 218
Divisional Supply Column 218
Divisional Trench Mortars 133, 156
Djebibina 245, 268
Dong Nai River 413–4
Doveli Cove 341
drafts 7, 86, 135, 147, 184, 269, 290, 292, 312, 326, 360, 362, 375, 391, 401–2
Drânoutre 139–40
dress 210, 335, 339, 364
Dreyer, Lt-Col Barry 416, 434, 448
Driver, HMS 22
Duff, Brig. Charles (Danny) 194, 208, 243, 332, 350, 353–4
Duigan, Maj. Gen. Sir John 169, 180, 217
Duke of Gloucester 168
Dumbéa 335
Dunedin 33, 36, 40, 47, 62, 65–6, 69, 83, 160, 163–4, 168, 315, 318–9, 322, 327, 357, 370–1, 435, 461
Dunedin, HMS 197
Dunkirk 105
Dunluce Castle 103
Düren 147
Durham Light Infantry 238
Dyson, Bert 163, 194, 217, 219, 230

E

East Timor 455–7, 461
Eaucourt Abbaye 117
Echelons, 2NZEF
 1st 194
 2nd 194, 197
 3rd 200
Ed Duda 228, 233
Edney, Maj. A.J. 172
Éfaté 338

Egypt 86, 89, 91, 102, 124, 148, 155, 188, 190, 192, 194–7, **198**, 200–1, 203, 214–7, 223–5, 241, 246–53, 255–9, 301, 353
Eighth Army 14, 230, 237–8, 246, 248, 250, 253, 258–9, 269, 271, 280, 288, 293, 298
El Adem 245, 263
El Agheila 225, 236, 259, 261
El Alamein 190, 248, 250, **253**, 255–7, 259, 288, 304, 308, 462
El Haseiat 261
El Mreir 251
Elands River 58
Elasson 206–8
Electric Light Section 366
Ellen Ballance 71, 366
Empress of Canada 194
Endymion, HMS 100
Enfidaville 267–9
Engineer Corps 367
Engineer of Defences 54
enlistment 191
entertainment 124, 133, 443
Escaillon River 144
Escault Canal 240
Esivo 330
Esk Valley 166
Esson, Col. J.J. 81
Estaires 118
Étaples 107, 113
Europe 10, 13, 17, 23, 86, 88, 157, 190, 297, 310, 429, 455, 462
evacuations 102–3, 208, 213, 222, 277
Ewshot Barracks 107, 186
examination batteries 71–2, 83–4, 310, 312–3, 319, 330, 368
Exercise Baseline 460
Exercise Brimstone 453
Exercise Golden Fleece 448
Exercise Hauraki Gulf 439
Exercise Herekino Safari 442
Exercise Ivanhoe 449
Exercise Kiwi III 454
Exercise Kiwi Tamasek 449
Exercise Northern Safari 442
Exercise Powderhorn 407
Exercise Southern Union 459
Exercise Suman Warrior 445
Exercise Sunny Post 450

Exercise Tasman   407
Exercise Thunder Warrior   449–50
Exercise Titan   461
Exercise Tropic Lightning   445–6

F
Fabriano   290, 292, 294
FACE (Field Artillery Computer Equipment)   452
Faenza   291, 293
Falamai   343–8
Falla, Lt-Col N.S.   88, 109, 138–9
Fanning Island   178, 328
Farinella   292
Featherston Military Camp   43, 135, **136**, 354
Fergusson, Governor-General Sir Bernard   410
field artillery   55, 66, 68–70, 152
    computer equipment   452
    weapons   34, 74, 151–2
Fiesler Storch spotter plane   223
Figueras   242
Fiji   84, 161, 187, 240, 313, 320, 323, 328–32, 334, 354–5, 365, 407, 428, 435, 447–8, 456
fire support bases   416, 418, 422–4
First World War   82–156
FitzRoy, Governor Robert   20
Fiumicino River   289
Five Power Defence Arrangement (FPDA)   15
flame-throwing   294–5
flash-spotting   259, **261**, 274–5, 291
Flers   114–5, 117
Fleurbaix   112, 118, 120–1
Florence   242, 284–5, **286**, 287, 290, 354, 360
Florida Island   339
Fontanaccia   288
food   103, 119, 210, 215, 250, 254, 263, 337, 345, 361
Foote, 2nd Lt John   342, 344
Forbes, Rt Hon George   171
Foret de Mormal   145–6
Forli   291
Forqloss   245–6
Forrester, Lt Leroy   450
Fort Ballance   70, 171, 314–5
Fort Britomart   **31**, 43
Fort Buckley   43
Fort Dorset   72, 83–4, 160, 163–4, 168, **171**, 172, 174, 176–7, **178**, 180, **181**, 184–5, 301, 313–4, 320–1, 324, 368–9, 430, 438, 462
Fort Jervois   **36**, **44**, 47

Fort Opau   311
Fort Rolleston   44
Fort Takapuna   174, 354, 365
Fortress Troops   169, 184–5
Fortunato   288
Fourka Pass   210
Fox, Col F.J. (Francis)   49–51, 78
Framework Force   436
France   79, 82–3, 98, 105, 107–8, 133, 145, 148–9, 167, 172, 186–7, 190, 195, 238–9
Frances, Capt. Brian   **451**
Fraser, Lt-Col K.W.   194, 207, 243
Fremicourt   142
French Resistance   242
Freyberg, Maj. Gen. Sir Bernard   188–90, 192, 203, 216, 218, 223, 227, 236, 245, 253, 257, 265–6, 271, 275, 290, 295, 298–9, 304, 402, 430
Freyberg Cup   244
Frezenberg   126
Fullarton, Capt. John   300
Futurist   321
fuzes   151–3

G
Gaba Tepe   91
Gabes   265–6
Gaiana Canal   296
Galatas   216–21
Gallagher, Bdr C.V.   262
Gallipoli   70, 79, 91–4, **95**, 96–105, 110–1, 145–7, 149, 155, 167, 241, 344
Galloway, Paul   449
gambling   263
Garawla   197
Gard'ner, Lt-Col M.M.   158, 166
gas shells   153
gas warfare   112–5, 328
Gascoigne, Maj. Frederick   55
Gauldie, Matt   239
Gawn, Lt-Col David   457
Gaza   454
Gazala   236
Geluveld   126, 132
Geraldine   351
Ghurkas   78, 100, 242
Gibraltar   78, 242
Gilbert, Jim   166, 176, 191, 196, 216, 266, 372–3
Gilbert and Ellice Islands   328

Gillard, Maj. Nick 456
Gillespie, George 382
Gisborne 26, 34, 44, 371
Glamoc 455
Glasgow, Lt-Col K.W.R. (Gussie) 223, 243
Glengyle, HMS 214
gliders 218
Glorious, HMS 242
Gneisenau 85
Godley, Maj. Gen. Alexander 73, 77, 98, 111, 126, 130, 149
Godley Head 356, 369
Golan Heights 454
Golden Bay 17
Gordon, Bdr John 226
Gordon Point 70–1, 83, 313–4
Gore 374
Gothic Line 287–90
Gouzeaucourt 143
GPS devices 452
Gravenstafel Spur 126–7
Great Barrier Island 319, 442
Greece 163, 190, 192, 201, 203–11, 213–5, 223, 226, 237–8, 268, 303, 332, 353
Green Island 349–51, **352**
Greytown 43, 326
Grigg, Maj. A.N. 231
Guadalcanal 334–5, 338, 340, 344, 349
Guardiagrele 272
Gueudecourt 117
Guildford 195
Gulf of Sirte 225, 263
Gulf War 448
gun carriages 12–3, 21–2, 29, 33, 40, 69, 79, 151, 180–1, 212, 214, 264, 290, 434
gun command posts 436
gun crew 87, 173, 176, 253–4, 383
gun position officers 154, 205, 420, 452
gun tractors **374**
gunpowder 10, 12, 69, 71
guns *see also* missiles, rockets, weapons
  2.95-inch 69
  3-inch **178**, 319, 330
  3.7-inch 317, **324**, 330, 333, 370, 375, 406
  4-inch 174–5, 177, 312–3, 319, 331
  4.7-inch 171, 315, **327**, 328–9
  5-inch 315
  5.5-inch 368, 370, 372, 405, 407–8, 440
  5.9-inch 127
  6-inch 29–30, 32–3, **36**, 47, 71–2, 74, 84, 163, 170–1, 174, 184, 311, 313, 315, 318, 328–9, 331, 335, 368
  7-inch 28–9, 33, **35**, 72
  8-inch 29–30, 32–3, 71
  9.2-inch 171, 176, 178, 316, **317**, **365**, 367, 370
  37-mm 330, 343
  40-mm 333
  65-mm 327
  75-mm 314
  90-mm 343, 345
  155-mm 316, 333, 335, 400, 440, 455, 466
  2-pr 193–5, 201, 204, 211–3, 223, **224**, 226–7, 233, 246, 314, 327, 334
  4-pr 22
  6-pr 22, 25–6, 30–1, 34, 36, 43, 68–9, 71, 84, 87, 163, 246–8, 250, 264, **293**, 306, **314**, 334, 360, 370, 372
  7-pr 24
  9-pr 22, 34, **38**, 66
  12-pr 21–2, 24, 27, 30–1, 34, **40**, 68–9, **70**, 71, 83, 86, 161, 163, 184, 195, 314, 319
  15-pr 58, 66, 68, 74, **76**, 84, 162
  17-pr 264, **265**, 272, 287, 290, 292, 294, 306, 370, 372
  18-pr 18, 31, 69–70, 88, 92, 94, **95**, 99, 105, 114, 120, 122–3, 127, 129–30, 134, **137**, 151, 159, 161–2, 166, 179, 181–2, 193–5, **198**, 212, 223, 230–1, 233, 314, 325, 327, 329–31
  24-pr 22, 25, 27, 34, 36–7, 42
  25-pr 30, 193, 195–6, 200–1, 207, 209, 212, 224, 226–8, 231, **232**, 233, 238, 248–9, 252, 257, 268, 270–1, 292, 325–7, 330, 333, 338, 345, 360, 370, 372, 379, 380, 400, 402, 405, 407–8, 435–6, 450, 465
  32-pr 22, 25, 27
  40-pr 24, 27, 29
  60-pr 127, 141, **159**, 161, 168, 174, 180, 204, 311, 315, 325, 330
  64-pr 28–9, **32**
  68-pr 22
  110-pr 25
  anti-aircraft 13–4, 157, 169–170, 175–6, **178**, 185, 193, 196, 211, 214, 218, 223–4, 236, 247, 249, 255, 263–5, 272, 275–6, 279, 290, 300, 316–7, 319–23, **324**, 326–7, 330, 332–3, 338–9, 342, 345, **346**, 350–1, 370, 375, 404–6, 465
  anti-submarine 87

anti-tank 193–5, 201, 204, 211–3, 223, **224**, 226–7, 233, 246–8, 250, 264, **265**, 279, 284, **286**, 287, 290–1, **293**, 294, 306–7, 314, 327, 334, **352**, 360, 370, 372

Armstrong 23–7, 29, 32, 34, **36**, 38, 39, **40**, 43, 53, 58, 66, 151

Bofors 193, 211, 214, 223, 230–1, 233–4, **253**, 255, 273, 289, 314, 316, 320–3, 330, 333, **337**, 344–5, 371, 374, 406, 465

breech-loading 11–2, 23, 29–30, 32, 34, 69

cannon 10, 17–20, 23, 25–6, 43

carronades 18–9, 22

disappearing 29, 33, **36**, 71, 163

drill 72

field 10, 13, 25–6, 44–5, 65, 69, **76**, 465

garrison 32

Gibson 246

Hotchkiss 31, **57**, 58

howitzers 11, 13, 23, 25, 36, 69, 92, 95, 98, 139, 141, 423, 425, 440

   3.7-inch 159, 217, 325, 328, 330, 334, 465

   4.5-inch 30, 69–70, 88, 120, 123, 127, 129, 152, 159, 181, 193–5, **198**, 325, 327, 330

   6-inch 161, 180, 182, 315, 325, 330, 370, 372

   8-inch 389, 400

   105-mm 285, 408, 411–2, 436, 440–1

   155-mm 445, 449

   24-pr 34

   FH2000 449–50

   L5 408, 411–2, 434, 436, 440, 459

   L118 441, 450, 460, 465

   L119 441

   M101A1 411–2, 436, 441

M10 anti-tank 284, **286**, 287, 290–1, 294, 307

M198 440

Maxim 44

mortars 11, 20–3, 25, 28, 290, 293, 396, 466

   4.2-inch 279, **280**, 306, 370–2, 405, 407–8, 442

   Coehorn 22, 26

   Minenwerfer 118, 120

   Newton 123, 150

   PIAT 360

   Royal 22, **31**

   Stokes 105, **106**, 120, 149, 150

   trench 13, 105, 118, 120, **121**, 123, 133, **140**, 144, 149–50

mountain 69, 70, 95

muzzle-loading 11, 29, 30, 33

naval 17–20, 22, 24–6, 312–3, 315–6, 319–20, 328–9

Nordenfelt 30–1, 44, 68–9, 71, 84–5

Noricum GHN-45 440

quick-firing 12, 30–1, 68–70, 87, 163

self-propelled 284, 307, 370, 455

swivel 17–9, 43

train-mounted 68, **70**

Vickers-Maxim 69

Gurkhas 78, 96, 100, 242, 266, 292, 408–9

Gustav Line 275

H

Hagley Park 168, 461

Haig, Fld Mshl Douglas 130

Hairini 25

haka 399, 402, 457

Halfaya Pass 227, 258

Hamilton 69, 164, 166–8, 243, 370, 437

Hamilton, Gen. Sir Ian 76, 91, 96

Han River 384, 390

Hankey, Sir Maurice 171–2

Hankins, Gnr Clarence 113

Hanna, Lt Phil **204**, 205

Hansen, Gnr Phil **383**

Haranui 86

Hargest, Brig. James 242

Harriet 18

Harrington Point Battery 314

Harwich 158

Hassell, Gnr Norman 110

Hassett, Maj. Gen. Ronald **463**, 464

Hat Dich 414

Havock, HMS 214

Havrincourt 143

Hawaii 445

Haweis 18

Hazebrouck 105–6, 140

Heathcote Hotel 62

Hébuterne 137, 141

Hédauville 137

height-finders 321, 323

helicopters 378, 402, 411–4, 422, 442, 452, 465

Heliopolis 89

Helwan 197–8, 200, 203, 223

Henderson, Jim 191, 226

Heraklion 216, 222

Heseltine, Gnr John 119

high explosives (HE) 12, 153

Hindenburg Line 143–5
Hiro Camp 391
Hiscocks, Gnr E.F. 238
Ho Chi Minh 409, 415
Hobo Woods 415
Hoengsong 384
Hokianga 18, 44
Holt, David 251
Holt 5 ton Caterpillar tractors 180
Home Guard 309, 313, 318, 327
Hone Heke 20
Honey tanks 266, 268
Hongch'on 385–6
Hongi Hika 18
Honnor, Maj. Harry 376, 416
Honshu 360
Hopuhopu military camp 185, 191–4, 223, 303, 443
Horokiri Hill 20, 22
Horrocks, Capt. John 313
horse-riding 176–7, **179**
Horsford, Col John 424
Hotchkiss 6-pr QF guns 31, **57**, 58
Howitzer Gully 92
Howlett Point 71, 83
Hughes, Lt David (Spike) 420
Hume, Lt-Col Arthur 46
Humphreys, Gnr Frank 104
Hutcheson, Bert 250
Hutcheson, Graeme 177, 226, 246
huts 107, 114, 133, 312, 324
Hynes, Gnr A.D. 230

I

Ich'on 380–1, 384
Île Nou 335
Imbros 103
Imjin River 383, 391–2, 402
Imperial General Staff 79
Imperial Reserve Force 73
incendiary shells 141, 153
India 170, 186, 194, 353
Indo-China 409
Indonesia 391, 408, 455–7
infantillery 195, 207, 216, 220–1, 223, 279, 282, 284, 350
Inspector of Coast Defences 158
instructors 35–6, 39, 50, 53, 65, 107, 164, 167, 176, 186, 191, 271, 321, 323–5, 328, 332, 372–3, 408, 420, 424
Integrated Expansion Force (IEF) 436–7, 440, 449, 461

Invercargill 28, 34, 44, 68–9, 164, 167, 370–1, 374, 435
Iraq 161, 466
Isernia 278
Ismailia 90, 102
Israel 454
Italy 190, 195, 197, 242, 244, 260, 269–299, 302, 326, 343, 351, 360, 362, 370, 400, 430

J

Jackson, Alan 213
Janie Seddon **71**, *366*
Japan 162, 169, 193, 298, 310, 359–62, 391, 430
Japanese threat to New Zealand 309–10
Jayforce 298, 360–2, 379, 430
Jellicoe, Viscount 162–3
Jervois, Sir William 28
Johannesburg 58
Johnson, Sgt James 300
Johnston, Lt-Col George Napier 148–9
Jones, Hon. Fred 178
Jordan 244
Joyce, Maj. John 191
Judgeford Camp 334
Junkers aircraft 218, 220, 247

K

Kaesong 391
Kaikoura 430
Kaipara Heads 453
Kaitaia airfield 442
Kaituna 187
Kaiwharawhara 33
Kalabaka 206
Kalamata 214–5
Kandahar 214
Kaponga Box 248–9
Kap'yong 386–90
Karehana Bay 325
Katerine 206
Katikara pa 24
Kauri Point 320
Kawau Island 316
Kawhia 24
Kayforce 378–402, 410, 462, 464
Kenning, Don 410, 414, 441
Kermadec Islands 87
Kimberley 58
Kinder, Gnr James 222

King Country 55
King's Own Scottish Borderers 390, 394–5, 397
Kippenberger, Maj. Gen. Howard 188, 219
Kittyhawk aircraft 265
Kolombangara Island 340
Korea, Republic of 378, 384, 387–8, 390, 392
Korean War 4, 9, 14, 343, 378–402, 403, 409, 411, 416, 426, 446, 462
Kroonstadt 57
Kure 391
Kwanam-ni 387

L

La Basseville 125–6
La Poggiona 286
La Romola 285
La Signy Farm 141
Labour government's defence policies 464
Lady Roberts 71, 83, 366–7
Ladysmith 58–9
Laifa Point 346
Lake Timsah 124
Lake Trasimene 283, 298, 360
Lambourn, Ernie 247, 270
Lami 329
Lamia 209–10
Lance Bombardier **366**
Land Force Command 438
landing craft 344, 348
Larisa 208–9
Larkhill School of Artillery 14, 353, 372, 407, 424, 464
Larkin, Sgt R.J. 300
Latham, Brig. H.B. 235–6
latrines 205, 250, 335
launches **366**, 367
Lautoka 329, 331
Le Havre 105
Le Quesnoy 145–7, 186
Lebanon 245, 454
Legion d'Honneur 79, 149
Lemnos Island 91, 102
Libya 197, 200, 203, 224–5, 232, 246, 259, 261–4
Lichtenburg 59
Line Benton 386
Line Jamestown 392, 394–5
Line Kansas 386–7, 402
Liri Valley 275–6, 281, 283
London 10, 101, 149, 303, 446, 463

Lone Pine 94, 98, 101, 186
Long Dien 422
Long Look exchanges 446
Long Tan 411, 416, **417**, 418, **419**, 422
Lough, Lt-Col David 448
Lower Hutt Racecourse 89
Luftwaffe 210, 219, 251
Lunga Point 338
Lyddite 12
Lyttelton (Harbour) 8, 33–5, 45, 62, 68, 83, 160–3, 168, 174, 176–7, 309, 312, 316, 318–9, 322

M

Maadi Camp 194, 197, 199, 200, 223, 250, 254, 269–70, 325, 463
Mace, Gen. John 447
Maclagan's Ridge 93
Mafeking 58–9
Mahfouz 200, 203
Maidstone 195
Mailly-Maillet 137
Maitland, Gen. Sir Henry 23, 203
Malay(si)a 14, 359, 399, 403, 408, 409, 434, 464
Maleme 216–20, 222
Malmani 59
Malone, Lt-Col William 99
Malsi 348
Malta 103
Mangere Airport 447
Manila 380, 403
Manukau Harbour 26, 319
Manurewa 332, 354
Maori 9, 11, 17–9, 23, 25–8, 33, 43, 99, 131, 196, 207, 220, 266, 276, 285, 398–9
Maori Pioneer Battalion 131, 399
Marandellas 58
Maravari 340
Marecchia River 288
Mareth Line 264–6
Marico River 58
Marion du Fresne, Marc-Joseph 17
Marjouram, Sgt William 22
Marquana Bay 342
Marseilles 105
Martin-Parry adapter kits 181
Martini Henry rifles 50
Massa Lombarda 295
Masters, John 87, 163–5, 187, 302, 372–3, 377, 408–9,

424–6
Matador gun tractors   374
Matawhero   55
Mateparae, Maj. Gen. Jerry   461
Matheson, James   192
Matu Soroto   341
Mau movement   79
Mauretania   200
Mauser rifles   58
Maxim machine guns   44, 99
McBeath, Bdr L.H.   254
McIntyre, Capt. Peter   238, **239**
McKinnon, Brig. Walter   **428**, 429
McLean, WO Rob   456
McQuarrie, Capt. R.S.   84
mechanisation   180–2
medals   24
Medenine   264–6, 298
media coverage   359, 423
Mediterranean Expeditionary Force (MEF)   91
Mekong Delta   414, 424
Menastir   226, 236
Meneksos Pass   208
Mennella   279
Menzies, Capt. H.G.   447
Mercer, Capt. Henry   23–4
Meremere   24
Mersa Matruh   247, 258
Messines   119, 122–3, 125–6, 132, 138–41, 147, 150
Metaxas Line   204
meteorology   436
Middlesex Battalion   384–5, 387–9
Miles, Brig. Reginald   241, **242**
Military Training Act 1949   363
Militia Act   33
Mills, Keith   311
Milne, George   315
minenwerfers   118, 120
Minqar Qaim   238, 246–8
Miramar Peninsula   33, 172
Miramare Hotel   297, 299
Miryang   380
missiles   14, 406, 452–3, 465
Mistral Detachment   461
Mistral rocket launchers   453, 465
Mitchell, Lt-Col Jack   243, 442
Miteiriya   255–7
Moa   87

Moascar   102
Modder River   60
Moindou   336
Molos   203, 209–11
Momi   329–31
Monastir Gap   206
Mono Island   343–4, **346–7**, 348
Monowai   84, 315
Monte Cassino   188, 275–81
Monte Trocchio   275
Montgomery, Fld Mshl Sir Bernard   250
Moodie, Lt-Col John   379, 395
Morbecque   132
Morris gun tractors   179, 181–2
Morse code   179, 182
Moruroa   453
Motuihe Island   87
Moturoa   26
Moturoa Island   311–2
Motutapu Island   171–2, 310, 312, 319, 368
Mounted Corps   25
Mounted Rifles   72
Mowat, Neville   281
Mrkonji Grad   455
Mt Cook barracks   **32**
Mt Olympus   **204**
Mt Tarawera   332
Mt White   **435**
Mudros Harbour   91–2
Muldoon, Gnr Wes   103
Munda   340
'murders'   211, 275–6, 280–1, 293, 298, 307–8
Murphy, Capt. Bruce   414
mustard gas   112, 328

N
Naech'on   387–8
Naegon-ni   381
Naia   335
Nancy Bell   316
Napier Guards   50
Naples   271, 360
Narrow Neck   443
Narrows   98, 100
Nathan, Capt. E.C.W.   279
National Military Reserve   184, 309, 326
National Service   **404**, 405, 427, 433, 435
NATO   408, 454–5

Nausori 448
Navula Passage 329, 331
Nebelwerfer rocket launchers 264, 275–8, 292, 296
Necal 333
Néméara 335–6, 351
Népoui 332, 335
Neuve Église–Ploegsteert sector 138–9
New Brighton 41
New Caledonia 41, 323, 332–6, **337**, 343, 351, 428
New Georgia 340, 348
New Hebrides 338
New Ireland 351
New Zealand, HMS 174–5, 312
New Zealand and Australian Division 92, 155
New Zealand Army Air Corps 378, 459
New Zealand Army Act 1950 363
New Zealand Artillery organisation
    1886 Volunteers Corps 48–9
    1900–1914 in New Zealand 67–8
    1915 at Gallipoli 155
    1917–1918 Western Front 156
    1920s reorganisation 160
    1937 in New Zealand 168
    1939–1945 in New Zealand 356–8
    1941 order of battle 202
    1941 Field and Anti–Tank North Africa 225
    1950–1953 in Korea 386
    1956 in New Zealand 369
    1961 in New Zealand 405
New Zealand Artillery units
    Colonial period
        New Zealand Field Artillery 28, 32–3, 46–8
        New Zealand Garrison Artillery 45–8, 50
        New Zealand Regiment of Artillery Volunteers 48
        1st (North Island) Brigade
            A Battery (Auckland) 41–2, 48
            D Battery (Wellington) 42–3, 48, 50
            F Battery (Napier) 48, 50
            J Battery (Cook County) 48
            O Battery (Parnell) 38, 45, 48
        2nd (South Island) Brigade
            B Battery (Dunedin) 34, 36, 38, **40**, 48
            C Battery (Timaru) 34, 48
            E Battery (Christchurch) 33, 37–8, 41, 44, 48
            G Battery (Invercargill) 48
            E Battery (Christchurch) 41, 48
            H Battery (Nelson) 43, 48
            I Battery (Oamaru) **38**, 48

            K Battery (Invercargill) 48
            L Battery (Port Chalmers) 45, 48
            M Battery (Queenstown) 48
            N Battery (Lyttelton) 33, 39–40, 45, 48
        Naval Artillery Volunteers 26, 33–4, 36, 39, 41, 43, **44**, 45–8, 50, 53
    pre-First World War
        New Zealand Field Artillery Volunteers 60, 65–7, 75
            A Battery (Auckland) 66–7, 69
            B Battery (Dunedin) 66, 68–9
            C Battery (Invercargill) 68–9
            D Battery (Wellington) 64, 66–7, 69, 78
            E Battery (Christchurch) **62**, 66, 68
            G Battery (Hamilton) 67, 69
            H Battery (Nelson) 68
            I Battery (Westport) **62**, 68–9, **70**
            J Battery (Palmerston North), 67, 69
            N Battery (Lyttelton) 68
        New Zealand Garrison Artillery Volunteers 60, 63, 65–7, 69, 72, 75, **76**, 80–1
        Naval Artillery Volunteers 62–3, 66–8, 80
        Coastguard Artillery Volunteers 62, 67
    First World War
        New Zealand Divisional Artillery 98, 121, 144, 146, 157–8
        New Zealand Field Artillery 88, **124**, 125, **134**, 145, 155, 158
        Artillery Headquarters 122, 147, 155–6
        1st Brigade 114, 117, 120, 122, 133–4, 142–3, 146, 155–6, 186–7
        2nd Brigade 114, 117–8, 120, 134, 140, 142, 146, 155–6
        3rd Brigade 114–5, 117, 119–20, 122, 124, 126, 133–4, 142–3, 146, 156
        4th Brigade 117, 120
        2 (Army) Brigade 120, 132, 138–9, 143–4, 156, 186
    between the Wars
        New Zealand Garrison Artillery 158, 160
        New Zealand Field Artillery 158, 160
        1st Artillery Brigade 160, 186
        2nd Artillery Brigade 160, 168
        3rd Artillery Brigade 160, 168
        Northern Coast Artillery Group 160–1
        Central Coast Artillery Group 160–1
    Second World War
        2 Division 188, 203, 269–70, 351, 376, 453
        Divisional Artillery HQ 201–3, 216, 232, 247, 265, 291, 297, **299**

INDEX

1 Survey Troop 202, 210, 216, 259
4 Field Regiment 188, 192–4, 197, 200–6, 209, 211, 214, 216–8, 221, 226, 228–9, 233, 236, 243–4, 246–50, 255–6, 264, 266–9, 272–4, 277–84, 288, 294, 296
5 Field Regiment 194–6, 201–9, 211, 214, 216–8, 231, 235–6, 243, 245, 247–9, 251, 255, 257, 262, 267–8, 271–2, 277–80, 282–5, 289, 295–6
6 Field Regiment 191, **198**, 200–5, 207, 211, 214–6, 227–8, 231–6, 243, 245, 247, 249–50, 255, 266–9, 272–3, 277–80, 282–3, 285, 288, 294–5, **297**
7 Anti-Tank Regiment 194, 200–2, 211, 213–4, 216, 223, 243, 245–6, 248, 255, 264, 287, 290
14 Light Anti-Aircraft Regiment 201, 223, 243, 245, 251, 255, 257, 289–90
32 Field Regiment 270
3 Division 14, 246, 270, 292, 309, 323, 325, 326, 330, 332–4, 336–8, 351–2
    Divisional Artillery HQ 332, 338, 351, 358
    4 Survey Troop 334, 358
    17 Field Regiment 332, 334, 338, 340, 350, 358
    28 Heavy Anti-Aircraft Regiment 333–4, 336, 358
    29 Light Anti-Aircraft Regiment 332–4, 336, **337**, 342–4, 350, 358
    33 Heavy Regiment 334, 336, 358
    37 Field Regiment 336, 358
    38 Field Regiment 336, 338, 342, **347**, 348, 358
6 Division 188
in New Zealand
    HQ Northern Military District 356
        1 Division 326, 356
            1 Field Regiment 356
            20 Field Regiment 356
        2 Fortress HQ 318–9, 356
            9 Heavy Regiment 318–9, 356
        15 Anti-Aircraft Brigade 323, 356
            15 Heavy AA Regiment 322, 356
            22 Light AA Regiment 356
    HQ Central Military District 357
        4 Division 326, 357
            2 Field Regiment 357
            12 Field Regiment (7 Brigade Group) 326, 357
        Wellington Fortress HQ 318, 357
            10 Heavy Regiment 318, 357
        16 Anti-Aircraft Brigade 323, 357
            16 Heavy AA Regiment 357
            22 Light AA Regiment 357
    HQ Southern Military District 357
        5 Division 326, 357
            3 Field Regiment 357
            18 Field Regiment 357
            19 Field Regiment (11 Brigade Group) 357
        Lyttelton Fortress HQ 318, 357
            11 Heavy Regiment 318, 357
        Dunedin Fortress HQ 318, 357
            13 Heavy Regiment 319, 357
        24 Heavy AA Regiment 357
        25 Light AA Regiment 357
post-Second World War
    1 Field Regiment 363, 369, 375, 405, 407
    2 Field Regiment 363, 369, 375, 403, 405, 407, 438
    3 Field Regiment 363, 369–70, 376, 405, 407, 427, 435–6, 438, 459
    4 Medium Regiment 363, 369–70
    5 Anti-Tank Regiment 363, 370
    5 Light Regiment 369–70, 374, 403
    6 Light AA Regiment 363, 369, 371, 403, 406
    12 Heavy Anti-Aircraft Regiment 369, 406
    13 Composite Anti-Aircraft Regiment 406
    14 Composite Anti-Aircraft Regiment 406
    15 Composite Anti-Aircraft Regiment 406
    16 Field Regiment 378–402, 404–5, **406**, 407, 411, 427, 433, 437–40, 442, 447–9, 456, 457, 461, 467
        161 Battery 409, **410**, 411–427, 434–5, 437–9, 447–9, 452–3, 458–9
    16 Heavy Anti-Aircraft Regiment 406
    Independent Regiment Signals Troop 369
    School of Artillery 369
    District Troops 369
        9 Coast Regiment 363, 367–9
        10 Coast Regiment 363, 368–9, 376
        11 Coast Regiment 363, 368–9
    1 Brigade 407
    3 Brigade 407–8
New Zealand Constabulary Force 28
New Zealand Corps 276, 278
New Zealand Defence Force 431, 463
New Zealand Division 104, 114–5, 118, 126, 141, 146–7, 149, 156
New Zealand Force South East Asia 434
New Zealand Garrison Artillery 48
New Zealand Infantry Brigade 96, 99
New Zealand Medical Corps 107

New Zealand Mounted Rifles Brigade 88, 96, 99–100, 102
New Zealand Permanent Force 60, **64**
New Zealand Permanent Militia 45–8, 51–5
New Zealand (Rifle) Brigade 102
Newall, Sir Cyril 335
Newtown Park *57*, **177**
Nga Puhi 17–20, 22
Ngai Tahu 18–9
Ngai Te Rangi 18–9, 25
Ngamotu 19
Ngaruawahia 21, 24, 191, 193, 301
Ngatapa 26, 55
Ngati Toa 18–9, 22
Ngati Tumatakokiri 17
Ngati Tumatauenga 399
Ngauranga 33
Nieuw Amsterdam 223
Nieuwpoort 132
night-bombing 289
Nile 86
Nissan Island 349–51, **352**
nitrocellulose explosives (cordite) 12
Niven, Bdr M.G. 230–1
Nofilia 244, 262–3
Nordenfelt guns 30–1, 44, 68–9, 71, 84–5
Norfolk Island 323, 333–5
North Africa 188, 223–236, **237**, 238–269, 304
North Head 171
North Vietnamese Army (NVA) 409, 416, 422–3
Northern District Ordnance Depot 376
Northern War (1845–46) 20–2
Norway 242
Nouméa 84, 332, 334–7
nuclear-free policy 446
Nui Dat 415–7, **419**, 422–5

O

Oakes Force 216, 218, 243
Oakes, Maj. Tommy 216
Oamaru 34, 37–8, 40–1, 162
observation posts 313, 367
observers 109, 138, 141, 143, 154, 348, 411, 420, 454, 460
O'Connor, Bdr Des 229
Officer Cadet School 373
O'Flynn, Hon. Frank 440
Ohaeawai 20, 22
Ohakea 357

Ohariu 64, 171–2, 176
Olphert, HMNZS 80
Olympus Pass 204–7
'One Army' concept 433, 460
Onehunga 26, 49, 161, 369, 375
Operation Buckland 293–5
Operation Commando 392–5
Operation Crimp 415
Operation Crusader 223–37, **239**, 242, 244, 304
Operation Dauntless 386
Operation Dickens 277
Operation Fargo 448
Operation Hardihood 415
Operation Hobart 418
Operation Hump 414
Operation Killer 385
Operation Marauder 414
Operation Minden 392
Operation New Life 414
Operation Platypus 423
Operation Radian 454
Operation Ripper 385
Operation Roundhouse 415
Operation Rugged 386
Operation Silver City 415
Operation Smash 414
Operation Spaniel 295–6
Operation Supercharge 257–8
Operation Tamborine 418–9
Operation Thunderbolt 381
Opotiki 26
Opua 315
Opunake 55
Orakau 25
Ormonde 200, 379–80
Orsogna 272–4, 278
Ostend 132
Otago Harbour 71, **76**, 313–4
Ottoman Empire 89
Ottoshoop 58–9
Oua Tom 335

P

Pacific Islands 328–352
Pacific War 87, 188
Padua 296
Paehak Reservoir 392
Pai Marire 25–6, 55

Palliser Bay 178
Palmer Head 171–3, 176, 178, 311–2, 368
Panmunjom 395
Panzer tanks 212, 231, 246–7, 287
Papakura Camp 223, 332, 334, 336, 379, 404, 411, 439, 449, 458–9
Parham, Brig. H.J. 308
Parihaka 28, 43–4
Park, Brig. Ronald 379
Parkes, 2nd Lt H.K. 211
Parkinson, Maj. Gen. Graham (Ike) 161, 187, **188**, 189
Passchendaele 125–7, **128**, 129–32, 147
Paterangi 24
Paterson, Lt-Col R.M. 395–6
Pauatahanui 325, 333–4
peacekeeping 15, 453–7, 461, 466–7
    Afghanistan 466–7
    Angola 454
    Bosnia–Herzegovina 454–5
    East Timor 455–7, 461
    Iraq 466
    Middle East 454
    Rhodesia 457
    Solomon Islands 457
Pearl Harbor 309, 318, 326, 331
Peloponnese Peninsula 214
Penton, Col A.P. 49, 51, 65, 73
Permanent Force 167–8, 186
Permanent Militia 45–7, 51–5
Pesaro 287
Pharsala 208–9
Philippines 449
Philp, Maj. W.D. 217, 219
phosgene gas 112, 115, 153
Phuoc Tuy 415–6
Piave River 296
pill boxes 131
Pinios Gorge 206, 209
Pinipel Atoll 351
Pipitea Point 27
Piraeus 203
Pirongia 55
Pisciatello River 289
Plaine des Gaiacs 335
Platamon Tunnel 204–6
Platanias 220
Plimmer, Sgt Harry 197
Ploegsteert Wood 122, 138

Plugge's Plateau **93**, 94, 96
Plumer, Lt-Gen. Sir Herbert 105–6, 122, 126
Po River 296
Poelcappelle 129
Point Britomart 27
Point Chevalier 24
Point Cruz 338
Point Jerningham 312
Point Tere 335
Pokonian plantation 350
Polderhoek 132–3, 150
police support 458–9
Poperinghe 107
Porirua 325
Port Chalmers 34, 45, 48, 62, 68, 83, 311, 315
Port Moresby 413
Port Tewfik 194, 200
Porto Rafti 214
Portsea 373
Powles, Lt-Col G.R. 336, 340
predictors **173**, 317, 321–3
Pretoria 58
Prieur, Capt. Dominique 459
prisoners 251, 266
projectiles 11, 22, 29, 30, 150, 152, 441
Prosecco 296
Puisieux-au-Mont 141–2
Puketakauere 23
Puketutu 20
Pukhan 390
Pusan 378, 380, 391, 402
Putaruru 369, 371, 374
Puttick, Brig. E. 161, 194, 216, 218

Q

Queen Charlotte Sound 162
Queree, Brig. Ray 189, 194, 203, 230, 292–3, 295, 299, 301, **302**, 430
Quetta 353
Qui Nhon 409

R

Rabaul 349, 351
radar 14, 223, 312, 322–3, 346, 350, 367, 371–2, 377, 406, 424, 428, 436, 438, 453–4
radio-telephones 182
radios 14, 84–5, 100, 143, 154, 157, 179, 182, **183**, 202, 227, 272, 295, 308, 320

336, 342, 388–9, 394, 396, 413, 417, 428
Raglan 425
Rahotu 43
Rainbow Warrior 459
Rangatira 330
range-finders 151, 313, 317, 452
range-scale indicators 262
range tables 154, 325
Rangihoua 18
Rangiriri 24
Rangitiki 196
Rangitoto Island 72, 314, 319
Rapido River 276
Rawene 44
Ready Reaction Force (RRF) 436–42, 445, 448, 452
Reed, Maj. C.K. 215, 296
Regular Force 362
Reinforcements, in World Wars 86, 88, 90, 124, 155, 223, 269, 271, 284, 290, 298, 326, 360, 391
Reno River 296
reorganisation 158–9, 168–9, 290, 324–7, 362, 364, 403–7, 427, 437–8, 440, 448–9, 458
Rerewahine Battery 311–3
Rerewhakaaitu 332
reservists 44, 161, 184, 312
rest and recreation 263, 294
Retimo 216, 222
Rhenoster Kop 58
Rhine 147
Rhodesia 58, 457
Rhodesian Field Force 58–9
Riccione 288
Richardson, Gnr Bert 104
Richardson, Sir George 46, 78–9
Richmond, Maj. J.M. 121, 145, 186
Rickard, Sgt L.J. 345
Rifle Volunteers 72
Rimini 288–90
Ripapa Island 33, 36, 44, 47, 71
RMT Company 218
Robin, Col Alfred 79
Robinson, Capt. E.L. 260, 449
Robinson's Pond 449
Robley, Lt H.G. 238
rocket launchers 14, 264, 275–8, 292, 296, 453
rocket tubes 20
rockets 14, 18, 277, 453, 465–6
Rodwell, Sir Cecil 161

Romagna 288
Rome 282–3, 290, 462
Rommel, Gen. Erwin 224–5, 230, 257–8
Rossignol Wood 141
round shot 18
Rout, Lt-Col John 438
Row, Brig. R.A. 343
Rowbotham, Col. W. 323
Royal Artillery 45, 78, 149, 364
Royal Australian Artillery 381, 384–5, 388, 396, 401, 409, 413–6, 418, 422–4
Royal Engineers 27
Royal Garrison Artillery 108
Royal Military Academy 11, 303
Royal Military College, Duntroon 13, 61, 157, 185, 187, 241, 301, 353, 373, 410, 416, 429, 462–3
Royal Military College, Sandhurst 301
Royal New Zealand Air Force 376–7
Royal New Zealand Engineers 60–1
Ruapehu 269
Ruapekapeka 21–2
Ruffell, Wally 182
rugby **64**, 124, 244, 332–3, 402, 425, 459
Russell, Maj. Gen. Sir Andrew 104, 111–2, 114, 121, 130, 133, 149
Russian scares 27, 32–3, 35, 40, 45
Rutherfurd, John 191, 251
Ruweisat Ridge 248–51

S
Saddle Battery **35**
Saigon 413, 415
Sailly-au-Bois 141
Salisbury Plain 14, 107, 165, 424
Salonika 79, 204
Salt, Maj. Harold George 354, **355**, 356
Salween 214
Samichon River 395
Samoa 79, 82, 84–6, 88
Samoa Expeditionary Force 66
Samoan Relief Force 124
San Casciano 285
San Michele 285
Sandown station **165**
Sangro River 271–3, **274**, 275, 300
Sangsok 385
Sant Angelo 271, 289
Santerno River 295

Sari Bair Range 98–9
Savage, Rt Hon. Michael Joseph 184
Savige Force 206, 209
Savio River 289
Sawyers, Maj. Huck 296
scattershot 19
Scharnhorst 82–3, 85
Schaw, Maj. Gen. H. 46
School of Artillery 13, 308, **324**, 325, **371**, 372, 405, 408, 419, 424, 438, 464
School of Instruction 51
Scott, Capt. Kevin 454
Scott, Robert 113
Scottish Borderers 390, 394–5, 397
Scratchley, Col Peter 28
searchlights 61, 100, 173, 176–7, 184, 313–4, 320–1, 328–9, 343, 345
SEATO 305, 431
Second World War 190–358
Seddon, Rt Hon. Richard John 49, 52, 73, 78
Seeadler 87
Seebees 344, 347
Selle River 144
Senio River/Line 291–3, 295, 299, 301, 432
Seoul 378, 380, 386, 390
Serbians 454–5
Servia Pass 204–7
Sfakia 222
Sfasciata Ridge 273
Shanghai 169
Shelly Bay **52**
Sherman tanks 284, 307
Shoeburyness 61, 78, 158
Shortland Islands 343, 347
shrapnel 11–2, 26, 34, 94–5, 99, 134, 136, 152–3, 166, 205, 465
Shrivenham 462
Sidi Azeiz 226, 230–1, 243, 258–9
Sidi Barrani 258
Sidi Rezegh 225, 227–31, **232**, 233–7
Siege Company 148
siege-warfare 10, 23, 82
sights 69, 70, 154, 313
signalling 182, **183**
Sillaro River 295
simulators 453
Sinclair-Burgess, Maj. Gen. William 170–2
Sinclair Head 312

Singapore 162, 175, 309, 330, 360, 433–5, 448–50, 453
Sinton, Capt. J.G. 444
Sioux helicopters 378
Sirot Island 350
Skyhawk fighter-bombers 442
Sling Camp 107
Smith, Brig. L. 362
smoke shells 153
Snadden, Capt. J.P. 217–8, 270
snipers 92, 103–4, 112, 277
Soanotalu 347–8
Sollum 227, 258
Solomon Islands 309, 335–49, 351–2, 457
Somes Island 320
Somme **106**, 111–2, 114–8, 122, 126, 134, 137–8, **139**, 142, 153, 241, 255
Sora Valley 283
SOS lines 111, 125
sound-ranging 146, 259, **260**, 274–5, 291, 371, 376, 436
South Africa 354
South African War 43, 56–61, 69, 74, 151–2
South-East Asia Treaty Organisation 305, 431
South Porton 188
Southern Military District 189, 364
Special Air Service (SAS) 403, 409, 447, 456, 466
Speight, Lt D.G. 362
Spencer, Maj. Spencer 286, 407
sport **64**, **113**, 124, 244, **245**, 332–3, 383, 402, 425, 459
St Clair beach **40**
Stanbridge, Lt Colin 375, 379
Stanford, Brig. H.M. 308
Stanley, Capt. Maurice 416–7
Steenwerck 107, 112
Steeple Rock 320
Stenbockfontein 59
Steward, Maj. Gen. E. Harding 148
Stewart, Clyde 373
Stewart, Maj. Gen. Keith 379
Stewart Island 162
Stirling Island 343–4, 346, 348
Stokes, Gnr Bert 107
'stonks' 262, 264, 266–8, 273, 281, 285, 291, 298, 308, 400
Strang, David 213, 226
stretcher carriers 443
strikes 47, 77, 161, 361, 458
Stukas 209, 273
Suani Ben Adem 263, 413

submarines 86, 175, 316, 319, 321, 337–8, 380
Suez Canal 89, 90, 102, 143–4, 245–6, 291, 296
Suva Battery **327**, 355
swivel guns 17–9, 43
Sydney Harbour 320
Sykes, Maj. S.B. 88, 98
Sylvia Park 376
Symon, Capt. Bob 186
Symon, Col Frank 186, **187**
Syria 244–7, 254, 308

T

Tahuna Park 135
Taiaroa Head 33, 71, 311
Taiwan 449
Takapuna 33, 83, 177, 311, 315, 331, 355, 438
Takrouna 260, 267–9, 432
Talavera Barracks 107
Tamaki, HMNZS 319
Tambama 342
Tangalan plantation 350
tanks 14, 115, 117, 125, 142, 144, 201, 205–9, 211–3, 225, 227, 229–34, 238, 243, 246–7, 249, 251, 256–8, 261–2, 264–6, 268, 272, 276–7, 285, 287–90, 294, 306, 327, 342, 349, 360, 388, 423, 454
Taom River 335
Taranaki War (1860–61) 22–3
Taranto 271, 294
Task Force Regions (TFR) 436–7, 439, 446
Tasker, Captain 177
Tasman, Abel Janszoon 17
Tauherenikau 75
Taupo 26, 284, 375
Tauranga 19, 25, 305, 370
Tauranga-ika 26, 55
Tavronitis River 218
Te Arei 23
Te Aroha 458
Te Atiawa 19, 23, 42
Te Awamutu 369
Te Kohia 23
Te Kooti 55
Te Kuiti 369–70
Te Mahurehure 44
Te Ranga 25
Te Rangihaeata 19, 22
Te Rauparaha 18
Te Rore 21, 24

Te Whiti o Rongomai 55
tear gas 153
Tebaga Gap 265
Tekapo 375
telephones 13, 70, 72, 154, 182
Tempe 206, 209
Territorial Force 56, 73, 75–7, 79, 81, 83–4, 88, 157, 163–5, 167, 169, 184–5, 193, 240, 303, 309, 318, 326, 329, 333, 362–3, 379, 405, 427, 432, **441**, 443, 467
    Regionalisation 460–1
    Special Reserve 157, 184
Tet Offensive 420, 422–3
Thailand 305, 449
Thames Estuary 61
Thermopylae 203, 206, 209–11, 216
Thornton, Lt-Gen. Sir Leonard 185, 189, 299, 429, **430**, 431
Tiger tanks 287
Timaru 34–5, 50, 315
Timaru Port Guards 50
Tirau 332
Tiritiri Matangi 312, 319
Tirnavos 208
Tito, Marshal 297
Titokowaru 26, 55
Tobruk 224–5, 227–8, 230, 233–4, 236–7, 246, 442
Tobruk, HMAS 442
Tohu Kakahi 43
Tokso-ri 390
Tokyo 361, 430
Tonga 312, 323, 331, 428
Tongan Defence Force 331
Tongariro draft 292
Tontouta 335
Torch 44
Torpedo Bay **366**
torpedoes 32, 51, **52**
training 13–4, 39–41, 50–3, 61, 65, 75–7, 107, 135–6, 157–8, 164–7, 179, 184, 191, 193–4, **198–9**, 270, 324–5, 372–3, 375–7, 403, 405, 407, 419, 424, 445–6
Transvaal 57–8
Treasury Islands 333, 343–5, **346**, 347–9, 351, 428
trench warfare 13, 110–1, 149, 152
Trentham Camp 14, 88, 135, 176–7, **179**, **183**, 184–5, 187, 240, 301, 324–6, 353, 372–3
Trescault Spur 143
Trieste 245, 270, 296, **297**, **299**, 301
Trigh Capuzzo 226–7, 243, 259

Tripoli 259, 261–4, 269
trumpeters 63, 443
Tudor Boddam, Maj E.M. 33, 54–5
Tuhawaiki 18
Tunisia 188, 263–9
Turanganui 55
Turkey 89–103, 161, 244
Tutanekai 86–7, 161
Tyrrhenian front 275

U

U-boat bases 122
Ulimaroa, HMNZT 86
Umbria 283
Unimogs 442, 452
United States Marines 324, 331, 334, 361, 386, 401, 429
upper-register shoots 278
Uren, Sgt Martyn 300
Uso River 289
Utah Line 386–7
Uzamba Beach 340

V

Vatican City 462
Vella Lavella 340, **341**, 342–3, 350
Venafro 278
Venice 296
veterans 188, 326, 362, 375, 379, 426–7
Via Balbia 226, 261
Victoria Cross medals 24
Viet Cong 409, 413–6, 418, 422
Vietnam War 14, 305, 359, 399, 403, 409–27, 429, 433–4, 445, 455, 457, 464
Vila 340
Vildebeeste aircraft 322
Viserba 288
Viti Levu 329
Vo Dat 414–6, 422–5
Völkner, Carl Sylvius 26
Volturno Valley 278–9
Volunteer Force Act 1865 33
Volunteers 13, 17, 26, 28, 32–9, 43–4, 48–9, 60–7, 72–3, 76, 81
 entertainment 40–3
 equipment 37, 49–50
 fines 38
 funding 37–9, 50
 officers 38–9, 51, 63–4

reorganisation 44–7, 49, 61–3
training 39–41, 50–3, 65–6
uniforms 43, 53
wages 37, 50
von Luckner, Count Felix 87
Vryburg 59
Vuda 330, 355
Vung Tau 415

W

Waaka, WO Carlyle 399
Wadi Akarit 261–2, 266
Wadi Matratin 261–2
Wadi Sedada 263
Waerenga-a-Hika 26
Wahine 391
Waiheke Island 316, 319, 368
Waikato, HMNZS 442
Waikato River **441**
Waikato War (1863–64) 21, 23, 25–6
Waiouru Camp 180, 182, 188, 192, 194, 239, 326, 371–3, 375, 379–80, 399, **404**, 405, 410, 424, 438, 443, 445, 448–9, 453, 461–2, 464
Waipa River 21
Waipapakauri 323
Waipukurau 177
Wairau incident 19
Wairoa redoubt 26
Waitara redoubts 23
Waitemata Harbour 27, 375
Walker's Ridge 94
Wallon Cappel 132
Wanganui 19, 22, 42
war artists 238–9
Warambari 342
Washington Naval Treaty 1922 162
water supplies 226
Watson Island 348
weapons 149–52, 174–5, 212–4, 306–7, 317–8, 367–8, 465
 coastal defence 10, 13–4, 18, 23–4, 29–31, 69, 70, 82, 85, 90, 98, 108, 112, 118, 151, 159, 163, 195, 209, 234, 246, 264–5, 284, 312, 317, 325, 328, 340, 355, 360, 368, 370, 405–6, 408, 415, 436, 448–50, 453, 456
Webb, Maj. Richard 379
Webber, Neville 300
Weir, Gen. Sir Stephen 200, 230, 232–5, 243, 245, 248, 250, 252–3, 255, 257–9, 267–9, 271, 273, 283, 298–9,

303, 304–5, 308, 406, 431
Weller, Joseph 18
Wellington 19, 22, 27–8, 32–4, 36, 39, 41–3, 46–7, 49, 50, 52–3, 57, 62–6, 69–72, 75, 77, 81, 83–5, 88, 99, 106–7, 109, 128, 140, 148, 157, 159–64, 168–72, 176–8, 185–7, 193–5, 198, 200, 224, 228, 232, 260–1, 311–4, 316, 318–20, 322–5, 334, 346–7, 365–8, 410, 461–2
Wellington, HMNZS 448
West Point 334
Western Front 102–149, 154, 186
Western Samoa *see* Samoa
Westhoek **137**
Westoutre 140
Westport 34, 47, 49, 62, 68–70, 83, 160
Whakatane 18
Whakatohea 26
Whakatu 83
Whangaparaoa 311–3, 316, 318, 355, 365, 370
Whangaroa 18, 315–6, 319
Whatawhata 21, 194
Whenuapai 323, 412, 425, 448
Williams, Maj. Alan 22, 27–8, 47, 91, 99, 162, 170, **187**, 191, 193, 240–1, 281
Wilson, Gen. Sir Henry 203–4, 210, 346, 348
wireless *see* radios
women 319, 323–4, 360–1, 438, **439**, 456, 466
Women's Auxiliary Army Corps (WAAC) 16, 313, 323, 333
World War I 82–156
World War II 190–358
Wrights Hill **317**, 368, 376
Wulverghem 138

Y

Yalu River 380
Yamaguchi 360–2
Yoju 384
Ypres 112, 122, 125–6, 132–3, **134**, 137–8, 150
Yugoslavia 204, 206, 245, 297

Z

Zaafran 234
Zeerust 58–9
Zeitoun 89, 90